W9-DFB-987

BORDEAUX

BORDEAUX

THE
DEFINITIVE
GUIDE TO THE
WINES OF
BORDEAUX
SINCE 1961

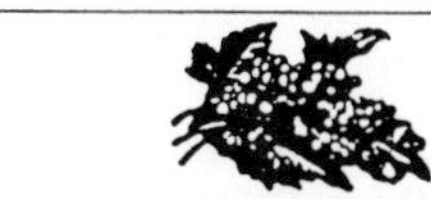

ROBERT PARKER

Drawings by
CHRISTOPHER WORMELL

DORLING KINDERSLEY · LONDON

First published in Great Britain in 1986 by
Dorling Kindersley Publishers Limited.
9 Henrietta Street, London WC2E 8PS
second impression 1987
third impression 1989

British Library Cataloguing in Publication Data

Parker, Robert
Bordeaux.
1. Wine and wine making – France – Bordeaux
I. Title
641.2'22"094471 TP553
ISBN 0-86318-193-7

ACKNOWLEDGMENTS

There are many people I would like to thank for going to so much trouble to obtain the endless wines needed for my tastings, for parting with the rare older vintages, and for simply providing time and encouragement.

First of all, I would like to thank my beloved wife, Patricia. This book is a direct product of my passion for wine, which she alone started by introducing me to my first glass of wine in Alsace in 1967. Little did she know I would take to the grape so passionately. However, without her endless assistance and remarkable charm as my loyal and faithful sidekick on so many forays into Bordeaux, I seriously doubt this book would have been possible. Second, I would like to thank several dear friends for parting with more perfectly stored, beautiful old vintages of wine than anyone could have ever imagined. Without their assistance, many of the rare 1961s could not have been tasted. To Karen and Joe Weinstock, and Paul Evans, I thank you dearly. Third, I owe a great deal of gratitude to my literary agent, Bob Lescher, whose encouragement and belief in what I do is eternally a great source of confidence and joy.

In Europe and Bordeaux, I owe a great indebtedness to so many people in obtaining the thousands of wines for tastings over recent years. The late Martin Bamford, Anthony Barton, Jean Claude Berrouet, Bill Blatch, Jean Eugène Borie, Christopher Cannan, Francis Dewavrin, Jean Delmas, Eric Fournier, Jean Paul Gardère, Peter Griffiths, Patrick Grubb, Phillippe Guyonnet-Duperat, Jean Paul Jauffret, Nathaniel Johnston, Archie Johnston, Dennis Johnston, Alain Maurel,

Jean-Pierre Moueix, Christian Moueix, Jean François Moueix, Yves Pardes, Bruno Prats, Dominique Renard, Michel Rolland, Pierre Tari, and Daniel Vergeley have all been immensely helpful in providing the necessary tastings for writing this book.

On this side of the Atlantic, I would like to thank the following people who have been instrumental in my career as a wine writer because of the support they have provided: Bill Rice, John and Elin Walker, Addy Bassin, Ed Sands, Frank Polk, Mary Mulligan, Steve Wallace, Thomas Hoving, Phyllis Richmon Chasanov, Steve and Barbara Jacoby, Stephen Gilbertson, Nick Poulos, Abdulah Simon, Elliott Staren, Dick Carretta, Jay Miller, Victor Morgenroth, and Alexis Bespaloff. I would also like to thank my secretary, Joan Passman, who for the last six months has had to be one of the most overworked people in the world. She never once complained. Thank you, Joan.

Lastly, I owe a great deal to both Dan Green and Carole Lalli at Simon & Schuster. Dan Green's enthusiasm and total support for this book and the extra effort he put forth to make this book what it is have made me feel incredibly fortunate and lucky. My editor, Carole Lalli, also was a wonderful asset with whom I found it a joy to work. All authors should be so lucky to have the kind of support, cooperation, and expertise I received from them and their assistants.

This book is dedicated to my beloved Pat, my mother and father, and to the memory of a dear friend, the late Martin Bamford.

CONTENTS

INTRODUCTION

Bordeaux holds the paramount position in today's world of wine. Never in the long history of this huge wine-producing region have Bordeaux wines been as popular or as well made as they are today. Certainly, recent history has been kind to Bordeaux. One suspects that 25 or 50 years from now, when wine writers look back upon the vintages from Bordeaux, the era of 1978–1983 will be widely regarded as Bordeaux's "Golden Age." During this period, Mother Nature provided textbook climatic conditions for making superb wine in bountiful amounts in every year but 1980.

There can be no question that the romance, if not downright mysticism, of opening a bottle of Bordeaux from a famous château has a grip and allure that are hard to resist. Writers for years have written glowing accounts of Bordeaux wines, giving them sometimes more respect and exalted status than they have deserved. How often has that fine bottle of Bordeaux from what was allegedly an excellent vintage turned out to

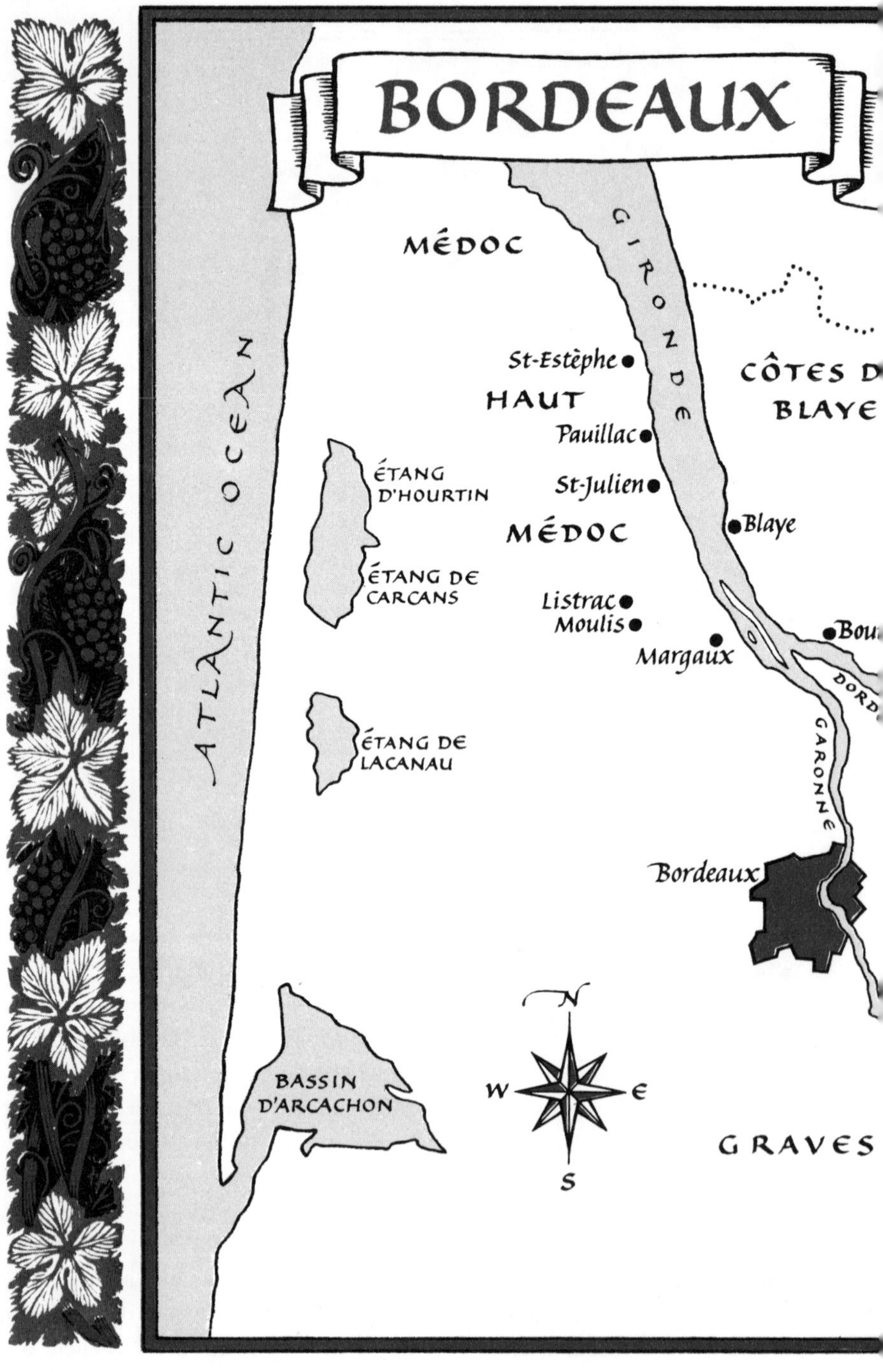
BORDEAUX
MÉDOC
GIRONDE
ATLANTIC OCEAN
St-Estèphe
HAUT
MÉDOC
CÔTES D
BLAYE
Pauillac
St-Julien
ÉTANG
D'HOURTIN
Blaye
ÉTANG DE
CARCANS
Listrac
Moulis
Margaux
ÉTANG DE
LACANAU
GARONNE
Bordeaux
BASSIN
D'ARCACHON
N
W
E
S
GRAVES

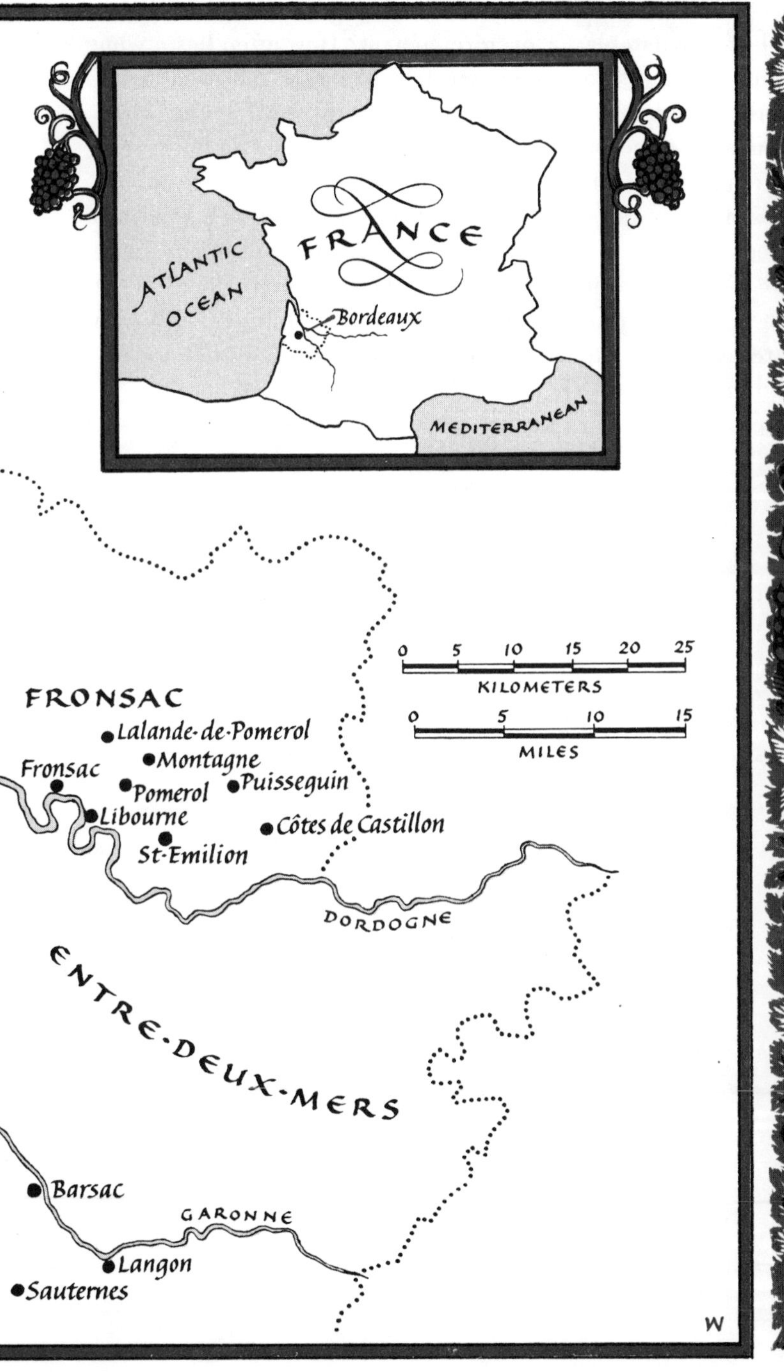
FRANCE
ATLANTIC OCEAN
Bordeaux
MEDITERRANEAN
0 5 10 15 20 25
KILOMETERS
0 5 10 15
MILES
FRONSAC
Lalande-de-Pomerol
Montagne
Fronsac
Pomerol
Puisseguin
Libourne
Côtes de Castillon
St-Emilion
DORDOGNE
ENTRE-DEUX-MERS
Barsac
GARONNE
Langon
Sauternes
W

be diluted, barely palatable, or even repugnant? How often has a wine from a famous château let you and your friends down when you tasted it? On the other hand, how often has a vintage written off by the critics provided you with some of your most enjoyable bottles of Bordeaux? And how often have you tasted a great wine from Bordeaux, only to learn that the name of the château is neither famous nor well known to you? This book is about just such matters. It is a wine consumer's guide to Bordeaux. Who is making Bordeaux's best and worst wines? What has a specific château's track record been over the last 20 years? Which châteaux are overrated and overpriced and, of course, which are underrated and underpriced? These are the issues addressed herein.

1: USING THIS BOOK

The comprehensive evaluations of the Bordeaux châteaux that follow are, I believe, the first extensive critiques of these wines to be published in a book on Bordeaux by someone outside the wine trade. They represent a contemporary consumer's point of view, since I have no other interest in the sale or promotion of Bordeaux wines. The evaluations that follow are the result of extensive tastings conducted in Bordeaux and in America. I have been visiting Bordeaux every year since 1970, and since 1978 I have gone to Bordeaux twice a year to conduct barrel tastings of the young wines, as well as to conduct comparative tastings of different wines and vintages that have been released for sale.

From 1970 onward, I have made approximately two to as many as six or more tasting critiques of all the major château-bottled wines of Bordeaux. From 1975 onward, I have made close to a dozen different tasting critiques of each specific vintage of wine for the great majority of the major châteaux that produce wine in this area. Except for several of the leading *négociants* in Bordeaux, I know of no one who tastes these wines as frequently as I do.

It is patently unfair to an estate to issue a final judgment about a wine when it has been tasted only one time. Consequently, when I do tastings of young Bordeaux, I try to taste them as many times as possible to get a clear, concise picture of the wine's quality and potential. I have often equated the tasting of an infant unbottled wine with that of taking a photograph of a long-distance runner. One look or tasting of such a wine is only a split-second glimpse of the moving object that is constantly changing and moving. To effectively evaluate its performance and quality in a given vintage, one must look at the wine time after time during its 16- to 24-month-prebottling evolution, and then evaluate it numerous times after its bottling to see if the quality or potential expected of a young wine is still present. Obviously, some wines as well as vintages are much more easy to assess than others. The 1975, 1978, and 1982 Bordeaux all showed various degrees of excellence at the top estates when first tasted in late March following the vintage. However, my first look at the 1979s in March 1980, and 1981s in March 1982, offered fewer clues as to what these wines were likely to turn out to be. Three months later, in June 1980 and June 1982, respectively, the direction and quality level of the 1979s and 1981s were much more apparent and easy to chart. For certain, tasting young wine requires total concentration and an extreme dedication to tasting the young wine as many times as possible in its youth, both at the individual châteaux and in comparative tastings against its peers. This is the only valid method by which to obtain an accurate look at the quality and potential of the wine. For this reason, I visit Bordeaux at least twice a year, spending altogether close to a month there, visiting all the major châteaux in all the principal appellations of the Médoc, Graves, Sauternes, St.-Emilion and Pomerol regions. The château visits and interviews with the winemakers are extremely important in accumulating the critical data about the growing season, the harvest dates, and vinification of the château's wines. Most of the winemakers at the Bordeaux châteaux are remarkably straightforward and honest in their answers, whereas the owners will go to great lengths to simply glorify the wine they have produced. I also request the leading *négociants* to assemble wines for tasting and evaluation. In addition to doing extensive visits to the specific Bordeaux châteaux in all appellations of Bordeaux in good, poor, and great vintages, I insist on comparative tastings of cask samples of the new vintages. For these tastings I call on many of Bordeaux's leading *négociants* to set up what most consumers would call massive comparative daylong tastings of 60–100 wines. Tasted in groups of 10–15 wines at a time, an entire vintage, from major classified growths to minor Crus Bourgeois, can be reviewed several times each over a course of two weeks of extensive tastings. Such tastings corroborated or refuted what quality I found to exist when I visited the specific château. Since I do these types of broad, all-inclusive tastings at least three times before the young Bordeaux wine is bottled, I am able to get numerous looks at the infant wine at 6, 9, and 18 months of age, which usually give a very clear picture of the quality of the wine.

Despite the fact that young Bordeaux wines are constantly changing during their evolution and aging process in the barrel, the great wines of a given vintage are always apparent. It has been my experience that some wines that ultimately turn out to be good or very good may be unimpressive or just dumb when tasted in their youth from the cask. But the true superstars of a great vintage are sensational, whether they are 6 months or 20 months old.

When I taste young Bordeaux from the cask, I prefer to judge the wine several weeks to a month after the final blend or *assemblage* has been completed. At this stage, the new wine has had only negligible aging in oak casks. For me, it is essential to look at a wine at this infant stage (normally in late March following the vintage) because the wine can be judged without the influence of oak, which can mask fruit and impart additional tannin and aromas to the wine. What one sees at this stage is a naked wine that can be evaluated for its richness and ripeness of fruit, its depth, its concentration, its body, its acidity, and its natural tannin content, unobscured by evidence of oak aging. The most important component I look for in a young Bordeaux is fruit. Great vintages, characterized by ample amounts of sunshine and warmth, result in grapes that are fully mature, and that produce rich, ripe, deeply fruity wines. If the fruit is missing, or unripe and green, the wine can never be great. In contrast, grapes that are allowed to stay on the vine too long in hot, humid weather become overripe and taste pruny and sometimes raisiny, and are also deficient in acidity. They too have little future. Recent vintages that have in their youth, throughout all appellations of Bordeaux, been marked by the greatest ripeness, richness, and purity of fruit have been 1970 and 1982, both great vintages for Bordeaux. The two vintages that exhibited the least fruit and an annoying vegetal character have been 1974 and 1977, both poor to mediocre vintages.

In late June following the vintage, I return to Bordeaux to get another extensive look at the wines. At this time the wines have settled down completely, but are also marked by the scent of new oak barrels. The intense grapey character of their youth has begun to peel away, as the wines have now had at least 3 to 4 months of cask aging. If extensive tastings in March or April give a clear overall view of the vintage's level of quality, comprehensive tastings in June and again the second March following the vintage are almost always conclusive evidence of where the vintage stands in relation to other Bordeaux vintages, and how specific wines relate in quality to each other.

With regard to vintages of Bordeaux in the bottle, I prefer to taste these wines in what is called a "blind tasting." A blind tasting can be either "single blind" or "double blind." This does not mean one is actually blindfolded and served the wines, but rather that in a single blind tasting, the taster knows the wines are from Bordeaux, but does not know the identities of the châteaux or the vintages. In a double blind tasting, the taster knows nothing other than that several wines from anywhere in the world, in any order, from any vintage, are about to be served.

For bottled Bordeaux, I prefer to conduct all my Bordeaux tastings under single blind conditions. I do not know the identity of the wine, but since I prefer to taste in peer groups, I always taste wines from the same vintage. Additionally, I never mix Bordeaux with non-Bordeaux wines, simply because whether it be California or Australia Cabernet Sauvignons, the wines are distinctly different, and while comparative tastings of Bordeaux versus California may be fun and make interesting reading, the results are never very reliable or especially meaningful to the wine consumer desirous of the most accurate information. It should be remembered that whether one employs a 100-point rating system or a 20-point rating system the objectives and aims of professional wine evaluations are the same—to assess the quality of the wine *vis-à-vis* its peers and to determine its relative value and importance in the international commercial world of wine.

In evaluating wines professionally, it goes without saying that proper glasses and the correct serving temperature of the wine must be prerequisites to any objective and meaningful tasting. The best glass for critical tasting is that approved by the International Standards Organization. Called the ISO glass, it is tulip-shaped and has been designed for tasting. As for the temperature of the wine, 60°F to 65°F is best for both red and white wines. Too warm a temperature and the bouquet becomes diffuse and the taste flat. Too cold a temperature and there is no discernible bouquet and the flavors are completely locked in by the overly chilling effect on the wine.

When I examine a wine critically, there is both a visual and physical examination. Against a white background the wine is first given a visual exam for its brilliance, richness, and intensity of color. A young Bordeaux wine that is light in color, hazy or cloudy, or both, has serious problems. For Bordeaux red wines, color is extremely important. Virtually all the great Bordeaux vintages have shared a very deep, rich, dark ruby color when young, whereas the poorer vintages often have weaker, less rich-looking colors because of poor weather and rain. Certainly, in 1961, 1970, 1982, and 1983, the general color of the red wines of Bordeaux has been very dark. In 1978 and 1975, it was dark but generally not nearly as deep in color as the four aforementioned vintages. In 1973, 1974, and 1980, the color was rather light.

In looking at an older wine, the rim of the wine next to the glass should be examined for amber, orange, rust, and brown colors. These are signs of maturity and are normal. When they appear in a good vintage of a wine under 6 or 7 years old something is awry. For example, young wines that have been sloppily made and exposed to unclean barrels or air will mature at an accelerated rate and take on the look of old wines when in fact they are in years still relatively young by Bordeaux standards.

In addition to looking at the color of the wines, I examine the "legs" of the wine, which are the tears or residue of the wine that run down the inside of the glass. Rich vintages of Bordeaux tend to have "good legs" because the grapes are rich in glycerol and alcohol, giving the wine a viscosity that causes this "tearing" effect. Examples of Bordeaux vintages which produced wines with good to excellent "legs" would be 1982, 1970, and 1961.

After the visual examination is completed, the actual physical examination of the wine takes place. The physical exam is composed of two parts, the smell of the wine, which depends on the olfactory sense, and the taste of the wine, which is tested on the palate. After swirling a wine, the nose must be placed into the glass (not the wine) to smell the aromas that the wine is giving off. This is an extremely critical step because the aroma and odor of the wine will tell the examiner the ripeness and richness of the underlying fruit, the state of maturity, and whether there is anything unclean or suspicious about the wine. The smell of a wine, young or old, will tell a great deal about the quality of the wine, and no responsible professional taster understates the significance of a wine's odors and aromas, often called the nose or bouquet. Emile Peynaud, in his classic book on wine tasting, *Le Goût du Vin* (Dunod, 1980), states that there are nine principal categories of wine aromas. They are:

1. animal odors: smells of game, beef, venison
2. balsamic odors: smells of pine trees, resin, vanilla
3. woody odors: smells of new wood of oak barrels
4. chemical odors: smells of acetone, mercaptan, yeasts, hydrogen sulfide, acidity and fermentation
5. spicy odors: smells of pepper, cloves, cinnamon, nutmeg, ginger, truffles, anise, mint
6. empyreumatic odors: smells of *crème brûlée*, smoke, toast, leather, coffee
7. floral odors: smells of violets, roses, lilacs, jasmine
8. fruity odors: smells of blackcurrants, raspberries, cherries, plums, apricots, peaches, figs
9. vegetal odors: smells of herbs, tea, mushrooms, vegetables

The presence or absence of some or all of these aromas, their intensity, their complexity, their persistence, all serve to create the bouquet or nose of a wine that can be said to be distinguished and interesting, or flawed and simple.

Once the wine's aroma or bouquet has been examined thoroughly, the wine is tasted, slushed or chewed around on the palate while also inhaled to release the wine's aromas. The weight, richness, depth, balance, and length of a wine are apparent from the tactile impression the wine leaves on the palate. Sweetness is experienced on the tip of the tongue, saltiness just behind the tongue's tip, acidity on the sides, and bitterness at the back. Most professional tasters will spit the wine out, although some wine is swallowed in the process. The finish or length of a wine, its ability to give off aromas and flavors even though it is no longer on the palate, is the major difference between a good young wine and a great young wine. When the flavor and the aroma of the wine seem to last and last on the palate, it is usually a great, rich wine that has just been tasted. The great wines and great vintages are always characterized by a purity, opulence, richness, depth, and ripeness of the fruit from which the wines are made. When the wines have sufficient tannin and acidity, the balance is struck. It is these facts that separate many a great 1982, 1970, or 1961 Bordeaux from a good 1981, 1978, 1975, or 1966 Bordeaux.

The rating system I employ in my wine journal, *The Wine Advocate*, is the one that I am utilizing in this book. It is a 100-point scale. The worst of all possible wines merits 50, and the most glorious, perfect gustatory experience is worth 100. I prefer it to the more widely quoted 20-point scale, called the Davis Scale, named after the University of California at Davis, because it permits more flexibility in scoring. It is easier to understand since it corresponds to the grading system most of us have experienced in high school, college, or graduate school, and it avoids the compression of scores from which the Davis Scale suffers.

For example, a review of scores given by wine critics who employ the Davis Scale will undoubtedly reveal the majority of wines falling between 15 and 18, so in effect the scale largely becomes a 4-point scale. The 100-point system rates wines as follows:

THE RATING SYSTEM

96–100	Extraordinary
90–95	Outstanding
80–89	Above average to very good
70–79	Average
50–69	Below average to poor

The score given for a specific wine reflects the quality of the wine at its best. Since the great majority of the wines reviewed in this text have been tasted numerous times, the score represents a sort of cumulative average of the wine's performance in tastings to date. However, the written commentary that describes the wine is a better source of information regarding the wine's style and personality, its relative quality level *vis-à-vis* its peers, its relative value in the overall Bordeaux hierarchy, and the aging potential that can be expected. The reader should realize that for the mature vintages of Bordeaux wines the score given reflects the status and quality of the wine today. For example, wines that were at their peak 2, 3, or 5 years ago, and have now begun to fade, obviously have received a lower score than if the wine had been evaluated when it was near or at its peak. For the young vintages, the score reflects the level of quality the wine should attain when it is fully mature. The written commentary gives an educated guess as to when full maturity will occur, assuming, of course, good storage.

In this book the rating for each wine can be found just under the vintage year. The easiest way for the reader to understand my scoring system is to think about the grades you received in school. Ninety to 100 is equivalent to an A, and it should be given for an outstanding or excellent special effort. There is a big difference between a 90 and 99, but both are top marks. Eighty to 89 is equivalent to a B in school, and such a mark, particularly in the 85–89 range, is very good. Seventy to 79 represents a grade school C, or an average mark, but obviously 79 is a much more desirable grade than 70. Below 70 is a D or F, depending on what school you went to, and for wine too it is a sign of an imbalanced, flawed, or terribly dull and diluted wine that should be of little interest to the wine consumer. My scoring system gives a wine 50 points to start with. The wine's general color and appearance merit up to 5 points. The aroma and bouquet merit up to 15 points. The flavor and finish merit up to 20 points, and the overall quality level and/or potential for further evolution and improvement merit up to 10 points for young wines.

Scores are important for the reader to sense the critic's overall qualitative placement of a wine, and I deem just as important the description of the wine's style, personality, and potential. It is also important to remember that no scoring system will ever adequately convey the enjoyment of a bottle of modest Bordeaux, served with the wonderful regional dish of *lamproie* from the Gironde River in a red Bordeaux wine sauce, in a restaurant overlooking the medieval town of St.-Emilion. In such a setting, a simple wine can become sublime and memorable. A good scoring system, applied unprejudicially and fairly, simply establishes different levels of wine quality. If done properly, it will guide you to the very finest wines, while not letting you miss the very finest wine values, but it cannot and should not be a hedonistic judgment that conveys the ambience, gorgeous settings, and gastronomic excellence, which can easily cause a modest wine to seemingly taste far superior to what it really is.

ABOUT THE BOOK'S ORGANIZATION

This book has been divided into the major geographical regions of Bordeaux. Within each region, the famous châteaux and many minor châteaux deserving recognition are reviewed. The emphasis, for obvious reasons, is on the major estates of Bordeaux that are widely available in this country and highly promoted. The quality of these wines over the period 1961 to 1983 is examined closely. For lesser-known châteaux, the selection process has been based on two factors, quality and recognition. High-quality, lesser-known estates are reviewed, as well as those estates which have gotten distribution into the export markets, regardless of their quality. I have made every effort over the last 15 years to discover and learn about the underpublicized châteaux in Bordeaux. Because older vintages of these wines are virtually impossible to find, the focus for most of these lesser-known Cru Bourgeois wines is on what they have accomplished in the period 1978–1983. I feel the châteaux that are reviewed are the best of these lesser-known estates, but to err is human, and it would be foolish for both you and me to believe that there is not some little estate making exquisite wine that I have omitted altogether.

At the beginning of each chapter on the appellations of Bordeaux is my classification of the wines from that appellation. This analysis is based on their overall quality *vis-à-vis* each other. This is not a book that will shroud quality differences behind skillfully worded euphemisms, so within each appellation the wines are reviewed in a qualitative rather than alphabetical order. For those who love lists, my overall classification of the top 103 wine-producing estates of Bordeaux may be found on p. 494.

With respect to the specific vintages covered, tasting emphasis has been given to only the good vintages. Vintages such as 1977, 1972, 1968, 1965, and 1963 are generally not reviewed because they were very poor years, and few Bordeaux châteaux made acceptable quality wine in those years. Furthermore, such vintages, with the exception of 1977, are not commercially available. As for the actual tasting notes, the "anticipated maturity" refers to the time period at which I believe the wine will be at its apogee. This is the time period during which the wine will be fully mature and should be drunk. These estimates as to anticipated maturity are conservative and are based on the assumption that the wine has been purchased in a sound, healthy condition, and has been kept in a vibration-free, dark, odor-free, relatively cool (below 65° F) storage area. For the wine-tasting terms I employ, and for the proper methods of cellaring Bordeaux wines, see Chapter 7, "A Glossary of Wine Terms," and Chapter 6, "A User's Guide to Bordeaux."

2: A SUMMARY OF BORDEAUX VINTAGES: 1961–1984

This chapter is a general assessment and profile of the Bordeaux vintages 1961 through 1984. While the very top wines for each good vintage are itemized, it should be remembered that the perception of a vintage should be regarded as a general view of that particular viticultural region. In mediocre and poor vintages, good wines can often be made by skillful vintners who are willing to make a careful selection of only the best grapes and *cuvées* of finished wine. In good, even great years, thin, diluted, characterless wines can be made by incompetent and greedy producers. For wine consumers, a vintage summary is important as a general guide to the level of potential excellence that could have been attained in a particular year by a conscientious grower or producer of wine.

1984
*(10–5–84)**

After three large and high quality crops in 1981, 1982, 1983, the euphoria that the Bordelais had been enjoying came to a sudden stop as the climatic events of the summer and fall of 1984 unfolded. The growing season for the grapes in Bordeaux started dramatically and positively with a warm, magnificently sunny month of April that got the vines off to a fast start. But, May was the wettest and coldest May in 25 years. The combination of a hot, sunny April and cold, wet May caused virtually a total destruction of the Merlot crop in all areas of Bordeaux. By the end of June, it was clear that after three successive large crops, 1984 was going to be small, particularly in the right-bank communes of St.-Emilion and Pomerol, which have extensive Merlot plantings. With regard to the other major red grape varieties, the Cabernet Franc was also damaged, but the hardy, tough Cabernet Sauvignon was totally unaffected and flowered well under good conditions.

July was dry and warm, and by the end of August there was the ever present optimistic talk of a 1961-style vintage. It should be remembered that 1961 was a small crop of primarily Cabernet Sauvignon because of the Merlot crop failures that year due to spring frosts. However, any comparisons with 1961 were quickly washed away with the cool, cloudy days of September and the torrential rains that fell between September 21 and October 4. On the latter date, a rare cyclone hit Bordeaux, causing further depressions if only because more damage was done to rooftops than to vines.

The harvest occurred throughout the month of October. The journalistic prophets of doom had declared 1984 a catastrophe long before the harvest commenced. So no doubt they cared little for the fact that the Cabernet Sauvignon grapes were picked in relatively ripe, healthy conditions.

Two weeks in late March 1985 spent tasting the infant 1984 wines left me with the following inescapable conclusion. This vintage, while not a great vintage like 1982, or even a very good vintage like 1983 or 1978, had produced a surprising number of good wines that have more concentration, tannin, and character than the 1980 vintage, another so-called "off" vintage, and in a few cases approach the quality of the charming medium-weight 1981s. The weakness of the wines is that they lack fatness and flesh, two of the personality traits that they would have

* Dates in parentheses denote actual day on which the Bordeaux harvest began, according to the French Ministry of Agriculture.

had had the Merlot flowered adequately. In general, the vintage is weakest in St.-Emilion, rather average in quality in Pomerol, Barsac and Sauternes, and Graves, yet certainly above average in quality for the Médoc.

In the Médoc, the top wines show surprisingly good color, are tannic, medium-bodied and, where the winemaker employed a warm, long fermentation, adequately rich and long on the palate. They will certainly outlast the 1980s as they are primarily 100% Cabernet Sauvignon wines, and should have a life span of at least 10–12 years.

I suspect that the dry white wines, particularly of Graves, will turn out quite well. Certainly they had a good measure of fruit and character when tasted from the cask in March 1985.

From a buyer's perspective, the top wines of 1984 are not likely to be of interest because they are expensive given their quality. This is simply because there is too much very fine Bordeaux to buy from the vintages 1978–1983, and 1984's cannot pretend to be of the same quality as the three vintages that preceded it. However, the vintage is not a catastrophe, unless one views it from a quantitative perspective in St.-Emilion and Pomerol.

The Best Wines

St.-Estèphe: Cos d'Estournel, Montrose, Meyney
Pauillac: Mouton-Rothschild, Lynch-Bages, Pichon Lalande, Latour
St.-Julien: Léoville-Las Cases, Gruaud-Larose, Talbot, Ducru-Beaucaillou, Léoville-Poyferré
Margaux: Margaux, Lascombes, d'Issan
Graves: Haut-Brion, La Mission-Haut-Brion
St.-Emilion: Cheval Blanc, Figeac
Pomerol: Pétrus, L'Eglise-Clinet, Trotanoy

1983
(9–26–83)

Nineteen eighty-three was one of the most bizarre growing seasons in recent years for the Bordelais. The flowering in June went well for the third straight year, ensuring a large crop. The weather in July was torrid and it turned out to be the hottest July on record. August became extremely hot, rainy, and humid, and as a result many vineyards began to have significant problems with mildew and rot. It was essential to spray almost weekly in August of 1983 to protect the vineyards. Those properties that did not spray diligently had serious problems with mildew-infected grapes. By the end of August, a dreadful month climatically, many pessimistic producers were apprehensively talking about a disastrous vintage like 1968 or 1965. September brought dry weather, plenty of heat, and no excessive rain. October provided exceptional weather as well, so the grapes harvested late were able to attain maximum ripeness under sunny, dry skies. Not since 1961 had the entire Bordeaux crop, white grapes and red grapes, been harvested in completely dry, fair weather.

Immediately, the Bordeaux wine trade began to stir up support for this vintage, calling it another great year. Some proprietors called it superior to 1982.

Now that I have had a chance to evaluate these wines on four separate trips to Bordeaux, I believe 1983 is indeed a great vintage for the wines of Margaux, some of the wines of St.-Emilion, and for the sweet wines of Barsac and Sauternes. In the other regions, there are of course some outstanding wines of great depth and richness, but the quality is extremely irregular.

In style and character, the 1983s are big, rich, alcoholic, full-bodied, aggressively tannic wines. The top wines are like the 1982 wines, rather atypically large-scaled by Bordeaux standards. In comparison with the 1982s, the wines tend to be less consistent and with much more aggressive, harsh tannins.

The best 1983s will be much less attractive in their youth than the 1982s. Nineteen eighty-three was also another excellent year for the Crus Bourgeois châteaux of Bordeaux. The greatest wines of the vintage at this early stage appear to be the following.

The Best Wines

St.-Emilion: Ausone, Canon, Cheval Blanc, Belair, Figeac, La Grave-Figeac, Clos des Jacobins, L'Arrosée, Pavie-Decesse

Pomerol: L'Evangile, Latour à Pomerol, Lafleur, L'Eglise-Clinet, Le Pin

Margaux: Margaux, Palmer, d'Issan, Prieuré-Lichine, Rausan-Ségla, Brane-Cantenac

St.-Julien: Léoville-Las Cases, Gruaud-Larose, Ducru-Beaucaillou, Léoville-Poyferré, St.-Pierre

Pauillac: Pichon-Lalande, Lafite-Rothschild, Mouton-Rothschild, Lynch-Bages

Southern Médoc: Cantemerle

Cru Bourgeois: Sociando-Mallet, Chasse-Spleen, d'Angludet, Haut-Marbuzet

Sauternes: Rieussec, Raymond-Lafon, Guiraud, Lafaurie-Peyraguey, Doisy-Daëne

With respect to anticipated maturity, most top 1983 red wines will need until 1993–1995 to develop properly. The dry white wines will drink well between 1985–1990, and the sweet wines will be at their best between 1990–2010.

In summary, 1983 is an abundant vintage of very good, sometimes outstanding wines that are quite large-scaled in size and weight. The vintage is, however, quite irregular, particularly in the northern Médoc, Pomerol, and Graves regions.

1982
(9–13–82)

Nineteen eighty-two is one of the greatest vintages of this century. The superb quality of the red wines produced in this vintage make it one vintage that must be held in the same class as the 1929, 1945, 1949, 1953, and 1961 vintages. From a purely hedonistic standpoint, the vintage has probably produced the most perfect and enjoyable wines in the post-World War II era. The vintage, in style and personality, is different from anything that preceded it, although many knowledgeable oldtimers in Bordeaux compare the 1982 Médocs to the 1953s, 1949s, and 1929s, the 1982 Graves to the 1959s, and the 1982 Pomerols to the 1947s. I am too young to have known what these great old vintages tasted like in their infancy, so I can neither confirm nor deny such statements. However, what I can be sure of is that never have technology and nature combined so dramatically and brilliantly to produce so many superlative wines. If some 1982s cannot claim to have the massive concentration of the top dozen or so 1961s, or if some cannot match up in sheer size, weight, and tannic ferocity with the top 1945s, they need not be ashamed. The 1982 Bordeaux overwhelm these two previous "vintages of the century" in most of the important criteria for greatness. The sheer magnitude in numbers of truly great wines that have been produced in this marvelous vintage is unparalleled in the history of Bordeaux.

Yet, for all its greatness, not every 1982 Bordeaux is miraculous. As in all vintages, there are wines which for reasons such as bad luck, overcropping, or just plain incompetence, have turned out to be less than special. In intensely studying this vintage over the last two and a half years, I have found that the major weakness is with the wines of Margaux, which are quite good. However, they will have to take a back seat to the excellent 1983s produced in this appellation. Nineteen eighty-two is also not a very good vintage for the sweet wines of Sauternes. There are a number of good wines from this region in 1982, but again 1983 is the vintage to get excited about for Barsacs and Sauternes. However, for the other major appellations of Bordeaux, Graves, St.-Julien, Pauillac, St.-Estèphe, Pomerol, and St.-Emilion, 1982 is unequivocally the finest Bordeaux vintage for red wines after 1961. If one compares the sheer number of great wines at all levels in Bordeaux with vintages such as 1961 or 1945, 1982 easily surpasses even those two vintages.

The reason why the 1982s are so remarkable was the outstanding weather conditions. The flowering occurred in remarkably sunny, dry, warm June weather, ensuring a large crop. July was very hot, and August slightly cooler than normal. By the beginning of September, everyone in Bordeaux was expecting excellent quality and a very large crop. However, in September a burst of intense heat, accompanied by dry, sunny days, sent sugars soaring in the grapes. In a span of three weeks, what looked to be a very good, very large vintage was transformed into a great vintage as the grapes were harvested at perfect maturity. The vinifications took place in hot wine cellars and were tricky as 24-hour monitoring of fermentations had to be maintained. However, the rumors of disasters from overheated fermentations have proved to be totally without substance, at least for the major estates that have the technology, equipment, and staff to monitor such things. Rain at the end of the harvest caught some Médoc properties with Cabernet Sauvignon still on the vine, but the extent of this has been of negligible effect on the final wine.

From the very beginning, the 1982s stood out as sensationally great wines. They were and continue to be characterized by the following personality traits that will no doubt follow them through their long lives.

1. They are very highly pigmented, densely colored wines with nuances of purple and dark ruby.
2. They are quite full-bodied, extremely concentrated wines that have masses of ripe, rich fruit.
3. They are very, very tannic, with the highest level of tannins of any

vintage since 1961. However, the tannins are ripe and round, thus creating a misleading impression that the wines are forward and will develop quickly.

4. They are high in alcohol, with an average alcoholic content of 12.5% for the Médocs, and 13.5% for the Pomerols and St.-Emilions.
5. They have average acidity levels, with a few St.-Emilions and Pomerols having below-average acidity levels.
6. They have remarkably penetrating aromas that are the most stunning I have ever experienced in a young Bordeaux wine.

On the negative side, those who love Bordeaux but did not move quickly to purchase these wines as wine futures in 1983 and 1984 must now pay a premium price that borders on the absurd for wines so young. As in any great vintage, insatiable worldwide demand and the entry of speculators into the market has been accompanied by shortages and astronomical price increases for the glamor wines of this vintage. Despite a very large crop, stocks of 1982s have dried up at an unparalleled rate.

There are so many great wines in this vintage that it may seem unfair to mention just the *crème de la crème*, but the following wines are certainly among the greatest wines produced in Bordeaux since 1945.

The Best Wines

St.-Emilion:	Cheval Blanc, Ausone, Canon, Figeac, Magdelaine, La Dominique, L'Arrosée
Pomerol:	Pétrus, La Grave Trigant de Boisset, Certan de May, Trotanoy, Lafleur, L'Evangile, Petit-Village, La Conseillante, Bon Pasteur, Le Gay, La Fleur-Pétrus
Margaux:	Margaux
St.-Julien:	Léoville-Las Cases, Gruaud-Larose, Ducru-Beaucaillou, Léoville-Barton, Branaire-Ducru, Léoville-Poyferré, Talbot
Pauillac:	Mouton-Rothschild, Latour, Lafite-Rothschild, Pichon Lalande, Lynch-Bages, Grand-Puy-Lacoste
St.-Estèphe:	Cos d'Estournel, Calon-Ségur, Haut-Marbuzet
Southern Médoc:	La Lagune
Graves:	Haut-Brion, La Mission-Haut-Brion, La Tour-Haut-Brion, Domaine de Chevalier
Cru Bourgeois:	Sociando-Mallet, Potensac
Sauternes:	Suduiraut, Raymond-Lafon, Bastor-Lamontagne

1981
(9–28–81)

This vintage has been labeled more "classic" than either 1983 or 1982. What classic means to those who call 1981 a classic vintage is that this year is a typically good Bordeaux vintage of medium-weight, well-balanced, graceful wines. Despite a dozen or so excellent wines, 1981 is in reality only a good vintage, surpassed in quality by both 1982 and 1983, and also by 1978 and 1979.

Nineteen eighty-one could have been an outstanding vintage had it not been for heavy rains that fell just as the harvest was about to start. There was a dilution of the intensity of flavor in the grapes as heavy rains drenched the vineyards between October 1 and 5, and again between October 9 and 15. Up until then, the summer had been perfect. The flowering occurred under excellent conditions; July was cool, but August and September hot and dry. One can only speculate, but had it not rained, 1981, as well as 1982, might well have also turned out to be one of the greatest vintages in the post-World War II era.

Nineteen eighty-one did produce a large crop of generally well-colored wines of medium body, medium weight, and moderate tannin. The dry white wines have turned out well, but the Barsacs and Sauternes suffered as a result of the rains.

The regions that seem to have turned out the best wines in the Médoc? Certainly St.-Julien, Pauillac, and Margaux lead the way with more successes than other Bordeaux appellations.

The 1981s are likely to mature quite rapidly. The wines have average to below average acidity levels, but nowhere near the concentration and tannin levels of the two subsequent vintages, 1982 and 1983. I would fully expect the great majority of red Bordeaux to be fully mature by 1990.

There are not many truly superb wines, but certainly the following are wonderfully made wines that represent the best of the bunch in 1981.

The Best Wines

St.-Emilion: Cheval Blanc
Pomerol: Pétrus, La Conseillante, Certan de May, Le Pin, Vieux Château Certan
Margaux: Margaux, Giscours, d'Issan
St.-Julien: Ducru-Beaucaillou, Léoville-Las Cases, Gruaud-Larose, St.-Pierre

Pauillac:	Latour, Lafite-Rothschild, Pichon Lalande, Mouton-Rothschild
St.-Estèphe:	Cos d'Estournel
Graves:	La Mission-Haut-Brion, Haut-Brion
Cru Bourgeois:	Haut-Marbuzet, Brillette, Chasse-Spleen
Sauternes:	d'Yquem, de Fargues, Rieussec, Raymond-Lafon, Lafaurie-Peyraguey

1980
(10–14–80)

Sandwiched in between a succession of fine vintages, the 1980 Bordeaux crop has been a forgotten stepchild. However, the adventurous wine enthusiast can probably tell a few tales about some surprisingly soft, supple wines that were much tastier than any critic led him or her to believe.

Nineteen eighty was a late harvest that suffered from a poor summer, particularly the terrible flowering that diminished the size of the Merlot crop. The weather improved dramatically in September, which allowed the grapes to mature; however, the vintage that commenced on October 14 met with rain once again.

The resulting wines are light, some are rather diluted and disappointing, but a number of sound, fruity, supple wines were produced that, if well chosen, offer immediate drinkability and charm. A great wine was made at Margaux, which continued its record of producing one of the finest wines of the vintage since the Mentzelopoulos family took over this estate in 1977. If the vintage was decidedly uninspiring for red wines, the late-harvest sweet wines of Barsac and Sauternes turned out quite well, with most properties picking into late November under ideal weather conditions.

Most 1980s are fully mature now, but only a handful of them will last until 1990. The best wines of the vintage include the following.

The Best Wines

St.-Emilion:	Cheval Blanc, La Dominique
Pomerol:	Pétrus
Margaux:	Margaux, Giscours, d'Issan
St.-Julien:	Langoa-Barton, Branaire-Ducru, Léoville-Barton, Talbot, Gruaud-Larose
Pauillac:	Pichon Lalande, Latour, Lafite-Rothschild

St.-Estèphe: Cos d'Estournel
Graves: Domaine de Chevalier, La Mission-Haut-Brion
Cru Bourgeois: Ramage La Batisse, Siran, Chasse-Spleen
Sauternes: d'Yquem, de Fargues, Climens

1979
(10–3–79)

Nineteen seventy-nine has proved to be one of the useful vintages of Bordeaux wines. Not only was the crop enormous in size, but the quality was quite good. I thought the wines were a trifle light when I first did my cask tastings of this vintage in late March 1980, particularly when tasted against the fuller-bodied, richer 1978s. However, the wines have continued to put on weight and richness during their time in both cask and bottle, and while not big, rich, full-bodied wines, the 1979s are graceful, nicely concentrated, well-balanced wines that are very pleasing.

The weather conditions that led up to the 1979 harvest were hardly exceptional. The summer was unusually cold, but thankfully quite dry. The harvest did not start until early October. The weather during the harvest was mixed, with generally good weather interlaced with showery periods. The grapes were considered healthy and mature in all regions of Bordeaux.

The initial reaction was that 1979 was a "Merlot year" and that therefore the top successes were in Pomerol and St. Emilion. One of the first Bordeaux experts to take exception to that point of view was the English Master of Wine, Clive Coates, who argued that it was the Médoc that had succeeded more than the right bank. Time has proved him to be right. The top wines seem to be concentrated in the appellations of Margaux, St.-Julien, and Pauillac.

The 1979 red wines have shown consistently well in tastings. They are not powerful wines, but rather fruity, medium-bodied wines with good concentration and moderate tannins. Most of these wines will be fully mature and ready to drink between 1988–1996. The top wines will of course last longer.

For the sweet white wines, the late harvest permitted enough botrytis to form so that some successful wines were made. However, most of the Barsacs and Sauternes are not as good as the 1980s.

The following are the top wines of the 1979 vintage that have consistently outperformed the others in my tastings.

The Best Wines

St. Emilion: Canon, Cheval Blanc, Ausone, Pavie
Pomerol: Pétrus, Certain de May, Lafleur, Trotanoy, L'Evangile, La Tour à Pomerol
Margaux: Margaux, Giscours, Palmer, du Tertre
St.-Julien: Gruaud-Larose, Léoville-Las Cases, St.-Pierre
Pauillac: Lafite-Rothschild, Latour, Pichon Lalande
St.-Estèphe: Cos d'Estournel
Graves: Haut-Brion, La Mission-Haut-Brion, Domaine de Chevalier, Haut-Bailly
Cru Bourgeois: Chasse-Spleen, Gloria, Meyney, Haut-Marbuzet
Sauternes: d'Yquem, de Fargues

1978
(10–7–78)

Nineteen seventy-eight turned out to be an excellent vintage for the red wines of the Médoc and Graves, a good vintage for the red wines of St.-Emilion and Pomerol, and a fair vintage for the sweet white wines of Barsac and Sauternes. Extremely poor weather throughout the spring, June, July, and the first part of August had many growers thinking of a repeat of the poor vintage of 1977. However, in mid-August the weather became sunny, hot, and dry. For the next 9 weeks this weather continued virtually uninterrupted except for some light rain. The harvest commenced very late, October 7, and the grapes were brought in under ideal conditions. The astonishing turnaround in the weather and the resulting excellent vintage caused Harry Waugh, the peripatetic English wine authority, to dub the vintage the "miracle vintage," a name that has stuck to it.

The top red wines of 1978 have almost always come from the Médoc and Graves. The wines of Pomerol and St.-Emilion, with a few exceptions, seem noticeably less successful, although they are certainly good. The 1978s at first appeared intensely fruity, very deeply colored, moderately tannic, and medium- to full-bodied. In style and character they seemed to resemble the lovely wines of the 1970 vintage. However, like most fine vintages of Bordeaux, the 1978s have closed up in the bottle and seem to really need at least another 4–5 years of cellaring to be at their best. Most of the top wines of 1978 should be fully mature by 1990–2000.

The lesser Crus Bourgeois of 1978 are less successful in this vintage than in more recent vintages such as 1982 and 1983.

As for the sweet wines in Sauternes and Barsac, this was a difficult year, and most of the wines lack the honeyed botrytis character.

There are numerous top 1978s and the following wines will provide tremendous enjoyment since they are the best of this vintage.

The Best Wines

St.-Emilion:	Cheval Blanc, Magdelaine, Figeac
Pomerol:	Pétrus, Latour à Pomerol, Trotanoy
Margaux:	Palmer, Margaux, Malescot St.-Exupéry
St.-Julien:	Ducru-Beaucaillou, Gruaud-Larose, Léoville-Barton, Beychevelle
Pauillac:	Latour, Mouton-Rothschild, Pichon Lalande, Lynch-Bages, Pontet-Canet
St.-Estèphe:	Montrose, de Pez, Cos D'Estournel
Southern Médoc:	Cantemerle
Graves:	La Mission-Haut-Brion, Haut-Brion, Haut-Bailly, Pape-Clément

1977
(10–3–77)

The worst vintage for Bordeaux between 1973 and 1985. A wet, cold summer played havoc with the crop. In addition, the Merlot crop was devastated by a spring frost. While warm, dry weather arrived prior to the harvest, there was just not enough of it to save the vintage, although given the raw materials several wines did turn out to be relatively decent. Nineteen seventy-seven was also a very poor year for the sweet-wine producers.

Should one find any of the 1977s listed below, the wine should be drunk over the next 2–3 years. They will not last. Most of the wines are rather high in acidity, with herbaceous, vegetal aromas and flavors. The following are some of the more successful wines produced for the vintage, although I cannot personally recommend any of them.

The Best Wines

St.-Emilion: Figeac
Margaux: Giscours, Margaux
St.-Julien: Ducru-Beaucaillou, Talbot, Gruaud-Larose
Pauillac: Pichon Lalande, Latour
St.-Estèphe: Cos d'Estournel
Southern Médoc: La Lagune
Graves: La Mission-Haut-Brion, Domaine de Chevalier

1976
(9–13–76)

Nineteen seventy-six was a very highly publicized vintage that has never quite lived up to its reputation. All the ingredients were present for a superb vintage. The harvest date of September 13 was the earliest harvest since 1945. The weather during the summer had been torridly hot, with the average temperatures for the months of June through September only exceeded by the hot summers of 1949 and 1947. However, with many *vignerons* predicting a "vintage of the century," very heavy rains fell between September 11 and 15, bloating the grapes.

The crop that was harvested was very large, the grapes were very ripe, and while the wines had good tannin levels, the acidity levels were low and the pH dangerously high. The top wines of 1976 offer wonderfully soft, supple, fruity drinking now and certainly can be said to have more charm than their much more publicized siblings (the 1975s) that preceded this vintage. At present, the top 1976s are among the most enjoyable clarets for drinking in 1985–1990 as these wines have matured very rapidly.

However, many 1976s, lacking color from the beginning and being very fragile, have taken on a disturbing brown cast to their color, while others have in fact lapsed into premature senility long before their tenth birthday. For the red wines, the vintage is strongest in St.-Julien, Pauillac, St.-Estèphe, and Margaux. It is weakest in Graves.

This vintage can offer wonderful wine for drinking now, but one must select his or her 1976s very, very carefully.

As for the sweet wines, it is an excellent vintage—rich, intense, full-bodied wines with plenty of botrytis and character.

The following are the top 1976s. With few exceptions, these are wines that are ideal for drinking over the next 4 years because few will still be alive by 1990.

The Best Wines

St.-Emilion: Ausone, Figeac, Cheval Blanc, Clos des Jacobins
Pomerol: Latour à Pomerol, Pétrus, Trotanoy, La Grave Trigant de Boisset
Margaux: Giscours, Palmer, d'Issan
St.-Julien: Branaire-Ducru, Ducru-Beaucaillou, Talbot, Beychevelle, Gloria, Léoville-Las Cases
Pauillac: Lafite-Rothschild, Pichon Lalande, Haut-Bages-Libéral, Latour
St.-Estèphe: Montrose, Cos d'Estournel
Southern Médoc: La Lagune
Graves: Haut-Brion
Cru Bourgeois: de Pez
Sauternes: d'Yquem, Suduiraut, de Fargues, Rieussec, Climens, Nairac, Guiraud

1975
(9–22–75)

Nineteen seventy-five was conceived in a climate in which Bordeaux had just had three large, generally poor or mediocre crops, 1972, 1973, and 1974. The 1975 crop was small as a result of spring frosts and because many growers zealously pruned their vines for fear of another big crop like 1974. July, August, and September were hot, but not excessively so. However, the latter two months were punctuated by several huge thunderstorms that delivered enormous amounts of rainfall. In fact, when one looks at the rainfall in the critical months of August and September, it was approximately the same as that of Bordeaux's worst vintages, 1969, 1968, and 1965. This caused some observers to question those who claimed that 1975 was the best Bordeaux vintage after 1961.

The harvest began on September 22 and continued until mid-October in good weather except for a hail storm that ravaged the central Médoc communes of Avensan, Moulis, Arcins, and Lamarque.

While the vintage has been highly touted, a thorough examination of all the top wines in April 1984 left me with the conclusion that while some very great wines were produced, 1975 is much more irregular in quality than initially believed.

The wines continue to be brutally tannic, full-bodied, and very backward and closed. The top wines have the richness and depth of fruit, and dark color to go along with the high astringent tannins. Other wines surprisingly lack color and seem to have an excess of tannin. Certainly, the 1975 vintage will provide some of the longest-lived Bordeaux wines in the last three decades, but unfortunately it will also provide a significant number of major disappointments.

Of all the major communes, the wines of Pauillac and Pomerol appear to be the most successful. These wines need a full 5–10 more years of cellaring as I do not expect most of the great 1975s to be mature before 1992–1995.

With regard to the Sauternes, this was an excellent vintage, with just about every estate producing a fine wine.

The following are the superb examples of this vintage.

The Best Wines

St.-Emilion: Cheval Blanc, Figeac, Magdelaine, Balestard-La-Tonnelle, Soutard, Cadet-Piola

Pomerol: Pétrus, Lafleur, Trotanoy, L'Evangile, La Fleur-Pétrus, Le Gay, L'Enclos, Vieux Château Certan

Margaux: Giscours, Palmer

St.-Julien: Léoville-Las Cases, Branaire-Ducru, Léoville-Barton, Gruaud-Larose, Gloria, Langoa-Barton

Pauillac: Latour, Lafite-Rothschild, Mouton-Rothschild, Pichon Lalande, Haut-Bages-Libéral

St.-Estèphe: Calon-Ségur

Southern Médoc: La Lagune

Graves: La Mission-Haut-Brion, La Tour-Haut-Brion

Cru Bourgeois: Haut-Marbuzet, Sociando-Mallet, Meyney

Sauternes: d'Yquem, de Fargues, Climens, Rieussec, Raymond-Lafon

1974
(9–20–74)

While the crop size was large in 1974 as a result of a good flowering and dry, sunny May and June, the weather from late August through October was rainy. Despite the persistent soggy conditions, some surprisingly good wines were made in Graves, which is clearly the vintage's most successful appellation. Most 1974s are rather hard, tannic, hollow wines that lack flesh and richness. They have kept fairly well because of their good tannin and acidity levels, but overall these wines have little to offer unless you can come across one of those listed below.

The vintage was terrible in the Barsac and Sauternes regions and many properties declassified their entire crop.

The Best Wines

St.-Emilion: Figeac
Pomerol: Trotanoy
St.-Julien: Branaire-Ducru, Gruaud-Larose, Ducru-Beaucaillou
Pauillac: Latour
Graves: La Mission-Haut-Brion, Domaine de Chevalier, Haut-Brion

1973
(9–20–73)

At one time in the mid-1970s, the 1973s had some value as agreeably light, soft, simple Bordeaux wines. Today, except for a handful of wines such as Latour and Pétrus, these wines have faded into oblivion.

Nineteen seventy-three was another Bordeaux vintage in which the summer had been just fine and all of Bordeaux was set for a big crop of good-quality grapes. However, as so often happens in the region, the heavens opened up, and in the course of the three weeks that followed the commencement date of the harvest on September 20, a good vintage was turned into a rain-bloated, swollen crop of mediocre grapes. The crop size was large, but the wines lacked color, extract, acidity, and backbone. The great majority of wines were ready to drink when released in 1976, and by 1979 many of them were beginning to fall apart. Nevertheless, there were some good, round, fruity wines to be found that had some concentration to them. However, buying any 1973s now would be extremely dangerous unless it were Pétrus (clearly the wine of the vintage) or Latour.

As a general rule, the sweet wines of Barsac and Sauternes turned out a little better, but most of them should have been drunk by now.

The Best Wines

Pomerol: Pétrus, Latour à Pomerol, Trotanoy
Margaux: Giscours
St.-Julien: Ducru-Beaucaillou, Beychevelle
Pauillac: Latour
St.-Estèphe: Montrose, de Pez
Graves: La Tour-Haut-Brion
Sauternes: d'Yquem

1972
(10–7–72)

The weather pattern of 1972 was one of unusually cool, cloudy summer months with an abnormally rainy month of August. While September brought dry, warm weather, it was too late to salvage the crop. Nineteen seventy-two produced the worst wines of the decade, acidic, green, raw, and vegetal tasting. Their high acidity has indeed kept many of them alive, but their deficiencies are too great for mere age to overcome. As with any poor vintage, some châteaux managed to produce wines far better than their neighbors'. In 1972 there were only a half-dozen or so wines worthy of consumer interest, and then only at very low prices. Certainly, no one appellation in 1972 did better or worse than any other.

The Best Wines

St.-Emilion: Cheval Blanc, Figeac
Pomerol: Trotanoy
Margaux: Rausan-Ségla, Giscours
St.-Julien: Branaire-Ducru, Léoville-Las Cases
Pauillac: Latour
Graves: La Mission-Haut-Brion
Sauternes: Climens

1971
(9–25–71)

Unlike 1970, 1971 was a rather small vintage because of a poor flowering in June that caused a significant reduction in the Merlot crop. By the end of the harvest, the crop size was a good 40% less than the huge crop of 1970.

Early reports of the vintage have proved to be overly enthusiastic. Some experts, relying on the small production yields when compared to 1970, even claimed that the vintage was better than 1970. This has proved to be totally false. Certainly the 1971s were forward and delicious, as were the 1970s when first released, but unlike the 1970s, the 1971s lacked the great depth of color, concentration, and tannic backbone. The vintage was rather mixed in the Médoc, but it was certainly a fine year for Pomerol, St.-Emilion and Graves.

Buying 1971s now is quite dangerous. There are only a few wines that are not fully mature, and even such superb wines as Pétrus, Latour, Trotanoy, La Mission-Haut-Brion, and Haut-Brion, all examples of very well-preserved wines from this vintage, are not likely to improve much more. Yet, when the top 1971s have been well cellared, they can provide the best *current* drinking of any vintage in the 1970s.

Nineteen seventy-one was originally portrayed as one of the really fine years that gets overlooked because of the publicity and hoopla given to the vintage that preceded it, in this case, the marvelous 1970. This is a vintage that is very irregular. There are a handful of really sensational wines to go along with a horde of mediocre ones. The sweet wines of Barsac and Sauternes were extremely successful, and contrary to their red siblings, the white wines have aged beautifully and will easily outlast the great majority of the red wines produced in 1971.

The Best Wines

St.-Emilion: La Dominique, Cheval Blanc
Pomerol: Pétrus, Trotanoy, Lafleur, La Fleur-Pétrus
Margaux: Palmer, Giscours
St.-Julien: Talbot, Beychevelle, Ducru-Beaucaillou
Paullac: Latour, Mouton-Rothschild
St.-Estèphe: Montrose
Graves: Haut-Brion, La Mission-Haut-Brion
Sauternes: d'Yquem, Climens, de Fargues, Coutet

1970
(9–27–70)

Between the two great vintages 1961 and 1982, 1970 has proved to be the best vintage. The wines are more attractive and charming than the austere 1966s and hard, tannic, big 1975s. Nineteen seventy was an unusual vintage in that it consisted of high volume and very high quality. It was a splendidly uniform and consistent vintage throughout Bordeaux, with every appellation being able to claim its share of superstars. It was also an outstanding year for the lesser growths of Bordeaux.

The weather conditions during the summer and fall of 1970 were perfect. There was no hail, no weeks of drenching downpours, no frost, and no spirit-crushing deluge at harvest time. Everything went well and the Bordelais harvested one of the biggest and healthiest crops of grapes ever.

From the earliest days the wines showed great color, an intense richness of fruit, full body, and good tannin. However, because the wines showed so well young, some writers began to say that these wines were precocious, that they were a product of the "*nouvelle vinification*" and would not last until 1980. History has recorded that some of the greatest Bordeaux vintages, 1929, 1947, 1949, 1953, and 1961, all showed extremely well young, causing many so-called experts to falsely assume that they would not last. Like these older vintages, the 1970s have slowed down in development, and in 1985 many of the top wines have still not reached their mature plateau.

With regard to the sweet wines, they were not as good as the 1971s, but certainly successful.

The 1970s will provide one of the greatest levels of enjoyment of high-quality Bordeaux for years to come. In the last 25 years, only two vintages, 1982 and 1961, can lay claim to being better than this marvelous vintage.

The Best Wines

St.-Emilion: Cheval Blanc, Figeac, Magdelaine, L'Arroseé
Pomerol: Pétrus, La Conseillante, Trotanoy, Latour à Pomerol, La Fleur-Pétrus, L'Evangile, Lafleur
Margaux: Palmer, Giscours, Rausan-Ségla, Lascombes
St.-Julien: Ducru-Beaucaillou, Léoville-Barton, Gloria, Gruaud-Larose, Branaire-Ducru, St.-Pierre, Langoa-Barton
Pauillac: Mouton-Rothschild, Latour, Pichon Lalande, Lynch-Bages, Haut-Batailley
St.-Estèphe: Montrose, Lafon-Rochet, Cos d'Estournel
Southern Médoc: La Lagune
Graves: La Mission-Haut-Brion, Domaine de Chevalier, Haut-Bailly
Cru Bourgeois: de Pez, Sociando-Mallet, Chasse-Spleen, Fourcas-Hosten, Poujeaux, Les-Ormes-de-Pez, Meyney
Sauternes: d'Yquem

1969
(10–6–69)

After Bordeaux has suffered through a disastrous vintage like that of 1968, there has always been a tendency to lavish false praise on the next vintage. No doubt Bordeaux, after a horrible year in 1968, badly wanted a fine vintage in 1969, but despite some overly optimistic proclamations by some leading Bordeaux experts at the time of the vintage, 1969 has turned out to be one of the least attractive vintages for Bordeaux wines in the last two decades.

The crop was small, and while the summer was sufficiently hot and dry to ensure a decent maturity, torrential September rains dashed everyone's hopes for a good vintage, except some investors who irrationally moved in to buy these insipid, nasty, acidic, sharp wines. Consequently, the 1969s, along with being extremely unattractive wines, were quite expensive when they first appeared on the market.

I can honestly say I have never tasted a red wine in 1969 I didn't dislike. Harsh and hollow, with no flesh, fruit, or charm, it is hard to imagine that any of these wines could have turned out palatable.

In the Barsac and Sauternes region, a few proprietors managed to produce acceptable wines.

1968
(9–20–68)

Nineteen sixty-eight was another of the very poor vintages the Bordelais had to suffer through in the decade of the '60s. The culprit, as usual, was heavy rains (it was the wettest year since 1951) that bloated the grapes. However, there have been some 1968s that I found much better than anything produced in 1969, a vintage with a "better" (I am not sure that is the right word to use) reputation. Should anyone run across these wines today, the rule of *caveat emptor* would seemingly be very applicable as I doubt that any of these wines would have much left to them.

The Best Wines

St.-Emilion:	Figeac
Margaux:	Giscours
St.-Julien:	Talbot, Gruaud-Larose
Pauillac:	Latour, Les Forts de Latour
Southern Médoc:	Cantemerle
Graves:	La Mission-Haut-Brion, Haut-Brion

1967
(9–25–67)

Nineteen sixty-seven can hardly be considered a great or even a very good vintage, but it was a useful, large vintage of soft, quick-maturing wines that provided agreeable drinking between 1970 and 1978. Most 1967s should have been consumed by the start of this present decade, although a handful of wines like Latour, Pétrus, Trotanoy, and Palmer should continue to give pleasure for at least another 5 years.

The strongest wines of 1967 were produced in the right bank communes of Pomerol and St.-Emilion, as well as the Graves and the Sauternes.

Should one find some of the top wines itemized below in large-format bottles (magnums, double magnums, etc.), they could well provide lovely drinking.

The Best Wines

St.-Emilion:	Cheval Blanc, Magdelaine, Pavie, Canon
Pomerol:	Pétrus, Trotanoy, La Fleur-Pétrus, La Violette
Margaux:	Palmer, Giscours
St.-Julien:	Gruaud-Larose, Ducru-Beaucaillou
Pauillac:	Latour, Pichon Lalande
St.-Estèphe:	Montrose, Calon-Ségur
Southern Médoc:	La Lagune, Cantemerle
Graves:	La Mission-Haut-Brion, Haut-Brion, Haut-Bailly
Sauternes:	d'Yquem, Suduiraut

1966
(9–26–66)

While there is general agreement that 1966 is the best vintage of the decade of the '60s after 1961, the vintage has not developed as well as many of its proponents would have liked. The wines, now coming up on their twentieth birthday, have never really blossomed. Many remain rather austere, lean, unyielding, tannic wines that seem to be in danger of losing their fruit before their tannin. This seems rather surprising in view of the early reports on the vintage which called the wines precocious, charming, and early maturing. Yet, if the vintage is not as consistent as believed, there were some wonderfully rich, well-balanced, medium-weight classic wines produced in 1966. The Médoc is clearly the strongest region for the top wines of this vintage, but there are many successes in Pomerol as well. It was a mediocre year for the wines of Barsac and Sauternes.

With regard to the climatic conditions that shaped the vintage, the flowering in June went slowly, July and August were intermittently hot and cold, and September dry and sunny. A large crop was harvested under sound weather conditions.

Most 1966s should continue to drink well for another decade, although I worry that the less-balanced wines will dry out. This is a very good vintage, but selection is extremely important.

The Best Wines

St.-Emilion: Cheval Blanc, Canon
Pomerol: Pétrus, Trotanoy, Latour à Pomerol
Margaux: Palmer, Giscours, Lascombes
St.-Julien: Léoville-Las Cases, Gruaud-Larose, Branaire-Ducru, Léoville-Barton, Beychevelle, Ducru-Beaucaillou
Pauillac: Latour, Mouton-Rothschild, Pichon Lalande
St.-Estèphe: Montrose
Southern Médoc: La Lagune, Cantemerle
Graves: La Mission-Haut-Brion, Pape-Clément, Domaine de Chevalier

1965
(10–2–65)

The vintage of rot and rain. I have had little experience tasting the 1965s. It is considered by most experts to be one of the worst vintages in the post-World War II era. A wet summer was bad enough, but what was the undoing of this vintage was an incredibly wet and humid September that caused rot to voraciously devour the vineyards. It should be obvious that these wines are to be avoided.

1964
(9–22–64)

One of the most intriguing vintages of Bordeaux, 1964 produced a number of splendid, generally underrated and underpriced wines in Pomerol, St.-Emilion, and Graves where many proprietors had the good fortune to have harvested their crops before the rainy deluge began on October 8. Because of this downpour, which caught many Médoc châteaux with unharvested vineyards, the vintage has never been regarded as a top Bordeaux vintage. While the vintage can be notoriously bad for some of the properties of the Médoc and the late-harvesting Barsac and Sauternes estates, the vintage is excellent to outstanding for the three appellations of Pomerol, St.-Emilion, and Graves.

The summer had been extremely hot and dry, and when the harvest commenced many proprietors thought that a great vintage was in the making. Since the Merlot grape ripens first, the harvest began in the areas where this is planted in abundance, St.-Emilion and Pomerol. When the rains came, not all of the Médoc properties were still picking. Consequently, there were some excellent wines made in the Médoc, but because of the famous failures such as Lafite-Rothschild, Mouton-Rothschild, Lynch-Bages, Calon-Ségur and Margaux, many wine enthusiasts have apprehensively shied away from the vintage.

The successful wines are quite rich, full-bodied, concentrated wines that are more deeply colored and significantly richer than the leaner, more austere 1966s. While most of the 1964s are now at full maturity, they will certainly hold another 5 years. Incredibly, I have enjoyed the best wines of 1964 more than the best wines of 1966, a vintage with a much greater reputation than 1964.

The Best Wines

St.-Emilion: Cheval Blanc, Figeac, Magdelaine, L'Arrosée, Soutard
Pomerol: Pétrus, Trotanoy, Vieux Château Certan, Lafleur, La Conseillante, L'Evangile
St.-Julien: Gruaud-Larose
Pauillac: Latour, Pichon Lalande
St.-Estèphe: Montrose, de Pez
Southern Médoc: La Lagune
Graves: La Mission-Haut-Brion, Haut-Brion, Haut-Bailly

1963
(10–7–63)

The Bordelais have never been able to decide whether 1963 or 1965 was the worse vintage of the '60s. Rain and rot, as in 1965, were the ruination of this vintage. I have not seen a bottle of 1963 (even in France) for over a decade.

1962
(10–1–62)

Coming after the great vintage of 1961, it could be expected that 1962 would be underrated, but this vintage would appear to be the most undervalued Bordeaux vintage of the last three decades. Elegant, supple, very fruity wines, the 1962s were neither too tannic nor too big, but consistently pleasurable and charming. Because of their balance, they have kept longer than anyone ever imagined, and while all the 1962s now require drinking up, the well-cellared top wines of the vintage can be kept for several more years.

The crop size was large in 1962 due to a hot and sunny summer with just enough rain. The wines drank well when young and surprised everyone that they still were going strong when they passed their tenth birthday in 1972.

Nineteen sixty-two is an especially good year for the sweet wines of Barsac and Sauternes, which are now at their decadently rich best.

The Best Wines

St.-Emilion:	Magdelaine, Figeac
Pomerol:	Trotanoy, Pétrus, Lafleur, La Violette
Margaux:	Palmer
St.-Julien:	Ducru-Beaucaillou, Gruaud-Larose
Pauillac:	Latour, Mouton-Rothschild, Lynch-Bages, Pichon Lalande
St.-Estèphe:	Montrose
Southern Médoc:	Cantemerle
Graves:	Haut-Brion, La Mission-Haut-Brion, Pape-Clément
Sauternes:	d'Yquem

1961
(9–22–61)

Until the advent of the 1982 vintage, there was little one could offer to refute the argument that 1961 was the finest vintage in the post-World War II era. Even though the 1982s are differently styled, the best of them will be able to hold their own with the finest 1961s. The 1961s have sensational concentration, magnificent penetrating bouquets of ripe fruit, rich, deep, long flavors, and outstandingly deep colors. Even though they are now 24 years old, the top wines can age for at least another decade, and the very best wines will still be marvelous by the year 2000.

The weather pattern was nearly perfect in 1961, with spring frosts reducing the crop size and then sunny, hot weather throughout the summer and the harvest, resulting in splendid maturity levels for the grapes. The small harvest guaranteed high prices for these wines, and today's prices for 1961s make them the equivalent of liquid gold.

The vintage was excellent throughout all appellations of Bordeaux except for the Barsacs and Sauternes, which have benefited greatly from the vintage's reputation, but are in reality quite mediocre. Some of the St.-Emilions are also not what they might have been because the vineyards there had not fully recovered from the killer freeze of 1956.

The Best Wines

St.-Emilion:	Cheval Blanc, Magdelaine, Figeac
Pomerol:	Pétrus, Latour à Pomerol, Trotanoy
Margaux:	Palmer, Margaux, Malescot St.-Exupéry
St.-Julien:	Ducru-Beaucaillou, Gruaud-Larose, Léoville-Barton, Beychevelle
Pauillac:	Latour, Mouton-Rothschild, Pichon Lalande, Lynch-Bages, Pontet-Canet
St.-Estèphe:	Cos d'Estournel Montrose, de Pez
Southern Médoc:	Cantemerle
Graves:	La Mission-Haut-Brion, Haut-Brion, Haut-Bailly, Pape-Clément

THE BORDEAUX VINTAGE GUIDE

A vintage chart should be regarded as a general overall rating of a particular viticultural region. Such charts are filled with exceptions to the rule—astonishingly good wines from skillful or lucky vintners in years rated mediocre, and thin, diluted, characterless wines from incompetent or greedy producers in great years.

My guide to Bordeaux vintages is divided into the six major or principal winemaking appellations for the simple reason that these six regions all have distinctive microclimates, different soil, and different percentages of the major grape varieties planted. The ratings and general comments about drinkability are based on the state of these wines today, and all of the ratings and statements about anticipated maturity are based on the assumption that the wine was purchased in a healthy, sound condition, and stored in a relatively cool (below 65°F), dark, vibration- and odor-free location.

REGION	*1984*	*1983*	*1982*	*1981*	*1980*	*1979*	*1978*	*1977*
Pomerol	72T	85T	98T	85T	75R	85R	83R	65C
St.-Emilion	60C	90T	95T	75R	72R	82R	84R	70R
Graves	75T	84T	95T	84T	75R	85T	90T	72R

REGION	*1984*	*1983*	*1982*	*1981*	*1980*	*1979*	*1978*	*1977*
S. Médoc, Margaux	78T	95T	88T	85T	78R	85T	90T	70R
N. Médoc, St.-Julien, Pauillac, St.-Estèphe	78T	88VT	98VT	85T	75R	85T	90T	72R
Sauternes	70C	95T	78R	84R	85R	80R	82R	65C

REGION	*1976*	*1975*	*1974*	*1973*	*1972*	*1971*	*1970*	*1969*
Pomerol	75VR	90T	79VR	75VR	65X	85VR	90R	55X
St.-Emilion	75VR	85R	72C	70X	60X	84VR	86R	55X
Graves	70VR	82T	83VR	68X	70C	85VR	90R	60X
S. Médoc, Margaux	83VR	87T	72VR	73X	62X	82VR	90R	60X
N. Médoc, St.-Julien, Pauillac, St.-Estèphe	84VR	88VT	74VR	75VR	60X	82VR	90T	60X
Sauternes	90R	93R	60C	73X	70C	87R	86R	65X

REGION	*1968*	*1967*	*1966*	*1965*	*1964*	*1963*	*1962*	*1961*
Pomerol	58X	86VR	82R	58X	90R	55X	84VR	90R
St.-Emilion	60X	84VR	82R	50X	89R	50X	84VR	88R
Graves	62X	85VR	87R	60X	90R	50X	84VR	98R
S. Médoc, Margaux	60X	80VR	85R	50X	75VR	50X	85VR	92R
N. Médoc, St.-Julien, Pauillac, St.-Estèphe	60X	78VR	86R	50X	75VR	50X	86VR	98R
Sauternes	50X	87R	80R	58X	60X	50X	87R	78R

KEY

T = Tannic; most wines need to age for 5–10 more years.
VT = Very tannic; most wines need a minimum of 10 more years.
R = Most wines are just entering their fully mature period. In vintages rated 85 or better, these wines can be expected to last 5–10 years at this plateau.
VR = Most wines have been mature for several years and should be consumed immediately over the next 4 years.
C = A very difficult vintage. The wine should be avoided, or chosen with great care.
X = Most wines are probably too old.

3: EVALUATING THE WINES OF BORDEAUX

The Haut-Médoc starts several miles north of the city of Bordeaux at the commercial town of Blanquefort, and runs north through the officially recognized appellations of Margaux, Moulis, Listrac, St.-Julien, Pauillac, and St.-Estèphe, where it ends. The area to the north is known as the Médoc, formerly called the Bas-Médoc.

The Haut-Médoc is Bordeaux's most famous region. A glance at a map reveals virtually all of the famous names of the aristocratic châteaux that have for more than a century dominated the wine talk coming from connoisseurs' lips. The first impression that a visitor gets after finding the famous Route du Vin (numbered D2) that runs through the heart of Bordeaux's vineyards is of a rather plain, flat, gravelly landscape that seems congested with famous châteaux and vineyards. In fact, the most obvious things are the absence of forests, the flat gravelly land, and utter congestion of one château sitting right next to another.

The close proximity of such famous vineyards is best exemplified by the half-mile stretch of D2 that runs from St.-Julien to the Pauillac border. The visitor is startled by the close proximity of such fabled château names. Within a three-minute drive are Léoville-Las Cases, Léoville-Poyferré, Pichon Lalande, Pichon Baron, and Latour, all sandwiched together on this short strip of road.

Haut-Médoc wines are not only Bordeaux's most famous wines, but also the most expensive. In the 1855 classification, 60 châteaux out of 61 châteaux listed in that historic classification as the best Bordeaux had to offer were from the Haut-Médoc.

ST.-ESTÈPHE

Of all the wines produced in the Haut-Médoc, those of St.-Estèphe have the reputation for being the slowest to mature, and the toughest, most tannic wines. While this generalization may have been true 20 or 30 years ago, the wines now being made in St.-Estèphe show an increasing reliance on the softer, fleshier Merlot grape, and a vinification aimed at producing more supple, earlier-maturing wines.

St.-Estèphe has the least prestige of all the well known Haut-Médoc appellations of Margaux, Pauillac, and St.-Julien. In the 1855 classification, only five wines were considered outstanding enough to be included. Of these five fortunate properties, two estates, Cos d'Estournel and Montrose, were ranked as second-growths, Calon-Ségur was classified as a third-growth, Lafon-Rochet a fourth-growth, and Cos Labory a fifth-growth. This commune, the most northern of the Haut-Médoc, is, however, blessed with numerous Cru Bourgeois châteaux. In fact, St.-Estèphe has a number of Cru Bourgeois châteaux that are currently making wine equal to many classified growths. Some of these Cru Bourgeois estates are certainly producing better wine than two of the five classified growths in St.-Estèphe. In any reclassification of St.-Estèphe, Cos Labory for one would be hard pressed to keep its standing, whereas

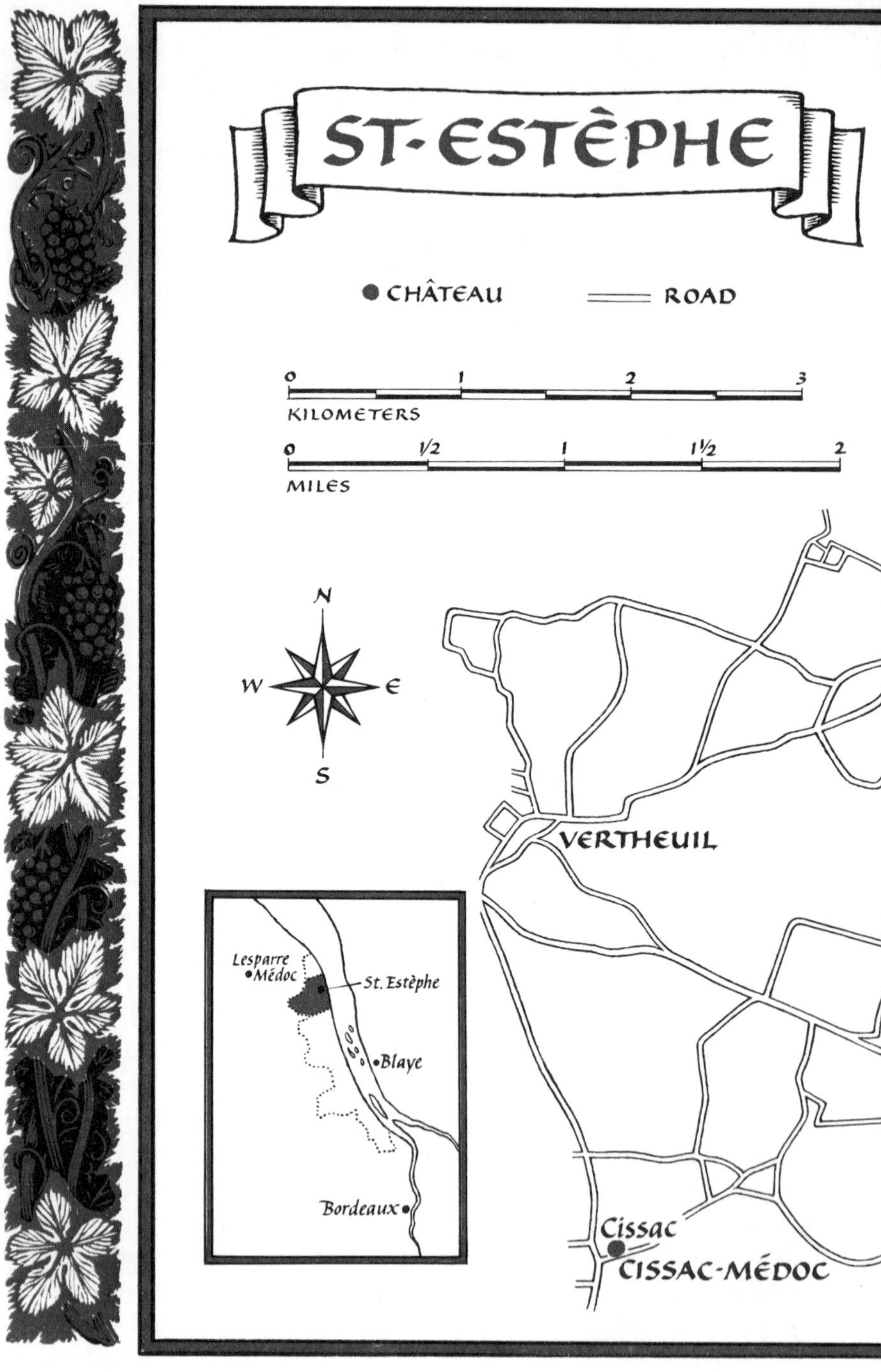
ST-ESTÈPHE
CHÂTEAU
ROAD
0
1
2
3
KILOMETERS
0
1/2
1
1½
2
MILES
N
W
E
S
VERTHEUIL
Lesparre
Médoc
St. Estèphe
Blaye
Bordeaux
Cissac
CISSAC-MÉDOC

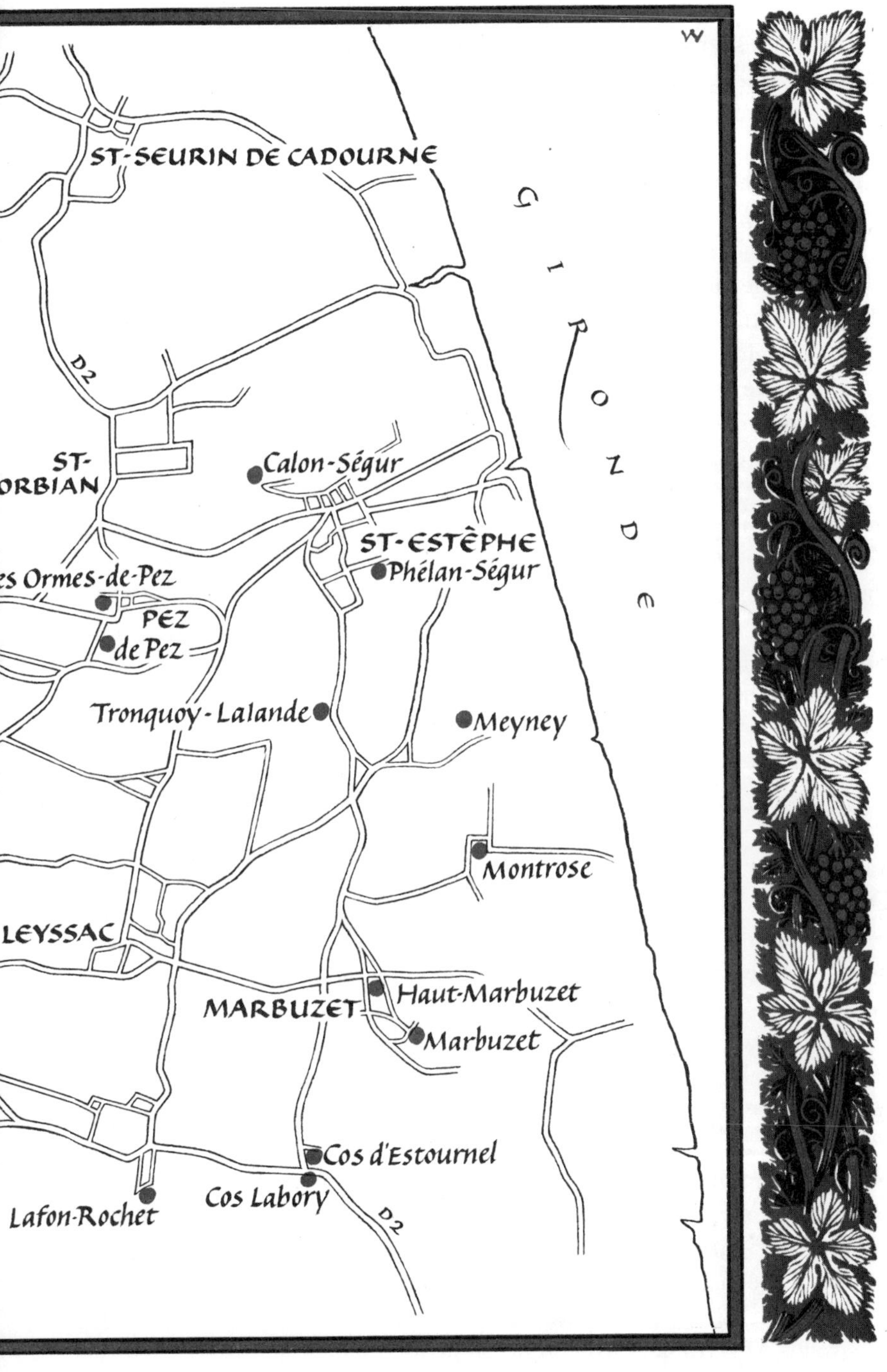

W
ST-SEURIN DE CADOURNE
GIRONDE
D2
ST-
ORBIAN
Calon-Ségur
ST-ESTÈPHE
Phélan-Ségur
es Ormes-de-Pez
PEZ
de Pez
Tronquoy-Lalande
Meyney
Montrose
LEYSSAC
MARBUZET
Haut-Marbuzet
Marbuzet
Cos d'Estournel
Cos Labory
Lafon-Rochet
D2

top-notch, lesser-known estates making excellent wine, such as de Pez, Haut-Marbuzet, Meyney, and Les-Ormes-de-Pez, would certainly merit serious consideration for elevation into the ranks of the classified growths.

Even with the growers of St.-Estèphe consciously trying to make a more supple style of wine, the wines of this region generally remain among the most backward and unyielding wines produced in Bordeaux. Certainly the soil is less gravelly in St.-Estèphe and it also has a higher clay content. Consequently, the drainage is slower, the wines relatively higher in acidity and lower in pH, and the textures of the wines chunkier and more burly than, for example, wines made in almost all gravel soil. Even with a heavier soil to work with, the individual winemaking styles of the châteaux are well delineated in St.-Estèphe.

At present, virtually everyone agrees that Cos d'Estournel is making this commune's finest wine, particularly since the mid-1970s. Coincidentally, it is also the first château one sees when crossing over the Pauillac boundary into St.-Estèphe. The eccentric pagoda-styled château sits on a ridge overlooking Pauillac's famous Lafite-Rothschild. Several recent vintages, particularly the 1982, would even suggest that Cos d'Estournel has first-growth aspirations. Cos d'Estournel's wine represents a brilliant combination of modern technology and respect for tradition. It is a wine supple enough to drink by age 5 or 6, but made to age and improve for as many as 10–20 years.

The chief rival to Cos d'Estournel is Montrose. Montrose is hidden on one of St.-Estèphe's tiny back roads, closer to the Gironde River. Until the mid-1970s, Montrose made one of Bordeaux's biggest, deepest, and slowest-maturing wines. Many Bordelais compared it to Latour because of its weight and richness. Since then, Montrose has curiously lightened its style and shown an increasing reliance on more Merlot in its final blend. Whereas older vintages of Montrose needed a good 15–20 years to shed their cloak of tannin, the more recent vintages of this wine have been drinking well within 5–6 years.

Potentially as good as any St.-Estèphe, as well as just about any Médoc, is Calon-Ségur, the white-walled château just outside the village of St.-Estèphe. When Calon-Ségur does everything right, as it did in 1982, 1953, and 1947, one cannot find a better wine. But Calon-Ségur has never been a model of consistency, and when looking at its wines made in the '80s, Calon's propensity for inconsistency is still clearly apparent. Nevertheless, the reputation of Calon-Ségur remains relatively untarnished, although smart *négociants* in Bordeaux always taste here before buying.

Lafon-Rochet continues to make a solid, tannic, backward style of wine that fanciers of hard, tough St.-Estèphe wines will find authentic. The fifth-growth Cos Labory is this commune's most overrated wine. Recent vintages have shown some modest improvements in quality, but this is a wine that continues to live off its 1855 reputation rather than modern-day quality.

One of the great attractions of St.-Estèphe is the glorious number of expertly made Cru Bourgeois wines in this appellation, some of which merit elevation to classified growths.

Haut-Marbuzet makes a splendid wine, overtly spicy and oaky, and filled with the flavors and aromas of blackcurrants. If one were to confuse it with Cos d'Estournel, I for one would not be surprised. The superb de Pez makes a wine that lasts as long as any wine of St.-Estèphe, and shrewd collectors have been beating a path to this property's wine for decades. For wine enthusiasts who do not have the patience to wait the 10 years for a wine like de Pez to reach maturity or who think that Haut-Marbuzet's style is too rich, Phélan-Ségur produces what must be St.-Estèphe's lightest and most supple wine. It is not an ager, but is meant rather to be drunk within its first decade of life. Meyney is another of St.-Estèphe's outstanding Cru Bourgeois properties. Its location north of Montrose near the river is superb, its production large, and its reliability for big, rich, deep, fine wines makes this St.-Estèphe a wine to seek out.

St.-Estèphes are not wines to look for and buy in mediocre or poor Bordeaux vintages. The two best performers of off-vintages are Cos d'Estournel and Haut-Marbuzet. However, the great vintages for this region are ones in which there are plenty of sunshine and heat, and all the grapes, particularly the Merlot, become fully mature. Since the drainage is not as good here as it is in other Médoc appellations, vintages in which there is plenty of rain are frequently less successful here than elsewhere. For example, 1983, 1980, 1977, and 1974 were less successful here than in other Médoc appellations. An important factor for the success of the vintage in St.-Estèphe is a healthy, very ripe Merlot crop that helps to cut the normally higher than average acidity and tannins in these wines. In 1982, 1976, and 1970, St.-Estèphe produced numerous outstanding wines because the Merlot was picked in excellent condition.

St.-Estèphes, being the least glamorous wines of the famous Médoc, offer excellent wine values. This pertains not only to the famous classified growths, but also to the appellation's excellent array of Cru Bourgeois wines.

A CONSUMER'S CLASSIFICATION OF THE CHÂTEAUX OF ST.-ESTÈPHE

OUTSTANDING

Cos d'Estournel

EXCELLENT

Montrose

VERY GOOD

Calon-Ségur
de Pez
Meyney
Les-Ormes-de-Pez
Haut-Marbuzet

GOOD

Lafon-Rochet
Phélan-Ségur
Tronquoy-Lalande

AVERAGE

Cos Labory

COS D'ESTOURNEL (Second-Growth) OUTSTANDING

Production: 20,000–22,000 cases	Grape varieties: Merlot—40% Cabernet Sauvignon—50% Cabernet Franc—10%
Time spent in barrels: 18 months	Average age of vines: 39 years
Evaluation of present classification: Should be maintained	

Under the inspired direction of Bruno Prats, Cos d'Estournel has risen to the top of its class in St.-Estèphe. Since 1976, the wines have improved going from one strength to another, and in most vintages, Cos d'Estournel can be expected to produce one of the best wines of the Médoc. This oriental-looking château, sitting on a ridge immediately north of the Pauillac border and its famous neighbor Lafite-Rothschild, is distinguished by the high percentage of Merlot used in the blend—40%. Not only is this one of the highest proportions of Merlot used in the Haut-Médoc, it no doubt accounts for the fleshy, richly textured character so noticeable in recent vintages of Cos d'Estournel. Bruno Prats, the manager and owner, is in the avant-garde of new wine technology, and this is one of the few major Bordeaux estates to be adamantly in favor of filtration of wine, both before cask aging and bottling. The results speak for themselves—Cos d'Estournel, after having to play the runner-up role to Montrose in the '50s and '60s, has in the '70s emerged as the leader in St.-Estèphe.

VINTAGES

1983—At first glimpse in March 1984, Cos was raw, tannic, angular
· and unyielding, although it had good color and weight on the
85 palate. Later in the year the wine was showing more richness
and fruit, but still decidedly tannic in a hard, lean way. Similar
to the 1975, the 1983 will need at least 10 years of cellaring.
Anticipated maturity: 1995–2010. Last tasted, 3/85.

1982—A monumental wine that has exhibited masses of explosive black-
· currant fruit from the very first cask samples tasted at the châ-
97 teau in March 1983. Unctuous, massive, rich, full-bodied, and
loaded with extract and tannin, this is the greatest Cos d'Estournel I have ever tasted. Anticipated maturity: 1995–2020. Last
tasted, 1/85.

1981—Deep ruby color, with a spicy, rich, briary, tightly knit bouquet,
· this wine is deeper and more promising than the 1983, but no
86 match for the exquisite 1982. Big, yet graceful, rich, but restrained, this wine will be at its best in 6–8 years. Anticipated
maturity: 1990–2020. Last tasted, 10/84.

1980—Unquestionably a success for the vintage, though obviously not
· a great wine, the 1980 Cos d'Estournel has medium ruby color,
83 an interesting, slightly spicy and herbaceous aroma, and well
above average, fruity flavors for the vintage. Drink now and over
the next 3–4 years; it will not be long-lived. Last tasted, 10/84.

1979—The best of the St.-Estèphes in 1979, Cos d'Estournel has a dark
· ruby color, with a developing bouquet of ripe cherries, cassis
86 and some vanillin, oaky scents. Full, rather corpulent for the
vintage, with surprising weight and depth, this wine needs another 4–6 years of bottle age to be fully mature. Anticipated
maturity: 1987–2000. Last tasted, 1/85.

1978—Very highly regarded by the château, I have found the wine to
· be very good, but not as graceful or as well balanced as the 1979.
85 Dark ruby with a moderately intense bouquet of black cherries,

spicy oak, and leather. On the palate, the wine is medium- to full-bodied with a dusty tannic texture. It needs 6–8 more years of cellar. Anticipated maturity: 1990–2005. Last tasted, 4/84.

1976—One of the better 1976s, Cos somehow succeeded in avoiding
· the feebleness and fragile character of many of the wines from
86 this early-maturing vintage. Now fully mature, but in no danger of collapse, this wine has a complex bouquet of fresh berries, fruit, spices, and good, supple, fruity taste, with just a trace of tannic astringence. Drink now and over the next 5 years. Last tasted, 11/84.

1975—Early in its life I had higher hopes for the 1975 Cos d'Estournel,
· but it is one of an increasing number of wines from this vintage
80 that will never live up to its potential. The color is medium ruby. The wine is still harshly tannic and angular, and while full-bodied, it lacks charm and fruit. It still needs 5–6 years of cellaring. Anticipated maturity: 1990–2005. Last tasted, 12/82.

1974—Adequate color, but this stalky, unripe wine still tastes green
· and hollow. Last tasted, 10/81.
67

1973—Five years ago the fruit had already faded and the sure signs of
· approaching senility (a brownish, pale color) were apparent.
65 Now best forgotten. Last tasted, 10/80.

1971—From a vintage which was very irregular in quality, the 1971 Cos
· d'Estournel is now fully mature. Medium to dark ruby, with an
84 orange/brownish edge, this wine has a silky, rather seductive quality with good, supple fruit. Drink over the next 2–3 years. It will not keep. Last tasted, 10/82.

1970—Still youthfully dark ruby with a reticent, yet promising plummy
· bouquet, a concentrated, deep, rich weighty feel on the palate,
88 and plenty of mouth-puckering tannin still showing, the 1970 remains an impressive but very young wine. Anticipated maturity: 1990–2010. Last tasted, 12/82.

1967—Now beginning to fade badly, this wine was at its prime in 1976–
· 1978, but never had the depth and concentration to remain there
73 very long. Brown at the edge, with the fruit quality drying up, this wine should be drunk now, if ever. Last tasted, 9/79.

1966—A very good 1966, yet not top-flight, the 1966 Cos d'Estournel is
· medium to dark ruby, with some browning, very good concentra-
85 tion, the somewhat lean, austere character of the vintage, and plenty of tannin in the finish. It does not yet seem to be mature,

but I would opt to drink it over the next 5–6 years while the fruit is still there. Last tasted, 10/84.

1964—Because of the heavy rains in this year, it was rather a hit-or-
· miss proposition with most Médoc châteaux. If the grapes were
72 picked early, then the château probably made good wine, but if the harvest was late, then the grapes were diluted by heavy rains. This wine, raw, ungenerous, yet surprisingly well colored, lacks fruit and complexity, and is not likely to improve any further. Last tasted, 10/78.

1962—This is a typical St.-Estèphe in the sense that wines from this
· commune are described as being hard and unyielding. Neverthe-
86 less, all the components are there, the dark ruby color, the very good concentration and weight, and the moderate tannin. Unlike most 1962 Bordeaux, the Cos d'Estournel has 2–5 more years of evolution ahead of it. Last tasted, 12/83.

1961—Typically dark and densely pigmented with no sign of browning
· at the edge, this big, intense, very concentrated, still very tannic
91 wine has decades of life ahead of it if well cellared. Very rich, deep and long on the palate, with masses of jammy fruit. Which is the greatest Cos d'Estournel—the 1961 or 1982? I'll take the latter. Anticipated maturity: 1986–2000. Last tasted, 9/81.

MONTROSE (Second-Growth) EXCELLENT

Production: 24,000 cases	Grape varieties: Cabernet Sauvignon—65% Merlot—30% Cabernet Franc—5%
Time spent in barrels: 22–24 months	Average age of vines: 29 years
Evaluation of present classification: Should be maintained	

One of the Médoc's best-situated vineyards and one of its most impeccably clean and well-kept cellars, Montrose was for years associated with huge, dense, powerful wines that needed several decades of cellaring to be soothing enough to drink. For example, Jean Paul Jauffret, the head of Bordeaux's CIVB, served me the 1908 Montrose in 1982, blind, to see if I could guess its age. The wine had plenty left in it and tasted as if it were at least 30 years younger.

The owner, the affable Jean Louis Charmolue, has obviously lightened the style of Montrose in response to his perception that the old style, dense, excruciatingly tannic wines are no longer popular with consumers. The change in style is particularly noticeable in the vintages of the late '70s and early '80s, as more Merlot has been introduced into the blend at the expense of Cabernet Sauvignon and Petit Verdot. Time will tell if the "nouveau" style is more successful, but for anyone who has the pleasure of drinking some of Montrose's greatest vintages, they are immensely impressive wines that show a style not unlike Latour, only more angular and aggressive. The wines of Montrose were especially strong in the period 1959–1971, when it was usually the best wine produced in St.-Estèphe. Since then, the quality has been surpassed by its rival, Cos d'Estournel.

VINTAGES

1983—Not nearly as big nor as tannic as I had expected, but neverthe-
· less well made, the 1983 Montrose has moderate tannin, medium
83 to dark ruby color, a spicy, plummy nose, and astringent finish.
Anticipated maturity: 1992–2005. Last tasted, 3/85.

1982—This is the finest wine made at Montrose since the glorious 1970.
· Very dark ruby, with a rich, intense aroma of spicy oak and ripe
87 fruit. This full-bodied wine has a deep, rich, unctuous texture,
plenty of round yet noticeable tannins, and a long supple finish.
Anticipated maturity: 1995–2010. Last tasted, 1/85.

1981—Montrose has produced an elegant, understated, somewhat shy
· medium-weight wine. This new streamlined version of Montrose
84 should be fully mature by 1990, but seems to lack the necessary
concentration and richness to last too far beyond that date. In
style it resembles the 1971, only slightly lighter. Anticipated
maturity: 1990–2000. Last tasted, 11/84.

1980—Lean, tannic, with a light ruby color, this wine will never be
· more than an expensive quaffing wine. One of the 1980s not
72 worth remembering. Last tasted, 2/84.

1979—A good wine, but rather a disappointing effort for Montrose. This
· medium ruby-colored wine has a light-intensity bouquet of
82 cherry fruit, intermingled with spicy oak. Quite dry and astringent in the finish because of aggressive tannins, this is a medium-bodied Montrose that will be ready soon. Anticipated
maturity: 1988–1996.

1978—Not unlike the 1979, although the color seems deeper, this aus-
· tere tannic wine shows good fruit, a stylish medium-weight tex-
82 ture on the palate, but lacks character, complexity, and

richness. The beginning of the new style by Montrose. How will it age? Anticipated maturity: 1988–1996. Last tasted, 3/83.

1976—Undoubtedly one of the successes for this vintage and destined
· to be one of the longest-lived wines of 1976, Montrose shows
85 very good dark ruby color, a spicy, vanillin oakiness, and a good, deep blackcurrant fruitiness. While many 1976s are browning badly, and beginning to lose their fruit, Montrose is still young-looking and promising. Anticipated maturity: 1986–1990. Last tasted, 12/84.

1975—Perhaps in an unflattering stage at present, the 1975 Montrose
· seems to have become very severe and tannic, but does have
85 full color, a ripe, deep weighty feel on the palate, and long finish. This wine needs a full 10 more years of cellaring. Impressive rather than enjoyable. Anticipated maturity: 1992–2015. Last tasted, 5/84.

1974—Not a bad effort in what has turned out to be a below average
· quality year for Bordeaux, the 1974 Montrose is too lean and
72 sinewy, but exhibits good color, some attractive fruit, oak and earthy scents in the bouquet, and an acidic finish. It is not likely to get any better. Last tasted, 5/82.

1973—Between 1976–1979 this was a pleasant, perhaps too woody
· wine, but one which could be deemed somewhat successful in a
65 year that produced far too many diluted, thin wines. Now it has lost its fruit with only the oak, alcohol, and tannin remaining. Drink up immediately. Last tasted, 6/84.

1971—At its peak, the 1971 Montrose is quite attractive, with a com-
· plete, leathery, cedary, ripe, fragrant fruity bouquet, supple,
86 smooth, moderately rich flavors, and medium body. Very charming and surprisingly soft for an old-style Montrose, this wine should be drunk over the next 2–3 years. Last tasted, 2/81.

1970—Undeniably the best Montrose since 1961, this massive, inky
· giant has exceptional concentration to go along with its hard
91 tannins. A wine for the year 2000 and beyond, and in size, weight, and life expectancy, not unlike the 1970 Latour. An outstanding wine for those with both patience and youth. Anticipated maturity: 1990–2020. Last tasted, 3/84.

1967—A surprisingly good wine for the vintage, Montrose was at its
· best between 1975 and 1979. Now in decline as the fruit recedes,
82 and the tannins and oak become more dominant, this medium ruby-colored wine still has good body and enough interest in the bouquet to hold most people's attention. Last tasted, 10/81.

1966—The 1966 is still dark ruby with a peppery, very spicy, yet tight,
· still relatively closed bouquet. The 1966 Montrose is austere and
86 tough on the palate, with good fruit and firm, dusty tannins.
Comparatively, it is not as massive or as rich as the 1970, 1964,
or 1961. Anticipated maturity: 1986–2010.

1964—With unexpected depth, richness and vigor, the 1964 of Mon-
· trose was one of just a few Médoc wines to be harvested prior to
89 the rains. Richer and more intense than the 1966, and better,
darker, more opaque in color, this huge, dusty, ripe wine is quite
a mouthful. Give it another 5 years of cellaring. Anticipated
maturity: 1990–2020. Last tasted, 1/85.

1962—At its peak in 1985, the 1962 Montrose should maintain its pla-
· teau for several more years. Dark ruby with a complex bouquet
88 of ripe, cedary, black cherry aromas, this lovely wine is surprisingly rich and deep on the palate, and supple and long in the
finish. Delicious now. Drink over the next 5 years. Last tasted,
5/82.

1961—A stunning wine from a stunning vintage, the 1961 Montrose is
· still a full decade or more away from maturity, but has intense,
93 deep, opaque dark ruby color, a huge bouquet of ripe fruit and
mineral scents, a full-bodied, dense richness and texture, and
gobs of tannin. A monumental bottle of wine for drinking over
the next 20–50 years. Last tasted, 11/84.

CALON-SÉGUR (Third-Growth) VERY GOOD

Production: 20,000 cases	Grape varieties: Cabernet Sauvignon—50% Cabernet Franc—25% Merlot—25%
Time spent in barrels: 24–26 months	Average age of vines: 38 years

Evaluation of present classification: Should be downgraded to a fourth-growth

Situated in the northernmost reaches of the commune of St.-Estèphe, Calon-Ségur, like Montrose, has a live-in owner. Philippe Capbern Gasqueton lives here, and his wine has for decades enjoyed one of the Médoc's finest reputations. As the tasting critiques demonstrate, the wines are not as deserving of their lofty reputation as they should be. Calon-Ségur was particularly strong in the late '40s and the '50s, but in the '60s and '70s the quality became quite uneven. I thought I detected a return to brilliance with the exceptional 1982 Calon-Ségur, but I believe the stunning quality in this year may have more to do with the vintage than any renaissance at Calon-Ségur. The wine of Calon-Ségur has a reputation for living a long time in the bottle. At least the textbooks on Bordeaux have said as much, but, quite to the contrary, I have found the vintages of the '60s and '70s to be precocious, and at their best within 8 to 10 years of the vintage. In contrast, the 1945, 1947, and 1948 tasted in 1984 were still vibrant, superb wines which clearly showed the great potential of this lovely vineyard.

The possible culprit in Calon-Ségur's spotty performance over recent years may be the *élevage*, or cellar treatment of the wine. More than one professional wine taster has said the wine always tastes better in its youth than in the bottle. Certainly the 1982 is fabulous, but other than this vintage, I find little else of special interest from recent vintages except for the 1975, which while excellent, varies considerably in quality from bottle to bottle.

VINTAGES

1983—When I first tasted this wine in the spring of 1984, it tasted
· surprisingly Rhône-like, with soft, grapey flavors, a hot, alco-
82 holic finish, and rather fragile framework. Later in the year, it was ripe and flavorful, but low in acidity, and again, quite alcoholic. In style, color, and texture, it reminded me of a 1976. It should mature early. Anticipated maturity: 1990–2000. Last tasted, 3/85.

1982—The best vintage of Calon-Ségur since 1947? Gasqueton thinks
· so, and I have no reason to disagree. This massive wine has
95 great color, with an opulent, intense, exotic, rich fruitiness, full body, significant tannins, and a silky, voluptuous texture on the palate. A classic wine that shows the great potential this estate has. Anticipated maturity: 1995–2015. Last tasted, 1/85.

1981—Rather light, but nevertheless charming, elegant and fruity, and
· clearly marked by new wood, the 1981 Calon-Ségur reflects both
83 the inconsistency of this famous estate and the 1981 vintage. Soft on the palate, it can be drunk now. Anticipated maturity: 1985–1992. Last tasted, 8/84.

1979—An elegant, charming, somewhat straightforward style of wine,
· with good, soft, supple fruit, light tannin, medium ruby color,
80 and a pronounced ripe Merlot character. Ready to drink now, it should last for 4–6 years. Last tasted, 10/84.

1978—A distinctly mediocre effort, with medium ruby color, a pleasing
· yet one-dimensional, ripe Merlot aroma, average flavor inten-
75 sity, and a short, simple finish. Some tannin is present, but this wine shows little potential for improvement beyond another 2 years. Last tasted, 12/82.

1976—A very pleasant, supple, deliciously fruity wine that is now fully
· mature. Medium garnet in color with brown at the edge, this
81 wine has a well-developed bouquet of hickory wood, ripe fruit, and spice. Soft, savory flavors are marked by low acidity. Drink immediately. Last tasted, 4/83.

1975—While the color shows some surprising brown at the edge, this
· is certainly the most mature and enjoyable 1975 St.-Estèphe. It
87 is virtually mature, with rich, savory, moderately rich, supple flavors, excellent concentration, and deep depth that is missing in some other well-regarded vintages of Calon-Ségur. However, the wine is notoriously inconsistent from bottle to bottle, and the score reflects the better bottlings. Drink over the next 10 years. Last tasted, 1/85.

1974—Somewhat typical of this vintage, Calon-Ségur produced a shal-
· low, though pleasingly colored wine with just enough fruit to
74 make it palatable. Still holding together, no doubt because of all the acidity present, the 1974 Calon-Ségur is hardly worth remembering unless you are in a pinch. Drink up. Last tasted, 10/80.

1973—In its prime in 1976–1978, this was one of the more pleasant
· 1973 Bordeaux wines. While not tasted recently, it would be
65 most shocking if the wine had much fruit left to it. Last tasted, 9/77.

1971—Fading badly, as evidenced by the brown color, the 1971 Calon-
· Ségur has a decaying mushroom aroma, soft, barely alive fla-
65 vors, and an acidic finish. My notes show I enjoyed a good bottle in 1977, but time has not been kind to this vintage of Calon-Ségur. Last tasted, 10/80.

1970—Another convincing piece of evidence that Calon-Ségur's repu-
· tation for producing long-lived wine is hardly justified by its
80 performance in the '60s and '70s. Fully mature in 1978, with an attractive, charming, moderately intense bouquet of ripe Merlot fruit and spicy oak, this garnet-colored, slightly brownish wine has soft, supple fruit, medium body, and little tannin remaining. Drink over the next 5 years. Last tasted, 3/85.

1967—Calon-Ségur made one of the best 1967s, which for several years
· outshone its more heralded older sibling, the 1966. Rich, soft,
84 supple, and deeply fruity, with a voluptuous texture—these are the reasons why this wine was so attractive. The bouquet offered ripe fruit and good cedary scents. The fruit has now begun to fade, so drink it immediately. Last tasted, 10/80.

1966—At its peak now, this wine has a lovely, full-intensity bouquet of
· cedar wood and ripe fruit. Very satisfying on the palate, with
85 good concentration and length, this is arguably the best Calon-Ségur of the '60s. Drink over the next 5 years. Last tasted, 11/82.

1964—Lacking fruit and coarsely textured, with a damp cellar aroma
· and modest flavors and proportions, this wine is still holding
75 together but seems to hold little promise for the future. Last tasted, 6/78.

1962—My one tasting experience, early in the '70s, found the 1962
· Calon-Ségur to be especially light, lacking richness and fat, and
76 to be browning at the edge. In all likelihood, this would be a bad gamble for anyone who crosses its path.

1961—A good, solid wine, but given the vintage and the overall quality
· of its two most famous neighbors, Montrose and Cos d'Estour-
83 nel, the 1961 Calon-Ségur is a disappointment. The color lacks the great depth and richness of this vintage, and this wine seems much less concentrated and less rich than others. Still drinking well in 1983, but not an especially noteworthy 1961. Drink over the next 5 years. Last tasted, 11/83.

DE PEZ (Cru Bourgeois) VERY GOOD

Production: 10,000 cases	Grape varieties: Cabernet Sauvignon—70% Merlot—15% Cabernet Franc—15%
Time spent in barrels: 16 months	Average age of vines: 30 years
Evaluation of present classification: Should be upgraded to a Médoc fourth-growth	

An excellent, virile, rather tough wine is made at de Pez that ages magnificently. Thanks to the Bordeaux restaurant Clavel's rather extensive list of old vintages, and the late Martin Bamford's fascination with the quality of this estate, I have had considerable tasting experience with vintages from the '40s and '50s, not to mention the more recent years.

Robert Dousson is the very capable manager of this château, and his meticulous care of the vineyard and the winery is very evident. Because Dousson believes his wine merits classified-growth status, he has refused to join the syndicate of Cru Bourgeois growers for fear that this would be an acknowledgment of an inferior-quality wine. The wines of de Pez are true St.-Estèphes, deeply colored, tannic, and extremely long-lived. Even in lighter vintages, the wine needs 8 or more years of bottle age to really show its true class. For high quality and excellent value, de Pez is a wine to seek out.

VINTAGES

1983—As good as any of the St.-Estèphes in 1983, de Pez has very dark
· color, dense, rich, ripe fruity flavors, a significant tannin con-
85 tent, and long finish. A very traditionally made wine which will require 10–15 years of cellaring by its owner. Not unlike the 1975 in style. Anticipated maturity: 1993–2010. Last tasted, 6/84.

1982—Much rounder and fruitier than the 1983, the 1982 is very dark
· ruby with an intense cassis bouquet, fat, rich, luscious flavors,
86 high but ripe round tannins, and an excellent long, opulent finish. A delicious 1982 that will be ready to drink by 1990. Anticipated maturity: 1990–2005. Last tasted, 6/84.

1981—The least successful de Pez in the trio of fine vintages, 1981,
· 1982, 1983, it is nevertheless well made. This medium-weight
81 wine is a trifle austere and unyielding, but has good fruit, and a firm, tannic, lean structure. This wine must be cellared until at least 1990. Anticipated maturity: 1990–2000. Last tasted, 3/84.

1979—A good rather than very good de Pez, with medium to dark ruby
· color, a spicy, rather evolved bouquet of spice, herbaceous, and
81 blackcurrant scents, this medium-bodied wine has good fruit, moderate tannins, and an astringent, moderately long finish. Anticipated maturity: 1987–1993. Last tasted, 6/82.

1978—An unqualified success for de Pez, the 1978, which has more
· Merlot than usual because of flowering problems with the 1978
85 Cabernet crop, is a rich, supple, deep, fruity wine with plenty of extract and tannin. Medium- to full-bodied, it is just now beginning to show some bottle bouquet. Anticipated maturity: 1990–2005. Last tasted, 10/84.

1976—From its birth, the 1976 de Pez showed excellent winemaking and a strict selection of only the best barrels in this copious vintage. Darker colored than most 1976 Bordeaux, with a ripe, rich, fruity aroma, and good underlying tannins, this wine is now approaching its apogee. A top-notch effort from this vintage. Anticipated maturity: 1985–1990. Last tasted, 7/83.
· 84

1975—Still brutally tannic and nowhere near ready to drink, this wine showed excellent concentration and fruit from the cask, but has been dormant and very closed during its life in the bottle. Will the fruit outlast the tannin? The crucial question for many 1975s is also a relevant concern here. Don't touch it until 1990. Anticipated maturity: 1990–2010. Last tasted, 2/84.
· 84

1973—Now beginning to fade, for a decade the 1973 was one of the most enjoyable wines of what I found to be a terribly weak, diluted vintage of frail, watery wines. Not so for the de Pez, which exhibited a lovely, charming, moderately intense, berry fruitiness, and soft, supple flavor. Drink up. Last tasted, 8/81.
· 82

1970—A classic of the vintage and for de Pez, the 1970, still a youthful wine with several more decades of aging potential, has dark ruby color, a spicy, rich blackcurrant aroma, the scent of leather, and a firm yet deep structure, with plenty of tannic flavors. One of my favorite wines of the vintage, it remains years away from maturity. Anticipated maturity: 1990–2005.
· 87

MEYNEY (Grand Bourgeois Exceptionnel) — VERY GOOD

Production: 25,000 cases	Grape varieties: Cabernet Sauvignon—70% Merlot—26% Cabernet Franc—4%
Time spent in barrels: 12 months	Average age of vines: 30 years

Evaluation of present classification: Should be upgraded to fifth-growth

Meyney, the large vineyard of over 125 acres immediately north of Montrose with a splendid view of the Gironde River, has made notably flavorful, robust wines that offer considerable value to the shrewd consumer looking for quality rather than prestige. If the wines never have the complex intensity and bouquet of a Cos d'Estournel, or the robust, massive richness of the pre-1978 wines of Montrose, it is not so shameful because Meyney rarely disappoints. The wine is fairly big-styled, with good fruit and excellent aging potential of 20–25 years, Since 1975 the wine seems to have achieved an even higher level of quality. Meyney is a wine to keep an eye on as it is owned by the highly reputable Cordier firm, a large *négociant* house that seems to offer both quality and value throughout its range of wines.

VINTAGES

1983—Meyney was extremely successful in 1983. The wine is very
· dense with a very ripe, roasted blackcurrant aroma, unctuous,
85 thick, rich flavors, average acidity, and moderate tannins. A fat,
fleshy wine, it is very concentrated and will probably mature within 10 years. Anticipated maturity: 1993–2010. Last tasted, 3/85.

1982—Bordering on too jammy a character, this wine is nevertheless
· loaded with intense, ripe blackberry fruit, a huge framework,
87 plenty of round, ripe tannins, and a long, big, alcoholic finish.
An extremely massive wine which will take at least a decade to mature. Anticipated maturity: 1992–2015. Last tasted, 1/85.

1981—Another example of Meyney's forte—chunky, densely flavored,
· powerful wines which have plenty of color, authority, and
85 weight. If they frequently lack complexity and elegance, the
wines of Meyney deliver oodles of ripe, blackcurrant fruit, and aging potential of 20 or more years. Anticipated maturity: 1991–2000.

1979—Undoubtedly a good wine for this prolific yet underrated vintage,
· the 1979 Meyney has dark ruby color, a rather simple, grapey,
81 spicy, stemmy aroma, moderately full body, and light tannins.
Anticipated maturity: 1986–1992.

1978—A textbook Meyney, dark-colored, chunky, fruity, loaded with
· flavors of blackcurrants and plums, this wine has plenty of ex-
84 tract, mouth-gripping tannins, and a 15- to 20-year life span. A
very good Meyney. Anticipated maturity: 1989–2010. Last tasted, 10/81.

1976—A mediocre effort from Meyney, this wine is palatable and good
· for uncritical quaffing, but is now in decline and destined for
74 senility if not consumed immediately, Drink up! Last tasted,
8/79.

1975—The best Meyney ever made? Perhaps. No doubt the 1982 will
· give this wine a run for the money, but this wine continues to
89 develop stunningly in the bottle. Very dark ruby with a powerful,

rich bouquet, and deep, tannic but very ripe fruity flavors. This full-bodied wine has virtually everything in its favor. While it is a superlative effort for Meyney in 1975, it may also be the best wine of this appellation in the 1975 vintage. Anticipated maturity: 1990–2010. Last tasted, 12/84.

1971—Still drinking nicely, the 1971 Meyney is dark ruby in color,
· chunky, "four square" as the English say, without much com-
80 plexity, but offering a good, robust mouthful of claret. At its peak now, it is best consumed over the near term of 1–3 years. Last tasted, 9/79.

1970—Approaching maturity, this dark ruby-colored wine with just a
· trace of orange/brown at the edges is full-bodied, firm, rather
83 austere on the palate, but generously flavored and fruity. It should last another 8–10 years. Last tasted, 8/83.

LES-ORMES-DE-PEZ (Grand Bourgeois) VERY GOOD

Production: 14,000 cases	Grape varieties: Cabernet Sauvignon—55% Merlot—30% Cabernet Franc—10% Petit Verdot—5%
Time spent in barrels: 14–18 months	Average age of vines: 25–30 years
Evaluation of present classification: Should be upgraded to a Médoc fifth-growth	

Les-Ormes-de-Pez is one of Bordeaux's most popular wines, due largely to the wine's generously flavored, plump, sometimes sweet and fat personality, as well as the extensive promotional efforts of its owner, Jean Michel Cazes. I find the wine rarely disappointing. The color of Les-Ormes-de-Pez tends to be quite dark, and since 1975, the flavors increasingly supple and rich, with less tannin. However, the wine can age for 10–15 years. Older vintages from the '40s and '50s that often can be found in several of Bordeaux's restaurants are notably good wines and good values.

Les-Ormes-de-Pez is a wine that consumers looking for high quality at modest prices should always give serious consideration.

VINTAGES

1983—Very deeply colored, with a fat, ripe, round, richly fruity char-
· acter, this full-bodied, well-made wine has good mouth-gripping
84 tannins and overall balance. Anticipated maturity: 1992–1997.
Last tasted, 3/85.

1982—A top-flight effort from Les-Ormes-de-Pez, this is a very concen-
· trated wine with a penetrating bouquet of ripe, blackcurrant
87 fruit, and spicy, oaky, thick, dense, powerful, fruity flavors
backed by significant tannins. Reminiscent of the gorgeous wine made by Les-Ormes-de-Pez in 1970, only softer, this wine will need 10 years to be fully mature. Anticipated maturity: 1990–2000. Last tasted, 10/84.

1981—This is a straightforward style of wine, which is not up to the
· excellent quality of the 1982, or very good 1983, but is still robust
82 and fruity, with a generous texture and a pleasing, rounded, soft
finish. Anticipated maturity: 1986–1992. Last tasted, 4/84.

1979—A mediocre effort from Les-Ormes-de-Pez, this wine is quite
· light in color, with a fully mature, light, intensely fruity bouquet,
75 some damp, oaky aromas, and soft, rather lean fruity flavors.
Drink now! Last tasted, 6/84.

1978—A very good wine, which exhibits deep, blackcurrant ripe fruit,
· a medium- and full-bodied feel on the palate, and good solid
85 tannins. The bouquet is fast beginning to reveal complex cedary,
spicy scents, yet the tannin is still very much in evidence. A fairly big, chunky, fleshy wine which should age well for 10–12 years. Anticipated maturity: 1987–1996. Last tasted, 10/82.

1976—Moderately intense jammy fruit suggests an overripe character
· on the palate. The wine is soft, with low acidity, and a diluted,
72 thinnish finish. Now fading. Drink up! Last tasted, 5/82.

1975—Successful for the vintage, and better than several of the more
· expensive classified growths, the 1975 Les-Ormes-de-Pez is
84 rich, full-bodied, with a leathery, ripe fruity bouquet, dusty,
spicy, fruity flavors, and some astringent tannins still present. Nevertheless, it's showing its best side now, and therefore should be drunk over the next 4–5 years. Last tasted, 5/84.

1971—Somewhat light and already fading when first tasted in 1977, this
· wine more recently has exhibited a harsh, biting acidity and lack
65 of fruit. It has no future. Drink up. Last tasted, 12/81.

1970—Les-Ormes-de-Pez is a massive, intense, ripe, rich wine, with
· an uncanny resemblance to the 1970 Lynch-Bages (which is co-
86 incidentally owned by the same Cazes family). This robust,

somewhat coarse, fleshy wine has tremendous extract, plenty of tannin, and an opaque, dark ruby color. What it lacks in finesse it makes up for in strength and richness. Anticipated maturity: 1986–2005. Last tasted, 10/84.

HAUT-MARBUZET
(Grand Bourgeois Exceptionnel) VERY GOOD

Production: 12,000 cases	Grape varieties: Merlot—50% Cabernet Sauvignon—40% Cabernet Franc—10%
Time spent in barrels: 18 months	Average age of vines: 28 years

Evaluation of present classification: Should be upgraded to a Médoc fifth-growth

Haut-Marbuzet is an immensely popular wine in western Europe, particularly in Belgium, Holland, and England where 90% of the wine is sold. It is a unique wine that I have had only limited experience tasting. From what I have sampled, the wine is characterized by an intense, almost opulent, rich fruitiness, a significant tannin content, and a very toasty, spicy, vanillin aroma and flavor due to the aging of the wine in 100% new oak barrels. This is a luxury that few châteaux other than first-growths can afford. Based on Haut-Marbuzet's performance in the '80s, this is clearly a château to keep an eye out for.

VINTAGES

1983—Extremely dense with an almost port-like, dark ruby color, ripe,
· rich, plummy nose, fat, intense, viscous flavor, and moderate
86 tannin, this young, generous wine should have quite a future
ahead of it. Anticipated maturity: 1988–1995. Last tasted, 1/85.

1982—A ravishing, luscious wine that seems to suggest a decadently
· rich Pomerol rather than a stiff, tannic St.-Estèphe. Very in-
92 tensely flavored with a gorgeous, perfumed bouquet of ripe, blackcurrant fruit and toasty oak, the 1982 Haut-Marbuzet seems to have produced the perfect marriage of exotic, spicy, vanillin, oak, and opulently rich fruit. Moderate tannins warrant cellaring it for at least 6–8 years. This wine is one of the most impressive Cru Bourgeois wines I have ever drunk. Anticipated maturity: 1990–1998. Last tasted, 1/85.

1981—Another intriguing wine, the 1981 Haut-Marbuzet is very deeply
· colored, with a ripe, plummy, spicy, oaky bouquet, full-bodied,
85 with plenty of concentration and moderate tannins. Anticipated
maturity: 1986–1992. Last tasted, 1/85.

LAFON-ROCHET (Fourth-Growth) GOOD

Production: 8,000–15,000 cases	Grape varieties: Cabernet Sauvignon—70% Merlot—20% Cabernet Franc—8% Malbec—2%
Time spent in barrels: 18–24 months	Average age of vines: 19 years
Evaluation of present classification: Should be downgraded to a Médoc fifth-growth	

One of the St.-Estèphes that seems to get little publicity these days is Lafon-Rochet. Located right on the Pauillac-St.-Estèphe border, with its vineyard adjacent to those of Lafite-Rothschild, Lafon-Rochet can make excellent wine, as it did in 1970. However, far too many other vintages have been very disappointing, and if a reclassification of the wines of the Médoc were done now, Lafon-Rochet would be hard pressed to hold its position in the Médoc's classification. Its owner, Guy Tesseron, has spent considerable sums of money to rebuild the château and improve the vineyard. Hopefully, the higher quality of the 1982 and 1983 Lafon-Rochets points to a renewed vigor in wine quality at this pretty estate.

VINTAGES

1983—In early tastings against the other top St.-Estèphes, this was
· right behind Cos d'Estournel. Very rich, full-bodied, deeply con-
86 centrated and loaded with fruit, this tannic, very dark-colored
wine shows excellent potential for extended aging. A top-notch effort. Anticipated maturity: 1995–2010. Last tasted, 6/84.

1982—Not a great 1982, but if taken out of the context of the vintage,
· it would be considered very good. Very dark, with the charac-
85 teristic ripe, intense plummy aroma of the 1982 vintage quite
evident, this wine is surprisingly lush and fat, even for a 1982. But don't be misguided; the wine has plenty of tannin. Give it

the 5–8 years it needs to develop bottle bouquet. Anticipated maturity: 1990–2000. Last tasted, 1/85.

1980—Adequate color, particularly in view of the vintage, however, the
· good 1980s have more charm and supple fatness than this wine,
70 which has an annoying vegetal character to it. Drink up. Last
tasted, 11/84.

1979—A successful wine was made by Lafon-Rochet in 1979. Dark
· ruby, with a pronounced aroma of new oak and black cherries,
85 this wine has plenty of stuffing, and curiously, may be a more
successful wine than the château's 1978, which is from a more acclaimed vintage. Needing 5 more years to shed its tannin, this wine may mark the beginning of an upward swing in quality at Lafon-Rochet. Anticipated maturity: 1986–1998. Last tasted, 4/83.

1978—This is a supple, straightforward, fruity wine that seems to lack
· direction and focus. Moderately dark in color, with an easygo-
82 ing, supple texture, pleasant, soft, fruity flavors, and a short
finish, Lafon-Rochet's 1978 is a good but rather undistinguished wine. Anticipated maturity: 1985–1992. Last tasted, 4/83.

1976—In this vintage, Lafon-Rochet produced a light, rather fragile
· wine which has been fully mature since 1980. Medium ruby,
74 with some brown at the edges, with diffuse and diluted flavors,
this wine should be drunk up. Last tasted, 7/81.

1975—The 1975 Lafon-Rochet is a big, surprisingly deeply colored,
· chunky wine which has the harsh, tannic, angular character of
82 many 1975s. Despite its color and intensity, it shows no com-
plexity or direction. A clumsy wine that has yet to prove its character. Anticipated maturity: 1988–2000. Last tasted, 4/84.

1973—Now pale, with a damp, faded, musty aroma, dissipated fruit
· flavors, and a washed-out short finish, the 1973 Lafon-Rochet is
64 best forgotten. Last tasted, 10/82.

1971—Light-bodied, yet somewhat charming and fruity in 1978, this
· wine was fully mature then, and one can only imagine that 7
76 more years of bottle age has seriously eroded any appeal it might
have had. Last tasted, 6/78.

1970—The 1970 is the best Lafon-Rochet made in the '70s. Still youth-
· fully rich, with a deep ruby color, this intensely concentrated,
87 deep, full-bodied wine has oodles of blackcurrant fruit, a heavy
overlay of chalky tannin, and a decade of life ahead of it. A rich, intense wine, and unquestionably one of the sleepers of the vintage. Last tasted, 11/84.

1966—Certainly an old-style Lafon-Rochet, the 1966 remains a dusty,
· tannic, briary wine, with good fruit, some browning at the edges,
83 and plenty of tannin still in evidence. It will live for at least
another half-dozen years, but is not likely to ever be very harmonious or graceful. Last tasted, 9/79.

1961—Bigger, richer and more concentrated than the 1966, with plenty
· of astringent tannins, this spicy, ripe, rather full-bodied and full-
86 flavored wine has plenty of extract, and a dusty, chalky finish.
A very good 1961 that can be drunk now or held for another 5–6 years. Last tasted, 8/84.

PHÉLAN-SÉGUR (Grand Bourgeois Exceptionnel) GOOD

Production: 17,000–20,000 cases	Grape varieties: Cabernet Sauvignon—50% Merlot—40% Cabernet Franc—10%
Time spent in barrels: 12 months	Average age of vines: 22 years
Evaluation of present classification: Should be maintained	

Phélan-Ségur is a well-regarded property that I have found to produce pleasant, round, early-maturing wines. The high percentage of Merlot used no doubt accounts for the wine's precocious personality. Generally a good value, but rather too inconsistent to merit serious attention. Phélan-Ségur's recent vintages, in the late '70s and early '80s, have not shown well in comparative tastings against their peers.

VINTAGES

1983—In three separate tastings from cask samples the wine tasted
· flawed. Judgment reserved.
?

1982—Overproduction seems to have given this wine, which has dark
· ruby color, less weight and richness than many of its peers. Soft,
78 forward and a trifle diffuse, but big, grapey and supple, yet
slightly unstructured, this wine seems to be a candidate for rapid maturation. Drink over the next 5 years. Last tasted, 10/84.

1981—Surprisingly better than the 1983, but nevertheless, rather shal-
· low, light, with a stemmy bouquet, the 1981 Phélan-Ségur has
74 just enough fruit to cover the wine's framework. Light tannins
and some ominous browning at the edge mandates drinking over the next 3 years. Last tasted, 9/84.

1979—Medium ruby in color with a charming, ripe, berry bouquet that
· shows full maturity at present. Soft, Merlot flavors dominate this
75 easy-to-drink, pleasant, one-dimensional wine. Drink over the
next several years. Last tasted, 6/81.

1978—Straightforward grapey flavors and a simple personality have
· given way to reveal some attractive, light-intensity, spicy, ripe,
74 cherry aromas. However, this medium-bodied wine finishes
short, and just seems to lack weight and grip. Drink up. Last
tasted, 10/82.

1976—Fully mature by 1980, this wine was pleasant, soft, fruity, and
· easy to drink. More recently, the wine has lost the medium ruby
75 color, replaced by a dull brownish cast. Drink now, if ever. Last
tasted, 10/80.

1975—The 1975 is the best wine of recent efforts of Phélan-Ségur. This
· wine shows good fruit intensity, weight, richness and direction
84 which have been missing in more recent vintages of Phélan-
Ségur. Fully mature, with moderately intense, cedary, ripe,
fruity bouquet, this is an attractively flavored wine that can be
drunk over the next 3 years. Last tasted, 5/84.

TRONQUOY-LALANDE (Grand Bourgeois) GOOD

Production: 5,000 cases	Grape varieties: Cabernet Sauvignon—65% Merlot—30% Cabernet Franc—5%
Time spent in barrels: 12 months	Average age of vines: 20 years
Evaluation of present classification: Should be maintained	

Tronquoy-Lalande is an historic property with a fine twin-towered château on the premises. It is a wine as highly regarded a century ago as it is today. I have followed the wine in every vintage since the late '70s, and the wine seems to lack consistency from vintage to vintage. At its best, it is a very dark, huge, clumsy sort of wine, with an earthy, distinctive character. The wine is distributed exclusively by the Bordeaux firm of Dourthe.

VINTAGES

1983—Dark ruby, with a pungent, ripe bouquet, this full-bodied wine
· has a very high level of astringent tannins present, good fruit,
80 but very backward and harsh. Will the fruit outlive the tannin?
Anticipated maturity: 1995–2000. Last tasted, 6/84.

1982—Quite black ruby in color, this is a huge, corpulent, rather fat wine that is high in concentration, high in tannin, but seems a trifle intense and exaggerated in style. Time may pull it together, but at present, a huge, clumsy wine. Anticipated maturity: 1992–2000. Last tasted, 1/85.
·
83

1981—This property can obviously make backstrapping, black purple wines with immense concentration as it did in 1982, but the 1981 is quite lean, severe, and tough. It will benefit from 4–5 years of cellaring, but I would like to see more richness of fruit. Anticipated maturity: 1987–1995.
·
78

COS LABORY (Fifth-Growth) AVERAGE

Production: 6,200 cases	Grape varieties: Cabernet Sauvignon—35% Merlot—35% Cabernet Franc—25% Petit Verdot—5%
Time spent in barrels: 12–16 months	Average age of vines: 26 years
Evaluation of present classification: Should be downgraded to a Cru Bourgeois	

One of the most disappointing wines of all the classified growths, Cos Labory is just one blatant example of the need for a more relevant classification than the 1855 classification of the wines of the Médoc. Ranked a fifth-growth in 1855, the wine would have a difficult time obtaining Cru Bourgeois status in any new order. The owners, François and Bernard Audoy, produce a fruity, bland, light, often feebly colored wine which lacks bouquet, flavor, concentration, and length. The wine is exposed to a rather cool vinification that minimizes flavor and color extraction, and is given two filtrations, one prior to barrel aging and the other prior to bottling, which can strip a wine if it is performed excessively.

The price for this low quality is high, no doubt because of Cos Labory's fifth-growth status. However, there are numerous Cru Bourgeois wines in St.-Estèphe that make much better and more interesting wine than Cos Labory. From a consumer's perspective, this is a wine to approach with a great deal of caution.

VINTAGES

1983—In tasting all the 1983 St.-Estèphes side by side, the Cos Labory
· was disturbingly light, innocuous, simple, and plain. A respect-
70 able *vin de table,* but hardly a wine of classified-growth quality.
Drink in 2–3 years. Last tasted, 6/84.

1982—In the context of the vintage, a rather mediocre wine, but in the
· context of Cos Labory's performance record, a solid, amply en-
75 dowed wine, with good concentration, very good color, and moderate tannins. Anticipated maturity: 1987–1994. Last tasted,
10/84.

1979—Medium ruby, with a shallow, faint, fruity aroma, this medium-
· bodied wine has a light intensity, dull fruitiness, simple flavors,
65 and few tannins. Drink now. Last tasted, 9/84.

1978—Fully mature, with a burnt, stemmy, leafy aroma, this light- to
· medium-weight wine has diluted fruit flavors and light to mod-
67 erate tannins. A very mediocre wine. Last tasted, 5/83.

1976—Faded, damp cellar aromas offer too little ripe fruit and too
· many wet earthy components for a good Bordeaux wine. Light
55 to medium ruby color now shows ample evidence of age as the
brown color sets in. Drink this thin, flawed wine now, if ever.
Last tasted, 2/80.

1975—A tannic, angular wine, with no charm, little fruit in evidence,
· and a severe, hard, tannic "bite" to it. Anticipated maturity:
64 1990–1995. Last tasted, 12/81.

1971—Poor winemaking, and perhaps overcropping as well, have ac-
· counted for a very mediocre, thin, green, nasty wine which
52 shows the ugliest side of Bordeaux. Last tasted, 4/78.

1970—An acceptable wine that provided decent, if hardly inspired
· drinking in the late '70s, this medium ruby wine exhibited a
70 simple yet straightforward fruitiness, some pleasing, spicy,
cherry components, and light to medium body. Drink immediately. Last tasted, 2/80.

PAUILLAC

There is no more famous appellation of the Haut-Médoc and Bordeaux than Pauillac. While the commune of Margaux has a more lyrical and romantic name, as well as a famous first-growth château of the same title, it is Pauillac's vineyards that lay claim to three of the Médoc's four first-growths. Yes, the fabled, fabulously expensive Pauillac trio of Lafite-Rothschild, Mouton-Rothschild, and Latour all reside here, and they are well backed up by a bevy of wines, some brilliant, some terribly overrated, and some seriously overlooked or forgotten. Seventeen wines from Pauillac were included in the original 1855 classification, and today only two or three estates would have trouble holding on to their position should an independent study of the quality of the wines be done.

If one had to describe the textbook Pauillac it would tend to have a rich, full-bodied texture, a distinctive bouquet of blackcurrants and cedary scents, and excellent aging potential. Since virtually all of the permitted vineyard acreage is controlled by the 17 classified growths, there are fewer Cru Bourgeois wines in Pauillac than in a commune such as St.-Estèphe. However, there is a wide diversity in the styles of Pauillac one is likely to encounter. Among the three famous first-growths, the styles of wine could not be more different. Certainly their soils all share the gravelly composition that reflects the sun's heat and affords excellent drainage. However, Lafite-Rothschild's vineyard, tucked in the northern part of Pauillac right on the St.-Estèphe border, has a limestone base, resulting in wines that are Pauillac's most aromatically complex and subtly flavored. Lafite's bouquet has of course the telltale Pauillac "cédarwood" aroma, but Lafite is never a match for Mouton-Rothschild for sheer opulence and power, or Latour for consistency. Of the other non-first Pauillacs, the lighter, aromatic Lafite style, albeit on a lower level, is best exemplified by the silky, light Haut-Batailley.

Mouton-Rothschild sits on a gravel ridge above the Médoc's largest town, Pauillac. In addition to the gravelly soil, Mouton has more sandstone in its soil base and combined with the abnormally high percentage of Cabernet Sauvignon used in making the wine, can, when everything works out right, produce the most decadently rich, fleshy, and exotic wine of not only Pauillac, but of the entire Médoc. In many ways, the wine of Mouton mirrors its flamboyant, bold owner, the Baron Philippe de Rothschild. Mouton is not the only Pauillac made in a big, rich, opulent style. Several kilometers south, on another slightly elevated ridge called the Bages plateau, Lynch-Bages makes a wine that can be splendidly deep and concentrated, clearly earning its reputation as the "poor man's Mouton."

Less renowned, but making a wine in this same style, is the reliable Haut-Bages-Libéral. Always dark ruby, fat, chunky, and oozing with the aromas of blackcurrants and cedarwood, this wine might well be called the "poor man's Lynch-Bages," as it is always a very fairly priced wine.

Latour is Pauillac's other first-growth, and this grand old estate, British owned yet French managed, has few if any peers when it comes to consistency from one vintage to the next. For most of this century, Latour, along with Montrose in St.-Estèphe, has been the slowest to mature and longest-lived wine made in Bordeaux. Its vineyard's location in southern Pauillac next to St.-Julien would seemingly suggest a more supple style of wine, but up until the late '70s, when a more supple style of Latour has seemingly and surprisingly emerged, Latour's wine had been as backward and as tannic as any. The soil at Latour is almost pure fine gravel soil that affords superb drainage, better than that enjoyed by Lafite-Rothschild or Mouton-Rothschild. That in itself may help explain why in rainy vintages such as 1968, 1969, 1972, and 1974 Latour easily outdistanced the other Pauillac first-growths. Latour is Latour, and in Pauillac there are no Latour "look-alikes" in style or character.

There are several other Pauillacs that have distinctive styles, making it difficult to generalize about the wine of this commune. Perhaps the most interesting wine of this group is Pichon-Longueville, Comtesse de Lalande, called Pichon Lalande by most that know her. Pichon Lalande sits adjacent to Latour, near the St.-Julien border. Unlike Latour, Pichon does indeed produce a St.-Julien-styled Pauillac, silky, spicy, supple, suave, and drinkable at a relatively young age. However, it would be foolish to assume that this precociously tasting wine does not age well—it does. The property has always made great wine, but over the last several decades this wine has been every bit as good as the other Pauillac first-growths, and certainly more consistent from vintage to vintage than Lafite-Rothschild and Mouton-Rothschild.

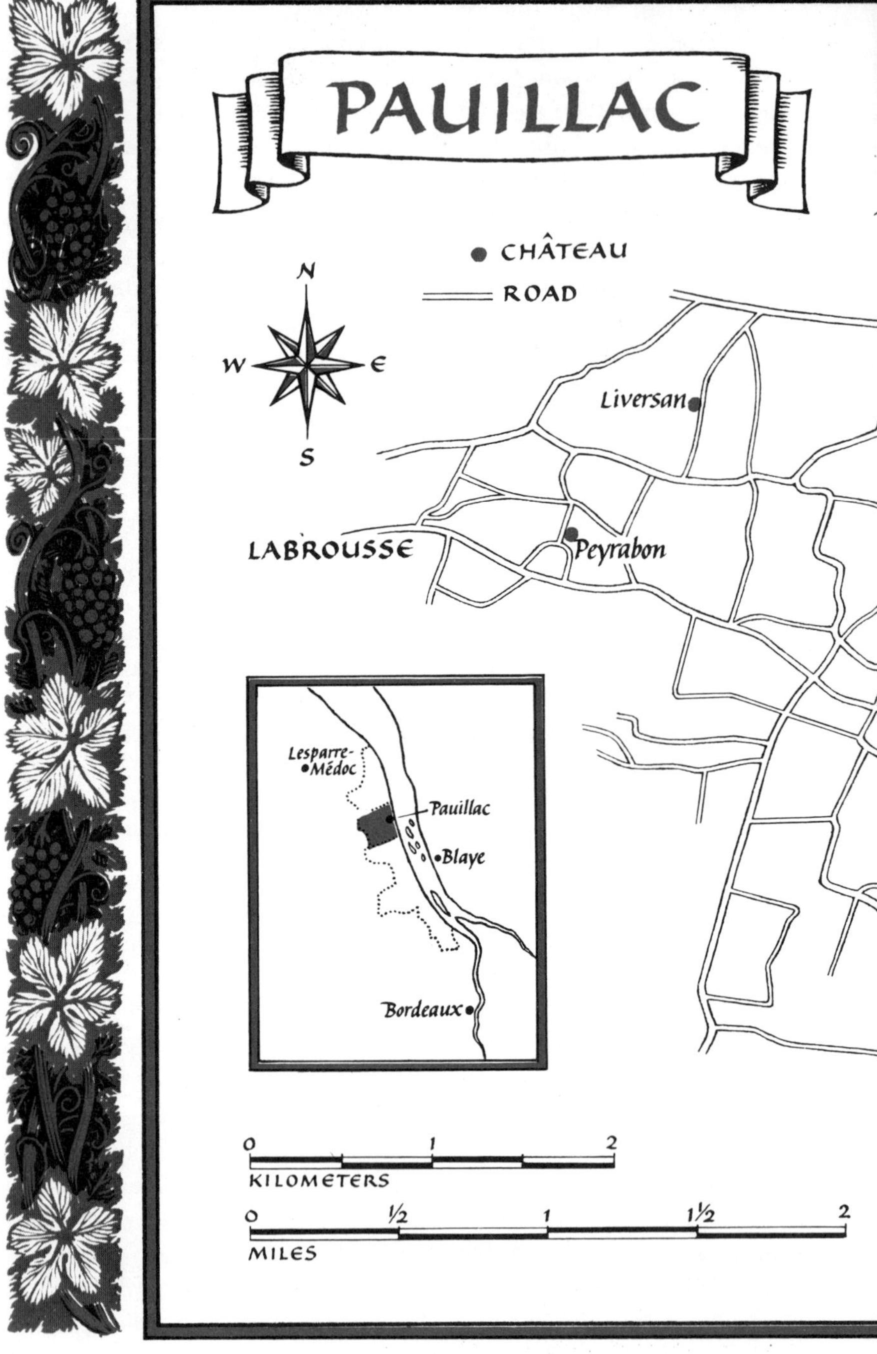
PAUILLAC
CHÂTEAU
ROAD
N
W
E
S
Liversan
LABROUSSE
Peyrabon
Lesparre-
Médoc
Pauillac
Blaye
Bordeaux
0
1
2
KILOMETERS
0
½
1
1½
2
MILES

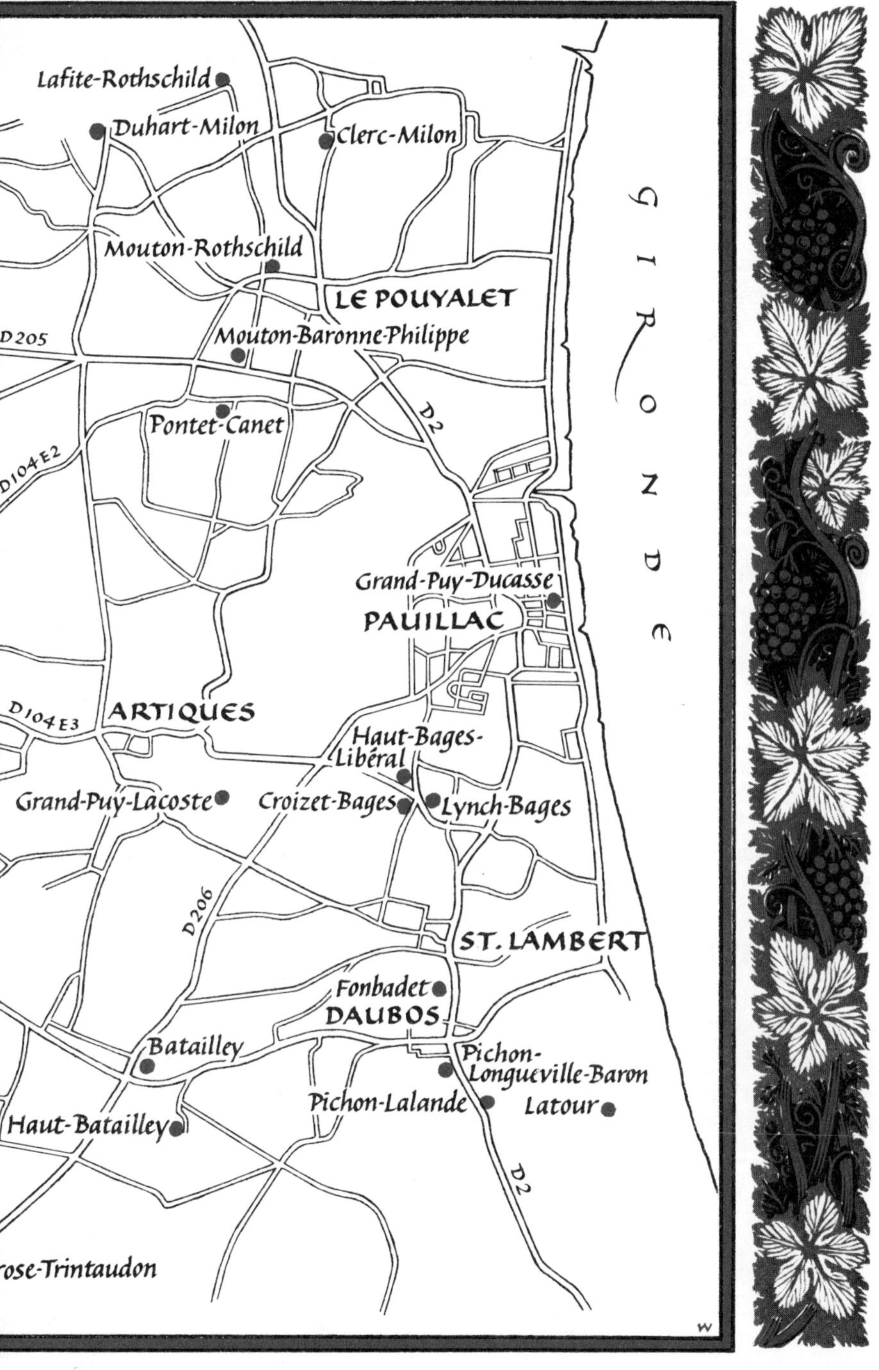
Lafite-Rothschild
Duhart-Milon
Clerc-Milon
GIRONDE
Mouton-Rothschild
LE POUYALET
D205
Mouton-Baronne-Philippe
D2
Pontet-Canet
D104E2
Grand-Puy-Ducasse
PAUILLAC
D104E3
ARTIQUES
Haut-Bages-Libéral
Grand-Puy-Lacoste
Croizet-Bages
Lynch-Bages
D206
ST. LAMBERT
Fonbadet
DAUBOS
Batailley
Pichon-Longueville-Baron
Pichon-Lalande
Latour
Haut-Batailley
D2
rose-Trintaudon

Grand-Puy-Lacoste never seems to receive the publicity that the other top Pauillacs do. For years this property, which sits well back from the Gironde River, was the joy of Bordeaux's leading gourmet (and from some accounts, gourmand as well), Raymond Dupin. Monsieur Dupin has died, but his reputation for holding lavish dinner parties remains unchallenged by anyone in Bordeaux today. Today the property, the wine cellars, and winemaking philosophy are under the capable, sure hand of Jean-Eugène Borie and his son, Xavier Borie. Their first vintage was a lovely 1978. You can be sure this is a property to watch, with a style unlike anything else described herein. It's a true Pauillac, cleaner, more consistent now than in the Dupin era, but still robust, tannic, and flavorful.

There are a bevy of other classified Pauillacs that generally merit their rating but rarely offer the excitement their price suggests they should have. Certainly Pichon-Longueville Baron has the most potential, but despite some recent improvements, Pichon Baron is a classic example of a Pauillac underachiever.

In contrast to St.-Estèphe, Pauillac has few well-known Cru Bourgeois properties. Certainly Fonbadet, which sits just north of Pichon Lalande and Latour, is a worthy entry into the new Médoc classification. The best non-classified-growth Pauillacs are the "second" wines of the famous first-growth estates Latour and Lafite, which are respectively Les Forts de Latour and Moulin des Carruades, and the second wine of Pichon Lalande called Reserve de la Comtesse. Les Forts is often better than the rank-and-file Pauillacs, and Reserve de la Comtesse can be very good (the 1983 is superb).

Vintages in Pauillac tend to be consistent. There are so many large estates here and so few Crus Bourgeois that the top properties should always be able to make very strict selections in years when Mother Nature is less than kind. Certainly, 1984 was a challenging year and some properties prevailed. Nineteen eighty-three was a very good year for Pauillac, 1982 of course superb, 1981 good, 1980 fair, 1979 very good, and 1978 quite good. Like St.-Estèphe, Pauillac is generally not a commune to buy blindly from in an off-vintage, unless you limit your purchases to the wine of Latour or Pichon Lalande, the two most consistent estates.

A CONSUMER'S CLASSIFICATION OF THE CHÂTEAUX OF PAUILLAC

OUTSTANDING

Latour
Mouton-Rothschild
Lafite-Rothschild
Pichon-Longueville, Comtesse de Lalande

EXCELLENT

Lynch-Bages
Grand-Puy-Lacoste

VERY GOOD

Haut-Batailley
Pontet-Canet
Duhart-Milon-Rothschild
Pichon-Longueville Baron de Pichon-Longueville
Les Forts de Latour

GOOD

Haut-Bages-Libéral
Batailley
Grand-Puy-Ducasse
Mouton-Baronne-Philippe
Clerc-Milon
Fonbadet

AVERAGE

Moulin des Carruades
Croizet-Bages

LATOUR (First-Growth) **OUTSTANDING**

Production: 20,000 cases	Grape varieties: Cabernet Sauvignon—80% Merlot—10% Cabernet Franc—5% Petit Verdot—5%
Time spent in barrels: 22–30 months	Average age of vines: 37 years
Evaluation of present classification: Should be maintained	

Impressively situated on the Pauillac-St.-Julien border, immediately north of the walled vineyard of Léoville-Las Cases, Latour's vineyard can be easily spotted from the road because of the fortress-like tower that is depicted on the label. This formidable tower, which overlooks the vineyards and the Gironde River, is a vestige of the 17th century, when it was built on the site of a 15th-century fortress used by the English to fend off attacks by pirates.

Latour is one of a handful of major Bordeaux châteaux to be controlled by foreign interests. Since 1963, Latour has been under English ownership with the French retaining a minority interest in the estate.

The wine produced here has been an impeccable and classic model of consistent excellence in great, mediocre, and poor vintages. For that reason, many consider Latour to be the Médoc's finest wine. Latour's reputation for making Bordeaux's best wine in mediocre or in poor vintages such as 1974, 1972, or 1960 seems totally justified, although in the two recent poor Bordeaux vintages of 1977 and 1980, Latour's wines were surprisingly light and were eclipsed in quality by a number of other châteaux. The wine of Latour also has a remarkable record of being a stubbornly slow developing wine, requiring a good 20–25 years of bottle age to shed its considerable tannic clout and reveal its stunning power, depth, and richness. This style, often referred to by commentators as virile, masculine, and tough, may be undergoing a subtle yet very perceptible softening up. This is adamantly denied by the staff at Latour, but my tastings of recent vintages, particularly those from 1979 on, seem to point to a more supple, more accessible, but still very great Latour. It is entirely too early to know if a change has in fact occurred, but subsequent vintages should be watched closely.

Even if a more supple, earlier-maturing Latour is now being crafted by the winemaking staff, the wine of Latour remains one of Bordeaux's most concentrated, rich, tannic and full-bodied wines which, when mature, has a unique bouquet of fresh walnuts and leather, blackcurrants, and gravelly, mineral scents. When comparing the great vintages of the famous first-growths of Pauillac over the years 1945–1975, it is interesting to note that regardless of the vintage, Latour will have the darkest color, the most reticent bouquet, and a restrained but rich, deep, full-bodied, muscular character and texture on the palate. Lafite-Rothschild tends to have the lightest color, and when vinified properly, the finest and most complex bouquet. Yet in Lafite-Rothschild, the surge of complex aromas is often followed by a wine that is sharper, more acidic, and less weighty on the palate. Mouton-Rothschild tends to be darker in color than Lafite, yet lighter than Latour. However, in a great vintage, it is the most silky and decadently opulent of the three wines. Since 1975, the wine of Lafite has taken on greater strength and vigor; consequently, generalizations about styles of these three great wines are less valid today than they were 10 years ago.

VINTAGES

1983—Tasted four times from the cask, the 1983 Latour is impressively
· dark-colored as one might expect, but on each occasion tasted
87 flabby, disjointed, and lacking firmness and structure. A sojourn in new oak barrels will no doubt help provide a much needed framework, but this wine is not likely to be one of Latour's great wines. At this early stage, the wine seems clearly outdistanced by the rival first-growth Pauillacs, Lafite-Rothschild and Mouton-Rothschild. Anticipated maturity: 1995–2010. Last tasted, 3/85.

1982—This is a very big, deep, rich, intense Latour with the 1982
· vintage's telltale personality traits—great dark ruby purple
97 color, a terrific ripe, fruity lushness and concentration, and significant tannin content. Somewhat surprisingly, the wine does not have the backward toughness usually associated with this wine. A very big, great wine that is undoubtedly the best Latour since the 1961. Anticipated maturity: 1995–2025. Last tasted, 1/85.

1981—The 1981 tastes remarkably velvety and supple for such a young
· Latour. Not that this is a malevolent occurrence, because the
90 excellence, complexity, and richness of the wine are still present. The color is dark ruby, the bouquet offers plenty of ripe cassis and spicy oak, the flavor is generous, silky, moderately tannic, and long in the finish. This Latour may turn out to be similar to the 1971. Anticipated maturity: 1991–2005. Last tasted, 10/84.

1980—In the mediocre vintages of the '50s, '60s, and early '70s, Latour
· frequently made the best wine in the Médoc. Not so in 1980.
83 The wine is clearly well above average for the vintage, but lacking weight and richness. Fruity, charming, supple, with a pleasant fruitiness, but short on the palate, this wine will be at its best over the next 6–7 years. Last tasted, 11/84.

1979—From cask samples, the 1979 Latour tasted typically tough,
· backward, and astringent, but now that it is bottled, it is sur-
88 prisingly precocious and forward, although not ready to drink. Dark ruby with an intense bouquet, filled with cassis fruit, some

scents of cedarwood and vanillin, this medium-bodied Latour has well-balanced, fleshy flavors, an underlying supple, smooth texture, and ripe, round tannin in the finish. Reminiscent of the 1971 Latour. Anticipated maturity: 1990–2000. Last tasted, 5/84.

1978 —The 1978 is a magnificent Latour, which may well turn out to be
· the best wine produced by Latour in the '70s. While it can't
95 match the incredible concentration of the massive 1970, or the pure strength of the powerful 1975, it is impeccably balanced with oodles of ripe blackcurrant fruit, fat, intensely concentrated flavors with a stunningly big bouquet and long, deep, very fine finish. Anticipated maturity: 1992–2010. Last tasted, 2/84.

1976 —I have had my share of arguments with Latour's staff over the
· relative merits of this wine, which I deem slightly shallow, lack-
83 ing depth, and somewhat hollow and angular on the palate for a Latour. Of course, the château thinks differently, but the proof is, as it is always, in the bottle. As a wine, it is a success for the vintage, but this Latour is not likely to get better, only worse as the fruit continues to fade and the harsh tannins ascend. Drink up! Last tasted, 1/85.

1975 —Of the recent vintages of Latour, this is the most backward as it
· begs for 20 or more years of cellaring. Still young, astringent,
93 and very impressive as it approaches its tenth birthday, this Latour has a splendid blackcurrant aroma, with a whiff of cedar, mineral scents, and walnuts. This wine will reward the patient collector with greatness at the turn of the century. Anticipated maturity: 2000–2030. Last tasted, 5/84.

1974 —In this mediocre vintage of rather green, stalky, hollow wines,
· Latour produced one of the very best wines of the vintage. Still
86 not fully mature, this dark ruby wine has good fruit, a medium body, surprising depth and ripeness for the vintage, and a sinewy, tannic finish. It avoids the telltale harshness and fruit deficiency found in so many 1974s. Anticipated maturity: 1988–1994. Last tasted, 1/84.

1973 —Very light for Latour, even considering the watery, diluted char-
· acter of most wines from this vintage, the 1973 Latour still offers
80 light, charming, somewhat complex drinking as it has held together much better than I would have suspected. Soft, ripe, moderately intense flavors seem dominated by Merlot and exhibit no tannin. Drink immediately! Last tasted, 11/82.

1972—A disastrous vintage for Bordeaux, yet Latour produced a rather
· big, deeply colored, somewhat disjointed and clumsy wine, but
75 one with good fruit, a herbaceous, cedary bouquet, and good
flavor concentration. Drink now! Last tasted, 12/83.

1971—Still not ready to drink, this dark ruby, tightly knit wine exudes
· blackcurrants, cedar, iron-like scents from a bouquet that is still
87 unfolding and continuing to develop. Dark ruby, with very good
concentration, a tannic finish, and fleshy, chewy texture, this
medium-weight Latour still needs time. Anticipated maturity:
1986–1998. Last tasted, 12/84.

1970—One of the most massive Latours produced in the post-World
· War II era, the 1970 is bigger and richer than any Latour in this
96 period except the 1945, 1959, 1961, and 1982. Extremely full-bodied, very, very concentrated, astonishingly backward, impenetrably dark ruby, and yet so, so promising. Dense, powerful, and overpowering on the palate. Anticipated maturity: 2000–2030. Last tasted, 1/85.

1969—In this ungracious vintage Latour produced an acceptable wine
· of average color and concentration, but lean, angular, and
74 charmless. Drink now! Last tasted, 6/76.

1967—Unquestionably the best wine produced in the Médoc in 1967,
· the Latour has dark ruby color with some browning at the edges,
88 a medium- to full-bodied feel, plenty of blackcurrant fruit, and
some light, soft tannins still present. Head and shoulders above the other first-growths, this wine has the classic Latour bouquet of black walnuts, blackcurrants, mineral scents, and cedarwood. Drink over the next 5–7 years. Last tasted, 1/85.

1966—A great wine, again the finest of all the Médoc first-growths in
· 1966, this wine has very dark ruby color, an amber edge, and a
95 top-notch bouquet of leather, spices, tobacco, and ripe fruit.
Quite concentrated, rich and powerful, this tannic wine is easily the best wine produced by Latour in the '60s, aside from the 1961. Anticipated maturity: 1988–2005. Last tasted, 1/85.

1964—In 1964, as in 1966 and 1967, Latour is the best Médoc. The
· 1964 is drinking beautifully now, but should hold for at least
92 another decade. Rich, round, supple, generous flavors show excellent concentration. Soft tannins and a silky, rich, very long finish make this a sumptuous Latour. Drink over the next 10 years. Last tasted, 5/84.

1962—Latour at its best, this is the best wine of the vintage. This hefty,
· powerful wine has a dense, almost opaque color, significantly
91 less charm and roundness than the 1964, but concentrated, thick, rich flavors that still exhibit mouth-watering tannins. An old-style, heavyweight Latour which still has a way to go. Anticipated maturity: 1985–1995. Last tasted, 3/84.

1961—A remarkably viscous, huge, intense wine that is one of the
· biggest and richest wines I have ever tasted from Latour, the
100 1961 is port-like, with an almost syrupy character, yet well balanced given its herculean proportions. A phenomenal bouquet of walnuts, cassis, and cedar inundates the nose. A wine with incredible concentration and length, the 1961 Latour has the potential to last 100 years. Anticipated maturity: 2000–2050. Last tasted, 10/83.

MOUTON-ROTHSCHILD (First-Growth) OUTSTANDING

Production: 22,500 cases	Grape varieties: Cabernet Sauvignon—85% Cabernet Franc—10% Merlot—5%
Time spent in barrels: 20–24 months	Average age of vines: 43 years
Evaluation of present classification: Should be maintained	

Mouton-Rothschild is the place and wine that the Baron Philippe de Rothschild single-handedly created. No doubt his aspirations for Mouton, at the age of 21 when he acquired the estate, were high. However, he has become, through the production of an opulently rich and remarkably deep and exotic style of Pauillac, the only person able to effectuate change in the 1855 classification of the wines of the Médoc.

In 1973 Mouton-Rothschild was officially classified a first-growth, which permitted the flamboyant Baron to change his defiant wine labels from "*Premier ne puis, second ne daigne, Mouton suis*" (First I cannot be, second I will not call myself, Mouton I am) to "*Premier je suis, second je fus, Mouton ne change*" (First I am, second I was, Mouton does not change).

There is no question that several of the greatest bottles of Bordeaux I have ever drunk have been Moutons. The 1945, 1947, 1949, 1953, 1959, 1961, and 1982 are stunning examples of Mouton at its best. However, I have also experienced too many mediocre vintages of Mouton that are embarrassing for a first-growth to produce, and obviously irritating for a consumer to purchase and taste. Certainly the record of the last 25 years is one in which great wines were produced only in 1961, 1970, possibly 1975, and undoubtedly in 1982. The 1980, 1977, 1976, 1974, 1973, 1967, and 1964 fell well below standards for a first-growth. Criticism of Mouton seems to have had an effect because Mouton's last three vintages have shown a consistency in top quality that was sometimes missing in earlier years.

The reasons for the success of this wine are quite numerous. The labels of Mouton are collectors' items. Since 1945, the Baron Philippe de Rothschild has commissioned an artist to do a painting which is depicted on the top of the label. There has been no shortage of great artists to appear on the Mouton-Rothschild label, from such Europeans as Miró, Picasso, Chagall, and Cocteau, to the Americans Warhol, Motherwell, and in 1982, movie director John Huston. Second, the opulence of Mouton in the great vintages differs significantly in style from the austere elegance of Lafite-Rothschild, and the powerful, tannic Latour. Third, the impeccably kept château itself, with its superb wine museum, is the Médoc's, and possibly the Bordeaux region's, top tourist attraction. And lastly, the Baron himself, who has done so much to promote not only his wines, but all the wines of Bordeaux.

VINTAGES

1983—A very fine Mouton for sure, but unless it suddenly develops
• more character, the 1983 will not be a great or legendary Mou-
89 ton. Dark ruby with a ripe, rich, full aroma of cassis, fruit, deep
and powerful on the palate, with plenty of noticeable tannin.
Bigger and richer than the 1981 or 1979, less elegant than the
1978, this Mouton may turn out to resemble the fine 1966. Anticipated maturity: 1992–2015. Last tasted, 3/85.

1982—One of the very greatest young wines I have ever tasted. Each
• time I have had an opportunity to evaluate this wine, I have
100 been apprehensive of finding less than pure perfection. However, on each new occasion I find a wine that seems to grow
more and more splendid. Nineteen eighty-two was a perfect
vintage for Mouton-Rothschild, which employed 600 pickers and
harvested this large vineyard in just 7 (versus the normal 21)
days. The 1982 Mouton presents a gustatory and olfactory smorgasbord. When tasting it, I recall what Michael Broadbent said
about the 1945 Mouton: "This is not claret, it is Mouton, a
Churchill of a wine." Incredibly rich on the palate, with an

opulence, weight and concentration that one can only compare to the very greatest Moutons, the 1929 and 1945, it will need a good 15 years, perhaps longer, to show all its considerable talents, but surely this wine is one of the legends of this century. Anticipated maturity: 1995–2025. Last tasted, 1/85.

1981—This is another very good Mouton that I prefer to the 1979, 1978,
· and 1976. It is not nearly as rich and concentrated as the 1982,
88 1975, or 1970, and not as tannic as the 1983. This wine may turn out to resemble the stylish and delicious 1971. Moderately dark ruby color, with an evolving bouquet of leather and blackcurrants, this wine has good firm tannins, very good richness, and an astringent finish. Anticipated maturity: 1990–2005. Last tasted, 10/84.

1980—This is an uninspiring effort from Mouton, notwithstanding the
· vintage conditions that were not favorable. Medium ruby color,
74 with a stemmy, stalky, unripe aroma, lean, austere, overly tannic flavors, and astringent finish. Time may help, but I have my doubts. Anticipated maturity: 1986–1990. Last tasted, 10/83.

1979—The 1979 is a very good wine which does not, however, compare
· favorably with the efforts turned in by the other first-growths in
85 1979. Rather high in acidity, with an austere, tight, hard, closed-in personality. On the palate, the wine shows good weight, some ripe blackcurrant fruit, but tails off in the finish. Somewhat perplexing to evaluate. Anticipated maturity: 1990–2000. Last tasted, 4/84.

1978—Quite tannic and unyielding but, nevertheless, exhibiting more
· richness, concentration and depth than the 1979, this dark ruby
87 wine is in a state of dormancy at the moment. Reticent aromas of ripe berry fruit and vanillin oakiness are present, as is a significant level of tannin. A promising Mouton which requires considerable patience. Anticipated maturity: 1995–2010. Last tasted, 6/83.

1977—Thin, vegetal, stemmy, and charmless, this medium ruby wine
· should have been declassified completely rather than sold as a
66 first-growth to unsuspecting consumers. Last tasted, 4/81.

1976—Medium to dark ruby with some browning at the edges, this wine
· is approaching maturity and exhibits an interesting, moderately
83 intense bouquet of ripe plums, spicy oak, and leather. Plenty of tannin is still evident, but the overall balance and depth of fruit suggests that the tannins will clearly outlive the fruit. Lacking

depth and concentration, this is a good Mouton for drinking over the next 5–6 years. Anticipated maturity: 1986–1992. Last tasted, 9/83.

1975—Still incredibly backward, yet for certain, the 1975 Mouton is
· loaded with chewy, blackcurrant fruit, a dusty, leathery texture,
90 and the hard tannins so typical of this vintage. Quite full-bodied and weighty on the palate, the dark ruby color shows no signs of maturity. The biggest Mouton of the '70s, but one must have considerable patience for this wine to become ready to drink. Anticipated maturity: 1995–2020. Last tasted, 4/84.

1974—A below-average effort from Mouton, this wine has the telltale
· hollowness of the vintage, a stale, flat bouquet, and deficiency
69 in rich fruitiness. Drink now and over the next 2–3 years. Last tasted, 5/81.

1973—The year Mouton was officially made a first-growth was cele-
· brated by a beautiful label done by Pablo Picasso. Whether one
65 is an art or a wine critic, the label clearly surpasses the wine. Very oaky and woody, with rapidly fading fruit, this is a wine worth having if only for the historic significance of the bottle's label. Last tasted, 2/82.

1971—Extremely enjoyable and mature by 1980, this medium-weight
· Mouton offers charm, elegance, and the classic Mouton "lead
86 pencil" bouquet. Moderately powerful and rich, this is a delightful Mouton for drinking over the next 2–3 years. Last tasted, 6/82.

1970—This vintage produced a classic Mouton that continues to de-
· velop at a snail's pace. Very dark ruby with a tight, closed-in
95 bouquet which reluctantly yields scents of walnuts, cassis, leather, and, of course, cedary, herbaceous aromas. Powerful on the palate with plenty of mouth-puckering tannin present, this wine has developed very slowly. Superlative length and depth suggest a 40–60-year life span. Anticipated maturity: 1995–2030. Last tasted, 10/84.

1967—I tasted an agreeably fruity, fairly simple, medium-weight, and
· fully mature 1967 Mouton in 1974. More recently the wine has
73 shown itself to be shallow, hollow, and in decline. Drink up! Last tasted, 4/79.

1966—This is a potentially outstanding Mouton that, while not in the
· class of the 1961, 1970, or 1982, can clearly be called one of the
92 half-dozen best '66s. Like many '66s, it has remained dry, austere, and buttoned-up for longer than most observers would have

liked. However, the dark ruby color, the evolving bouquet of tobacco, cedar, spices, and mineral scented Cabernet Sauvignon fruit, and rich yet tightly restrained flavors, as well as a long finish, all point to a promising future. Anticipated maturity: 1990–2010. Last tasted, 11/84.

1964—The 1964 Mouton is a notable failure because it was picked late
· in the deluge of rain that wiped out those châteaux who were
55 waiting for extra ripeness. One wonders why Bordeaux's best
châteaux do not declassify the entire crop when they produce a
wine this miserable. Last tasted, 5/78.

1962—Noticeable bottle variation, always a plague when tasting older
· wines, and most likely caused by different storage conditions,
90 has been the one common characteristic that I find in my 1962
Mouton tasting notes. The score reflects the well-kept bottles that are now fully mature. A huge bouquet of blackcurrant fruit, spices, and leather all combine to captivate the olfactory senses. Silky, soft, nicely concentrated flavors are supple, round, and long. Delicious now; drink up. Last tasted, 6/83.

1961—Still remarkably backward for its age, this dark, densely colored
· Mouton has a rich, multiscented bouquet of cedar, leather, cin-
96 namon, and ripe fruit. Big, tough, and fat on the palate, with
exceptional concentration, this wine just lingers and lingers. There is still plenty of tannin remaining to preserve this big wine for another 20 or 30 years. Anticipated maturity: 1992–2020. Last tasted, 9/83.

LAFITE-ROTHSCHILD (First-Growth) OUTSTANDING

Production: 22,000–30,000 cases	Grape varieties: Cabernet Sauvignon—70% Merlot—20% Cabernet Franc—5% Petit Verdot—5%
Time spent in barrels: 24–30 months	Average age of vines: 44 years
Evaluation of present classification: Should be maintained	

Bordeaux's most famous property and wine, Lafite-Rothschild, with its elegant, undersized, and understated label, has become a name synonymous with wealth, prestige, history, respect, and wines of remarkable longevity.

While the vintages since 1975 have witnessed the production of a succession of superlative Lafites, the record of Lafite between 1961 and 1974 was one of surprising mediocrity for a first-growth. It has always remained a mystery to me why more wine critics did not cry foul after tasting some of the Lafite wines made during this period. The official line from the château has always been that the wines were made in such a light, elegant style that they were overmatched in blind tastings by bigger, more robust wines. Certainly such things do indeed happen, but the mediocrity of Lafite was exemplified by wine from very fine vintages (1966, 1970, 1971) that were surprisingly deficient in color, very dry and overly oaked, and quite high in acidity. Several vintages were complete failures (1964, 1967, 1974), yet released for high prices under the Lafite name.

The reasons for such occurrences are not likely to ever be admitted by the Rothschild family, but given the great record of successes since 1975, the problems in the '60s and early '70s seems to be related to the following. First, there were absentee and casually interested owners who lived in Paris and loosely supervised the goings-on at Lafite. Certainly the management of Lafite since 1975 has been diligent and active by both Eric and Elie Rothschild. Second, the wine at Lafite was kept too long in oak barrels. In the past, the wine was often kept a minimum of 32–36 months in oak barrels, whereas now 24–30 months is maximum. This change has undoubtedly caused Lafite to taste fruitier and fresher. Third, the current winemaking staff at Lafite seems to be consciously picking the grapes later to obtain greater ripeness and lower acidity in their wines. Lastly, all Lafite is being bottled at the same time. In the past there have always been unsubstantiated rumors that Lafite often dragged out the bottling operation over many months. If true, then more than acceptable levels of bottle variation would exist.

Regardless of the record of the immediate past, Lafite-Rothschild is now producing great wines, and the turnabout in quality clearly occurred with the magnificent 1975.

VINTAGES

1983—The 1983 is an unbelievably tannic wine that I am sure will
• require at least several decades to mature. A very dark-colored
92 wine, with excellent concentration, and a surprisingly tough, fleshy texture, it seems to have more in common with the wines made at Latour. A very impressive wine, yet only the very patient will be interested in this wine, because it must be cellared. Anticipated maturity: 2005–2035. Last tasted, 3/85.

1982—Similarly tannic and incredibly backward like the 1983 Lafite,
· the 1982 is a bigger, more concentrated wine than the 1983.
96 Opaque, with a dark ruby color, a huge unevolved bouquet of ripe blackcurrants, violets, and vanillin, spicy oaky scents, this is an uncommonly "big" wine for Lafite. In recent vintages, only the 1959 is of similar power and style and had the same enormous potential. Anticipated maturity: 2000–2030. Last tasted, 2/85.

1981—The classic Lafite bouquet, perhaps the most interesting and
· complex of all the Médocs save Palmer and Margaux, is just
93 beginning to emerge. Ripe with blackcurrant fruit, intermingled with cedary scents and spices, it is extremely promising. On the palate the wine is hard, quite tannic, rich, and full-bodied, with long length and a multidimensional personality. Another big Lafite which has obviously been vinified to last decades. Anticipated maturity: 2000–2025. Last tasted, 11/84.

1980—A lightweight, agreeable wine from Lafite, it has a moderately
· intense aroma of cassis and fresh tobacco, and soft, charming
83 flavors. A success for the vintage. Anticipated maturity: 1986–1990. Last tasted, 4/84.

1979—Not quite the size of the 1981, but graceful and perhaps more
· "typically" Lafite than the 1982 or 1983, this wine has a dark
90 ruby color, a tight but complex bouquet of blackcurrants, spice and vanillin oakiness, medium body, firm tannins, and a long crisp finish. Anticipated maturity: 1988/2005. Last tasted, 10/84.

1978—If vintage charts were always correct, the 1978 would be con-
· sidered far superior to the 1979 Lafite. However, I tend to per-
90 sonally prefer the 1979, but qualitatively both wines appear equal. Dark ruby, with pronounced ripe, savory, fruity, cedary, slightly herbaceous bouquet, surprisingly approachable, velvety flavors, and a long supple finish, this moderately tannic wine seems to be developing quickly. Anticipated maturity: 1988–2005. Last tasted, 2/84.

1976—The wine of the vintage with nary a challenger in view, the 1976
· Lafite clearly stands far above the crowd in 1976. A beautiful
96 bouquet of seductive cedarwood, spices, and ripe fruit is followed by a very concentrated, darkly colored wine, with excellent concentration and great length and texture. A stunning wine which may turn out to be the best Lafite of the '70s. Anticipated maturity: 1990–2010. Last tasted, 11/84.

1975—Nineteen hundred seventy-five was a watershed vintage for
· Lafite-Rothschild. Emile Peynaud, Bordeaux's famed oenolo-
96 gist, oversaw the vinification while Lafite was in search of a new winemaker. The first great Lafite since 1959, in weight, power, and style it coincidentally resembles the 1959. An intense, cedary, ripe, rich, fruity, tobacco-scented bouquet seems at times to suggest a great Graves. On the palate, the wine explodes with deep fruit, full body, remarkable texture and length. A great wine that seems less intense but more powerful and lighter in color than the superb 1976. Anticipated maturity: 1990–2010. Last tasted, 4/84.

1974—It was very difficult to make good wine in 1974, but certainly a
· first-growth is expected to make a strict selection of its best lots
56 and sell only the best. This wine is browning badly, has a tired, stale, flat taste, and is inexcusably diluted, as well as very short and thin on the palate. Quite poor. Last tasted, 11/82.

1973—One of the charming 1973s, this light, somewhat watery, thin
· wine has Lafite's classic perfumed bouquet, short, compact,
72 agreeable flavors, and little tannin. That was in 1980, the last time I tasted it. Drink it up, as it most likely is in complete decline. Last tasted, 12/80.

1971—Another disappointment for Lafite, the 1971 has always tasted
· flat, is quite brown in color, with a stewed, slightly dirty, rusty,
60 nondescript bouquet suggesting a poor *élevage* (the French term for bringing up the wine). Now close to its demise, this wine is of no value except to those who care only for labels. Last tasted, 11/82.

1970—Upon my graduation from law school, my parents gave me a
· case of this wine. I was simply overjoyed to get it, knowing the
83 château's reputation and the excellence of the 1970 vintage. Tastings from my own supply, and elsewhere, have always left me questioning the wine's lack of intensity and richness. The bouquet is richly perfumed with the scent of cedarwood and ripe fruit, but on the palate the wine tastes slightly sour, acidic, and looks surprisingly light in color for the 1970. A perplexing wine that with time has seen the bouquet grow more complex and the flavors more shallow and acidic. Perhaps it has fooled me, and my parents made the right choice, but until proved otherwise, I will stick to the score. Anticipated maturity: 1986–1998. Last tasted, 10/83.

1969—The 1969 Lafite has been consistently unusual to smell, with a
· cooked, burnt aroma, short flavors that suggested coffee and
62 herbs, and a hollow framework. This is a poorly made, ungracious wine which is best drunk up. Last tasted, 11/78.

1967—A vintage in which Lafite could certainly have done better. Light
· ruby with browning very much in evidence, this wine, in the
72 mid-1970s, had a fragrant, spicy, charming bouquet, easygoing, simple fruity flavors, and light tannins. Now it is quite tired, with old, faded fruit flavors. Drink up! Last tasted, 12/80.

1966—The 1966 is a very highly regarded vintage in which the 1966
· Lafite is a mirror image of the 1970. It is highly acclaimed in
84 certain corners, but I have the same problems with the 1966 Lafite as I did with the 1970. The bouquet is complex enough, although not particularly deep or intense, but on the palate the wine is disturbingly light, a trifle too acidic, and very dry, astringent, and austere in the finish. Furthermore, the color is quite pale when compared with other top 1966s. Certainly good, but hardly a notable success, given the vintage's reputation. Drink over the next 5 years. Last tasted, 11/84.

1964—Given the overblown praise for the 1961, 1966, and 1970 Lafites,
· it seems as though the 1964, a wine obviously made after the
80 rains, is a wine which has taken more criticism than it deserved. Not that it is sublime or profound, but it has consistently shown a chunky, fruity character, and a whiff of some of Lafite's fabulous bouquet. Drink up. Last tasted, 7/82.

1962—Like an old lady whose makeup can no longer conceal the ever
· increasing wrinkles, the 1962 Lafite is beginning to crack up,
84 but still offers a lovely, complex yet quickly evaporating bouquet of cedar, mineral scents, spices, and ripe fruit. Soft and silky, yet the acidity and alcohol are becoming more assertive as the fruit fades. The 1962 Lafite is still enjoyable, but it should be consumed quickly. Last tasted, 11/82.

1961—This wine has a phenomenal reputation. However, I have tasted
· the wine on five separate occasions where I found it to be un-
84 yielding, too acidic, disturbingly austere, and surprisingly ungenerous for a 1961. In several tastings, the wine was clearly drying out. The color is not terribly dense or dark for a 1961, but rather medium ruby with some amber at the edges. The wine does have a penetrating "cigarbox" Lafite bouquet, yet even it seems shy, given the legendary status of this wine. Lacking the

weight, concentration, and majesty of the great 1961s, this is a wine about which far too many writers have euphemistically said that it "needed time," was "elegant," or "not properly understood," when they should have used the word "overrated." In the context of the vintage and the estate of Lafite-Rothschild, it is a disappointment. Anticipated maturity: 1985–2000. Last tasted, 1/84.

PICHON-LONGUEVILLE, COMTESSE DE LALANDE
(Second-Growth) **OUTSTANDING**

Production: 18,000 cases	Grape varieties: Cabernet Sauvignon—45% Merlot—35% Cabernet Franc—12% Petit Verdot—8%
Time spent in barrels: 18–24 months	Average age of vines: 22 years
Evaluation of present classification: Should be upgraded to a Médoc first-growth	

At present, Pichon-Longueville, Comtesse de Lalande (Pichon Lalande) is unquestionably the most popular and consistently successful Pauillac. In many vintages it rivals and occasionally surpasses the three famous first-growths of this commune. The wines of Pichon Lalande have been very successful since 1961, but there is no question that in the late '70s and early '80s, under the energetic helm of Madame de Lencquesaing, the quality has risen to an extremely high plateau. This has been particularly true in the vintages since 1978.

The wine is made in what is a very intelligent manner, darkly colored, supple, fruity, and smooth enough to be drunk young. Yet Pichon Lalande has the requisite tannin, depth, and richness to age gracefully for 10–20 years. The proportion of Merlot (35%) here is the highest for any Pauillac, and no doubt accounts for part of the wine's soft, fleshy characteristic. Pichon Lalande belongs on the shopping list of any serious Bordeaux wine enthusiast as the commitment to quality here is as high as one can find in Bordeaux.

VINTAGES

1983—One of the great wines of the vintage, Pichon Lalande's 1983 is
· quite exceptional; and better than several of the Pauillac first-
94 growths, most notably Latour. Especially powerful and rich for Pichon Lalande, with more aggressive tannins than any vintage since 1975, this dark ruby wine has an intense bouquet of blackcurrants, violet-scented fruit, and vanillin oak, a full-bodied and excellent concentration, good acidity, and sensational length. A superstar of the vintage. Anticipated maturity: 1995–2015. Last tasted, 3/85.

1982—In the first 12 months of this wine's life I had given the wine
· very good but not outstanding marks. I deemed it a trifle too
94 flabby and soft. During the second year in the cask, the wine strengthened in character, firmed up in texture, and displayed more mid-range richness than I originally thought. Since it has been bottled, it has become nothing less than marvelous, and even in the context of the great 1982 vintage, it is one of the truly great wines. Very dark, very rich, and quite concentrated, this big, intensely fruity, viscous wine has excellent concentration, and is probably the best Pichon Lalande since the 1961. Anticipated maturity: 1992–2010. Last tasted, 1/85.

1981—The 1981 is a deliciously supple, fat, silky wine which exudes
· ripe flavors of blackcurrants and huge aromas of spicy oak and
91 violets. A lovely, full-bodied wine which is somewhat precociously styled, and probably best consumed over the next 12 years while waiting for some of the more tannic and backward 1981s to mature. Deep ruby in color, and deliciously fruity, this Pichon Lalande is a top success for the vintage. Anticipated maturity: 1988–1998. Last tasted, 11/84.

1980—A lovely, medium-weight wine which has been very well vinified,
· the 1980 Pichon Lalande is a delightful wine for drinking over
84 the next 2–3 years. The bouquet offers spicy, cedary aromas intermingled with copious ripe aromas of blackcurrants. Soft, velvety, very nicely concentrated, this supple, fruity, complex wine, from a vintage considered poor to mediocre, must be tasted to be believed. Anticipated maturity: 1985–1990. Last tasted, 10/84.

1979—Another top success for the vintage, and a worthy challenger to
· the outstanding 1978 which preceded it, the 1979 Pichon La-
93 lande is dark ruby in color, with a ripe, full-intensity, blackcurrant-scented bouquet that in some bottles seems to also show

a slight herbaceousness. Quite velvety, rich and gentle on the palate, and developing quickly, this round, generous, yet stylish and elegant wine has impeccable balance. Anticipated maturity: 1987–1998. Last tasted, 1/85.

1978—More tannic than the 1979 or 1981 Pichon Lalandes, this wine is
· among the deepest and richest wines produced at this château
94 in recent years. The telltale vanillin, spicy, blackcurrant, violet scents are present, but this medium- to full-bodied wine, despite a lush, deep velvety texture, shows some unresolved firm tannins in the finish. Anticipated maturity: 1988–2005. Last tasted, 4/84.

1976—Lacking the concentration and character of the best years, this
· wine is still very successful for the vintage. The color is medium
82 ruby, showing a little brown and amber at the edges. A gentle, light, interesting, mature bouquet, and soft, round flavors suggest this wine will last for several more years, but is at its peak now. Last tasted, 1/85.

1975—In an extensive blind tasting of the 1975 clarets in spring 1984
· at Sotheby's in London, I mistook this wine for a Pauillac first-
92 growth. It is a rather big-boned, full-bodied Pichon Lalande with more flesh and robustness than seen in recent vintages. A superlative bouquet of cedar, tobacco, and ripe plummy fruit is followed by a big wine with deep flavors, long length, and moderately hard tannins. Anticipated maturity: 1990–2010. Last tasted, 5/84.

1974—Now past its prime by a good 3–4 years, the 1974 Pichon La-
· lande is light ruby/amber in color with a frail, dissipated bou-
67 quet, and soft, very faded flavors. Last tasted, 9/80.

1973—Again completely gone, the light ruby, brown-colored wine was
· at its best in 1978, but like so many light, diluted 1973s, it is
62 now thin and empty. Last tasted, 10/80.

1971—An attractive wine that I have had several times recently, but
· only from a magnum which, of course, would be slower to evolve
81 than a regular bottle. From a magnum, the wine had a very mature, yet very alive, spicy, caramel-scented, ripe, complex bouquet. Soft, gentle, spicy flavors exhibit good concentration, low acidity, and very light tannins. Quite pleasant, but one should drink it up. Last tasted, 2/83.

1970—Just beginning to come into its own, the 1970 Pichon Lalande is
· a bigger, fuller, more robust wine than normally seen from Pi-
91 chon Lalande. Its bouquet offers ripe, almost exotic, chocolatey,

cedary aromas. Big, ripe, rich, and flavorful, this is a very impressive Pichon Lalande. Anticipated maturity: 1986–2000. Last tasted, 12/84.

1967—The 1967 was at its best in 1975, when it had some charm, and
· just enough fruit to balance out the acidity and tannins. Not
75 tasted recently, but given its light, frail character, the wine is
most likely to have faded badly. Last tasted, 7/78.

1966—Still not ready to drink, but quite dark in color with a rich,
· toasty, peppery, somewhat minty bouquet and big, yet firm,
88 fleshy, tannic flavors, this medium- to full-bodied wine has
plenty of concentration and length on the palate, as well as
obvious potential. One of the top wines of the vintage. Anticipated maturity: 1987–2000. Last tasted, 11/83.

1964—A delicious, yet rather uncomplex wine, the 1964 Pichon La-
· lande continues to evolve well in the bottle, It exhibits solid,
85 chunky, blackcurrant fruit, an earthy, spicy, almost Graves-like
bouquet, and soft, nicely endowed, fruity flavors. It is now fully mature. Drink up. Last tasted, 2/79.

1962—Quite flavorful, elegant, and deliciously charming as so many of
· the 1962s have proved to be, this fully mature wine has a mod-
85 erate to full intensity bouquet of ripe blackcurrant fruit, cedar,
and mineral scents. It is medium weight on the palate with a good measure of fruit and charm still in evidence. It should continue to drink delightfully for the next 3–4 years. Last tasted, 2/82.

1961—In 1978 I had the 1961 Pichon Lalande from a magnum in which
· it was quite unready, but since then I have had the wine several
95 times from the regular bottle where it was equally impressive,
but clearly approaching its apogee. Dark, almost opaque in color, with a huge, ripe, plummy bouquet with savory scents of toffee and chocolate, the 1961 Pichon Lalande is rich, full-bodied, viscous and incredibly deep on the palate, with amazing length. This wine will continue to drink well for 10–15 years. Last tasted, 6/84.

LYNCH-BAGES (Fifth-Growth) EXCELLENT

Production: 25,000 cases	Grape varieties: Cabernet Sauvignon—70% Merlot—15% Cabernet Franc—10% Petit Verdot—5%
Time spent in barrels: 18–20 months	Average age of vines: 34 years
Evaluation of present classification: Should be upgraded to a Médoc second-growth	

As one drives north on Bordeaux's château-studded "Route du Vin" (D2), immediately south of the dull, tiny commercial town of Pauillac is a plateau situated to the west called the Bages Plateau. Here lies Château Lynch-Bages, a modest building which has benefited enormously from a recent renovation project.

Bordeaux wine enthusiasts the world over have made Lynch-Bages one of Pauillac's most popular wines. Usually impressively colored, rather substantial and full-bodied, quite chunky and fruity, Lynch-Bages has fulfilled the role of the hulking yeoman, if Lafite and Pichon Lalande were the graceful, impeccably dressed aristocrats, and Latour and Mouton the powerful and well-mannered royalty.

Lynch-Bages is a straightforward, rich, chewy wine that offers loads of blackcurrant fruit, a chewy texture, and full, solid, substantial finish. If it lacks the grace and charm of Pauillac's best wines, it compensates for its deficiency in elegance with its generosity, roundness, and warmth.

Lynch-Bages's style between 1961 and 1983 reflects an inconsistency that was especially critical in the early '70s when the wine was poorly made in mediocre vintages such as 1972, 1973, 1974, and 1977. Even in good vintages such as 1971 and 1976, Lynch-Bages was not as good as it should have been. In addition, the wines made in the era between 1976 and 1981 exhibited a noticeably lighter and less forceful style than previous efforts. If Lynch-Bages was flirting with a lighter, more elegant style of wine, the shift to such a style was apparently discontinued in 1982 and 1983, as both wines recall the big, rich, hefty Lynch-Bages wines of 1970, 1962, and 1961.

Jean Michel Cazes is the proprietor at Lynch-Bages and is one of

Bordeaux's most effective ambassadors of good will for the region's wines. His affable personality and warm hospitality make Lynch-Bages one of the Médoc's friendliest spots for the wine tourist.

VINTAGES

1983—A top success for this very good, yet surprisingly inconsistent
· vintage, the Lynch-Bages 1983 is a full-blown, big, ripe, gutsy
90 Pauillac, with a rather intense bouquet of blackcurrant fruit, and deep, rich, briary flavors. Quite full-bodied, alcoholic and long, this substantial wine has a massive finish with mouth-puckering tannins present. A big, chewy wine. Anticipated maturity: 1995–2005. Last tasted, 3/85.

1982—In its first 6 months of life, I thought the 1982 Lynch-Bages to
· be a very good, yet a somewhat flabby, fat example of the 1982
93 vintage. After one year in the cask, the wine deepened, began to show significant tannin content, as well as the structure that was missing early in its life. From the bottle, Lynch-Bages is a massive, huge, densely colored wine, with an intense bouquet of ripe cassis fruit intermingled with scents of hot tar and vanillin oakiness. Viscous, rich, very full and concentrated on the palate, with plenty of tannin, this big-framed extroverted Lynch-Bages is in the same league as the outstanding 1970 and 1961 wines produced at this château. Anticipated maturity: 1994–2010. Last tasted, 1/85.

1981—After a period in the late '70s where Lynch-Bages seemed to be
· taking suppleness in winemaking too far, I detected a gradual
85 return to the very rich, robust, ripe, huge extract style of the great Lynch-Bages wines like the 1970, 1962, and 1961 with the 1981 Lynch-Bages. Certainly the monumental 1982 and excellent 1983 will eclipse the 1981 in stature, but this wine is quite good, and the best Lynch-Bages since 1975. Very dark ruby, with a strong, aggressive bouquet of blackcurrants, cedar, and new oak, this ripe wine has surprising density on the palate, and with plenty of tannin, this wine shows plenty of gutsy character. Anticipated maturity: 1990–1998. Last tasted 11/84.

1980—Somewhat variable from bottle to bottle, this lightweight Lynch-
· Bages has a cedary, fruity, somewhat stalky, herbaceous aroma,
78 light intensity flavors, and short, greenish, unripe finish. Anticipated maturity: 1985–1988. Last tasted, 3/85.

1979—Made in a period when Lynch-Bages was flirting with a lighter,
· more precocious, supple style, this wine is attractive but atypi-
83 cal for what fans of Lynch-Bages expect. Medium-bodied with soft, crisp, berryish flavors, light tannins, and some pleasing spicy, oaky notes, it is quite drinkable now. Anticipated maturity: 1985–1991. Last tasted, 4/84.

1978—Very similar to the 1979 in that it is round, fruity, and straight-
· forward in style, with soft, spicy blackcurrant flavors of moder-
84 ate intensity. Ready to drink now, it should continue to drink well for 4–5 years. A good, but not particularly noteworthy effort from Lynch-Bages. Anticipated maturity: 1985–1992. Last tasted, 11/84.

1976—Fully mature and somewhat frail-tasting, the 1976 Lynch-Bages
· is currently still charmingly fruity, a trifle too soft and diffuse,
75 with no grip or "attack," and showing disturbing browning at the edge. Owners of this vintage of Lynch-Bages should run, not walk, to the wine cellar, and consume it immediately. Last tasted, 9/82.

1975—The 1975 is one of the few classified-growth 1975s that can be
· drunk with some degree of pleasure. This precociously styled
85 Lynch-Bages is chocolatey, with ripe blackcurrant and cedar aromas, dusty, fat, savory flavors, and ripe tannins which are quietly falling away. Interestingly, it lacks the excellent depth of color of many 1975s. Anticipated maturity: 1988–1995. Last tasted, 5/84.

1974—A surprisingly weak effort from Lynch-Bages, this watery hollow
· wine fades remarkably fast in the glass, and the shallow, pale
60 colors suggest a wine which was diluted significantly by rain and perhaps overcropping. Drink up. Last tasted, 2/80.

1973—Disappointing for Lynch-Bages, this light, feeble wine has a
· washed-out color, a chaptalized bouquet of hot, burnt fruit, and
55 thin, nondescript flavors. It was at its best in 1978. Last tasted, 2/80.

1971—Lynch-Bages was clearly in a slump in the period 1971–1974
· because 1971 was a good vintage and a number of very fine,
58 graceful, fruity Pauillacs were produced. Not at Lynch-Bages. Now decrepit and very brown, with a musty, faded, dead vegetal bouquet, and short, sharp acidic flavors. A failure for the vintage. Last tasted, 10/79.

1970 · 90—The 1970 is a massive, inky-colored wine with gobs of blackcurrant, cedary, leathery flavors and aromas. This huge, ponderous wine is still youthfully aggressive and powerful. While it lacks finesse and elegance, it offers an immensely enjoyable robust-styled "big" wine which will last for at least another decade. Anticipated maturity: 1990–2010. Last tasted, 1/85.

1966 · 84—Impressively dark ruby with a slight amber edge, this wine seems to have the requisite concentration and structure to be more impressive, yet for whatever reason the wine seems to lack complexity and character. Rather one-dimensional, plump and fat, and capable of aging, but clearly missing something. Anticipated maturity: 1985–1995. Last tasted, 1/84.

1964 · 58—The 1964 Lynch-Bages is a failure, not so much because of faulty winemaking, but as a result of the château's decision to pick late to obtain maximum ripeness in the grapes. Such decisions always run the risk of foul weather, and in 1964 Lynch-Bages was one of the châteaux to get caught badly in the deluge that ensued. Thin, old, watery and uninteresting. Last tasted, 8/80.

1962 · 86—One of the all-time popular wines of Lynch-Bages, this wine has been drinking beautifully since 1970, and is still a delightful wine. However, the regular bottle size seems to be losing some of its exuberant, unabashed, gutsy fruitiness. Cedary and blackcurrant aromas still prevail, and this wine still has a wonderful, silky voluptuousness that has made it so pleasurable. Owners of it are advised to catch its wonderment now, or risk losing its pleasure altogether. Last tasted, 10/83.

1961 · 93—Perhaps the best Lynch-Bages ever made, the rich, cedary, massive aromas of blackcurrants and leather are present in plentiful amounts. Not terribly refined, but very deep, powerful, concentrated, and extremely long on the palate. This huge wine is at its apogee now, but will hold for a decade. Anticipated maturity: 1985–2000. Last tasted, 5/84.

GRAND-PUY-LACOSTE (Fifth-Growth) EXCELLENT

Production: 10,000–14,000 cases

Grape varieties:
Cabernet Sauvignon—75%
Merlot—25%

Time spent in barrels: 20–22 months

Average age of vines: 35 years

Evaluation of present classification: Should be upgraded to a Médoc third-growth, particularly since 1978

I never had the pleasure of meeting Raymond Dupin, the late owner of Grand-Puy-Lacoste. Dupin had a monumental reputation as one of Bordeaux's all-time great gourmets. According to some of his acquaintances, he was a gourmand as well. Prior to his death in 1978, he sold Grand-Puy-Lacoste to the highly talented and respected Jean-Eugène Borie, who installed his son Xavier at Grand-Puy-Lacoste to "run the show," and began a remodeling program for Grand-Puy's ancient and somewhat dilapidated cellars.

The château has been completely modernized. The resurgence of Grand-Puy-Lacoste to the forefront of leading Pauillacs, expected to take several years, was immediately apparent with Xavier's first vintage at Grand-Puy-Lacoste, the 1978.

Grand-Puy-Lacoste, which sits far back from the Gironde River on the Bages plateau, has enjoyed a solid reputation for big, durable, full-bodied Pauillacs, not unlike its neighbor a kilometer away, Lynch-Bages. However, the wines of the '60s and '70s, like those of Lynch-Bages, showed an unevenness in quality that in retrospect may have been due to the declining health of its owner. For example, highly regarded vintages such as 1961, 1966, 1970, and 1975 were less successful at Grand-Puy than its reputation would lead one to expect. Other vintages during this period, particularly the 1976, 1971, 1969, and 1967, were close to complete failures for some unexplained reason, but probably due to inattentiveness to detail.

However, since 1978 Grand-Puy-Lacoste has been making excellent wines, and no doubt the 1982 will be long remembered as one of the greatest wines of this château's long history. The price of Grand-Puy-Lacoste has not kept up with the recent strides in quality, so it is often a very fine value.

VINTAGES

1983—Fairly big-styled with a dark ruby color, rich blackcurrant
· aroma, this big, tannic wine shows very good concentration,
86 typical power, and an astringent finish. It will take time to mature. Anticipated maturity: 1993–2005. Last tasted, 3/85.

1982—This is a stupendous vintage, with the remarkable richness,
· intensity of fruit, and powerful, long finish that usually mark a
91 first-growth. Very dark, almost opaque, with a huge aromatic
bouquet of ripe blackcurrants, this velvety, very concentrated
wine shows tremendous fruit extract, but also mouth-gripping
tannins. Anticipated maturity: 1995–2015. Last tasted, 1/85.

1981—Surprisingly light in style for Grand-Puy, the 1981 has more in
· common with the 1979 than either the substantial 1982 or full-
80 bodied 1978. An elegant mixture of ripe berry fruit and spicy
oak overlaid with soft tannins makes this wine very easy to drink
now. Anticipated maturity: 1986–1991. Last tasted, 12/84.

1979—Quite precocious, with a surprisingly mature bouquet of ripe
· berry fruit, spicy oak, and flowers. Medium-bodied, with soft
83 flavors, a gentle, round texture, and pleasant yet short finish,
this wine is quite well made in a somewhat light style. Anticipated maturity: 1986. Last tasted, 2/85.

1978—The first vintage made under the expert management of Jean-
· Eugène Borie and his son Xavier, the 1978 is a very good wine
87 with long-term cellaring potential. Dark ruby, with a ripe, yet
tightly closed bouquet of cassis, fruit, and vanillin oakiness, full-
bodied, rich and deep on the palate, with plenty of astringent
tannin present, this big, attractive Pauillac begs for time. Anticipated maturity: 1990–2005. Last tasted, 12/83.

1976—An acceptable wine for certain, but this Grand-Puy-Lacoste is
· surprisingly jammy, overripe, with a scent of fresh tea. Soft,
72 flabby, and loosely knit on the palate, this wine is now fully
mature. Drink up! Last tasted, 7/80.

1975—A mediocre wine, particularly in view of the vintage and prop-
· erty, the 1975 Grand-Puy-Lacoste lacks weight, richness, and
74 character. Rather soft and one-dimensional, without the grip
and length of many of the 1975s. Ready to drink now. Last
tasted, 5/84.

1971—Beginning to fall apart, this wine was fully mature by 1977. Quite
· brown in color, with an oxidized, stale, faded bouquet, soft,
62 dissipated, fruity flavors, and no tannin present. This wine does
possess plenty of sharp acidity. Last tasted, 7/77.

1970—Extremely inconsistent from bottle to bottle, I have found bottles
· of the 1970 Grand-Puy-Lacoste that were ripe, deeply colored,
74 rich on the palate, with oodles of lovely blackcurrant fruitiness, but little tannin. Other bottles have displayed an unpleasant barnyard aroma and tannic, acidic, sharp flavors. Now fully mature. In either case, the wine is not up to the standards of the vintage. Last tasted, 6/84.

1967—Premature senility, a problem which seems to have plagued
· Grand-Puy-Lacoste in the '60s and early '70s, is again the culprit
65 here. Quite brown, with a decaying, leafy aroma, and shallow, feeble flavors. Last tasted, 2/83.

1966—A successful wine was produced by Grand-Puy-Lacoste in 1966.
· Now fully mature, with a moderately intense, smoky, cassis-
84 dominated bouquet, soft, savory flavors, and somewhat of a short finish, this is a wine to enjoy over the next several years before it fades. Last tasted, 11/84.

1964—Quite successful in this very uneven rain-plagued vintage, the
· 1964 Grand-Puy-Lacoste offers rather robust, chunky, generous
84 blackcurrant flavors, a somewhat coarse texture, but good length and weight. Now fully mature. Last tasted, 9/81.

1962—Just beginning to fade, this wine has a lovely bouquet of ripe
· fruit, caramel, and spices. Soft, savory, fruity and lush on the
82 palate, but it clearly tails off in the glass. Last tasted, 9/81.

1961—Certainly not in the top league of 1961s, this moderately dark
· ruby wine seems to be lacking great concentration, as well as
85 density of fruit and color, which are the two hallmarks of this great vintage. Nevertheless, the wine is still very good and now at its apogee, with a fine bouquet and ripe, cedary, blackcurrant flavors which still have some tannin to lose. Drink over the next 5–6 years. Last tasted, 9/81.

LES FORTS DE LATOUR (Unclassified) VERY GOOD

Evaluation: The quality equivalent of a Médoc fifth-growth

The staff at Latour have always maintained that the "second" wine of Latour was equivalent in quality terms to a second-growth in the 1855 classification. In fact, they claim that blind tastings of Forts de Latour are held at Latour against the wines produced by the second-growths.

If Forts de Latour does not do extremely well, then a decision must be made whether to declassify it as regional Pauillac.

Forts de Latour is excellent, particularly in the top vintages like 1966, 1967, 1970, 1975, and 1978. Undeniably, the wine can, in such vintages, compete favorably with many of the second-growths, but not the "super" second-growths such as Léoville-Las Cases, Ducru-Beaucaillou, Pichon Lalande, Léoville-Barton, or Cos d'Estournel.

The wine, which is vinified exactly the same way as Latour, comes from three vineyards called Petit Batailley, Comtesse de Lalande, and Les Forts de Latour. Additionally, selected lots of Latour (often from young vines) not considered quite "grand" enough are also blended into the wine produced from the aforementioned vineyards. The character of Forts de Latour is astonishingly similar to Latour itself, only lighter and quicker maturing. The château does not release the wine until it is deemed close to maturity. Les Forts de Latour is certainly the finest of the second labels or "*marques*" produced by the well-known châteaux in Bordeaux. It is not inexpensive, but given its similarity to the great Latour at half the price, it merits consideration.

VINTAGES

1978—(Not Yet Released)—tasted from the cask twice, this wine cer-
• tainly has the potential to be the best Forts de Latour since the
87 wine was first made in 1966. Quite dark with a rich, intense, cassis, oaky nose, ripe, moderately tannic yet supple flavors, and excellent length and depth, all combine to make this a wine to keep an eye and palate out for whenever it is eventually released by Latour. Anticipated maturity: 1988–2000. Last tasted, 3/81.

1976—The margin of quality difference between Latour and Forts de
• Latour seems especially minute in this vintage of high yield and
78 early maturing, somewhat frail wines. In fact, I find the wines almost equal in quality. Forward, smooth, and showing ripe fruit and less tannin than its big brother, this wine can be drunk now, but is quite ordinary in the total Bordeaux scheme of things. Last tasted, 6/82.

1975—True to the vintage and to Latour, this wine is tannic, lean,
• aggressive and in need of bottle age. The color is impressive,
85 the richness and depth seem to be present, only time is necessary. Anticipated maturity: 1990–2000. Last tasted, 1/85.

1974—Latour made one of the top wines of the vintage, so it is not
· surprising to find Forts de Latour better than many a more fa-
70 mous classified growth. A trifle austere and lean, but spicy, with
good fruit, a hard, tough personality, yet short, soft finish, this
wine seems to suggest potential for improvement, but the personality of the vintage scares me off. Respectable for the vintage. Drink over the next 5 years. Last tasted, 1/83.

1972—Surprisingly dark-colored, with an amber/brownish edge, this
· soft, chunky, somewhat rugged wine offers good chocolatey,
74 herbaceous, stemmy fruit, a good palate impression, and a short
finish. Drink up. Last tasted, 4/80.

1970—Close to really hitting the mark, this very fine wine is fully ma-
· ture, but should have no problem aging well for another 2–4
84 years. Very dark ruby, with a smooth, round, ripe blackcurrant
and cedar bouquet, savory, full, generous flavors, and a slightly
tart, acidic finish that detracts from an otherwise fine performance in 1970. Drink now. Last tasted, 1/85.

1967—The 1967 is now beginning to fade in the decade of the '80s. For
· a number of years, this wine could lay claim to giving wine
84 enthusiasts on a budget a good introduction to the style of Latour. Drink up. Last tasted, 3/82.

1966—The 1966 Forts de Latour is a textbook Pauillac, whish displays
· near perfectly proportioned scents of blackcurrants, spices,
leather and cedar, ripe yet supple flavors, a long fruity texture
and palate impression, and light tannins. It is now at its zenith.
Drink up! Last tasted, 4/83.

HAUT-BATAILLEY (Fifth-Growth) — VERY GOOD

Production: 6,000–8,500 cases

Grape varieties:
Cabernet Sauvignon—65%
Merlot—25%
Cabernet Franc—10%

Time spent in barrels: 18–20 months

Average age of vines: 32 years

Evaluation of present classification: Should be maintained

Haut-Batailley is not one of the better-known estates in Pauillac. The vineyard is owned by the reputable and well-known Jean-Eugène Borie, who lives at Ducru-Beaucaillou in St.-Julien and also owns Grand-Puy-

Lacoste. Perhaps the reasons for its obscurity in the Pauillac firmament are the modest production, the lack of a château on the estate, and its secluded location on the edge of a woods, far away from the Gironde River.

While recent vintages of Haut-Batailley have demonstrated the full potential of the property under the expert winemaking team of Borie and his son, the wines of this estate have not always been the model of consistency one would expect. In general, the weakness is a tendency toward lightness and softness in style. Most wines of Haut-Batailley are fully mature long before their first decade of life ends, an anomaly for a Pauillac. Nevertheless, the last several vintages, particularly the 1982, have shown greater concentration and grip than ever before. However, the wines are still more St.-Julien in personality than true Pauillacs.

VINTAGES

1983—A good vintage for Haut-Batailley, the wine exhibits youthful,
· dark ruby color, attractive, fat, soft flavors, moderate tannins,
84 and a certain astringent dryness on the palate. It is not quite in harmony yet. Anticipated maturity: 1990–1995. Last tasted, 3/85.

1982—The best Haut-Batailley I have tasted. Voluptuous, almost
· sweet, ripe, rich berry fruit, and vanillin oakiness jump from the
88 glass. Quite intense, supple, and unbelievably concentrated on the palate, this wine, despite its stunning show of deep, almost jammy fruit, has plenty of tannin in evidence. A great Haut-Batailley wine. Anticipated maturity: 1990–2000. Last tasted, 1/85.

1981—This is my favorite Haut-Batailley between 1971 and 1981. Silky
· on the palate and quite perfumed, with a pronounced oaky bou-
85 quet, this velvety, round, pleasant wine is quite delicious. It will mature rapidly. Anticipated maturity: 1987–1993. Last tasted, 11/84.

1979—Lacking a bit in depth and concentration, this light to medium
· ruby colored wine has a pleasant, round, supple texture, me-
80 dium body, and a light finish. Drink over the next 3 years. Last tasted, 2/84.

1978—A very charming, supple wine that is a delight to drink now, the
· 1978 Haut-Batailley is a straightforward, effusively fruity wine,
82 with a nice touch of spicy oak, light tannins, and a warm, round finish. Ready now. Last tasted, 4/84.

1976—Fully mature with soft, supple, rather modest flavors, low acid-
· ity, an amber/ruby color, and short finish. Drink immediately!
74 Last tasted, 9/80.

1975—The astringency of the 1975 vintage has obviously given this
· wine more backbone and firmness than one usually finds in
81 Haut-Batailley. Good, dark ruby color, with a ripe, plummy, rather open-knit bouquet, somewhat dominated by the smell of new oak and decaying vegetation. Medium-bodied, with moderate tannins, adequate depth and texture, this is a 1975 without much complexity. Anticipated maturity: 1986–1992. Last tasted, 4/84.

1973—Shallow, watery, and now quite decrepit, this wine was at its
· meager best in 1978. Of little interest now.
64

1970—The 1970 is a top-flight effort for Haut-Batailley, and a wine
· which in personality and character behaves like a true Pauillac,
87 rather than a St.-Julien. Rather rich and full for Haut-Batailley, with a good, firm underpinning of tannins still evident, this dark ruby wine has a complex bouquet and fine long finish. Anticipated maturity: 1986–1995. Last tasted, 10–83.

1966—Solid, firm, true in style to the 1966 vintage that has evolved so
· slowly, this Haut-Batailley seems to be at its apogee. A modest
84 bouquet of spices and blackcurrant fruit is quite attractive. Medium-bodied with good, rather than excellent concentration, and a solid finish. Anticipated maturity: 1986–1992. Last tasted, 4/82.

1962—A charming, fruity wine that continues to hold well in the bottle.
· This moderately fruity wine has soft, round, easygoing flavors,
84 a good finish, and a fully developed bouquet. Drink now! Last tasted, 3/83.

1961—In the context of the vintage's great reputation, this wine seems
· to be atypical and more akin to the style of the 1962. Soft, ripe,
84 spicy fruit on the nose shows maturity, but none of the intense ripeness that exists in many 1961s. Soft, round, and plump, with rather fat, fruity flavors overlaid with oak, this medium-bodied wine is fully mature. Drink over the next 4 years. Last tasted, 7/83.

PONTET-CANET (Fifth-Growth) VERY GOOD

Production: 25,000–40,000 cases	Grape varieties: Cabernet Sauvignon—70% Merlot—20% Cabernet Franc—8% Malbec—2%
Time spent in barrels: 18–24 months	Average age of vines: 34 years
Evaluation of present classification: Should be maintained	

With the largest production of any classified-growth wine of the Médoc, and with its enviable vineyard position directly across from Mouton-Rothschild, one would expect the quality and stature of the wines of Pontet-Canet to be quite high. A close look at the track record of Pontet-Canet over the period 1961–1983 is certainly one of sound wine quality, but in general, the wines have usually lacked excitement. In the last several years a renewed vigor and commitment under a new ownership has commenced. Hopefully, the wine's quality will increase.

Until 1975, the famous Cruse firm owned Pontet-Canet and tended to treat the wines as simply a brand name rather than a distinctive, individual, estate-bottled wine from Pauillac. The wine was not château-bottled until 1972, and for years lots of the wine were sold to the French railways without a vintage date under the name Pontet-Canet. In 1975 the Cruse firm was forced to sell Pontet-Canet as a result of a trial that had found the firm negligent in its blending and labeling practices. Guy Tesseron, a well-known Cognac merchant, purchased Pontet-Canet. I believe everyone in Bordeaux agrees that Pontet-Canet is a vineyard with enormous potential, should it be carefully managed and exploited properly. If the initial wines from Guy and Alfred Tesseron lacked the character expected of them, I feel confident that the Tesseron family will reestablish respect for the name of Pontet-Canet.

VINTAGES

1983—An impressive vintage for Pontet-Canet, the 1983 is quite dark ruby in color, with a sweet, ripe blackcurrant fruitiness, deep,
·
86 briary, concentrated flavors that linger on the palate, and quite a powerful kick from both the tannins and alcohol. One of the best Pontet-Canets in the last two decades. Anticipated maturity: 1993–2008. Last tasted, 3/85.

1982—The vintage's telltale deep ruby, almost purple color is present,
· as well as the fabulous ripe aromas of ripe black cherries, spicy
85 oak, and fresh tar. Quite fat and plump on the palate, with a viscous, very ripe character, adequate acidity, and long, alcoholic, tannic finish. A big, corpulent wine that tastes juicy, but also a bit dull and overweight. It has the tannin to last for 10–15 years. Anticipated maturity: 1992–2005. Last tasted, 1/85.

1979—The 1979 is a straightforward sort of Pauillac, with a bland,
· moderately intense, blackcurrant aroma, soft, charming, round
80 flavors, medium body, and light tannins in the finish. Anticipated maturity: 1985–1990. Last tasted, 4/82.

1978—In contrast to the 1979, a much more tannic, reserved wine for
· long-term cellaring, the 1978 Pontet-Canet has dark ruby color,
82 a spicy, ripe, yet generally tight and closed bouquet. While certainly a good wine, it seems to be missing length and complexity. Anticipated maturity: 1990–2000. Last tasted, 4/81.

1976—Not particularly outstanding, the Pontet-Canet, like so many
· 1976 Bordeaux, is quite mature, with an amber, brownish color.
75 Medium-bodied, with good, soft, round, fruity flavors, this wine is slightly deficient in acidity and length, but very agreeable. It requires immediate drinking. Last tasted, 10/84.

1975—A good, solid, slightly rustic 1975 with a well-developed, toasty,
· spicy, caramel-scented bouquet, Pontet-Canet lacks the tre-
84 mendous grip and size of the best 1975 Pauillacs, but has good fruit, and a firm, long finish. Perhaps the best Pontet-Canet of the '70s. Anticipated maturity: 1986–1995. Last tasted, 5/84.

1971—An ambivalent sort of wine, with both positive and negative
· attributes, this fully mature, somewhat brownish-colored wine
81 has an interesting, spicy, fruity, complex bouquet, and a savory, satisfying, sweet palate impression. However, sharp acidity in the finish detracts considerably from the overall impression. Drink up. Last tasted, 7/82.

1970—Good dark ruby color still exists. The bouquet of wood and ripe
· plums is enjoyable, but lacks complexity. In the mouth, the wine
82 has plump, chunky, fruity flavors of good intensity, but seems to miss the mark when it comes to interest and length. Hopefully, it will get better, but I am unsure. Anticipated maturity: 1985–1992. Last tasted, 6/84.

1966—The 1966 Pontet-Canet is a leaner-styled, tight, hard wine which
· to this day remains firm, closed, and unready. The wine is mod-
83 erately dark ruby, with a restrained, cedary blackcurrant bou-

quet, and a somewhat austere, astringent finish. Anticipated maturity: 1986–1992. Last tasted, 5/82.

1964—I prefer the 1964 Pontet-Canet to the 1966 simply because of the
· supple, lush fruitiness, and its straightforward, gustatory plea-
84 sure. Browning at the edge, with virtually all of the tannin gone, this wine requires drinking up immediately. Last tasted, 5/83.

1961—Pontet-Canet produced a great 1961, although quality variation
· as a result of the numerous English bottlings is undoubtedly a
90 problem. The best bottles exhibit rich, deep color, with a full-blown, ripe, deep bouquet of spices and plums, viscous, round, supple flavors, and the sumptuous length that typify this great vintage. Now fully mature, the good examples of this wine will last a decade. Certainly the best Pontet-Canet I have ever tasted. Last tasted, 12/81.

DUHART-MILON-ROTHSCHILD
(Fourth-Growth) VERY GOOD

Production: 10,000–16,000 cases	Grape varieties: Cabernet Sauvignon—70% Merlot—20% Cabernet Franc—5% Petit Verdot—5%
Time spent in barrels: 24–28 months	Age of vines: 16 years
Evaluation of present classification: Should be downgraded to a Médoc fifth-growth	

The "other" Pauillac château owned by the Rothschilds of Lafite-Rothschild fame, Duhart-Milon-Rothschild was purchased by them in the early '60s, and its poorly cared for vineyards totally replanted during the mid- and late '60s. Because the vineyard is extremely young, particularly for a classified growth, the wines of the late '60s and '70s have not lived up to the expectations of wine enthusiasts who assume the Rothschild name is synonymous with excellence. Since 1978, the quality has dramatically improved, and certainly the 1982 and 1983 are the best Duhart-Milons made under the current ownership.

VINTAGES

1983—The 1983 Duhart has excellent color, a solid, firm structure, with
· an expansive, ripe fruity, cassis dominated aroma, astringent,
86 very concentrated flavors, and a hard, tough finish. This is a very good, rich, quite full-bodied Duhart which at the moment

is quite big and aggressive. Anticipated maturity: 1996–2010. Last tasted, 3/85.

1982—The best Duhart-Milon in the last two decades, the 1982 is rich,
· full-bodied, with a very dark ruby color, rich viscous fruit, gobs
88 of tannin, and a long finish. Impressive, yet quite unready to
drink. Anticipated maturity: 1995–2010. Last tasted, 1/85.

1981—All of the Lafite domaines were successful in 1981. Quite back-
· ward in development, this deep ruby colored wine has an attrac-
84 tive bouquet which suggests crushed blackcurrants, fresh
leather, and new oak. Relatively big, quite tannic, concentrated,
astringent, and dry in the finish, this backward wine begs for
time. Anticipated maturity: 1992–2005. Last tasted, 1/85.

1979—Quite an elegant wine, Duhart-Milon has good, dark ruby color,
· with a moderately intense, complex, cedary bouquet, medium
83 body, restrained power and richness, but good balance and harmony. The precocious development of the bouquet and amber
color at the edges suggests early maturity. Anticipated maturity:
1987–1992. Last tasted, 4/83.

1978—A medium-bodied wine with a well-developed, ripe fruity, spicy,
· toasty, iron-scented bouquet, and soft, savory, round flavors,
84 the 1978 Duhart-Milon is the first wine in a succession of vintages to follow that correctly reflects the style and character of
its famous sibling, Lafite-Rothschild. The 1978 Duhart is approaching maturity, but will hold for 5–6 years. Anticipated maturity: 1986–1992. Last tasted, 12/82.

1976—Ruby garnet, with a fully developed, moderately intense, ce-
· dary, vanillin, fragrant bouquet, this forward-styled wine has
80 soft, round, attractive flavors, light tannins, low acidity, and a
casual resemblance to Lafite, particularly in the bouquet. Duhart has produced a charming wine in this uneven vintage. Drink
up. Last tasted, 9/81.

1975—A disappointing vintage, the 1975 Duhart-Milon has a big,
· herbal, almost minty aroma, a spicy, vegetal fruitiness, and a
75 sweet burnt quality that suggests over-chaptalization. Fully mature, but disjointed and unique in style. Last tasted, 5/84.

1974—A poor, watery wine. Very disappointing. Last tasted, 1/78.
·
62

1970—In this vintage which produced such wonderfully balanced,
· richly fruity wines, Duhart-Milon has made a wine with an at-
70 tractive, earthy, spicy, oaky bouquet, but it lacks fruit, and

finishes short, acidic, and quite harshly. Rather unpleasant to drink. Last tasted, 2/82.

1966—The 1966 has a dusty texture with dry, slightly acidic flavors, yet
· perplexingly, a rather attractive, cedary, ripe fruity bouquet that
75 promises much more than the meager flavors deliver. Fully mature. Last tasted, 11/79.

PICHON-LONGUEVILLE BARON DE PICHON-LONGUEVILLE (Second-Growth) VERY GOOD

Production: 11,000 cases	Grape varieties: Cabernet Sauvignon—75% Merlot—23% Malbec—2%
Time spent in barrels: 18–20 months	Average age of vines: 25 years

Evaluation of present classification: Should be downgraded to a Médoc fifth-growth

This noble-looking château opposite Pichon-Longueville, Comtesse de Lalande and Latour has made a modest comeback in wine quality in the early '80s, but the wine remains considerably overrated, and is equaled and/or surpassed in quality by a number of other lower-ranked classified growths, not to mention top Cru Bourgeois wines in the Médoc.

The vineyard is superbly situated, and one can only surmise that the lack of brilliance in many of the Pichon Baron wines in the '60s and '70s was a result of both casual viticultural practices and poor cellar management. Some observers have pointed to an inexperienced and youthful Bernard Bouteiller, who had little experience when he was first put in charge of Pichon Baron. His *maître de chai* was eventually replaced in 1974, and I have been told that it was a result of poor viticultural practices and sloppy handling of the wine when it was in cask that led to his dismissal.

Since 1979, the wines here have lightened up in style considerably. Pichon Baron has become what some might say is a shockingly supple, fruity, commercial-styled wine. Currently, the wine is bottled and released on the market prior to any other classified growth. Certainly, this is a wine which must be watched very closely over the coming years to ascertain if the quality is really improving, as I believe it is.

VINTAGES

1983—Perhaps the best Pichon Baron since the 1961, the 1983 is cer-
· tainly the best-structured, most powerful wine in some time
86 from this estate. Very dark ruby, with a rich, dense, deeply concentrated feel on the palate, this wine has plenty of tannin for the long haul. Anticipated maturity: 1993–2005. Last tasted, 1/85.

1982—In several tastings from the cask, the wine was impressively
· black/ruby in color, with a very ripe cassis, oaky, toasty bou-
84 quet. However, despite its massive color and fruity intensity, it always tasted flat and lacked acidity. From the bottle, the wine is much better balanced, still big, brawny and opaque in color, but slightly deficient in acidity. Very rich and full as well as supple, this moderately tannic wine will last 8 years. Anticipated maturity: 1990–1998. Last tasted, 1/85.

1981—The 1981 is a trifle overoaked, perhaps consciously to disguise a
· lack of concentration and depth. However, there is no denying
83 the lovely, aromatic oaky scents. Average to above average concentration of fruit, and somewhat short in the finish, this Pichon Baron is a charming, agreeable, precociously styled wine for consumption over the near term. Anticipated maturity: 1985–1990. Last tasted, 11/84.

1980—Thin, vegetal, unripe fruity flavors reveal a nastiness that is not
· likely to fade with aging. Last tasted, 2/83.
60

1979—Was 1979 a watershed vintage for Pichon Baron, indicating bet-
· ter quality in the future, or just the luck of a winemaker? What-
84 ever the reason, this Pichon Baron, which is amazingly supple and ready to drink already, has ample, velvety, blackcurrant fruit, a spicy, tarry, oaky bouquet, and soft, precocious flavors. Anticipated maturity: 1985–1992. Last tasted, 11/84.

1978—Fat, plump, jammy and quite one-dimensional, the 1978 Pichon
· Baron lacks grip and backbone, has a loosely knit structure, and
78 a sweet, short finish. Will it develop? Anticipated maturity: 1986–1990. Last tasted, 12/84.

1975—A very medicinal, unusual nose suggesting burnt coffee is
· offputting. Chaptalized, sweet, unstructured flavors dissipate
70 and fade in the glass. A soft, uncharacteristic wine for 1975. Drink up. Last tasted, 5/84.

1971—A very poor effort from Pichon Baron, this dried-out, rather
· hollow wine has a very old brown color, little ripeness or fruit,
65 and a poor, astringent tannic finish. Quite disappointing. Last tasted, 9/78.

1970—Decently colored, but rather light in weight with an astringent,
· very tannic feel on the palate, this medium-bodied wine does
73 not appear to have the fruit to outdistance the tannin. Only a gambler would bet on it. Anticipated maturity: 1985–1992. Last tasted, 1/81.

1966—Rather imbalanced and perplexing to taste, the 1966 Pichon
· Baron has good, dark ruby color, with just a little amber at edge,
82 a spicy aggressive, cedary, blackcurrant bouquet intermingled with decaying vegetation smells. Big, fleshy, but disjointed on the palate, with a heavy finish, this wine can be drunk now or aged for 5–6 years. Last tasted, 4/80.

1961—After having several mediocre bottles of this wine, the last time
· I tasted it, it showed quite well. Dark ruby, with an orange edge,
86 the 1961 Pichon Baron has a big, spicy, earthy, cedary bouquet, and rich, fat, substantial but somewhat straightforward flavors. Fully mature, Pichon Baron should hold well for 5–8 more years. Not one of the leaders in 1961, but quite good. Last tasted, 1/81.

HAUT-BAGES-LIBÉRAL (Fifth-Growth) GOOD

Production: 8,000 cases	Grape varieties: Cabernet Sauvignon—78% Merlot—17% Petit Verdot—5%
Time spent in barrels: 16–18 months	Average age of vines: 23 years
Evaluation of present classification: Should be maintained	

This modestly sized château sitting just off Bordeaux' main road of wine (D2) has been making consistently fine wine since the mid '70s, and today represents one of the great values in Pauillac. Fortunately for consumers, the price has not yet caught up with the new level of high quality at Haut-Bages-Libéral. As the name suggests, part of this estate's vineyard sits on the Bages plateau, but more important is the fact that the major portion of the vineyard is adjacent to the main Latour vineyard.

The Cruse family has thoroughly modernized Haut-Bages-Libéral. Replanting was done in the early '60s and the vines are now coming into their mature, adult stage. No doubt the young vines accounted for the mediocre quality of the wine in the '60s and early '70s. However, in 1975 an outstanding wine was produced, and this success has been followed by the more recent vintages which have also exhibited high quality.

Haut-Bages-Libéral produces a strong, ripe, rich, very blackcurranty wine, no doubt as a result of the unusually high percentage of Cabernet Sauvignon used here. In 1983; the Cruse family sold Haut Bages Liberal to a Paris-based firm. The current manager is Bernadette Villars who also makes the excellent wine at Chasse Spleen in Moulis.

VINTAGES

1983—A big, brash, aggressive sort of wine, with intense color, a full-
· blown bouquet of ripe blackcurrants, deep, full, tannic, thick,
87 fruity flavors, and a long, astringent finish. A brawny wine that
will need plenty of time. Anticipated maturity: 1994–2005. Last
tasted, 3/85.

1982—This is a very good 1982, with a voluptuous, rich, silky texture,
· layers of blackcurrant fruit, and some attractive vanillin oaky
87 scents. This fat, densely colored, tannic wine should develop
quite well over the next decade. Anticipated maturity: 1992–
2005. Last tasted, 11/84.

1981—The 1981 is typical in style for Haut-Bages-Libéral. Dark ruby,
· with a big, spicy, smoky, blackcurrant bouquet, dense, rich,
85 tannic flavors, full body, and a tannic, rough finish, this is a
gutsy, big, chewy mouthful of wine that has plenty of crowd
appeal. Anticipated maturity: 1991–2003. Last tasted, 4/84.

1980—One-dimensional, this wine has a spicy, light-intensity, some-
· what skinny bouquet, and underendowed flavors, but it is sup-
74 ple, with a pleasant fruitiness. Drink over the next 3 years. Last
tasted, 11/83.

1979—The 1979 is another full-flavored, robust wine from Haut-Bages-
· Libéral. Quite dark ruby, with an appealing ripe cassis, spicy
83 bouquet, a full-bodied meaty texture, this wine has enough tannin to warrant cellaring. Not refined or elegant, but rather robust
and straightforward. Anticipated maturity: 1988–1993. Last
tasted, 7/83.

1978 · 75 — The 1978 is a solid wine, but given the recent string of successes for Haut-Bages-Libéral, a bit of a disappointment. Dark ruby, with a rather stemmy, smoky, somewhat burnt bouquet, the wine is a trifle weedy and herbaceous on the palate, and perhaps too acidic in the finish. Anticipated maturity: 1986–1991. Last tasted, 5/81.

1976 · 84 — The 1976 is a notable success in this mixed vintage. Haut-Bages-Libéral is approaching maturity, but will certainly hold for a good 4–5 more years. Dark ruby, with some amber at the edge, this big, spicy, cedary, blackcurrant-scented wine has very good concentration, a juicy, rich, fruity texture, and surprising length. Anticipated maturity: 1985–1990. Last tasted, 10/84.

1975 · 90 — The best Haut-Bages-Libéral in memory, this wine has impressive dark ruby color, a complex, cedary, ripe fruity bouquet, sweet, rich, intense flavors, excellent length, full body, and tremendous potential. The hard tannin of the 1975 vintage has yet to fully resolve itself, but this is a very fine wine, and one of the top wines of the vintage. Anticipated maturity: 1988–2000. Last tasted, 5/84.

1974 · 55 — Thin, hollow, and harsh on the palate, this wine lacks fruit and charm. Last tasted, 3/79.

1970 · 70 — Dark ruby, with a spicy, vegetal aroma of celery and cloves, this wine tastes out of balance, with an emerging flavor of herbal tea. Drink up. Last tasted, 4/77.

BATAILLEY (Fifth-Growth) — GOOD

Production: 20,000 cases	Grape varieties: Cabernet Sauvignon—70% Merlot—22% Cabernet Franc—5% Petit Verdot—3%
Time spend in barrels: 18 months	Average age of vines: 29 years
Evaluation of present classification: Should be maintained	

Batailley is an attractive château located well inland from the Gironde River. Its vineyards are situated between those of Haut-Batailley to the south, and Grand-Puy-Lacoste to the north.

Batailley produces wines that have never been in the top class of Pauillacs. They are solid, well-colored, somewhat rustic wines that are inclined to be rather bland and one-dimensional. Nevertheless, Batailley can be a satisfying wine which no doubt can handle long-term cellaring quite well. If never terribly exciting as a wine, Batailley is reliable, and generally very fairly priced.

VINTAGES

1982—Soft, relatively fat, fruity flavors lack the great concentration of
· the very best 1982s, but nevertheless offer juicy blackcurrant
87 flavors nicely mixed with a pleasing vanillin oakiness. Moderate
tannin dictates cellaring for 5–6 years. Anticipated maturity:
1990–2005. Last tasted, 1/85.

1980—Light, thin and lacking fruit, this shallow, short-tasting wine is
· clearly not one of the better efforts from this mediocre vintage.
67 Ready now. Last tasted, 3/83.

1979—Good dark ruby color, with a ripe, but hard closed-in aroma of
· light intensity cassis fruit, oak, and earthy scents. This aggres-
76 sively hard and tannic wine is far from maturity, and seems to
lack much of the charming round fruit that typifies the best
wines of this vintage. Anticipated maturity: 1990–1995. Last
tasted, 4/82.

1978—A solid, durable wine, the 1978 Batailley is quite attractive, with
· an exotic, moderately intense bouquet of cassis, anise, and spicy
84 components. Full-bodied, with surprisingly soft, supple fruit,
round, ripe tannins, and good length, this is a very good effort
from Batailley. Anticipated maturity: 1988–2000. Last tasted,
2/84.

1976—A straightforward sort of wine that is fully mature, this medium
· ruby-colored wine has a spicy, plump, fruity bouquet, medium
81 body, attractive, gentle, almost polite flavors, and a rather short
yet soft finish. Drink now. Last tasted, 4/84.

1975—An unusual yet enjoyable wine, the 1975 Batailley has a full-
· blown bouquet of ripe, chocolatey fruit, a sweet, ripe palate
83 impression, and astringent, tannic finish. Somewhat at odds
with itself, with the ripe, sweet, round flavors suggesting maturity, and hard tannin dictating future aging. I like this wine, but
have a difficult time projecting whether it will get better or
worse. Anticipated maturity: 1987–2000. Last tasted, 4/84.

1971—An aroma highly suggestive of freshly brewed tea and ripe tan-
· gerines suggests overripeness, yet on the palate the wine is dif-
73 fuse, lacking direction, and somewhat watery and uninteresting.

A curious and unappealing rendition of Batailley. Fully mature. Last tasted, 2/79.

1970—In many respects, this wine typifies Batailley and the style of
· wine so often produced there. Dark ruby, with a bouquet that
82 offers ripe fruit, some mild oaky notes, but not much complexity. On the palate, the wine is chunky and fleshy, with good concentration, firm tannins, yet little complexity. Anticipated maturity: 1986–1997. Last tasted, 2/83.

1966—The 1966 Batailley is now entering its mature period. The bou-
· quet offers modest, ripe blackcurrant aromas. The flavors are
82 plump and solid, but the wine, which is satisfying, still leaves one wanting just a little bit more. Drink over the next 5 years. Last tasted, 3/84.

1962—Fading now, the 1962 Batailley shows the telltale brown at the
· edge, the dissipated, fruity flavors on the palate, and the sugary,
74 acid sharpness in the finish that almost always signifies a wine on the brink of collapse. Last tasted, 10/82.

1961—In this great vintage, I have found Batailley to be a nice, com-
· pact, fruity wine, with good color, a robust, dusty texture on the
84 palate, but not the best example of what the 1961 vintage was all about. Drink over the next 5 years. Last tasted, 3/79.

GRAND-PUY-DUCASSE (Fifth-Growth) GOOD

Production: 14,000 cases	Grape varieties: Cabernet Sauvignon—70% Merlot—25% Petit Verdot—5%
Time spent in barrels: 12–14 months	Average age of vines: 24 years
Evaluation of present classification: Should be maintained	

I don't see enough of Grand-Puy-Ducasse on the market and in the last several years have had few opportunities to taste it. However, I have always enjoyed this fifth-growth Pauillac, which has been largely ignored by consumers and the wine press. Unquestionably, the current prices for vintages of Grand-Puy-Ducasse are below most other Pauillacs, making it a notable value given the quality.

Unlike the other Pauillac châteaux, Grand-Puy-Ducasse is located next to the main road of Pauillac that runs parallel to the river. The château serves also as the "Maison du Vin de Pauillac."

Grand-Puy-Ducasse is owned by Mestrezat-Preller, the same firm which runs the excellent Bordeaux estate Chasse-Spleen in the commune of Moulis, as well as the well-known Sauternes property, Rayne-Vigneau. Extensive renovations and replanting have occurred since 1971, and the future looks encouraging for Grand-Puy-Ducasse. Undoubtedly, Grand-Puy-Ducasse is a château to keep an eye on.

The style of wines here is quite fruity and supple rather than tannic, hard, and backwards. Most vintages of Grand-Puy-Ducasse are drinkable within 5 years of the vintage, but do last considerably longer.

VINTAGES

1979—The 1979 is medium to dark ruby, with a spicy, ripe fruity bou-
· quet, and attractively silky, soft flavors which show noticeable
82 maturity. This is a charming, quite fruity wine with medium
body. Anticipated maturity: 1985–1990. Last tasted, 2/84.

1978—Good solid color, a ripe blackcurrant, somewhat herbaceous
· bouquet, and round, generous flavors characterize the 1978
82 Grand-Puy-Ducasse. Quite precocious for the vintage, and
showing quite well at present, this is a wine to drink over the
next 6–7 years. Last tasted, 5/84.

1976—Quite mature, with a loosely knit, jammy, somewhat overripe
· aroma of plummy fruit and spicy oak, this soft velvety wine lacks
80 concentration and acidity, but is soft, very round, and ready.
Drink up. Last tasted, 5/81.

1975—The 1975 is dark ruby in color, with a stalky, vegetal note to an
· otherwise attractive bouquet. Ripe, round, deep fruit has an
84 aggressive, rustic texture to it, and despite the wine's concentration and hefty proportions, the overall impression is one of
coarseness. A good wine which just misses being excellent. Anticipated maturity: 1987–1994. Last tasted, 4/84.

1971—One of my favorite wines from Grand-Puy-Ducasse, this lovely,
· round, charming, effusively fruity wine was fully mature by
85 1978, but has continued to remain at that plateau without fading
or losing its fruit. A complex, cedary, ripe fruity bouquet is
seductive and complex. Soft, round, velvety flavors are satisfy-
ingly rich and lengthy. A total success for Grand-Puy-Ducasse.
Drink up. Last tasted, 3/84.

MOUTON-BARONNE-PHILIPPE (Fifth-Growth) GOOD

Production: 18,000 cases	Grape varieties: Cabernet Sauvignon—65% Merlot—30% Cabernet Franc—5%
Time spent in barrels: 20–24 months	Average age of vines: 33 years
Evaluation of present classification: Should be maintained	

Twelve years after purchasing Mouton-Rothschild, the Baron Philippe Rothschild purchased Mouton-d'Armailacq, which he renamed Mouton-Baronne-Philippe after his beloved wife (who died in 1976). Adjacent to Mouton-Rothschild, this property has traditionally produced lighter, quicker-maturing wines, without the richness and opulence of Mouton-Rothschild.

However, recent vintages, starting with the good 1981, have begun to show more stuffing, concentration, and character, and while it may be a little too early to tell, Mouton-Barrone-Philippe appears to be a property on the move upward in quality.

VINTAGES

1983—Amply proportioned when tasted from the cask, the 1983 Mou-
· ton-Baronne-Philippe is less concentrated and richly fruity than
85 the 1982, but still impressively full, well structured and concentrated. Anticipated maturity: 1990–2000. Last tasted, 6/84.

1982—While no one should confuse this wine with Mouton-Rothschild's
· legendary 1982, this wine is quite good, and clearly the best
86 effort I have tasted from this vineyard. Dark ruby, with a cedary, ripe blackcurrant bouquet of moderate intensity, this wine is full-bodied, with very good concentration, plenty of dusty yet ripe tannins, and very fine length on the palate. Anticipated maturity: 1992–2005. Last tasted, 1/85.

1981—Dark ruby, with a rather closed, tight bouquet of currants and
· plums, this moderately tannic wine shows good, ripe fruit, me-
83 dium body, and fine length. Lighter than Mouton-Rothschild, but the stylistic similarities are there. Anticipated maturity: 1988–1996. Last tasted, 12/84.

CLERC-MILON (Fifth-Growth) GOOD

Production: 9,500 cases	Grape varieties: Cabernet Sauvignon—70% Merlot—20% Cabernet Franc—10%
Time spent in barrels: 22–24 months	Average age of vines: 20 years
Evaluation of present classification: Should be maintained	

Another of the Baron Philippe Rothschild estates, Clerc-Milon was acquired in 1970. While there is no château, the vineyard is brilliantly placed next to both Mouton-Rothschild and Lafite-Rothschild, immediately adjacent to the huge oil refinery that dominates the tranquil town of Pauillac. The wine produced here has to my taste always been light and undistinguished. Recent vintages have shown more of a lush fruity quality, and I believe I detect a higher level of quality starting with the 1981 vintage. However, in comparison with the Baron's other wines, Clerc-Milon is significantly less concentrated and opulent.

VINTAGES

1983—A pleasant, rather lightweight wine which seems to offer high
· hopes with its sensual, ripe fruity, oaky bouquet, but on the
83 palate, the wine tends to tail off. A good, medium-bodied wine that will mature quickly. Anticipated maturity: 1988–1994. Last tasted, 3/85.

1982—The 1982 Clerc-Milon is a charming, forward, ripe fruity wine,
· with an open-knit, lovely bouquet of ripe berry fruit, and oaky,
84 vanillin scents. Medium- to full-bodied, with soft, light tannins, this wine will be ready to drink soon. Anticipated maturity: 1987–1993. Last tasted, 3/85.

1981—Perhaps the best Clerc-Milon of the three most recent vintages,
· the 1981 exhibits good, dark color, medium to full body, a classy,
85 complex, cedary, oaky, ripe blackcurrant bouquet, and surprisingly full, rich flavors. Anticipated maturity: 1988–2000. Last tasted, 11/84.

FONBADET (Unclassified) GOOD

Production: 8,500 cases

Grape varieties:
Cabernet Sauvignon—60%
Merlot—19%
Cabernet Franc—15%
Malbec, Petit Verdot—6%

Time spent in barrels: 15–18 months

Average age of vines: 40 years

Evaluation of present classification: Should be upgraded to a Médoc fifth-growth

Should any reclassification of the wines of the Médoc be done, Fonbadet would have to be elevated to the rank of fifth-growth. This is an expertly vinified wine that can, in vintages such as 1982 and 1978, surpass many of the classified growths of Pauillac. In style it is always very darkly colored, with a very rich, blackcurrant bouquet, an intense concentration of flavor, and full body. I find it similar to the style of the two fifth-growth Pauillacs, Lynch-Bages and Haut-Bages-Libéral.

VINTAGES

1983—This looks to be a real top-notch wine from Fonbadet. As dark
· as the opaque 1982, just slightly less concentrated, this rich,
86 full-bodied, moderately tannic wine should surprise many a
taster with its quality. Anticipated maturity: 1990–1996. Last
tasted, 3/85.

1982—A gorgeous wine, very deep and rich, concentrated and well
· structured, the ripe, rich, blackberry aromas surge from the
87 glass. On the palate, the wine is full-bodied, moderately tannic,
opulently fruity, and very long. A sleeper of the vintage. Anticipated maturity: 1990–2000. Last tasted, 1/83.

1981—Another successful wine from Fonbadet, the 1981 is richly
· fruity, darkly colored, more precocious and earlier maturing
84 than either the 1982 or 1983. It is a wine that is charming, well
balanced, and very satisfying. Drink over the next 5 years. Last
tasted, 2/84.

1978—A textbook Pauillac, the 1978 Fonbadet has a well-developed
· bouquet of cedar, ripe plums and currants, and well-balanced,
86 deeply fruity flavors. Drinking well now, it should hold well for
5–6 years. Quite impressive. Last tasted, 2/84.

MOULIN DES CARRUADES (Unclassified) AVERAGE

Evaluation: The quality equivalent of a Médoc Grand Bourgeois Exceptionnel

The second wine of Lafite is produced from the youngest parts of the vineyard, as well as from lots of wine not considered of high enough quality for Lafite. The wine benefits from the same vinification as Lafite and of course the same cellar treatment, except that a smaller percentage of new oak barrels are utilized. Despite the care given the wine, I have never considered Moulin des Carruades to be anywhere near the class and quality of the Forts de Latour, the second wine of Château Latour, or the Pavillon Rouge de Margaux, the second wine of Château Margaux. Nevertheless, it is a good wine, but the quality level is more akin to a good Cru Bourgeois than a top classified growth. However, the price, because of the association with a name as great as Lafite-Rothschild, is quite high, making Moulin des Carruades a rather poor wine value from a consumer's perspective.

VINTAGES

1982—The 1982 Moulin des Carruades is a riper, richer wine than
· expected, with dark ruby color, plenty of spice and extract, full
83 body, some astringent tannin in the finish, and good length. Anticipated maturity: 1988–1994. Last tasted, 6/85.

1981—Medium ruby color, with an attractive, fruity, cassis-scented
· bouquet, supple, soft, moderately intense flavors, and a pleasant
81 yet undistinguished finish. Anticipated maturity: 1986–1994. Last tasted, 6/84.

CROIZET-BAGES (Fifth-Growth) AVERAGE

Production: 8,000 cases

Grape varieties:
Cabernet Sauvignon—37%
Cabernet Franc—30%
Merlot—30%
Petit Verdot—3%

Time spent in barrels: 12–18 months

Average age of vines: 34 years

Evaluation of present classification: Should be downgraded to a Grand Bourgeois

Croizet-Bages is owned and managed by the Quié family that also owns the well-known Margaux estate, Rauzan-Gassies, and the reliable St.-Estèphe Cru Bourgeois, Bel-Orme-Tronquoy-de-Lalande. I have always found Croizet-Bages to be one of the lightest and quickest maturing Pauillacs. No doubt the abnormally high percentage of Merlot and Cabernet Franc used in the wine accounts for this wine's lightness. Never terribly deep or spectacular, Croizet-Bages is a sound, gentle, soft, fruity wine, which is generally fully mature within 4–5 years. While it is not of classified-growth quality, the wine is never very expensive.

VINTAGES

1983 · 68 —From the cask, the wine was light, innocuous, dull, and bland. While some fruit was present, the color and weight suggested a wine which was overcropped and diluted. Anticipated maturity: 1985–1988. Last tasted, 3/84.

1982 · 75 —For whatever reason, this wine is not what it should be. Medium ruby, with a very developed, spicy, ripe cherry, earthy bouquet, soft, rather flabby flavors, and a short, rather clumsy finish, the 1982 Croizet-Bages is acceptable, but given the vintage, not what it should be. Drink over the next 5 years. Last tasted, 1/85.

1981 · 72 —Disappointingly light, already fully mature, the 1981 Croizet-Bages should be drunk over the next 2–3 years, before it fades into oblivion. Last tasted, 6/84.

ST.-JULIEN

If Pauillac is famous for having the Médoc's largest number of first-growths, and Margaux, the Médoc's most widely known appellation, St.-Julien is the Médoc's most underrated commune. The winemaking in St.-Julien, from the lesser-known Cru Bourgeois châteaux such as Terrey-Gros-Cailloux and Lalande Borie, to the three flagship estates of this commune, Léoville-Las Cases, Ducru-Beaucaillou, and Gruaud-Larose, is consistently both distinctive and brilliant. St.-Julien starts where the commune of Pauillac stops, and this is no better demonstrated than where Léoville-Las Cases and Latour meet at the border. South of Pauillac, Léoville-Las Cases is on the right, followed by Léoville-Poyferré on both the left and right, Langoa and Léoville-Barton on the right, Ducru-Beaucaillou on the left, Branaire-Ducru on the right, and Beychevelle on the left. At normal driving speeds, the time necessary to pass all of these illustrious properties is no more than five minutes. Further inland and lacking a view of the Gironde are the two large Cordier properties, Gruaud-Larose and Talbot, as well as Lagrange and St.-Pierre-Sevaistre.

There is no commune in the Médoc where the art of winemaking is practiced so highly as in St.-Julien. Consequently, the wine consumer has the odds stacked in his/her favor when purchasing a wine from this commune, a fact that cannot be said elsewhere in the Médoc. In addition to a bevy of fine wines from the Cru Bourgeois châteaux of St.-Julien, the 11 classified growths are all turning out wonderfully crafted wines, yet all are so very different in style.

Léoville-Las Cases is the most Pauillac-like of the St.-Juliens, not only because its vineyards sit next to those of Pauillac's famous first-growth, Latour, but because owner Michel Delon makes a deeply concentrated, tannic wine marked by the scent of vanillin oakiness and, in most vintages, needing a minimum of a decade to shed its cloak of tannin. No other St.-Julien is this stubbornly backward at the outset, as the other top properties seem to make wines that don't require as much patience from the consumer.

Léoville-Las Cases is one of three St.-Julien estates with the name Léoville. It is the best of the three, largely because its proprietor is a perfectionist. Of the other two, Léoville-Poyferré has more potential. Like Léoville-Las Cases, its office and wine *chai* sit in the tiny, sleepy town of St.-Julien-Beychevelle. Poyferré's record had been less than brilliant in the '60s and '70s, but a new manager, M. Cuvelier, was brought in and the first several vintages of the '80s are superb, showing much greater strength and richness, and a noticeably darker color. Perhaps Poyferré is about to challenge Léoville-Las Cases.

The other Léoville is Léoville-Barton. It is an outstanding wine, sometimes inconsistent, particularly in the vintages that produce lighter, more elegant wines, but when Bordeaux has an excellent vintage, Léoville-Barton is a wine to seek out. Léoville-Barton reeks of cedarwood when mature and is a classic, very traditionally made St.-Julien. The owner of Léoville-Barton, Anthony Barton, also has another St.-Julien property, Langoa-Barton. This impressive château sits right

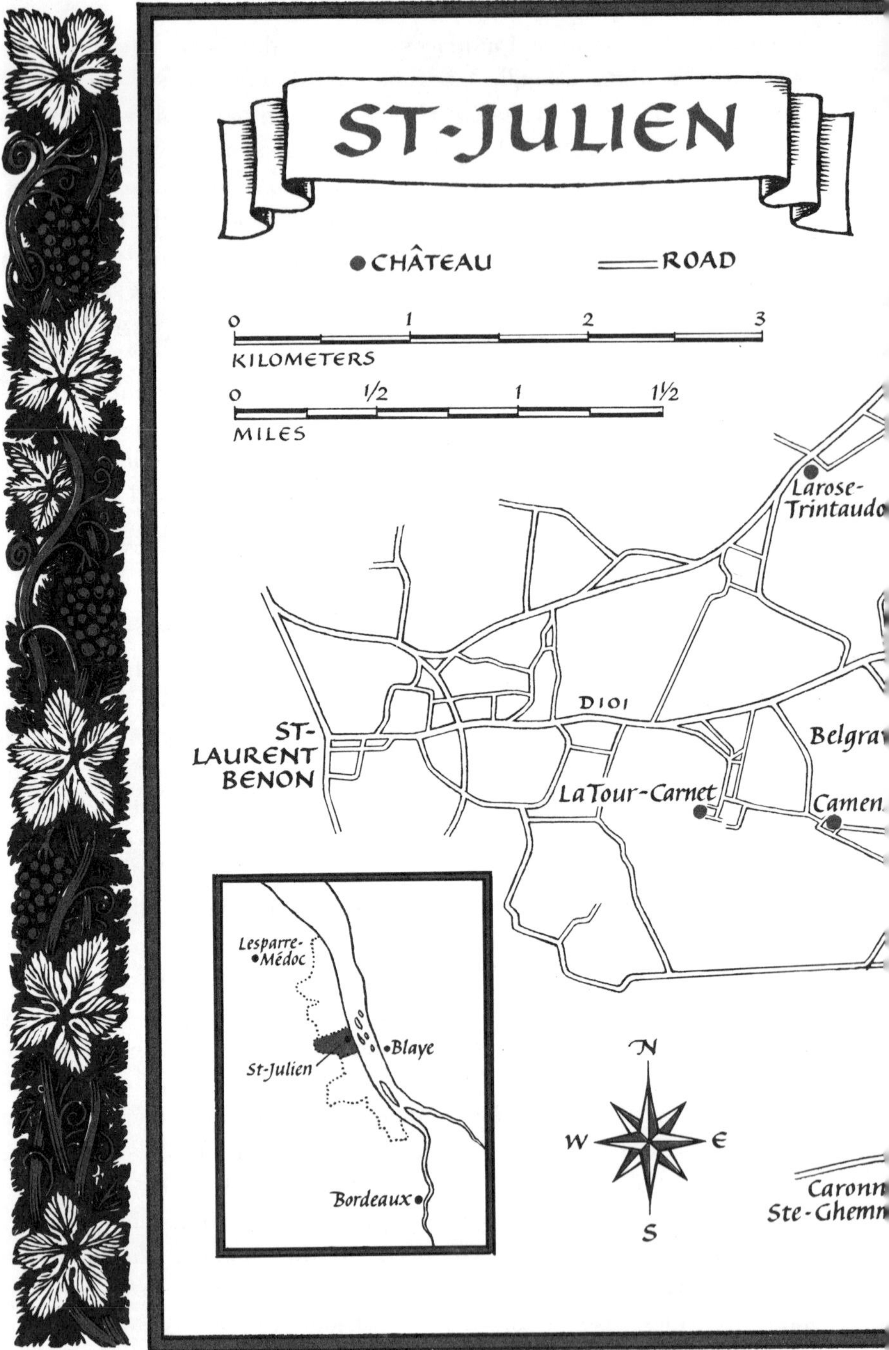

ST-JULIEN
CHÂTEAU
ROAD
0
1
2
3
KILOMETERS
0
1/2
1
1½
MILES
Larose-
Trintaudo
D101
ST-
LAURENT
BENON
Belgra
LaTour-Carnet
Camen
Lesparre-
Médoc
St-Julien
Blaye
Bordeaux
N
W
E
S
Caronn
Ste-Ghemn

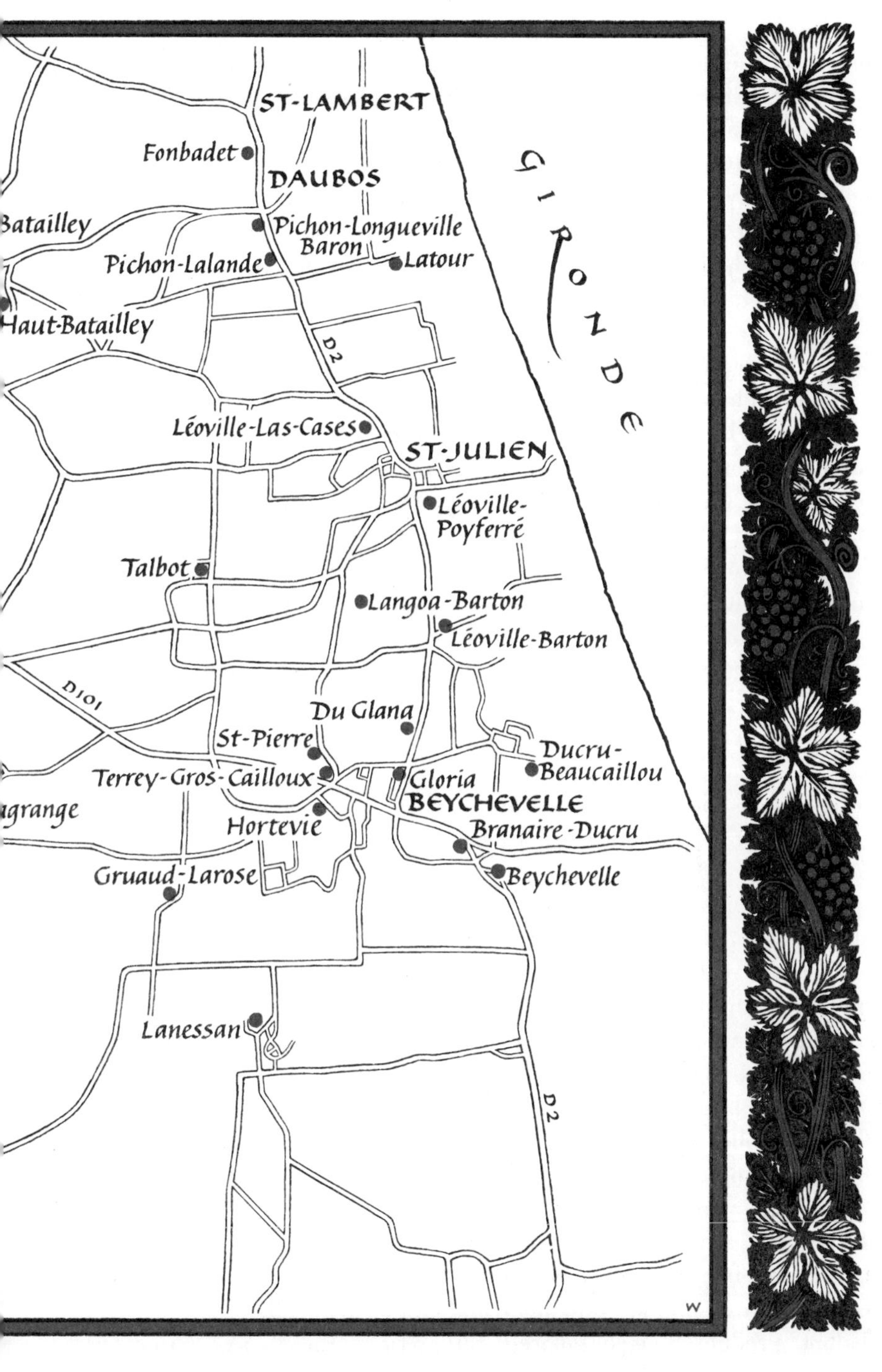

ST-LAMBERT
Fonbadet
DAUBOS
Batailley
Pichon-Longueville
Baron
Latour
Pichon-Lalande
Haut-Batailley
GIRONDE
D2
Léoville-Las-Cases
ST-JULIEN
Léoville-
Poyferré
Talbot
Langoa-Barton
Léoville-Barton
D101
Du Glana
St-Pierre
Ducru-
Beaucaillou
Terrey-Gros-Cailloux
Gloria
BEYCHEVELLE
agrange
Hortevie
Branaire-Ducru
Gruaud-Larose
Beychevelle
Lanessan
D2
W

on top of the heavily traveled Route du Vin (D2) and houses the winemaking facilities for both Léoville-Barton and Langoa-Barton. Not surprisingly, Langoa is very similar in style to Léoville-Barton—cedary, rich, and flavorful. It is often difficult to pick a favorite, but my tasting notes usually show that I give Léoville-Barton the edge.

The great St.-Julien estate of Ducru-Beaucaillou is usually the property that challenges both Léoville-Las Cases and the Médoc first-growths in quality each year. I remember vividly my first visit to Ducru-Beaucaillou in 1970 when I asked the old cellarmaster, M. Prévost, what the secret to Ducru's remarkable consistency was. He simply stated, "Selection, selection, selection." This is an expertly run property in which the owners, the genteel Borie family, oversee every step of the winemaking procedure. The château has a gorgeous location overlooking the Gironde, and the style of wine made here, while less massive and tannic than Léoville-Las Cases and less overtly fruity than Gruaud-Larose, is a classic St.-Julien that needs 8–10 years to reveal its rich, fruity, elegant, suave flavors. If Léoville-Las Cases is the Latour of St.-Julien, Ducru-Beaucaillou is St.-Julien's Lafite-Rothschild.

Within shouting distance of Ducru-Beaucaillou are Branaire-Ducru and Beychevelle, the two most southern St.-Juliens. Beychevelle is widely known, perhaps because tourists love the Médoc's most photogenic gardens, and the wine is supple, fruity, light, and quick to mature. While good, and sometimes excellent, Beychevelle has always had a better reputation than its performance record would lead one to believe.

Just the opposite is the case with Branaire-Ducru, the rather drab, sullen-looking château across the road from Beychevelle. Few consumers seem to realize just how good Branaire's wines can be. Furthermore, the price for Branaire is one of the lowest for a wine of its quality. Branaire is a bigger wine than its neighbor, Beychevelle, always darkly colored and usually possessed of an exotic, richly scented bouquet of cedar and chocolate. Branaire will never have the aging potential of the three Léovilles or Ducru-Beaucaillou, but between the ages of 8 and 20, Branaire can be an opulently rich, distinctive style of wine.

Two other great wines of St.-Julien are made at Gruaud-Larose and Talbot, two very large estates owned by the Cordier family. Gruaud-Larose sits back off the river behind Beychevelle and Branaire-Ducru. Gruaud-Larose and its stablemate and immediate neighbor to the north, Talbot, produce densely colored, rather rich, fruity wines. Gruaud is usually superior to Talbot, which has a tendency to sometimes be lean, but the quality of these two wines, while historically quite good, has been brilliant since 1978. Furthermore, since they both produce in excess of 32,000 cases of wine, and the price charged seems remarkably modest, Gruaud-Larose and Talbot immensely satisfy both the purse and the palate. In particular, Gruaud-Larose has performed at what is certainly a first-growth level since 1961, although one hears critics of Gruaud-Larose suggest that it lacks the great complexity and staying power of a true first-growth. Both of these points have proved baseless when it is compared in blind tastings against the first-growths.

The remaining two St.-Julien classified growths, Lagrange and St.-Pierre-Sevaistre, both are undergoing significant changes in personality. Lagrange, a rather little-regarded wine these days, has taken on new owners from Japan, and with some expert advice from Michel Delon of Léoville-Las Cases, the 1982 will prove to be a great step forward in quality, and the 1983 an improvement on even the 1982. Since Lagrange's low price reflects years of mediocrity and the trade's lack of confidence in this wine, shrewd Bordeaux enthusiasts might do well to take an interest in this up-and-coming property.

St.-Pierre-Sevaistre has for me always been a terribly underrated property. Until recently it was Belgian-owned and the style of wine produced here was rich in color and extract, full-bodied, sometimes a bit rustic, but always satisfying fat, robust, and fruity. Now the property and the wine are under the watchful eye of Henri Martin, the owner of St. Julien's most famous Cru Bourgeois, Gloria. The transition to a "Martinized" style of St.-Julien is clearly apparent with the 1983, a richly fruity, almost sweet, easy to drink, supple wine that has huge popular appeal.

St.-Julien is not without some excellent Cru Bourgeois properties. In addition to the excellent Gloria, there are the very good Terrey-Gros-Cailloux and Hortevie, both made at the same property; the stylish, elegant Lalande Borie; the rather commercial, sometimes dull, sometimes good du Glana; and a bevy of good "*deuxième*" or second wines from the major châteaux. The best of these is the Clos du Marquis from Léoville-Las Cases.

St.-Julien is a good commune in which to go treasure hunting when Bordeaux has a poor or mediocre vintage. Since most of the major vineyards are close to the Gironde, they tend to have excellent, well-drained, deep beds of gravel soil. In 1984, 1980, and 1977, all difficult years, St.-Julien produced more acceptable wines than elsewhere in Bordeaux. For the moment, the two Cordier estates, Gruaud-Larose and Talbot, as well as Branaire-Ducru, Ducru-Beaucaillou, and Léoville-Las Cases seem to do the best job in the so-called off-vintages.

In the excellent to great vintages, St.-Juliens are quintessential Médocs. The 1982s, 1978s, 1970s, and 1961s from St.-Julien are the truly great vintages for this appellation, followed by 1966, 1981, 1983, 1975, 1979, and 1976.

A CONSUMER'S CLASSIFICATION OF THE CHÂTEAUX OF ST.-JULIEN

OUTSTANDING

Ducru-Beaucaillou
Léoville-Las Cases
Gruaud-Larose

EXCELLENT

Branaire-Ducru
Léoville-Barton

VERY GOOD

Beychevelle
Talbot
Langoa-Barton
Léoville-Poyferré
Gloria
St.-Pierre-Sevaistre

AVERAGE TO GOOD

Lagrange

OTHER NOTABLE ST.-JULIEN PROPERTIES

Terrey-Gros-Cailloux
Hortevie
Lalande Borie
du Glana
La Bridane

DUCRU-BEAUCAILLOU (Second-Growth) OUTSTANDING

Production: 18,000 cases	Grape varieties: Cabernet Sauvignon—65% Merlot—25% Cabernet Franc—5% Petit Verdot—5%
Time spent in barrels: 20 months	Average age of vines: 35 years

Evaluation of present classification: Should be upgraded to a Médoc first-growth

Ducru-Beaucaillou, sitting amongst an outcropping of trees, directly on the road, with a splendid view of the Gironde River, has one of the great settings in the Médoc. It is the property of Jean-Eugène Borie, who inherited it from his father. Borie is one of an ever decreasing number of live-in proprietors. In the last three decades, he has brought the quality of Ducru-Beaucaillou up to a level where vintages such as 1961, 1966, 1970, 1973, 1976, 1978, 1981, 1982, and 1983 can challenge any of the Médoc first-growths. His passion for his wine, his obsessive commitment to quality, his numerous trips abroad as ambassador for Bordeaux, and his remarkable modesty have made him one of this region's most respected wine personalities.

The wine of Ducru-Beaucaillou is the essence of elegance, symmetry, balance, breed, class, and distinction. It is never one of the most robust, richest, or fruitiest wines of St.-Julien, and by its nature, a stubbornly slow developer. Ducru-Beaucaillou usually takes 10 years to show its stunning harmony of fruit and power. In great vintages, this wait can take as long as 15 years.

Ducru-Beaucaillou is a great wine for a number of reasons. The meticulous attention to detail, the brutal selection process whereby only the finest grapes and finest barrels of wine are permitted to go into the bottle, and the conservative viticultural practices followed, all play major roles in the success of this wine.

Ducru-Beaucaillou is one of Bordeaux's most expensive second-growths, reflecting the international demand for the wine and its consistently high quality. Does the St.-Julien vineyard merit first-growth status? Many wine enthusiasts, including this writer, would argue that Ducru-Beaucaillou, Léoville-Las Cases, and Gruaud-Larose merit elevation because of their exceptional performance over the last 25 years.

VINTAGES

1983—1983 is a very good, rather than great vintage for Borie's Ducru-
· Beaucaillou. The 1983 has a deep, dark ruby color, an expansive
88 bouquet of ripe blackcurrant fruit, and a moderate oakiness. Aggressively tannic, rather hard, quite youthful and backward, this is a more forceful-styled, full-bodied rendition of Ducru-Beaucaillou than most of us usually expect. Bottle age should tame it down a trifle. Anticipated maturity: 1996–2010. Last tasted, 3/85.

1982—Along with the 1953 and 1961, this is the greatest Ducru-Beau-
· caillou I have ever tasted. A sensational bouquet surges upward
96 from the glass displaying youthful cassis, oaky vanillin, and ripe

blackberry aromas. Voluptuous, extremely concentrated, with a stunning density of fruit extract, this full-bodied wine has plenty of tannins and a finish which must last at least a minute. A great success, even considering the vintage. Anticipated maturity: 1994–2015. Last tasted, 1/85.

1981—Another undeniable success for the vintage, the 1981 Ducru-
· Beaucaillou will require 8–10 years of cellaring because of its
90 tannic bite, but offers deep, dark ruby color, plenty of concentrated, blackcurrant flavors, a deft touch of oak aging, and an expansive, very long finish. A beautifully crafted wine, obviously vinified with care and made to last. Anticipated maturity: 1993–2008. Last tasted, 11/84.

1980—Ducru can often be counted on in off-vintages, but the 1980 lacks
· charm and fruit, has good structure, but finishes short and a bit
74 harsh. Anticipated maturity: 1987–1990. Last tasted, 1/84.

1979—Ducru has produced so many exceptional wines in the last sev-
· eral decades that when the château does not produce a wine that
84 is among the top dozen or so best wines of the Médoc, it is quite a surprise. This offering is a good but not great Ducru. Medium ruby in color, and noticeably lighter in style than previous efforts, this moderately intense, soft, pleasant wine should evolve quickly. Anticipated maturity: 1986–1991. Last tasted, 12/83.

1978—The 1978 is one of the finest wines of the vintage. Dark ruby,
· with a deep, rich, spicy, multidimensional bouquet of fresh cas-
90 sis, new oak, and subtle earthy scents. Full-bodied, with a degree of ripeness and richness which is only evident in the finest winės. Deep, savory flavors, moderate tannins, and a very long, clean finish have combined to make excellent wine with extended aging potential. Anticipated maturity: 1990–2015. Last tasted, 4/84.

1977—One of the more attractive 1977s, with surprisingly good fruit
· and not marred by too much acidity or vegetal aromas,the 1977
78 Ducru will continue to improve. Good solid fruit, yet not complex, this medium-bodied wine has some charming attributes to it. Anticipated maturity: 1985–1989. Last tasted, 2/84.

1976—This is a lovely Ducru that retains much of the silky, elegant
· personality of a top-class St.-Julien. However, it does not have
85 the concentration and richness of the 1982, 1978, 1970, or 1961. Still not fully mature (an anomaly for a 1976) this medium-weight, firm, yet rich, savory, and well-constituted 1976 has

plenty of character and elegance. Anticipated maturity: 1987–1994. Last tasted, 1/84.

1975—A very traditional, old-style claret with oodles of dusty tannins,
· the 1975 Ducru-Beaucaillou has a hard, muscular, sinewy per-
85 sonality, deep, ripe fruit, and perhaps an excessive amount of astringent, aggressive tannins. Needing plenty of time, this wine may ultimately deserve a higher score, but I wonder about the level of tannins which are so apparent. Anticipated maturity: 1995–2015. Last tasted, 4/84.

1974—A bit hollow, a trifle vegetative, but spicy, palatable, and softly
· fruity. Drink now. Last tasted, 10/81.
70

1973—Ducru is certainly one of the best wines of this watery vintage.
· It is still drinking well, although holding it any longer would be
83 senseless. The 1973 Ducru was fully mature by 1978, but has miraculously retained its fruit for the last 7 years. Drink up. Last tasted, 6/84.

1971—For whatever reason, the 1971 vintage for Jean-Eugène Borie's
· Ducru-Beaucaillou was not as good as it should have been. Now
78 fully mature, the bouquet exhibits light intensity, cedary, vanillin aromas. The flavors are satisfying, but not very concentrated or interesting. A rather straightforward Ducru-Beaucaillou. Last tasted, 9/79.

1970—The 1970 is a great Ducru-Beaucaillou, certainly the best after
· 1961 and before 1982. In 1970, it ranks as the best of the St.-
91 Juliens, just ahead of Léoville-Barton and Gruaud-Larose. The deep rich color shows a few signs of aging. On the palate, the wine is intense, with layers of ripe fruit admirably complemented by spicy oak. An intense, highly perfumed bouquet and great length give this wine wonderful charm and appeal. Anticipated maturity: 1986–2000. Last tasted, 10/84.

1967—For Ducru, the 1967 is a rather coarse, bland, obviously chap-
· talized wine, without the graceful fruit and spicy exuberance
74 normally found in wines from this estate. It is beginning to fade badly. Drink up. Last tasted, 10/78.

1966—A very flavorful wine, just now entering its prime of life, this
· 1966 Ducru-Beaucaillou defines such wine adjectives as ele-
87 gance, balance, and breed. Medium dark ruby with an amber edge, the bouquet is spicy, cedary, and subtly herbaceous. Velvety, round, spicy flavors show good concentration, as this wine

finishes soft and smooth. Drink over the next 5 years. Last tasted, 6/83.

1964—Solid, rustic, amiable, and pleasantly full and firm, the 1964
· Ducru-Beaucaillou lacks complexity and character, but offers a
82 rather robust, round mouthful of claret. Drink over the next 5 years. Last tasted, 3/84.

1962—Never among my favorite 1962s, but overall a success for the
· vintage, this wine is now starting to lose its fruit. Light to me-
78 dium ruby, with a mature, fruity, damp cellar, woody bouquet, and soft flavors that seem to be just beginning to fade, the wine should have been drunk up 5 years ago. Last tasted, 5/82.

1961—Fully mature, and I suspect showing as well as it possibly can,
· this dark ruby wine has amber/orange edges, a big, almost exotic
93 bouquet of ripe fruit, vanillin, caramel, mint, and cedar. Fat, rich, and capable of caressing the palate with its luxurious, silky fruit, this beautifully crafted wine finishes very long, and should be drunk over the next 5 years. Last tasted, 10/84.

LÉOVILLE-LAS CASES (Second-Growth) OUTSTANDING

Production: 30,000 cases	Grape varieties: Cabernet Sauvignon—65% Merlot—17% Cabernet Franc—13% Petit Verdot—5%
Time spent in barrels: 18 months	Average age of vines: 32 years

Evaluation of present classification: Should be upgraded to a Médoc first-growth

Léoville-Las Cases is unquestionably one of the great names and wines of Bordeaux. Situated next to Latour, Léoville-Las Cases's main vineyard of over 100 acres is a picturesque, enclosed vineyard that is also pictured on the label. The estate is one of Bordeaux's largest, and while the meticulous and passionate commitment to quality here may be equaled by several other estates, it is rarely surpassed. The man in charge here is Michel Delon, who has followed in the steps of his father, Paul, and is widely regarded as one of Bordeaux's strictest and most perfectionist managers.

The wines of Léoville-Las Cases have been excellent in the post-World War II era, yet the period from 1975 onward has witnessed the production of a string of wines which are close to perfection in vintages such as 1975, 1978, 1981, 1982, and 1983. In fact, these wines are as good as most of the Médoc's first-growths in these vintages.

In comparison to Ducru-Beaucaillou, its chief rival in St.-Julien, the wines of Léoville-Las Cases tend to be a shade darker in color, more tannic, bigger structured, slightly deeper, and of course built for an extended cellaring. They are traditional wines, designed for connoisseurs who must have the patience to wait the 10 to 15 years necessary for them to mature properly. Should a reclassification of Bordeaux's 1855 classification take place, Léoville-Las Cases, like Ducru-Beaucaillou and Gruaud-Larose, would get serious support for first-growth status.

VINTAGES

1983—This is unquestionably one of the top wines of the vintage. However, interested buyers should keep in mind that this dark ruby, deep, extremely tannic and raw wine will require 15 or more years of cellaring to reach its peak. Very dark in color, explosively fruity, with excellent depth and length, but mouth-shocking tannins, this is an infant giant of a wine. Anticipated maturity: 1998–2020. Last tasted, 3/85.
· 90

1982—In this special vintage, Léoville-Las Cases produced a monumental wine, which is not only one of the great wines of the vintage, but also of our times. From its birth it has shown a dimension of richness and length on the palate that is truly unbelievable. It is black ruby, with an astonishingly rich, blackberry, vanillin, oaky bouquet, intense, very concentrated flavors, full body, and, of course, the standard Las Cases mouth-puckering tannins. In France, this must be called an "*objet d'art.*" Anticipated maturity: 2000–2030. Last tasted, 1/85.
· 97

1981—This wine will no doubt live in seclusion given the herculean effort turned in by Las Cases in 1982, but make no mistake about it, the 1981 is very, very good. Quite dark ruby, with a spicy, oaky, ripe, berryish bouquet of moderate intensity, this big, tannic, full-bodied, amply endowed wine has outstanding length and concentration. Anticipated maturity: 1994–2010. Last tasted, 11/84.
· 88

1980—A solid, respectable effort for the year, but like many wines from this vintage, there is just not enough fruit to cover the bones. Drink this medium-weight wine over the next 3 years. Last tasted, 10/84.
· 75

1979—Not dissimilar in style to the excellent 1978, but slightly less
· concentrated and more supple, the 1979 Las Cases has a spicy,
86 cedary, ripe fruity bouquet, medium to full body, moderate tannin, and good texture, balance, and length. Anticipated maturity: 1988–2010. Last tasted, 5/84.

1978—The 1978 is a great Las Cases that appears to have immense
· potential. It certainly is one of the greatest wines of this highly
92 regarded vintage. Very dark ruby, with an intense cassis, vanillin, spicy bouquet, rich, full, deep flavors which coat the palate. This beautifully crafted wine offers the promise of greatness if cellared for 8–10 years. A stunning and gorgeous example of the 1978 vintage. Anticipated maturity: 1994–2015. Last tasted, 3/84.

1976—Showing extremely well, and ideal for drinking over the next
· several years, the 1976 Las Cases has shed its tannin and
84 exhibits ripe, berryish fruit, some subtle, spicy, oaky, vanillin aromas, and a plump, soft, round texture. A surprisingly concentrated yet mature 1976. Last tasted, 4/84.

1975—The 1975 is a classic Léoville-Las Cases that is loaded with
· potential, but still stubbornly young. Dark ruby, with a spicy,
92 oaky, very tight, but deep, ripe bouquet of black cherries on the palate, the wine is quite full, still aggressively tannic, but very concentrated and long. It will be one of the longest lived of all the Las Cases wines produced in the last 25 years. Anticipated maturity: 1995–2030. Last tasted, 12/84.

1974—The color is quite sound and still youthful-looking, but the prob-
· lem this wine has is the lack of fruit, which gives it a short finish
74 and rather empty taste on the palate. Time will help soften the harshness, but I suspect the fruit will fade as well. Last tasted, 2/82.

1973—Still drinkable, but clearly losing its freshness and lively, fruity
· character, the 1973 Las Cases is light, supple, and pleasant, but
70 quite one-dimensional, and now beginning to fade. Drink up! Last tasted, 5/80.

1971—The 1971 is an unbalanced Léoville-Las Cases, exhibiting too
· much tannin, a loosely knit structure, and fruity flavors that
77 seem to dissipate rapidly in the glass. An austere, unyielding wine in which the tannin clearly has the edge over the fruit. Nevertheless, there is interest in the bouquet, and the color remains sound. Anticipated maturity: 1986–1990. Last tasted, 10/84.

1970—A wine with a considerable reputation; however, I have found
· the Léoville-Las Cases 1970 on each occasion I tasted it to be
82 rather lean, angular, and light for the vintage, still quite dry, austere, and surprisingly compact for a 1970. Lacking in the rich fruitiness so typical of the vintage, this wine, while good, is a disappointment in the context of the vintage. Anticipated maturity: 1985–1995. Last tasted, 11/84.

1966—A classic Léoville-Las Cases, as well as textbook St.-Julien, this
· dark ruby-colored wine has no amber at the edges, a rich, full-
90 intensity bouquet of ripe blackcurrants, spices, and vanillin oakiness. The wine is perfectly balanced on the palate, with an excellent fruity intensity, and long, lingering, silky flavors. An extremely satisfying wine that is fully mature but will keep for at least another decade. One of the great wines of the 1966 vintage. Last tasted, 3/84.

1964—I never tasted this wine when it was supposedly at its best (1970–
· 1973), but recent examples have been dry, astringent, acidic,
71 and showing a glaring deficiency of fruit. A wine that will only grow more unattractive. Last tasted, 11/80.

1962—A lovely wine, not quite in the top flight of 1962s, but neverthe-
· less, charming, round, and gentle, with soft fruit, and a moder-
85 ately intense, fully developed bouquet. It requires drinking up over the next 5 years. Last tasted, 1/85.

1961—A highly regarded wine that has always proved somewhat of a
· letdown to me, the 1961 Las Cases has excellent, dark ruby color
86 with some amber at the edge, a briary, yet surprisingly compact bouquet, and rather dusty, spicy, coarse flavors which have nowhere near the depth, concentration, and complexity one expects from one of Bordeaux's great estates in a great vintage. A dry, austere, tannic finish suggests that better things may come with aging, but I believe the wine is fully mature. Drink up. Last tasted, 11/84.

GRUAUD-LAROSE (Second-Growth) OUTSTANDING

Production: 32,000 cases	Grape varieties: Cabernet Sauvignon—63% Merlot—25% Cabernet Franc—9% Petit Verdot—3%
Time spent in barrels: 18–24 months	Average age of vines: 40 years
Evaluation of present classification: Should be upgraded to a Médoc first-growth	

Gruaud-Larose is St.-Julien's most popular wine. The production is large and the quality is consistently very high. The wine is vinified in a style that is easy for most consumers to appreciate, and most important, the price Gruaud-Larose sells for is remarkably modest given both its official position in the Bordeaux hierarchy and its outstanding quality. Gruaud-Larose is an impressive château that is not likely to be seen unless the visitor to the Médoc turns off the main Route du Vin (D2) at the town of Beychevelle, and takes route D101 in a westerly direction. The great portion of the huge vineyard holdings of Gruaud-Larose are directly west of Beychevelle and Branaire-Ducru.

Gruaud-Larose is owned by the large *négociant* firm of Cordier, which also owns the neighboring Château Talbot in St.-Julien and a bevy of other fine estates in both the Médoc and St.-Emilion. Gruaud-Larose is frequently compared with its neighbor Talbot, since both wines are under the same ownership, and Cordier's highly respected oenologist, Georges Pauly, oversees the vinification and upbringing of both wines. Certainly the comparison in quality between the two wines over recent vintages makes for a lively topic of conversation. In my opinion, Gruaud-Larose has had the edge in most vintages, especially 1983, 1982, 1981, 1979, 1978, 1975, 1974, 1970, 1966, 1964, 1962, and 1961. In 1980, 1976, and 1971, I think Talbot made the better wine of these two St.-Juliens.

Critics of Gruaud-Larose argue that the wine is too chunky, too obviously fruity, and often does not fulfill the high expectations given the wine when it is young. I think all such arguments are easily rebuffed. Certainly the style of Gruaud-Larose is deeply fruity, and the wine often does show more color, fruit, and exuberance than the stylish, more tannic and reserved wines of Ducru-Beaucaillou and Léoville-Las Cases, but most wine enthusiasts seem to enjoy this fruitier style of wine. It certainly has the advantage of being drinkable at an earlier age. As for aging potential, the vintages of Gruaud-Larose in the '50s, '60s, and '70s have time and time again exhibited rich, savory fruit and excellent aging capacity.

Lastly, along with the Latour in Pauillac and La Mission-Haut-Brion in Graves, Gruaud-Larose is one of the most consistently successful wines that is produced in Bordeaux, regardless of the vintage conditions.

VINTAGES

1983—An unctuous, rather viscous, deep, plummy wine, with great
· extract of fruit, an opaque, dark ruby color, superb concentra-
90 tion, sound acidity, and plenty of alcohol, the 1983 Gruaud-Larose is a very big and very promising wine, with considerable tannin in the finish. Anticipated maturity: 1995–2015. Last tasted, 3/85.

1982—A rather huge, massive, incredibly rich and concentrated wine,
· the 1982 Gruaud-Larose is full, fat, deliciously viscous, but ex-
96 tremely tannic, with an amazingly long finish. This wine has plenty of tannin and alcohol, and will have no trouble living for at least 25 years, although it will be approachable in 10 years. The greatest Gruaud-Larose since the 1961. Anticipated maturity: 1995–2015. Last tasted, 1/85.

1981—A great success for the vintage, the 1981 Gruaud-Larose is quite
· good but it does not come close to challenging the splendid 1982
88 and 1983 wines produced by this property. Very dark ruby, with a full-intensity bouquet of ripe blackcurrants, spicy oak, plums, and violets, this wine is very concentrated on the palate, with rich, tannic, lingering flavors. Anticipated maturity: 1990–2005. Last tasted, 11/84.

1980—Unusually variable from bottle to bottle, the 1980 Gruaud-Larose
· can be soft, fruity, spicy, and attractive, if a bit too short in the
80 finish and too lean, but it can also be overly herbaceous, and too hard and acidic. The good examples are much deeper in color with surprising intensity and a soft, supple, weedy blackcurrant fruitiness. The rating reflects the better bottles. Anticipated maturity: 1985–1990. Last tasted, 3/85.

1979—This is a typical Gruaud-Larose, darkly colored, ripe, with fat,
· fruity flavors suggesting plums and black cherries, full body,
86 and medium tannins. Very full and supple, this is clearly a top success for the vintage. Because of its forward charms, it is

destined to be drunk young. Anticipated maturity: 1987–1998. Last tasted, 12/84.

1978—In 1978 Gruaud-Larose produced a very dark-colored wine with
· plenty of tannin for long cellaring, a big, briary, tarry-scented
87 bouquet, deep, intense, ripe, relatively supple flavors loaded with fruit, and a full-bodied, long finish. The 1978 will take longer to mature than the 1979, and probably be slightly superior in quality. Anticipated maturity: 1990–2010. Last tasted, 6/84.

1976—Not one of the better efforts for Gruaud-Larose, the 1976 lacks
· the rich, soft, silky fruitiness which characterized the top wines
73 of this irregular vintage. It seems to have an imbalance of tannin, and an annoying acidity in the finish. Anticipated maturity: 1985–1989. Last tasted, 2/83.

1975—The 1975 Gruaud-Larose is potentially greater than the score
· here may reflect. The only reservation I have about the 1975 is
90 the high level of mouth-puckering tannins that exist in this otherwise big, very impressive wine. Opaque in color, with a tight, yet rich, promising bouquet, and a deep, weighty feel on the palate, it has exceptional length, and while this wine is too good to pass by, one must wait at least another decade for it to mature. Anticipated maturity: 1995–2025. Last tasted, 5/84.

1974—Gruaud-Larose is an unquestioned success for the vintage. Now
· fully mature, and not likely to hold together for many more
80 years, this off-year Gruaud is surprisingly dark ruby, with a pleasingly mature, moderately intense bouquet of cassis and spices, medium body, and is soft and fully ready to drink. Last tasted, 2/83.

1973—Soft, fruity, and somewhat charming, this wine has held together
· longer than I would have expected. It requires immediate drink-
72 ing, but offers simple, straightforward, one-dimensional flavors that are a little watery, but certainly clean and pleasant. Last tasted, 2/82.

1971—Gruaud-Larose is a good example of the 1971 vintage which is
· now fully mature, and just beginning to show some telltale brown
83 color. This vintage of Gruaud is fruity, plummy, spicy, soft, and quite agreeable. It lacks the great concentration of a 1975, 1978, or 1982, but offers a graceful, fruity character. Drink up! Last tasted, 11/84.

1970—This wine has consistently shown well throughout its evolution,
· yet is still not ready to drink. Quite dark ruby in color, with
87 Gruaud's typical chunky, plummy fruitiness on display, this full-

bodied wine has plenty of tannin, a fairly hefty constitution, and long finish. Anticipated maturity: 1986–2005. Last tasted, 4/84.

1967 —This wine was at its peak in the mid-'70s and was quite effu-
· sively fruity, ripe, round, and sweet. Now the color has taken on
75 a brownish cast, the flavors seem to be at odds with each other,
and the wine tastes like it is cracking up. Drink immediately.
Last tasted, 10/81.

1966 —A classic vintage for Gruaud-Larose, the 1966 is still very young,
· relatively unevolved, but beautifully balanced, with plenty of
88 ripe, blackcurrant, cedary fruit, firm, yet not excessive tannins,
and a long, tight finish. In style and texture, the 1966 Gruaud-
Larose tastes more like a Pauillac than in any other vintage I
have sampled. Anticipated maturity: 1988–2015. Last tasted,
6/84.

1964 —One of the few successes in the Médoc, Gruaud-Larose is un-
· commonly fruity, deep, and very round. There is no evidence of
86 dilution from the heavy rains that ruined many a Médoc vineyard, but rather fat, generous, perfumed fruity flavors, and medium to full body. The 1964 Gruaud-Larose is fully mature and
should be drunk over the next 5 years. Last tasted, 9/83.

1962 —A surprisingly big, darkly colored wine that continues to steadily
· improve in the bottle, the 1962 Gruaud-Larose remains quite
87 concentrated for a wine of this vintage, with deep, blackcurranty
flavors, full body, and a good finish. A robust, intensely fruity
wine that is ideal for drinking over the next 4–5 years. Last
tasted, 11/84.

1961 —To my way of thinking, this is the greatest Gruaud-Larose I have
· ever drunk, with the exception of the 1982. This big, powerful,
95 rich, densely concentrated wine remains young, fresh, and vigorous, with a full 10–20 years of life ahead of it. It continues to
exhibit a very dark color, with a wonderful perfumed quality,
viscous texture, sensational depth of fruit, and a fabulous finish.
Anticipated maturity: 1987–2020. Last tasted, 10/84.

BRANAIRE-DUCRU (Fourth-Growth) **EXCELLENT**

Production: 20,000 cases

Grape varieties:
Cabernet Sauvignon—60%
Merlot—25%
Cabernet Franc—10%
Petit Verdot—5%

Time spent in barrels: 18–24 months

Average age of vines: 18 years

Evaluation of present classification: Should be upgraded to a Médoc second-growth

I have always found Branaire-Ducru to be curiously underrated, undervalued, and somewhat forgotten when Bordeaux enthusiasts discuss their favorite wines. (Certainly the château is not hard to miss; it is directly opposite Beychevelle on the Médoc's main wine road.) This is a pity, and no doubt likely to change once the wines of Branaire receive the publicity they merit. Several of the recent vintages, particularly 1975, 1976, and 1982, have been magnificently scented, deep, rich wines that are as good as most of the first-growths in those years, not to mention the other top wines of St.-Julien.

The vineyards of Branaire, like many Bordeaux châteaux, are spread out in a morseled fashion throughout the commune of St.-Julien. The wine is made uncompromisingly, in a very traditional manner. Branaire is one of the few non-first-growth châteaux to use 75% new oak barrels every year, and, in contrast to many châteaux that are making shorter *cuvaisons* to produce a more supple wine, Branaire keeps the skins in contact with the grape juice for a full month, a practice that is quite rare in Bordeaux today.

The wines of Branaire have a distinctive character. For a St.-Julien they are particularly spicy, with exotic aromas of spice, oak, and vanillin. On the palate, the wine often has a pronounced, distinctive chocolatey component that makes Branaire relatively easy to spot in blind tastings. This personality trait is especially noticeable in the great vintages of 1975, 1976, and 1982.

VINTAGES

1983—Somewhat soft for Branaire, with a medium-weight texture and relatively lush fruit, the 1983 is a moderately tannic, compact wine that is similar to the 1981 Branaire, only less elegant and charming. Anticipated maturity: 1990–1996. Last tasted, 3/85.
· 84

1982—The 1982 is a superlative wine from a vintage where Branaire
· attained perfection. The 1982 is the finest example of this châ-
93 teau's wine I have drunk, and a great success in the vintage. From the very first cask tastings in March following the vintage, this wine has consistently exhibited an explosive blackcurrant, chocolatey fruitiness, great concentration and length, full body, moderate tannin, and a spicy, smoky, opulent, exotic quality that makes it sensational on the palate. A gustatory smorgasbord. Anticipated maturity: 1992–2000. Last tasted, 2/85.

1981—Somewhat understated in personality, the 1981 Branaire is quite
· successful, but forward, precociously supple, and fruity. The
85 bouquet is already showing expansive, complex, chocolatey, cedary components. Anticipated maturity: 1988–1998. Last tasted, 11/84.

1980—A pleasant, fruity, soft, round wine without any of the vintage's
· unripe vegetal greenness present, the 1980 Branaire-Ducru is
78 fully mature now but will keep until 1986–87. Last tasted, 2/83.

1979—Almost ready to drink as full maturity seems very close, the
· 1979 Branaire has a full intensity, spicy, cedary, ripe blackcur-
84 rant bouquet. On the palate, the wine is soft, supple, with a generous silky fruitiness, light to moderate tannins, and good length and weight. A very stylish, round, elegant wine. Anticipated maturity: 1986–1993. Last tasted, 3/84.

1978—A good wine for certain, but the 1978 is not up to the quality
· level of either the 1979 or 1976 Branaires. The wine has good
80 color, an attractive, spicy, ripe bouquet, but on the palate the wine has a sharpness and angular quality which detracts from the overall quality. Anticipated maturity: 1987–1994. Last tasted, 1/84.

1976—The 1976 Branaire is fully mature, and one of my favorite wines
· from this vintage, which was much more irregular than most
86 consumers were led to believe. Medium ruby, with some browning at the edge, the 1976 Branaire has a full-blown, captivating bouquet of spicy oak, ripe fruit, caramel, and toffee scents. In the mouth, the wine is soft, silky, and admirably concentrated for a 1976. It finishes round and generously. A delicious wine for drinking over the next 2–4 years. Last tasted, 11/84.

1975—A great Branaire, just behind the monumental 1982 in quality,
· the 1975 is still a few years away from maturity but has a full-
90 intensity bouquet of spicy, vanillin oakiness, ripe fruit, and cedarwood. In the mouth, the wine is chocolatey, quite concen-

trated, rich and spicy, with aggressive tannins still in evidence. A great success for the vintage. Anticipated maturity: 1988–2005. Last tasted, 10–84.

1974—One of the very best St.-Juliens produced in this poor vintage,
· the 1974 Branaire is now fully mature and quite good. A complex
82 bouquet of spicy oak, flowers, and ripe blackcurrant fruit has
the depth of a much better vintage. Medium-bodied, with good fruit, and just a trace of brown at the edge, this is a noteworthy success for the vintage. Drink now! Last tasted, 3/80.

1971—A mediocre wine for Branaire, with a diffuse, somewhat watery
· character, rust/brown-colored at the edges, and light in body
71 and extract. It was best drunk up by 1978–80, as now it is
entirely too old. Last tasted, 10/79.

1970—The 1970 is a dark ruby wine that is now approaching maturity.
· Branaire is a plump, somewhat fat wine, with good, chewy fruit,
84 some coarse, dusty tannins, and plenty of oak aromas. Big and
powerful rather than elegant, the 1970 Branaire is a good but not excellent wine for this château. Anticipated maturity: 1985–1992. Last tasted, 2/83.

1966—A beautiful Branaire that is now fully mature but in no danger of
· falling off for at least another couple of years, the 1966 is dark
87 ruby, with a big, intense, spicy, blackcurrant, tarry, truffle-
scented bouquet, soft, silky, ripe, rich, deep, savory flavors, and a long finish. A lovely success from St.-Julien for the 1966 vintage. Last tasted, 7/82.

1964—The 1964 has been tasted only once, and that was in the early
· '70s. At that time, the wine was chunky and fruity, without much
70 direction or character, and browning prematurely. Probably well
past its prime. Last tasted, 4/72.

1962—Branaire usually can be counted on to age extremely well; how-
· ever, this wine was brown, fading badly, and very sweet and
60 sugared when last tasted in 1978. It had little redeeming interest
then, and I suspect it has completely collapsed by now.

1961—This is a very good Branaire, but to my thinking, not as good as
· the fine 1966 or nearly as successful as the outstanding wines
83 made in 1975 and 1982. Good dark ruby color with amber at the
edges indicates maturity. On the palate, the wine is full-bodied, quite flavorful and deep, but the tannins are coarse, and the dusty texture lacks elegance and finesse. Anticipated maturity: 1985–1995. Last tasted, 2/83.

LÉOVILLE-BARTON (Second-Growth) EXCELLENT

Production: 16,000 cases	Grape varieties: Cabernet Sauvignon—70% Merlot—15% Petit Verdot—8% Cabernet Franc—7%
Time spent in barrels: 24 months	Average age of vines: 30 years

Evaluation of present classification: Should be maintained

Léoville-Barton is generally acknowledged to have an edge on its sibling, Langoa-Barton. Both properties are owned by Anthony Barton, whose conservative, traditional winemaking is well displayed at both Léoville and Langoa-Barton. Unlike other proprietors, Barton uses only a small amount of the supple, fleshy Merlot in the blend, whereas the proportion of Cabernet Sauvignon and Petit Verdot, two more tannic and astringent grapes, is high not only for the commune of St.-Julien, but for the Médoc.

Léoville-Barton is made at Langoa-Barton since there is no château at Léoville. The main vineyard for Léoville-Barton sits immediately behind the town of St.-Julien-Beychevelle, and runs in a westerly direction where it intersects with the large vineyard of Château Talbot.

Like Langoa, Léoville-Barton can excel in the great Médoc vintages like 1982, 1975, and 1970, but is often somewhat more irregular than its peers in lighter weight, mediocre-quality vintages.

VINTAGES

1983—Extremely tannic and hard, with a very deep color, plenty of
· alcohol, and a rich, ripe, weighty fruitiness, this big wine will
86 require plenty of cellaring. All the component parts are present, but this is a very traditionally made wine for long-term cellaring. Anticipated maturity 1996–2005. Last tasted, 1/85.

1982—An outstanding wine was produced by Léoville-Barton in 1982.
· Extremely dark in color, very tannic, rich, intensely fruity, with
92 ripe aromas and flavors of blackberries and spicy oak, this full-bodied wine has superb length, and it is the best Léoville-Barton since the 1959. Anticipated maturity: 1995–2010. Last tasted, 1/85.

1981—Not dissimilar to the Langoa-Barton, this medium-bodied wine
· has an attractive, spicy, blackcurrant fruitiness, medium body,

84 moderate tannin, and an average finish. The 1981 is a good wine, but is clearly outdistanced by several other St.-Juliens in this vintage. Anticipated maturity: 1990–1996. Last tasted, 6/84.

1980—A lovely wine and outstanding success for the vintage, the 1980
· Léoville-Barton has a surprisingly good color, a spicy, caramel-
83 scented, deep bouquet, soft, ripe fruity flavors, moderate tannins, and a good finish. This wine should be drunk over the next 2–3 years. Last tasted, 10/83.

1979—Surprisingly light and precociously fruity, with little grip or
· backbone, this medium-bodied, moderately fruity wine has
75 charm and a savory, easygoing character, but tastes a bit watery. Drink over the next 5 years. Last tasted, 4/83.

1978—This is a very attractive Léoville-Barton that seems to be devel-
· oping at a more accelerated pace than I had initially expected.
86 A lovely, rather full, big bouquet of smoky, berryish, ripe fruit is first class. On the palate, the wine shows a good cedary, spicy, deep fruity constitution, moderate tannins, and a long finish. It is just about ready. Anticipated maturity: 1987–1993. Last tasted, 10/84.

1977—A trifle weedy and herbaceous to smell, however, the 1977 Léo-
· ville-Barton is well above average in quality for this vintage with
78 soft, flavorful, fully mature flavors. It should be drunk up. Last tasted, 10/82.

1976—A very successful wine, Léoville-Barton obtained much more
· fruit and stuffing in its 1976 than did Langoa. Rich, fully mature,
85 with a plummy fruitiness, and fat, lush finish, this wine's bouquet seems to jump from the glass. Sweet, ripe, velvety fruit caresses the palate. A little low in acidity, and some tasters might say it's too soft, but the 1976 Léoville-Barton is delicious for drinking over the next 2–3 years. Last tasted, 4/84.

1975—The 1975 Léoville-Barton is a big-styled wine with an uncanny
· resemblance to a Pauillac rather than to a suave, gentle St.-
88 Julien. Quite dark ruby, with a trace of amber at the edge, this full-bodied Léoville has a deep, spicy, long, hefty amount of fruit, mouth-puckering tannins, a bouquet which develops cedary aromas as it sits in the glass, and excellent length. Patience is required. Anticipated maturity: 1990–2000. Last tasted, 4/84.

1971—Now fading badly, and best drunk up immediately, the 1971
· Léoville-Barton has a sweet caramel candy-like nose, soft, shal-
70 low flavors that show no tannins, and a watery, weak finish. It is a disappointing effort from this château. Last tasted, 2/82.

1970—It seems that Léoville excels in years like 1970. Dark ruby with
· an amber edge, the wine is rich and quite full on the palate, with
87 excellent concentration, a full-intensity bouquet of blackcurrants and cedar wood, and moderate tannins still in evidence. A wine that can be drunk now, but will take at least 2–3 more years to reach its apogee. Anticipated maturity: 1987–2000. Last tasted, 4/83.

1966—The 1966 is a good, reliable wine that, in view of the vintage,
· could perhaps have been better. A moderately intense, spicy,
84 fruity bouquet that exhibits plenty of oak is seductive enough. However, the palate impression is one where austerity dominates the fruit. Fully mature, but capable of holding, this is a good but hardly top-rank 1966. Last tasted, 4/83.

1964—Darker in color, richer in flavor, and longer on the palate than
· the 1966, this hunky, fleshy wine shows impressive fruit, soft
85 yet noticeable tannins, and a ripe, fruity bouquet. Drink over the next 5 years. Last tasted, 4/83.

1962—Too angular, dry, and austere, with the fruit beginning to fade
· and the tannins becoming dominant, this medium ruby, moder-
75 ately intense wine should be consumed immediately. Last tasted, 4/83.

1961—A good wine, but given the greatness of the vintage—the normal
· excellence of Léoville in years when the Cabernet Sauvignon
85 attains great maturity—this wine could have been better. Medium ruby with brown at the edge, this wine has an attractive, spicy, cedary, ripe berry bouquet, good concentration, soft, round tannins, but not nearly the weight, richness, and length of other top 1961 St.-Juliens, such as Gruaud-Larose and Ducru-Beaucaillou. Fully mature. Drink over the next 5 years. Last tasted, 4/83.

BEYCHEVELLE (Fourth-Growth) **VERY GOOD**

Production: 30,000 cases	Grape varieties: Cabernet Sauvignon—72% Merlot—25% Cabernet Franc—2% Petit Verdot—1%
Time spent in barrels: 20 months	Average age of vines: 24 years

Evaluation of present classification: Should be upgraded to a Médoc third-growth

For the tourist visiting Bordeaux, Château Beychevelle is not likely to be missed since it is the first major château passed on the D2 road leading into the commune of St.-Julien. Furthermore, the beautiful flowering gardens that face the road have caused many a speeding driver to stop and take a photograph of them.

The wines of Beychevelle can be as beautifully produced as the property's flower gardens. However, the lack of consistency from vintage to vintage has been a problem. Additionally, the wine tends to be quite disappointing in mediocre years. In the '60s and '70s, the wine of Beychevelle tasted uncommonly smooth, supple and drinkable at a very young age, causing some to wonder if the vinification had changed. Most good vintages of Beychevelle have been fully mature by the time they are 10 years old, but have shown an alarming tendency to decline rapidly thereafter.

The current owners seem to have sensed that the ultra-smooth style of Beychevelle was as the English say "not making old bones," since there has been an increasing reliance on the firmer, more muscular Cabernet Sauvignon in the new vineyard plantings. Furthermore, there has been a change in the all-important *cuvaison* period, (the time period the skins are kept in contact with the grape juice). It has been lengthened by a full week to gain greater extraction of color and tannins for longevity. Beychevelle, which would be described as a light, supple, elegant, quick-maturing wine on the basis of the wines produced in the '60s and '70s, has in 1982 and 1983 made a deeper, more firmly constructed, and more tannic wine.

Beychevelle is one of St.-Julien's most expensive wines, often selling at a price level near or just below the price of Léoville-Las Cases and Ducru-Beaucaillou. Until recently, such high prices seemed out of line with the quality in the bottle.

VINTAGES

1983—The new, firmer style of Beychevelle is no better displayed than
· in Beychevelle's 1983. Quite dark in color, with a ripe, intense,
85 cassis smell, this wine is rich and tannic on the palate, with very
good depth, an aggressive texture, and long, rough finish. An
impressive wine for long-term cellaring. Anticipated maturity:
1995–2005. Last tasted, 3/85.

1982—The 1982 has been tasted numerous times, yet my notes are
· marked by tremendous inconsistency. In the spring following
87 the vintage, at the château, the wine tasted rather lean, austere
and unimpressive, particularly in view of the vintage. Four
months later, the wine was typical of many top 1982s—decadently rich, with a sensual, glossy fruitiness, excellent color and
concentration, as well as enough tannin to age for 10–15 years.
Just recently, from the bottle, the wine has been very good, but
a trifle unyielding, severe, and tannic, and rather atypical for
the vintage. Nevertheless, it remains an impressive Beychevelle, if not an impressive 1982. Anticipated maturity: 1995–
2010. Last tasted, 1/85.

1981—The last supple, light-bodied, finesse-styled Beychevelle? For
· certain, the 1982 and 1983 are more muscular and aggressive
84 wines. The 1981 is forward, quite fruity, with a rather obvious
taste of new oak apparent. Medium-bodied with good color, this
is a supple, soft, charming wine which tends to resemble the
1979. Anticipated maturity: 1987–1993. Last tasted, 4/84.

1979—Slightly diffuse and overly soft in style, this medium-bodied,
· moderately dark ruby wine is very drinkable now, and should
81 continue to drink well for 3–5 years. Some structure, depth and
firmness seem to be missing, but the wine has appeal. Last
tasted, 10/83.

1978—Dark ruby/garnet with some amber at the edge, the 1978 Bey-
· chevelle seems very close to maturity. A lovely bouquet of ripe
85 berry fruit is followed by a wine which is slightly sweet, soft and
savory, with some unresolved tannins. A bit chunky, but overall
very satisfying and flavorful. Anticipated maturity: 1986–1993.
Last tasted, 10/82.

1976—Technically, not the most perfect wine—the acidity is low, the
· pH high. But technical data aside, this is an immensely enjoy-
84 able, plummy, fat, fruity wine that has a wonderful sweetness of
fruit and chunky texture. In stylistic terms, it leans toward the
plump style of Gruaud-Larose rather than a Léoville-Las Cases

or Ducru-Beaucaillou. Drinking well now, it should continue to develop well for 4–5 more years; however, it will not be long-lived. Last tasted, 11/84.

1975—Early in this wine's life, it tasted precocious and forward for the
· normally tannic, hard wines of this vintage. This wine has now
86 firmed up, and I have no doubts it will be the longest-lived
Beychevelle of the decade. Dark ruby, with a ripe, rich, spicy, blackcurrant bouquet, full body, weighty, deep, tannic flavors, and a long finish, this big Beychevelle begs for more cellaring. Anticipated maturity: 1988–2000. Last tasted, 4/84.

1974—Beychevelle made a good showing in 1974, producing a supple,
· easygoing, fruity, gentle wine that has been fully mature for
80 several years. Drink up! Last tasted, 3/79.

1973—Now totally faded and dissipated, this light wine should have
· been drunk by 1980. Last tasted, 2/81.
65

1971—Quite attractive and fully mature, the 1971, while not classically
· structured, being rather loosely knit and too soft, nevertheless
83 has a savory, spicy, fruity character, with moderately intense
flavors and light tannin. Drink up! Last tasted, 2/83.

1970—Fully mature with a spicy, plum-like bouquet, and some caramel
· aromas, the 1970 Beychevelle is round, fruity, quite silky and
84 soft, and nicely concentrated. It lacks the complexity and depth
of the best 1970s, but is still quite attractive. Drink over the next 3–4 years. Last tasted, 9/84.

1967—In the early and mid-1970s, this wine was quite attractive, fla-
· vorful, spicy, with above-average fruity intensity for the vintage.
70 Now, the wine has lost its exuberant fruitiness and has faded
badly since 1977. Some fruit still remains, but this wine should have been drunk up prior to 1980. Last tasted, 3/81.

1966—One of my favorite Beychevelles, this wine has constantly shown
· well in tastings of the 1966s. Quite mature, with an expansive,
85 complex, ripe, fruity, spicy, cedary bouquet, and supple, soft,
velvety flavors, this Beychevelle displays the kind of concentration, consistency, firmness, and character that some of the more recent vintages of Beychevelle have lacked. Drink over the next 5 years. Last tasted, 1/79.

1964—Beginning to crack up ever so slightly, the 1964 Beychevelle still
· has a good measure of chunky fruitiness, a rustic, medium- to
83 full-bodied feel on the palate, and a creeping brownish caste to
the color. The bouquet is particularly spicy for Beychevelle.

Drink over the next several years; it will not improve. Last tasted, 1/81.

1962—Another example of a Beychevelle that has not stood the test of
· time. My notes show I had a good example in a Bordeaux restau-
78 rant in 1970, but more recent tastings have displayed a tired and
fatigued wine, with some fruit and character still remaining, but
most definitely on the slide. Drink up! Last tasted, 7/79.

1961—Certainly a very fine example of the vintage, the 1961 Beyche-
· velle is not in the top league of 1961s, but overall is a very fruity,
87 concentrated wine that has a voluptuous character, no tannins,
and just enough acidity to prevent the wine from tasting heavy.
A very good wine that is fully mature. Last tasted, 1/79.

TALBOT (Fourth-Growth) — VERY GOOD

Production: 38,000 cases	Grape varieties: Cabernet Sauvignon—70% Merlot—20% Cabernet Franc—5% Petit Verdot—5%
Time spent in barrels: 18–24 months	Average age of vines: 28 years
Evaluation of present classification: Should be upgraded to a Médoc third-growth	

The sibling château of Gruaud-Larose, the famous fourth-growth Talbot is also owned by the *négociant* firm of Cordier. The huge single vineyard of Talbot is situated inland from the Gironde River, well behind the tiny hamlet of St.-Julien-Beychevelle and just north of Gruaud-Larose.

Talbot, named after the English commander, John Talbot, the Earl of Shrewsbury, who was defeated in battle at Castillon in 1453, makes consistently fine, robust yet fruity, full-bodied wines which should be moved upward should any new reclassification of the wines of the Médoc be done. The wine is vinified in the same manner as Cordier's Gruaud-Larose, but the two wines do not resemble each other except for this enviable record of high-quality consistency. Gruaud-Larose always tends to be fruitier, less austere, usually darker in color, and in the really top vintages, more tannic and bigger-framed. Talbot usually has to take a second seat to Gruaud-Larose in head-to-head competition, but in certain vintages Talbot can surpass its more prestigious sibling. For example, the 1982 Talbot is almost a match for the brilliant

Gruaud-Larose of that year, and in 1980, 1976, and 1971 Talbot can be said to have bested Gruaud-Larose in head-to-head competition.

Talbot is a wine that needs 8–10 years to show its class and character, and like Gruaud-Larose tends to be undervalued in the current-day Bordeaux wine market. Of particular significance is the fact that Talbot has been consistently brilliant since the 1975 vintage. The 1977 is the only weak wine produced in this period.

VINTAGES

1983—Quite full-bodied, with a deep, almost opaque ruby/purple color,
• and a cassis-scented aroma, with rich, full-bodied, tannic fla-
89 vors, the 1983 Talbot is quite a big wine that will require a long
evolution in the bottle. It is one of the great successes of the
vintage. Anticipated maturity: 1998–2010. Last tasted, 3/85.

1982—The 1982 is massive, with dense, ruby/purple color, a viscous,
• ripe, very fruity, powerful taste, and firm, yet round, ripe tan-
89 nins. The big, rich flavors linger and are huge on the palate. The
1982 Talbot is the biggest and richest Talbot I have ever tasted,
and potentially the best wine from this estate since the 1953.
Anticipated maturity: 1995–2010. Last tasted, 1/85.

1981—Quite attractive and well made, the 1981 Talbot shows surpris-
• ing elegance and suppleness for this property. Very dark ruby,
85 with a moderately intense bouquet of cassis and tarry aromas.
Full-bodied, with very good concentration and body, this moderately tannic wine should be drinkable soon. Similar in style to
the 1979, only a shade deeper and fruitier. Anticipated maturity:
1989–2000. Last tasted, 11/84.

1980—As successful as Gruaud-Larose in 1980, this wine offers solid,
• straightforward, fruity flavors, none of the vegetal character
82 found in the worst 1980s, and a solid, round, flavorful finish.
Drink over the next 3–4 years. Last tasted, 6/83.

1979—A richly fruity Talbot, with a precocious, forward appeal, this
• medium-bodied wine has a velvety texture, and a soft, round
84 finish. Drink over the next 6 years. Last tasted, 2/84.

1978—Developing very nicely in the bottle, the 1978 Talbot has concen-
• trated, ripe, round, rich, blackcurrant fruit, a bouquet sugges-
86 tive of plums and subtle herbaceous notes, a full-bodied,
generous texture, and some tannin to lose. It is not nearly as
backward as some 1978s are. Anticipated maturity: 1987–1998.
Last tasted, 6/84.

1976—The variable 1976 vintage reached its greatest heights in the
· commune of St.-Julien where a number of fine wines were pro-
85 duced. Talbot is one of them. Now fully mature, but capable of
holding for 2–4 years, this immensely enjoyable wine has a
lovely cedary, spicy, ripe plummy bouquet, soft, round, nicely
concentrated flavors, and a velvety, satisfying finish. Last
tasted, 9/84.

1975—When young it was not impressive, as it seemed to lack concen-
· tration, grip, and character. However, the 1975 Talbot has
86 shown surprisingly well in recent tastings. Not that darkly colored for a 1975, but medium dark ruby with some amber, this
wine has a well-developed bouquet of spicy, vanillin, blackcurrant fruit, a dusty, tannic, rather weighty texture, and good
length. It is much more evolved than its sibling, the 1975
Gruaud-Larose. Anticipated maturity: 1986–2000. Last tasted,
4/84.

1971—One of the most stylish and complete wines of the vintage, the
· 1971 Talbot is now fully mature and showing no signs of fading.
85 It has good concentration, a lively, berryish, fruity quality, a
deft touch of vanillin oakiness, and medium to full body. Very
well structured for a 1971, without any brown color or soupy
softness that afflicts many of the wines of this vintage, the 1971
Talbot is certainly a wine to look for from this vintage. Last
tasted, 10/84.

1970—The 1970 Talbot is good, but not up to the quality level expected.
· Too austere, a trifle harsh and unyielding, this wine lacks one of
80 the telltale characteristics of the 1970 vintage—a rich, glossy
fruitiness. The bouquet shows Médoc breeding, iron-like mineral scents, oak, and blackcurrants, but the tannin overwhelms
the fruit. Time may help, but this is one wine where the tannin
has the edge. Anticipated maturity: 1985–1992. Last tasted,
12/84.

1967—One of the more attractive wines of the vintage, the 1967 Talbot
· is now cracking up. Short, compact flavors now show little of
75 the rich, fruity, robustness exhibited in the mid-'70s. Drink up!
Last tasted, 1/83.

1966—Age has given this wine some complexity as a result of bottle
· bouquet; however, this vintage did not produce a good example
77 of Talbot. Hard, austere, lean flavors show little evidence that
rich, ripe fruit is hidden behind a shield of tannin and acidity.

The color is light, the fruit just adequate, the finish short. Drink up! Last tasted, 9/84.

1964—An attractive if uncomplex 1964, Talbot is adequately fruity,
· chunky, a trifle hard and coarse in the finish, but overall, a good
82 mouthful of claret. Drink up! Last tasted, 3/79.

1962—An elegant Talbot, finely etched and reminiscent of the style of
· the 1971, this medium-bodied, flavorful, fully mature wine is
84 holding up nicely in the bottle. A fragrant, spicy, cedary bouquet is interesting and shows good fruit. Rather reserved on the palate, with polite flavors, some unresolved tannins still present, and above-average length, this is a good but not a great Talbot. Last tasted, 2/83.

1961—One would naturally expect the 1961 Talbot to completely over-
· whelm the 1962. When tasted side by side, the similarities are
85 quite abnormal, given the different styles of these two vintages. The 1961, like the 1962, is a bit austere and lean, has medium to full body, a rather stern, unyielding texture, and good rather than excellent concentration. The wine lacks the color and richness of the best 1961s, but is still a good wine, yet certainly a disappointment in the context of the vintage. Drink over the next 5–6 years. Last tasted, 1/85.

LANGOA-BARTON (Third-Growth) VERY GOOD

Production: 8,000 cases	Grape varieties: Cabernet Sauvignon—70% Merlot—15% Petit Verdot—8% Cabernet Franc—7%
Time spent in barrels: 22–24 months	Average age of vines: 30 years
Evaluation of present classification: Should be maintained	

Langoa-Barton is an impressively large château that sits directly on the well-traveled D2, or Médoc Route du Vin. The wine of the well-known second-growth, Léoville-Barton, is also made here. Both Langoa and Léoville-Barton are the properties of Anthony Barton, an Irishman, whose family has had an interest in the Bordeaux area since the 1820s.

Ronald Barton, the former owner, and his nephew, Anthony, produce top-class wine that critics should and do call uncompromisingly traditional and classic. Both are St.-Julien wines with a distinctive Pauillac character and personality. Since the wines are made in the same wine cellar, by the same staff, the first question someone always asks is in what ways they are different. A few years ago, Anthony Barton put on a vertical tasting (back to 1948) of most of the vintages of both châteaux. In most years, Léoville-Barton edged out Langoa, but it was quite close. Both wines are big, ripe, concentrated, spicy wines, which frequently lack in their youth the suppleness and cunning fruit of some of their neighbors. Nevertheless, they age extremely well, and when mature, seem to combine the savory, complex, graceful fruitiness of St.-Julien with the cedary toughness and virility of Pauillac.

Neither Léoville nor Langoa-Barton has ever had the reputation of Léoville-Las Cases or Ducru-Beaucaillou. Much of the consumer's lack of knowledge regarding the quality of these two Barton estates had been a result of a less than perfect distribution system abroad. Heretofore, the wines were difficult to find. Now more of the wine can be found and both wines, for the time being, offer truly superb values from St.-Julien.

My only criticism of Langoa Barton and Léoville-Barton is that in some of the lighter Bordeaux vintages (e.g., 1979, 1971, 1974, and 1973) the wines of these two châteaux seem less successful than perhaps they should be. Whatever the reason, both châteaux do indeed excel in such great vintages as 1982, 1975, and 1970. As for Langoa-Barton, the track record in the 1980s, starting with a surprisingly good 1980 from an otherwise mediocre vintage, may well be a harbinger of better and more consistent things to come.

VINTAGES

1983—From the cask, the Langoa-Barton was impressively deep in
· color, full-bodied, admirably concentrated, but extremely
85 tannic. However, it appears to have the fruit to outlast the aggressive tannins. Anticipated maturity: 1995–2005. Last tasted, 6/85.

1982—A great Langoa-Barton, and probably better than the excellent
· 1975, 1970, 1959, 1949, and 1948, the 1982 has a rich, deep ruby
88 color, an intense, ripe, blackcurrant bouquet, big, tough, full-bodied framework, and exceptional potential. Very rich, very tannic, very big, and very promising. Anticipated maturity: 1995–2010, Last tasted, 1/85.

1981—Like many vintages for the Barton-owned pair of Léoville and
· Langoa, it is often difficult to conclude which is the better wine
84 since they are made and handled in identically the same way. The 1981 Langoa is medium-bodied, with good color, a spicy, moderately fruity bouquet, and solid, firm tannin. A trifle austere, but well made. Anticipated maturity: 1992–2000. Last tasted, 11/84.

1980—One of the very delicious wines of the vintage, the 1980 Langoa
· can be consumed now or held for 3–4 years. This wine is quite
83 savory and spicy, with soft, round, attractively ripe, fruity flavors, nicely balanced by a touch of oak. Not a big wine, but it is very flavorful and attractive. Last tasted, 6/84.

1979—An appealing wine for certain, but for whatever reason, the huge
· yield perhaps, the wine lacks concentration and tastes rather
78 supple and light for Langoa-Barton. Medium ruby garnet, with a forward, supple, spicy bouquet, soft, average-intensity flavors, and a short finish. Anticipated maturity: 1986–1990. Last tasted, 9/84.

1976—Very easy to drink, and soft, slightly sweet, with no abrasive
· tannin present, the 1976 Langoa is fully mature, has some brown
81 creeping in at the edges, and should be drunk up should one have stocks of it on hand. Last tasted, 4/84.

1975—An excellent Langoa, the 1975 has an open-knit, full-intensity,
· seductive bouquet of cedarwood, vanillin spices, and ripe fruit.
87 On the palate, the wine is quite full-bodied, loaded with tannin as well as rich fruit, and has real length. A big, complex St.-Julien that wants to be a Pauillac. Anticipated maturity: 1990–2005. Last tasted, 4/84.

1971—Langoa is an obviously chaptalized wine that unfortunately is
· now browning quite a bit. The 1971 Langoa seems to be quite
69 flabby and unknit, and finishes quite diffusely. It was fully mature when last tasted. My notes do show that a surprisingly rich, flavorful bottle was tasted in 1982, so perhaps some bottle variation exists with this wine. Now probably badly in decline. Last tasted, 4/83.

1970—A wonderfully successful wine, the 1970 Langoa smells like a
· first-class Pauillac, and tastes like one too. A big yet restrained
88 bouquet of cedar and blackcurrants is first-rate. On the palate, the wine is ripe, weighty, rich, tannic, full-bodied, and several years away from its zenith. One of the top Langoas. Anticipated maturity: 1986–2000. Last tasted, 4/85.

1966—Another unquestioned success for Langoa, the 1966, while very
• good, is not up to the 1975 or 1982 quality level. Amber at the
87 edge, with a solid ruby color, the 1966 has a full-intensity, spicy, cedary, rich bouquet, lean, somewhat austere flavors, but a good, round, generous finish. Fully mature. Last tasted, 4/85.

1964—The tannin and acid seem to clearly outbalance the fruit in the
• 1964 Langoa. Chunky, but a trifle lean and thin on the palate,
72 the wine's attractively spicy, complex bouquet leaves the palate unfulfilled. Fully mature. Last tasted, 4/83.

1961—Tasted next to the 1959 at Anthony Barton's extravagant vertical
• tasting at the International Wine Center in New York City, it
89 was hard to pick which wine was the best. The 1959 perhaps was more alcoholic, but the 1961 was filled with a richly scented smell of cedar, oak, vanillin, and ripe fruit. On the palate the rich, round, sweet, ripe fruitiness of the vintage was capably displayed. Fully mature, but will no doubt hold for 5–6 more years prior to fading. Last tasted, 10/82.

LÉOVILLE-POYFERRÉ (Second-Growth) VERY GOOD

Production: 23,000 cases

Grape varieties:
Cabernet Sauvignon—65%
Merlot—30%
Cabernet Franc—5%

Time spent in barrels: 18–22 months

Average age of vines: 25 years

Evaluation of present classification: Should be downgraded to a Médoc fourth-growth

Talk to just about any knowledgeable Bordelais about the potential of the vineyard of Léoville-Poyferré, and they will unanimously agree that Poyferré has the soil and capacity to produce one of the Médoc's greatest red wines. In fact, some will argue that Léoville-Poyferré has better soil than any of the other second-growth St. Juliens. But the story of Léoville-Poyferré since 1961 is one of unrealized potential. At present, the wine is nowhere close to the quality of Léoville-Las Cases or Ducru-Beaucaillou, or even Léoville-Barton, Branaire-Ducru, Gruaud-Larose, Talbot, Langoa-Barton, or Gloria. However, the most recent two vintages, 1982 and 1983, do indeed show the depth and richness that this property is capable of attaining. If these two wines are indicative of a new era for Léoville-Poyferré, as many Bordelais believe, this will be a property with unlimited potential, and one to take seriously from now on.

VINTAGES

1983—Perhaps a match for the excellent 1982 made by Léoville-
· Poyferré, the 1983 has been consistently impressive from the
89 cask. Very dark ruby, with a classic bouquet of blackcurrants, plums, and new oak, this wine shows very good to excellent concentration of fruit, very hard, astringent tannins, and a long finish. A wine for long-term cellaring. Anticipated maturity: 1998–2010. Last tasted, 1/85.

1982—Broodingly black ruby in color, with a young yet expansive bou-
· quet of ripe, rich, blackcurrants and spicy oak, this is a partic-
92 ularly big-styled Poyferré. Full-bodied, with rich, ripe fruit very much in evidence, as well as tough, plentiful tannins, this wine, like the 1983, will require long-term cellaring. Anticipated maturity: 1995–2010. Last tasted, 1/85.

1981—Consistently perplexing to judge, the 1981 Poyferré has ade-
· quate tannin and acidity, a soft, jammy mid-range, and a short
83 finish. Surely a good wine with 4–5 years of evolution ahead of it, but certainly not one of the leading St.-Juliens in 1981. Anticipated maturity: 1986–1992. Last tasted, 10/84.

1979—Medium to dark ruby with an amber edge, this wine has an open-
· knit, ripe, rather port-like bouquet. Soft, flabby flavors have
78 modest appeal, but the wine is quite loosely knit and diffuse in the finish. Drink over the next 5 years. Last tasted, 5/84.

1978—An easygoing wine, with soft, charming, above-average-inten-
· sity flavors, medium body, and very light tannins, this is a wine
80 that has obviously been vinified for near-term consumption. Drink over the next 5 years. Last tasted, 4/82.

1976—Very soft, flabby, almost soupy, fruity flavors show good ripe-
· ness but little structure, grip, or balance. A sweet, simple, fruity
75 wine which can be quaffed easily, but it does not deliver classified-growth breed or character. Drink up. Last tasted, 6/83.

1975—Several outstanding performances of this wine in early tastings
· of the 1975s proved to be an unreliable guide to its potential
? quality. Dark ruby, with a spicy, closed, woody bouquet, the 1975 Poyferré has a flavor suggestive of ripe black cherries. There is significant tannin that will require patience to resolve. Very inconsistent from bottle to bottle, which suggests a sloppy approach to the blending of the different barrels prior to bottling.

Some bottles can be superb, while others are merely good. Unfortunately, the latter seem to predominate. Anticipated maturity: 1988–2000. Last tasted, 5/84.

1971—Fully mature, simple, straightforward, with a bouquet reminis-
· cent of cranberry juice, medium-bodied, somewhat compact and
75 lean, this is a pleasant but hardly inspiring wine. Drink up. Last
tasted, 6/79.

1970—Foul barnyard aromas have long beset this wine which otherwise
· shows a good, dark ruby color, ripe, savory fruit, moderate tan-
65 nins, and a decent finish. I had once hoped that time would
cause dissipation of the stinky smells, but they have only gotten
worse. Last tasted, 10/83.

1966—Given the listless management that Poyferré was under during
· this period, it is a wonder that the 1966 turned out as well as it
83 did. Now fully mature, this medium-bodied, stylish wine has
good blackcurrant fruit, a complex yet restrained bouquet of
cedar and spices, and a good, crisp, clean finish. Drink over the
next 2–3 years. Last tasted, 9/84.

1964—Some fruit can be found, but first one's palate must fend off
· abnormally high acidity and harsh tannins. It is memorable only
55 because of its obvious deficiencies. Last tasted, 11/75.

1962—Much of the Léoville-Poyferré vineyard was replanted in 1962,
· and while the young, infant vines may have been the reason for
67 some of the lackluster wines produced in the late '60s and early
'70s, they had nothing to do with the mediocre 1962. Light,
overly acidic, with some redeeming fruit flavors, this light- to
medium-weight wine should be drunk up. Last tasted, 9/77.

1961—The 1961 is very good but not in the top class of wines from this
· vintage. Certainly rich, flavorful, and concentrated with fruit,
87 this wine represents a rather rare phenomenon for Poyferré during a period of mediocrity. Dark ruby, with an attractive, cedary,
spicy, mature bouquet, on the palate the 1961 Léoville-Poyferré
is deep, supple, ripe and long, but fully mature. Drink up. Last
tasted, 3/80.

GLORIA (Unclassified) VERY GOOD

Production: 20,000 cases	Grape varieties: Cabernet Sauvignon—65% Merlot—25% Cabernet Franc—5% Petit Verdot—5%
Time spent in barrels: 16 months	Average age of vines: 20 years

Evaluation of present classification: Should be upgraded to a Médoc fourth-growth

Gloria has always been used as an example of why the 1855 classification of the wines of the Médoc is so outdated. Gloria has made wines over the last two and a half decades that in vintages such as 1961, 1966, 1970, 1971, 1975, and 1976 are certainly as good as many of the wines produced by many of the classified growths. Shrewd merchants and consumers have long known Gloria's quality, and the wine has been widely merchandized abroad.

Henri Martin, Gloria's owner, is one of the Médoc's legendary figures. His wines at Gloria are no doubt made for sheer crowd appeal. They are round, generous, slightly sweet, with wonderful cedary, spicy, almost exaggerated bouquets. They show well young, but age well for up to 12–15 years. The Gloria style of the '60s and '70s seems to have changed in recent years. It may be premature to say so, but recent Gloria vintages, such as 1978, 1979, 1980, 1981, 1982, and 1983, definitely appear to be wines that are lighter, more obviously fruity, and less tannic than those that were made previously. Well made, stylish, delicious wines they continue to be, but there is no question that recent vintages are not made to last as long as the wines made in 1975, 1971, 1970, 1966, and 1961. Nevertheless, this is still a wonderfully fruity, delicious St.-Julien that continues to sell at a price well below its actual quality level.

VINTAGES

1983—A forward, typically spicy, fruity wine, the 1983 Gloria has more
· noticeable tannin than the 1982, but less rich, glossy fat fruit.
82 Gloria is moderately tannic, somewhat herbaceous to smell, but attractive in its own distinctive way. Anticipated maturity: 1989–1995. Last tasted, 3/85.

1982—A gloriously fruity, spicy, almost grapey Gloria, the 1982 is
· charmingly drinkable already, has the telltale spicy, cedary bou-
85 quet, and soft, lightly tannic flavors. It lacks the great depth of the best vintages of Gloria, but is still a very attractive, deliciously fruity wine. Anticipated maturity: 1987–1996. Last tasted, 1/85.

1981—Very similar to the stylish yet mature 1979 Gloria, this wine
· offers supple, cedary, olive-tinged flavors, medium body, a more
80 austere character than the 1979. The Gloria telltale sweetness on the palate is present. Drink over the next 5 years. Last tasted, 4/84.

1980—Light, slightly vegetal, and lacking the roundness and fruity
· character one expects from Gloria, the 1980 is a very mediocre
73 wine from a mediocre vintage. Last tasted, 3/84.

1979—Very forward and quite ready to drink, this wine has an attrac-
· tive fruity character, a medium-bodied, nicely ripe, savory,
82 sweet, ripe, lush texture, and little or no tannins present. This wine will hold for 5 years, but other than some further bottle bouquet development, it is ready now. Last tasted, 9/84.

1978—Round, flavorful, fruity, with a bouquet suggestive of cinnamon,
· this wine is deliciously mature now, but will hold for 4–5 more
83 years. The sweetness and fruitiness on the palate are almost burgundian. Last tasted, 10/84.

1976—Gloria's huge, plummy, spicy bouquet is very enticing. Dark
· ruby/garnet, with plenty of sweet, ripe fruit in evidence, this
84 medium- to full-bodied wine is deep, very fruity, and ready to drink. It will last for 5–6 years. One of the top 1976s. Last tasted, 10/84.

1975—The 1975 is an older, more traditional, powerful-styled Gloria
· than we are used to seeing in more recent vintages. A big, volup-
87 tuous bouquet of spicy oak, ripe plummy fruit, and chocolate is first-rate. In the mouth, the wine is quite full-bodied with a big, alcoholic, ripe, deep, rich texture, and a long finish. Anticipated maturity: 1986–1996. Last tasted, 10/84.

1973—In the mid-'70s, this wine could be enjoyed for its light, fruity,
· simple charms. It has now faded badly. Drink up immediately.
72 Last tasted, 4/81.

1971—A beautiful wine, the 1971 Gloria has been fully mature since
· 1979, but has not lost a thing, although amber, brownish colors
86 are becoming more and more apparent. The bouquet is highly

perfumed, exhibiting scents of cedar, plums, vanillin spice, and sweet oak. On the palate, the wine is silky, gentle, and very fruity and sweet. An unquestioned success. Drink up. Last tasted, 10/84.

1970—Another triumphant success for Gloria, the 1970, richer and
· fuller than the lovely 1971, with more long-term keeping possi-
88 bilities, is a really classy, complex wine. Dark ruby in color, with a full mature bouquet of sweet fruit and vanillin oakiness, this wonderful, rich, fruity, medium-bodied wine impresses the palate with a long, gentle, soft finish. A voluptuous, decadently fruity wine. Drink over the next 5 years. Last tasted, 10/84.

ST.-PIERRE-SEVAISTRE (Fourth-Growth) VERY GOOD

Production: 8,000 cases	Grape varieties; Cabernet Sauvignon—63% Merlot—20% Cabernet Franc—15% Petit Verdot—2%
Time spent in barrels: 24 months	Average age of vines: 34 years
Evaluation of present classification: Should be maintained	

St.-Pierre is the least-known of the classified-growth St.-Julien châteaux. Much of the production of St.-Pierre is sold to eagerly awaiting wine enthusiasts in Belgium, no doubt because the former owners, Monsieur Castelein and Madame Castelein-Van dan Bussche, are themselves Belgian.

The vineyards of St.-Pierre are well located right behind the town of St.-Julien-Beycheville, and a drive past them will reveal quite a few old and gnarled vines, always a sign of quality.

The style of wine of St.-Pierre tends to be quite robust in almost a coarse way. Always deeply colored, sometimes opaque, St.-Pierre is a big, rustic, dusty-textured wine, without the finesse and charm of many St.-Juliens. It seems to have all the components and ages well, but the wine is rarely sold in America, and almost never shown by *négociants* in Bordeaux at comparative tastings. Consequently, my experience tasting St.-Pierre has been extremely limited.

However, this should all change, as St.-Pierre was purchased in 1982 by Henri Martin, the dynamic owner of Château Gloria in St.-Julien. Because of the distinctively sweet, ripe, round style of Gloria, one would expect the hefty, beefy style of St.-Pierre to change with future vintages. The name has been shortened on the new labels to St.-Pierre.

VINTAGES

1983—Surprisingly similar in style to the 1982, fat, succulent, and very
· concentrated with a soft, rich, almost jammy concentration, this
87 full-bodied, robust wine has a seductive lushness and will make excellent drinking. Anticipated maturity: 1990–1998. Last tasted, 3/85.

1982—A lovely, supple, ripe, savory, richly fruity wine with medium to
· full body, a moderately intense bouquet of vanillin oakiness and
86 ripe fruit, the 1982 St.-Pierre seems forward and lush, but exhibits sufficient underlying tannin to develop nicely. Anticipated maturity: 1990–2000. Last tasted, 1/85.

1981—A top-notch wine, certainly one of the most successful wines of
· this vintage, the 1981 St.-Pierre is impressively dark ruby, very
87 aromatic, with the scent of ripe berry fruit, cedarwood, and caramel. On the palate, it is quite rich, medium- to full-bodied, long, lush, and moderately tannic. A rather big, extroverted St.-Julien, with considerable personality. Anticipated maturity: 1988–2000. Last tasted, 2/85.

1979—A rather robust, virile wine for a 1979, St.-Pierre has impressive
· color, a chunky, satisfying, rich fruity character, some whiffs of
85 cedarwood, and a solid, moderately tannic finish. Not elegant, but nevertheless substantial and flavorful. Anticipated maturity: 1988–1995. Last tasted, 2/84.

1975—Impressive for sure, but like so many 1975s, one wonders
· whether it will live up to its potential. Quite dark in color, with
86 no signs of aging, this full-bodied wine has ripe, chocolatey fruit, but also mouth-lashing high tannins that are quite severe. The 1975 St.-Pierre is a robust, muscular wine which most definitely requires time in the bottle. Anticipated maturity: 1990–2005. Last tasted, 5/84.

1971—Ready to drink, this wine is quite spicy, with a plummy, cedary
· nose, that offers high expectations on the palate. The wine is
83 good, but less promising than the fine bouquet suggests. The somewhat coarse, rough flavors are heavy-handed and too aggressive. Drink over the next 5–6 years. Last tasted, 6/82.

1970—A sleeper of the vintage, the 1970 St.-Pierre is very dark ruby,
· loaded with spicy, blackcurrant fruit, has full body, plenty of
87 round, ripe tannins, and substantial length on the palate. Still

youthfully exuberant and obviously made in a style to last and last, the 1970 St.-Pierre can rival many of Bordeaux's best vineyards in 1970. Anticipated maturity: 1987–2010. Last tasted, 6/84.

1961—This is a very fine 1961, with a fully mature, sweet, savory,
· plummy spiciness, medium to full body, dark garnet color, and
86 good length. Drink over the next 5–8 years. Last tasted, 3/82.

LAGRANGE (Third-Growth) — AVERAGE TO GOOD

Production: 10,000 cases	Grape varieties: Cabernet Sauvignon—58% Merlot—40% Petit Verdot—2%
Time spent in barrels: 18–20 months	Average age of vines: 25 years
Evaluation of present classification: Should be downgraded to Grand Bourgeois Exceptionnel	

Lagrange, a third-growth, has suffered numerous blows to its reputation as a result of a mediocre track record in the '60s and '70s. The vineyards are large, over 100 acres of well-situated, unmorseled property adjacent to Gruaud-Larose, so there is no reason why good wine should not be produced. The future may be more promising for Lagrange because the property and château were sold to the large Japanese firm of Suntory, which has stated that greater and stricter quality controls and management of the vineyard's winemaking will be employed. Certainly, the first example of the new Japanese commitment to quality, the 1983, was extremely impressive from the cask.

VINTAGES

1983—Potentially a sleeper of this vintage, Lagrange is quite deep in
· color, spicy, and rich, with full-bodied, briary, cassis flavors,
86 good firm tannins, and a long finish. If the wine resembles the style of Léoville-Las Cases, it's not surprising because Michel Delon, the gifted winemaker at Las Cases, oversaw the vinification of Lagrange in 1983. Anticipated maturity: 1993–2000. Last tasted, 1/85.

1982—Nineteen eighty-two was a very successful vintage for Lagrange.
· Perhaps the 1982 is not the equal of the excellent 1983, but it is
85 still a dimension above in quality over recent efforts from Lagrange. Very dark ruby, with a well-developed bouquet of ripe

berry fruit and vanillin oak, the wine is also precocious on the palate, displaying rich, lush, nicely concentrated flavors, and full body. Anticipated maturity: 1990–2000. Last tasted, 1/85.

1979—The 1979 is a bit too herbaceous and stalky, but once past the
· rather unimpressive bouquet, the wine shows good ripe fruit, a
78 supple, soft texture, and spicy finish. It will be ready early. Anticipated maturity: 1986–1990. Last tasted, 3/83.

1978—Dark ruby in color, with a ripe berry bouquet suggestive of Mer-
· lot, the 1978 has generous, straightforward, fruity flavors, light
80 to moderate tannins, medium body, and a pleasant finish. A good, if unexciting wine. Anticipated maturity: 1986–1990. Last tasted, 3/83.

1975—The color is dark ruby, yet one is hard pressed to find any fruit
· behind the wall of abrasive tannins. Very severe and bitter on
70 the palate, with an excess of tannins, this will require a lengthy stay in the cellar, just to soften. However, my guess is that the fruit will never be adequate enough to balance out the harsh qualities of this wine. Anticipated maturity: 1990–1998. Last tasted, 4/84.

1973—A total failure—no fruit, no charm, just watery, thin flavors with
· entirely too much acidity and tannin. Last tasted, 10/79.
50

1971—A little wine, compact, a bit tannic, lean and short in the finish,
· the 1971 Lagrange is the kind of claret that is an embarrassment
65 to the commune of St.-Julien, as well as Bordeaux. A charmless, coarse wine. Last tasted, 10/78.

1970—The 1970 is the best Lagrange of the '70s, as nothing of this
· quality level was seen again until 1982 and 1983. Dark ruby,
84 chunky flavors, with good, ripe, blackcurrant fruit, a solid, moderately long finish, and potential for further evolution, this is a respectable effort from Lagrange. Anticipated maturity: 1985–1992. Last tasted, 4/81.

1966—Light, fruity, simple and one-dimensional, the 1966 Lagrange
· has been fully mature for a number of years, and seems totally
72 devoid of the complexity, breadth of character, and the length one expects in a third-growth St.-Julien. Drink up. Last tasted, 4/80.

1964—Lagrange's 1964 was pale in color, and very stringy and skinny
· on the palate when I tasted it in 1980 for the first and only time.
60 It is a dubious effort for certain in this mixed, rainy vintage. Drink up.

1962—While the 1962 was reportedly a success for the vintage, my
· experience (two separate tastings) has shown the wine to have
70 adequate color, but too much acidity, a harsh, aggressive finish,
and little of the rich fruity charm one expects from a St.-Julien.
Drink up. Last tasted, 2/81.

1961—Produced in a period when the wines of Lagrange were quite
· mediocre, the 1961 is a surprisingly good effort. Dark ruby with
85 amber at the edge, this is a chunky, flavorful wine, with some
delicious blackcurrant fruit, a pleasant oaky spiciness, and very
good suppleness and length on the palate. Fully mature, it
should hold for 5–7 more years. Last tasted, 2/84.

OTHER NOTABLE ST.-JULIEN PROPERTIES

Henri Martin's Gloria is the most famous and widely distributed non-classified-growth property of St.-Julien, but there are other properties that also make fine wine.

Certainly, shrewd consumers looking for high quality St.-Juliens at modest prices should remember the names Terrey-Gros-Cailloux, Hortevie, Lalande Borie, du Glana, and La Bridane.

TERREY-GROS-CAILLOUX (Unclassified)

Evaluation: The quality equivalent of a Grand Bourgeois Exceptionnel

One of the best of the lesser-known St.-Juliens, Terrey-Gros-Cailloux can make surprisingly good St.-Juliens. The 1979 is fully mature, supple, and very fruity. The 1980 and 1981 are not as successful as other St.-Juliens, but the 1982 is quite rich, a trifle too jammy, but a big, meaty mouthful of wine. The best recent vintage looks to be the 1983, which is quite full and tannic, but shows very good concentration and aging potential of at least a decade.

HORTEVIE (Unclassified)

Evaluation: The quality equivalent of a Grand Bourgeois Exceptionnel

Hortevie is produced at Terrey-Gros-Cailloux, and is an exclusive of the well-known and highly respected Bordeaux *négociant* Nathaniel Johnston et Fils. In theory it should be a better wine than Terrey-Gros-Cailloux since it represents a selection of wine produced from the oldest vines at Terrey-Gros-Cailloux. All of the most recent vintages, 1983,

1982 and 1981, are very attractive, silky, lush, rich, and flavorful wines which typify a good St.-Julien. Of this trio, the 1982 looks to be the real standout, with dense, ripe, jammy, blackberry flavors, full body, and enough acidity and tannin to last for 5–8 years.

LALANDE BORIE (Unclassified)

Evaluation: The quality equivalent of a Grand Bourgeois Exceptionnel

The highly respected Jean-Eugène Borie produces this wine from a relatively young vineyard he planted in 1971 and 1972. Contrary to what some people have claimed, this is not the second wine of any of M. Borie's prestigious estates in St.-Julien and Pauillac. The 1981 Lalande Borie is supple and soft, a charmingly fruity wine that is quite well made. The 1982 is dense and gorgeously colored, with rich, fat, deep blackcurrant flavors, and the 1983, full-bodied as well as the most tannic of this trio.

DU GLANA (Grand Bourgeois Exceptionnel)

Evaluation: Should be maintained

Du Glana is a sizeable vineyard of 110 acres that has had a very spotty record of achievement until 1978. Since then, reliable wines have been made. The 1978 is a fully mature, cedary, generously fruity wine. The 1979 and 1981 are light, particularly so in view of the vintages, but the 1982 is a real winner, fat, concentrated, full-bodied, and quite supple. The 1983 seems somewhat diffuse, as well as slightly diluted, but is fruity, soft, and ready to drink.

LA BRIDANE (Unclassified)

Evaluation: Should be maintained

La Bridane produces a solid, reliable yet rarely exciting style of St.-Julien. Combined with the fact that it tends to be rather expensive in this country, it is therefore a wine I largely ignore. The 1982 looks to be the clear-cut winner among the vintages of the '80s. In the '70s, the 1970 and 1975 are the two vintages to seek out. It is not terribly complex, but fruity, ripe, medium-bodied, and satisfying. Most vintages of La Bridane are best drunk within 5–6 years. La Bridane produces 6,500 cases of wine made from a blend of 55% Cabernet Sauvignon and 45% Merlot.

MARGAUX AND THE SOUTHERN MÉDOC

Margaux is certainly the most sprawling of all the Médoc's principal wine-producing communes, although the acreage under vine (2,579 acres) is just a little less than St.-Estèphe's 2,660 acres farther north. The first-time tourist to Margaux immediately realizes just how spread out the châteaux of Margaux are. Only a few sit directly on Bordeaux's Route du Vin (D2), and these are Dauzac, Prieuré-Lichine, Palmer and Malescot St.-Exupéry. Château Margaux is just off the main road in the town of Margaux, but the other major châteaux are spread out through the five principal communes of this appellation, Arsac, Labarde, Cantenac, Margaux, and Soussans.

Margaux has the greatest number of classified-growth châteaux (Crus Classés) in the 1855 classification. A total of 21 Margaux châteaux made the so-called grade, which is four more than Pauillac's 17 châteaux that were included, 10 more than St.-Julien's 11 châteaux that were classified, and 16 more than St.-Estèphe's 5 châteaux that were listed in the 1855 classification.

From an outsider's view, Margaux thus appears to have the highest number of quality wine producers; however, nothing could be further from the truth. From 1961–1983, there are at least a half-dozen estates in Margaux that have a dreadful record of performance, and at least another four or five properties that should be downgraded to fifth-growth status should any revised classification of the wines of the Médoc be done and the five-tiered hierarchy maintained. Even the regal first-growth queen herself, Château Margaux, went through a period of mediocrity that was dramatically reversed when the Mentzelopoulos family purchased Château Margaux in 1977 from the Ginestets, who had through neglect permitted this grande dame to slip considerably in quality (not price however) below first-growth quality standards.

Despite the irregularity and lackluster track record of many Margaux châteaux over the last two and a half decades, the fragrant bouquet and seductive charm of a few great Margaux wines are what set these wines apart from a St.-Julien or Pauillac. The bouquet of a fine Margaux is unquestionably greater than what one can find in the wines of St.-Julien, Pauillac, and St.-Estèphe. This has been well chronicled in virtually all the writings on Bordeaux wine, but what one has not been told is that the great wines of Margaux are really limited to Château Margaux, Palmer, and Giscours. These three estates have been consistently the best over the last 25 years, followed by d'Issan, Boyd-Cantenac, Lascombes, Prieuré-Lichine, and Malescot St.-Exupéry.

No one will argue that properties such as Rausan-Ségla, Rauzan-Gassies, Brane-Cantenac, Durfort-Vivens (all second-growths), and Cantenac-Brown (a third-growth) have great soils, superb vineyards, and immense potential, but except for the quite recent turnabout in quality for several of these estates, the wines of these estates over the period 1961–1980 have been terribly inconsistent and, in far too many vintages, very mediocre or poor in quality.

The great diversity of soils and quality level of wines produced in Margaux is challenging for even the most devoted Bordeaux wine enthusiast. Certainly the soils in Margaux are the lightest and most gravelly of the Médoc, and when one gets down to Ludon where La Lagune is located, a high percentage of sand appears in the soil base.

Since 1977, Château Margaux has made unquestionably the greatest and most powerful wine of this appellation. Rather virile, very concentrated and densely colored, only Giscours produces a similarly rich and full-bodied, very concentrated wine like the style Château Margaux is aiming for today. Boyd-Cantenac can produce a rather powerful, dark colored wine, but it comes nowhere close to the quality of either Margaux or Giscours.

Château Margaux's chief competitor is not Giscours, but Palmer. However, Palmer's style of wine is different. It shares a dark color and deep concentration of flavor with Château Margaux, but it is a more supple, rounder, less tannic wine as a result of a rather high percentage of Merlot used in the blend at Palmer. Palmer does have a fabulously complex bouquet that in certain vintages—1961 and 1966 come to mind immediately—is hauntingly perfect.

Closest in style to that of Palmer is the wine of d'Issan. D'Issan, like Haut-Bages-Libéral in Pauillac and Branaire-Ducru in St.-Julien, is curiously overlooked when great Margaux wines are mentioned. However, d'Issan, which is almost a totally Cabernet Sauvignon–based wine, produces a gloriously perfumed, stylish wine that is usually supple and quite round. Not surprisingly, the property abuts that of both Palmer and Margaux.

Another recognizable style of Margaux wine would be typified by

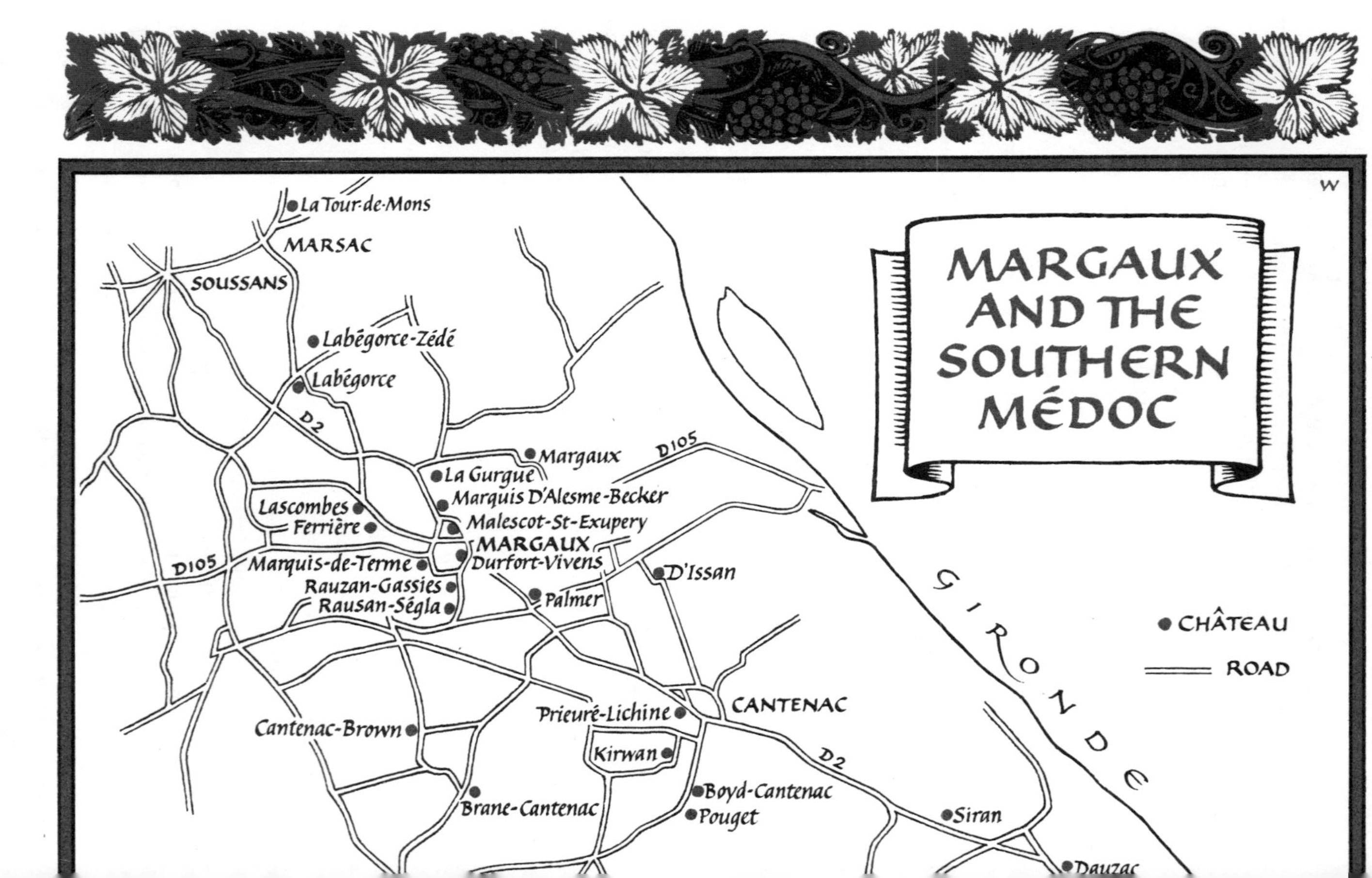

MARGAUX AND THE SOUTHERN MÉDOC
W
CHÂTEAU
ROAD
GIRONDE
La Tour-de-Mons
MARSAC
SOUSSANS
Labégorce-Zédé
Labégorce
D2
Margaux
D105
La Gurgue
Marquis D'Alesme-Becker
Lascombes
Ferrière
Malescot-St-Exupery
MARGAUX
Durfort-Vivens
D105
Marquis-de-Terme
D'Issan
Rauzan-Gassies
Rausan-Ségla
Palmer
Prieuré-Lichine
CANTENAC
Cantenac-Brown
Kirwan
D2
Boyd-Cantenac
Pouget
Brane-Cantenac
Siran

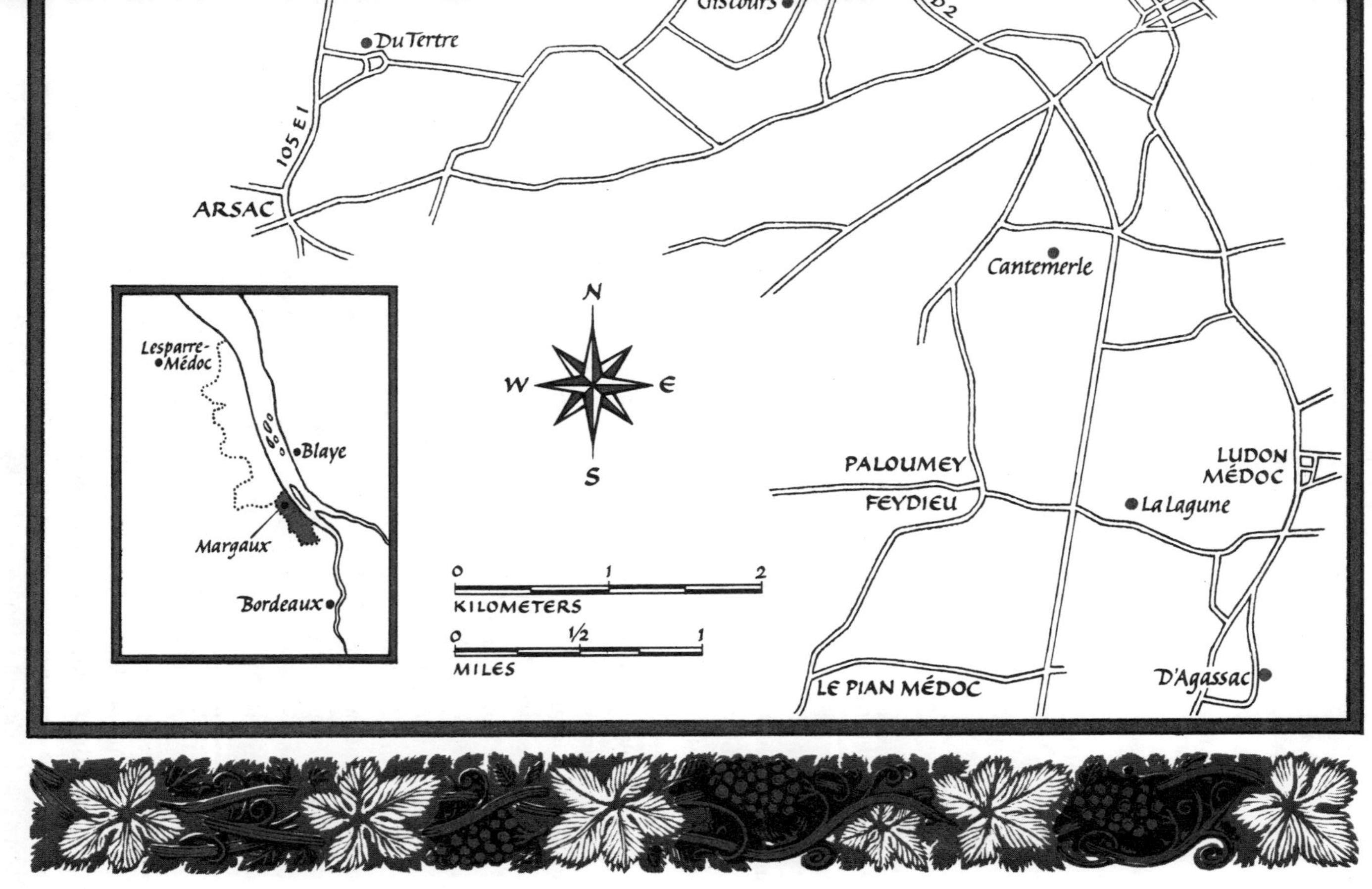

Giscours
Du Tertre
105 E1
ARSAC
Cantemerle
N
W
E
S
Lesparre-Médoc
Blaye
Margaux
Bordeaux
PALOUMEY
FEYDIEU
LUDON MÉDOC
La Lagune
0
1
2
KILOMETERS
0
1/2
1
MILES
LE PIAN MÉDOC
D'Agassac

wines with an intense fragrance, but lighter in weight, less concentrated, and less tannic. Certainly Prieuré-Lichine, Lascombes, and Malescot St.-Exupéry all produce wines in this manner.

Prieuré-Lichine, the home of Alexis Lichine, can produce very stylish, elegant, fragrant wines. The property has generally been much more consistent than many of its more famous neighbors. Certainly Lascombes, a wine that I adore when it is made well, has been like a yo-yo in terms of quality. The reports of a renewed vigor and commitment to higher quality from its corporate owners is apparently true if the wines Lascombes produced in 1982 and 1983 are any indication.

Malescot St.-Exupéry has a great reputation and I have tasted a few great bottles from this property, yet it is overrated, but not overpriced.

Despite the number of mediocre, even poor wines produced by such noteworthy Margaux estates as Brane-Cantenac, Durfort-Vivens, Dauzac, Rausan-Ségla, and Kirwan in the 1961–1980 period, the encouraging thing is that all of these properties have halted their nose dives, and in the '80s turned in some of their best winemaking efforts in more than a decade.

Both Brane-Cantenac and Durfort-Vivens have provided far too many disappointing, often shabbily produced wines. As much as I enjoy the company of Lucien Lurton, the proprietor, the wines from these two estates throughout the '60s and '70s were terribly inconsistent and sometimes undrinkable. However, with the help of Emile Peynaud and, I suspect, a more careful selection process, the 1981s have turned out well, the 1982s excellent, and the 1983s superb.

Dauzac's wines have also made progress since the late '70s, as have those of Kirwan. Even Rausan-Ségla, considered to have one of the greatest vineyards in all of the Médoc, yet which consistently turned out drab, feebly colored, dull wines, has turned in surprisingly good efforts in both 1982 and 1983. However, Rausan-Ségla still has a long way to go in quality before it regains the reputation that it had in 1855 as the best wine in the Médoc after the first-growths.

There are a handful of other classified-growth Margaux estates. The most promising estate is du Tertre, which has since 1978 been making excellent wine under the capable hand of Philippe Capbern-Gasqueton. Cantenac-Brown continues to produce rather rustic, tannic, hard wines that appeal to those with 19th-century tastes. Rauzan-Gassies can be quite good, but leans toward a chunky, full-bodied, St.-Estèphe style of wine rather than a true Margaux. In contrast, Marquis d'Alesme-Becker, hardly known and rarely seen, makes a rather light wine, while

Marquis-de-Terme produces an earthy, rather coarse yet flavorful Margaux.

Among the Crus Bourgeois in Margaux, most observers would say that four properties consistently make fine wine. D'Angludet, Labégorce-Zédé, Siran, and Labégorce are very good estates making typically elegant, perfumed, aromatic wine. Labégorce-Zédé's wine tends to be the most robust and richest of this quartet.

Lastly, two major properties and classified growths to the south of Margaux both make excellent wine. La Lagune is one of my favorite wines. Brilliantly made by Madame Boyrie, the wine can resemble both a Pomerol and a burgundy, but it is always deliciously rich, round, fruity, and complex. The quality seems to get better with each passing vintage. Cantemerle is the other treasure of the southern Médoc and after an uneven period in the late '70s, Cantemerle has been making superb wine, with the 1983 as its crowning achievement. Both La Lagune and Cantemerle, no doubt because they are not in the famous Médoc appellation, are considerably undervalued in the scheme of Bordeaux wine pricing.

Vintages for Margaux and southern Margaux can often be different from those for the communes of St.-Julien, Pauillac, and St.-Estèphe, which sit a good distance to the north. This is not a region in which to look for good wines in off-vintages. The thin soil seems to produce thin wines in rainy years, although there are always exceptions. Both Margaux and Giscours produced excellent wines in 1980. However, the best vintages for Margaux wines have been 1983, 1982, 1979, 1978, 1970, 1966, and 1961. In both 1975 and 1976, the number of disappointments clearly exceeded the number of successes in Margaux.

A CONSUMER'S CLASSIFICATION OF THE CHÂTEAUX OF MARGAUX AND THE SOUTHERN MÉDOC

OUTSTANDING

Margaux
Palmer

EXCELLENT

Giscours
La Lagune

VERY GOOD

Boyd-Cantenac, Cantemerle, d'Issan, Lascombes, Prieuré-Lichine, Malescot St.-Exupéry

ABOVE AVERAGE TO GOOD

Rausan-Ségla, Brane-Cantenac, Rauzan-Gassies, du Tertre, Pouget, Kirwan, Cantenac-Brown, Durfort-Vivens, Marquis d'Alesme-Becker, Marquis-de-Terme, Dauzac

OTHER NOTABLE MARGAUX PROPERTIES

d'Angludet, Siran, Labégorce-Zédé, Labégorce, La Tour-de-Mons, Desmirail, Ferrière, La Gurgue, Bel-Air-Marquis d'Aligre, Tayac, Paveil de Luze, Canuet

MARGAUX (First-Growth) — OUTSTANDING

Production: 20,000 cases	Grape varieties: Cabernet Sauvignon—75% Merlot—20% Cabernet Franc—5%
Time spent in barrels: 23–24 months	Average age of vines: 35 years
Evaluation of present classification: Should be maintained	

After a period of mediocrity in the '60s and '70s, when far too many wines lacking richness, concentration, and character were produced under the loose administration of Pierre and Bernard Ginestet, Margaux was sold in 1977 to André and Laura Mentzelopoulos. Lavish amounts of money were immediately spent on the vineyards and the winemaking facilities. Emile Peynaud was retained as a consultant to oversee the vinification of the wine. Apprehensive observers expected the passing of several vintages before the new financial and spiritual commitments to excellence would be exhibited in the wines. It took just one vintage, 1978, for the world to see just how great Margaux could be. Unfortunately, André Mentzelopoulos died before he could see the full transformation of a struggling first-growth into a brilliantly consistent wine of stunning grace, richness, and complexity. His wife Laura and daughter Corinne run the show now with the renewed vigor and expertise of the winemaking team of director Paul Pontallier, *régisseur* Philippe Barré, *maître de chai* Jean Grangerou, and consulting oenologist Emile Peynaud. The immediate acclaim for the 1978 has been followed by a succession of even more brilliantly executed wines, so stunning, so rich and balanced that it is not unfair to suggest that today there is no better wine made in all of Bordeaux than that of Château Margaux.

The style of rejuvenated wine at Margaux is one of opulent richness, a deep, multidimensional bouquet with a fragrance of ripe blackcurrants, spicy vanillin oakiness, and violets. The wine is now considerably darker in color, richness, body, and tannin than the wines made under the pre-1977 Ginestet regime.

Margaux also makes a tiny quantity of white wine. Produced entirely from Sauvignon Blanc, it is fermented in new oak barrels and bottled after several months' aging under the name Pavillon Blanc de Margaux. While it is the Médoc's finest white wine, crisp, fruity, subtly herbaceous and oaky, it is quite expensive, and not, in my opinion, worth its lofty price tag.

VINTAGES

1983—The 1983 Margaux is a remarkable wine which, at this early
· stage, looks quite clearly to be the top wine of the vintage. The
96 staff at Margaux achieved perfect maturity in the Cabernet Sauvignon grapes in 1983, and the result is an astonishingly rich, concentrated, atypically powerful and tannic Margaux. The color is very dark ruby, the aromas exude ripe cassis fruit, violets, and vanillin oakiness, and the flavors are extremely deep and long on the palate with a clean, incredibly long finish. This will certainly be a monumental wine. Anticipated maturity: 1998–2030. Last tasted, 3/85.

1982—At the time of the vintage, rumors abounded in Bordeaux wine
· circles that 1982 was disastrous for Margaux—that fermenta-
96 tions stuck and could not be restarted, that the crop had become overripe, etc. Jealousy of owners who are willing to spare no expense or who do not hesitate to eliminate any batch of grapes or wine not perfect enough to produce only the best is not uncommon in Bordeaux. The 1982 Margaux, because of such a rigid selection process, is a celestial wine. Deep dark ruby/purple with an undeveloped but explosive bouquet of blackcurrants, spicy oak and ripe, intense, fruity flavors, this full-bodied wine has layers and layers of richly textured fruit, round yet significant tannins, and a finish that must be experienced to be believed. Anticipated maturity: 1995–2025. Last tasted, 2/85.

1981—In weight and texture, the 1981 Margaux is close in style to the
· 1979 but seems a trifle more precocious and less weighty. It is a
92 stunning wine for sure, even in the company of the monumental wines of 1982 and 1983, although it does not have the power and weight of these other two vintages. The bouquet of the 1981 Margaux suggests ripe cassis fruit, spicy vanillin oakiness, and

violets. On the palate, the wine is very concentrated, tannic, and extremely long. Anticipated maturity: 1991–2010. Last tasted, 10/84.

1980—Margaux is unquestionably the best wine produced in this vin-
· tage. A wine of uncommon power, concentration, richness, and
89 beauty, the Margaux is deep in color, deep in fruit extract, and shockingly long on the palate. Medium-bodied and moderately tannic, this wine has no challengers for the best of 1980. Anticipated maturity: 1989–2000. Last tasted, 10/84.

1979—Like the 1980, the 1983, and possibly the 1981, the 1979 Mar-
· gaux is again the finest wine of the vintage. Dark ruby with a
93 deeply scented bouquet of spicy, vanillin oak, ripe blackcurrant fruit, and the telltale haunting violet aromas, this wine has a great texture and sensational length. This medium- to full-bodied wine has quite a future. Anticipated maturity: 1990–2005. Last tasted, 11/84.

1978—Developing in the bottle as expected, the 1978 Margaux is
· slightly fuller-bodied and more powerful than the 1979, but less
94 fruity. It has a gorgeous, seductive bouquet of ripe fruit and spicy oak, and tarry, truffle aromas. A wonderful harmony of oak, fruit, acidity and tannin, and a finish which just lingers and lingers all combine to make this a truly great wine. The 1978 Margaux is again one of the superstars of the vintage. Anticipated maturity: 1990–2015. Last tasted, 10/84.

1977—Fully mature, the 1977 Margaux is soft, has a herbaceous, black-
· currant fruitiness, no hollowness or bitterness, and a soft, sup-
78 ple, pleasant yet undistinguished finish. Drink over the next 5 years. Last tasted, 4/81.

1976—A pre-Mentzelopoulos wine for certain, the 1976 is light, a trifle
· jammy and fruity, but straightforward in style and terribly un-
70 complex. Drink up! Last tasted, 2/82.

1975—Given the vintage, the excellent must weights measured at Mar-
· gaux, one would have expected this wine to be outstanding. It is
68 not even attractively fruity. Quite a disappointment, the 1975 Margaux is extremely lean and acidic, with shallow flavors, a washed-out color and, quite truthfully, not much concentration to it. It should be drunk up. Last tasted, 4/84.

1973—Now in complete decline, this light brownish, ruby wine had
· some light-intensity fruit and charm in 1978, but when last
55 tasted in 1980, it was decrepit and bland.

1971—Another mediocre wine produced during the Ginestet reign, the
· 1971 is best consumed immediately for what little fruit it has
70 remaining. Light ruby, browning badly at the edges, the simple, light fruity bouquet and diluted flavors are hardly inspirational, and definitely not what one expects from one of Bordeaux's fabulously expensive first-growths. Last tasted, 6/79.

1970—The 1970 is better than the 1971 or 1975, but certainly exceeded
· in quality by most of the classified growths of the Médoc, not to
76 mention a goodly number of Cru Bourgeois. From a great vintage this is certainly the type of wine to foster consumer ill-will toward expensive, presumably "great" first-growth Bordeaux. Compact, austere, lacking fruit and richness, this wine has adequate color and tannins, but not much flesh to cover the bones. Time may help, but then again, it may not. Last tasted, 9/83.

1967—Light, charming, and fruity in 1974, beginning to thin out and
· drop its fruit in 1978, the 1967 Margaux is now way past its
67 prime. Last tasted, 11/80.

1966—One of the best examples of Margaux during its period of medi-
· ocrity, the 1966 is too light for a first-growth-quality wine, but
84 has some of the fabulous bouquet fragrance this wine is famous for, as well as good, soft, round fruity flavors with a hint of cedar and plums. Fully mature, this wine should be drunk over the next 5 years. Last tasted, 11/84.

1964—The 1964 Margaux is a chunky specimen, with good color but a
· rather dumb, old grapey aroma, a fleshy, tannic texture, but
78 quite curiously, no real resemblance to a wine from Château Margaux. Perplexing, but drinkable. Last tasted, 9/77.

1962—This wine should be enjoyed now for its gorgeous, fully mature,
· and quickly evaporating bouquet. It is beginning its decline for
84 sure, but the full, intensely cedary, fruity bouquet has its merits. The flavors are soft, and I detect some acidity beginning to poke its ugly head through. Drink up! Last tasted, 4/81.

1961—The 1961 is a top-flight wine and unquestionably the last great
· Margaux until the Mentzelopoulos era began its remarkable
92 string of great Margauxs in 1978 through 1983. An intense bouquet filled with the scents of ripe plums, flowers, toasted walnuts, and oak is divine. The wine is silky, rich, very generously flavored, long, and full-bodied on the palate. Fully mature, but there is little chance of this wine falling apart for at least another 4–5 years. Last tasted, 4/84.

PALMER (Third-Growth) **OUTSTANDING**

Production: 12,000 cases	Grape varieties: Cabernet Sauvignon—45% Merlot—40% Petit Verdot—10% Cabernet Franc—5%
Time spent in barrels: 18–24 months	Average age of vines: 27 years

Evaluation of present classification: Should be upgraded to a Médoc first-growth

The impressive turreted château of Palmer, which sits right on top of Bordeaux's D2 or Route du Vin, is a worthy photogenic spot to stop for a picture. More important to wine enthusiasts is the fact that the château also produces one of Bordeaux's greatest wines.

Palmer can often be every bit as grand as any of the first-growths. In vintages such as 1961, 1966, 1967, 1970, and 1975, it can be better than many of them. While Palmer is officially a third-growth, the wine sells at a price level between the first-growths and second-growths, no doubt reflecting the high respect and reliability Bordeaux merchants and importers throughout the world have for this wine.

Palmer is a very traditionally made wine, and its enviable track record of success is no doubt attributable to a number of factors. First, there is the dedication of the Chardon family, who have been making the wine and caring for the vineyard for over a century. Second, the *encépage* (blend of grapes) at Palmer is unique in that a very high percentage of Merlot (40%) is used to make the wine. This high proportion of Merlot no doubt is the reason for Palmer's richness, suppleness, and generous, fleshy character. Third, Palmer has one of the longest maceration periods, wherein the grape skins stay in contact with the grape juice. This explains the richness of color, excellent extract, and abundant tannins that are found in most vintages of Palmer.

Palmer consistently made the best wine of the Margaux appellation between 1961 and 1977, but the resurgence of Château Margaux in 1978, which has seen that property take its place at the top of the Margaux hierachy, has for the moment left Palmer in the runner-up spot in the commune of Margaux.

The style of Palmer's wine is one that is characterized by a sensational fragrance and bouquet. I have always felt that the great vintages of Palmer, 1961, 1966, and 1970, can often be identified in blind tastings by smell alone. Palmer's bouquet has the forward, fruity richness of a great Pomerol and the complexity and character of a Margaux. The wine's texture is rich, often supple and lush, but always deeply fruity and concentrated.

VINTAGES

1983—Nineteen eighty-three is the best vintage for Palmer since 1979.
· Very dark ruby with a full-intensity, plummy, rich bouquet, fat,
90 chewy, deep concentrated flavors, and a powerful alcoholic finish, the 1983 is an especially successful vintage for the commune of Margaux, and Palmer is certainly one of the best. Anticipated maturity: 1995–2010. Last tasted, 1/85.

1982—In this legendary vintage, one could have expected Palmer to be
· among the great wines of the vintage. It is very good for sure,
85 but the huge production at Palmer seems to have caused a certain lack of grip, direction, and concentration that is not missing in the great wines of 1982. Palmer's 1982 is a precocious, soft, fat, oaky wine, with a kinship in style to the 1976, only slightly fuller and deeper. Anticipated maturity: 1990–1998. Last tasted, 1/85.

1981—Not as good as it should be, the 1981 Palmer lacks the charac-
· teristic richness, flavor interest, and generous fleshy character
82 that has made Palmer so much in demand. The wine has been given a healthy dosage of new oak aging which partially disguises a lack of concentration and short finish. For Palmer this is a minor disappointment for the 1981 vintage. Anticipated maturity: 1988–1995. Last tasted, 12/84.

1980—Light, fruity, and straightforward, the 1980 Palmer is ready to
· drink and should be appreciated for its simple charms. One
72 might call it a picnic Palmer. Drink over the next 3 years. Last tasted, 2/84.

1979—Especially outstanding in the 1979 vintage, Palmer is rich and
· concentrated, with slightly less body than the 1978 but perhaps
89 more charm and finesse. Quite dark in color, with an opulent bouquet of ripe fleshy fruit, cedar, and tarry, truffle scents, this is moderately tannic and quite flavorful. Palmer's 1979 is one of the best wines of the vintage. Anticipated maturity: 1988–2000. Last tasted, 4/84.

1978—Developing beautifully in the bottle, the 1978 Palmer from its
· birth is a superstar of this vintage. The wine is now exhibiting a
91 very complex, peppery, rich, cedary, earthy, ripe, quite spicy

bouquet, concentrated, round, velvety flavors, moderate tannins, and a long finish. A full-bodied Palmer which is approachable now, it will be even better with bottle age. Anticipated maturity: 1989–2005. Last tasted, 11/84.

1977—Rather thin, ungenerous, and too vegetal and herbaceous, the
· 1977 Palmer is medium-bodied, somewhat fruity, lightly tannic,
70 and shows no harsh or bitter qualities. Drink up. Last tasted, 4/81.

1976—A deliciously supple, fruity, plump 1976 with a smooth, soft
· nature and little tannins, Palmer is fully mature, has adequate
83 fruit, but unlike many frail, somewhat diluted wines of this vintage, it should hold nicely for 3–4 years. Last tasted, 8/84.

1975—The 1975 Palmer is a brilliant success in a year where a number
· of great wines were made, but also a surprising number of fail-
92 ures. Quite dark in color with no sign of aging, this full-bodied wine is uncommonly powerful and rich, even for Palmer. Loaded with both fruit and tannin, this wine has a very long evolution ahead of it, but it will be very special. Anticipated maturity: 1990–2020. Last tasted, 4/84.

1974—In this poor tintage, Palmer produced a very mediocre wine with
· brownish color, a stringy, lean, weak, bland character, and little
64 fruit in evidence. Last tasted, 2/78.

1971—While certainly not in the same class as the 1979, 1975, 1970,
· and 1966, Palmer's reputation for quality and finesse is hardly
86 in danger as a result of this effort. Fully mature, with a good dark ruby color, the highly touted Palmer bouquet of mulberries, flowers, and cassis is readily perceptible. A silky, lush wine that is now at its peak. Drink over the next 5–7 years. Last tasted, 11/83.

1970—A very great Palmer with a splendidly deep, dark ruby/purple
· color, this wine is just beginning to evolve and open. Intense
94 berryish aromas, which are married brilliantly with vanillin oak, ascend profusely from the glass. Quite full-bodied and rich, yet amazingly youthful, this is a prodigious bottle of Palmer. Anticipated maturity: 1988–2005. Last tasted, 6/84.

1967—The 1967 Palmer reached its zenith several years ago, but seems
· to be holding its own without losing any of its marvelous per-
86 fumed bouquet and soft, spicy, attractive, medium-weight flavors. A very charming, complex wine, but it should be drunk up. Last tasted, 6/84.

1966—For the fortunate owners of this wine, it has developed magnifi-
· cently, and seems to be reaching a point of perfection that rivals
96 Palmer's legendary 1961. In its haunting bouquet it expresses the greatness of claret and Palmer. It is as good a Palmer as I have ever drunk, including the much ballyhooed 1961. Simply stated, the bouquet is sensational. On the palate, the wine has a velvety richness, excellent concentration, and an extremely long finish. This is a very great wine. Anticipated maturity: 1986–2000. Last tasted, 10/84.

1964—A straightforward, somewhat awkward wine with none of Pal-
· mer's best qualities—the great bouquet, the fleshy texture, the
75 generous, plummy fruitiness—apparent in this medium-bodied, coarsely made wine. Drink up. Last tasted, 2/78.

1962—Now expressing the full eloquence of Palmer, this medium-bod-
· ied wine has a full-intensity bouquet of violets, cedar, and ripe
85 fruit, soft, mature, voluptuous flavors, and a long, smooth finish. It may not be as profound and as concentrated as the 1961 or 1966, but it clearly outclasses several of the first-growths in this vintage. Drink up. Last tasted, 12/82.

1961—For many wine enthusiasts, the 1961 Palmer is the wine of the
· vintage. I am in the minority because I prefer the 1966, as I
96 believe the 1961 is beginning to fade ever so slightly. It remains a very great wine, its hallmark an extraordinary perfumed character which is still one of the greatest wine bouquets I have ever smelled. On the palate, the wine has an opulent, multidimensional richness, and silky, expansive flavors which are both powerful and refined. This is a great wine which should be drunk over the next 5 years. Last tasted, 5/84.

GISCOURS (Third-Growth) EXCELLENT

Production: 25,000 cases	Grape varieties: Cabernet Sauvignon—66% Merlot—34%
Time spent in barrels: 18–28 months	Average age of vines: 28 years

Evaluation of present classification: Should be upgraded to a Médoc second-growth

Giscours is a vast estate of over 600 acres (only 25% of which are under vine) in the most southern portion of the Margaux commune known as Labarde. The estate has had a resurgence in quality and prestige since its purchase by the Tari family in 1952. Pierre Tari has taken over from his father, Nicholas, and is one of the leading spokespeople for Bordeaux. He is frequently seen in America with Bordeaux's Union des Grand Crus, an association of châteaux banded together for one common cause, to promote the virtues of Bordeaux wines.

The château of Giscours is one of the most impressive, and well worth a visit. The style of wine produced here has been consistently excellent in the last two decades. Furthermore, Giscours's record of "off" vintages such as 1980, 1974, 1973, and 1972 is far superior to most other Bordeaux châteaux. Those who drink Giscours regularly know it to be a very dark-colored wine, with an intense, chewy, robust richness and full body. It is quite a big, fleshy wine for Margaux, powerfully scented in great vintages, and often quite tannic. I have heard Giscours called both "Pomerol-like" and "Californian" because of the wine's dark color and full-bodied, chewy, richly fruity character. Because of the wine's quality and consistency over the last 20 years, Giscours should be elevated to a second-growth if a new classification of the wines of the Médoc were done. For Bordeaux wine enthusiasts, this is a wine to buy since the price has not yet caught up with the excellent quality.

VINTAGES

1983—Giscours was not as successful as many other Margaux châteaux
· in this vintage. Medium ruby with a soft, fruity, silky texture,
86 light tannins and medium body, the 1983 Giscours will evolve
very quickly as the acidity is low, the pH high, and the wine
lacking tannin and great depth. Anticipated maturity: 1990–
1998. Last tasted, 6/84.

1982—A rather precocious-styled wine for the vintage, the 1982 Gis-
· cours is dark ruby in color, with a very ripe, rich, berryish
87 bouquet, full-bodied, fat, deep flavors, a good deal of alcohol,
and lush, silky finish. Very flavorful, but a trifle loosely knit, I
expect the 1982 Giscours to develop early. Anticipated maturity:
1990–2000. Last tasted, 1/85.

1981—The 1981 Giscours is a totally charming wine with a supple,
· graceful fruitiness, a rich, spicy, berry fruit bouquet, lush, deep
86 flavors, light to moderate tannins, and a long finish. A very well-

balanced wine, it can be drunk now, but will age well for a decade. Anticipated maturity: 1988–1996. Last tasted, 11/84.

1980—An outstanding success in this mediocre vintage, the 1980 Gis-
· cours is sweet, ripe, round, flavorful, with no scent or taste of
85 unripe vegetal fruitiness. Surprisingly concentrated and dark in color, this wine is fully mature, but will last for 5–6 more years. A wine to buy and drink. Last tasted, 6/84.

1979—Beautifully full, voluptuous aromas of ripe plums, vanillin oak,
· and floral fragrances jump from the glass. On the palate, this
87 wine has very good concentration, medium to full body, and moderate, round, ripe tannins. The 1979 Giscours is a noteworthy success for the vintage. Anticipated maturity: 1989–2003. Last tasted, 1/85.

1978—A big, broodingly dark ruby-colored wine, with a huge bouquet
· of ripe blackcurrants, truffles, and wood, this tannic, very
90 chunky, fleshy, full-bodied Giscours has very impressive extract and concentration, and a long, youthful finish. It has excellent potential. Anticipated maturity: 1990–2005. Last tasted, 6/84.

1977—Giscours has a habit of excelling in Bordeaux's off-years, but
· nothing special was made in 1977. It is medium ruby, with dry,
70 vegetal, lean, skinny flavors, and enough tannin in the finish to outlast the fruit by a decade. Last tasted, 6/82.

1976—Always one of my favorite 1976s, Giscours produced a deeply
· colored, plump, quite round, generously fruity wine, with me-
85 dium to full body and a lush texture. Fully mature, this Giscours will hold for 3–4 years. Last tasted, 6/84.

1975—The best Giscours in the last two decades, the 1975 remains a
· young and powerful rich wine that is loaded with potential. Still
91 dark ruby with no amber, this wine has a deep, full, tight bouquet of blackcurrant fruits and spicy tarry scents. Full-bodied, quite tannic, but possessed with layers of fruit, this is a wine for the patient. Anticipated maturity: 1990–2010. Last tasted, 4/84.

1974—An above-average wine, yet quite attractive for the vintage, the
· 1974 Giscours has a medium ruby color, a fragrant, spicy, fruity
78 bouquet, and soft, moderately intense flavors. Drink up. Last tasted, 2/81.

1973—At its prime in 1976–1979, this was one of the top wines of this
· watery, light vintage. Now in decline, but hanging on to its
80 charming, soft berry fruitiness and straightforward, easygoing style, this remains a pleasant wine to drink. Last tasted, 2/80.

1971—An impressively dark-colored wine for the vintage, the 1971 Gis-
· cours is rather robust and chunky, but lacking in polish and
84 finesse. It makes a big palate impression with its dusty, ripe, substantial fruit and weight, but it finishes a trifle coarse. An interesting, enjoyable, but brawny, oafish example of Giscours. Anticipated maturity: 1985–1990. Last tasted, 2/85.

1970—A big, dark ruby, dense, rich, fat wine, with oodles of ripe fruit,
· a good lashing of tannin, the 1970 Giscours is approachable now,
88 but its big framework and gutsy, meaty texture suggest full maturity is several years away for this full-bodied, very concentrated wine. Anticipated maturity: 1986–2000. Last tasted, 6/84.

1967—Now fading and just past its prime, the 1967 Giscours was quite
· rich, savory, and flavorful in the period between 1975 and 1979.
84 However, the fruit is now beginning to drop off, the acidity is emerging from the wine's structure, and the color is taking on more and more brown. Drink up. Last tasted, 6/84.

1966—Just beginning to tire a bit, this wine represents perfectly the
· Giscours style of Margaux. Quite dark ruby, with some amber
85 at the edges, the expansive bouquet of tarry, ripe, plummy fruit is first-rate. On the palate, the wine is chunky, profusely fruity, and tannic, with a long, fat finish. It is a big, tasty, corpulent mouthful, but it should be drunk over the next 4 years. Last tasted, 6/84.

1962—Like the 1966 and 1967, this wine is past its prime. However,
· the bouquet still exhibits spicy, floral-scented, ripe fruit. In the
80 mouth, the wine lacks the plump, rich, fruity character of other Giscours, and tails off in the finish. Drink up. Last tasted, 1/81.

1961—Opaque in color, with a full-intensity, ripe blackcurrant, cedary
· bouquet, this wine is somewhat heavy and thick on the palate,
86 but has plenty of rich, chunky, deep fruit, a toasty, tarry flavor, and long, somewhat unrefined finish. This is an old-style, hefty Giscours that is quite a mouthful. Drink up over the next 5–8 years. Last tasted, 6/84.

LA LAGUNE (Third-Growth) **EXCELLENT**

Production: 25,000 cases

Grape varieties:
Cabernet Sauvignon—55%
Merlot—20%
Cabernet Franc—20%
Petit Verdot—5%

Time spent in barrels: 18–22 months

Average age of vines: 26 years

Evaluation of present classification: Should be upgraded to a Médoc second-growth

La Lagune is one of Bordeaux's shining success stories. In the 1950s the property was so run down that numerous potential buyers, including Alexis Lichine, refused to accept the herculean task of replanting the vineyards and rebuilding the winery to reestablish La Lagune as a truly representative member of Bordeaux's elite group of 1855 Crus Classés châteaux. In 1958, George Brunet, an entrepreneur, acquired the property and totally replanted the vineyard and constructed what today remains one of the most sophisticated wineries in the Médoc. Brunet did not stay long enough to reap the accolades from his massive investment in the property; he moved to Provence where he now runs one of the area's best wineries, Château Vignelaure. He sold La Lagune in 1962 to the Ayala Champagne firm which has continued to manage La Lagune with the same fervor and passion.

La Lagune is the very first classified growth that one encounters on the road to the Médoc from Bordeaux. La Lagune was also the first château to position a woman, Jeanne Boyrie, as manager of the estate in 1964. In the male chauvinist-dominated Bordeaux, this was (and continues to be) a revolutionary development. However, no one will deny that the stern, formidable, meticulous Madame Boyrie is undoubtedly one of the most conscientious and competent managers in all of Bordeaux. Much of the credit for the high quality and consistency of the wines of La Lagune over recent vintages must go to her.

The style of wine produced at La Lagune has been described as both Pomerol-like and Graves-like. One other notable connoisseur has called it very burgundian. All three of these descriptive stylistic analyses have merit. It can be a rich, fleshy wine, with sometimes an overpowering bouquet of vanillin oak (it is one of the only non-first-growths to use 100% new oak barrels in almost every vintage), and black cherries. The wine of La Lagune is usually fully mature by the tenth year of its life, but will certainly keep 15 or 20 years. The quality and strength of La Lagune have improved significantly since 1966. With the vineyard getting older every year, and the hawklike eyes of Madame Boyrie aware of every detail, La Lagune will continue to emerge as one of the great wines of the Médoc. The price of La Lagune remains quite reasonable, so cost-conscious consumers should certainly make themselves aware of this well-made wine.

VINTAGES

1983—Following the monumental wine produced at La Lagune in 1982, it is easy to overlook the 1983, which is a very good rather than great wine. Madame Boyrie compares it to the 1981, but with more substance and vigor. I agree. It is dark ruby, with a full-bodied texture, rich plummy fruit, and moderate tannins present. Anticipated maturity: 1993–2000. Last tasted, 1/85.
· 86

1982—As close to a perfect La Lagune as one can hope to find, this very dark ruby-colored wine has a sensational aroma of roasted nuts, ripe black cherries, and vanillin oak that gushes from the glass. Quite full-bodied on the palate, with significant tannin present, this wine fills the mouth with incredibly rich cassis fruit. A powerful tannic finish lasts and lasts. This is a fantastic La Lagune, with a 25-year evolution ahead of it. Anticipated maturity: 1995–2010. Last tasted, 1/85.
· 92

1981—Bottle variation at first seemed a problem, but recent tastings of this wine have been consistent. A medium-bodied, spicy, plummy, cherryish-flavored wine, with good extract, an appealing texture, and pleasant finish. Anticipated maturity: 1988–1995. Last tasted, 9/84.
· 83

1979—After an initial dumb period following the bottling, the 1979 La Lagune is opening up and showing good, glossy, ripe plummy fruit, a moderately intense, spicy, vanillin aroma, and a clean, crisp, dry finish. Fat and plump, but very satisfying and long, this is the type of wine that is easy to confuse with a good burgundy. Anticipated maturity: 1987–1995. Last tasted, 11/84.
· 84

1978—A top-rank success, the 1978 La Lagune is splendidly deep in color, with an expansive bouquet suggestive of plums and fresh new oak. On the palate, the wine is tannic, but lush and silky, with oodles of fruit present. Just beginning to open up after a period of dormancy, this excellent, brilliantly made wine will have a long evolution. Anticipated maturity: 1990–2000. Last tasted, 9/84.
· 88

1977—Stalky and light, yet soft, fruity and one-dimensional, the 1977
· La Lagune is best consumed over the next 2–3 years. Last
72 tasted, 1/82.

1976—In a vintage that produced numerous frail, diluted, fragile wines,
· the 1976 La Lagune is a firmly made, concentrated, very suc-
86 cessful wine. Not yet mature, this medium to dark ruby wine has a rather full-intensity bouquet of vanillin oak and ripe cherries. On the palate, it has an elegant, stylish texture, medium to full body, ample fruit, and a good, solid finish. Anticipated maturity: 1986–1993. Last tasted, 10/84.

1975—Quite successful, the 1975 La Lagune is a chunky specimen,
· with plenty of deep, ripe fruit, a firm tannic underpinning, and
87 long, youthful finish. It is an atypically big wine for La Lagune. Anticipated maturity: 1990–2005. Last tasted, 4/84.

1971—Fully mature, with an open-knit, aromatic, complex bouquet of
· cedarwood and ripe fruit, this medium-bodied wine is silky,
85 lush, and quite seductively round and fruity. Drink up. Last tasted, 3/82.

1970—Surprisingly not yet ready to drink, the 1970 La Lagune is dark
· ruby, with a big, plummy, woodsy bouquet, full-bodied, with
87 deep, concentrated, berryish fruit flavors, firm tannin, and a long finish. This is a very, very fine La Lagune. Anticipated maturity: 1987–2000. Last tasted, 6/82.

1967—One of the best 1967s, which was at its apogee by 1976, this
· wine has a soft, round, burgundian character, quite a complex
83 bouquet of truffles, caramel, and raspberry fruit, and little tannin. Drink up. Last tasted, 1/80.

1966—Fully mature, but certainly capable of holding for 4–5 years, the
· 1966 is supple and fleshy, with an attractive plummy fruitiness,
84 medium body, and a soft, easy finish. Drink up. Last tasted, 4/78.

1962—Tasted only once, the 1962 La Lagune was browning badly, and
· was quite soft on the palate, with dissipated, washed-out, fruity
55 flavors. It seemed to be clearly coming apart at the seams. Pass it by. Last tasted, 8/78.

1961—An unusual wine, very peppery and Rhône-like, with an odd
· medicinal nose, disjointed flavors, and a hot, alcoholic finish,
60 this vintage represents a strange style of La Lagune made ostensibly from very young vines. Last tasted, 10/77.

BOYD-CANTENAC (Third-Growth) **VERY GOOD**

Production: 6,500 cases	Grape varieties: Cabernet Sauvignon—67% Merlot—20% Cabernet Franc—8% Petit Verdot—5%
Time spent in barrels: 24 months	Average age of vines: 38 years
Evaluation of present classification: Should be maintained	

The wines of Boyd-Cantenac are rarely seen in the United States, This is unfortunate in view of the wine's quality and reasonable price. Belgium, Holland, Great Britain, and Switzerland, rather than America, remain the top markets for Boyd-Cantenac.

The style of wines produced at Boyd-Cantenac is supposedly changing to a lighter, more supple wine that can be drunk earlier. At least this is what the proprietor, Pierre Guillemet, claims. However, I continue to find Boyd-Cantenac to be a deeply flavored, rather full-bodied, rich, plump, and aggressive wine for a Margaux, and quite long-lived. It certainly merits significantly more interest from wine enthusiasts in this country than it has heretofore received.

VINTAGES

1983—In this very good vintage, Boyd-Cantenac has clearly produced
· one of the top wines. Quite dark ruby in color, with a full-blown,
87 spicy, ripe plummy aroma, rich, full-bodied, concentrated flavors, and plenty of tannin, this big robust Margaux will need every bit of 10 years to mature. Anticipated maturity: 1995–2005. Last tasted, 3/85.

1982—Virtually identical in quality to the 1983 Boyd-Cantenac, but
· differently styled, the 1982 is quite dark ruby, with a rich, fra-
86 grant, ripe black cherry bouquet, unctuous, fat, fleshy flavors, full body and moderate tannins. Anticipated maturity: 1992–2005. Last tasted, 1/85.

1981—Whether I have been unlucky or whether Boyd-Cantenac's 1981
· is simply inferior, the fact remains that the several bottles of
70 this wine I have sampled have been consistently mediocre to below average in quality. Soft, diluted flavors show a vegetal character and uncharacteristic lightness for this property. It will mature very rapidly and fade even more quickly. Last tasted, 10/84.

1979—A flavorful, beefy, corpulent wine, with good concentration, a
· precocious, soft, round personality, and attractively supple fla-
84 vors, the 1979 Boyd-Cantenac should be fully mature by 1986,
but is easy to drink now. It is medium to full-bodied and typically
dark in color. Last tasted, 1/85.

1978—Not as powerful as the 1982, 1983 or 1975, but bigger and richer
· than the 1979, this darkly colored wine has plenty of blackcur-
85 rant fruit, an earthy, spicy bouquet, and rich, medium- to full-
bodied flavors, backed up nicely by firm, somewhat aggressive
tannins. Anticipated maturity: 1990–2000. Last tasted, 10/82.

1975—The most powerful and large-scaled wine from Boyd-Cantenac
· over the last several decades, this broodingly dark-colored wine
86 is still mouthfully hard and tight but shows promising maturity.
Very dark, with a spicy, mineral-scented aroma and big, ripe,
yet mouth-puckering tannic flavors that make quite a big impression. Boyd-Cantenac's 1975 is a long-distance runner for sure,
as it remains severe and unyielding. Anticipated maturity: 1995–
2010. Last tasted, 5/84.

1971—Fully mature, with a damp cellar, earthy, plummy, spicy bou-
· quet, the 1971 Boyd-Cantenac has above-average, soft, round
82 flavors, medium body, some browning at the edge, and a pleasing finish. Drink up. Last tasted, 6/82.

1970—A textbook Boyd-Cantenac, beefy, fat, richly textured, with
· plenty of blackcurrant fruit, this medium- to full-bodied wine
84 has very good extract and a savory richness. While fully mature
now, it will hold for 5–8 more years. Last tasted, 7/81.

1966—A complex bouquet of vanillin spices, mineral, gravelly aromas,
· and ripe black cherries is quite satisfying. On the palate, the
83 wine is a trifle lean and austere, with a short, tannic finish. It is
not likely to get better. Drink over the next 5–6 years. Last
tasted, 2/81.

1961—Only tasted once, the 1961 Boyd-Cantenac was impressively big,
· aggressive, ripe, and concentrated, with a rather coarse, dusty
85 texture, gobs of mouth-watering tannin still present, and a long,
robust finish. Lacking finesse, but robust and virile, this wine
will continue to drink well for at least a decade. Last tasted,
11/80.

CANTEMERLE (Fifth-Growth) **VERY GOOD**

Production: 8,000–10,000 cases	Grape varieties:
	Cabernet Sauvignon—45%
	Merlot—40%
	Cabernet Franc—10%
	Petit Verdot—5%
Time spent in barrels: 18 months	Average age of vines: 25 years

Evaluation of present classification: Should be upgraded to a third-growth

Cantemerle is the second major château that the tourist passes heading north on Bordeaux's famous Route du Vin. The château cannot be seen from the road for it sits amidst a charming, heavily wooded park.

The wines of Cantemerle have always enjoyed an excellent reputation for quality. However, it was no secret in Bordeaux that the old wine cellars and ancient wood fermentation tanks were not in the best of condition for making consistently good wine. A drop in quality as well as consistency was clearly discernible in the wines produced in the '60s and '70s. The culmination of owner neglect and the increasing trend toward mediocrity resulted in the sale of Cantemerle in 1980 to a syndicate, of which the famous Cordier family is a partner. While Cordier's interest is not a majority one, the renovation of the winemaking facilities and making of the wine is now carried out by the Cordier staff. Extensive new plantings in the vineyards of Cantemerle commenced in 1981, and in 1983 a totally new winemaking facility was completed.

The style of Cantemerle has changed beginning with the 1981 vintage. In accordance with the Cordier philosophy of making wine, the color of the wine has darkened, and the wine seems to have taken on an extra measure of fatness and rich fruity intensity. From a consumer's perspective, the wines of Cantemerle are undervalued and frequently represent excellent bargains, particularly vintages such as 1982 and 1983.

VINTAGES

1983—The first vintage to be produced in the new *chai*, the 1983 is a
· very special wine, and undoubtedly destined to become one of
91 the very great wines of this vintage. The color is very dark ruby/purple and the bouquet explodes from the glass with scents of ripe plums, flowers, and oak. On the palate, the wine is very concentrated, extremely long in the finish, and moderately

tannic. This is an extremely lush, rich, ripe, intensely concentrated wine. Anticipated maturity: 1994–2010. Last tasted, 3/85.

1982—A very good Cantemerle, precociously supple, fat and fruity, the
· 1982 should be drinkable at quite a young age. Certainly not one
85 of the great wines in this legendary vintage, Cantemerle is however loaded with soft, berry fruit, has a lush texture, and long, round, generous, elegantly wrought flavors, and good length. Anticipated maturity: 1992–2000. Last tasted, 1/85.

1981—The 1981 has deep ruby color, a pronounced vanillin, oaky com-
· ponent, a ripe cassis, fruity taste, moderate tannin, and a good
84 finish. This is a good yet unspectacular wine. Anticipated maturity: 1988–1995. Last tasted, 11/84.

1979—Surprisingly ready to drink, Cantemerle's 1979 is charmingly
· fruity, soft, pleasant and round, but seems to lack grip and
82 length. Drink over the next 5 years. Last tasted, 2/83.

1978—Not unlike the 1979, only darker in color, with a more pro-
· nounced richness discernible in the bouquet and taste, this me-
84 dium-bodied wine is quite fruity, soft, round, elegant, and attractive. The flavor suggests ripe black cherries. Drink over the next 5–6 years. Last tasted, 7/83.

1976—Unfortunately, the 1976 Cantemerle is in decline, exhibiting a
· very brownish color, pale, weak, washed-out flavors that taste
60 cooked and highly chaptalized. Coming apart at the seams, this is a wine to drink up quickly. Last tasted, 4/84.

1975—Like most classified growths, the 1975 Cantemerle is not nearly
· ready and is still tannic and hard. Dark ruby with no signs of
85 aging in the color, this is a rather full-bodied, tough, brawny Cantemerle, with very good concentration, medium to full body, and a dusty, sinewy texture. It needs time. Anticipated maturity: 1995–2005. Last tasted, 5/84.

1971—Now fully mature, but unlike many 1971s Cantemerle is capable
· of holding in the bottle for another 4–5 years. Medium ruby with
83 some amber orange color at the edges, this wine has a light-intensity fragrant bouquet suggestive of berry fruit and oak. On the palate, the flavors show adequate fruit and concentration, but the acidity is a bit sharp in the finish. Drink up. Last tasted, 10/83.

1970—This is a much more substantial effort from Cantemerle. The
· 1970 is still not quite fully mature, but shows a good plummy,
86 spicy, rich fruit in both its bouquet and flavors. Medium-bodied and nicely concentrated, this wine is the best Cantemerle made

in the decade of the '70s. Anticipated maturity: 1986–1995. Last tasted, 10/83.

1967—Now in decline, in the mid-1970s this was a pleasingly fruity yet
· firm wine that had good concentration, a savory, round, plummy
74 character, and adequate finish. I suspect the acidity and tannins now overwhelm what fruit is left. Last tasted, 6/76.

1966—Like many 1966s, the Cantemerle has been slow to evolve. It is
· now beginning to lose its fruit rather than open up and blossom.
84 This medium-weight wine has a stylish, elegant bouquet filled with the scents of truffle and blackcurrant fruit. On the palate the wine is impressively structured but a trifle lean, unyielding, and ungenerous. Drink over the next 5–6 years. Last tasted, 2/82.

1962—Still gorgeously perfumed after so many years, the 1962 Cante-
· merle has a lovely, seductive full-blown bouquet, round, gener-
86 ous, pleasingly fruity, savory flavors, and no tannins present. It is elegant, ripe, delicious wine for drinking now. Last tasted, 4/81.

1961—Along with the 1983, the 1961 is the best Cantemerle in the last
· 20 years. Very dark-colored with some amber at the edge, the
90 bouquet explodes from the glass with the scent of toasted nuts, rich blackcurrant fruit and plums, as well as a vanillin oakiness. On the palate, the wine is very concentrated, rich and fat, with plenty of tannin still remaining. Drink over the next decade. Last tasted, 6/84.

D'ISSAN (Third-Growth) — VERY GOOD

Production: 10,000–12,000 cases	Grape varieties: Cabernet Sauvignon—85% Merlot—15%
Time spent in barrels: 18 months	Average age of vines: 22 years
Evaluation of present classification: Should be maintained	

When I think of d'Issan, I am often more inclined to talk about the beautiful château and its setting than the wines produced there. This is not because of a lack of quality, but rather because d'Issan is not seen terribly much in the marketplace. Additionally, it rarely appears in comparative tastings sponsored by *négociants* in Bordeaux. The relative obscurity of the wines of d'Issan has kept them relatively inexpensive for a third-growth château of Margaux, a point worth remembering since the quality is so good.

In style, the wines are quite unique. First, the remarkably high percentage of Cabernet Sauvignon (85%) in the blend and absence of any Petit Verdot and Cabernet Franc is quite unusual. From such a high percentage of Cabernet Sauvignon, one would expect a tannic, hard, tough wine, but that is not the case. The wines of d'Issan that I have tasted have been very darkly colored, rich and plummy with plenty of fruit, but surprisingly forward and supple, and usually ready to drink within 6–8 years of the vintage. I have found them to be quite high in quality, clearly justifying their classification.

VINTAGES

1983—The most impressive d'Issan I have tasted, the 1983 is quite
· concentrated with an almost exotic, rich, spicy, plummy bou-
89 quet and rich, viscous, cherry, fat, fruity flavors. It is a trifle low
in acidity, but moderately tannic, very lush and richly fruity,
and should be ready to drink early. Anticipated maturity: 1990–
2000. Last tasted, 3/85.

1982—Very dark ruby in color with an expansive, rich, spicy earthy
· bouquet, the 1982 d'Issan seems successful for the vintage, but
86 certainly not one of the leaders. On the palate, the wine displays
good black cherry fruit, a supple richness, and moderate tannins. Anticipated maturity: 1988–2000. Last tasted, 1/85.

1981—This underrated property has produced a lovely wine in 1981,
· with dark ruby color, a ripe berryish, oaky, plummy bouquet,
86 moderate tannins, sweet, rich, deep, concentrated fruit, and a
stylistic resemblance to the wine of Palmer. Anticipated maturity: 1988–2000. Last tasted, 1/85.

1979—Medium to dark ruby with a straightforward berryish bouquet,
· soft, ripe, somewhat jammy flavors and little tannin, this light-
83 to medium-bodied wine is ready to drink, but will hold for 4–5
years. Last tasted, 4/84.

1978—Dark ruby in color with a very fragrant ripe berry aroma, soft,
· corpulent, round, ripe fruity flavors, medium body, and light
87 tannins, this is a harmonious, pleasant, very charming, rather
rich wine for drinking now and over the next 5 years. It is somewhat reminiscent of Palmer in this vintage. Last tasted, 1/85.

1976—Browning in color and somewhat stinky in aroma, this fairly
· mature wine is quite light, has adequate fruit, but seems very
70 fragile and on the brink of a rapid descent into oblivion. Drink
up. Last tasted, 6/82.

1975—One of the few classified growths that can be drunk now, d'Issan has a good, dark ruby color, a spicy, chewy, muscular texture,
84 good ripeness of fruit and medium body, but tastes somewhat dull. It is a good wine for drinking over the next 5–8 years. Last tasted, 5/84.

1970—Atypically tightly knit and still closed, the 1970 d'Issan has a good, dark ruby color, medium body, a spicy, dusty fruitiness
82 and plenty of firm tannins still in evidence. Will the fruit outlast the tannins? Anticipated maturity: 1990. Last tasted, 1/82.

LASCOMBES (Second-Growth) VERY GOOD

Production: 35,000–40,000 cases	Grape varieties: Cabernet Sauvignon—46% Merlot—33% Petit Verdot—12% Cabernet Franc—8% Malbec—1%
Time spent in barrels: 18 months	Average age of vines: 20–25 years
Evaluation of present classification: Should be downgraded to a fourth-growth	

Lascombes is one of the largest estates in the Médoc, with almost 240 acres of vineyards. The vineyards are not contiguous, but consist of in excess of 40 separate plots of vines spread throughout the Margaux appellation. Because of this, the harvest at Lascombes can be one of the most difficult to manage.

Lascombes's current fame and popularity are no doubt a result of the herculean efforts made by Alexis Lichine, who directed Lascombes between 1952 and 1971. He oversaw a thorough renovation of the wine cellars, as well as an aggressive plan of vineyard acquisition from surrounding properties. Because of Lichine's commitment to high-quality wines, a succession of very good vintages of wine from Lascombes resulted.

Since 1971, when Lascombes was sold to the English firm of Bass Charrington, the quality and consistency of Lascombes has noticeably dropped. However, the two recent vintages, 1982 and 1983, hopefully reflect a renewed dedication to top-notch quality wine at Lascombes. The post-Lichine vintages of Lascombes were characterized by far too many wines that were inexcusably light and lacking depth and dimension. In spite of the very successful 1982 and 1983 Lascombes, this is an estate that is not making wine of second-growth quality, and the price now charged for Lascombes reflects a deterioration in trade and consumer confidence in this wine.

VINTAGES

1983—Very impressive from the cask with excellent dark ruby color, a
· rich spicy, berrylike aroma of deep intensity, rather fat concen-
87 trated tannin flavors, the 1983 Lascombes appears to be the best wine made at the property in over a decade. Anticipated maturity: 1993–2000. Last tasted, 3/85.

1982—Hopefully, the 1982 is a sign that higher-quality wines from Las-
· combes will be forthcoming. Dark ruby with a very fragrant,
87 rich, ripe, intense bouquet of vanillin oak and ripe fruit. On the palate, the wine is plump, richly fruity, full-bodied with a long finish and moderate tannin. The 1982 is somewhat reminiscent of the 1970, only better. Anticipated maturity: 1990–2000. Last tasted, 1/85.

1981—The 1981 is light to medium ruby in color with a simple, some-
· what herbaceous aroma, modest, rather meagerly endowed fla-
74 vors, and a short tannic finish. Anticipated maturity: 1988–1992. Last tasted, 2/83.

1980—Green and vegetal with an annoyingly high acidity level and
· shallow, diffuse, washed-out flavors. Ignore. Last tasted, 8/83.
60

1979—While the commune of Margaux seemed to have produced a
· number of fine wines in 1979 (Margaux, Palmer, Giscours) the
78 Lascombes tastes very light and diluted with not much character. Moderately concentrated fruit and plenty of oak and alcohol leave one yearning for something more. Anticipated maturity: 1986–1990. Last tasted, 8/83.

1978—Surprisingly lean and acidic without any of the plump, round,
· generous, ripe, rich fruit that is one of the landmarks of this
76 vintage, the 1978 Lascombes lacks depth and richness, and seems quite mediocre given the high quality of the vintage. I have also detected some barnyard aromas in the bouquet of this wine. Anticipated maturity: 1987–1990. Last tasted, 8/83.

1977—Extremely thin, stalky, and vegetal, this nasty little wine has
· very little to like. Last tasted, 1/82.
60

1976—Extremely disappointing, light, diffuse, overly ripe flavors, low
· acidity and now browning badly, this wine should be consumed
66 over the next year before it deteriorates any further. Last tasted, 4/81.

1975—Consistently inconsistent, one never seems to know what to ex-
· pect from a bottle of 1975 Lascombes. At its best, it is a big,
82–87 ripe, rich, full-bodied, intensely flavored wine which, except for the infant 1982 and 1983 Lascombes wines, is this property's best wine in several decades. Other bottles were quite delicious but distinctly minty in style, with little tannin present. An enigma to say the least. Last tasted, 5/84.

1971—In the mid to late '70s this was one of my favorite vintages of
· Lascombes. Now it has begun to tire and lose some of its supple,
84 intense fruitiness, but this elegantly wrought wine still retains a complex, spicy, earthy, ripe, plummy bouquet and soft, rich yet fading flavors. Drink up. Last tasted, 5/81.

1970—A fine example of Lascombes, darkly colored, ripe, full-bodied,
· richly fruity and fleshy, the 1970 is now fully mature but has the
86 concentration of fruit and structure to hold for 4–6 more years. It is a spicy, fragrant, and altogether satisfying mouthful of wine. Last tasted, 5/84.

1966—A top-notch effort from Lascombes, the 1966 is better than the
· 1970, certainly more consistent than the 1975, and probably
87 longer-lived than either the 1982 or 1983. Dark ruby with just a slight amber edge to its color, on the palate this wine has very good richness and length to go along with its voluptuous, seductive bouquet. Ready to drink, but it will hold for 5–6 years. Last tasted, 6/82.

1962—A beautiful wine, fragrant, spicy, with a certain fat sweetness to
· its taste, this textbook Margaux has a big, intense bouquet and
87 wonderfully silky, lush flavors. It has been fully mature since 1976, so it requires drinking. Last tasted, 11/81.

1961—A substantial Lascombes, but seemingly lacking complexity and
· the great depth associated with this vintage, the 1961 Las-
85 combes is quite dark in color with an amber edge. It possesses a smoky, earthy, ripe bouquet, a touch of raw acidity in the finish, and a good but unspectacular finish. Fully mature, the wine will hold for 5–7 more years. Last tasted, 10/79.

PRIEURÉ-LICHINE (Fourth-Growth) VERY GOOD

Production: 23,000–30,000 cases	Grape varieties: Cabernet Sauvignon—52% Merlot—31% Cabernet Franc—12% Petit Verdot—5%
Time spent in barrels: 16–18 months	Average age of vines: 33 years
Evaluation of present classification: Should be maintained	

The only major château in the Médoc open 7 days a week every week of the year to accept tourists, Prieuré-Lichine is the home of Alexis Lichine, a world-famous wine writer, wine authority, and promoter of the wines of Bordeaux. Lichine purchased Prieuré in 1951 and began an extensive program of improvements that included tripling the vineyard area. I have always thought that harvest time here must be an incredibly complex operation because Prieuré-Lichine's vineyard is one of the most morseled in the Médoc, with in excess of 25 different parcels spread out from the southern portion of the appellation to the northern portion.

The wine of Prieuré tends to be made in a modern yet intelligent style. It is supple and fast-maturing, but has enough tannin—and in good vintages, substance—to age well for 8–12 years. The price of Prieuré seems surpisingly low, and in vintages such as 1978, 1982, and 1983 it can represent one of the great bargains of the Médoc.

VINTAGES

1983—This wine may well turn out to be the best wine Lichine has ever produced. Tasted from the cask, it was extremely dark in color for Prieuré with a huge, intense aroma of ripe blackcurrants, a viscous, chewy texture, full body, rather high alcohol, and a long, rich, moderately tannic finish. Anticipated maturity: 1990–2005. Last tasted, 3/85.
· 89

1982—More austere and slightly less concentrated than the 1983, the 1982 Prieuré has a beautifully fragrant, ripe plum-scented bouquet, just the right touch of oak, and a moderately intense blackcurrant aroma. On the palate, the wine is forwardly rich, sumptuous, and has oodles of ripe fruit. It is medium-bodied
· 87

and moderately tannic. Anticipated maturity: 1992–2000. Last tasted, 3/85.

1981—Rather light but attractively fruity and pleasant when young, this
· wine seems to have lost some fruit and taken on a lean, rather
78 light-bodied and underendowed personality. It is pleasant, but the light ruby color and shallow flavors suggest that drinking this wine over the next 2–3 years is advisable. Last tasted, 6/84.

1980—A light ruby-colored wine with very shallow, light-intensity fla-
· vors that suggest strawberries, the 1980 Prieuré is soft, one-
70 dimensional, and ready to drink. Last tasted, 6/84.

1979—Prieuré tastes particularly light in this vintage. Nevertheless,
· the wine is medium-bodied with soft, pleasant flavors; however,
80 it finishes short and seems destined to begin its decline in 2–4 years. Drink up. Last tasted, 6/84.

1978—One of the best efforts from Prieuré-Lichine, the 1978 is not yet
· fully mature, but exhibits a ripe, rather rich, fruity, oaky bou-
86 quet, good concentration, moderate tannins, and a long, substantial finish. An extremely harmonious wine, the 1978 Prieuré-Lichine should be drunk over the next 7–8 years. Last tasted, 4/84.

1977—An acceptable level of quality was reached by Prieuré in this
· vintage. The wine has medium ruby color, a slight vegetal aroma
73 that is commonplace in 1977, and is deficient in rich, fleshy fruit. However, the wine is palatable. It should be drunk over the next 2–3 years. Last tasted, 4/83.

1976—This wine tasted rather unknit when young, but with age it has
· pulled itself together (unlike many 1976s), and shows a good,
82 ripe, cedary, fruity, spicy bouquet, and soft, rather fat, nicely concentrated flavors. Drink over the next 3–4 years. Last tasted, 11/84.

1975—A typical 1975, tough, hard, and backward, the Prieuré has a
· leathery, ripe fragrance. Rather full-bodied and astringent with
83 hard, tannic flavors, this wine is just beginning to show signs of shedding its tannins and revealing some ripe, fleshy fruit. Anticipated maturity: 1987–1998. Last tasted, 11/84.

1971—One of the most enjoyable Prieuré-Lichines, the 1971 has for
· the last several years provided immensely satisfying drinking.
86 Fully mature and possibly just beginning to decline a trifle, the 1971 is very perfumed and aromatic, with a bouquet redolent of spices, berry fruit, and oak. On the palate, it is soft, supple and so, so velvety. Drink up. Last tasted, 3/82.

1970—A delightfully fat, fruity, concentrated velvety Margaux, with
· soft, lush berryish, plummy flavors, some spicy oak, and light
86 tannins. Fully mature, but capable of holding for 3–5 more
years, this well-made, elegant wine is quite attractive. Last
tasted, 6/82.

1967—Not tasted since 1980, the 1967 Prieuré-Lichine was a note-
· worthy success in a year when many more famous properties
84 made wine not nearly as good as Prieuré. Quite aromatic and
plummy with a ripe, fruity richness, this wine should be drunk
up. Last tasted, 1/80.

1966—The 1966 Prieuré is a restrained, elegant, somewhat austere
· wine with a moderately intense, spicy, berryish, ripe, fruity bou-
85 quet. On the palate, it shows less of the 1966 leanness and
reserved character, but rather soft, rich fruit, medium body, and
a good finish. Drink over the next 4 years. Last tasted, 12/80.

1962—I last tasted the 1962 in 1975 and my notes say it was pleasant,
· stylish, and fully mature. It is probably still quite palatable and
80 fruity if well stored, but this is a wine that clearly merits immediate consumption. Last tasted, 6/75.

MALESCOT ST.-EXUPÉRY (Third-Growth) VERY GOOD

Production: 12,000 cases

Grape varieties:
Cabernet Sauvignon—55%
Merlot—30%
Cabernet Franc—10%
Petit Verdot—5%

Time spent in barrels: 18 months

Average age of vines: 33 years

Evaluation of present classification: Should be downgraded to a fifth-growth

Malescot St.-Exupéry sits right in the town of Margaux, a few blocks north of Château Palmer on Bordeaux's main Route du Vin, D2. Malescot has long enjoyed a very favorable reputation, particularly for long-lived, traditionally made, firmly styled wines.

The proprietors, the Zuger family, claim that the style of Malescot will not be changed so as to be more supple and drinkable when released. However, it seems to me that recent vintages, particularly those in the '70s and '80s, are nowhere near as tannic and as hard as the wines of the '60s. Malescot, like a number of other Margaux châteaux that fail to receive much notoriety or publicity, is somewhat undervalued in price when compared to some of the other top Margaux châteaux; however, the quality of the wine here is not as good as its lofty position in Bordeaux's 1855 classification would suggest.

VINTAGES

1983—The 1983, tasted from the cask, was not very impressive, partic-
· ularly in view of the vintage and overall success of the wines of
83 the southern Médoc. The 1983 Malescot has moderately dark ruby color, a ripe berryish, bouquet, hard, very astringent tannins present, medium body and severe, compact finish. This wine requires a lot of time, but I doubt the fruit will outlast the tannins. Anticipated maturity: 1995. Last tasted, 3/85.

1982—Rather atypical for Malescot, the 1982 is quite fat, round, lus-
· ciously fruity, yet not as deep or as profound as some of the
85 other wines from this vintage. Dark ruby in color with wild berrylike bouquet, and medium to full body, this is a very good but not great Malescot. Anticipated maturity: 1992–2000. Last tasted, 1/85.

1981—The 1981 is a rather lean, tight, unyielding wine which may
· develop better than I anticipate. However, the wine seems to be
78 deficient in fruit, although the color is sound and the bouquet hints at an underlying ripeness. Anticipated maturity: 1990–2000. Last tasted, 11/84.

1979—Soft, ripe fruity, oaky aromas are quite charming and appealing
· on the palate. This offering from Malescot is medium-bodied,
83 rather oaky, moderately tannic, surprisingly soft and accessible, and well balanced. It is a lighter-styled, rather graceful wine for drinking over the next 4–6 years. Last tasted, 6/84.

1978—Ripe blackcurrant fruit and plenty of spicy vanillin oak dominate
· the bouquet of this medium-bodied, stylish, generally well-made
84 wine. In the mouth, the oak is quite apparent, the wine is plump and round, a little low in acidity, but attractively forward. Anticipated maturity: 1989–1998. Last tasted, 11/84.

1976—A very sound, fruity, straightforward 1976, with a ripe berrylike
· fruitiness, medium body, a soft, round texture, and short, yet
78 adequate finish. Fully mature, the 1976 Malescot should be drunk over the next 1–2 years. Last tasted, 6/84.

1975—Not as darkly colored as expected, this medium-body wine has
· a predominantly oaky, spicy bouquet that exhibits very little
84 fruit. Medium-bodied and fruity with a ripe Merlot component, good length, and a slightly chaptalized flavor, this is a good wine

which is just beginning to approach maturity. Drink over the next decade. Last tasted, 5/84.

1970—This is a coarse wine with plenty of punch and power, but a
· dusty, rough texture, a closed bouquet, and just no real finesse
78 or complexity. It remains surprisingly young and severe, but the color is quite deep, so perhaps the future will reveal qualities that are now hidden. Anticipated maturity: 1988–2000. Last tasted, 2/80.

1967—The color is still surprisingly deep for a 1967, but the fruit is now
· drying out, and the tannins and acidity are becoming quite
75 overbearing. At one time, a good wine from this mixed sort of vintage, but other than this wine's pleasant, spicy bouquet, it lacks real substance and depth to be interesting. Last tasted, 11/79.

1966—Rather light and insubstantial, the 1966 Malescot has a pleasing
· enough bouquet of oak, plums and spices, but on the palate it is
83 lean, a trifle austere and severe. Medium-bodied with firm tannins in the finish, this wine is likely to lose its fruit before the tannin completely resolves itself. Drink over the next 5–6 years. Last tasted, 6/83.

1964—The 1964 Malescot is an uncomplicated style of wine, but given
· the number of failures in the Médoc in 1964, it is a satisfactory
82 wine. Chunky and darkly colored with a briary, spicy, cedary bouquet, tough yet substantial flavors, and a coarse finish, this gutsy wine is best drunk over the next 5–6 years. Last tasted, 10/78.

1961—The best Malescot I have tasted, the 1961 has a rich, deep,
· blackcurrant, spicy, cedary bouquet, long, fat, yet still tannic,
89 concentrated flavors, full body, and an excellent finish. Still remarkably young and behaving more like a Pauillac than a Margaux, this wine has at least another 10–15 years of evolution ahead of it. Its only flaw is a slight touch of excessive acidity in the finish. Malescot has turned in an excellent effort in a great vintage. Anticipated maturity: 1988–2005. Last tasted, 6/83.

RAUSAN-SÉGLA (Second-Growth) ABOVE AVERAGE TO GOOD

Production: 14,000 cases	Grape varieties: Cabernet Sauvignon—55% Merlot—32% Cabernet Franc—11% Petit Verdot—2%
Time spent in barrels: 20 months	Average age of vines: 25 years

Evaluation of present classification: Should be downgraded to a fifth-growth

In 1855 Rausan-Ségla was considered Bordeaux's best wine after the quartet of Premiers Grands Crus Lafite-Rothschild, Latour, Margaux, Haut-Brion, and the top-ranked second-growth, Mouton-Rothschild. In 1973 Mouton-Rothschild was elevated and now Rausan-Ségla sits at the head of the class of the remaining 14 second-growths. Its position hardly seems justified by the wines produced there between 1961 and 1983. Perhaps the exclusive contract for the sale and distribution of the wines through the Eschenauer shipping firm has resulted in a lessening of quality control, as well as overproduction.

Whatever the reasons, there is no doubt that Rausan-Ségla's wines do not merit their current price or status. Between 1973 and 1981, a number of very mediocre wines were produced. The 1975 and 1978 vintages, both excellent years, resulted in two very poor wines that are simply inexcusable. However, the 1982 and 1983 vintages of Rausan-Ségla exhibit high quality and offer renewed hope for enthusiasts of this property's wines.

VINTAGES

1983—This is the best vintage of Rausan-Ségla since 1970. Deeply
· pigmented, with a rich, spicy, intense aroma of ripe grapes and
86 oak. On the palate, the wine is quite full-bodied, concentrated, very tannic, and in need of a full decade of cellaring. This is a very encouraging effort from Rausan-Ségla. Anticipated maturity: 1995–2005. Last tasted, 3/85.

1982—Softer and fatter than the 1983, but not as classically structured,
· the 1982 Rausan-Ségla is dark ruby in color, with a ripe black-
86 currant, oaky, very fragrant bouquet of considerable class, medium to full body, and a lush, soft finish. Anticipated maturity: 1988–1995. Last tasted, 12/84.

1981—This mediocre wine is light, fruity, round, and one-dimensional.
· Hardly a wine representative of its official Bordeaux pedigree,
65 this meager Rausan-Ségla should be drunk over the next 4 years.
Last tasted, 6/84.

1980—The very thin, watery flavors, vegetal aroma, as well as little
· depth or length all combine to make this a very undistinguished
60 effort. Last tasted, 3/83.

1979—Quite light, round and fruity, the 1979 Rausan-Ségla resembles
· a simple Bordeaux Superieur. Drink over the next several years.
72 Last tasted, 4/84.

1978—True to form for many of the wines that Rausan-Ségla produced
· in the '70s, the 1978 is fruity, round, and slightly charming, but
74 devoid of flavor interest and complexity. Drink over the next 2–
3 years. Last tasted, 10/82.

1977—Intensely vegetal and thin, the 1977 Rausan-Ségla is a failure.
· Last tasted, 11/81.
50

1976—A leafy, weedy-scented wine, with light-intensity flavors, light
· to medium ruby/garnet color, and an awkward, unbalanced feel
60 on the palate, this wine lacks richness and seems very sloppily
vinified. Last tasted, 4/80.

1975—Very light in color, with a suspicious brownish cast to the color,
· the 1975 Rausan-Ségla has a burnt, cooked-fruit aroma, shallow,
55 very tannic and astringent flavors, and a short, nasty finish. This
is a pitiful effort in such a fine vintage. Last tasted, 5/84.

1972—Ironically, in this disastrous vintage Rausan-Ségla made one of
· the more successful wines. Surprisingly dark, yet now showing
75 a brownish-orange cast, the chunky, one-dimensional wine has
good fruit, medium body, and is still quite palatable. Drink up.
Last tasted, 7/82.

1971—The 1971 is a light, elegant, supple, fruity wine that now requires
· immediate drinking. Medium ruby with an orange rim, this fra-
80 grant, medium-bodied wine is beginning to tire, but has elegance
and charm. Drink up. Last tasted, 6/83.

1970—This is a complete wine, and certainly the finest Rausan-Ségla
· produced between 1961 and 1983. The 1970 is still impressively
86 dark ruby in color, with a tight, spicy, blackcurrant bouquet,
medium to full body, excellent ripeness and concentration, and
a long finish. Anticipated maturity: 1987–2000. Last tasted,
4/84.

1966—Similar in style to the 1970, only more austere and not quite as
· concentrated, the 1966 has a ripe plummy, oaky fragrance of
84 moderate intensity, and graceful, yet still tough and firm flavors. Drinkable now, this fully mature wine will hold for 6–8 more years. Last tasted, 4/79.

1962—This is an uncharacteristic wine for the 1962 vintage that pro-
· duced so many elegant, charming, round, fruity wines. Hard,
75 lean, and austere, without much richness or charm, this wine's fruit has no chance of ever outdistancing the considerable tannins that are still present. Drink up. Last tasted, 2/78.

1961—Not a noteworthy 1961, Rausan-Ségla is ripe, fruity, a somewhat
· awkward and disjointed wine. While the wine tastes jammy,
81 diffuse, and finishes flat, it nevertheless has appeal, as well as plenty of concentration and power. Drink up. Last tasted, 9/79.

BRANE-CANTENAC (Second-Growth) ABOVE AVERAGE TO GOOD

Production: 30,000–35,000 cases	Grape varieties: Cabernet Sauvignon—70% Merlot—17% Cabernet Franc—13%
Time spent in barrels: 18–20 months	Average age of vines: 20 years
Evaluation of present classification: Should be downgraded to a Médoc fifth-growth	

One of the Médoc's largest vineyards, Brane-Cantenac's extensive vineyards (just over 200 acres) lie west of the village of Cantenac and well inland from the Gironde River. Given the fact that Brane-Cantenac was classified a second-growth in 1855, its large production, and I suspect also because of its very friendly and charming owner, Lucien Lurton, the wines of Brane-Cantenac have enjoyed a large measure of commercial success throughout the world. This has occurred notwithstanding a record of mediocrity that was particularly acute throughout the period 1967–1977. Most wine writers seem to have turned the cheek in the other direction rather than point out what were obvious flaws in the makeup of Brane-Cantenac's wines during this era. First, the wine was entirely too light in style for either a Margaux or a second-growth. Second, far too many vintages suffered from a distressing barnyard aroma which no doubt was the result of poor management in the wine cellars.

However, things seem to have been straightened out in the '80s. The famous "professor," Emile Peynaud, was brought in to supervise the vinification starting with the 1981 vintage, and in both 1982 and 1983 Brane-Cantenac has produced its best wines since 1961.

Even with this renewed level of quality, the wines of Brane-Cantenac are made in a very forward, fruity, soft style which makes the wine easily appreciated when young. Recent vintages have been fully mature within 5–6 years after bottling.

VINTAGES

1983—Rather forward for the vintage, but quite seductive and flavorful,
· ripe and richly fruity, the 1983 Brane-Cantenac has a fragrant,
89 plummy bouquet, a sweet, savory, round texture, and light to moderate tannins. Quite delicious and generously flavored, this wine will develop early. It is certainly one of the great successes of this vintage. Anticipated maturity: 1988–1996. Last tasted, 3/85.

1982—Undoubtedly, the finest Brane-Cantenac since the 1961 and to
· my palate much better than that wine, the 1982 is a marvelously
87 rich, deep, fat, intensely perfumed wine, with very lovely fruity flavors, plenty of round, ripe tannins, and a precocious personality. Medium-bodied and almost decadently fruity, this wine will drink well young, but will last well as there are moderate tannins present. Anticipated maturity: 1989–1996. Last tasted, 2/85.

1981—This Brane-Cantenac is a charming, fruity wine, with medium
· body and a spicy, clean, light-intensity bouquet, a soft texture,
83 and light tannins in the finish. Anticipated maturity: 1985–1990. Last tasted, 10/84.

1980—Light, with an innocuous, faintly fruity aroma, this light-bodied
· wine has shallow yet clean, fruity flavors, and a short finish.
78 Drink over the next 2 years. Last tasted, 10/84.

1979—A respectable effort from Brane-Cantenac, the 1979 is medium
· to dark ruby, with a herbaceous, fruity, spicy bouquet. Medium-
78 bodied and quite soft and supple on the palate, it is best drunk over the next 3–4 years. Last tasted, 4/82.

1978—Made in a period when the wines of Brane-Cantenac were quite
· spotty in quality, the 1978 is a success for the château, but
82 hardly an inspired effort for a second-growth property. Medium ruby with a moderately intense, berryish, earthy bouquet, very soft, round, plump flavors with little acidity or tannin present,

this is one 1978 that is close to full maturity. Drink over the next 5 years. Last tasted, 6/83.

1977—Light, faintly fruity, with shallow, somewhat herbaceous flavors,
· this medium-bodied wine is medium ruby, with some tannin in
67 the finish. Drink up. Last tasted, 4/81.

1976—Fully mature and beginning to show some brown at the edges,
· this loosely knit wine lacks firmness, concentration and struc-
75 ture, but does offer round, pleasant, soft, somewhat flabby, fruity flavors, with a hint of the barnyard dirtiness sometimes found in the wines of Brane-Cantenac. Drink up. Last tasted, 6/83.

1975—Now approaching full maturity, the 1975 Brane-Cantenac has a
· generous, earthy, spicy, interesting bouquet, sweet, relatively
83 soft, fruity flavors, medium body, and good length. A noteworthy effort in a period when Brane-Cantenac was notoriously mediocre. Drink over the next 5–6 years. Last tasted, 5/84.

1971—Very dirty, farmyard smells predominate. On the palate, the
· wine is diffuse, frail, very tannic and lean, weakly concentrated,
62 and just barely palatable. Avoid. Last tasted, 3/84.

1970—This is a distressingly poor wine, particularly in view of the
· vintage. The 1970 has quite a foul aroma and dirty barnyard
65 scent. On the palate, the wine is beginning to fall completely apart. Lacking fruit and concentration, this is a vivid example of a very poorly and sloppily made wine. Last tasted, 3/82.

1967—When it was at its peak in 1975–76, the 1967 Brane-Cantenac
· was not a bad wine. However, its charm then was a soft, easy-
70 going fruitiness. It has now faded and the wine tastes hollow and austere. Last tasted, 10/80.

1966—The best Brane-Cantenac between 1961 and 1982, the 1966 has
· been fully mature since 1976, and is now beginning to tire. A
84 stylish bouquet of cedary, plummy fruit is still very fine, but on the palate, the round, sweet fruit is fading, and the tannin and acidity are more and more noticeable. Drink up. Last tasted, 2/82.

1964—Not tasted recently, but my notes from 1978 indicate that the
· wine was attractively fat and sweet, surprisingly ripe and fruity,
80 with the tannin no longer evident. Drink up. Last tasted, 2/78.

1961—Unlike most other 1961s, Brane-Cantenac is a little past its
· prime. Nevertheless, there is still plenty of fruit and flesh left to
85 enjoy. It is medium dark ruby, with a full-intensity bouquet of ripe, rich fruit, toasty oak, and a subtle herbaceousness. The

wine is plump, quite round and generous, with light tannins and medium body. Not a great 1961, but quite flavorful. Drink over the next 5 years. Last tasted, 2/79.

RAUZAN-GASSIES (Second-Growth) ABOVE AVERAGE TO GOOD

Production: 10,000 cases	Grape varieties: Cabernet Sauvignon—40% Merlot—35% Cabernet Franc—23% Petit Verdot—2%
Time spent in barrels: 12–18 months	Average age of vines: 33 years
Evaluation of present classification: Should be downgraded to a Médoc fifth-growth	

The vineyards and wines of Rauzan-Gassies and Rausan-Ségla share a number of common characteristics. First, and most important, neither is making wine worthy of its position in the 1855 classification. However, both properties seem to be rebounding with more conscientious efforts in recent vintages.

Historically, Rauzan-Gassies has always been a more inconsistent wine than Rausan-Ségla. In style, it tends toward heaviness and corpulence for a Margaux, without the fragrance or finesse normally associated with the better wines of this commune. However, it can make fairly concentrated, powerful wines. In most vintages, the wines of Rauzan-Gassies have reached maturity surprisingly fast for a classified growth, usually within 7–8 years of the vintage. Reports continue to emanate from Bordeaux that the quality of wines produced at Rauzan-Gassies is on the upswing. I remain rather skeptical of such statements, but hopefully they are true.

VINTAGES

1983—The 1983 is not a complex wine, but very fat, grapey, quite
· tannic and astringent, with surprising power and presence in the
84 mouth. This is a rather chunky, typical Rauzan-Gassies, but
much more powerful and tannic than expected. Anticipated maturity: 1993–2000. Last tasted, 3/85.

1982—Rather fat, plummy, velvety and very precocious, with low acid-
· ity, moderate tannin, and a very forward, precocious personal-
85 ity, this is a charmingly fruity and straightforward Rauzan-
Gassies. Anticipated maturity: 1987–1995. Last tasted, 1/85.

1981—Surprisingly diffuse, flabby, and lacking depth, richness, and
· structure, the 1981 is quite mediocre. Drink over the next 5
74 years. Last tasted, 3/85.

1979—A corpulent, straightforward, plausible wine, with good dark
· ruby color, a ripe black cherry, oaky bouquet of moderate inten-
82 sity, and soft, round, somewhat jammy flavors. Anticipated maturity: 1986–1992. Last tasted, 4/83.

1978—This is a strong effort from Rauzan-Gassies, quite rich and full-
· bodied, with plenty of blackcurrant fruit, some attractive vanil-
84 lin oakiness, good length and depth, and the promise of better
things to come if cellared. Anticipated maturity: 1988–1995.
Last tasted, 4/82.

1976—Diluted flavors and a lack of structure and grip have resulted in
· a wine that tastes shallow, simple, and uninteresting. Browning
72 badly at the rim, this wine is fully mature. Drink up. Last tasted,
4/83.

1975—A sleeper in this vintage, Rauzan-Gassies may well be the best
· wine produced in the Margaux appellation after Palmer and Gis-
86 cours. It has excellent dark ruby color, a deep, rich, oaky,
blackcurrant fragrant bouquet, a chewy, full-bodied, very concentrated feel on the palate, and a tannic, long finish. Anticipated maturity: 1990–2000. Last tasted, 5/84.

1970—The 1970 is a simple, one-dimensional, somewhat dull wine
· which has adequate color, a compact bouquet of fruit and wood,
78 and soft, average, concentrated flavors. Drink up. Last tasted,
4/83.

1966—Still quite lively, crisp, richly fruity and full on the palate, the
· 1966 Rauzan-Gassies has a spicy, mushroom-like aroma, robust,
81 rather aggressive flavors, and a rather hard, coarse finish. It is
an interesting, rather rustic-style wine. Drink over the next 4
years. Last tasted, 4/83.

1961—Certainly not to be passed by if one should come your way, the
· Rauzan-Gassies is, however, less successful in this vintage than
85 many of its second-growth peers. Dark ruby, with significant
browning at the edges, the wine has an open-knit, fully mature,
spicy, oaky, plummy, toffee-scented bouquet, moderately rich,
soft, fruity flavors, and a supple, velvety finish. It is very attractive but lighter in style than most 1961s. It should be drunk up.
Last tasted, 4/83.

DU TERTRE (Fifth-Growth) — ABOVE AVERAGE TO GOOD

Production: 14,000 cases	Grape varieties:
	Cabernet Sauvignon—80%
	Merlot—10%
	Cabernet Franc—10%
Time spent in barrels: 24 months	Average age of vines: 24 years
Evaluation of present classification: Should be maintained	

Virtually everyone in Bordeaux agrees that Château du Tertre is a property that is producing better and better wine with each new vintage. The proprietor, Philippe Capbern-Gasqueton, acquired the property in 1962 and began an extensive replantation of the vineyard. Gasqueton, who is one of Bordeaux's few resident proprietors (he owns and resides at the famous St.-Estèphe château, Calon-Ségur), is a very traditional winemaker, believing in long fermentations and a lengthy stay of the new wine in oak barrels.

His success with du Tertre, which is located well inland from the Gironde River in a secluded area north of the town of Arsac, has been especially noteworthy in the late '70s, when he turned out two brilliant back-to-back successes in the vintages of 1978 and 1979. Du Tertre is clearly a property to take note of, as it is already outperforming many of its more expensive and more renowned Margaux peers.

VINTAGES

1983—Tasted from the cask, the color was quite impressive and the
· bouquet was rich and ripe, but the full-bodied flavors were in-
87 tensely tannic and tough. This should be a very good rather than exceptional wine from the 1983 vintage. Anticipated maturity: 1995–2005. Last tasted, 6/84.

1982—A wonderful, fragrant bouquet of violets, cedarwood, blackcur-
· rants, and vanillin oak jumps from the glass. On the palate, the
88 wine is tannic, full-bodied, and very concentrated, with rich, ripe fruity flavors. The finish is very promising. This is one of the top Margaux wines of the vintage. Anticipated maturity: 1992–2002. Last tasted, 1/85.

1981—Medium to dark ruby in color, with a moderately intense, spicy,
· perfumed bouquet, the 1981 du Tertre is much leaner than the
83 fat, generously flavored 1982 or excellent 1979. It has plenty of tannin, medium weight, and a short finish. Anticipated maturity: 1988–1994. Last tasted, 4/84.

1979—A sleeper of the vintage, the 1979 du Tertre has a marvelous,
• tarry, rich, deep, mulberry-scented bouquet, fat, supple, very
89 concentrated, fruity flavors, medium body, very fine length, and
enough tannin to age gracefully for 5–7 years. Anticipated maturity: 1987–1996. Last tasted, 4/84.

1978—Perhaps the equal of the excellent 1979, only more backward
• and a trifle more tannic and reserved, the 1978 has an impressive
88 dark ruby color, a tight but promising bouquet of ripe berry fruit,
and a pronounced vanillin oakiness. On the palate, the wine is tannic, well structured, and very concentrated. Anticipated maturity: 1989–2000. Last tasted, 11/83.

1976—A well-made, solidly put together 1976, du Tertre has a healthy,
• medium to dark ruby color, a spicy, full, floral, tarry bouquet,
84 moderate tannins, and good savory fruit. Quite drinkable now,
it should hold nicely for 4–5 years. Last tasted, 11/80.

1975—Surprisingly close to maturity for a 1975, the du Tertre is fruity,
• pleasant, with above-average ripeness and concentration, but
81 nowhere near the depth, dimension, and complexity of later
vintages, notably the 1978, 1979, and 1982. Drink over the next 5–7 years. Last tasted, 2/84.

POUGET (Fourth-Growth) — ABOVE AVERAGE TO GOOD

Production: 3,500 cases	Grape varieties: Cabernet Sauvignon—85% Merlot—10% Petit Verdot—5%
Time spent in barrels: 22–24 months	Average age of vines: 28 years

Evaluation of present classification: Should be downgraded to a fifth-growth

Pouget is owned and managed by Pierre Guillemet, the proprietor of Boyd-Cantenac, a much more sizable and better-known Margaux estate. Pouget's wines are vinified in exactly the same way as Boyd-Cantenac's and therefore it is not surprising that the style of Pouget is one in which the wine is sturdy and robust, deeply colored, and richly concentrated, although not always the model of consistency.

VINTAGES

1978—A rather perplexing wine, the 1978 Pouget has a very deep,
· richly pigmented color. On the palate, the wine offers little of
? the deep, rich fruit implied by the color, but rather has very woody, hard, tough flavors which seem unusually severe and backward. A big, rather awkward wine that has not yet come together. Anticipated maturity: 1988–1994. Last tasted, 11/83.

1975—An intriguing bouquet of ripe blackcurrant fruit, spicy oak, and
· mineral scents is top notch. In the mouth, the wine is typically
84 1975, very tannic, severe, hard and remarkably backward. The color is dark and a good concentration of fruit is present, but one must wait a very long time for this wine to mature. Anticipated maturity: 1992–2000. Last tasted, 5/84.

1974—A surprisingly good wine for this vintage, the 1974 Pouget has
· good fruit, a chunky texture, some hard tannins to lose, but a
80 healthy ruby color, a good, spicy, curranty bouquet, and adequate yet firm finish. Drink over the next 3 years. Last tasted, 1/81.

1971—A lightweight, less tannic, less intense version of the 1970, the
· 1971 Pouget is quite mature, velvety, still holding its fruit, and
84 very attractive, as well as being well made. Drink up. Last tasted, 2/81.

1970—A big, rich, solidly constructed, deep, flavorful, somewhat force-
· ful wine, the 1970 Pouget has still not reached its mature pla-
83 teau. Lacking finesse in favor of power and robustness, this is a gutsy, rustic-styled Margaux. Anticipated maturity: 1986–1992. Last tasted, 3/83.

KIRWAN (Third-Growth) — ABOVE AVERAGE TO GOOD

Production: 10,000–16,000 cases	Grape varieties: Merlot—30% Cabernet Sauvignon—40% Cabernet Franc—20% Petit Verdot—10%
Time spent in barrels: 20 months	Average age of vines: 20 years

Evaluation of present classification: Should be downgraded to a Médoc fifth-growth

Kirwan is another Margaux estate that would have a hard time holding its position in Bordeaux's 1855 classification should a reclassification take place. Like many other Margaux classified growths, Kirwan has not had a very distinguished track record. I have been a continual critic of Kirwan's wines, which I have consistently found too light, dull, and bland to justify its lofty classification and price tag. However, the Schÿler family began an extensive rehabilitation program at Kirwan in 1972 and recent vintages since 1978 clearly show more promise than what heretofore existed in the past, particularly the 1979, 1982, and 1983.

VINTAGES

1983—Certainly the best Kirwan produced in recent memory, the 1983
· is quite dark ruby in color with a moderately intense, rich, oaky,
85 curranty aroma. Solidly tannic on the palate, with aggressively rich, plummy, fruity flavors and good length, the 1983 Kirwan is quite youthful and no doubt destined to have a relatively long evolution. Anticipated maturity: 1992–2000. Last tasted, 3/85.

1982—A rather loosely knit wine with very good color, jammy, grapey
· fruit, low acidity and a lush, supple texture, this medium- to full-
84 bodied wine has a precocious personality, a charming fruitiness, and will evolve rapidly. Anticipated maturity: 1986–1993. Last tasted, 2/85.

1981—This vintage of Kirwan has been better received by others than
· by me. I have found the wine to be soundly colored and rather
75 chunky, but quite one-dimensional and bland. Anticipated maturity: 1988–1993. Last tasted, 1/85.

1980—Very light, thin, feeble and simple, this pale-colored wine should
· be consumed immediately. Last tasted, 3/84.
64

1979—An unspectacular but overall solid effort from Kirwan, this dark
· ruby wine has a moderately intense, herbaceous, fruity, oaky
83 aroma, straightforward cherryish flavors, medium body, good acidity, and light tannins. Anticipated maturity: 1988–1994. Last tasted, 4/84.

1978—Impressively colored, but a trifle jammy and loosely knit, the
· 1978 Kirwan borders on overripeness, but has a pleasingly fat,
82 supple fruitiness, and medium body. Drink over the next 5 years. Last tasted, 11/84.

1975—Medium to dark ruby in color with a very tight and closed bou-
· quet, this wine is quite severe and austere with high acidity and
72 tannin. There is barely enough fruit to cover its frame. It is not

unpleasant to drink, but my suspicion is that time will only make matters worse. Anticipated maturity: 1986. Last tasted, 4/84.

1971—Fully mature and beginning its decline, the 1971 Kirwan is a
· light, simple, fruity wine without much character, depth, or
73 complexity. It must be consumed immediately. Last tasted, 4/79.

1970—The 1970 has more stuffing than the 1971, but tastes rather light
· and meagerly endowed for a 1970. Now fully mature, the wine
75 has a spicy, berrylike bouquet, medium body, and average concentration. Drink over the next 5 years. Last tasted, 2/82.

CANTENAC-BROWN (Third-Growth) ABOVE AVERAGE TO GOOD

Production: 15,000 cases	Grape varieties: Cabernet Sauvignon—75% Merlot—15% Cabernet Franc—8% Petit Verdot—2%
Time spent in barrels: 16–20 months	Average age of vines: 25 years
Evaluation of present classification: Should be downgraded to a fifth-growth	

Cantenac-Brown is another one of the Margaux properties that one hears very little about these days. The wine is rarely seen in America, and even more curiously, it is hardly ever seen in comparative tastings set up by Bordeaux *négociants*. Consequently, my experience in tasting Cantenac-Brown is much more limited than with other Bordeaux wines. The wines that I have tasted have displayed a rather coarse, dusty texture, seem quite robust, severely tannic and dry, and all too frequently very charmless. The wine has a reputation for taking a long time to come around, but I suspect that in reality the wine never quite develops as well as it should because of its excess of tannin and acidity. Certainly that has been my experience to date.

VINTAGES

1983—A typical effort from Cantenac-Brown, darkly colored, ripe, ro-
· bust, rich, full-bodied, coarsely structured, with very good con-
84 centration, plenty of power, but lacking charm and finesse. Perhaps long cellaring will reveal more character. Anticipated maturity: 1993–2005. Last tasted, 3/85.

1981—Surprisingly good, the 1981 Cantenac-Brown has impressive
· color, a chocolatey, rich, smoky bouquet, dusty, coarse, tannic
84 flavors, and full body. Quite tannic, it will need a long time to come around. Anticipated maturity: 1991–2004. Last tasted, 1/85.

1978—The predominant impression left by this wine is one of vanillin
· oakiness. On the palate, the wine is not deep or terribly concen-
76 trated, but light and lacking in substance. Drink over the next 3–4 years. Last tasted, 9/79.

1976—Soft berryish aromas intermingle with oak to create a very light-
· intensity bouquet. On the palate, the wine is shallow and pale,
67 relatively light-bodied and quite short in the finish. Last tasted, 11/80.

1975—A good effort for certain, yet far from the top league of 1975
· Bordeaux, Cantenac-Brown has a rather complex, oaky, smoky
84 bouquet, with attractive, relatively sweet, tannic, fruity flavors. It is medium- to full-bodied and much more precocious than most wines from this vintage. Anticipated maturity: 1986–1995. Last tasted, 5/84.

1971—A thin, angular, muscular wine which lacks richness and flesh,
· the 1971 Cantenac-Brown tastes hollow and austere, and is best
64 drunk up before the meager fruit dissipates even more. Last tasted, 12/78.

1970—Still dense ruby/purple in color, with a big, blackcurranty, cin-
· namon-and mineral-scented bouquet, this massive wine has
86 huge tannic flavors and is very full-bodied. This is a very young, relatively raw yet impressive wine that overwhelms one with its power and toughness. Anticipated maturity: 1990–2010. Last tasted, 2/84.

1966—A compact, muscular, firm wine, with a dusty, rather coarse
· texture, some spice and leathery aromas, medium to full body,
83 but deficient in richness and just too acidic and austere. Drink over the next 5 years. Last tasted, 4/80.

DURFORT-VIVENS (Second-Growth) ABOVE AVERAGE TO GOOD

Production: 8,000 cases
Grape varieties:
Cabernet Sauvignon—82%
Cabernet Franc—10%
Merlot—8%
Time spent in barrels: 20 months
Average age of vines: 23 years
Evaluation of present classification: Should be downgraded to a Médoc fifth-growth

In spite of the fact that Durfort-Vivens' proprietor, Lucien Lurton, appears to have put this famous property back in the correct direction for making wines representative of its placement in the Bordeaux hierarchy, the track record of Durfort between 1961 and 1981 is inexcusably poor.

There is no question that the relatively recent acquisition by Lurton of the vineyard in 1961, when it was already in poor condition, certainly slowed efforts to revitalize this estate. However, it has taken until 1982 for Durfort-Vivens to produce a vintage of very good wine. Far too frequently the wines of Durfort-Vivens have been characterized by thin, herbal, washed-out flavors, annoyingly high levels of acidity and tannins, and a persistent lack of concentration of fruit.

VINTAGES

1983—A well-balanced, nicely constructed wine, the 1983 Durfort-Vivens is leaner and more austere than many of its Margaux counterparts, but has very good concentration, plenty of aggressive tannins and good length, and an excellent ripe, rich fruitiness. Anticipated maturity: 1995–2005. Last tasted, 3/85.
· 86

1982—Unquestionably one of the finest Durfort-Vivens I have tasted, the 1982 has a big, lovely, ripe, rich blackcurrant bouquet, deep, supple, concentrated flavors, a long finish and plenty of tannin for aging. This is not a great or even excellent 1982, but certainly a very fine Durfort-Vivens. More importantly, it marks a dramatic turnabout in the quality of wines from this estate. Anticipated maturity: 1992–1998. Last tasted, 1/85.
· 85

1981—This is a rather typical pre-1982 Durfort-Vivens. Sinewy, lean, angular, this wine needs additional fruit and flesh to balance out the excessive tannins and acidity. Rather charmless. Anticipated maturity: 1990–1995. Last tasted, 6/84.
· 74

1980—The 1980 is thin, herbaceous, watery, and quite unattractive.
· Time will only make matters worse for this meagerly endowed
64 wine. Last tasted, 1/85.

1978—A solid effort from Durfort, the 1978 has a light-intensity bou-
· quet of raspberry cherry fruit and new oak. On the palate, the
75 wine is a little austere and harshly tannic, but has adequate
fruit, medium body, and a decent finish. Anticipated maturity:
1988. Last tasted, 3/84.

1976—This is straightforward, fruity wine, with a chunky texture, and
· spicy, woody, rather closed bouquet. Medium-bodied, supple,
75 and attractively long and fruity in the finish, it is a rather good
effort from Durfort-Vivens. Drink over the next 5 years. Last
tasted, 6/84.

1975—Extremely disappointing in the vintage, Durfort-Vivens is quite
· light in color, disturbingly brown at the edges, and has a very
52 pronounced, stinky, barnyard aroma. Furthermore, it tastes surprisingly diluted, feeble, and thin on the palate. A miserable
effort. Last tasted, 6/84.

1974—The 1974 Durfort-Vivens is a very poor wine even taking into
· consideration the mediocrity of the vintage. Harshly tannic, vir-
50 tually devoid of fruit, this hollow wine has no fruit, no charm,
and no future. Last tasted, 3/84.

1973—As bad as the 1974, but totally different in style. Watery, hollow,
· thin, and barely resembling a wine, this unbelievably shallow,
50 brown-colored wine has lost any fruit it may have once possessed. Last tasted, 10/79.

1971—The 1971 is an attractive wine that is still holding a plummy,
· spicy, moderately endowed, rich fruitiness. This medium-
75 bodied wine is fully mature and showing no signs of falling apart.
Drink over the next 4–5 years. Last tasted, 3/84.

1970—A tough, angular, rustic sort of wine, the 1970 is medium- to
· full-bodied, quite tannic, has good color, but seems to lack sup-
74 pleness and the rich, glossy fruitiness so prevalent in this vintage. Anticipated maturity: 1986–1992. Last tasted, 11/79.

1966—Austere, tight, hard, and unyielding, with good grip and harsh
· tannins still very much in evidence, this severe style of wine
70 lacks both finesse and charm. Drink over the next 5 years. Last
tasted, 10/78.

1962—High acidity, thin, tart, short flavors and a harsh finish make
· this a very unattractive wine which is likely to get only more out
62 of balance as the fruit continues to fade. Last tasted, 10/78.

MARQUIS D'ALESME-BECKER

(Third-Growth) ABOVE AVERAGE TO GOOD

Production: 3,500 cases	Grape varieties: Cabernet Sauvignon—29% Merlot—29% Cabernet Franc—29% Petit Verdot—13%
Time spent in barrels: 12–16 months	Average age of vines: 24 years

Evaluation of present classification: Should be downgraded to a Médoc Grand Bourgeois Exceptionnel

The wine of Marquis d'Alesme is rarely seen in America. The production is tiny, the name little known, and the quality solid but rarely special. The château itself is located just north of the road to Château Margaux in the town of Margaux. The estate is owned by the Zuger family, who are better known for their more famous Margaux property, Malescot St.-Exupéry.

The little experience I have had with Marquis d'Alesme left me with the distinct impression that the wine is no better than one of the better Bourgeois growths of the Médoc. It seems always to be a well-colored wine, but always rather simple and one-dimensional.

VINTAGES

1982—Rather than spectacular, this wine is solid and reliable, with
· good dark color, a moderately intense blackberry, oaky bouquet,
84 and medium body. Anticipated maturity: 1990–2000. Last
tasted, 1/85.

1979—Attractive dark ruby color, with an open, flowery, ripe curranty
· bouquet intermingled with the scents of new oak, this medium-
83 bodied wine is fruity, supple and flavorful. This wine should be
drunk over the next 5–6 years. Last tasted, 4/83.

1978—A solid effort, the 1978 has an old woodsy aroma, a faint perfume
· of berry fruit, a round, charming, forward fruitiness, and some-
80 what short finish. Anticipated maturity: 1986–1990. Last tasted,
6/84.

1975—An average quality wine, but somewhat bland and plainer-scaled
· given the quality of the vintage, the 1975 has straightforward
77 fruity flavors, some spicy oak aromas, and a rather hard, sharp
finish. Anticipated maturity: 1988–1995. Last tasted, 5/84.

MARQUIS-DE-TERME
(Fourth-Growth) **ABOVE AVERAGE TO GOOD**

Production: 12,000 cases	Grape varieties: Cabernet Sauvignon—45% Merlot—35% Cabernet Franc—15% Petit Verdot—5%
Time spent in barrels: 18–24 months	Average age of vines: 28 years

Evaluation of present classification: Should be downgraded to a Grand Bourgeois

Despite the sizable production, Marquis-de-Terme is even more difficult to find in commercial wine channels than other esoteric, hard-to-locate Margaux wines such as Pouget, Ferrière, Marquis d'Alesme-Becker, and Desmirail. The reason is that nearly three-fourths of Marquis-de-Terme's production is sold directly to European wine enthusiasts. What wine remains usually finds its way to Belgium and Holland, and on rare occasions, to the United States.

VINTAGES

1979—Given the château's reputation for producing rather tough,
· brawny wines, I would have expected this wine to be more back-
82 ward and tannic. Not so. Fragrant, earthy, berrylike aromas jump from the glass. Precocious, fruity, and soft, this medium-bodied wine should be drunk over the next 5–6 years. Last tasted, 4/84.

1978—This is a rather unimpressive wine from a vintage that was gen-
· erally excellent for the wines of the Médoc. Dirty, musty, un-
50 clean aromas suggest an unkempt wine cellar. On the palate, the wine is thin, tastes of mold, and is quite unattractive. A flawed effort. Last tasted, 6/83.

1971—Pungent, earthy, smoky aromas intermingle with ripe blackcur-
· rant scents to provide a rather exotic bouquet. On the palate,
80 the wine is fully mature, soft, much lighter than one would expect, and ready to drink. Drink up. Last tasted, 2/80.

1970—Very backward, almost opaque ruby in color, with a rich, deep,
· intense bouquet of spicy oak, smoky fruit, and earthy scents.
84 Dense, powerful, and tannic, and perhaps too robust for its own good, this full-bodied wine should age well for another 5 years. Anticipated maturity: 1985–1990. Last tasted, 4/82.

DAUZAC (Fifth-Growth) **ABOVE AVERAGE TO GOOD**

Production: 15,000 cases

Grape varieties:
Cabernet Sauvignon—70%
Merlot—20%
Cabernet Franc—5%
Petit Verdot—5%

Time spent in barrels: 16–18 months

Average age of vines: 15 years

Evaluation of present classification: Should be downgraded to a Grand Bourgeois

Despite a new ownership in 1978 that has invested considerable sums of money, Dauzac remains among the most mediocre of all the Médoc classified growths. Surely, the estate would be demoted should any new classification take place. However, the technology and commitment to quality representative of its historic reputation are present, and perhaps Dauzac will regain the respect and esteem that it has lost.

The impressive new winery is one of the first major classified growths the visitor to the Médoc encounters on the famous D2 heading north. The improvements made since 1978 by the new owners, the Chatellier family, include installation of stainless steel fermentation tanks in 1981, an extensive program of new vineyard plantings, and the increased usage of new oak barrels, now representing 50% of the total cooperage used to age the wine. This may be a wine to watch over future vintages.

VINTAGES

1983—Given the vintage and the rather high number of very successful
· wines made, particularly in the Médoc, Dauzac's 1983 is good,
80 but hardly a top success for the vintage. Medium ruby, with a spicy, vanillin-scented aroma, rather ripe, uncomplex, cherryish flavors, and medium body, the wine is light for a 1983 and should mature rapidly. Drink between 1988–1994. Last tasted, 6/84.

1982—An enjoyable, rather charming, plump, fruity wine with good
· color, a spicy, savory, fat character on the palate, and soft, ripe
82 tannins in the finish. Good as it is, it is hardly a noteworthy effort in this sensationally great vintage. Anticipated maturity: 1988–1995. Last tasted, 1/85.

1981—The 1981 is more elegant and distinctly lighter in style than the
· 1982, with light to medium body, a spicy, oaky component, and
80 moderately intense, cherrylike flavors. Anticipated maturity: 1986–1992. Last tasted, 11/84.

1979—The 1979 is a solid, one-dimensional wine, with a sense of dull-
· ness and blandness pervading its bouquet and flavors. The wine
75 is dark ruby in color but very simple. Anticipated maturity:
1985–1992. Last tasted, 6/84.

1978—A light, delicate, yet fragrant wine that suffers from lack of
· concentration and depth, the 1978 Dauzac does offer a pleas-
76 antly fragrant bouquet of fruit and oak, and straightforward, soft
flavors. Drink over the next 4 years. Last tasted, 10/83.

1971—The 1971 is a washed-out, diluted, very simple wine which has
· little interest and character left to it. Light ruby, with dull,
55 acidic, fruity flavors that seem very meager, the 1971 Dauzac is
well past its prime. Last tasted, 3/80.

1966—Lean, austere, tight, and compact, the 1966 has some interest-
· ing, woodsy, mushroom-like aromas in its bouquet, but it is
74 lacking in concentration, complexity and character. Last tasted,
1/79.

OTHER NOTABLE MARGAUX PROPERTIES

The large commune of Margaux has a number of properties that can produce wine at a level of quality that can match the classified growths. Several of these estates are even producing wine better than several of the classified growths of Margaux. For example, d'Angludet, Labégorce-Zédé, and Siran are three estates that can be counted on to produce good, sometimes very good wine at prices which do not yet reflect their high quality. The following estates appear in order of my estimation of their quality.

D'ANGLUDET (Unclassified)

Evaluation: The quality equivalent of a Médoc Grand Bourgeois Exceptionnel

The highly respected Bordeaux wine broker and part owner of the famous Margaux estate of Palmer, Peter A. Sichel, resides at d'Angludet. He has been responsible for taking this modest but well-placed property from virtual obscurity to international prominence by making a wine that can rival some of Margaux's more famous names. An average of 9,000 cases of spicy, moderately colored, supple, moderately elegant wine are produced at d'Angludet from a vineyard planted with 55% Cabernet Sauvignon, 35% Merlot, 8% Cabernet Franc, and 2% Petit Verdot.

The wines seem to be getting better and better as the vineyard, which was replanted in the '60s, gets older and older. Of recent vintages, the 1975 is a notable success, but still youthfully tannic and closed. The 1976 is quite mediocre, the 1978, 1979, 1981, and 1982 good, and the 1983 truly superb. In fact, the 1983 may well be the finest wine ever produced at d'Angludet. In most vintages, d'Angludet will be mature after 5–8 years of bottle age. Despite its increasing fame and popularity, particularly in England, the wine remains a good value. While d'Angludet has the potential to be considered a fifth-growth, at present the quality is more akin to the Grand Bourgeois Exceptionnel.

SIRAN (Unclassified)

Evaluation: The quality equivalent of a Médoc Grand Bourgeois Exceptionnel

This outstanding property in Labarde in the southern part of the Margaux appellation is making consistently delicious, fragrant, deeply colored wines that are in quality on a par with the best Grands Bourgeois Exceptionnels.

The estate is owned and managed by William Alain B. Miailhe, a meticulous grower, who produces in an average year 12,000 cases of rich, flavorful, polished wine that admirably reflects its Margaux appellation. The wine is also distinguished by a Mouton-Rothschild-like label which has a different artist's painting on it each year.

Siran's wine usually needs 5 to 6 years of bottle age to mature properly. The recent vintages have all been quite successful, even the light, mediocre vintage of 1980 where Siran outperformed virtually all of its Margaux peers save Margaux and Giscours. Bordeaux wine enthusiasts looking for excellent value and high-quality wine should take special note of the powerful, densely colored, rather big 1983, the lush, rich, supple 1982, the elegant, richly fruity, stylish 1981, the solid, light but pleasant 1980, the charming 1979, and the rich, tannic, full-bodied 1978.

If a new classification of the wines of the Médoc were ever done, Siran would surely be given significant consideration for inclusion as a fifth-growth, but in all likelihood, it deserves status as a Grand Bourgeois Exceptionnel. If and until such a restructuring of this classification takes place, consumers will find the wine of Siran uncompromisingly made, and a fine value.

LABÉGORCE-ZÉDÉ (Unclassified)

Evaluation: The quality equivalent of a Médoc Grand Bourgeois Exceptionnel

Labégorce-Zédé produces a solid, plump, chunky, quite flavorful style of Margaux wine, but I have never found the wine to have the finesse and fragrance of Siran or d'Angludet. Nevertheless, it is one of the best-made wines of the Margaux commune.

Approximately 10,500 cases are produced each year from a vineyard planted with 50% Cabernet Sauvignon, 35% Merlot, 10% Cabernet Franc, and 5% Petit Verdot.

The Belgian Thienpont family own and manage Labégorce-Zédé, and like their famous Pomerol estate of Vieux Château Certan, this is a very traditionally made wine. Labégorce-Zédé usually requires 5 to 6 years to reach maturity, but once there, will retain its fruit and harmony for 5 to 8 more years in top vintages. Recent vintages to look for include the brawny, deeply fruity, tannic 1983, and the ripe, robust, more supple, yet still ageworthy 1982.

LABÉGORCE (Unclassified)

Evaluation: The quality equivalent of a Médoc Grand Bourgeois Exceptionnel

Consumers no doubt find it confusing that there are several châteaux with Margaux appellations bearing the name Labégorce. Château Labégorce is another reliable property which produces just over 10,000 cases of wine from a vineyard planted with 60% Cabernet Sauvignon and 40% Merlot. The wine is lighter in color and body than Labégorce-Zédé, and generally matures more quickly, with a more pronounced, intense Margaux fragrance. Some vintages tend to be quite light and meagerly endowed, and for that reason I have found the wines of Labégorce to be less consistent than Labégorce-Zédé. The 1981 is rather light and bland, the 1982 supple, soft and fruity, and distinctly less concentrated in the bottle than it was from the cask. The 1983 is above average in quality, but not very exciting.

Labégorce can be a delightful, lightish, fruity wine that is ideal for lighter dishes. When it is fairly priced, as it almost always is, it is also a good value.

LA TOUR-DE-MONS (Unclassified)

Evaluation: The quality equivalent of a Médoc Grand Bourgeois

One of the most famous Médoc Cru Bourgeois growths, La Tour-de-Mons in Soussans has a history traceable to 1615. The production of 8,000-plus cases from a vineyard planted with 45% Cabernet Sauvignon, 40% Merlot, 10% Cabernet Franc, and 5% Petit Verdot is managed by the Clauzel family, who until 1980 had also managed the nearby classified-growth estate of Cantemerle. La Tour-de-Mons is a very popular wine in Europe, where it is well regarded for its very dark color, ripe, rich plummy fruitiness, and aging potential of 10 to 15 years. However, the wine has not been a model of consistency, and my major objection has been an annoyingly high level of acidity in certain bottlings. Two great vintages for La Tour-de-Mons are 1970 and 1975, particularly the latter, wherein this property produced an uncommonly powerful and rich wine for drinking in 1990 and later. The 1978 is soft, rich, and round, and the 1981 rather light, herbaceous, and slightly too high in acidity. From an overall Bordeaux quality perspective, La Tour-de-Mons has the quality of a Grand Bourgeois.

DESMIRAIL (Third-Growth)

Evaluation: The quality equivalent of a Médoc Grand Bourgeois

From its inclusion in the famous Médoc classification of 1855, we know that the wines of Desmirail were highly esteemed. However, the vineyards and château were sold in parcels to the owners of Palmer and Malescot St.-Exupéry.

The dynamic owner of Brane-Cantenac, Lucien Lurton, has decided to revive the wine of Desmirail from 4 specific vineyard locations that comprise just over 25 acres. The wines of the first three vintages, 1981, 1982, and 1983, are uncomplicated, fruity wines, with adequate depth and richness, but not yet up to the standards of a classified growth. With Lucien Lurton apparently giving more attention than ever before to the quality of winemaking at his bevy of estates, and with the assistance of the famed oenologist Emile Peynaud, the future of Desmirail may prove to be a promising one.

FERRIÈRE (Third-Growth)

Evaluation: The quality equivalent of a Médoc Grand Bourgeois

An obscure and very tiny property, Ferrière's vineyard has been leased to Château Lascombes since 1962, and the wine vinified and sold exclusively by Lascombes to a French restaurant chain, the Relais de Campagne. Since none of the wine is exported or routinely exhibited at major tastings sponsored by *négociants* in Bordeaux, my experience with Ferrière is limited to just one vintage—the 1966, which when tasted in 1982 was quite robust and powerful, with a personality more akin to Pauillac or St. -Estèphe than Margaux.

LA GURGUE (Unclassified)

Evaluation: The quality equivalent of a Médoc Grand Bourgeois

Located right in the village of Margaux, this obscure property that produces only 2,000 cases of wine has been totally revitalized by the owner of one of Bordeaux's best Cru Bourgeois wines, Chasse-Spleen in Moulis. The results of extensive renovations and top-notch management of the vineyard and wine cellar are obvious in the 1982 and 1983 wines. The 1982 is ripe, rich, chunky, and full of fruit. The 1983 is an even bigger wine, with a blackcurrant, chocolatey, intense fruitiness, as well as plenty of body and tannin.

La Gurgue is currently an unknown wine which I predict is about to win many a wine lover's palate with its high-quality wines.

BEL-AIR-MARQUIS D'ALIGRE (Unclassified)

Evaluation: The quality equivalent of a Médoc Cru Bourgeois

A well-situated vineyard and winery that was highly regarded in the 19th century, Bel-Air-Marquis d'Aligre is a wine which, in my limited experience with it, I have found to be impressively colored, but coarse, astringent, and lacking harmony and finesse. About 4,200 cases are produced. The wine is primarily marketed in Europe.

TAYAC (Cru Bourgeois)

Evaluation: Should be maintained

Tayac produces supple, easy-to-drink wines, which are generally meant to be consumed upon their release by the château. Interestingly, the vineyard is composed of 73% Cabernet Sauvignon, 25% Merlot, and 2% Petit Verdot, which would seemingly suggest that the wines would be firmer than they are. Both the 1978 and 1979 are charming, well-made, medium-weight, fruity wines. The 1981 is similar to the 1979, only more austere, whereas the 1982 is supple, very fruity, and surprisingly concentrated. Tayac's wines, like many Cru Bourgeois wines, are sound values.

PAVEIL DE LUZE (Grand Bourgeois)

Evaluation: The quality equivalent of a Cru Bourgeois

Paviel de Luze's wines are widely available in Europe, and seem to be most enjoyed by consumers who want rather supple, easy-to-drink, straightforward wine. I have found both the 1978 and 1979 to be compact, rather bland wines, with short finishes and uninteresting bouquets and flavors.

CANUET (Unclassified)

Evaluation: The quality equivalent of a Cru Brougeois

A small estate of just over 20 acres, producing approximately 3,500 cases of wine, Canuet is a property to keep an eye on. The 1981 was rather light and unexciting, but the 1982 showed a precocious, sumptuous fruitiness, a first-class, rich bouquet, and a good finish. If priced fairly, Canuet can be a good value. The style of the wine seems to be one that is aimed at providing immediate gratification, as neither the 1981 nor 1982 had much tannin.

THE LESSER-KNOWN WINES OF THE MÉDOC: THE MOULIS, LISTRAC, HAUT-MÉDOC, AND MÉDOC APPELLATIONS

There are hundreds of châteaux in the vast Médoc that produce notable wines of quality, character, and interest. They frequently offer astonishing wine values in good vintages, and sensationally great values in excellent vintage years. A few of these estates make wine as good as, and in a few instances better than, many of the famous classified growths. However, most of these properties make solid, reliable wines, which if never spectacularly exciting, are nevertheless sound and satisfying. In the very good to great vintages of Bordeaux, 1961, 1970, 1975, 1982, and 1983, the wines from the best of these properties should be especially sought out.

THE HAUT-MÉDOC

Immediately at the northern edge of the Médoc appellation of Margaux is the town of Soussans. Starting here, and heading north in the direction of St.-Julien, is a 12-kilometer stretch of road that traverses a large area where a great many of these properties are situated. No one will argue that the best wines come from the three villages just slightly west and north of Soussans called Grand Poujeaux, Moulis, and Listrac. Tourists on Bordeaux's Route du Vin rarely venture over into this area, which is only a 10-minute drive from Margaux, but shrewd wine importers and *négociants* are frequently encountered in the central region of Médoc because of the high quality-to-price ratio so many of the wines here represent.

In these villages, the top estates in Moulis are Chasse-Spleen, Poujeaux, Brillette, and Maucaillou, and in Listrac, Fourcas-Hosten.

The wines of Moulis tend to be densely colored, rather big, full-bodied and tannic wines that start off life tough and stern, but in a decade mellow out to become quite rich and complex clarets. Chasse-Spleen and Poujeaux both consistently perform on the same level as a classified growth, and can even be spectacular on occasion. Brillette, Maucaillou, and Fourcas-Hosten are also the quality equivalent of a classified growth. Maucaillou is the most elegant and quickest to mature, Brillette the most dependent on the toasty, vanillin, oaky aromas of new barrels for its personality, and Fourcas-Hosten a St.-Julien look-alike in texture and taste. The wines of Listrac and Moulis have become much better known over the last several years as shrewd wine consumers have realized that the quality here was well above the price asked for the wines. Of recent vintage, 1978, 1982, and 1983 were in different ways all spectacularly successful for the wines of Moulis and Listrac.

If one stayed on the famous D2, the towns of Arcins, Lamarque, and Cussac would be encountered before arriving at the southern border of St.-Julien, where the famous properties of Beychevelle and Branaire-Ducru sit nobly confronting each other on a high plateau. There are numerous well-run properties in this section making good, reliable wine for modest prices. All of the wines from this region are entitled to the Haut-Médoc appellation.

In Arcins, a tiny village just north of the commune of Margaux, the top property of the moment is Arnauld, which produces a well-colored wine with a kinship to a fuller-bodied Margaux. The 1983 is particularly good. In the town of Lamarque, a good spot for taking the car ferry across the Gironde to the right bank town of Blaye, is the château of Lamarque. It makes especially appealing wine that is round, fruity, and capable of living for a decade. Two properties just south of the town of Lamarque that produce good, open-knit, easy-to-drink claret at fair prices are Malescasse and Moulin Rose. Malescasse makes light, fragrant wine, Moulin Rose, rather forceful, rich, well-colored wine not unlike a St.-Julien.

Leaving Lamarque for the 10-minute drive north to St.-Julien, Beaumont is the best estate between the tiny, nondescript villages of Vieux-Cussac and Cussac. Beaumont produces a sound, commercial wine

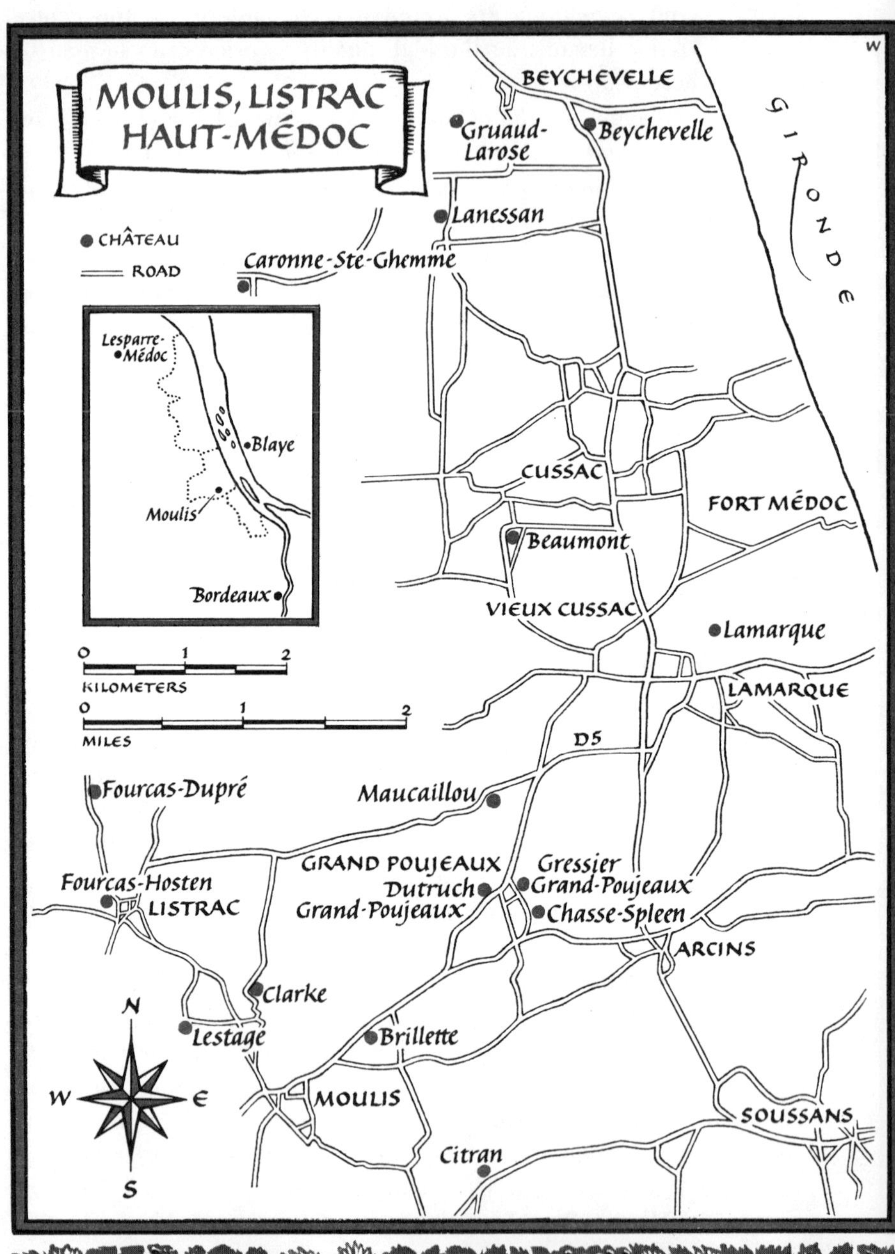
MOULIS, LISTRAC
HAUT-MÉDOC
CHÂTEAU
ROAD
BEYCHEVELLE
Gruaud-Larose
Beychevelle
GIRONDE
Lanessan
Caronne-Ste-Ghemme
Lesparre-Médoc
Blaye
Moulis
Bordeaux
CUSSAC
FORT MÉDOC
Beaumont
VIEUX CUSSAC
Lamarque
LAMARQUE
0 1 2
KILOMETERS
0 1 2
MILES
D5
Fourcas-Dupré
Maucaillou
GRAND POUJEAUX
Gressier
Grand-Poujeaux
Fourcas-Hosten
Dutruch
LISTRAC
Grand-Poujeaux
Chasse-Spleen
ARCINS
Clarke
N
Lestage
Brillette
W
E
MOULIS
SOUSSANS
Citran
S

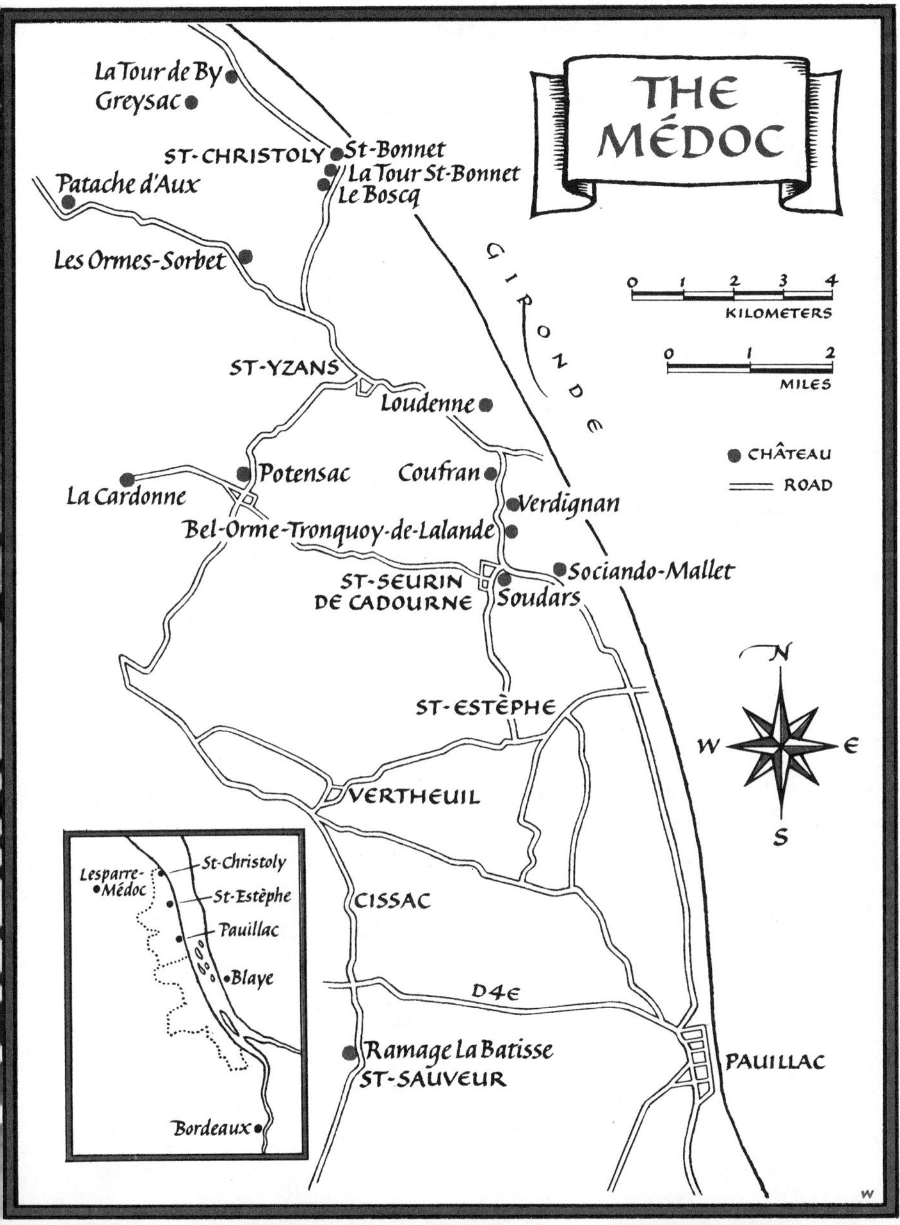

THE MÉDOC

La Tour de By
Greysac
ST-CHRISTOLY
St-Bonnet
La Tour St-Bonnet
Le Boscq
Patache d'Aux
Les Ormes-Sorbet
GIRONDE
0 1 2 3 4
KILOMETERS
0 1 2
MILES
ST-YZANS
Loudenne
CHÂTEAU
ROAD
Potensac
Coufran
La Cardonne
Verdignan
Bel-Orme-Tronquoy-de-Lalande
ST-SEURIN
DE CADOURNE
Soudars
Sociando-Mallet
N
W
E
S
ST-ESTÈPHE
VERTHEUIL
Lesparre-
Médoc
St-Christoly
St-Estèphe
Pauillac
Blaye
Bordeaux
CISSAC
D4E
Ramage La Batisse
ST-SAUVEUR
PAUILLAC
W

with a pleasing, supple fruitiness. It, like most of these wines, is meant to be drunk young. At Cussac, the last village passed before entering St.-Julien, the wine of Lanessan is produced. Lanessan is an excellent wine, consistently of classified-growth quality, and in the excellent Médoc vintages, Lanessan has the color, power, richness, and aging potential of a fine Pauillac. It is a terribly undervalued wine, so wine consumers wanting the finest quality/price rapport for the wine, take note.

St.-Laurent (also part of the Haut-Médoc appellation), located to the west of the St.-Julien appellation and well inland from the Gironde, is another Médoc region that can be counted on to produce very fine wine. St.-Laurent's reputation for top-rank Bordeaux is not new, as three of the châteaux included in the 1855 classification were from this region, Belgrave, Camensac, and La Tour-Carnet.

Only Camensac would, in my opinion, merit retaining its current status. However, Belgrave and La Tour-Carnet, two properties that slipped in quality in the '60s and '70s, have both been revitalized in the '80s, again producing wine that one could call classified-growth quality. Two other St.-Laurent properties worth a serious look from wine enthusiasts are Larose-Trintaudon and Caronne-Ste.-Gemme. Larose-Trintaudon is the Médoc's largest vineyard, and the wine produced is consistently supple, fruity, soft, and often resembles a lighter-styled St.-Julien. If it never quite hits the heights, it is a delicious, modern-style claret that is always sold at a reasonable price. In contrast, Caronne-Ste.-Gemme is a backward, often aggressively tannic wine with more of a resemblance to some of the wines of Listrac and Moulis than of St.-Laurent.

North of St.-Julien, on the back side of Pauillac, is the commune of St.-Sauveur. This area has a few notable properties. Ramage La Batisse is the top property of St.-Sauveur, followed by Peyrabon and Liversan. If one goes farther north and inland, parallel with St.-Estèphe, one will find extensive numbers of properties making fine wines. In and around the towns of Cissac (directly west of the famous Cos d'Estournel), in Vertheuil, and St.-Seurin-de-Cadourne are numerous moderately sized estates making good wine. These properties are also entitled to the Haut-Médoc appellation.

Cissac and its immediate neighbor several kilometers to the north, Vertheuil, are good towns in which to seek out some of the lesser-known Crus Bourgeois, but no village is richer with treasures than St.-Seurin-de-Cadourne. The gravel and clay soil here is similar to St.-Estèphe and many excellent wines at prices that make them exceptional bargains are produced in St.-Seurin-de-Cadourne. One can argue quite convincingly that there is no better Cru Bourgeois property than Sociando-Mallet in St.-Seurin-de-Cadourne. This estate has been totally resurrected since 1969 by its passionate owner, and in vintages such as 1970, 1975, 1976, 1978, 1982, and 1983, Sociando-Mallet has produced one of the truly outstanding wines of the Médoc. While Sociando-Mallet is made to last and last, two fine wines made in a supple, very fruity style to drink when young are Coufran and Verdignan, two properties run by the President of the Syndicate of the Crus Bourgeois, Jean Miaihle. Bel-Orme-Tronguoy-de-Lalande is another good Cru Bourgeois in the Saint-Seurin-de-Cadourne area.

In Cissac, the top property is Château Cissac, an impeccably made wine that offers excellent value.

THE MÉDOC

North of St.-Seurin-de-Cadourne the Bas-Médoc or Médoc region begins at the town of St.-Yzans and continues to run north to Soulac. All of the properties in this region are entitiled to the appellation "Médoc" rather than "Haut-Médoc." The best vineyards in this region are centered around the towns of St.-Yzans, Potensac, Bégadan, and St.-Christoly-Médoc.

In St.-Yzans, there is the lovely, pink-colored Loudenne, clearly the showpiece château of this region of the northern Médoc. Farther north in St. Christoly-Médoc, the top properties are Le Boscq, St.-Bonnet, and La Tour St.-Bonnet, three estates that offer excellent wines at shockingly low prices. All of these wines will last a good 10–15 years in an excellent vintage.

Heading east and away from the Gironde, the wines of Greysac, La Tour de By, and Patache d'Aux are expertly made year in and year out. Finally, in the town of Potensac, the wine of the same name is superbly made and is still a remarkably good value, notwithstanding the fact that more and more consumers realize that it is the equivalent of a Médoc classified growth.

The wines of the Haut-Médoc and Médoc should be especially sought after in the excellent vintages. In rainy years, most of these proprietors cannot afford to make a severe selection of only the best lots, as can the top classified growths. Consequently, in lesser years, the wines of these properties are more risky. However, in vintages such as 1970, 1975, 1978, 1982, and 1983, the top Cru Bourgeois estates excelled and it is in these years that numerous vinous treasures can be found.

A CONSUMER'S CLASSIFICATION OF THE CHÂTEAUX OF THE HAUT-MÉDOC

VERY GOOD

Chasse-Spleen (Moulis), Sociando-Mallet (Haut-Médoc), Poujeaux (Moulis), Brillette (Moulis), Maucaillou (Moulis), Fourcas-Hosten (Listrac), Camensac (Haut-Médoc), Lanessan (Haut-Medoc)

GOOD

Cissac (Haut-Médoc), Larose-Trintaudon (Haut-Médoc), La Tour-Carnet (Haut-Médoc), Pichon (Haut-Médoc), Coufran (Haut-Médoc), Lamarque (Haut-Médoc), Ramage La Batisse (Haut-Médoc), Verdignan (Haut-Médoc)

AVERAGE

Dutruch-Grand Poujeaux (Moulis), Gressier Grand-Poujeaux (Moulis), Clarke (Listrac), Fourcas-Dupré (Listrac), Lestage (Listrac), Beaumont (Haut-Médoc), Belgrave (Haut-Médoc), Soudars (Haut-Médoc), d'Agassac (Haut-Médoc), Caronne-Ste.-Gemme (Haut-Médoc), Bel-Orme-Tronquoy-de-Lalande (Haut-Médoc), Citran (Haut-Médoc), Peyrabon (Haut-Médoc), Villegeorge (Haut-Médoc)

CHASSE-SPLEEN (Grand Bourgeois Exceptionnel) Moulis — VERY GOOD

Evaluation of present classification: The quality equivalent of a Médoc fifth-growth

An outstanding property, Chasse-Spleen has consistently produced fine wine which for the last three decades has been as good as a fourth- or fifth-growth in Bordeaux's 1855 classification. The wine, even in poor and mediocre vintages, is characterized by a very pronounced, deep ruby color, a bouquet of plummy ripeness, and rich, round, substantial flavors. In style, it tends to resemble a rich, fat, plump style of Margaux, such as Giscours or Siran.

The production at Chasse-Spleen is normally around 18,500 cases in a good, average year, and the vineyard is planted with 50% Cabernet Sauvignon, 40% Merlot, and 10% Petit Verdot. The wine is vinified very traditionally, with only egg white fining used and an adamant policy against filtration being standard procedures here.

The great vintages for Chasse-Spleen, in which the wine can compare favorably with most of the Médoc classified growths, are 1966, 1970, 1975, 1978, 1979, 1982, and 1983.

The 1966, now fully mature, has a splendid bouquet of roasted chestnuts and plummy fruit. The 1970 is just now entering its mature period, and has excellent concentration and depth. The 1975 is a huge wine, massive, full-bodied, extremely concentrated and tannic; it may turn out to be the best wine made at Chasse-Spleen in the last 20 years. The 1978 is more supple and precocious, but loaded with blackcurrant fruit.

More recently, the 1979 is lighter in style and precocious, as is the 1981. Both the rich, chewy, full-flavored, ripe, big-framed 1982, and the large-scaled, alcoholic, and massive 1983 show enormous potential.

In a good to excellent vintage, Chasse-Spleen requires at least 6–8 years to shed its tannic clout, and will have no problem lasting for 10–20 years. Chasse-Spleen is unquestionably one of the top wines of the central Médoc, and frequently represents a splendid value.

SOCIANDO-MALLET (Grand Bourgeois)
Haut-Médoc VERY GOOD

Evaluation of present classification: The quality equivalent of a Médoc fifth-growth

Located in St.-Seurin-de-Cadourne, Sociando-Mallet is making uncompromising wines of extremely high quality that are meant to age and improve for 10 to 20 years. The vineyards are superbly situated overlooking the Gironde, and the style of wine produced here by its meticulous owner, Jean Gautreau, is inky black ruby in color, extremely concentrated, quite full-bodied, and loaded with mouth-puckering tannin. The production has gradually increased to just over 10,000 cases, as Gautreau, since his purchase of the property in 1969, has fervently worked to restore what was then a run-down, poorly kept vineyard. The vineyard, planted with 60% Cabernet Sauvignon, 30% Merlot, and 10% Cabernet Franc, renders a rich, tannic wine, which receives a long sojourn in oak barrels (50% of which are new in each vintage) before bottling.

Sociando-Mallet is easily the equal of most classified growths, and its surging reputation among France's wine connoisseurs has already assured that not much of it is exported. It has become a particular favorite of two of France's greatest temples of cuisine, the Paris restaurants of Taillevent and Robuchon. All of the recent vintages since the mid-'70s have been successful, but the really magnificent wines are the superb

1970, the still backward, powerful 1975, the rich, flavorful, intense 1976 and 1978, the massive, huge, very, very concentrated, great wine Sociando-Mallet produced in 1982, and the excellent 1983. Should consumers have the good fortune to run across a bottle of Sociando-Mallet, one should never hesitate to try it.

POUJEAUX (Grand Bourgeois Exceptionnel) Moulis — VERY GOOD

Evaluation of present classification: The quality equivalent of a Médoc fifth-growth

Château Poujeaux, sometimes referred to as Poujeaux-Theil after its recently deceased owner, Jean Theil, sits close to Chasse-Spleen and makes a similarly rich, rather full-bodied, deeply colored wine which can be consistently counted on for both quality and value. If it does not quite match the brilliance of Chasse-Spleen or Sociando-Mallet, it is not far behind.

Poujeaux's large vineyard of over 120 acres is planted with the following grape varieties: 35% Cabernet Sauvignon, 35% Merlot, 15% Cabernet Franc, and a surprisingly high 15% of Petit Verdot. The wine is consistently well-made as well as fairly priced, and generally is widely available in commercial markets.

Poujeaux's style is typical of the wines of Moulis. It is dark ruby in color, tannic, sometimes astringent and hard, and usually needs a minimum of 6–8 years to soften and mature. It is one of the slowest developing wines of Moulis, yet has the potential to be one of the longest-lived. A splendid bottle of 1928 was served to me in March 1985. The most successful recent vintages include the chunky, fruity, full-bodied 1978, the lighter, yet elegant 1981, the dark, brooding, rich, tannic, superb 1982, and a very good yet backward 1983.

BRILLETTE (Grand Bourgeois) Moulis — VERY GOOD

Evaluation of present classification: The quality equivalent of a Médoc fifth-growth

Just about one kilometer north of the town of Moulis in Medoc is the vast, 374-acre estate of Brillette, which has only 80 acres under vine, producing approximately 9,500 cases. The wines of Brillette are not yet well known, but the quality of winemaking here is very high, and the wines produced are made in a spicy, oaky, richly fruity style that appeals to so many tasters.

Brillette's vineyard is still relatively young, with the great majority of it planted in the early 1960s. The composition of the vineyard is 55% Cabernet Sauvignon, 40% Merlot, and 5% Petit Verdot.

Brillette always seems to possess a good blackcurrant fruitiness and deep dark ruby color. With regard to the recent vintages, particularly the fine 1979, 1981 and truly excellent, richly textured 1982, I have found the wines also characterized by an intense vanillin, oaky character which obviously indicates that a good percentage of new oak barrels are being used for aging the wine.

Both the 1981, which is as good as if not better than many classified growths costing twice the price, and the rich, full-bodied, concentrated 1982 are excellent examples of the high quality wine that can be obtained for a modest price.

I have little experience with older vintages of Brillette, but my reaction to the most recent vintages is that these wines will mature in 4–6 years after the vintage, and hold for another 4–5 years before fading. Brillette is an up-and-coming Moulis estate that is currently making excellent wine.

MAUCAILLOU (Unclassified) Moulis — VERY GOOD

Evaluation of present classification: The quality equivalent of a Médoc fifth-growth

Another of the very fine wines produced in Moulis, Maucaillou is a large property, with a lovely château which today makes over 20,000 cases of wine. The vineyards are planted with 45% Cabernet Sauvignon, 35% Merlot, 15% Cabernet Franc, and 5% Petit Verdot. Since 1921, the wine has been produced and marketed exclusively by the large firm of Dourthe. The style of wine sought seems to put a premium on suppleness and early drinkability. For that reason, Maucaillou is the earliest-maturing wine from Moulis.

In addition to its savory, supple character, the wines of Maucaillou share a spicy, oaky, rather fragrant bouquet, which also develops much faster than other wines of Moulis. In most years, Maucaillou can easily be drunk 3 to 4 years after the vintage, yet will hold together nicely in the bottle for up to 8 years.

The supple, elegant, mature 1978, the lighter, soft, yet deliciously fruity, fragrant and graceful 1979, the fat, intensely fruity and spicy

1982, and the ripe, rich yet tannic 1983 are all serious wines meriting consumer interest. Maucaillou's style reflects the lighter, more precocious style of Moulis wine, but it achieves very good flavor interest and character, and is a wine that should enjoy a great deal of commercial success.

FOURCAS-HOSTEN (Grand Bourgeois Exceptionnel) Listrac VERY GOOD

Evaluation of present classification: The quality equivalent of a Médoc fifth-growth

At present, Fourcas-Hosten is the leading vineyard of Listrac, the commune and town that sits along the major highway, D1, that traverses the central portion of the Médoc. In 1972 Fourcas-Hosten was sold to a syndicate dominated by American investors that began an extensive plan of renovation in both the vineyard and wine cellars. The vineyards have now grown to 96 acres, and their composition is 55% Cabernet Sauvignon, 40% Merlot, and 5% Cabernet Franc. Approximately 8,500 cases of wine are produced here, with most of it sold to England and, not surprisingly, America.

The style of wine of Fourcas-Hosten has changed with the new ownership. The old Fourcas-Hosten wines tended to be hard, tannic, rather robust, coarse wines, with impressive color and body, but often excessive tannins. The best of the old-style Fourcas-Hosten is the 1970, which is a big, rich, generously flavored wine which is just now approaching maturity. Starting with the light vintage of 1973, the wines have taken on a pronounced suppleness and fruitiness, with less abrasive tannins in evidence. The 1975 is perhaps the finest example of the new style Fourcas-Hosten, possessing both rich, deep, blackcurrant fruit, and aging potential of 10–20 years. The 1978 is very drinkable now, quite soft and flavorful, as is the lighter, more delicate 1979. After 1975, the next best vintage will surely be the 1982, which has a rich, glossy, fat texture, oodles of fruit, moderate ripe tannins, and aging potential of at least 10 years. The 1981 is also a noteworthy effort from Fourcas-Hosten, revealing a lovely berry fruitiness and excellent balance.

This is a wine to take note of, as the price has not kept pace with the increased quality.

CAMENSAC (Fifth-Growth) Haut-Médoc VERY GOOD

Evaluation of present classification: Should be maintained

Camensac is among the least known of the 1855 classified growths. No doubt its location well inland and west of St.-Julien in the commune of St.-Laurent explains in part its relative obscurity. In addition, the record of mediocrity, unchanged until the decade of the '70s, certainly added to a general lack of interest. However, things have changed for the better for Camensac.

The dynamic individual behind the revival of Camensac is M. Forner, who purchased the estate in 1965. Forner, who also owns Larose-Trintaudon, a huge St.-Laurent property, and oversees the making of a red wine from Spain's Rioja region called Marqués de Cáceres, believes in progressive, modern vinification techniques that produce a wine that can be drunk young.

With the help of the omnipresent Bordeaux oenologist, Emile Peynaud, Camensac's wines have lightened up in style and emphasize more suppleness and fruit. The production of 18,000 cases comes from a 150-acre vineyard composed of 60% Cabernet Sauvignon, 20% Merlot, and 20% Cabernet Franc.

Camensac is making wines true to its classification, neither above it nor below it. The wines have a St.-Julien-like personality, with good fruit, medium body, and enough tannin to warrant a decade of cellaring in the good vintages. The 1970, now mature, was the first good example of a Peynaud-Forner style of wine. This was followed by an excellent 1975 which is just now beginning to open, but can challenge many a top St.-Julien in this vintage. The 1978 is attractively forward, fruity, and supple, but will age well, and the 1982 is richly concentrated, with plenty of blackcurrant fruit, and an obvious spicy, vanillin oakiness. Camensac is a good fifth-growth.

LANESSAN (Unclassified) Haut-Médoc VERY GOOD

Evaluation of present classification: The quality equivalent of a Médoc fifth-growth

Lanessan is one of the outstanding wines of the Haut-Médoc appellation. The wine could probably be given serious consideration for fifth-growth status should any reclassification of the wines of the Médoc take place.

Lanessan, which is located in Cussac immediately south of the commune of St.-Julien, opposite the big vineyard of Gruaud-Larose, makes intensely flavored wines, with deep color, a robust, large-scaled frame, and chewy texture. If they can be criticized for lacking finesse, they more than compensate for that weakness with rich, gutsy, blackcurrant flavors.

The 106 acres, which are being augmented each year with new plantings, produce in excess of 17,500 cases of wine, which is usually a blend of 70% Cabernet Sauvignon, 25% Merlot, and 5% Cabernet Franc. The property is owned and managed by the Bouteiller family, who also own the famous second-growth Pauillac, Pichon-Longueville Baron, a property which until recently rarely made wines as good as its less highly regarded sibling, Lanessan.

Lanessan ages extremely well, as attested by a delightful but tired 1920 I shared with a friend in 1983. Of more recent vintages, the top successes include the 1975, 1978, and 1982. All three are quite powerful, individualized wines that are somewhat similar in style and character to the fifth-growth Pauillac, Lynch-Bages. Of the three, the 1982 appears to have the greatest concentration and length on the palate. All of these three vintages need at least a full 7–8 years of cellaring to reach their potential.

CISSAC (Grand Bourgeois Exceptionnel) Haut-Médoc GOOD

Evaluation of present classification: Should be maintained

The proprietor of Cissac, Louis Vialard, is one of Bordeaux's most dedicated proprietors. Consequently, his beloved Château Cissac produces one of the best Bourgeois wines of the central Médoc.

Located just north of the town of Cissac, this property produces approximately 14,000 cases of very traditional, full-bodied, tannic, interesting, darkly colored wine from a vineyard planted with 75% Cabernet Sauvignon, 20% Merlot, and 5% Petit Verdot. Normally unyielding and reserved when young, Cissac begins to show its true character at around age 8, and can easily age and improve in the bottle for 10–15 years.

The wine of Cissac is especially popular in England, and seems to have a growing popularity among American connoisseurs who have the patience to wait for its slow but sure evolution.

In looking at the recent vintages, the 1971, 1973, and 1976 are all fully mature, but not quite up to the high standards set by Vialard for

Cissac. However, the 1970 is very good and now drinking nicely. The 1975 is still stubbornly backward and youthful, but loaded with potential, as well as oodles of blackcurrant fruit. The 1978 is equally successful but differently styled, more supple, fruity, and precocious. The 1979 is good but not exciting, the 1981 is tannic, austere, and perhaps too lean, and the 1982 is quite rich, full-bodied, powerful, and clearly the most promising Cissac since 1975.

Cissac is one of the best-made Bourgeois wines, and merits considerable attention from enthusiasts of Bordeaux.

LAROSE-TRINTAUDON (Grand Bourgeois)
Haut-Médoc GOOD

Evaluation of present classification: The quality equivalent of a Grand Bourgeois Exceptionnel

The same Forner family that rejuvenated the Cru Classé Camensac also owns Larose-Trintaudon. After purchasing this property in St.-Laurent, extensive replantings of the vineyard took place, as well as improvements to the winery.

Larose-Trintaudon now has an enormous production by Médoc standards. Over 65,000 cases of wine from its huge vineyard holdings of just under 400 acres are produced each year. The vineyard is planted with 60% Cabernet Sauvignon, 20% Cabernet Franc, and 20% Merlot.

The style of wine produced at Larose-Trintaudon has proved to be an immensely popular one. Silky, supple, blackcurrant flavors intermingled with aromas of vanillin oakiness, medium body, and light tannins are all telltale characteristics of the wine of Larose-Trintaudon. Made to be drunk young, preferably within 6 to 8 years of the vintage, the wines of Larose-Trintaudon have proved in good vintages that they can also age for at least a decade. As this young vineyard gets older, the quality of wine should get even better.

The 1975 and 1978 are two vintages that can be drunk now, but will continue to age and improve gracefully for at least another 4–5 years. The 1976, 1979, and 1981 are very pleasant, supple, charming, lighter-styled wines which are cleanly made and easy to drink. More recently, both the 1982 and 1983 look to be real winners. The 1982 is surprisingly powerful and rich for a Larose-Trintaudon and quite well made. It will certainly age well for at least 10 years. The 1983 is less powerful, but quite well made.

LA TOUR-CARNET (Fourth-Growth) Haut-Médoc GOOD

Evaluation of present classification: Should be downgraded to a Grand Bourgeois Exceptionnel

La Tour-Carnet is also located in St.-Laurent, and despite its inclusion in the 1855 classification, it too has remained largely anonymous. This beautiful property has been restored completely, and boasts a real moated medieval castle which alone makes it unique in the Médoc. The wine suffered considerably from, I suspect, extensive replanting in the '60s. Certainly the 1970, 1971, and 1976 proved to be thin, rather bland, uninteresting wines that were hardly worthy of the estate's classification. The 1975 is good, rather than special, the 1978 and 1979 are slightly herbaceous and stalky, but the 1982 and 1983 are very promising. It is these two latter vintages that I believe will make many observers begin to once again take La Tour-Carnet seriously. Based on this property's performance to date, it does not merit its fourth-growth classification, as the quality of the wine is no better than a Grand Bourgeois Exceptionnel.

The vineyard of 80 acres is planted with the following varieties: 53% Cabernet Sauvignon, 33% Merlot, 10% Cabernet Franc, and 4% Petit Verdot. The current production is 16,000 cases.

PICHON (Unclassified) Haut-Médoc GOOD

Evaluation of present classification: The quality equivalent of a Médoc Grand Bourgeois Exceptionnel

An up-and-coming star in the southernmost portion of the Médoc in the town of Parempuyre, Pichon is one of the most beautiful châteaux, as well as one of the first vineyards tourists encounter as they head north from the city of Bordeaux. The wealthy Bordeaux contractor, Clément Fayat, a man passionate about making excellent wine as witnessed by the top-flight wine made at his St.-Emilion estate, La Dominique, had to replant Pichon and spend considerable sums of money modernizing the estate. The first three vintages, 1981, 1982, and 1983, are surprisingly good, and each vintage has been stronger as the vines get older.

Pichon's wine, which is made by one of Bordeaux's brilliant new oenologists, Michel Rolland, is quite supple, rich, concentrated, moderately tannic, and deeply colored. Château Pichon, because of both the financial commitment by its owner, and because its winemaking is meticulously looked after by one of the best oenologists of Bordeaux, is a new name to watch for high-quality wines. The production is currently 2,500 cases, and the price is moderate.

COUFRAN (Grand Bourgeois) Haut-Médoc GOOD

Evaluation of present classification: Should be maintained

The wines of Coufran, an estate located in St.-Seurin-de-Cadourne, have long enjoyed a good reputation for their fleshy, forward, fruity, supple character. The proprietor, Jean Miailhe, has chosen to plant his 150 acres of vineyards that produce 25,000 cases of wine on an average, with 85% Merlot, 10% Cabernet Sauvignon, and 5% Petit Verdot. The abnormally high percentage of Merlot is unusual for the Médoc and accounts for this wine's telltale richly fruity, precocious personality.

I have generally found Coufran's wines to be quite loosely knit and sometimes diluted in character which to me suggests overcropping. Fruity and soft they were, but many vintages like 1971, 1976 and 1980 tasted like Bordeaux Beaujolais. However, the 1981 is above average in quality, and the 1982 certainly the best Coufran I have ever tasted. Nineteen eighty-two was a great year for many properties, but it was a superb year for the Merlot grape. With Coufran's high percentage of Merlot, it is not surprising that the wine is so successful in this vintage. The 1983 is also a very good Coufran, so perhaps this estate is beginning to show more consistency than it has in the past.

Coufran is best drunk within 5–6 years of a vintage although in the top vintages such as 1970, 1975, and 1982, it can last for 10 years or more; however, in most vintages Coufran has rarely had the stamina and depth for prolonged cellaring.

LAMARQUE (Grand Bourgeois) Haut-Médoc GOOD

Evaluation of present classification: Should be maintained

One of the outstanding medieval fortress castles in the Bordeaux region, Lamarque, named after the town of the same name, sits just off the main Route du Vin (D2) of the Médoc directly on the road to the ferry boat that traverses the Gironde to Blaye.

The entire vineyard has been reconstituted since the early '60s and is planted with 50% Cabernet Sauvignon, 25% Merlot, 20% Cabernet Franc, and 5% Petit Verdot. The production from the 124 acres is approximately 25,000 cases, and the wine is widely seen in the export channels.

Lamarque is a typically good, middle-weight, central Médoc wine. It seems to have a touch of the St.-Julien elegance mixed with round, supple, soft, ripe fruity flavors. The owners, the Gromand family, make the wine with great care. Certain vintages, for example, the luscious, rich, fully mature 1970, powerful, tannic 1975, and supple 1978, are wines well worth searching out for the consumer who wants high quality for modest prices.

Both the 1981 and 1982 were successes at Lamarque, yet curiously, they taste slightly softer than the wines produced in 1970, 1975, and 1978. Lamarque is usually quite drinkable within 5 years after the vintage, but in the best vintages the wine will age gracefully to 8–10 years without any difficulty.

RAMAGE LA BATISSE (Bourgeois) Haut-Médoc — GOOD

Evaluation of present classification: The quality equivalent of a Médoc Grand Bourgeois

The vineyards of Ramage La Batisse are located in St. Saveur, a small wine-producing region which sits well inland to the west of the commune of Pauillac. The vineyard has been completely replanted since 1961 and the production is now in excess of 20,000 cases. The wines from the late '70s, particularly the 1978 and 1979, were very impressive, supple, oaky, richly fruity wines of real style and character. The 1980 was also a notable success in this mediocre vintage. However, both the 1981 and 1982 seemed inexplicably unimpressive. Both of these two recent vintages tasted quite tannic, lean, austere, with perhaps too much oakiness in the bouquet and flavor. Nevertheless this is a well-run modern property which can normally be counted on to produce good wines at fair prices. Most vintages of Ramage La Batisse drink best between 5 and 10 years of age.

VERDIGNAN (Grand Bourgeois) Haut-Médoc — GOOD

Evaluation of present classification: Should be maintained

Another one of the solidly run properties that are located in and around the northern Médoc village of St.-Suveur-de-Cadourne, Verdignan is owned and managed by the well-known Miailhe family. A large property of 116 acres, Verdignan produces in excess of 25,000 cases from a blend of 60% Cabernet Sauvignon, 35% Merlot, and 5% Cabernet Franc.

A wine that I have consistently enjoyed, it is ripe, supple, richly fruity, and possesses a powerful blackcurrant aroma. Verdignan is usually a wine to drink between 5 and 8 years after the vintage.

In recent years, the wine seems to have gotten measurably richer and more distinctive. The 1978 drinks as well today as it did in 1980. The 1981 is charming and elegant, but the two powerhouse Verdignans are the 1982 and 1983.

The 1982 is almost black purple in color, with a very rich, dense concentration of fruit, full body, supple, long-lasting flavors and 5 to 8 years of positive development ahead of it. The 1983 is equally good, even more supple, and intensely packed with blackcurrant fruit.

Verdignan is a very satisfying and enjoyable wine that is ideal for those who do not have the patience to wait 10 or 15 years for a wine to reach maturity.

DUTRUCH-GRAND POUJEAUX
(Grand Bourgeois Exceptionnel) Moulis — AVERAGE

Evaluation of present classification: Should remain the same

Very little of this wine seems to be exported, as I have only encountered it in restaurants in France. While my experience with it is limited, the modest vineyard of just over 60 acres produces around 10,000 cases of what I find to be a rather backward, stubborn, hard wine which seems to have an excess of tannin. The hard 1970, very tannic and severe 1975, and rather coarse 1978 seem to be wines more notable for their roughness on the palate than for their finesse and rich, fleshy fruit.

GRESSIER GRAND-POUJEAUX
(Unclassified) Moulis — AVERAGE

Evaluation of present classification: The quality equivalent of a Grand Bourgeois

Gressier Grand-Poujeaux is the smallest of the Moulis properties with Poujeaux as part of their name. On just under 40 acres of vineyard, Gressier produces 5,000 cases of wine that has a reputation for being more supple and fruity than Dutruch-Grand Poujeaux, and significantly lighter than Poujeaux. The wine is rarely exported, and I have no more recent tasting notes than the 1961, which is excellent, and the 1970, which was pleasant and somewhat charming in 1976, but hardly exciting. Certainly the label of Gressier may be its most noticeable characteristic. It resembles the label of the well-known Listrac estate of Fourcas-Hosten, only it has added a coat of arms which many would no doubt find in poor taste.

CLARKE (Cru Bourgeois) Listrac — AVERAGE

Evaluation of present classification: The quality equivalent of a Grand Bourgeois

One of the most remarkable and newsworthy recent developments in the Médoc has been the complete restoration and rejuvenation of the old vineyard of Château Clarke, which has a history dating back to 1750. It took the considerable resources of a wealthy member of the famous Rothschild family, Baron Edmond de Rothschild, to resurrect this property. In 1973 the work began, and in the following 5 years the area under vine increased dramatically to 346 acres, which has the potential to produce over 25,000 cases of wine. The present composition of the vineyard is 49% Cabernet Sauvignon, 37% Merlot, 10% Cabernet Franc, and 4% Petit Verdot. The first wines released, a 1978 and 1979, were given a great deal of hoopla from the wine press, but in actuality they were rather light, medium-bodied wines, which clearly tasted like the product of a young vineyard. However, the commitment to high quality, the financial resources, and the management are all present, so as the vineyard matures, Château Clarke has the potential to become one of the best wines made in Listrac. Certainly, the stylish, elegant, supple 1981 showed more character than either the 1978 or 1979, and the 1982 should prove to be the best wine yet from the dynamic Baron Edmond de Rothschild. The 1983 is also promising, but very, very tannic, and clearly a wine for long-term cellaring or, as the French say, a "*vin de garde*." The promise is here, but unfortunately the Rothschild name has meant that the price is at present higher than the quality.

FOURCAS-DUPRÉ (Grand Bourgeois Exceptionnel) Listrac — AVERAGE

Evaluation of present classification: Should be maintained

Fourcas-Dupré is located directly on the main route (D1) to Lesparre, and it makes a good Listrac wine that, while never as exciting as the best vintages of Fourcas-Hosten, or as loaded with potential as Clarke, nevertheless is sound and consistent.

The jovial Guy Pagés is the manager and part owner of Fourcas-Dupré, and he has actively promoted this inexpensive, well-made wine. The wine, made from a blend of 50% Cabernet, 38% Merlot, 10% Cabernet Franc, and 2% Petit Verdot, is usually at its best 4 to 6 years after a vintage. It is at this time that Fourcas-Dupré usually displays a light-intensity, cedary, spicy bouquet, and moderately intense, somewhat tightly knit flavors. It is never a particularly fragrant wine, nor does it have a great deal of richness. However, it is a typical central Médoc, a touch austere and lean, but reliable and sturdy. The best recent vintages have been the fine 1982, an even better 1978, and the very good 1975. Among these three, I have to give the nod to the 1978 which has an extra measure of richness and charm, and gets my vote as the best Fourcas-Dupré in the last 15 years.

LESTAGE (Cru Bourgeois) Listrac — AVERAGE

Evaluation of present classification: Should be maintained

Lestage produces very fruity, supple, straightforward wine from its 136 acres of vineyards just northwest of the village of Moulis in Médoc. Made from 58% Merlot, 38% Cabernet Sauvignon, and 4% Petit Verdot, Lestage is a wine to drink within the first 5 to 7 years after the vintage, as it rarely has the tannin to warrant further aging. The 1982 is the most recent vintage worthy of serious interest, as it is a darkly colored, fat, fruity wine, with a glossy, velvety texture, not much complexity, but quite satisfying. The owner of Lestage, the Chanfreau family, also owns another historic property, Château Fonréaud, whose wines are lighter and less interesting than those of Lestage.

BEAUMONT (Grand Bourgeois) Haut-Médoc — AVERAGE

Evaluation of present classification: Should be maintained

One of the most important Bourgeois estates of the central Médoc, Beaumont is located just to the southwest of the small town of Cussac, which sits right on the D2 or the Médoc Route du Vin.

I have very fond memories of the 1975 Beaumont, a wine of depth, dimension, and complexity that is just now reaching its apogee. The man who was responsible for this wine, M. Bolivar, died in 1978 and his widow sold the property to Bernard Soulas, who has augmented the vineyards considerably and renovated the wine cellars. The first vintages I tried, the 1979 and 1981, were slightly herbaceous and definitely lighter in style and texture than the wines made by Soulas's predecessor. The 1982 shows more depth, fruit, and character, but is made in a very quick-maturing, soft, commercial style. However, it is the best Beaumont since the 1975.

Beaumont is a wine to drink young, preferably within 5 to 6 years of the vintage. It is an ideal wine for restaurants who want a good estate-bottled Bordeaux on their wine list at a reasonable price and which can be drunk immediately upon release.

The production of Beaumont is approximately 13,500 cases in a good year, and it is made from 56% Cabernet Sauvignon, 36% Merlot, and the balance, Cabernet Franc and Petit Verdot.

BELGRAVE (Fifth-Growth) Haut-Médoc AVERAGE

Evaluation of present classification: Should be downgraded to a Grand Bourgeois

Classified a fifth-growth in 1855, Belgrave's wines have been consistently mediocre over the last several decades. They have rarely been even equal in quality to the better Crus Bourgeois. This, however, should change as a new ownership took over Belgrave in 1980 and invested considerable sums of money in the new wine cellars and vineyards. Bordeaux wine observers are optimistic that this infusion of much-needed capital and talent will resurrect Belgrave to the original position of respect it had in 1855.

The vineyard of 110 acres produces just over 25,000 cases of wine from the following grape varieties: 40% Cabernet Sauvignon, 35% Merlot, 20% Cabernet Franc, and 5% Petit Verdot.

The style aimed for by the new owners is a fruity, supple, early-maturing wine. So far, the results have been mixed. The 1982 is the best vintage for the "new" Belgrave, fruity, supple, with good concentration, and an 8- to 10-year life span. The 1983 is disappointing, thin, light, and lacking richness and depth.

Belgrave, located in St.-Laurent just slightly to the west of the St.-Julien vineyards of Lagrange, has promise, but as yet this potential has not been realized.

SOUDARS (Bourgeois) Haut-Médoc AVERAGE

Evaluation of present classification: The quality equivalent of a Médoc Grand Bourgeois

A relatively new estate in the St.-Seurin-de-Cadourne, Soudars is sure to establish a good reputation for well-colored, rich, flavorful, tannic wines.

This young, small vineyard of 34 acres, planted with 55% Cabernet Sauvignon and 45% Merlot, is run by M. Eric Miailhe. The two most recent vintages I tasted both showed very good concentration of fruit, and rich, ripe flavors. The 1982 is lovely to drink now, supple, fruity, smooth, and quite charming. The 1983 is even better, fat, ripe, round, and very flavorful. It, like the 1982, should be drunk within 5 to 6 years of the vintage. As this vineyard gets older, one suspects the name Soudars will become much better known.

D'AGASSAC (Grand Bourgeois Exceptionnel) Haut-Médoc AVERAGE

Evaluation of present classification: Should be downgraded to a Grand Bourgeois

Located in Ludon, the very southern part of the Haut-Médoc, the lovely, moated, medieval Château d'Agassac belongs to the Capbern-Gasqueton family who own and manage several other Médoc properties, the two most famous being the classified growths, du Tertre in Margaux and Calon-Ségur in St.-Estèphe.

Until recently I have always found the wines of d'Agassac to be very light, almost innocuous and bland for a Médoc. In some vintages, the wine can have a fragrant bouquet, but rarely does d'Agassac produce more than a sound, light, soft, fruity wine.

Traditionally made, the wine was highly regarded in the 19th century, given the number of awards it received. Nothing but organic fertilizer is used on the vineyard, which is planted in equal proportions of Cabernet Sauvignon, Merlot, and Cabernet Franc.

While vintages in the late '70s seemed unusually uninspired, the first several vintages of the '80s, particularly the 1982 and 1983, offer encouraging enough evidence for some observers to begin once again to sing the praises of d'Agassac. Certainly, the coincidental reemergence of Capbern-Gasqueton's other two major properties, du Tertre in 1978 and Calon-Ségur in 1982, may signal that Philippe Capbern-Gasqueton is now in complete control of his family's estates.

CARONNE-STE.-GEMME (Grand Bourgeois Exceptionnel) Haut-Médoc

AVERAGE

Evaluation of present classification: Should be downgraded to a Grand Bourgeois

This little-seen estate in St.-Laurent gets little publicity these days. For both tourists and writers desiring to visit it, the property is virtually impossible to find on the back roads of the Médoc. The wine is hardly an inspiring gustatory pleasure. My limited experience with this wine has found it to be generally dark in color, with surprisingly little bouquet, a solid, rather rustic, almost coarse taste, and an excess of tannin. The wine in vintages such as 1975, 1978, and 1981 is very austere and tannic, and seems to taste like a high percentage of Cabernet Sauvignon is used in the blend. In practice, the estate tries to make a wine from a blend of 67% Cabernet Sauvignon, 30% Merlot, and 3% Petit Verdot, so the wine should be more supple. The best vintage of Caronne-Ste.-Gemme that I have tasted is the 1982, which is a powerful, big, and fortunately richly fruity wine that begs for 5 to 8 years of cellaring.

BEL-ORME-TRONQUOY-DE-LALANDE (Grand Bourgeois) Haut-Médoc

AVERAGE

Evaluation of present classification: Should be maintained

A highly respected property in the northern reaches of the Haut-Médoc, Bel-Orme-Tronquoy-de-Lalande has a solid reputation for producing one of the most tannic and long-lived Bourgeois wines.

Owned and managed by the Quié family who also own the two Crus Classés, Rauzan-Gassies in Margaux and Croizet-Bages in Pauillac, Bel-Orme is made in such a backward style that I have often dismissed it as lacking fruit when young, only to be pleasantly surprised when it is 10 or 15 years old.

Certainly the 1945, drunk on New Year's Day, 1985, was in remarkably good health and held its own against many much more famous wines in a 1945 tasting I attended that day. Other notes of mine showed that a 1962 tasted in 1979 was also impressive. Therefore, it is with some trepidation that I share my notes which found the 1975, 1978 and

1979 Bel-Orme wines to be unyielding and terribly tannic. Perhaps these wines will need several decades to reveal their true character.

This traditionally run property produces approximately 10,500 cases of wine from a rather atypical blend of 30% Cabernet Sauvignon, 30% Cabernet Franc, 30% Merlot, and 10% Petit Verdot.

CITRAN (Grand Bourgeois Exceptionnel) Haut-Médoc

AVERAGE

Evaluation of present classification: Should be downgraded to a Cru Bourgeois

Citran is a very large estate in the southern part of the Haut-Médoc. It is located inland and west of the commune of Margaux. The vineyard, planted with 60% Cabernet Sauvignon and 40% Merlot, produces in excess of 25,000 cases of a wine that is highly promoted. The wine has a good reputation; however, I have found it to be overrated. Often dilute and diffuse, overcropping, and I suspect an overzealous reliance on filtering equipment, seems to give Citran an emaciated taste and texture. The last interesting vintage was 1970, which I suspect is now in decline. Other vintages of Citran, particularly the 1975, 1978, 1981, and 1982, have been quite mediocre, lacking in both style and richness.

At present, this is a wine on the decline that is living off a past reputation.

PEYRABON (Grand Bourgeois) Haut-Médoc

AVERAGE

Evaluation of present classification: Should be downgraded to a Cru Bourgeois

Peyrabon, in St.-Sauveur, is a wine which has rarely come my way. The production in a good, average year is largely exported to the Benelux countries, Germany, and Switzerland.

The vineyard of 168 acres produces approximately 14,000 cases of soft, supple, fruity wine, from 50% Cabernet Sauvignon, 27% Merlot, and 23% Cabernet Franc.

The only vintages I have tasted include a round, harmonious, fruity 1975, and an even more supple, ripe, fresh, charming 1978.

VILLEGEORGE (Not Classified) Haut-Médoc

AVERAGE

Evaluation: The quality equivalent of a Cru Bourgeois

The property of Lucien Lurton, the proprietor of two famous Margaux châteaux, Brane-Cantenac and Durfort-Vivens, Villegeorge is located in the southern Médoc commune of Avensan.

The vineyard encompasses almost 40 acres, and is planted with 60% Merlot, 30% Cabernet Sauvignon, and 10% Cabernet Franc.

The wine apparently has a good reputation in Europe, but up until the promising 1983 vintage, I have found the wines of Villegeorge to be quite mediocre. The 1978 has good color, but a lean, hard, herbaceous personality. In 1980 the tannin totally overwhelmed the meager fruit. The 1981 is spicy, but very astringent and a little hollow. The 1982 is charming, fruity, but light and shallow for the vintage. The 1983 is generously fruity, supple, spicy, with good concentration, and an easy-going, supple, smooth texture. It will drink well over the next 5 years.

Villegeorge is a well-situated property which, aside from a good 1983, has a track record of mediocrity.

A CONSUMER'S CLASSIFICATION OF THE CHÂTEAUX OF THE MÉDOC

VERY GOOD

Potensac

GOOD

Greysac
Loudenne
La Tour St.-Bonnet
La Tour de By
St.-Bonnet
Patache d'Aux

AVERAGE

La Cardonne
Les Ormes-Sorbet
Le Boscq

POTENSAC (Grand Bourgeois) — VERY GOOD

Evaluation of present classification: The quality equivalent of a Médoc fifth-growth

Potensac, located in the village of the same name, is, at the moment, the top wine with a Médoc appellation. Potensac, in recent vintages such as 1978, 1982, and 1983, can challenge many a classified-growth estate in quality. Since its price is modest, Potensac represents a great Bordeaux bargain.

Potensac is owned and managed by Michel Delon, whose considerable winemaking talents include making the wine at the great St.-Julien estate, Léoville-Las Cases. It is not surprising to find that the wine of Potensac has more than a coincidental resemblance to that of Léoville-Las Cases. Very dark in color, rich, full-bodied, and tannic, Potensac is a serious wine meant for aging. The production of Potensac has crept up to almost 30,000 cases, as Delon and his staff have expanded the vineyard to 124 acres. The grape varieties planted at Potensac are 55% Cabernet Sauvignon, 25% Merlot, and 20% Cabernet Franc.

Recent vintages of Potensac have shown enormous potential, a result of brilliant winemaking. The 1983 is excellent, rich, firm, deep, and a likely candidate for 10 years of positive development in the bottle. The 1982 is a superb wine by any standards. Extremely rich and concentrated, with a wonderful bouquet of blackcurrants and spicy oak, it will last for 20 years. The 1981 is lighter, but elegant and charming, and the 1978 is very, very good.

Unquestionably, Potensac belongs in any serious Bordeaux enthusiast's wine collection.

GREYSAC (Grand Bourgeois) GOOD

Evaluation of present classification: The quality equivalent of a Grand Bourgeois Exceptionnel

In recent years, Greysac has become one of the most popular Bourgeois wines in the United States. High quality and the dynamic personality and marketing ability of its recently deceased proprietor, the gregarious Baron François de Gunzburg, were totally responsible for this wine's acceptance by Americans, normally so label and classification conscious when it comes to wine.

Greysac is one of several well-run properties in the Bédagan region of the northern Médoc. The vineyards here have been expanded considerably to the present limit of 150 acres. The grape varieties planted are 50% Cabernet Sauvignon, 38% Merlot, 10% Cabernet Franc, and 2% Petit Verdot.

The style of wine at Greysac is one that I have always found very elegant, smooth, medium-bodied, with a complex bouquet filled with currant fruit, and a true, mineral, soil-like aroma. Never an aggressive or overly tannic wine, Greysac is usually fully mature by its sixth or seventh year, and keeps well for up to 12 years.

There have been some splendid successes at Greysac in the '70s. The 1975, while still not fully mature, is my favorite wine from this estate. Rich, full-bodied, complex, and powerful, it is an excellent example of a Bourgeois wine. The 1976 is drinking beautifully now, supple, sweet and ripe, yet well balanced, it is better than many classified growths in this vintage. The 1978 is also ready to drink, but will hold until 1986 or so. Supple, ripe, and soft, it is very tasty. The 1979 is a favorite, elegant, complex, and richly flavored, it is a medium-weight wine, with a good 10-year life span.

For whatever reasons, the vintages of the early '80s, 1981, 1982, and 1983, seem to be less successful, but still good wines. 1982 looks to be the best of this trio, but I can't help wondering if the failing health of the late Baron, plus the expanded production at Greysac, have caused quality to slip a bit this decade.

LOUDENNE (Grand Bourgeois) GOOD

Evaluation of present classification: The quality equivalent of a Grand Bourgeois Exceptionnel

I suspect it is very difficult for many wine writers to write totally objectively about Loudenne because so many of us owe so much in gratitude to the late Martin Bamford, the energetic, meticulous, and dynamic gentleman of taste and refinement who made Loudenne the showpiece château of the northern Médoc. Martin Bamford died tragically on September 24, 1982, at the age of 42. However, his legacy was one that will not be easily erased. In addition to upgrading the quality of Loudenne's red wine, Martin Bamford introduced modern technology at Loudenne, which was especially instrumental in making the white wine of Loudenne one of the best dry wines of the Médoc.

The red wine, which is supple, elegant, fragrant, and complex, is produced from 53% Cabernet Sauvignon, 40% Merlot, and 7% Cabernet Franc. I usually find the red Loudenne to be at its peak by age 6 or 7, but with surprising holding power. The best recent vintages for the red wine of Loudenne are the 1978 and 1982. Both vintages produced rich, nicely concentrated wines that are supple, elegant, and have at least a 10-year life span.

The white wine of Loudenne resembles a good white Graves, only less oaky, remarkably fresh and elegant, and always a little lighter than a Graves. Produced from 50% Sauvignon Blanc and 50% Semillon, it is an extremely attractive, dry, fresh, crisp wine, which is ideal as an *apéritif* or complementary beverage for fish or fowl dishes. The last three vintages, 1981, 1982, and 1983, have all been very successful for this wine.

LA TOUR ST.-BONNET (Bourgeois) GOOD

Evaluation of present classification: The quality equivalent of a Grand Bourgeois Exceptionnel

The wines of this estate in St.-Christoly have yet to become well known in America, but I have found the quality to be quite good. The price is also very reasonable.

The vineyard of 100 acres is well situated on a gravel ridge adjacent to the Gironde River. The style of wine produced is deeply colored, firm, tannic, full-bodied, and usually quite concentrated. It is not a supple or early-maturing wine, but a wine which is best at ages 6–8 years, though it will keep for over a decade. Of recent vintages, the 1975 is a classic, rich, multidimensional, and very long on the palate. The 1976 is above average in quality, the 1978 very good, and the 1982 the best vintage produced so far in the decade of the '80s.

La Tour St.-Bonnet produces serious, traditionally made Bordeaux that scores high on a price/quality scale of judgment.

LA TOUR DE BY (Grand Bourgeois) GOOD

Evaluation of present classification: The quality equivalent of a Grand Bourgeois Exceptionnel

Located in Bédagan, La Tour de By produces drinkable, flavorful, solid wines, with good color, and 8–10 years' aging potential in the best vintages.

The proprietor, Marc Pagés, makes his 30,000 cases of wine in a good yielding year from 150 acres of gravelly soil near the Gironde, planted with 65% Cabernet Sauvignon, 33% Merlot, and 2% Cabernet Franc. La Tour de By's only flaw is its noticeable lack of a rich, fragrant bouquet. Even the older vintages seem to be unyielding in bouquet. Nevertheless, the wine always has plenty of flavor, although vintages from 1976 onward seem lighter and more supple. La Tour de By made outstanding wine in 1970 and 1975. Both wines are just beginning to open up and develop. The 1978, 1979, 1981, and 1982 are well above average, well-colored, fruity wines, with firm backbones, and 5 to 8 years of life ahead of them. Of this quartet, I would opt for the fat, fruity, rich 1982 if I were to choose just one for drinking circa 1988.

Like other good estates in the Bédagan region of the Bas-Médoc, La Tour de By is quite a good value.

ST.-BONNET (Bourgeois) GOOD

Evaluation of present classification: The quality equivalent of a Grand Bourgeois

A modestly sized vineyard of 80 acres in St.-Christoly, St.-Bonnet's wines are rarely seen in America. However, based on the excellent quality of the two vintages I have tasted, the rich, full-bodied, large-scaled 1982, and equally impressive 1983, this is an estate capable of producing quite rich and concentrated wines full of flavor. M. Solivères is the proprietor, and he lists the production in a good year at 23,000 cases. St.-Bonnet's wines look to be real winners, so this is a name to watch in the future. I shall look forward to tasting more vintages of St.-Bonnet.

PATACHE D'AUX (Grand Bourgeois) GOOD

Evaluation of present classification: Should be maintained

An important estate in Bédagan, but at the moment eclipsed in quality by the wines produced at the neighboring Greysac and La Tour de By, Patache d'Aux makes solid, firm, somewhat one-dimensional wines. The vineyard is planted with 70% Cabernet Sauvignon, 20% Merlot, and 10% Cabernet Franc. The production from the estate's 94 acres totals 25,000 cases.

Of recent vintages, the 1975, 1976, 1978, and 1979 are very acceptable, yet somewhat bland. The 1981 is meagerly endowed; however, the 1982 is a very rich, flavorful wine, and certainly the best example of Patache d'Aux I have encountered. It should have a cellar life of at least 8–10 years. The 1983 also looks to be quite good, so if Patache d'Aux's record in the '70s was uninspiring, the wines made in 1982 and 1983 hopefully portend a new, higher level of quality.

LA CARDONNE (Grand Bourgeois) AVERAGE

Evaluation of present classification: Should be maintained

Immense optimism sprung forth in 1973 when the Rothschild family (owners of Lafite-Rothschild and Duhart-Milon) acquired this property in Blaignan. Significant investments were made in expanding the vineyards and renovating the wine cellars.

In spite of all the investment, the wines have continued to be rather bland and uninteresting. Palatable, clean, and technically correct they are, but these wines lack character, richness, and flavor. Overcropping and a heavy reliance on filtering machines seem probable causes for the lack of character to date.

LES ORMES-SORBET (Grand Bourgeois) AVERAGE

Evaluation of present classification: Should be maintained

Les Ormes-Sorbet, in the sleepy town of Couqueques, makes one-dimensional, solid, deeply colored wine, which lacks both finesse and richness, but is pleasant and generally cleanly made. I have found the vintages of the '70s, particularly the 1975, 1976, and 1978, to be more flavorful than the recent vintages of 1979, 1980, and 1981. Both the 1979 and the 1981 had a distinctive herbal character, and lean, tannic, ungenerous flavors. The 1982 is more promising, and may signal that the 1979–1981 period of mediocrity has passed quickly.

Les Ormes-Sorbet produces 11,500 cases of wine from 50 acres of vineyard planted with 55% Cabernet Sauvignon, 35% Merlot, 5% Cabernet Franc, and 5% Petit Verdot.

LE BOSCQ (Bourgeois) AVERAGE

Evaluation of present classification: Should be maintained

Another reliable wine from the village of St.-Christoly, Le Boscq is made by the Lapalu family at their château in Bédagan, Patache d'Aux.

Le Boscq is a wine dominated by the Cabernet Sauvignon grape. The two vintages I have tasted were both impressive examples of a Bourgeois wine. Both the rich, intense, supple 1982 and the equally rich but more tannic 1983 will reward the shrewd consumer who has the good fortune to purchase this reasonably priced wine and cellar it for 4–5 years.

THE RED AND WHITE WINES OF GRAVES

The history of wine production in Bordeaux has recorded that it was the wines of Graves that were the first Bordeaux wines to be made and exported. Barrels of Graves wine were shipped to England during the English reign over this region of France between 1152 and 1453. Even the Americans, led by the multi-talented Thomas Jefferson in 1785, were great enthusiasts of the wines of Graves.

Times have changed, and no wine-producing region in Bordeaux has lost more ground, literally and figuratively, than the region of Graves.

The region of Graves, which gets its name from the gravelly soil, a vestige of Ice Age glaciers, is totally different from the other wine regions of Bordeaux. It begins in what most tourists would think is still the city of Bordeaux, but which is actually the congested southern suburbs of Bordeaux known as Talence and Pessac, two high-rise, modern, heavily populated centers of middle-class Bordelais and University of Bordeaux students. The major vineyards in the Pessac and Talence areas happen to be the best in the Graves region, but since the last century they have had to fight off both urban sprawl and blight. A visit to these "suburban" vineyards will offer a noisy contrast to one's visit to the tranquil, quiet, pastoral settings of the vineyards in the Médoc, Pomerol, and St.-Emilion.

Heading south from Talence and Pessac for the better part of 20 kilometers are the other widely scattered vineyards of Graves. The region, once past the commercial suburb of Gradignan, does become pastoral and rural, with vineyards intermingled with pine forests and small farms. The two southern areas of Graves that produce the best wine are Léognan and Martillac, two small bucolic towns that seem much further away from the bustling city of Bordeaux than they actually are.

The entire Graves region is famous for both red and white wines. The top white wines of this region are rare and expensive, and in a few cases, capable of rivaling the finest white wines produced in France. They are produced from two basic grape varieties, the Sauvignon Blanc and Semillon. However, the greatest wines of Graves are its red wines. Graves' most famous estate, the American-owned Château Haut-Brion in the northern suburb of Pessac, was the first great wine of Bordeaux to get international recognition. It was referred to in 1663 by the English author Samuel Pepys and between 1785 and 1789 by America's Thomas Jefferson. The international acclaim for the wines of Haut-Brion no doubt was the reason why this property was the only non-Médoc to be included in the 1855 classification of the wines of the Médoc. Along with Haut-Brion, the other great red wines produced in Graves are Haut-Brion's cross-street rival, La Mission-Haut-Brion, and the great estate in the southern Léognan region, the curiously named Domaine de Chevalier.

There are other fine Graves wines, most notably Pape-Clément in Pessac, La Tour-Haut-Brion in Talence, and Haut-Bailly in Léognan, but the overall level of quality winemaking, looked at from a consumer's perspective, is not as high as in such Médoc communes as St.-Julien, Pauillac, and St.-Estèphe.

The wines of Graves, like the Médoc, have their own quality classification. It too falsely serves as a quality guide to unsuspecting wine enthusiasts. The first classification occurred in 1953, and the most recent classification in 1959. The 1959 classification (see pages 487–88) listed 13 châteaux producing red wine with Haut-Brion appearing first, and the remaining 12 listed alphabetically. For the white wine producers (often the same châteaux), there were 8 châteaux listed in alphabetical order, with Haut-Brion's minuscule production of white wine originally excluded, but it was added to this list in 1980.

For the great red wines of Graves, their personality traits are quite individualistic and unique, and not difficult to decipher when tasted blind in a tasting with Médoc wines. While top wines such as Haut-Brion and La Mission-Haut-Brion differ considerably in style, they do share a rich, earthy, almost tobacco-scented character, which seems to taste like a blend of a great St.-Emilion from the *graves* section of that appellation, and a great Pauillac, with a toasted, smoky component added for additional complexity.

This particular personality trait of Graves red wines reaches its most intense level in the wines of Haut-Brion and La Mission-Haut-Brion, the two internationally recognized superstars of this appellation, yet these wines cannot be more dissimilar.

Like two hostile championship fighters staring each other down before a match, La Mission-Haut-Brion and Haut-Brion face each other across Route NP650. Neither the proprietors nor winemakers of each

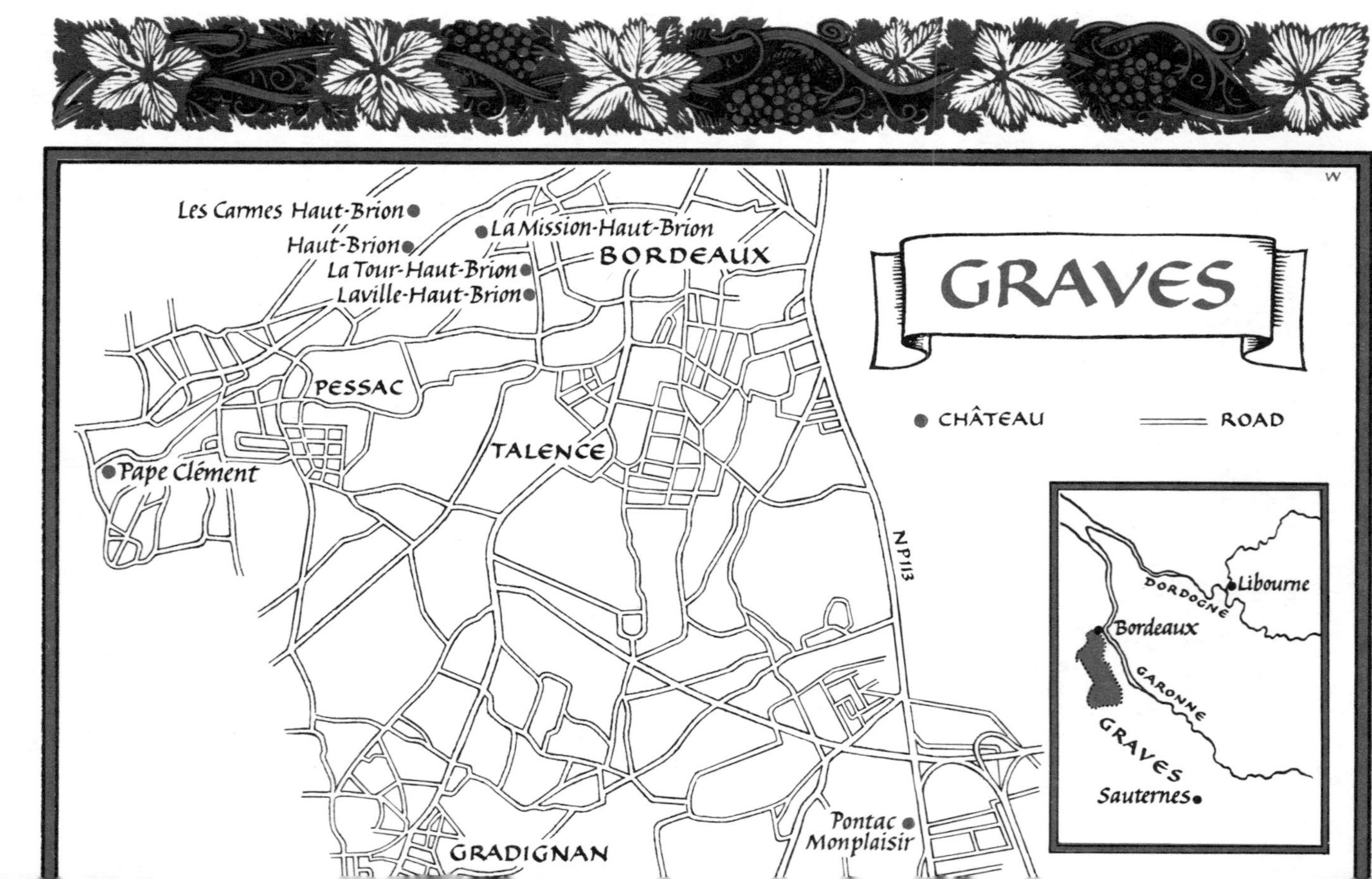
GRAVES
CHÂTEAU
ROAD
Les Carmes Haut-Brion
Haut-Brion
La Mission-Haut-Brion
La Tour-Haut-Brion
Laville-Haut-Brion
BORDEAUX
PESSAC
TALENCE
Pape Clément
NP113
Pontac Monplaisir
GRADIGNAN
Libourne
DORDOGNE
Bordeaux
GARONNE
GRAVES
Sauternes

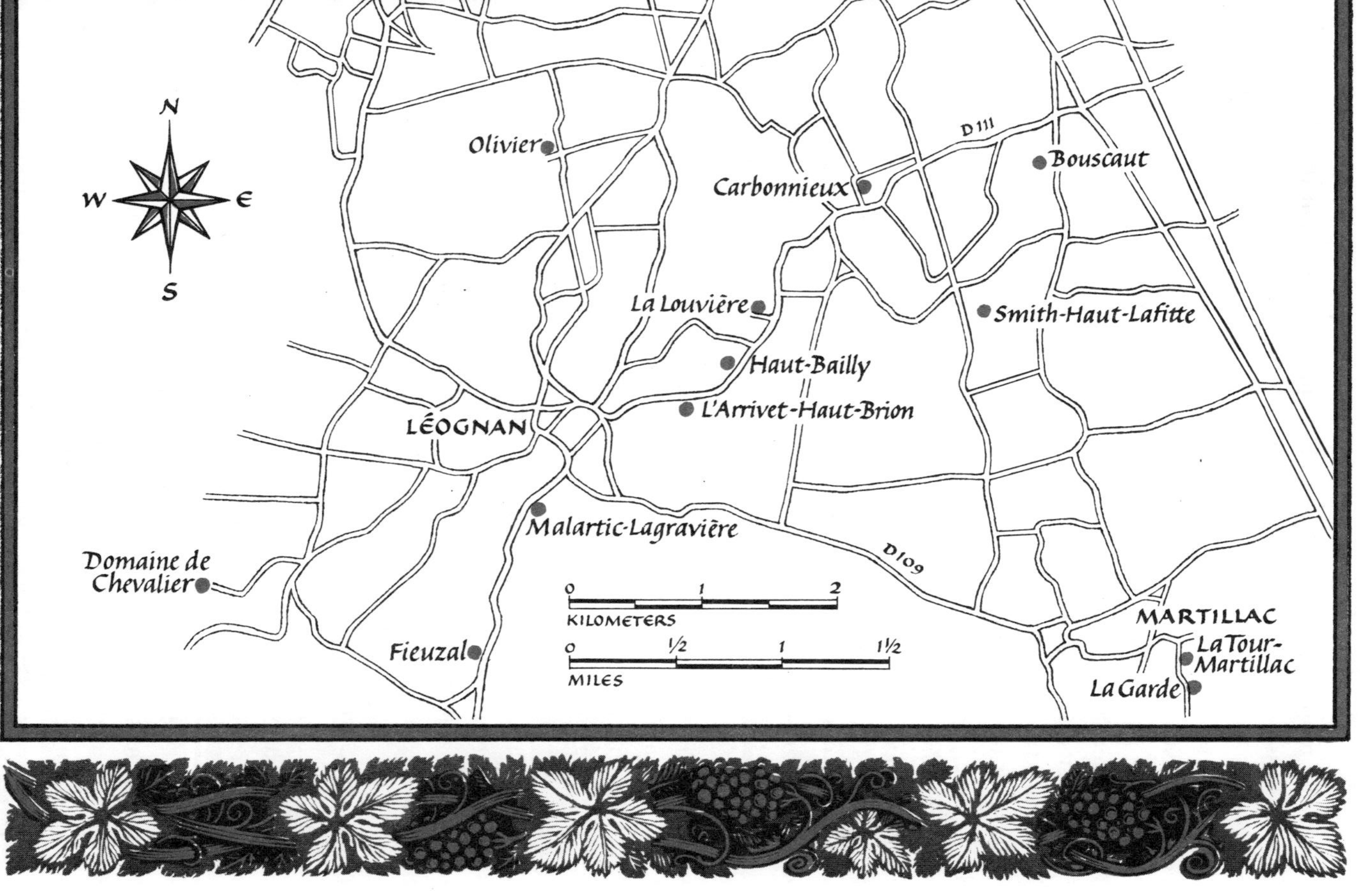
N
W
E
S
Olivier
D111
Bouscaut
Carbonnieux
La Louvière
Smith-Haut-Lafitte
Haut-Bailly
L'Arrivet-Haut-Brion
LÉOGNAN
Malartic-Lagravière
D109
Domaine de Chevalier
0 1 2
KILOMETERS
0 1/2 1 1 1/2
MILES
Fieuzal
MARTILLAC
La Tour-Martillac
La Garde

respective property ever had many kind things to say about the other, the La Mission winemaking team calling Haut-Brion's wine too light, overpriced, and overmanipulated, the Haut-Brion team accusing La Mission of making overly big, alcoholic, sometimes volatile wines that lacked finesse. This long-standing dispute came to an end in 1983 when Haut-Brion purchased La Mission, but the truth is that both properties produce great wine, but very different wine.

La Mission-Haut-Brion is certainly a bigger, richer, more deeply colored wine than Haut-Brion. It has also been one of Bordeaux's most successful wines in mediocre to poor vintages. The 1957, 1958, 1960, 1967, 1972, 1974, and 1977 are vivid proof of that fact. When mature, it has the classic Graves bouquet of tobacco and earthy, mineral scents. Haut-Brion is noticeably lighter, particularly in the period 1966–1976, but before and after this period Haut-Brion has been a textbook Graves, still lighter than La Mission, often marked by the scent of new oak, but remarkably complex and rich.

No other Graves wine from the Pessac or Talence areas comes close to matching these two great wines unless you consider the second wines of both properties, the Bahans-Haut-Brion and La Tour-Haut-Brion (actually a separate estate, but in practice the second wine of La Mission).

Pape-Clément in Pessac has afforded me some superb wines, but at present this property is in a slump that is reflected by some rather uninspired wines from recent vintages.

Once away from the overly noisy, traffic-laden roads of Pessac and Talence, the Graves region takes on more charm. This is the southern Graves and the wines are less earthy, less smoky and tobacco-scented than the Graves from Pessac and Talence. They are also lighter. Léognan is the heart and center for the best southern Graves. The tiny Domaine de Chevalier, a relatively obscure vineyard hidden by thick forests, performs splendidly well, making minuscule quantities of outstanding white Graves and moderate quantities of a smooth, very flavorful rich and complex red wine. Domaine de Chevalier is a connoisseur's favorite the world over.

Nearby is Haut-Bailly. Haut-Bailly produces an intensely fruity Graves wine that is usually ready to drink within 5–7 years of the vintage. Some of this château's wines can be long-lived, but this is one wine for which patience is not required.

There are of course numerous other Graves wines, yet most of the other classified growths making red wine tend to produce light, rather one-dimensional wines that can be satisfying but will rarely offer much excitement. The reds of Carbonnieux, Malartic-Lagravière, and Smith-

Haut-Lafitte would fit this mold nicely. De Fieuzal and Bouscaut are more interesting and to my taste have the potential to be higher-quality wines.

Among the Cru Bourgeois properties of Graves, La Louvière is clearly the best and in the vintages since 1978 frequently better than many of the more famous Graves. I recommend it enthusiastically. Les Carmes Haut-Brion in Pessac, Larrivet-Haut-Brion in Léognan, Pontac-Monplaisir in Villenave-D'Ornon, and Pique-Caillou in Merignac are all capable of producing light but complex, savory Graves wines.

Graves is one region to look carefully at when Bordeaux has a mediocre or poor vintage. The drainage is excellent here and in years like 1974, 1964 and 1958, when the wines of the Médoc were generally diluted and disappointing, properties like La Mission-Haut-Brion, Domaine de Chevalier and Haut-Brion produced excellent wines from healthy, fully mature grapes. Recent outstanding vintages for Graves have been 1982, 1979, 1978, 1971, 1970, 1964, and 1961.

A CONSUMER'S CLASSIFICATION OF THE RED WINE PRODUCING CHÂTEAUX OF GRAVES

OUTSTANDING

La Mission-Haut-Brion
Haut-Brion

EXCELLENT

La Tour-Haut-Brion

VERY GOOD

Domaine de Chevalier, Haut-Bailly, Pape-Clément, La Louvière

AVERAGE

Bouscaut, de Fieuzal, Malartic-Lagravière, Smith-Haut-Lafitte, Carbonnieux, La Tour-Martillac, Olivier

LA MISSION-HAUT-BRION (Cru Classé) OUTSTANDING

Production: 5,000 cases

Grape varieties:
Cabernet Sauvignon—60%
Merlot—35%
Cabernet Franc—5%

Time spent in barrels: 20 months

Average age of vines: 29 years

Evaluation of present classification: Should be upgraded to a first-growth

La Mission-Haut-Brion in Talence is one of the greatest wines in the entire Bordeaux region. This estate sits across the road from its long-time rival, Haut-Brion, and has a record of virtually unmatched brilliance that predates the scope of this book by a good 40 years.

The Woltner family, particularly the late Frederic and his son Henri, were responsible for the ascendancy of La Mission-Haut-Brion's wine quality to a level that matched and frequently surpassed the first-growths of the Médoc and neighboring Haut-Brion.

Woltner's genius was widely recognized in Bordeaux. He was known as a gifted taster and oenologist, and was a pioneer in installing easy-to-clean, metal, glass-lined fermentation tanks in 1926, which even today are among the most unusual looking in all of Bordeaux. Many observers attribute the dense, rich, powerful, fruity character of La Mission to these short, squat vats which, because of their shape, tend to increase the grape skin-to-juice contact during the fermentation.

La Mission-Haut-Brion's style of wine has always been one of intense richness, full body, great color and extract, and plenty of tannin. I have had the pleasure of tasting all of the best vintages of La Mission back to 1921, and it is a wine that can easily last 30 or 40 years in the bottle. It has always been a much richer and more powerful wine than its arch rival, Haut-Brion, and for that reason, plus its remarkable consistency in poor and mediocre vintages (along with Latour in Pauillac, it has the best record in Bordeaux for good wines in poor vintages), La Mission has over the years become a more popular wine than Haut-Brion.

Henri Woltner passed away in 1974, and until the sale of La Mission-Haut-Brion to the present owners of Haut-Brion in 1983, La Mission was managed by Françoise and Francis Dewavrin-Woltner. Internal family bickering over the administration of this property ultimately led to the sale of La Mission and its two sister properties, La Tour-Haut-Brion and the white-wine-producing estate of Laville-Haut-Brion.

The speculation now is how many changes in winemaking will be made by the staff at Haut-Brion. There is no doubt that the philosophy of winemaking and their techniques are quite different. Most observers seem to share the view that La Mission will change in style, but not quality, starting with the 1983 vintage.

La Mission is a true first-growth in quality if not in name, and this fact is reflected in the prices fetched for the wine, which are very, very close to those of the Médoc first-growth châteaux.

VINTAGES

1983—The first La Mission-Haut-Brion produced under the manage-
· ment of Haut-Brion, the 1983 will represent a change in style
88 from previous wines of La Mission. Very dark colored, quite spicy, with the scent of vanillin, this medium- to full-bodied wine has plenty of tannin, a more austere structure than usual, and a good, solid finish. It is a very good, potentially excellent La Mission. Anticipated maturity: 1996–2000. Last tasted, 3/85.

1982—A monumental bottle, unbelievably black/purple in color, with a
· huge and enormous feel on the palate, with rich, spicy, very fat,
95 tannic flavors, this full-bodied wine will need plenty of time. Anticipated maturity: 1994–2015. Last tasted, 1/85.

1981—The 1981 is a big, ruby/purple, densely colored wine, with layers
· and layers of cassis fruit. Some prominent vanillin notes emerge
90 as a result of aging in new oak barrels. Fairly full-bodied, yet not nearly as powerful as the 1982, the 1981 should require 8–10 years of cellaring. Anticipated maturity: 1991–2000. Last tasted, 10/84.

1979—The 1979 is one of the few vintages in the '70s in which I find La
· Mission to be less successful than its neighbor, Château Haut-
88 Brion. Nevertheless, in this bountiful year, La Mission made a wonderfully elegant, surprisingly concentrated wine which resembles in style the 1971. While it lacks the extraordinary depth and complexity that La Mission is capable of achieving in great years like 1982 or 1978, the 1979 is still a very fine wine, with a life expectancy of 15 years. Anticipated maturity: 1990–2005. Last tasted, 1/85.

1978—One of the great wines of this vintage, this is the best La Mission
· of the '70s after the 1975. Quite full and concentrated, with a
94 very rich, gravelly-scented bouquet, full body, layers and layers of cassis, fruity flavors, and a superb finish, this big, powerful wine will need 5 more years of cellaring. Anticipated maturity: 1990–2010. Last tasted, 12/84.

1977—One of the modest successes of the vintage, La Mission-Haut-
· Brion's 1977 is surprisingly well colored, has a herbaceous, ce-
80 dary, spicy bouquet, medium body, and rather good, supple, ripe flavors that finish a little short, but are satisfying. Drink over the next 5 years. Last tasted, 3/84.

1976—One of the most disappointing La Mission Haut-Brions of the
· '70s, the 1976 looked prematurely brown when only 4 years old,
74 and has continued to lose its ruby color at an accelerated pace.

Rather diffuse and watery on the palate for La Mission, this medium-bodied wine has an earthy, spicy, burnt aroma, and flabby flavors. Drink up. Last tasted, 6/82.

1975—A monumental and magnificent bottle of a wine that is certainly
· one of the very greatest young wines I have ever tasted. Cer-
100 tainly this wine has it all. Very dark ruby, it has a sensational bouquet of cassis, cedary, iron-like mineral scents, and smoky oak. Very concentrated, rich and deep, this exceptional wine needs another decade of cellaring to develop further. It is a perfect wine, and is arguably the best La Mission since 1929. Anticipated maturity: 1990–2025. Last tasted, 12/84.

1974—A mediocre year for all regions of Bordeaux, but for La Mission
· an unqualified success. The 1974 is unquestionably the top wine
88 of the vintage. La Mission succeeded in utilizing its close proximity to the University of Bordeaux to obtain hundreds of student pickers to gather in the grapes prior to the deluge which drowned the prospects for an excellent vintage at other châteaux. While most 1974s are ready to drink now, La Mission needs another 5–8 years of cellaring. Dark ruby, with a beautiful, full-intensity bouquet of mineral scents, blackcurrants, and earthy, smoky scents. It is rich, fully-flavored wine, with a good measure of tannin. Anticipated maturity: 1989–2000. Last tasted, 12/84.

1973—A very poor La Mission-Haut-Brion, watery, light, flabby, and
· loosely knit, this wine is in serious decline, and should be drunk
60 immediately. Last tasted, 2/79.

1971—The 1971 is a wonderfully delicious La Mission that is now ap-
· proaching its apogee. An unqualified success for this variable
89 vintage, La Mission is dark ruby (darker than most 1971s), with a medium to full intensity, spicy, earthy, cigar box, iron-like aroma, and full, rich, moderately intense, soft, generous flavors. It will hold for another 5–10 years, but is best drunk while waiting for the really big La Missions like 1970, 1975, and 1978 to develop. Anticipated maturity: 1986–1992. Last tasted, 1/85.

1970—One of the great attributes of La Mission is its consistency from
· bottle to bottle in a given vintage. For some reason, 1970 seems
92 to be a vintage that produced some significant bottle variation. I have had bottles with very prominent volatile acidity, which suggests a growing danger to the wine's health. However, other bottles are pure, richly fruity, massively concentrated, and years away from maturity. I am convinced that there must have

been a problem with at least one vat of this wine, but the château has consistently denied any "variation" or volatile acidity problems with this vintage. The good bottles are great wines in the making, full, rich, deep, spicy, quite full-bodied, and very tannic. The score reflects the good bottles, which I have tasted considerably more times than the bad ones. Anticipated maturity: 1990–2005. Last tasted, 12/84.

1967—Still holding its fruit, the 1967 La Mission has been fully mature
· since the mid-1970s. Medium to dark ruby, with some amber
85 edges, the 1967 has a very spicy, earthy, tobacco-scented bouquet, and soft, supple, very attractive flavors. Holding this wine any longer will be tempting fate, so drink it up. Last tasted: 3/82.

1966—Considered by most authorities as a classic vintage for La
· Mission-Haut-Brion, I have always admired this wine, but gen-
91 erally have found the 1964 La Mission to be even better. This is certainly the minority point of view. The 1966 is still not fully mature, although it is currently displaying a complex, cedary tobacco-scented aroma, some interesting herbaceous elements, and full, rich, firm flavors which are still held together by tight acidity and plenty of tannin. An excellent, but for me not a great, La Mission. Anticipated maturity: 1986–1995. Last tasted, 10/84.

1964—Curiously overlooked when great La Missions are discussed,
· 1964 was another variable year throughout Bordeaux, with the
93 fall rains washing out many of the famous vineyards, particularly in the Médoc. The 1964 is a big, powerful, rich, tannic La Mission, with an enormous concentration of fruit, and full-intensity, spicy, cedary, earthy bouquet. Along with Pétrus and Cheval Blanc, it is one of the three best wines of the vintage. Drink over the next 10 years. Last tasted, 12/84.

1962—Unquestionably a very good La Mission, but given the vintage
· and usual brilliance of La Mission, it is not as special a wine as
85 it could have been. Medium weight, with a moderately intense, berryish, earthy bouquet, soft, nicely concentrated flavors, and supple finish, the 1962 should be drunk over the next 4–5 years. Last tasted, 9/83.

1961—The 1961 is an extraordinary wine, with a fabulous bouquet of
· huge, spicy, tobacco, cedary, blackcurrant scents. Full-bodied,
96 with viscous, rich, highly concentrated flavors, this big, fleshy wine seems capable of another 10–20 years of longevity. The

bouquet suggests an approaching maturity, but there is plenty of tannin to go along with the great depth of fruit. La Mission's 1961 is a big, mouth-filling wine which is certainly one of the 10 best wines of the vintage. It can be drunk with great enthusiasm now, but should peak in 4–8 years. Anticipated maturity: 1987–2010. Last tasted, 12/83.

HAUT-BRION (First-Growth) OUTSTANDING

Production: 12,000–15,000 cases	Grape varieties: Cabernet Sauvignon—55% Merlot—25% Cabernet Franc—20%
Time spent in barrels: 24–26 months	Average age of vines: 30 years
Evaluation of present classification: Should be maintained	

Haut-Brion, the only non-Médoc estate to be included in the famous 1855 classification of the wines of the Médoc, was, in the 17th century, Bordeaux's first internationally acclaimed winemaking estate.

Located in the bustling commercial suburb of Pessac, Haut-Brion is the only first-growth to be American-owned. The Dillon family purchased Haut-Brion in 1935 in a very poor condition, and invested considerable sums of money in the vineyards and wine cellars. This lovely property is now one of the showpiece estates of Graves.

The making of wine at Haut-Brion is expertly managed by the articulate Jean Delmas, who believes fervently in a rather hot, short fermentation. As Bordeaux wines go these days, Haut-Brion is kept a rather long time in new oak barrels. It is often the last château to bottle its wine.

The style of wine at Haut-Brion has changed. The magnificently rich, earthy, almost sweet wines of the '50s and early '60s gave way in the period 1966–1974 to a lighter, leaner, easygoing, somewhat simplistic style of claret that lacked the richness and depth one expects from a first-growth. Whether this was intentional, or just a period in which Haut-Brion was in a bit of a slump, remains a mystery. I know personally that the staff at Haut-Brion remain quick-tempered and sensitive about such a charge. Starting with the 1975 vintage, the wines have again taken on more of the customary earthy richness and concentration that previously existed in the pre-1966 era, and today Haut-Brion is undoubtedly making wine that merits its first-growth status, particularly the wines from 1978 onward, which consistently have been among the finest wines produced in those vintages.

Certainly, the wines of Haut-Brion and La Mission-Haut-Brion offer a dramatic contrast in styles. La Mission is deeper in color, richer, and more powerful, while Haut-Brion is lighter, less tannic, and to some people's taste, more elegant and balanced.

Haut-Brion produces a wine under a secondary label called Bahans-Haut-Brion. It is a wine that I have found to be quite supple and delicious, but little is exported to America.

VINTAGES

1983—Haut-Brion's 1983 is a very good, perhaps excellent wine which has an impressive depth, rich, soft, fat, lush fruit, a good measure of tannin in the finish, but is overall forward, ripe, and voluptuous. It is not as rich and multidimensional as the 1982, but clearly superior to the 1981. Anticipated maturity: 1992–2005. Last tasted, 3/85.
·
88

1982—The best Haut-Brion since the magnificent 1959, this very darkly colored wine has a gorgeous bouquet of ripe fruit and vanillin oakiness. On the palate, the wine is unctuous, with layers and layers of fruit, full body, moderate tannins, and astonishing length. Approachable now, it would still be infanticide to drink it before 1992. Anticipated maturity: 1995–2015. Last tasted, 1/85.
·
96

1981—My notes on the 1981 Haut-Brion are terribly inconsistent. From the cask on three occasions, I found it to be mediocre. From the bottle, it has varied from moderately rich, overtly oaky and tannic, to quite tannic, angular, and lean. The rating reflects its better showings. Anticipated maturity: 1990–2000. Last tasted, 1/85.
·
84

1979—One of the very best wines of the vintage, the 1979 Haut-Brion continues to develop splendidly in the bottle, although it remains a good decade away from maturity. It is very dark in color, with a closed, but very complex bouquet of ripe fruit, tobacco, and mineral, earthy scents. Rich, ripe, medium- to full-bodied, and extremely well structured, this is a wine that seems to balance power and elegance, richness and harmony perfectly. Anticipated maturity: 1992–2005. Last tasted, 12/84.
·
90

1978—The 1978 is a seductively rich, very fruity, well-colored Haut-
· Brion that is presently more accessible than the 1979, no doubt
90 due to its very ripe fruit and lower acidity level. A young but complex bouquet of very ripe fruit and oak shows enormous potential. On the palate, the wine is supple, round and very generous, creating a misleading impression that it will mature early. However, there is plenty of tannin in the finish. A very impressive Haut-Brion. Anticipated maturity: 1990–2000. Last tasted, 6/84.

1977—Haut-Brion was clearly outperformed by its neighbor, La Mis-
· sion-Haut-Brion, in this poor vintage. Medium ruby, with an
74 aromatic, spicy, somewhat vegetal aroma, and lightish flavors with some harshness in the finish, this wine is best drunk up over the next 5 years. Last tasted, 9/83.

1976—Medium ruby in color, with some amber creeping in at the
· edges, the 1976 Haut-Brion is fully mature. A spicy, earthy,
84 oaky, moderately fruity bouquet offers elegance. On the palate, the wine is very soft, round, medium-bodied, and quite charming. Drink over the next 5 years. Last tasted, 3/83.

1975—Surprisingly forward and mature-looking for a 1975, this wine
· has a full-blown "burnt wax," tobacco-scented bouquet, round,
86 alcoholic, relatively rich, deep flavors, and a long finish. Full-bodied and not very tannic, this very interesting wine should be drunk over the next 5–8 years. Last tasted, 5/84.

1974—Given the vintage, the Haut-Brion could be considered a modest
· success. Now fully mature and a bit short in fruit, this wine has
76 an open-knit, spicy, earthy bouquet, somewhat angular, medium-bodied flavors, and a short finish. Drink up. Last tasted, 3/79.

1971—For me, the 1971 is the best Haut-Brion produced between 1966
· and 1975, a point the château will not argue. This fully mature
88 1971 has a sumptuous, sweet, ripe, earthy, richly fruity flavor, medium to full body, a big, full-intensity, spicy bouquet, and silky, supple texture. Very stylish, and very delicious, this wine should be drunk over the next 4–5 years. Last tasted, 4/82.

1970—This is a good Haut-Brion, but in the context of the vintage, and
· the fact that so many châteaux in Graves made excellent wine
83 in 1970, it is a disappointment. Surprisingly compact, medium-bodied, and not nearly as concentrated or as rich as it should be, this tannic, rather lean Haut-Brion may turn itself around in

time, but I am doubtful. Anticipated maturity: 1985–1990. Last tasted, 4/81.

1966—At its apogee, the 1966 Haut-Brion has an attractive, earthy,
· moderately intense, fruity bouquet. In weight and richness, it is
86 medium-weight and bordering on being too lean and light. It is a satisfying, lighter-styled Haut-Brion which is quite attractive, but not really of first-growth proportions. Drink over the next 5–8 years. Last tasted, 11/84.

1964—Nineteen hundred sixty-four, while a mixed vintage for the wines
· of the Médoc as a result of many properties being caught by the
90 heavy rains, was a very good year for the Graves châteaux. Haut-Brion's 1964 is fully mature, and has a splendidly rich, earthy, tobacco- and mineral-scented bouquet. Ripe, deep, supple, voluptuous flavors are present on the palate. This full-bodied wine should be drunk over the next 5–7 years. Last tasted, 4/83.

1962—Another smashingly delicious wine from Haut-Brion, the 1962 is
· fully mature and not likely to hold its intensity of rich, earthy,
88 spicy fruit for much longer. However, for the lucky few who own a bottle of this wine, it is quite soft and round, with an opulent richness that resembles a Pomerol. Drink up. Last tasted, 1/81.

1961—This is a great Haut-Brion, but it is eclipsed in my view by its
· predecessor, the 1959, and more recently by the monumental
93 1982. Not as dark colored as many 1961s, with surprisingly more amber/brown at the edge, this rich, luxurious wine has an intense, earthy, ripe, cedary, spicy bouquet. On the palate, the wine has excellent intensity of fruit, a long, rich, alcoholic finish, and chewy texture. Fully mature for the last 5–7 years, this wine will drink well for at least 5 more years. Last tasted, 12/83.

LA TOUR-HAUT-BRION (Cru Classé) EXCELLENT

Production: 3,000 cases	Grape varieties: Cabernet Sauvignon—60% Merlot—35% Cabernet Franc—5%
Time spent in barrels: 24 months	Average age of vines: 29 years

Evaluation of present classification: The quality equivalent of a third-growth

La Tour-Haut-Brion, while a separate vineyard and château, was, until 1983, owned by the Woltner family, who also owned La Mission-Haut-Brion. In 1983 these two properties, plus the white-wine-producing Woltner property Laville-Haut-Brion, were sold to the American owners of Haut-Brion.

The wines of La Tour-Haut-Brion up to 1983 were vinified at La Mission-Haut-Brion and handled identically. After both wines were completely finished with the secondary or malolactic fermentation, a selection process was made in which the most promising barrels were chosen for the wine of La Mission-Haut-Brion, and the others reserved for La Tour-Haut-Brion. In vintages such as 1982 and 1975, the difference in quality between these two wines was very negligible. To give La Tour-Haut-Brion its unique personality, the wine has added to it more of the black/purple-colored, very tannic, press wine than La Mission-Haut-Brion. This makes La Tour-Haut-Brion a wine with more size, tannin, color and grip than even La Mission-Haut-Brion. While all of this is likely to change under the new ownership, this is how La Tour-Haut-Brion was produced until 1983. In effect, it is the second wine of La Mission-Haut-Brion, but the extra measure of tannin and color given it has always made it a fuller, coarser, more rustic wine than La Mission-Haut-Brion.

The addition of press wine has resulted in most vintages of La Tour-Haut-Brion being very slow to evolve. In a few vintages, notably 1973 and 1976, the wine incredibly turned out better than its more famous sibling.

VINTAGES

1983—A potentially good La Tour-Haut-Brion, but lighter and more supple in texture than previous vintages of this wine, the 1983 is
· 84
a product of the different approach to winemaking employed by the staff at Haut-Brion who controlled the vinification for the first time in this vintage. Good medium to dark ruby color, spicy, soft, supple, and very approachable, this wine should mature fairly quickly. Anticipated maturity: 1990–1996. Last tasted, 3/85.

1982—Deep ruby black in color, with a very intense blackcurrant, tarry, earthy bouquet, the 1982 La Tour-Haut-Brion is a great
· 94
success. Rather massive on the palate, with great depth and concentration, full body, significant tannin content, and excep-

tional length, grip, and richness, this is a bigger, more tannic wine than its more famous sibling, La Mission-Haut-Brion. It is a great success in this vintage. Anticipated maturity: 1996–2015. Last tasted, 2/85.

1981—The 1981 La Tour-Haut-Brion is a robust, aggressive, rather
· tannic wine, with plenty of power and guts, but lacking finesse.
85 The color is impressively dark, the weight of fruit and body on the palate considerable, but this is not a wine for Bordeaux enthusiasts who want immediate gratification. Anticipated maturity: 1991–2005. Last tasted, 12/84.

1980—Rather light, slightly bitter and underendowed, the 1980 La
· Tour-Haut-Brion has a smoky, earthy, interesting bouquet,
75 straightforward flavors, and should be drunk over the next 3 years. Last tasted, 4/83.

1979—Somewhat similar in style to the 1981, only less tannic, more
· open-knit and fruity, yet darkly colored, the 1979 La Tour-Haut-
85 Brion has a spicy bouquet, good weight, richness, medium to full body, and length on the palate. The bouquet is beginning to mature, revealing earthy, Graves, smoky, mineral scents. This is an attractively forward La Tour-Haut-Brion that can be drunk now but will be better in 1988. Last tasted, 10/84.

1978—After the great 1975 La Tour-Haut-Brion, the 1978 is certainly
· the best wine from this property in the decade of the '70s. Very
89 dark ruby, with a rich, ripe blackcurrant, earthy, spicy, tarry bouquet of excellent intensity and penetration. On the palate, the wine is quite full-bodied, aggressively tannic, rich, slightly low in acidity, but immensely satisfying. It is just beginning to open up and develop. Anticipated maturity: 1988–2005. Last tasted, 9/84.

1976—Clearly better than the diffuse and diluted La Mission-Haut-
· Brion, yet really not very deep or complex for La Tour-Haut-
80 Brion, this fully mature wine has an open-knit, smoky, earthy bouquet, soft, rather diffuse flavors, medium to full body, and a short, rather coarse finish. Drink over the next 4 years. Last tasted, 10/80.

1975—By far the greatest La Tour-Haut-Brion I have ever tasted, this
· magnificent wine has a bouquet of great penetration, revealing
96 intense, spicy, chocolatey, earthy, tobacco aromas. In the mouth, this big, ripe, rich wine explodes with layers and layers of fruit. Quite full-bodied, with enormous potential, this is a

monumental wine which will not be fully mature until 1995 or later. Anticipated maturity: 1995–2020. Last tasted, 5/84.

1974—Like its sister château, La Mission, La Tour-Haut-Brion is an
· unqualified success for the vintage. Beginning to reach its apo-
83 gee, this wine is a robust, somewhat rustic, unpolished, rich, hefty wine that lacks finesse but delivers plenty of punch and taste. Medium- to full-bodied, with good concentration, this wine should be drunk over the next 4–5 years. Last tasted, 7/82.

1971—More firm and tough than La Mission, with perhaps a little too
· much tannin and acidity for its own good, the 1971 La Tour-
84 Haut-Brion is now approaching maturity. A textbook, mineral-scented, burnt tobacco bouquet offers a lot of interest. On the palate, the wine is medium- to full-bodied, a trifle austere and hard, but big and robust. Drink over the next 6 years. Last tasted, 2/83.

1970—Still impenetrably closed, broodingly dark in color, with little
· sign of maturity, this big, robust, hefty wine has tremendous
86 power and weight, but borders on being too tannic and a trifle overdone. Certainly, fanciers of massive, tannic wines will want to have some of this wine in their collection. Anticipated maturity: 1992–2020. Last tasted, 10/83.

1966—Fully mature, with the telltale dark ruby, dense color of La Tour-
· Haut-Brion, punctuated only slightly by amber, this big, rich,
88 spicy wine has a voluptuous bouquet of rich fruit, and earthy, tobacco aromas. On the palate, it is less massive than some La Tour-Haut-Brions, but has more finesse and overall balance. It is a very attractive Graves. Drink over the next 6–8 years. Last tasted, 3/81.

1961—Only tasted once, the 1961 La Tour-Haut-Brion showed remark-
· able concentration and richness, and seemed to have a full 20
95 years of life ahead of it. Very dark in color, with just a touch of amber, this big, chewy, viscous wine had an opulent and exotic bouquet of ripe currants, cinnamon, tobacco, and truffles. Massively proportioned, with layers of fruit and oodles of tannin still present, the 1961 La Tour-Haut-Brion was a gustatory *tour de force*. Anticipated maturity: 1990–2030. Last tasted, 3/79.

DOMAINE DE CHEVALIER (Cru Classé) VERY GOOD

Production: 5,000 cases	Grape varieties: Cabernet Sauvignon—65% Merlot—30% Cabernet Franc—5%
Time spent in barrels: 20–24 months	Average age of vines: 17 years
Evaluation of present classification: The quality equivalent of a third-growth	

The tiny estate of Domaine de Chevalier, tucked away in the midst of a forest on the southwest outskirts of Léognan, is a true connoisseur's wine. The production is tiny, the wines highly sought after, and most important, the quality very, very high.

Although the estate was recently sold, the man who is still responsible for these hand-crafted, expertly made wines is Claude Ricard. The wines of Domaine de Chevalier do not resemble the intense, rich, earthy style of Graves best exemplified by Haut-Brion and La Mission-Haut-Brion. They possess a subtle, mineral, earthy aspect, but are generally lighter in body and more Médoc-like in style than the Graves wines from Pessac and Talence. An important trend to watch is what I perceive to be a conscious effort to produce a bigger, more fiercely tannic style of wine. This is a common personality trait of the 1981, 1982, and 1983 wines, which are all noticeably harder and oakier than previous vintages. Domaine de Chevalier can be surprisingly good in off-vintages for Bordeaux (note the 1974, 1977, and 1980), and of course produces a glorious white wine which is reviewed later in this chapter. Until the recent trend to make longer-lived wines began, most vintages of Domaine de Chevalier were fully mature by age 7, and in decline by the time they were 15 years old.

Domaine de Chevalier is an expensive wine as a result of its lofty reputation and small production.

VINTAGES

1983—Typically hard, tough, and tannic, the 1983 Domaine de Chevalier was quite unyielding on each of the occasions I tasted it
·
86 from the cask. Rather classically proportioned, with a very good concentration of fruit, a very firm structure, and medium to full body, this is a wine that will require a good decade more of cellaring. Anticipated maturity: 1996–2006. Last tasted, 1/85.

1982—Here is a wine that showed very good potential from the cask,
· but was always uncommonly hard, tannic, and unyielding. From
90 the bottle, however, the incredible intensity of fruit and depth can now be ascertained, and this wine has jumped from very good to one of the great wines of the vintage. Still very tannic, the 1982 Domaine de Chevalier will require extended cellaring, but this wine, from one of Bordeaux's best-run estates, is the best wine made here in over 25 years. Anticipated maturity: 1995–2010. Last tasted, 1/85.

1981—The 1981 Domaine de Chevalier is very well made. Still quite
· tannic and closed, this medium-bodied wine has a pronounced
85 vanillin oakiness, aggressive tannins, good dark ruby color, and a lean, but long finish. Anticipated maturity: 1992–2000. Last tasted, 11/84.

1980—A notable success in this mediocre vintage, Domaine de Cheva-
· lier has made a deeply fruity, spicy, open-knit wine, with a
84 bouquet dominated by the scent of new vanillin oakiness. Medium-bodied, with surprising concentration and light tannins, this supple, classy wine is ideal for drinking over the next 5–6 years. Last tasted, 10/84.

1979—Very agreeable and drinkable now, the 1979 Domaine de Che-
· valier will get better; it is charmingly supple, fruity, and me-
84 dium-bodied. A fragrant bouquet of ripe berry fruit is also quite alluring. On the palate, the wine is medium-bodied, fruity, and lightly tannic. Drink over the next 5–6 years. Last tasted, 10/84.

1978—Along with the 1970, this is my favorite wine from Domaine de
· Chevalier in the decade of the seventies. Quite dark ruby in
88 color, with a quite rich, blackcurrant, spicy bouquet, medium to full body, a lush, ripe, fruity texture, and long, moderately tannic finish, the 1978 Domaine de Chevalier is seductively charming now, but ideally should be cellared until 1988. Last tasted, 2/84.

1977—One of the better 1977 wines, the Domaine de Chevalier is soft
· and fruity, with moderately intense, medium-bodied flavors that
76 exhibit a pleasant berry fruitiness. Drink over the next 4 years. Last tasted, 3/81.

1976—An open, spicy, rather earthy, ripe, almost burnt bouquet is
· followed on the palate by a wine that is fully mature, soft, less
78 concentrated than normal, but fruity. Drink over the next 4 years. Last tasted, 11/84.

1975—For some reason I have yet to ascertain, perhaps the hail that
· afflicted the Léognan area, the 1975 Domaine de Chevalier is
73 quite disappointing. I have seen more favorable accounts of the wine elsewhere, but I have consistently found the wine surprisingly light in color, very tannic and lean, and lacking fruit and substance. The finish is coarse and unimpressive. Last tasted, 5/84.

1974—This is a flavorful, supple, fruity 1974, without any of the harsh-
· ness or hollowness that afflicts so many wines from this vintage.
76 Drinkable now, the tannins and overall balance will keep this wine from declining for another 3–4 years. Last tasted, 6/80.

1971—Quite disappointing, this decrepit, prematurely senile wine has
· a very brown color, hot, almost cooked flavors, and a lean, short
67 finish. It is now past its prime. Last tasted, 3/81.

1970—The 1970 is a wonderfully rich, fragrant, exquisitely scented
· wine, with ripe fruit interlaced with aromas of roasted nuts and
89 vanillin oak. On the palate, the wine is soft, quite mature, very supple, and generously fruity, and ready to drink. It is a top-notch effort from Domaine de Chevalier, but one must drink it over the next 5 years. Last tasted, 10/82.

1966—Still holding tenuously on to its fruity component, the 1966 is
· beginning to show a great deal of brown in its color, and tastes
84 a trifle dried out. However, it still retains an elegant, aged, savory richness and spiciness that gives it plenty of appeal. Drink up. Last tasted, 8/82.

1964—Now quite mature and fading badly in the glass, if opened and
· served immediately, the wine will exhibit an aged, brownish,
83 ruby color, an earthy, truffle-like bouquet, and soft, graceful, ripe yet faded, fruity flavors. Quite soft in the finish, this medium-bodied wine requires drinking. Last tasted, 3/79.

1961—Not unlike the 1964, the 1961 has better color, but a coarser
· texture, and enough signs to suspect that it was in its prime in
84 the early '70s. The complex, aged bouquet of roasted fruit and nuts is classy, but on the palate the wine does not deliver the expected richness and depth that characterize this vintage. Last tasted, 12/80.

HAUT-BAILLY (Cru Classé) VERY GOOD

Production: 8,500 cases	Grape varieties Cabernet Sauvignon—36% Merlot—30% Cabernet Franc—10% Mixed parcel of old ungrafted vines, mostly Cabernet Sauvignon—24%
Time spent in barrels: 18–20 months	Average age of vines: 38 years

Evaluation of present classification: The quality equivalent of a fourth-growth

Haut-Bailly is located in the southern Graves region, just a kilometer northeast of the town of Léognan. The wine has a considerable following in Europe and England, but is yet to be widely known and appreciated in America. The late Daniel Sanders was responsible for the modern era of Haut-Bailly since his acquisition of the property in 1955. His son, Jean, now looks after the wine.

Haut-Bailly can produce an opulently fruity, silky wine, which is never too tannic or too commercially soft. Some vintages of Haut-Bailly have been quite exceptional, for example, the 1961, 1966, 1979, and 1982. However, the property has also had a propensity for inexplicably falling on its face. The 1975 and 1976 are extremely disappointing. When Haut-Bailly does it right, which fortunately has been most of the time recently, the wine seems to have an uncanny resemblance to a St.-Emilion from the Graves section of that appellation on the Pomerol border. The wine is usually ready to drink within 6 to 8 years of the vintage, but has demonstrated the cunning ability to age well in the bottle in the very good vintages despite its forward fruitiness and charm.

VINTAGES

1983—A typical Haut-Bailly, the 1983 is dark ruby in color, with a rich,
· voluptuous, ripe, blackcurrant bouquet, and some attractive va-
85 nillin oaky aromas. On the palate, the wine is lush, silky, with good, ripe, round tannins in evidence. Medium- to full-bodied, with a Pomerol-like silky, fat texture, this will be a precocious and delicious 1983. Anticipated maturity: 1990–1996. Last tasted, 3/85.

1982—A Pomerol/St.-Emilion look-alike, this lush, ample, round, and
· generously fruity wine has layers of berrylike fruit, a very pene-
87 trating bouquet of spicy oak, vanillin, and currants. Medium-bodied, moderately tannic, and quite long in the finish, many tasters will opt for drinking this deceptively charming, precocious wine too soon, but I will keep mine until 1990. Anticipated maturity: 1990–2000. Last tasted, 2/85.

1981—The 1981 Haut-Bailly is neither profound nor intensely concen-
· trated, but rather perfumed, elegant, spicy, soft, and deliciously
84 fruity. It does not have the punch and depth of either the 1982, 1983, or 1979, but is very agreeable and pleasant. Drink over the next 6 years. Last tasted, 10/84.

1979—One of the most delicious wines of this somewhat overlooked
· vintage, the 1979 Haut-Bailly has excellent deep ruby color, a
86 rich, moderately intense, spicy, ripe fruity bouquet, soft, silky, fat, plump, fruity flavors, light to moderate, non-aggressive tannins, and a good finish. It is totally harmonious and lovely. Anticipated maturity: 1986–1993. Last tasted, 1/85.

1978—For whatever reason, the 1978, while now mature, fruity, quite
· charming and soft, never quite had the depth and dimension of
83 the 1979. Medium-bodied and quite fragrant, this is a good, rather than very good, Haut-Bailly. Drink over the next 6 years. Last tasted, 9/82.

1976—Haut-Bailly is not a success in 1976. The intense heat prior to
· the harvest caused the grapes to become overripe. The wine is
62 now quite mature, even old-looking, with a loosely-knit structure, very low acidity, and diluted flavors. Last tasted, 9/79.

1975—Another problem vintage for Haut-Bailly, the 1975 is light in
· color, weight, and body. The herbaceous, spicy bouquet shows
69 none of the expected ripeness that is present in the better 1975s. It is a thin, meager, and skinny wine, with very little charm or personality. Drink up; it will not improve. Last tasted, 5/84.

1971—Charming, but a little light and flabby, the 1971 Haut-Bailly is
· now in decline, taking on an even deeper and pronounced
75 brownish cast. The velvety, soft, fruity flavors are likable, but fade quickly in the glass. Drink up. Last tasted, 12/83.

1970—The 1970 is a strong effort from Haut-Bailly. Decadently ripe
· and fruity, with a top-flight bouquet of spicy oak, this lush wine
87 has flavors that suggest caramel, tobacco, and blackcurrant fruit. On the palate, the wine is round, plump, quite long, and

extremely satisfying. The wine is now at its apogee. Drink over the next 5–8 years. Last tasted, 3/81.

1966—Fully mature, quite fruity, yet a little more reserved and sterner
· than the richer, more opulent 1970, the 1966 shows a little
85 browning at the edge, good concentration, earthy, fruity flavors, and a soft, round finish. Drink over the next 5 years. Last tasted, 4/82.

1961—An intensely rich, almost pungent bouquet of earthy, smoky
· tobacco and ripe berry fruit is first-class on the palate. The wine
90 is atypically huge and massive for a Haut-Bailly, with layers of very rich, full-bodied, powerful flavors. A lot of alcohol creates a bit of hotness in the finish, but this is a splendidly rich, uncommonly strong, herculean-sized wine from Haut-Bailly. Drink over the next 10 years. Last tasted, 2/85.

PAPE-CLÉMENT (Cru Classé) — VERY GOOD

Production: 10,500 cases

Grape varieties:
Cabernet Sauvignon—67%
Merlot—33%

Time spent in barrels: 22–24 months

Average age of vines: 33 years

Evaluation of present classification: The quality equivalent of a fifth-growth

Pape-Clément is clearly one of the leading Graves estates. It is located in the northern Graves region, within the Bordeaux suburb of Pessac. It is several kilometers from Haut-Brion. Pape-Clément's rise to prominence among the leading wines of Graves is relatively recent in spite of the fact that the vineyard's history predates that of Haut-Brion. While the estate enjoyed a good reputation in the 1920s, the vineyard was devastated by hail in the late '30s, and it was not until the late '50s that top-quality wines were again made.

The vineyard is somewhat unusual in that no Cabernet Franc or Petit Verdot are planted. To my knowledge, Pape-Clément is one of the few red Graves wine-producing vineyards to utilize only two grape varieties.

The style of the wine here is significantly lighter and less tannic than Haut-Brion, La Mission-Haut-Brion, and La Tour-Haut-Brion. Vintages of Pape-Clément tend to mature quite rapidly, with most wines fully mature by the time they are 7 or 8 years old. In fact, the only criticism of the estate seems to be a failing of the wines of Pape-Clément to hold up in the bottle. Recent vintages, particularly those in the '70s, have demonstrated a predilection to turn brown earlier than expected and to fade early. Nevertheless, the wines can be quite delicious in their youth. However, a word of caution is in order. In recent vintages, particularly 1979–1983, Pape-Clément has performed surprisingly poorly in tastings I have done in Bordeaux.

VINTAGES

1983—This will be a good Pape-Clément, with perhaps more staying
· power than other recent vintages of this wine. The wine is me-
80 dium ruby, with an attractive, spicy, ripe fruity nose somewhat
dominated by vanillin oak, and tight, rather hard, unyielding
flavors. Anticipated maturity: 1990–1996. Last tasted, 3/85.

1982—Surprisingly variable, I have both poor tasting notes from cask
· samples, as well as notes showing the wine to be very concen-
68 trated, cleanly made, supple, and typically Graves, with a textbook, earthy, tobacco-like bouquet. The poor examples shared
a common dirty, musty, unclean, old barrel smell. From the
bottle, the wine has been rather disappointing. Will the real 1982
Pape-Clément please come forth? Last tasted, 2/85.

1981—Disappointingly light, musty, and frail, this medium-bodied wine
· tastes uncommonly weak and diluted. It will age very rapidly.
68 Drink over the next 3–4 years. Last tasted, 4/84.

1979—Ready to drink now, this is a lightweight, somewhat shallow, but
· overall simple, supple, fruity wine. Drink over the next 4 years.
76 Last tasted, 9/84.

1978—One of the better efforts from Pape-Clément in recent vintages,
· the 1978 has medium to dark ruby color, and an open-knit,
80 expansive, Graves bouquet of smoky tobacco. This medium-
bodied wine has above average to good concentration, round,
ripe tannin, and an adequate finish. Drink over the next 5–6
years. Last tasted, 12/84.

1976—Quite mature, and exhibiting a great amount of brown color, this
· medium-bodied wine is flabby, diluted, and poorly structured,
67 without much concentration of fruit or tannin. Drink up. Last
tasted, 11/81.

1975—The best Pape-Clément of the '70s, but it too has performed
· rather inconsistently over the last decade. A smoky, roasted
86 chestnut, earthy bouquet is top-class. On the palate, the wine is
medium-bodied and lighter than most 1975s, but has very good
concentration, a surprising suppleness, and good finish. It is

reaching its apogee. Drink over the next 6–7 years. Last tasted, 9/84.

1971—Fully mature and beginning to show the telltale signs of old age
· (a significant brown color), the 1971 still remains an elegant,
80 cedary, spicy, soft, fruity wine which should be drunk up immediately. Last tasted, 12/84.

1970—While the 1970 was impressive when young, it has, like most
· recent vintages of Pape-Clément, not stood the test of time. Now
84 becoming loosely knit and losing some fruit, this medium-bodied, very soft and supple wine has a classy, earthy, cedary, spicy bouquet, and good flavors, but both fade quickly in the glass. It is still very attractive, but it must be drunk up. Last tasted, 12/84.

1966—Fully mature, but exhibiting much more sustained holding power
· than more recent vintages, the lovely, classy 1966 Pape-Clément
87 reached its zenith in 1978, but has continued to rest at this plateau. A classic bouquet of smoky tobacco and earthy, cedary, currant fruit is quite complex and alluring. On the palate, the wine has good structure, an elegant, balanced, fruity texture, and long, soft finish. Drink up. Last tasted, 3/83.

1964—Extremely enjoyable and tasty in 1975, it is now beginning to
· fade badly. Brown at the edge, soft, with the hint of caramel and
78 decaying vegetation, there is not much left of this once lovely yet now tired wine. Last tasted, 11/79.

1961—Still at its apogee, the 1961 Pape-Clément has a full-blown,
· earthy, rich, cedary, spicy bouquet, ripe, round, rich, deep,
88 gravelly flavors, medium to full body, and a long, lush, silky finish. This wine is delicious for drinking over the next 5–6 years. Last tasted, 10/84.

LA LOUVIÈRE (Unclassified) VERY GOOD

Production: 16,000 cases	Grape varieties: Cabernet Sauvignon—80% Merlot—20%
Time spent in barrels: 12 months	Average age of vines: 25 years

Evaluation of present classification: The quality equivalent of a fifth-growth

While not technically classified, La Louvière in Léognan is now making red wines superior to many of the Crus Classés of Graves, and vintages since 1981 have certainly been on a quality level with a fifth-growth.

André Lurton has revitalized this estate, and the results have been impressive.

While the red wine can still not match the brilliance of the white wine produced here, the red wine in stylistic terms is becoming more dominated by the taste of Merlot, as Lurton gradually increases the percentages used in the blend. Unlike the tannic, rather tough wines produced at La Louvière in the early '70s, the recent vintages have been generously fruity, fleshy wines, with considerable character. La Louvière is at the moment notoriously undervalued, so wine consumers have an opportunity to stock up on a delicious wine that will only become more expensive once the word gets out on the quality of La Louvière.

VINTAGES

1983—A notable success in 1983, La Louvière had the darkest color of
· all the wines in a tasting of major Graves wines put on for me by
87 the Union des Grands Crus. A lot of tannin is present in this
medium- to full-bodied wine, which exhibits wonderful ripeness,
excellent balance, deep, concentrated flavors, and aging potential. Anticipated maturity: 1990–2000. Last tasted, 3/85.

1982—This wine has the telltale dark ruby color of this vintage, and a
· very expressive bouquet suggesting ripe fruit, and toasty, vanil-
86 lin oak. On the palate, the wine is quite full-bodied, silky and
velvety, with layers of fruit and plenty of ripe, round tannins in
the sumptuous finish. Anticipated maturity: 1986–2000. Last
tasted, 1/85.

1981—The least successful of the La Louvière vintages of the early
· '80s, the 1981 is lean, a trifle austere, medium-bodied, and rel-
75 atively compact and bland in taste. Moderate tannins suggest
that 2–3 years of cellaring may be helpful. Anticipated maturity:
1986–1990. Last tasted, 6/84.

1978—Almost ready to drink, the 1978 La Louvière is charmingly
· fruity, soft, round, and supple, with a pleasing, ripe berry, to-
83 bacco-scented character. Medium- to full-bodied, with little tannins present, this precocious, easy-to-drink wine should drink
well for another 3–5 years. Last tasted, 12/84.

BOUSCAUT (Cru Classé) AVERAGE

Production: 10,000 cases	Grape varieties: Merlot—60% Cabernet Sauvignon—35% Cabernet Franc—5%
Time spent in barrels: 20–24 months	Average age of vines: 33 years
Evaluation of present classification: The quality equivalent of a Grand Bourgeois Exceptionnel	

Bouscaut has gone through several changes of ownership in the last two decades. However, the current ownership should provide the right ingredients for Bouscaut to regain a degree of reputation and respect. Jean Bernard Delmas, the manager of Haut-Brion, looks after the winemaking here, and Lucien Lurton, the agreeable proprietor of the two famous Médoc estates, Brane-Cantenac and Durfort-Vivens, is now the owner.

In the past, the wines of Bouscaut have had a tendency to be too dry, severe, and tannic, somewhat of a surprise in view of the abnormally high percentage of Merlot used in the blend. However, the vintages since 1981, under the Delmas-Lurton banner, have represented the best efforts from Bouscaut in more than a generation. Despite the recent turnabout in quality, this is a wine which tends to be overrated and overpriced.

VINTAGES

1983—This is an extremely supple, fleshy, medium-weight Graves, with plenty of style and charm. Fortunately, it lacks the abrasive tannin so common in many wines of this vintage. Quite spicy on the nose, and nicely colored, this wine will be an early maturing 1983. Anticipated maturity: 1989–1996. Last tasted, 3/85.
· 84

1982—The best Bouscaut in two decades, the 1982 is quite dark in color for this wine, with a vividly rich, ripe berry aroma, fat, lush, concentrated flavors, plenty of tannins in the long finish, and good aging potential of 10–12 years. This is a big-styled, impressive Bouscaut. Anticipated maturity: 1992–2000. Last tasted, 1/85.
· 85

1981—The 1981 has a light-intensity, spicy, rather reserved bouquet, followed by flavors that are quite unyielding, hard, and austere. Is there enough fruit to outlast the abrasive tannins? Probably not. Anticipated maturity: 1990–1996. Last tasted, 6/84.
· 74

1980—Not terribly different from the 1981, only lighter in color and
· body, the 1980 Bouscaut is an acceptable but quite one-dimen-
72 sional wine. Drink now. Last tasted, 2/83.

1978—An average-quality Bouscaut, with a light-intensity, spicy, oaky
· aroma and modest, fruity, berryish flavors, this wine has a mod-
78 erately tannic, firm finish. Anticipated maturity: 1987–1992.
Last tasted, 12/82.

1975—Very closed, unyielding, and painfully tannic and harsh on the
· palate, the 1975 Bouscaut has above-average color and good
75 weight, but I see no possibility that the fruit can outlive the
tannin. Anticipated maturity: 1990–1996. Last tasted, 5/84.

1970—Hard and severe when young, this wine has not developed any
· richness or character, but remained sternly tannic, woody, and
72 ungenerous, with little charm or fruit. Last tasted, 2/80.

DE FIEUZAL (Cru Classé) AVERAGE

Production: 7,000 cases	Grape varieties: Cabernet Sauvignon—70% Merlot—20% Petit Verdot and Malbec—10%
Time spent in barrels: 18–20 months	Average age of vines: 30 years

Evaluation of present classification: The quality equivalent of a Grand Bourgeois Exceptionnel

De Fieuzal is located in the rolling countryside just south of the town of Léognan. It is one of the least-known Graves properties. The care and meticulousness of the winemaking here is noteworthy, and unlike many of the nearby Graves properties, de Fieuzal has a vineyard composed primarily of relatively old vines.

The red wine of de Fieuzal seems to be quite elegant and much more harmonious and fleshy than many of the Graves from this region. Supple in its youth, with good concentration, de Fieuzal shows every indication of aging well for 8 to 12 years. Perhaps underrated and undervalued, this could well be a property to watch in the future.

VINTAGES

1983—Elegant, spicy, richly fruity, and balanced by good, firm tannins,
· this medium-bodied 1983 has good structure and length. De
83 Fieuzal is a well-made, polished, refined sort of wine. Anticipated maturity: 1990–1996. Last tasted, 7/84.

1982—Quite attractive and deceptively forward, the 1982 de Fieuzal is
· dark ruby, with a rich, berrylike aroma, a prominent oakiness,
84 and full body. A big, more intense style of de Fieuzal than usual, this wine should age well for at least a decade. Anticipated maturity: 1990–1998. Last tasted, 12/84.

1981—The 1981 is light and elegant, with a pleasant herbaceous, ber-
· rylike bouquet, good acidity, medium weight, and moderate tan-
83 nin. De Fieuzal's 1981 is a polite, restrained style of wine. Anticipated maturity: 1988–1994. Last tasted, 7/84.

1978—Good-intensity flavor of plums and an aroma of oak and mint
· intermingles nicely to create an interesting, supple, richly fruity,
84 and harmonious wine. Anticipated maturity: 1985–1990. Last tasted, 3/84.

MALARTIC-LAGRAVIÈRE (Cru Classé) AVERAGE

Production: 6,000 cases

Grape varieties:
Cabernet Sauvignon—50%
Merlot—25%
Cabernet Franc—25%

Time spent in barrels: 20–22 months

Average age of vines: 15 years

Evaluation of present classification: The quality equivalent of a Grand Bourgeois

One of the numerous estates in the southern Graves region of Léognan, Malartic-Lagravière is a property that makes much better white wine than red wine. The production per hectare at this estate is quite high as the proprietor, Jacques Marly, holds the minority point of view that young vines and high yields produce a better wine than low yields and old vines.

In stylistic terms, the red wine of Malartic-Lagravière is rather light, quite stern and tannic, and generally lacking richness and depth. Since it is unappealing when young, one would hope that with age it will fill out and develop. That has not been the case. Whether the recent retention of Bordeaux's famous oenologist, Emile Peynaud, will change what has been a history of mediocrity for the red wine will have to be answered in the future.

VINTAGES

1983—A decent effort from this property, the 1983 is a light to medium
· weight Graves, with a dry, tannic finish, an attractive spicy,
80 cherry-like bouquet, and moderately intense flavors. Anticipated maturity: 1990–1995. Last tasted, 6/84.

1982—Certainly the best recent vintage of wine from Malartic-Lagra-
· vière, the nicely colored 1982 has more flesh and fruit than one
82 normally finds from this property. On the palate, the wine has stiff, hard tannins, good fruit, and medium body. Anticipated maturity: 1990–1995. Last tasted, 6/84.

1979—Medium ruby in color, with some amber, the 1979 has an open-
· knit bouquet of light, berry fruit as well as some herbaceous
74 elements. In the mouth, the wine is light, too tannic for its depth of fruit, but pleasant in a rather tough, austere way. Drink over the next 6 years. Last tasted, 2/82.

1978—The bouquet is quite herbaceous and overly oaky. This medium-
· bodied wine is very hard, closed, and not very attractive as a
62 result of severe, mouth-puckering tannins that obscure any hint of ripe fruit. It is quite a disappointing effort. Last tasted, 2/82.

1975—Typically backward, stiff, unyielding, and seemingly incapable
· of ever developing well, this medium-ruby wine is a very tannic,
70 high strung, skinny wine without much flesh or fruit. Will it age? Last tasted, 2/82.

1970—This is the best Malartic-Lagravière of the '70s that I have
· tasted. Hardly inspirational, but fruity, with a good color, a one-
78 dimensional bouquet of black cherries and oak, and not too tannic, the 1970 should be drunk over the next 5–8 years. Last tasted, 2/82.

SMITH-HAUT-LAFITTE (Cru Classé) AVERAGE

Production: 20,000 cases	Grape varieties: Cabernet Sauvignon—73% Merlot—16% Cabernet Franc—11%
Time spent in barrels: 16–18 months	Average age of vines: 19 years

Evaluation of present classification: The quality equivalent of a Cru Bourgeois

An overrated and overpriced wine, Smith-Haut-Lafitte is made by the well-known shipping firm of Louis Eschenauer. The white wine tends to be more interesting than the red wine, but my experience with numerous vintages of Smith-Haut-Lafitte is limited.

The style of red wine at Smith-Haut-Lafitte is certainly sound and reliable, but generally is quite light, one-dimensional, fruity, and soft. In recent vintages, the wine has been quite drinkable and close to maturity when released two years after the vintage.

VINTAGES

1983—A cleanly made, medium-bodied, spicy, moderately tannic wine,
· which is obviously made in a lighter style, but shows a good,
82 supple fruit, and a pleasant, satisfying finish. Drink over the next 7–8 years. Last tasted, 1/85.

1982—The 1982 is the best Smith-Haut-Lafitte I have tasted; however,
· don't get your hopes too high. This is a pleasant, spicy, supple,
82 medium-weight wine, with attractive fruit, a pleasing ripeness, and light tannins. Drink over the next 6–8 years. Last tasted, 1/85.

1975—A diffuse, herbaceous bouquet hints at some good, ripe fruit
· underneath. On the palate, the wine is lean, a trifle hard and
74 severe, and short and coarse in the finish. Will it get better? Not in my opinion. Last tasted, 5/84.

1970—Bland, simple, and one-dimensional, this wine is not over the
· hill, but straightforward, shallow, and rather atypical for this
67 excellent vintage. Drink up. Last tasted, 5/80.

CARBONNIEUX (Cru Classé) AVERAGE

Production: 15,000 cases	Grape varieties: Cabernet Sauvignon—50% Merlot—30% Cabernet Franc—10% Petit Verdot and Malbec—10%
Time spent in barrels: 20 months	Average age of vines: 28 years

Evaluation of present classification: The quality equivalent of a Cru Bourgeois

One of the largest estates of the Graves region, Carbonnieux seems to fit into the pattern I have delineated for most of the estates in the southern Graves region—the white wines can be delicious, the red wines innocuously light and bland. The Carbonnieux red is a wine meant for consumption upon release, and rarely improves beyond 7 to 8 years of age.

VINTAGES

1983—The 1983, tasted from cask samples, is an attractive, plump, spicy, juicy wine, with an elegant cherry fruitiness, soft, savory texture, light tannins, and a supple finish. Drink over the next 6 years. Last tasted, 11/83.
· 80

1982—The 1982 Carbonnieux has a trifle more punch than the 1983, better color and more concentration than the 1981, but in the company of other 1982s tastes too soft, fruity, and surprisingly mature. It is a lightweight yet charming wine. Drink over the next 6 years. Last tasted, 1/85.
· 82

1981—A light ruby-colored wine, the 1981 Carbonnieux is quite one-dimensional, with spicy, soft, jammy fruit, a light-intensity bouquet, and weak finish. Drink now. Last tasted, 11/84.
· 73

LA TOUR-MARTILLAC (Cru Classé) AVERAGE

Production: 7,500 cases

Grape varieties:
Cabernet Sauvignon—65%
Merlot—25%
Cabernet Franc—6%
Petit Verdot and Malbec—4%

Time spent in barrels: 18–30 months

Average age of vines: 33 years

Evaluation of present classification: The quality equivalent of a Cru Bourgeois

A property owned by the shipping firm of Jean Kressman, La Tour-Martillac is better known for its high-quality white wine than its red wine. I have had little chance to see many vintages of La Tour-Martillac, but of those I have, the wine has tasted stubbornly hard, tannic, and deficient in fruit. The wine is traditionally made, and one is apt to admire the dedication of Jean Kressman, who believes in old vines and the use of only organic fertilizer. However, in spite of such good intentions, the red wine is mediocre, although the quality of the 1982 and 1983 wines looks encouraging.

VINTAGES

1983—Quite tannic and spicy, with fortunately enough fruit in the
· background to handle the tannin, this medium-bodied, deeply-
82 colored wine has more substance and depth than usual. It will
require a long wait. Anticipated maturity: 1993–2000. Last
tasted, 6/84.

1982—Back-to-back good vintages from La Tour-Martillac may suggest
· a brighter future for the red wines from this estate. The 1982 is
83 medium to dark ruby, with a ripe cherryish, oaky bouquet, and
chunky, moderately tannic flavors. Anticipated maturity: 1988–
1995. Last tasted, 1/85.

1975—Far too tannic, austere, and thin, with an abrasive, coarse tex-
· ture and too little fruit, this medium-bodied, charmless wine has
64 an earthy Graves-like aroma, but that is its only redeeming quality. Last tasted, 5/84.

1970—A little wine, with straightforward, simple, soft, fruity flavors,
· no complexity, and not much of a finish. Drink up. Last tasted,
68

OLIVIER (Cru Classé) AVERAGE

Production: 9,000 cases	Grape varieties: Cabernet Sauvignon—65% Merlot—20% Cabernet Franc—15%
Time spent in barrels: 16–18 months	Average age of vines: 14 years
Evaluation of present classification: The quality equivalent of a Cru Bourgeois	

Like Château Smith-Haut-Lafitte, its neighbor to the east, Olivier is owned and managed by Jean-Jacques de Bethmann. This is another average-quality, rather overrated and overpriced red wine of the southern Graves region. The wine produced here is usually simple, fruity, and quite light. The owners have consistently argued that better things were to be expected as the vineyard matures, but so far the red wine has rarely exceeded the quality of a shipper's Bordeaux blend.

VINTAGES

1983—Extremely tannic, rather coarse, and roughly textured, the 1983
· Olivier has adequate fruit, but is basically an austere, hard, lean
72 wine. Anticipated maturity: 1990–1995. Last tasted, 6/84.

1982—A little more fruit helps to give this wine slightly more appeal
· than the tart, sinewy, green and raw 1983, but the overall
78 impression is that this wine still lacks enough fruit to carry the tannin. Olivier has acceptable quality in this vintage and is fruity, but it is not very distinctive. Anticipated maturity: 1990–1995. Last tasted, 6/84.

1979—Light, diluted, rather hollow and graceless, this medium-bodied
· wine has light intensity, strawberry, cherry fruitiness, and a
67 short finish. Drink up. Last tasted, 6/84.

A CONSUMER'S CLASSIFICATION OF THE WHITE WINE PRODUCING CHÂTEAUX OF GRAVES

OUTSTANDING

Laville-Haut-Brion, Haut-Brion Blanc, Domaine de Chevalier

VERY GOOD

Carbonnieux, La Tour-Martillac, Malartic-Lagravière, La Louvière, de Fieuzal, Pontac-Monplaisir

GOOD

Bouscaut, Smith-Haut-Lafitte, Olivier

LAVILLE-HAUT-BRION (Cru Classé) OUTSTANDING

Only 1,200 cases of this remarkable yet very expensive wine are produced in a good, average year. Made from 60% Semillon and 40% Sauvignon Blanc, Laville-Haut-Brion is the finest white wine of Graves, although Domaine de Chevalier and Haut-Brion Blanc are often as superb. The estate was owned until 1983 by the Woltner family, but was sold that year to the owners of Haut-Brion. Until 1983, the style of Laville-Haut-Brion was one of opulent, intense richness and fullness with astonishing fruit and body. Under the management at Haut-Brion, it is expected that the wine will be less powerful and rich, but more elegant.

Laville-Haut-Brion has had incredible aging potential. Just recently, I had the pleasure to taste the 1961, 1962, 1966, and 1970, all of which were filled with fruit and were still astonishingly fresh, rich, and deep.

Of recent vintages, the 1975, 1978, 1981, 1982, and 1983 are extremely successful, with the 1982 and 1975 being the most powerful wines of this group, and the 1981 and 1983 the most elegant.

The 1976 has a considerable reputation, but I have consistently found it to be overripe, overbearing, and just too heavy to really enjoy with food.

HAUT-BRION BLANC (Cru Classé) OUTSTANDING

Initially excluded from the 1959 classification of the white wine producers of Graves, Haut-Brion Blanc was later added to the classification. Approximately 1,500 cases are produced from a blend of 50% Sauvignon Blanc and 50% Semillon. Haut-Brion Blanc is different from Laville-Haut-Brion, primarily because it is aged in brand-new oak casks, whereas Laville is aged in old casks and tanks. Additionally, the grapes for Haut-Brion Blanc are generally picked earlier and are less ripe than those at Laville-Haut-Brion. In comparing the two wines, the contrast was quite apparent. Laville would always have more of a golden color, a ripe, more opulent taste, and Haut-Brion, oakier aroma and flavors, as well as lighter color and a more restrained, less obvious personality.

Haut-Brion Blanc, like Laville-Haut-Brion, is very rare, and the price charged for it is absurdly expensive, usually 40–50% more than Haut-Brion's excellent red wine. Of the recent vintages, the 1982 and 1981 are both marvelous wines. The 1982 is lush, intense, powerful, and quite full-bodied. The 1981 is oaky but extremely graceful, with a steely firmness. The 1983 is lighter than both the 1982 and 1981, but shows promise. Of older vintages, the one that stands out in memory, and in my notes, is the 1976 Haut-Brion Blanc, which had all of the richness and power of the Laville-Haut-Brion that year, better overall balance, and a refreshing acidity.

DOMAINE DE CHEVALIER (Cru Classé) OUTSTANDING

The rarest of the top white Graves wines, Domaine de Cheavlier makes only about 24 barrels (600 cases) of long-lasting, brilliant, white wine. The blend of grape used shows a preference for Sauvignon Blanc, which represents 70% of the blend; Semillon provides the remaining 30%. The wine is fermented in new oak barrels and aged rather a long time, 16 to 18 months. The wine when first released can be overpoweringly oaky, with little of the ripe fruit revealing itself. Five years later, the fruit seems to emerge, and at 10 years Domaine de Chevalier can be an exquisite gustatory pleasure that combines power and finesse with richness and balance.

The 1983 is the greatest young Domaine de Chevalier I have tasted, and undeniably the best white wine produced in Graves in that vintage. The 1982 and 1981 are also excellent.

In the decade of the '70s, the 1979, 1978, and 1975 stand out; however, I have been disappointed with the 1971, and the 1970 tasted compact and short. These last two wines have been praised elsewhere, so perhaps some bottle variation does exist.

Domaine de Chevalier is quite expensive and very difficult to find. It has become a favorite of leading restaurants in France, and it is there that most people will have the best chance of finding a bottle.

CARBONNIEUX (Cru Classé) VERY GOOD

Carbonnieux is a very large estate, producing close to 15,000 cases of white wine from a 65% Sauvignon Blanc, 35% Semillon blend. This is a modern-style white Graves, bottled early after several months in new oak, and put on the market immediately. It is a very medium-bodied, fresh, crisp, austere yet satisfying wine which is always drunk young, but really needs 2 to 3 years of bottle age to be at its best. A recent bottle of 1971 was outstanding, proving that in certain vintages, it can age well.

The 1983, 1981, and 1978 are the most successful recent vintages for Carbonnieux. Prices for Carbonnieux are quite reasonable, as this is one of the most sensibly priced classified-growth white wines of Graves.

LA TOUR-MARTILLAC (Cru Classé) VERY GOOD

While the red wine of La Tour-Martillac offers little excitement, the white wine of this property can be among the best in Graves. One thousand five hundred cases are produced from a blend of 50% Semillon, 45% Sauvignon Blanc, and 5% very old mixed vines. The style of white wine made is one of the most robust and deeply concentrated of the white Graves, if the last three vintages are typical. The 1983 is a very impressive white Graves, with an intense, spicy character, deep, ripe, rich fruit, and excellent crispness and acidity. The 1982 is ripe, supple, and a trifle fatter, and the 1981 a marriage in style between the very fine 1983 and good 1982. This is a rich, flavorful wine, with plenty of body, no oak aging whatsoever, and a deep, fruity finish. One wishes there were more white La Tour-Martillac produced.

MALARTIC-LAGRAVIÈRE (Cru Classé) VERY GOOD

This is another Graves property with a deservedly much higher reputation for its white wine than its red wine. Interestingly, the tiny production of 600 cases of white Malartic-Lagravière is made from 100% Sauvignon Blanc, aged three months in new oak casks, and then bottled. Because there is no Semillon in the blend, Malartic is often discernibly lighter and distinctively different from other white Graves. Its bouquet is more pungent, with noticeably more grassy, herbaceous scents. On the palate, the wine is lemony and spicy, with a refreshing lightness and crispness.

The 1981 is my favorite of recent Malartic-Lagravière wines. It has a steely, lemony character, a pungent, earthy, grassy bouquet, and excellent balance. The 1983 is very similar, only a trifle lighter, whereas the 1982 is fatter and richer, but somewhat less interesting.

LA LOUVIÈRE (Unclassified) VERY GOOD

An up-and-coming property for both red and white wine, this good-sized estate produces 7,500 cases of white wine from a blend of 85% Sauvignon Blanc and 15% Semillon. Virtually all of the recent vintages have shown considerable style, charm, and richness. They are made in an early-maturing, rather rich, supple style, and therefore should be drunk within 4 years of the vintage.

The 1983 is especially rich, ripe, almost unctuous, with supple, deep flavors. The 1982 is full-bodied and fat, the 1981 more elegant, and the 1978 a top-notch success that can rival the best of the white wines of Graves. La Louvière's price has not yet caught up with the great strides in quality made here by owner André Lurton, so consumers should look for this modestly priced, high-quality white Graves.

DE FIEUZAL (Unclassified) VERY GOOD

De Fieuzal's white wine was not included in the 1959 classification of the Graves. However, it continues to be one of the better wines, exhibiting stylish, well-knit flavors, and a highly perfumed, fragrant bouquet. Very little white de Fieuzal (500 cases) is made, so it remains difficult to find. The white grape varieties employed at de Fieuzal are 60% Sauvignon Blanc and 40% Semillon. Both the 1983 and 1982 are quite good, and compete very favorably with the Crus Classés of Graves.

PONTAC-MONPLAISIR (Unclassified) VERY GOOD

This little-known estate in the wooded countryside near Villenave d'Ornon makes approximately 1,800 cases of delicious, stylish, crisp, white Graves, which sells at ridiculously low prices given the quality. In a recent tasting, both the 1983 and 1982 Pontac-Monplaisir wines bested most of the competition, which consisted of several Cru Classé estates in Graves. This is a wine that is clearly a great bargain, and has yet to be discovered by white Graves enthusiasts.

BOUSCAUT (Cru Classé) GOOD

A very traditionally made white Graves, Bouscaut, a blend of 70% Semillon and 30% Sauvignon Blanc, is fermented in oak barrels, and given 8 months of oak aging prior to bottling. The production is said to be 2,500 cases.

The Bouscaut white wine, like the red wine, receives meticulous care from people who both love and know wine. Yet, for whatever reason, the final product is somewhat uninspiring and of average quality. Both the 1982 and 1981 white Bouscaut wines have shown satisfactorily in comparative tasting against their peers, but they were hardly exciting, distinctive wines. However, the 1983 was impressive from the cask, showing excellent ripeness and fruit, with perhaps the best potential of any white Bouscaut I have tasted.

SMITH-HAUT-LAFITTE (Unclassified) GOOD

An unclassified white wine of Graves, Smith-Haut-Lafitte's recent vintages from 1981 onward have shown as much quality as its more renowned neighbors; 2,500 cases of white wine from 100% Sauvignon Blanc are produced that, to my palate, show more character and style than this property's mediocre red wine. The 1983 is quite good, with a highly perfumed bouquet of freshly mowed grass, and very fine concentration of ripe fruit. The 1982 is softer, and a trifle low in acidity, but still fruity and satisfying. Finally, the 1981 is very stylish, with a pungent, earthy, grassy bouquet, and well-balanced flavors.

OLIVIER (Cru Classé) GOOD

In excess of 9,000 cases of white Graves, from a blend of 65% Semillon, 33% Sauvignon Blanc, and 2% Muscadelle, are made at Château Olivier in Léognan. The wine is bottled after aging in vats (approximately 30% is barrel-fermented and aged six months in new oak), and is meant to be consumed within 3 to 4 years of its vintage. I have found Olivier to be a sound, reliable, usually fresh, fruity wine, which makes no pretensions of greatness, but is satisfying and never very expensive. The 1983 is quite good, if on the light side for a white Graves from this vintage.

OTHER NOTABLE GRAVES PROPERTIES

FERRANDE (Unclassified)

Evaluation of present classification: The quality equivalent of a Grand Bourgeois Exceptionnel

Ferrande produces easy-to-drink, supple, round, warm, soft, red wines, and stylish, earthy, white wines. The quality is certainly as good as most Crus Classés of Graves, yet the price is remarkably low. The red wine is a blend of 40% Cabernet Sauvignon, 40% Merlot, and 20% Cabernet Franc. It usually reaches maturity 2 to 4 years after the vintage. The recent vintages to consider include the 1982, 1981, and 1979. The white wine is a blend of 60% Sauvignon Blanc and 40% Semillon. The 1981 is quite good, but the star at a tasting of white Graves that I attended in Bordeaux was the 1983, which had wonderful fruit, style, and concentration.

LES CARMES HAUT-BRION (Unclassified)

Evaluation of present classification: The quality equivalent of a Grand Bourgeois Exceptionnel

A small producer of only 1,800 cases of red wine from an unusual blend of 50% Merlot, 40% Cabernet Franc, and 10% Cabernet Sauvignon, Les Carmes Haut-Brion is a neighbor of Haut-Brion and Pape-Clément in the bustling Bordeaux suburb of Pessac. This is an underrated wine which seems to always have a great depth of color, robust, rich structure, and plenty of substance and tannin. If the wine has a flaw, it is a certain coarseness that never quite mellows out with aging. My first exposure to Les Carmes Haut-Brion was a big, robust, chewy 1959, and recent vintages show that the style of wine has not changed. The supple, rich, lush 1982, stylish 1978, and flavorful 1975 all are wines that are better than many Crus Classés of Graves.

L'ARRIVET-HAUT-BRION (Unclassified)

Evaluation of present classification: The quality equivalent of a Grand Bourgeois

This estate in Léognan has a reputation for solid, well-colored wines which are supposedly among the best of the unclassified Graves properties. Unfortunately, I have had very limited tasting experience with this estate. While a small amount of white wine is made, which I have never tasted, the primary production here is red wine. 6,000 cases are produced from a 60% Cabernet Sauvignon, 40% Merlot blend. A 1973 and 1981 tasted in 1984 both exhibited good, plummy fruit, a spicy, vanillin, oaky character, and aging potential of 5 to 8 years.

LA GARDE (Unclassified)

Evaluation of present classification: The quality equivalent of a Grand Bourgeois

A large property in the Martillac region that produces 20,000 cases of red wine and 2,000 cases of white, La Garde is owned and managed by the Bordeaux *négociant* firm of Eschenauer. I have never tasted the white wine, but have had a half-dozen vintages of the red. It is made in an open-knit, soft, fruity, medium-bodied, fleshy style, which is best consumed before it reaches its eighth birthday. Of those vintages I have tasted, all were quite sound, but the 1978 and 1979 pleased me the most.

RAHOUL (Unclassified)

Evaluation of present classification: The quality equivalent of a Grand Bourgeois

Australian wine writer Len Evans has taken the ultimate risk for a wine critic and that is to make wine. His estate, Rahoul, produces both white wine (300 cases) and red wine (5,500 cases). As little white wine as there is, it has been remarkably good, rich, and flavorful, with a pronounced oakiness, no doubt attributable to the use of a high percentage of new barrels. The 1981 was elegant, the 1982 opulent and exotic, and the 1983 powerful, oaky, and rich.

The red wine is a blend of 80% Merlot and 20% Cabernet Sauvignon, and it seems to get better with each vintage. Fleshy, savory, and marked by oak, it is a supple, exuberant wine for drinking within its first 8 years of life. The 1982 leads the pack with regard to recent vintages, followed by the 1979 and 1981. Rahoul is a property to watch.

RESPIDE (Unclassified)

Evaluation of present classification: The quality equivalent of a Cru Bourgeois

Respide has a growing reputation for both its red and white wines. For some unknown reason, I have not seen these wines on the American market for the last several years. However, the red wine from vintages such as 1970, 1971, and 1978 showed a round, accessible fruitiness, medium body, and fragrantly pleasing bouquets. I have never tasted the white wine.

PIRON (Unclassified)

Evaluation of present classification: The quality equivalent of a Cru Bourgeois

Piron is primarily a white wine producer, although a little red wine (1,000 cases) is made. The white wine from the last three vintages, 1981, 1982, and 1983, has been consistently good, flinty, dry, crisp, and very stylish. Piron appears to be an underrated property, making reliable wine and selling it at attractive prices.

There are a number of other small properties in Graves that certainly merit a few comments. As for red wines, I have enjoyed the wines of Cheret-Pitres in the town of Portets, particularly the rich, flavorful 1978 and opulent, spicy 1982. Millet, in the same vicinity, also makes a stylish, yet rather lightweight wine. Red wine producers that have left rather bland impressions on me included Baret in Villenave-d'Ornon, La Tour-Bicheau in Portets, and in more recent vintages, de France in Léognan.

As for the white wine producers in Graves, de Courbon in Toulenne, Domaine la Grave in Portets, Magence in St.-Pierre-de-Mons, and de Chantegrive in Podensac can all make sound, crisp, refreshing examples of white Graves wines.

THE WINES OF POMEROL

For those wine enthusiasts who put their faith in rigid classifications of wine quality like the 1855 classification of the wines of the Médoc, the little, flat countryside of Pomerol must appear like an unwanted stepchild of its more famous neighbor to the southeast, St.-Emilion. Yet, as the true connoisseur of wine knows so well, unclassified Pomerol wines have a habit of upstaging dinner parties where wine lovers inexplicably let out more cries of joy for the Pomerol on the table than for the famous Médoc classified growth that "was supposed to be" the pinnacle of gustatory delight.

The wines of Pomerol have never been classified as have the red wines of the Médoc, Graves, and St.-Emilion. Yet the region's wines have never enjoyed more popularity, and their recently achieved respect shows no signs of abating as more and more wine lovers learn of the sumptuous, opulent joys of so many wines from this bucolic region that is no bigger than the size of one Médoc commune.

Today, the Bordeaux wine most in demand is not a Médoc first-growth such as Margaux, Lafite-Rothschild, Mouton-Rothschild, or Latour, but a Pomerol called Pétrus. It fetches prices a good 50% more than a Médoc first-growth when young, and with age, will usually sell for twice the price. No doubt its minuscule production of roughly 4,000 cases is responsible for the high prices, but the sheer magnitude of this colossal wine's power and richness, and its position as the spiritual head of the Pomerol family, make it so unique that I seriously doubt that even if 20,000 cases were available, the price or demand would be any different.

Pétrus sits at the summit of Pomerol. While it may have no challengers for pure strength and richness, there is a fleet of decadently rich, opulent wines right below it in quality.

What is the key to the telltale characteristic traits of Pomerol wines? The deep, dark ruby color, the intense, plummy, sometimes truffle-scented but always deep fruity bouquet, and lush, voluptuous, almost unctuous texture these wines possess is a result of the Merlot grape.

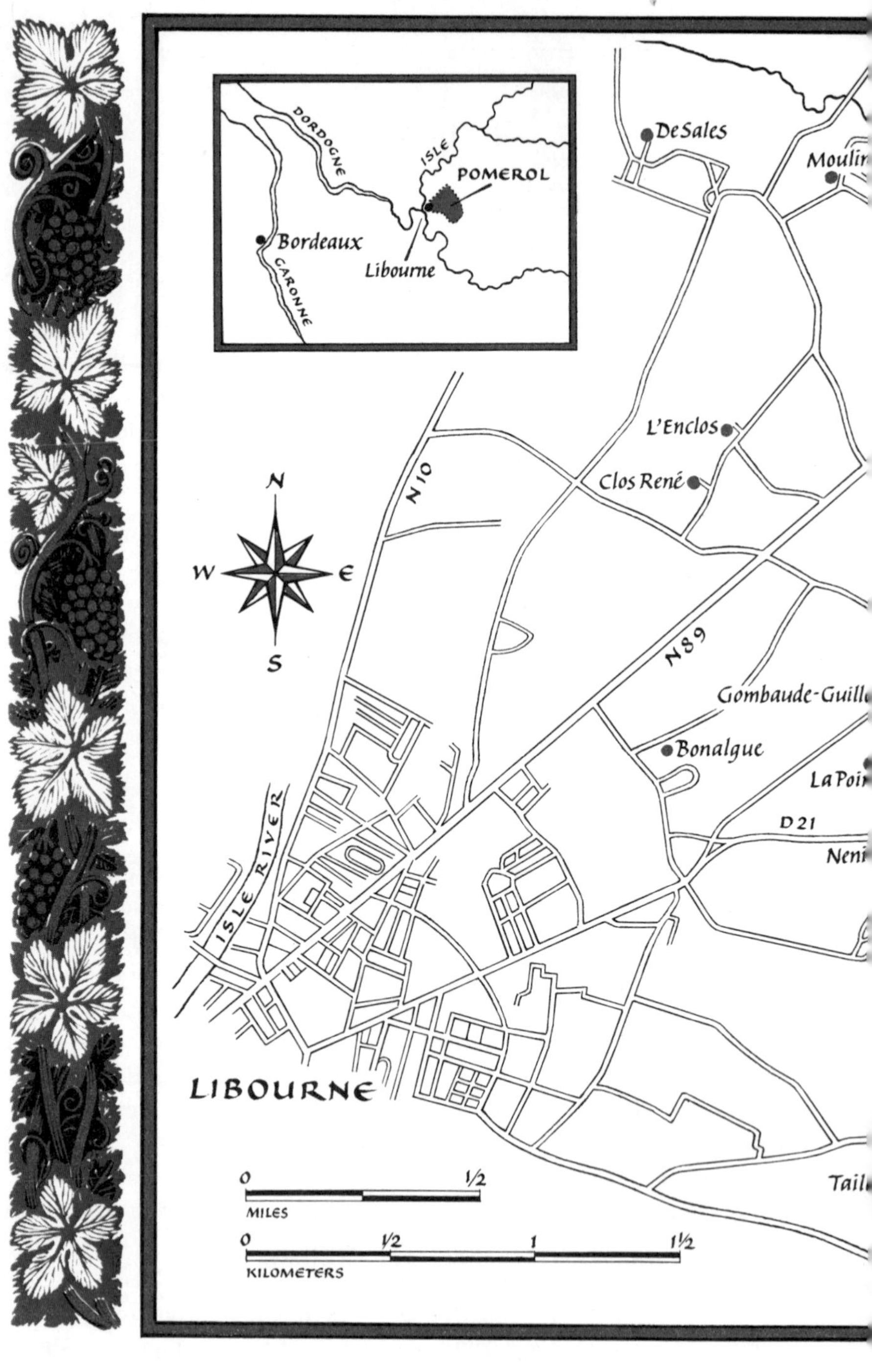
DORDOGNE
ISLE
POMEROL
Bordeaux
GARONNE
Libourne
De Sales
L'Enclos
Clos René
N10
N
W
E
S
N89
Gombaude-Guill
Bonalgue
La Poi
D21
Nen
ISLE RIVER
LIBOURNE
Tail
0
1/2
MILES
0
1/2
1
1½
KILOMETERS

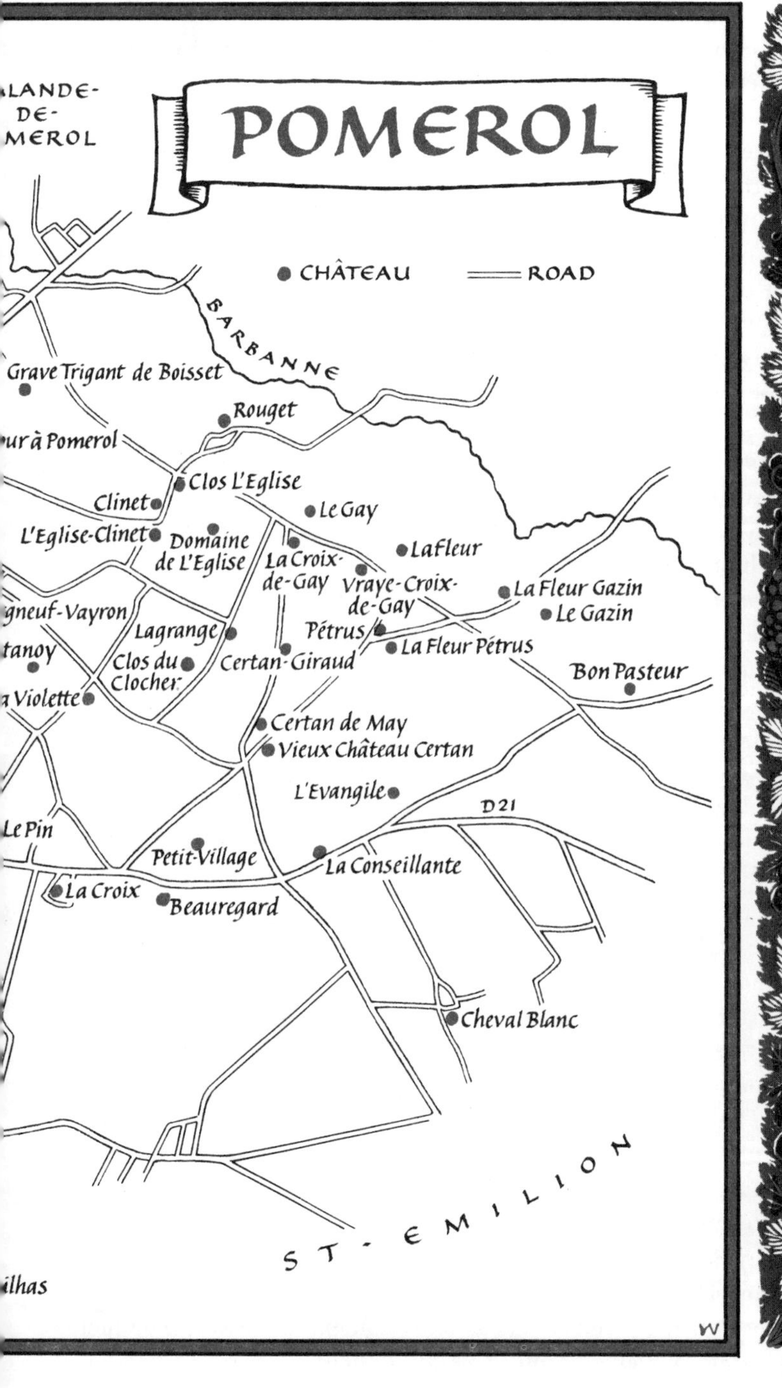

LANDE-
DE-
MEROL
POMEROL
CHÂTEAU
ROAD
BARBANNE
Grave Trigant de Boisset
Rouget
ur à Pomerol
Clos L'Eglise
Clinet
Le Gay
L'Eglise-Clinet
Domaine de L'Eglise
La Croix-de-Gay
LaFleur
Vraye-Croix-de-Gay
La Fleur Gazin
Le Gazin
gneuf-Vayron
Lagrange
Pétrus
La Fleur Pétrus
tanoy
Clos du Clocher
Certan-Giraud
Bon Pasteur
a Violette
Certan de May
Vieux Château Certan
L'Evangile
D21
Le Pin
Petit-Village
La Conseillante
La Croix
Beauregard
Cheval Blanc
ST-EMILION
ilhas
W

Merlot grows elsewhere in Bordeaux, where its supple, fleshy personality helps cut and smooth out the rough, astringent Cabernet Sauvignon. But in Pomerol, Merlot is king. Planted in abundance, and usually representing at least 50%, and at Pétrus 95% of the grapes used in making the wine in Pomerol, Merlot has proved to be the perfect grape variety for the heavy, clay subsoil that dominates most of this region.

The first-time visitor to Pomerol is struck by not only the smallness of this region, but also by its modest châteaux that are more like houses than the aristocratic, sprawling châteaux that exist in the Médoc. The area is quite flat, although a small ridge does rise to an elevation of 130 feet above sea level. Not surprisingly, Pétrus and a number of other Pomerols sit on this plateau. In the Médoc, many classified growths produce 15,000 to 20,000 cases of red wine, and a few produce 35,000 to 40,000 cases. In Pomerol, the largest two producers are Nenin and de Sales, who make respectively 7,000 and 16,000 cases of wine. Most Pomerol properties produce only between 1,200 cases and 3,600 cases of wine. The appellation is planted to the maximum, and there is no hope for increased quantities of Pomerol's succulent, round, and generous wines. As the wine world continues to discover the top Pomerol estates, prices will only get higher because the supply never has (and never will) kept pace with the demand for these luscious wines.

The overall quality of winemaking in Pomerol is extremely high. Only in the Médoc appellation of St.-Julien is there as brilliant an overall level of quality winemaking present throughout both the lesser- and the well-known properties.

As for the styles of wine produced in Pomerol, it is true if one says generally that these are Bordeaux's most gentle, smooth, silky, lush and richly fruity wines. However, that does not explain the diversity of styles that one can find here. Pétrus is of course this appellation's greatest wine, as well as the most massively concentrated, rich, and long-lived. The heavy clay soil that the vineyard of Pétrus sits on results in a powerful wine. Yet Trotanoy is often indistinguishable from Pétrus in blind tastings and is clearly the most complete and demanded Pomerol after Pétrus. Not surprisingly, Pétrus is made from 95% Merlot and Trotanoy 85%, and they are treated identically by the same winemaking team. The only other Pomerol that can rival the massive concentration of Pétrus as well as its complex, opulent, and exotic bouquet is the tiny estate of Lafleur. Interestingly, Lafleur's vineyard sits adjacent to that of Pétrus and it too has the extremely old vines that render such small quantities, yet give such concentrated juice. These three vineyards refused to tear out their vines after the killing freeze in 1956.

If Pétrus, Trotanoy, and Lafleur make Pomerol's richest, deepest colored, most massive wines, L'Evangile, La Conseillante, Petit-Village, La Fleur-Pétrus, and L'Eglise-Clinet produce this appellation's most graceful, smooth, elegant, burgundian-like wine. None of these properties can lay claim to making as massive or as rich a wine as Pétrus, Trotanoy, or Lafleur, but no Pomerol enthusiast would dare pass up the opportunity to lay away a few bottles or cases of any of these wines.

L'Evangile and La Conseillante have two of Pomerol's greatest reputations and despite some irregular performances, usually produce excellent wine. La Conseillante tends to be rather light and precocious for a Pomerol, but has the cunning ability to age well. L'Evangile is inconsistent, but can make spectacularly perfumed wines suggestive of violets and ripe blackcurrants. Its 1975, 1982, and 1983 are among the greatest wines of those top vintages.

La Fleur-Pétrus has the right name for fame, yet it seems to rarely get the accolades it should. It is usually a superb Pomerol, velvety, rich, savory, quick to mature, but complex and delicious. Its vineyard sits on very gravelly soil, which no doubt contributes to its precocious personality.

Petit-Village has the same type of soil, but until recently the wine did not have the most meticulous care and ownership. This is a potentially great vineyard of Pomerol that until the late 1970s had performed well below its potential level. Now the wine is very carefully made with no compromises and Petit-Village is one of the up-and-coming Pomerols to watch. The trio of vintages in the '80s, the fine, racy 1981, incredibly rich, exotic 1982, and the robust 1983, are reason to take Petit-Village more seriously than ever before.

L'Eglise-Clinet is another budding superstar of this appellation. Possessed of some of Pomerol's oldest vines, this traditionally run property produces an explosively fruity, darkly colored Pomerol that always seems to have the taste of rich, velvety fruit.

A third style of Pomerol wine might well be called the "Médoc" style. Two top Pomerol estates, Vieux Château Certan and Clos L'Eglise, do indeed make a wine with a high percentage of Cabernet Sauvignon rather than Merlot, and their wines often have more Médoc-like characteristics than other Pomerols. Both properties employ between 30% and 40% Cabernet Sauvignon and Cabernet Franc in their blends, which is abnormally high for a Pomerol. Vieux Château Certan has the greater reputation of the two and for years was considered the best

Pomerol after Pétrus. However, this property's wines passed through an uninspired period in the '60s and '70s that caused a drop in the reputation of Vieux Château Certan. Hopefully, the wines of the '80s signal a return to the style and quality Vieux Château Certan had in the '40s and '50s.

A fourth school of Pomerols produces wines that are light, supple and immediately drinkable, and which rarely last more than a decade. Most of these Pomerols are located in the western part of the appellation on neither clay nor gravelly soil, but on light, sandy soils. These Pomerols rarely have the reputations that the bigger, tannic, more massive wines do, but they offer immediate drinkability, charm, and excellent value. Three of the best estates in this area are de Sales, L'Enclos, and Clos René. All three make very fine wines with the wine of L'Enclos usually the most complete.

There are two other groups of superb Pomerols that make some of this appellation's finest wines. Sitting together alongside Pétrus on the famous plateau of Pomerol are Certan de May, Certan-Giraud, and Le Gay. These properties have gravelly soil, but produce totally different styles of wine. Certan de May's wine since 1976 has been not only one of the great wines of Pomerol, but of all Bordeaux. This is a tiny property meticulously and impeccably looked after by the proud Madame Odette Barreau and her son. The wine produced here is a fragrant, very rich, deep, quite tannic wine that will keep and improve for 15–20 years in the top vintages. Certan-Giraud is a neighbor, but its wine is made in a forwardly fruity, lush, Pomerol style with oodles of fruit present. While Certan de May has been discovered and the prices demanded for its splendid 2,000–2,200 cases of wine are quite high, Certan-Giraud has not yet gotten the acclaim it deserves and therefore its prices are somewhat lower than what they will ultimately be. Le Gay, the third property on this plateau, is run by another woman, Marie Robin, who produces a tannic, deeply scented, surprisingly rich, virile wine from very old vines. Le Gay has a notorious reputation for inconsistency, but recently the 1975 and 1982 have been brilliant.

Less than a kilometer to the west sits one of the top-flight Pomerols, Latour à Pomerol. Its vineyard is situated on a mixture of sandy and gravelly soil, and is consistently one of the top Pomerols. It is always hard to find as connoisseurs, knowing that Latour à Pomerol can produce one of the greatest wines in all of Bordeaux as it did in 1961, 1970, 1982, and 1983, scramble to grab up the few cases of this rather big, brawny, yet rich, velvety Pomerol.

Like all appellations of Bordeaux, Pomerol too has its crop of potential new stars, as well as perennial underachievers meriting interest (for different reasons) by any Bordeaux enthusiast. Old properties sporting new, hopeful images are such up-and-coming estates as Bon Pasteur, Rouget, La Violette, and La Grave Trigant de Boisset. A totally new, tiny property that looks to have a great future is Le Pin.

Historically well-regarded properties that are not living up to their reputations include Gazin, Nenin, Clinet, and Domaine de L'Eglise.

The best vintages for Pomerol tend to be those where the Merlot grape has flowered and ripened well. When the Merlot has problems, as it did in 1984, Pomerol is not an appellation to search for good values. The great recent vintages for Pomerol have been 1982 (a year most growers consider the best since 1947), 1975, 1971, 1970, 1967, 1964, and of course 1961. Because the growers harvest the earlier-ripening Merlot one to two weeks sooner than the later picking properties in the Médoc, Pomerol can sometimes complete its harvest in excellent weather long before the Médoc, which may be caught by fall rains. Classic cases in point would be 1964 and 1967, where the Pomerols were very good to excellent, and the Médocs generally rather diluted and weak.

In off-vintages for Pomerol, one wine has consistently performed the best and that has been Trotanoy. Trotanoy's soil drains better than the heavy clay soil at Pétrus, and in relatively poor Pomerol vintages like 1972, 1974, and 1984, Trotanoy can be a surprising revelation.

Much of the success and current prestige Pomerol's wines have received has only come about in the last 30 years. Until the early 1950s, Pétrus was not even known in America. It was the English, Belgian, and Dutch who first promoted these wines and chronicled their beauty. Their task was made much easier by the fact that the quality of many Pomerols was so high. Much of the credit for that belongs to one man, Jean-Pierre Moueix, a gentleman of taste who championed the virtues of Pomerol's wines, and in the process built up a firm that now owns or controls most of the top Pomerol wines of this appellation. Jean-Pierre Moueix's vision of greatness for these wines, combined with his fanatical commitment to the highest quality, has not only guaranteed that Pomerols are no longer regarded as the stepchildren of Bordeaux, but has ensured that they are Bordeaux's new superstars.

A CONSUMER'S CLASSIFICATION OF THE CHÂTEAUX OF POMEROL

OUTSTANDING

Pétrus, Trotanoy

EXCELLENT

Lafleur, Latour à Pomerol, L'Evangile, La Conseillante, Certan de May, Vieux Château Certan, La Fleur Pétrus

VERY GOOD

Le Gay, L'Enclos, L'Eglise-Clinet, de Sales, Rouget, Bon Pasteur, Petit-Village, Clos René, Certan-Giraud, La Grave Trigant de Boisset, Le Pin

ABOVE AVERAGE TO GOOD

La Croix

OTHER NOTABLE POMEROL PROPERTIES

Nenin, Gazin, Lagrange, La Fleur Gazin, Plince, Taillefer, Domaine de L'Eglise, Tailhas, La Violette, Vraye-Croix-de-Gay, Clos L'Eglise, Clos du Clocher, Clinet, Beaurenard, La Pointe, Bourgneuf-Vayron, Bonalgue, Gombaude-Guillot, Moulinet, La Croix de Gay

PÉTRUS (Unclassified) OUTSTANDING

Production: 3,800–4,000 cases	Grape varieties: Merlot—95% Cabernet Franc—5%
Time spent in barrels: 22–28 months	Average age of vines: 42–45 years
Evaluation of present classification: The quality equivalent of a first-growth	

The wines of Pétrus have taken on legendary proportions, yet in spite of an almost mystical allegiance connoisseurs give this wine, it seems to deserve all the superlatives attributed to it. This small, modest estate, jointly owned by Jean-Pierre Moueix and Mme. L. P. Lacoste-Loubat, produces Bordeaux's most intensely concentrated, richly flavored, and unique red wine. In great vintages, it has a jammy viscosity and such a powerful presence on the palate that comparisons with vintage port are not too far-fetched. Yet for all its power, depth, and richness, the secret to the greatness of Pétrus is its remarkable balance and penetrating aroma which set it so much apart from not only other Pomerols, but all of Bordeaux's finest wines.

The reasons why Pétrus is what it is are mostly a result of the soil. The composition of the topsoil and the subsoil at Pétrus is almost all clay, whereas at adjacent properties the soil is either a gravel-sand mixture or clay-sand mixture. The Merlot flourishes in this soil, and for that reason, Pétrus's vineyard is planted with 95% Merlot. In addition to the soil, the vines at Pétrus are unusually old, and are only replanted after they reach 70 years of age. Unlike many Pomerol estates that tore out their vines and replanted after the devastating killer freeze suffered by this region in 1956, Madame Loubat, the owner then, refused to replant, and simply waited several years for the vines to recover.

Even with the unique clay soil and old vines, Pétrus would not be the wine it is without brilliant management of the vineyard and expert winemaking. Under the passionate direction of Jean-Pierre's son, Christian, and this family's brilliant oenologist, Jean-Claude Berrouet, Pétrus receives the care of a spoiled and pampered child. The grapes are picked only in the afternoon, when the morning dew has evaporated, so as not to risk even the slightest dilution of quality. When the wine has finished its fermentations, a severe selection of only the finest lots are chosen to go into Pétrus itself. Like a first-growth in the Médoc, Pétrus is aged completely in new oak casks, and never filtered for fear of removing some of its remarkable richness.

Pétrus is a wine that in great vintages needs and requires 12 to 15 years of cellaring. Because of its incredible opulence and almost decadent richness, far too much of Pétrus is drunk long before it even reaches its tenth birthday. It ages as well as any Médoc first-growth, always retaining its incredible sweetness, as well as ripe, rich, Merlot fruitiness. Pétrus is better made now than ever before, and its performance in recent vintages attests to its remarkable popularity and celestial price.

VINTAGES

1983—The 1983 Pétrus, while quite excellent, is a very big, jammy,
· densely colored wine which has considerable power and author-
89 ity on the palate, but is lacking a bit in finesse and balance. Quite full-bodied, viscous, and chewy, with outstanding ripeness, and plenty of tannin, this is a rather gawky Pétrus that

needs time to completely pull itself together. Anticipated maturity: 1993–2015. Last tasted, 3/85.

1982—The 1982 Pétrus will no doubt be regarded as one of the great
· wines of this century. It embodies all of the greatest elements of
100 legendary wines and legendary vintages of Pétrus. Consistently "perfect" from the cask and bottle, words hardly do justice to such a rare achievement. First, the color is sensationally dark, the bouquet explodes upward from the glass within penetrating aromas of ripe mulberry, blackcurrant fruit, and spicy vanillin oak. The wealth of fruit overwhelms the palate with a luxuriance and richness that I have never encountered before. Even the considerable tannic clout of this monumental wine seems to be buried by what is simply a tidal wave of voluptuous, decadently concentrated fruit. In March 1983, when I first tasted this wine, I thought it was the most perfect and symmetrical wine I had ever experienced. Later that day, Christian Moueix called it his "legacy." In an age when "the greatest ever" seems to lack significance and sincerity, this is truly the best wine ever produced for this remarkable property. Anticipated maturity: 1995–2030. Last tasted, 1/85.

1981—A monumental bottle of wine, and unquestionably the wine of
· the vintage, the 1981 Pétrus is the best wine produced by the
95 property since 1975, until the 1982 was conceived. Christian Moueix likens it to the marvelous 1971, but it tastes bigger and more tannic than that wine. The color is dark ruby/purple, the bouquet explodes upward from the glass inundating the nose with ripe cassis scents, spicy vanillin oak, grilled almonds, and toffee. Incredibly rich, viscous and full-bodied, this amazing, multidimensional wine will need a good 15 years of cellaring to mature fully. What fun millionaire collectors will have 20 years from now comparing the 1981 to what appears to be the wine of the century, the 1982 Pétrus. Anticipated maturity: 1997–2025. Last tasted: 1/85.

1980—A difficult vintage, but Pétrus, while lighter and less powerful
· than usual, has made a wine with good ripeness of fruit, medium
85 body, a spicy, open-knit bouquet and supple, round flavors. Drink over the next 6–7 years. Last tasted, 3/85.

1979—Nineteen seventy-nine was a very successful vintage for the
· Merlot grapes; consequently most of the wines of Pomerol
92 turned out quite well. The 1979 Pétrus is the top wine of Pomerol in this vintage. Quite rich and powerful with a dense dark-ruby

color, Pétrus has a bouqet of ripe blackcurrants, spicy oak, and a hint of toffee. On the palate the wine is of typically Pétrus proportions—large-framed, concentrated, tannic, and very long and voluptuous. Not the size and weight of the 1975, 1981, or 1982, the 1979 is still a very impressive Pétrus. Anticipated maturity: 1993–2015. Last tasted, 11/84.

1978—I have never found the 1978 Pétrus to be typical of this estate's
· wines. It enjoys a good reputation and sells at stratospheric
82 prices, but it has consistently tasted loosely knit, a trifle flabby
and overripe, and distinctively vegetal- and herbaceous-scented. Rather soft, with round, ripe, moderate tannins, this is a Pétrus I would monitor closely and opt for drinking over the next 6–8 years. Last tasted, 4/83.

1977—In retrospect, I would imagine that if Christian Moueix and his
· father had to do it over again, they would not have released the
69 1977 Pétrus. Not that it is unpalatable, but it is a disappointing
wine, stalky, vegetal tasting, and ungenerous, thinnish flavors. Drink up. Last tasted, 1/83.

1976—A good but not special Pétrus, this wine is now fully mature with
· a full-blown bouquet of herbaceous tobacco aromas, spicy oak,
84 and overripe fruit. Somewhat loosely knit and unstructured, and
lacking the firmness of the best vintages, this is a big, alcoholic wine without much finesse. Drink over the next 5 years. Last tasted, 4/83.

1975—One of the two greatest wines of the vintage, as well as the most
· concentrated tannic and concentrated Pétrus of the decade of the
98 '70s, the 1975 is a blockbuster wine, opulently rich, broodingly
dark in color, and rather massive, yet so, so backward on the palate. Layered with sweet, ripe blackcurranty fruit, this huge wine is oozing with tannin as well. This is a monumental Pétrus that must be kept. It will keep for 50 years. Anticipated maturity: 2000–2050. Last tasted, 12/84.

1973—The wine of the vintage, this is the best Pétrus for immediate
· consumption from those wines produced in the '70s. Given the
87 prolific yield in 1973 and the diluted, thinnish quality of many
wines, the Pétrus is sensationally concentrated, rich, supple, fat and so, so flavorful. Ready to drink, it will keep for at least another 5–6 years. Last tasted, 12/84.

1971—A sensational Pétrus, rich, velvety, full-bodied, with layers of
· silky ripe fruit, the 1971 must surely be the best wine of the
95 vintage. Light to moderate tannins and high alcohol will pre-

serve this plump unctuous wine for another decade, but this is a Pétrus that one can begin to drink as it is close to its apogee. Anticipated maturity: 1987–2000. Last tasted, 1/85.

1970—I believe I have always been in the minority, preferring the
· velvety, voluptuous and sensual 1971 to the more massive-
93 framed 1970. The 1970 is still young and has, I am sure, quite a long future ahead of it, but to my taste, it has always had less distinction and character. However, it is an excellent wine, rich, jammy, typically loaded with fruit, and like so many wines of Pétrus, extremely rich, full-bodied and long on the palate. Anticipated maturity: 1990–2020. Last tasted, 10/84.

1967—In this vintage which produced so many lightweight wines, only
· the stablemate of Pétrus, Trotanoy, can compete with the great
90 Pétrus. Fully mature with good, dark ruby color and minimal browning, this chunky, fleshy, warm and generous wine has plenty of ripe Merlot fruit, a viscous, weighty texture, and fast-fading tannins. A lovely Pétrus, it is best drunk over the next 5–6 years. Last tasted, 12/83.

1966—Excellent, but even more highly regarded elsewhere than by me,
· the 1966 Pétrus is quite full-bodied, with very good, viscous,
89 ripe, berry flavors. A big, almost syrupy wine that seems just a trifle out of synch, the 1966 Pétrus has plenty of tannin, alcohol, and flavor, but they have not yet fully meshed. Anticipated maturity: 1986–1996. Last tasted, 11/84.

1964—A massive, even mammoth wine, the 1964 has extraordinary
· concentration and weight. The bouquet gushes from the glass
97 carrying with it intense aromas of ripe fruit, caramel, framboise, and vanillin oak. Incredibly dense, powerful, and viscous, this multidimensional wine should be drunk over the next 10 years. Last tasted, 12/84.

1962—This is a very good Pétrus, yet I have never found it to have the
· great richness and individual personality so prevalent in other
87 vintages of this great wine. Quite fruity, but rather straightforward and lacking direction, this plump, chunky wine has attraction, but tastes short in the finish for Pétrus. Drink now. Last tasted, 10/83.

1961—A perfect wine, the 1961 Pétrus has an unforgettable bouquet of
· ripe blackcurrants, warm-melted buttery caramel, and toasty
100 vanillin oak. Massively proportioned, yet so impeccably balanced, this wine has exotic, opulent, astonishingly concentrated flavors. Extremely dense, with a port-like viscosity, this stagger-

ing wine is just entering a period of maturity that will take it well into the next century. It is an awesome wine. Last tasted, 1/85.

TROTANOY (Unclassified) OUTSTANDING

Production: 3,500–3,800 cases	Grape varieties: Merlot—85% Cabernet Franc—15%
Time spent in barrels: 20–24 months	Average age of vines: 35 years
Evaluation of present classification: The quality equivalent of a first-growth	

Trotanoy is one of the great wines of both Pomerol and Bordeaux. It is at least the quality equivalent of a Médoc second-growth, and in most vintages every bit as good as a first-growth. Trotanoy has been owned since 1953 by the firm of Jean-Pierre Moueix. This modest estate lies a kilometer to the west of Pétrus on a mixed soil of clay and gravel. The wine is vinified and handled in exactly the same way as Pétrus, except only 33% to 50% of the barrels used each year at Trotanoy are new.

Trotanoy is an opulently rich, intense, full-bodied wine which usually needs a full decade of cellaring to reach its zenith. In some vintages, its power, intensity, and concentration come remarkably close to matching that of Pétrus. It has an enviable track record of producing good, sometimes brilliant wines in poor Bordeaux vintages. The 1967, 1972, and 1974 are three examples of vintages where Trotanoy was among the best two or three wines of the entire Bordeaux region.

In the late '70s, 1976–1979, Trotanoy seemed to lighten up a bit in style, perhaps a result of replanting done in the early '70s. However, the wines of the first three vintages of the '80s have been typically rich, savory, full-bodied examples of Trotanoy at its best.

Trotanoy is an expensive wine since it is highly regarded by connoisseurs the world over. Yet it rarely sells for more than half the price of Pétrus, a fact worth remembering since it does in certain vintages have more than just a casual resemblance to the great Pétrus itself.

VINTAGES

1983—A powerful, tannic, rather big-boned Trotanoy, the 1983 has
· impressively deep color, hard, dry tannins in ample quantities,
87 very good concentration of fruit, and an assertive, aggressive

personality. It needs extended cellaring to mellow and lose some of its coarseness. Anticipated maturity: 1995–2010. Last tasted, 3/85.

1982—One of the greatest Trotanoys ever produced, the 1982 is almost
· black purple in color, with a reticent, but powerful, rich, deep
96 bouquet of ripe blackcurrants and a hint of fresh leather. On the palate, the wine is massively proportioned à la Pétrus, with an avalanche of rich, ripe fruit and plenty of mouth-searing tannins. Has there ever been a greater Trotanoy? Probably not. Anticipated maturity: 1997–2020. Last tasted, 1/85.

1981—Lighter than either the stupendous 1982 or very fine 1983, the
· 1981 Trotanoy is an elegantly wrought, yet authoritative, rich
87 wine with good, deep, ripe fruit, a spicy, oaky, leathery bouquet, full body, very good concentration, and plenty of tannin in the finish. It will have a slow, long evolution. Anticipated maturity: 1994–2010. Last tasted, 11/84.

1979—Surprisingly precocious, charmingly supple and fruity, the 1979
· Trotanoy continues to develop well in the bottle. Quite drinkable
86 now, this is not a big or massive Trotanoy, but rather a round, ample, elegant wine with good overall balance. It should drink and age well for another 8–10 years. Last tasted, 11/84.

1978—The 1978 Trotanoy has matured quite rapidly. Ready to drink
· now, it has a full-blown bouquet suggestive of herbs, fresh to-
84 matoes, and blackcurrants. On the palate the wine is medium-bodied, soft and velvety, without the depth of fruit normally found in this wine. Little tannin remains in this rather exotic-styled Trotanoy. Drink over the next 4 years. Last tasted, 11/84.

1976—I have enjoyed the 1976 Trotanoy, generally very highly re-
· garded by other critics, but it is now fully mature, showing signs
84 of overripeness, and has a jammy, low acid character. Quite plummy, fat, even peppery, with a lovely lush structure, this is an exotic style of Trotanoy that is quite delicious, but lacking backbone and structure. Drink up! Last tasted, 10/83.

1975—The 1975 Trotanoy is a great success. It is very concentrated
· with broad, deep, rich, long ripe fruity flavors, and a bouquet
93 that combines scents of tobacco, toffee, leather, and mulberries to reveal sensationally complex aromas. Fleshy, full-bodied and still tannic, but beginning to open and shed some astringence, this is an excellent Trotanoy. Anticipated maturity: 1988–2010. Last tasted, 1/85.

1974—One of the best wines of the vintage (clearly the best Pomerol),
· Trotanoy's 1974 is now fully mature and should be drunk over
87 the next 2–3 years. Uncommonly concentrated and surprisingly
ripe and fruity, this medium to full-bodied wine has good concentration, and a smooth, very satisfying finish. Last tasted, 12/84.

1971—The 1971 is a controversial Trotanoy. Virtually everyone agrees
· that it is wonderfully fruity and rich, but the disagreement cen-
92 ters over whether it is mature. Despite its gobs of velvety, ripe,
decadent Merlot fruit, I think the wine is still young and will continue to evolve for at least another 5–6 years. Quite concentrated, with a voluptuous, lush texture, and ripe, intense bouquet, this is an excellent Trotanoy. Anticipated maturity: 1985–1992. Last tasted, 12/84.

1970—A broodingly dark, powerful, closed Trotanoy, the 1970 is large
· proportioned, very full-bodied and concentrated, but also quite
90 tannic and hard. Loaded with potential, but stubbornly back-
ward, this is a wine for the patient. Anticipated maturity: 1990–2005. Last tasted, 11/84.

1967—Only Pétrus is a better wine in 1967. Fully mature, the 1967
· Trotanoy has good dark ruby color, a fleshy, warm, generous
89 constitution that is loaded with savory, ripe Merlot fruit.
Medium-bodied, silky and rich, this is a lovely wine. Drink up! Last tasted, 2/84.

1966—I am beginning to wonder when this wine, still tannic, tough,
· closed in, impressively colored and concentrated, will open up.
85 It is a big, brawny Trotanoy that may very well lose its fruit
before its tannin. Anticipated maturity: 1988–1992. Last tasted, 1/83.

1964—An impressively big, deep, darkly colored Trotanoy, but its
· weight, ripeness, and concentration notwithstanding, the 1964
86 Trotanoy has a persistent touch of bitterness in the finish that
somewhat detracts from an otherwise noteworthy effort. Nevertheless, don't ever pass up the opportunity to taste it. Drink over the next 6–8 years. Last tasted, 9/84.

1962—The top Pomerol of the vintage, Trotanoy is still quite attractive
· with a big, spicy, cedary, tobacco-scented bouquet, and soft,
88 generous, round flavors which linger on the palate. Quite har-
monious and attractive, this wine should be drunk up over the next 3–4 years. Last tasted, 1/83.

1961—One of the greatest Pomerols in this vintage, Trotanoy has mas-
· sive richness, huge body, a ripe, unctuous texture, still plenty
95 of tannin, but extremely long, sweet, and ripe. The 1961 Tro-
tanoy is a gorgeously rich, full-bodied wine which is just now approaching maturity. It will keep for 10–20 more years. Last tasted, 12/84.

LAFLEUR (Unclassified) EXCELLENT

Production: 1,500 cases	Grape varieties: Merlot—50% Cabernet Franc—50%
Time spent in barrels: 20–24 months	Average age of vines: 40 years
Evaluation of present classification: The quality equivalent of a second-growth	

One of the least-known and obscure of the Pomerol properties, Lafleur's tiny vineyard of just over 9 acres sits just to the north of Pétrus on the gravelly clay plateau of Pomerol. The age of vines is among the oldest in Pomerol, as this vineyard was not torn up after the devastating freeze in 1956.

The history of Lafleur's wines has been one of mixed results. None of the Pomerol cognoscenti will argue with the fact that the vineyard of Lafleur is the only one in Pomerol that produces wine that can challenge the power and richness of the wine of Pétrus. This is a fact that even the owner of Pétrus, Jean-Pierre Moueix, readily acknowledges. However, Lafleur in many vintages has suffered from sloppy management problems, including old dirty barrels and a wine cellar that did double duty as a chicken house. The rumors have always been that great wines were made but that some barrels of the wine became flawed in such a miserably kept cellar.

The co-proprietors of Lafleur, Marie and Therese Robin (now deceased), were extremely dedicated to quality, yet in their advancing age refused to modernize or even listen to advice about making Lafleur and their other Pomerol, Le Gay, in more receptive and cleaner surroundings. Since 1981, the brilliant team of Christian Moueix and Jean-Claude Berrouet have overseen the making of the wine. As the following tasting notes demonstrate, Lafleur can be a sensationally and consistently great wine.

In style, Lafleur is easily the match for Pétrus in power and weight.

It remains to be seen if Lafleur can match Pétrus for complexity and balance, but there is no doubt that a bottle of Lafleur from a very good vintage is a massive, monumental wine of great richness and presence.

VINTAGES

1983—The 1983 is a powerful, rich, alcoholic (over 14%) wine with
· tremendous presence, richness, and power on the palate. Typi-
90 cally Lafleur, it is a brawny, ripe, intense wine with considerable
concentration and tannin. Anticipated maturity: 1995–2010.
Last tasted, 3/85.

1982—According to the firm of Jean-Pierre Moueix, the 1982 is the
· greatest Lafleur ever made, even better than the majestic 1975
95 and legendary 1947. I cannot disagree, although this wine does
not quite have the sheer weight and power of these two previous
vintages. Consistently impressive from the cask and bottle, this
is a titan of a wine. Black ruby purple in color, with an amazing
concentration of rich, layered, plummy, blackcurrant fruit and
an enormous bouquet of oak and plums, this is a terrific, yet
quite tannic wine of immense proportions. Anticipated maturity:
1995–2010. Last tasted, 1/85.

1981—Considerable bottle variation seems to be the culprit with the
· 1981 Lafleur. The good examples exhibit a savory, supple,
? chewy, spicy, velvety, concentrated fruitiness, medium body,
and light tannins. The others, an annoying musty aroma which
refuses to dissipate with aeration. Drink over the next 5 years.
Last tasted, 11/84.

1979—One of the top two Pomerols in this vintage, Lafleur's power and
· richness are readily apparent. Very dark ruby, almost opaque,
90 Lafleur's bouquet is tight and unyielding, but reluctantly renders
aromas of plums, mineral scent, and blackcurrants. On the palate the wine is quite full-bodied, very tannic, extremely long in
the finish and concentrated. This wine is an atypical 1979 because of its backwardness and size, but for Lafleur, quite normal. Anticipated maturity: 1990–2000. Last tasted, 2/84.

1978—I have always been astonished that the elderly, frail, small-
· framed Robin sisters could produce such robust, intense, pow-
86 erful wine. The 1978 lacks the overall balance and promise of
the 1979, and is very straightforward and big rather than interesting, but this is another quite rich, full-bodied, intensely
tannic, very darkly colored wine. Anticipated maturity: 1988–
2000. Last tasted, 5/82.

1976—Like many Pomerols of this vintage, which was marked by the
• intense heat and drought of that year's summer, Lafleur's 1976
78 shows an overripe character. Diffuse in its structure, with a flabby, soft texture, the flavors of the 1976 Lafleur are pleasingly plump and ripe, but the acidity is quite low, and the tannins fading quickly. Drink up! Last tasted, 9/82.

1975—This splendid wine recalls some of the old-style, heavyweight,
• right-bank wines of the late '40s. Very dark with an unbelievable
96 bouquet of ripe fruit, spices, tobacco, and leather, this huge, full-bodied, tannic, opulent, viscous wine lingers and lingers on the palate. A great old-style Pomerol that is well worth the long wait it requires. Anticipated maturity: 1990–2015. Last tasted, 1/85.

1971—Fully mature, this wine has an opulent, savory, cedary, spicy,
• slightly jammy, herbal bouquet. Soft, supple, broad flavors show
83 a lot of ripe fruit and little tannins. Drink up! Last tasted, 2/84.

1970—Brawny, beefy, full-bodied and stubbornly backward and tannic,
• the 1970 Lafleur is just beginning to open up. The bouquet shows
86 good ripe fruit and an earthy, mineral-scented bouquet with the smell of roasted chestnuts. On the palate the wine is rich, quite tannic, well structured, and long. It is a solid, rustic, robust wine. Anticipated maturity: 1990–2010. Last tasted, 2/84.

1964—Still dark colored with just a slight rim of amber, the 1964 La-
• fleur is quite a big, rich, full-bodied, intense wine with oodles of
87 extract and body. Still tannic, but beginning to open up, this old-style, chewy, powerful wine is lacking in complexity, but delivers quite a mouthful. Drink over the next 10 years. Last tasted, 6/84.

1962—One of the three best Pomerols of the vintage, Lafleur lacks the
• complexity and elegance of the 1962 Trotanoy, but is a more
87 substantial wine than the Pétrus. Surprisingly dark in color, with a full-intensity, waxy, ripe black cherry bouquet, this wine is much tougher and tannic than most 1962s. It is still in excellent condition. This wine should drink well for 5–10 more years. Last tasted, 11/83.

1961—For whatever reason, this wine has never been impressive in the
• two tastings of it I have had. The wine is dark in color with some
70 browning, the bouquet has a hot, charred aroma, and the flavors are astringent and out of balance. There is fruit present, but it is buried behind a wall of bitterness. Last tasted, 3/82.

LATOUR À POMEROL (Unclassified) EXCELLENT

Production: 3,500 cases	Grape varieties: Merlot—80% Cabernet Franc—10% Malbec—10%
Time spent in barrels: 20–24 months	Average age of vines: 32 years

Evaluation of present classification: The quality equivalent of a second-growth

Latour à Pomerol produces splendidly dark-colored wine with typical Pomerol power and opulence, and fleshy, ripe Merlot fruit. The vineyard is situated on gravelly soil just to the north of the tiny village of Catusseau. The vineyard is owned by Mme. L. P. Lacoste-Loubat, the co-owner of Pétrus; however, the wine is vinified, handled, and marketed by the famous Libourne firm of Jean-Pierre Moueix.

Latour à Pomerol can be a majestic Pomerol, and from certain vintages not only one of the great wines of this bucolic commune, but also of all Bordeaux. The 1961, 1970, 1982, and 1983 offer convincing examples of that. Some Pomerol observers have suggested that it comes closest in weight and structure to Pétrus, but except for the 1961 or 1983, I would disagree with such a statement.

Like other top Pomerols, Latour à Pomerols have the glossy, fat, rich fruitiness and texture that deceptively causes people to think they should be drunk young. However, most good vintages often need a full decade of cellaring before consumption.

Latour à Pomerol is usually about one-third the price of Pétrus and about 40–50% less expensive than Trotanoy or Lafleur. For a limited-production Pomerol of high quality, it is a relative bargain.

VINTAGES

1983—Not for the fanciers of light-hearted, streamlined wines, the 1983
· Latour à Pomerol was among the richest, most powerfully con-
90 structed, broodingly opaque and enormous wines I sampled from the cask when doing my early assessments of this vintage. It has remained big, brawny, ripe and muscular, with enough tannins to carry it along for quite some time. Anticipated maturity: 1994–2005. Last tasted, 3/85.

1982—This is a great Latour à Pomerol, black purple in color, ex-
· tremely full-bodied, with a rich, superbly scented bouquet of
93 ripe plums and currants. Decadently rich and multidimensional, with explosive power and plenty of tannins, this big, viscous wine needs a good decade of cellaring. Anticipated maturity: 1992–2010. Last tasted, 1/85.

1981—The 1981 is the best Latour à Pomerol since 1970. However, its
· fame has subsequently been eclipsed by both the 1982 and 1983
87 wines. Very dark in color for a 1981, with a dense, ripe, rich, full-bodied texture on the palate. Quite tannic, well balanced, this big wine will prove to be quite a mouthful in 8–10 years. Last tasted, 10/84.

1979—Precociously fat, supple, and easy to drink, this vintage of La-
· tour à Pomerol seems to have produced an amply endowed,
85 charming, silky wine without much tannin. I would drink this wine—medium-bodied, dark ruby in color, and quite forward—over the next 6–7 years. Last tasted, 10/84.

1978—Jammy, soft, ripe and quite round, the 1978 Latour à Pomerol is
· ready to drink. Like many Pomerols of this vintage, I detect a
83 degree of overripeness and shortness in the finish, nevertheless, this is a pleasant, fruity wine. Drink over the next 4–5 years. Last tasted, 2/83.

1976—My favorite 1976 Pomerol. This estate managed to produce a
· rich, flavorful, spicy, concentrated wine while avoiding the
85 overripe character that afflicted so many Pomerol estates. Lush, silky, creamy and fruity, this medium-bodied wine is complemented nicely by spicy oak. Fully mature with no discernible tannins remaining, this wine should be drunk over the next 3 years. Last tasted, 12/83.

1975—In a vintage where a number of Pomerols are superb, the 1975
· Latour à Pomerol is inexplicably disappointing. Severe, tannic,
67 hollow, and totally charmless, this wine lacks fruit, substance, and color. Last tasted, 10/83.

1971—Beginning to fade ever so slightly, this lovely wine peaked in the
· mid-'70s. With some brown at the edges, the 1971 is soft, round,
82 medium-bodied, with no tannins left. The classy bouquet still shows some cedary, spicy fruit, but fades in the glass. Drink up! Last tasted, 10/82.

1970—A very big, successful vintage for Latour à Pomerol, the 1970,
· while still young and evolving, has been very impressive from its
88 earliest days. It is dark ruby with an expansive bouquet of ripe

Merlot fruit, spicy, vanillin oak, and grilled chestnuts. In the mouth, the wine is full-bodied, ripe, very long and concentrated, and still quite tannic in the finish. Anticipated maturity: 1986–1994. Last tasted, 12/83.

1966—The 1966 is an atypically ripe, rich, powerful, rather dense wine,
· which in style seems an anomaly in this vintage, which produced
87 rather lean, elegant, restrained wines. Still quite dark in color with an orange rim, this wine has a bouquet of ripe, deep fruit, oak, and a tarry, truffle-scented aroma. Powerful, full-bodied, and rich, this wine should be drunk over the next 10 years. Last tasted, 4/81.

1961—One of the greatest wines from this great vintage, the 1961 La-
· tour à Pomerol has it all. A sensational bouquet of rich, mature,
98 blackcurrant fruit inundates the nose. Viscous, ripe, incredibly concentrated, this sweet, succulent wine has a staggering level of concentration and amazing length. Drink over the next 10 years. Last tasted, 11/84.

L'EVANGILE (Unclassified) EXCELLENT

Production: 3,500 cases	Grape varieties: Merlot—67% Cabernet Franc—33%
Time spent in barrels: 20–24 months	Average age of vines: 32 years
Evaluation of present classification: The quality equivalent of a second-growth	

Universally regarded as one of the very top Pomerols, L'Evangile can indeed produce superb wines. However, they have tended to lack consistency with wines from vintages such as 1971, 1976, and 1981, not nearly as good as they should have been.

The recently deceased Louis Ducasse, who owned L'Evangile, was quite blunt in telling visiting wine critics that his wine was every bit as good as Pétrus. However, I have never found L'Evangile to have the power and body of Pétrus. In recent vintages, it has exhibited a very refined, polished elegance, with a deep, rich, distinctive bouquet of raspberries and violets. It is soft and lush, and recent vintages since 1966 have matured quite rapidly, usually within 7–8 years. This style may well be moving toward a deeper, fuller-bodied, more tannic wine. The excellent Libourne oenologist, Michel Rolland, was brought in to make the 1982 and 1983 wines, and both are powerful, outstanding Pomerols.

L'Evangile remains one of the most sought after Pomerols. The vineyard is superbly located facing on the St.-Emilion border, where it sits adjacent to another top-notch Pomerol, La Conseillante.

VINTAGES

1983—Destined to be recognized as one of the top Pomerols, maybe the best of this vintage, L'Evangile's 1983 is quite dark ruby in color with an intense bouquet of ripe, crushed blackberries. Quite full-bodied, the dense, lush, very concentrated flavors lack a little acidity, but exhibit excellent richness and moderate tannins. A deep, unctuous big-styled L'Evangile, this wine looks to be one of the greats of the vintage. Anticipated maturity: 1990–2005. Last tasted, 3/85.
·
91

1982—Potentially one of the greatest wines ever from L'Evangile, the 1982 is astonishingly dark in color with an explosive, jammy, blackcurrant bouquet which also smells of violets and cedarwood. Intense, rich, full-bodied, and unctuous on the palate, this voluptuous wine has considerable tannins buried beneath a mountain of fruit. A superb effort. Anticipated maturity: 1992–2005. Last tasted, 3/85.
·
96

1981—Unexpectedly light, diffuse, and inadequately concentrated, the 1981 is well below the standard for this excellent estate. It is medium ruby and just too bland, without much concentration to it. Drink up! Last tasted, 4/84.
·
73

1979—Approaching full maturity, the 1979 L'Evangile is a seductive, sensual wine with a soft, raspberry, blackcurrant fruitiness, a wonderful bouquet of violets and spice, medium body, and a smooth, velvety finish. It is almost reminiscent of a fine Chambolle-Musigny. Drink over the next 5–6 years. Last tasted, 1/85.
·
86

1978—Attractively plump, spicy, and solid, but for whatever reason, not terribly complex, the 1978 L'Evangile has always struck me as a good, straightforward, nicely concentrated wine, but nothing special. Drink over the next 6–7 years. Last tasted, 4/84.
·
84

1975—Until the appearance of the 1982 and 1983, this was the greatest L'Evangile in the last two decades. This gorgeously opulent, concentrated wine has a bouquet of flowers, grilled nuts, and oodles of rich, berry fruit. It is very dark in color with multidimensional flavors, a very lush, rich, savory texture, and superb finish. This full-bodied, perfectly balanced wine can be drunk now and over the next 10–12 years. Last tasted, 6/84.
·
92

1971—Beginning to decline, the 1971 L'Evangile is showing an increas-
· ing brown color and its bouquet has begun to suggest decaying
70 vegetation. The wine is also a trifle unstable on the palate. Medium ruby brown with a spicy, minty, somewhat burnt aroma and short, medicinal flavors, this wine should be drunk up. Last tasted, 3/80.

1970—Fully mature, quite round, fruity, soft, elegant, and charming,
· with L'Evangile's telltale violet, raspberry-like bouquet, this
84 medium-bodied, velvety wine should be drunk over the next 5–6 years. Last tasted, 3/81.

1966—Fully mature, yet seemingly longer-lived than the 1970, the 1966
· has more body and tannin, a vividly brilliant dark ruby color
85 with just a touch of amber, and a long, satisfying rich, plummy finish. It is a harmonious, supple, very fruity wine. Last tasted, 3/79.

1964—Quite full-bodied and robustly styled for L'Evangile, this fleshy,
· meaty wine is ready to drink, has a big, rich, toasty, spicy,
84 blackcurrant bouquet, and soft, fat, slightly rough-edged, big flavors. Drink over the next 5–6 years. Last tasted, 1/80.

LA CONSEILLANTE (Unclassified) EXCELLENT

Production: 4,000 cases	Grape varieties: Merlot—45% Cabernet Franc—45% Pressac—10%
Time spent in barrels: 22–24 months	Average age of vines: 45 years

Evaluation of present classification: The quality equivalent of a second-growth

A very highly regarded Pomerol estate, La Conseillante produces some of this appellation's most elegant, lush, and delicious wines. On the negative side, this estate in some vintages has had a tendency to turn out wines that are too light and mature at an overly rapid rate. However, these problems seem to have been corrected with the first three vintages of the '80s. La Conseillante is owned by the Nicholas family, and the estate is well situated in eastern Pomerol next to L'Evangile and right across from the St.-Emilion border.

La Conseillante is a meticulously made wine. It is vinified in stainless steel tanks and aged in oak barrels of which 50% are new each year. In style, the wine is not nearly as powerful as Pétrus, Trotanoy, Lafleur, or Latour à Pomerol, but it is always more supple and ready to drink sooner. Recent vintages have as a general rule reached full maturity within 6–8 years. Presently, the long-lived, great vintages for La Conseillante have been 1970, 1981, and 1982. La Conseillante is an expensive wine, normally selling at a price above most Médoc second-growths.

VINTAGES

1983—The third straight top-notch success for La Conseillante, the
· 1983 has excellent ripeness and big, creamy, velvety, concen-
86 trated flavors nicely complemented by a toasty oakiness. There
is moderate tannin present, but the overall impression created
by this wine is one of voluptuousness and decadently ripe fruit.
Anticipated maturity: 1990–2000. Last tasted, 3/85.

1982—Rather massive and backward for La Conseillante, with a ripe,
· intense nose of framboise and cassis fruit, this wine has the rich,
90 creamy, toasty flavors that make La Conseillante so popular.
Endowed with a boatload of tannin, this is the biggest and dens-
est La Conseillante since the 1970. Anticipated maturity: 1992–
2008. Last tasted, 1/85.

1981—A great success for La Conseillante, this wine does not have the
· weight, power and authority of Pétrus, Certan de May, or Tro-
90 tanoy in 1981, but it is a remarkably elegant, balanced wine with
layers of gorgeous, plummy, sweet, spicy, ripe fruit. The right
touch of new oak adds complexity without overwhelming the
rich, savory, supple, lush fruitiness. Drink over the next 8 years.
Last tasted, 12/84.

1979—Rather light and insubstantial, the 1979 La Conseillante is ready
· to drink, has little tannin, not much body, and rather soft, some-
78 what diluted flavors, but it is attractive and pleasant. Drink over
the next 5 years. Last tasted, 4/83.

1978—The 1978 is not terribly different from the 1979, and suffering
· from the same ills—lack of depth, grip, and body. Medium ruby
75 with some amber at the edge, this medium-bodied wine tastes
soft, ripe, a trifle diffuse and unstructured, and short and bland
in the finish. Drink up! Last tasted, 4/83.

1976—The 1976 is very brown and on the verge of complete collapse.
· If one rushes to drink the 1976 La Conseillante there is still
72 enough overripe, jammy, soft fruit and velvety texture to produce enjoyment, but please hurry. Drink up! Last tasted, 6/84.

1975—The 1975 La Conseillante, which had such impressive creden-
· tials when young, has not developed terribly well. Now ap-
84 proaching full maturity, as the telltale brownish cast to the color indicates, this is a very evolved 1975. It is a spicy, ripe, open-knit, elegantly wrought wine that inexplicably seems to lack the depth and richness of the top Pomerols of this year. Drink over the next 5 years. Last tasted, 5/84.

1971—Quite charming, fruity, and seductively easy to drink in 1976,
· the 1971 La Conseillante has now begun to fade, taking on more
80 and more brown color and losing its fruit. It still offers a supple, round mouthful, but the prime of its life is but a fleeting memory. Drink up! Last tasted, 6/82.

1970—The 1970 is a magnificent La Conseillante that is just now enter-
· ing its mature period, where it should remain for a good decade.
92 Still very dark in color, with a sensational bouquet of ripe black cherries and violets, this wine is lush and deep, with powerfully concentrated flavors that are firm and admirably balanced. An intense, big, very rich style of La Conseillante, it is a wine that should be drunk over the next 10 years. Last tasted, 11/82.

1966—Almost Médoc-like, with a cedary, tobacco-scented bouquet, the
· 1966 La Conseillante has reached its apogee. However, it is
85 unlikely to decline for several years because of its firmness and structure. Medium ruby with some amber color, this is a rather restrained La Conseillante, yet complex and interesting. Drink up. Last tasted, 5/84.

1964—A trifle fleshier and more substantial than the 1966, the 1964 La
· Conseillante has excellent color, a toasty, tarry, richly fruity
86 aroma, medium to full body, some hard tannins, and a generous, long finish. Drink over the next 4 years. Last tasted, 5/84.

CERTAN DE MAY (Unclassified) — EXCELLENT

Production: 1,600 cases	Grape varieties: Merlot—70% Cabernet Franc—30%
Time spent in barrels: 20–26 months	Average age of vines: 35 years

Evaluation of present classification: The quality equivalent of a second-growth, particularly since 1976

An up-and-coming superstar in the Pomerol firmament, Certan de May's vineyard is superbly located on the highest ground of Pomerol, right between Vieux Château Certan and Pétrus. For years the wine was made by another château, but since 1974 the present proprietors, Mme. Barreau-Badar and her son, have been responsible for every detail. The result has been a series of remarkably rich, concentrated Pomerols that make Certan de May one of this appellation's top new stars.

This is a very traditionally made Pomerol, vinified in stainless steel tanks, but aged entirely in new oak. Interestingly, the wine macerates on the skins for almost a month, which no doubt accounts for its sensational concentration and black purple color. This is a wine for connoisseurs who are willing to wait the minimum 10 years for it to shed its considerable tannic clout.

VINTAGES

1983—Perhaps too tannic, oaky, and astringent for its own good, the
· 1983 Certan de May is a brawny, very powerful wine with a
86 tough texture and excellent concentration, but tastes coarse in
the finish. The wine will take a long, long time to shed its tannins. Anticipated maturity: 1998–2010. Last tasted, 3/85.

1982—A fantastic wine, the 1982 Certan de May has an enormous
· bouquet of spices, vanillin oak, ripe, rich blackcurrants, and
97 plums. On the palate it is overwhelming in its richness, depth,
concentration and multidimensional personality. Very full-bodied, viscous, and not unlike the great Pomerols of 1947 in size and weight, this is a colossal effort from the tiny, soon-to-be famous Certan De May. Anticipated maturity: 1995–2010. Last tasted, 1/85.

1981—A wine for the the student and connoisseur of Bordeaux, this
· authentic "*vin de garde*" is deep, broodingly dark, with a big,
90 spicy, blackcurrant bouquet, full body, a powerful, rich, concen-
trated fruity texture, and excellent length. Anticipated maturity: 1994–2005. Last tasted, 11/84.

1979—The 1979 Certan de May produced a wonderfully rich, brawny,
· broad wine with layers of ripe fruit, a top-rank bouquet of spicy
90 oak and caramel scents. This well-crafted wine is full-bodied
and rich, impeccably balanced, and has a finish which lingers and lingers on the palate. Anticipated maturity: 1990–2005. Last tasted, 11/84.

1978—Unusually spicy, slightly peppery and herbaceous, but rich, dusty, ripe, and full-bodied, the 1978 Certan de May has dark ruby color, very good extract, but rather pungent Rhône-like flavors. Anticipated maturity: 1986–1993. Last tasted, 1/85.
·
85

1976—The 1976 Certan de May is an opulent, very ripe, rich, dense, full-bodied wine that has much more structure and richness than many wines of this vintage. Very drinkable now, but showing no signs of losing its fruit, this big, corpulent wine is a delight to drink now and over the next 5–6 years. Last tasted, 6/84.
·
87

VIEUX CHÂTEAU CERTAN (Unclassified) EXCELLENT

Production: 6,500–7,000 cases	Grape varieties: Merlot—50% Cabernet Franc—25% Cabernet Sauvignon—20% Malbec—5%
Time spent in barrels: 20–22 months	Average age of vines: 27 years
Evaluation of present classification: The quality equivalent of a third-growth	

One of the most renowned estates of Pomerol, the Belgian-owned Vieux Château Certan has produced a number of superb vintages of wine, particularly in the '40s and '50s. Beautifully situated on the Pomerol plateau just adjacent to Pétrus and Certan de May, Vieux Château Certan has for years been considered by experts to be second in quality only to Pétrus. While this may have been true in the first 20 years following World War II, Vieux Château Certan has been overtaken in quality by a number of Pomerols from the stable of Jean-Pierre Moueix as well as its immediate neighbor, Certan de May. Always distinctly lighter in style than other Pomerols, and somewhat Médoc-like as a result of the abnormally large percentage of Cabernet Sauvignon used, Vieux Château Certan has been inconsistent in the decades of the '60s and '70s, but in 1981, 1982, and 1983 the wine has been close to top form again.

Vieux Château Certan is an expensive wine because it does have an historic reputation of excellence, and like most Pomerols, a small production.

VINTAGES

1983—This vintage is quite successful. The wine is dark ruby, with a
· rich, berrylike, slightly minty, oaky bouquet, plump, round, fat
88 flavors, good round tannin content, and medium to full body. Like most Pomerols of 1983, it is slightly deficient in acidity, but is round, generously flavored, and precocious. Anticipated maturity: 1990–1998. Last tasted, 3/85.

1982—While lighter than the other top Pomerols from this vintage, the
· 1982 Vieux Château Certan is still a very rich, deep, quite per-
87 fumed wine, with layers of lush, ripe, concentrated fruit. Medium- to full-bodied and moderately tannic, this elegantly wrought wine should have a very good evolution ahead of it. Anticipated maturity: 1990–2000. Last tasted, 1/85.

1981—The 1981 is extremely good, richly fruity, with a blackcurrant,
· cedary bouquet interlaced with subtle, herbaceous scents.
87 Rather Médoc-like in its firm, well-structured feel, medium body, and tough tannins, this wine is quite well made. Anticipated maturity: 1991–2005. Last tasted, 10/84.

1979—Rather light for a wine of its reputation, the 1979 Vieux Château
· Certan is medium ruby, with a moderately intense, cherryish,
78 oaky bouquet, medium body, soft, light tannins, and an adequate finish. Drink over the next 3 years. Last tasted, 7/83.

1978—The 1978 has much more color than the 1979, with better con-
· centration, a relatively rich, supple, medium-bodied texture,
82 light tannins, and a round, attractive finish. This vintage should be drunk over the next 5 years. Last tasted, 7/83.

1976—Quite one-dimensional, with soft, ripe plummy fruit, and some
· oaky aromas, the 1976 has average concentration, no noticeable
75 tannin, and a pleasant yet uninteresting finish. Drink up. Last tasted, 7/83.

1975—The best Vieux Chàteau Certan of the '70s, the 1975 has the
· power and richness one expects from wines with excellent rep-
90 utations, as well as complexity and balance. Medium to dark ruby, with a fragrant, ripe, rich, plummy, cedary, spicy bouquet, full body, big concentrated flavors, and moderate tannin, the wine is just beginning to reach its apogee. Anticipated maturity: 1990–2000. Last tasted, 5/84.

1971—The 1971 is a little wine, pleasant enough, but lacking concen-
· tration, richness, character, and length. It has been ready to
74 drink for some time and now seems to be losing its fruit. It should be immediately consumed. Last tasted, 9/79.

1970—A burgundian aroma of cherry fruit and earthy, oaky, spicy com-
· ponents is satisfactory enough. On the palate, the 1970 Vieux
80 Château Certan is moderately concentrated, light, fruity, and
charming. However, it has little of the power, richness, and
depth expected. Drink up. Last tasted, 4/80.

1966—The 1966 Vieux Château Certan is browning badly, but is still
· solid and is showing moderately ripe fruit, medium body, a
74 rather severe, unyielding texture and a short finish. Some astringent tannin still remains. This wine is very Médoc-like in character, but not very impressive. Last tasted, 2/82.

1964—A lovely wine which is round, generous, velvety, and deeply
· fruity, the 1964 has a very sweet, ripe bouquet of fruit, oak, and
86 truffles, soft, amply endowed flavors, medium to full body, and
a long, silky finish. It requires drinking up. Last tasted, 5/83.

1961—This wine has gotten mixed reviews in my notes. Several years
· ago it was big and powerful, but coarse, dumb, and totally lack-
86 ing in finesse. More recently, at a vertical tasting of Vieux Château Certan, it was still a little rough around the edges, but
showed rich, deep, youthfully scented fruit, full body, plenty of
weight and power, and impressive length. The score reflects the
better effort. Drink over the next 5–6 years. Last tasted, 5/83.

LA FLEUR PÉTRUS (Unclassified) EXCELLENT

Production: 2,500 cases	Grape varieties: Merlot—80% Cabernet Franc—20%
Time spent in barrels: 20–24 months	Average age of vines: 28 years
Evaluation of present classification: The quality equivalent of a third-growth	

Located on the eastern side of the plateau of Pomerol where so many of the best estates are found, La Fleur Pétrus is one of the very top Pomerols. Virtually replanted in its entirety since the mid-'50s, the vineyard is still rather young by standards employed by its owner, the firm of Jean-Pierre Moueix. The wine at La Fleur Pétrus is lighter in weight and texture than other Moueix Pomerols such as Pétrus, Trotanoy, and Latour à Pomerol, but it has tremendous elegance, and a supple, smooth, silky texture. It usually matures faster than the aforementioned three wines, and can normally be drunk 5 or 6 years after the vintage. Recent vintages have been generally quite consistent in quality, and as the vineyard gets older, the quality should continue to improve.

Because of its name, quality, and small production, La Fleur Pétrus tends to be quite expensive.

VINTAGES

1983—Rather light and fruity, but nevertheless charming, with medium
· body, an open-knit, fruity, plummy, spicy, somewhat oaky bou-
83 quet, this is a good effort from La Fleur Pétrus. I expect it to develop rapidly, and be ready to drink by 1988–89. Last tasted, 3/85.

1982—In a year when so many Pomerols were outstandingly great, La
· Fleur Pétrus is merely excellent. Atypically big, dense, full-
90 bodied, rich, and tannic, this is one vintage of La Fleur Pétrus that will atypically need most of a decade to reach maturity. Very dark, with a full-intensity bouquet of vanillin spice and ripe plums, this rich, full wine is quite promising. Anticipated maturity: 1992–2000. Last tasted, 1/85.

1981—Very soft, a trifle jammy, and too supple, the 1981 La Fleur
· Pétrus is still a deliciously fruity, savory, medium-bodied wine
84 that is ideal for drinking over the next 5–6 years. Last tasted, 10/84.

1979—The 1979 is an elegant, supple, very fruity wine, with the smell
· of ripe plums and spicy, vanillin oak very prominently displayed.
85 Medium-bodied, with medium to dark ruby color, a lush, nicely concentrated texture, this is not a big, hefty, rich Pomerol, but rather a suave, delicate yet fruity, interesting wine. Drink over the next 5 years. Last tasted, 2/83.

1978—Quite similar to the 1979, yet showing a more perceptible amber,
· brownish edge to it, the 1978 La Fleur Pétrus has a supple, rich,
84 fat, ripe Merlot fruitiness, medium to full body, and light, round tannins. Drink over the next 5–6 years. Last tasted, 2/85.

1977—This poor vintage produced a decent, soft, fruity wine with me-
· dium body, not too much annoying vegetal stalkiness, and a
73 pleasant, clean bouquet. Drink up. Last tasted, 4/82.

1976—The 1976 La Fleur Pétrus is quite mature, with some browning
· at the edges. It is a charming, open-knit, very soft, round wine,
83 with considerable appeal, but like the great majority of 1976 Bordeaux, it is a trifle diluted and flabby, with quite low acidity. Drink up. Last tasted, 1/80.

1975—A very impressive wine that has just begun to open up and
· become drinkable, the 1975 La Fleur Pétrus is quite concen-
90 trated, with rich, ripe plummy fruit, full body, plenty of tannin, and unusual power for this Pomerol. Long and deep, this wine is every bit as good as the exceptional 1982. Drink over the next 10 years. Last tasted, 5/84.

1970—A top-notch success for the vintage, the 1970 La Fleur Pétrus is
· now at its apogee. It is very round and richly fruity, with medium
88 to full body, a lush, velvety texture, and a long finish. Drink over the next 5–7 years. Last tasted, 4/82.

1966—Fully mature, the 1966 La Fleur Pétrus has a bouquet of oak,
· truffles, and soft, ripe, Merlot fruit. Medium-bodied and amber
84 at the edge, this is a wine which can be kept, but is best drunk up over the next 3–4 years. Last tasted, 1/80.

1964—Nineteen sixty-four was a wonderful vintage for the wines of
· Pomerol, and for the properties of the firm of Jean-Pierre
85 Moueix. Chunky and a trifle rustic for La Fleur Pétrus, this is a corpulent, jammy, ripe wine, full and flavorful, with good body, but a touch of coarseness does come through on the palate. Drink over the next 3–5 years. Last tasted, 4/78.

LE GAY (Unclassified) VERY GOOD

Production: 2,000 cases	Grape varieties: Cabernet Franc—50% Merlot—50%
Time spent in barrels: 18–22 months	Average age of vines: 35 years

Evaluation of present classification: The quality equivalent of a fifth-growth

Just to the north of the Pomerol plateau is the run-down property of Le Gay, with its unkempt and rather poorly lit and cleaned wine cellar. Le Gay and the adjacent vineyard of Lafleur are owned by the Robin family, and now managed by Marie Robin since the death of her sister, Therese, several years ago. Since 1982, the wine has been made under the guidance of the Libourne firm of Jean-Pierre Moueix, which also controls its commercialization.

Le Gay is a vineyard of enormous potential, with old vines and a well-situated location, but its history has been one of inconsistency. Great raw materials from the vineyard were often translated into mediocre wine as a result of very old and sometimes dirty barrels. At Le Gay the aging wine had to share space with flocks of chickens and ducks. Under the meticulous eye of the Moueix management, Le Gay is a property to watch, as the successful vintages should occur with a greater degree of frequency.

The style of winemaking at Le Gay results in a powerful, rich, tannic, often broodingly dark-colored wine. In some years, it can be coarse and a little overbearing, whereas in other vintages the power of Le Gay is in harmony, well balanced against ripe fruit, firm acidity, and tannin. Le Gay is a big, powerful wine that remains somewhat undervalued when compared to other Pomerols.

VINTAGES

1983—The 1983 is a good Le Gay, alcoholic, tannic, a little clumsy and
· awkward, but powerful and ripe. Low acidity may prevent a
83 long, graceful evolution, but this wine will please many a buyer
for its direct, full-bodied, rich, aggressive style. Anticipated maturity: 1990–2000. Last tasted, 3/85.

1982—The 1982 Le Gay is an extremely powerful, very rich and con-
· centrated wine, with a big, deep, blackberry, earthy, almost
89 peppery bouquet. It is dense, almost opaque in color, with great
depth of fruit, full body, mouth-gripping tannin, and excellent potential for long-term cellaring. Very impressive. Anticipated maturity: 1995–2015. Last tasted, 1/85.

1981—The deliciously fruity, supple, and deep cask samples of the
· 1981 Le Gay were impressive, but in the bottle it has shown a
? remarkable degree of variation. Some bottles have dirty, flawed
bouquets, while others are rich, fruity, and clean. It is impossible to tell which bottle is the clean one, so this wine is best avoided. Last tasted, 11/84.

1979—A success for Le Gay, the 1979 is richly fruity with the smell of
· blackcurrants and violets, and earthy, truffle-scented aromas.
84 This medium- to full-bodied wine has light to moderate tannins
and a good finish. Anticipated maturity: 1987–1994. Last tasted, 6/82.

1975—An outstanding effort from Le Gay, the 1975 is a very rich,
· powerful, concentrated, tannic, deeply scented wine, with a
88 very long evolution ahead of it. Quite dark ruby, with a full-
blown bouquet of ripe berry fruit, violets and iron-like mineral scents, this full-bodied wine is rich, tannic, and has excellent potential. Anticipated maturity: 1987–2005. Last tasted, 11/84.

1966—Now mature and fully ready to drink, the 1966 Le Gay has an
· amber, moderately dark ruby color, an earthy, austere, Médoc-
83 like, restrained bouquet, medium body, and a solid, somewhat
rustic finish. Drink over the next 5 years. Last tasted, 9/82.

1962—Still firm, but now entering its mature period, Le Gay's 1962 has
· a moderately intense bouquet of ripe plums and mineral scents.
85 On the palate, the wine is concentrated, surprisingly well balanced, and interesting. Drink over the next 5 years. Last tasted,
11/79.

1961—A disappointment in this great vintage, Le Gay has a bizarre,
· medicinal bouquet and a loosely knit structure, harsh fruity fla-
68 vors, and little balance. Drink up. Last tasted, 11/79.

L'ENCLOS (Unclassified) — VERY GOOD

Production: 3,600 cases	Grape varieties: Merlot—80% Cabernet Franc—19% Malbec—1%
Time spent in barrels (and vats): 20 months	Average age of vines: 27 years

Evaluation of present classification: The quality equivalent of a fifth-growth

Located in the most western portion of the Pomerol appellation, L'Enclos is a property that produces very good wine, but it receives very little publicity. Perhaps I have been very lucky and only seen the best vintages of L'Enclos, but I have been very favorably impressed with this wine for its consistently smooth, velvety, rich, supple, nicely concentrated, blackberry fruitiness, and for its overall harmony. In most vintages, L'Enclos seems to need only 3–4 years of bottle age to show its opulent, rich, silky fruitiness.

VINTAGES

1983—The 1983 L'Enclos is a succulent, fat, juicy wine, with a very
· forward, exuberant grapey appeal, round, ripe, lush flavors, and
86 a velvety finish. Delicious now, this wine should be drunk over
the next 6 years. Last tasted, 3/85.

1982—More concentrated than the 1983, but equally forward and pre-
· cociously styled, the 1982 has medium to dark ruby color, a full-
87 blown, ripe blackberry bouquet, a wonderfully lush, deep, unc-

tuous texture, and a sweet, velvety finish. Seemingly quite drinkable now, this wine should continue to provide pleasure for up to a decade. This wine is a real crowd pleaser. Last tasted, 1/85.

1979—Deliciously fruity with a lovely perfumed quality suggesting
· blackcurrants, this medium-bodied wine has a silky, velvety tex-
84 ture, light tannins, and a round, generous finish. An extremely enjoyable style of wine. Drink over the next 5 years. Last tasted, 2/85.

1975—This is an outstandingly sweet, ripe, round, gentle, smooth wine,
· with oodles of blackberry fruitiness, a complex berry and truffle-
89 scented bouquet, and a velvety finish. The 1975 L'Enclos is medium- to full-bodied and is drinking well now, but this beautifully made wine can be kept for at least another 5–6 years. It is a sleeper in this vintage. Last tasted, 1/85.

1970—The 1970 L'Enclos is very similarly styled to the 1975 and 1982.
· Perhaps more tannic, but nevertheless, velvety, ripe, smooth,
86 and polished, this dark ruby wine is loaded with fruit and has a finish that caresses the palate. Drink over the next 5–6 years. Last tasted, 1/85.

L'EGLISE-CLINET (Unclassified) — VERY GOOD

Production: 1,500 cases	Grape varieties: Merlot—60% Cabernet Franc—30% Malbec—10%
Time spent in barrels: 20 months	Average age of vines: 50 years

Evaluation of present classification: The quality equivalent of a fifth-growth

One of the least-known Pomerol estates, L'Eglise-Clinet often produces a typically fat, succulent, juicy, richly fruity style of Pomerol. The wine is admirably and traditionally made, but because of the tiny production, simply not well known.

L'Eglise-Clinet is one of the few Pomerol vineyards that was not replanted after the 1956 killing freeze, and consequently it has very old vines, a few of which exceed 100 years in age.

Pierre Lasserre, the owner of the bigger and better known Pomerol property of Clos René, farms this vineyard under the *metayage* system (a type of vineyard rental agreement), and obtains a wine that is both rich and well balanced, supple and firm, and always well vinified.

Rarely does one ever encounter a bottle of L'Eglise-Clinet that is not well made and interesting. The cost for a bottle of L'Eglise-Clinet is high, as the European connoisseurs are already aware of the wine's quality.

VINTAGES

1983—A top-notch success in 1983, L'Eglise-Clinet is very dark ruby,
· with a dense, ripe, fat, black cherry bouquet, chewy, dense,
86 ripe flavors, full body, low acidity, and moderate tannin. This
big wine will mature quickly. Anticipated maturity: 1989–1995.
Last tasted, 3/85.

1982—The 1982 is very dark in color, with an emerging bouquet of
· black cherries and truffles. On the palate, the wine shows ex-
86 cellent concentration, full body, a vivid cranberry, plummy fruitiness, and moderate tannin. It is a plump yet well-structured
wine. Anticipated maturity: 1989–1998. Last tasted, 1/85.

1981—Less powerful and less rich than the 1982 and 1983, the 1981
· L'Eglise-Clinet is a light yet still very fruity, supple, spicy wine,
84 with medium to full body, moderate tannin, and a good finish.
Anticipated maturity: 1987–1992. Last tasted, 6/84.

1978—The 1978 is fully mature, with a chocolatey, somewhat smoky,
· fruity bouquet. It is a soft, round, moderately concentrated wine
82 that is pleasant, but lacks a little weight and richness. Last
tasted, 1/85.

DE SALES (Unclassified) VERY GOOD

Production: 12,500–16,000 cases	Grape varieties: Merlot—66% Cabernet Franc—17% Cabernet Sauvignon—17%
Time spent in barrels: 16–22 months	Average age of vines: 30 years

Evaluation of present classification: The quality equivalent of a fifth-growth

De Sales is the largest vineyard in Pomerol, and it has that appellation's only grand château. The owners and managers are the de Lambert family. The wines are increasingly among the most enjoyable of the Pomerols. They are prized for their sheer, supple, glossy, round, generous, ripe fruitiness, and lush, silky personalities. De Sales has always made good wine, but the recent vintages have been particularly strong. It is never a powerful, aggressive, oaky, or big wine, and always offers immediate drinkability. In spite of its precocious style, it has a cunning ability to age well for 10–12 years.

De Sales is a consistently good but not great Pomerol that has rarely ever disappointed me. Its price remains quite modest, making it an excellent value.

VINTAGES

1983—Perhaps a little atypical for de Sales, the 1983 is a fat, jammy,
· rather alcoholic wine, with an opulent fruitiness, a very ripe
85 bouquet of black cherries and peaches, and a soft, viscous texture. Low acidity seems to suggest that this wine should be drunk when it is young. Anticipated maturity: 1987–1994. Last tasted, 3/85.

1982—The 1982 is an exceptionally elegant, supple, richly fruity,
· round, and generous wine, with very good concentration, excel-
87 lent balance, a long, velvety, silky finish, and a wonderfully fruity, spicy bouquet. Simply delicious to drink now, this wine will be even better if cellared for 2–5 years. Anticipated maturity: 1986–1994. Last tasted, 1/85.

1981—The 1981 de Sales is a notable success for the vintage. Quite
· lush and concentrated, with ripe, rich fruit, some spicy oak,
86 medium body, and a long finish, this graceful, savory wine should be drunk over the next 6 years. Last tasted, 11/84.

ROUGET (Unclassified) — VERY GOOD

Production: 5,500 cases	Grape varieties: Merlot—40% Cabernet Franc—30% Cabernet Sauvignon—30%
Time spent in barrels: 24 months	Average age of vines: 35 years

Evaluation of present classification: The quality equivalent of a fifth-growth

Historically, Rouget is one of Pomerol's most illustrious estates. In one of the early editions of Cocks et Féret's *Bordeaux et ses Vins*, the vineyard was ranked fourth among all the Pomerols. At present, its reputation has been passed by numerous properties, but there is no question that Rouget can be a very rich, very interesting wine. For example, just last year I tasted both the 1945 and 1947 wines of Rouget, which were dazzling examples of just how superb this wine can be.

Since 1974, François Jean Brochet has run this old yet beautiful estate that sits in the northernmost part of the Pomerol appellation, with a lovely view of the Barbanne River visible through the trees. The wine is very traditionally made by Brochet. He is unique in Pomerol, for he maintains an immense stock of old vintages of Rouget wines. Consequently, it is not unusual to see old vintages of Rouget appearing on the market at what can be remarkably good prices.

The style of Rouget is one that makes no concessions to consumers who want to drink their wine young. It is darkly colored, rich, full-bodied, often very tannic wine that usually needs a minimum of 8–10 years of cellaring. It can sometimes border on being a little coarse and rustic, but is almost always a very delicious, rich, ripe, spicy wine. The vintages of the early '80s seem to show less of the aggressive tannins that were present in older vintages, and more fleshy, rich, chewy fruit, so perhaps the new management is moving toward a slightly more supple style.

Rouget is an outstanding value among the wines of Pomerol, with even the old vintages being very fairly priced.

VINTAGES

1983—Richly fruity, spicy, fat, and quite concentrated, the 1983 Rouget is a rather big, full-bodied, moderately tannic wine that will make quite a fine bottle of wine when it matures. Anticipated maturity: 1989–2000. Last tasted, 3/85.
· 83

1982—A top-notch effort from Rouget, the 1982 is a big, corpulent, concentrated, moderately tannic, full-bodied wine, with layers of fleshy fruit, a voluptuous texture, good grip and attack, and a long, tannic finish. Anticipated maturity: 1987–2005. Last tasted, 1/85.
· 88

1981—Rouget's 1981 is good, but seems to suffer in comparison with the powerful, rich 1982 and grapey, fat, succulent 1983. Nevertheless, it has good fruit, rather hard, aggressive tannin, and an adequate, but uninspiring finish. Last tasted, 6/83.
· 80

1978—A chunky, spicy, fruity, medium- to full-bodied wine, the 1978 Rouget is attractive, but a trifle awkward and clumsy on the palate. Moderate tannin is present, so perhaps the wine will pull itself completely together. Anticipated maturity: 1985–1992. Last tasted, 6/83.
· 82

1971—Fully mature, the 1971 Rouget has a dusty texture, a spicy,
· earthy, cedary bouquet, nicely concentrated flavors, but a some-
80 what coarse texture. This medium amber, ruby-colored wine
should be drunk over the next 2–3 years. Last tasted, 6/84.

1970—A big, rather fat, well-endowed wine, with full body, a cedary,
· rich blackcurrant fruitiness, the 1970 Rouget has roughly tex-
84 tured flavors and moderate, aggressive tannin still very much in
evidence. Anticipated maturity: 1985–1995. Last tasted, 6/84.

1964—The 1964 is a total success for Rouget in which its predilection
· for wines with a rough, big, tannic structure has in the vintage
87 resulted in a wine with more balance and harmony. Very deeply
fruity, with earthy, blackcurrant flavors in abundance, this full-
bodied wine has power, symmetry, and surprising length.
Rouget is one of the top Pomerols in this vintage. Drink over the
next 10 years. Last tasted, 1/85.

BON PASTEUR (Unclassified) VERY GOOD

Production: 2,500 cases	Grape varieties: Merlot—90% Cabernet Franc—10%
Time spent in barrels: 18–20 months	Average age of vines: 37 years

Evaluation of present classification: The quality equivalent of a fifth-growth

Bon Pasteur is owned and managed by one of the up-and-coming oenologists in Bordeaux, Michel Rolland. Rolland, along with a highly capable wife who is also an oenologist, not only makes the wine at Bon Pasteur, but also provides significant consultation and advice to a bevy of fine Pomerol estates such as L'Evangile and La Conseillante.

The wine of Bon Pasteur has improved in quality dramatically since Michel Rolland took over. It is a round, richly fruity, very harmonious, medium- to full-bodied wine without excessive tannin. Its great appeal is its suppleness and consistency, which has even extended to off-vintages such as 1980. Bon Pasteur is another Pomerol estate to keep an eye out for. Although it does not yet have the glamorous reputation of estates such as Pétrus, Trotanoy or L'Evangile, the quality of the wine here is very fine. Fortunately the price has not yet caught up with Bon Pasteur's quality.

VINTAGES

1983—The 1983 Bon Pasteur is a richly fruity wine, with a lovely per-
· fumed bouquet of blackcurrants. Quite supple, lush, and pre-
85 cocious, despite the presence of moderate tannins, this is a wine
that will be very pleasing over the near term. Anticipated maturity: 1988–1993. Last tasted, 1/85.

1982—An atypically powerful wine for Bon Pasteur, the 1982 is dark
· ruby, with a wonderful bouquet of ripe black cherries, toffee,
90 and oak. On the palate, the wine is unctuous, rich, lush, and
gorgeously fruity and concentrated. Anticipated maturity: 1987–
2000. Last tasted, 1/85.

1981—Supple, richly fruity, elegant, spicy, and soft, this medium-bod-
· ied wine has a jammy, blackcurrant fruitiness, a harmonious,
85 lush texture, and immediate accessibility. It should be drunk
over the next 7–8 years. Last tasted, 1/85.

1980—Very well made in this difficult vintage, Bon Pasteur is a soft,
· medium-weight wine with good ripeness and a savory, mellow
82 personality. Drink over the next 2–3 years. Last tasted, 6/84.

1979—The 1979 Bon Pasteur has always lacked the generous, ripe,
· richly fruity character I enjoy and associate so much with the
78 wine from this estate. Well made, but austere and a little lean,
it should be drunk over the next 5 years. Last tasted, 6/84.

1978—A surprisingly successful 1978, the Bon Pasteur is somewhat
· dominated by the smell of toasty, new oak. The wine is deep and
85 concentrated, with layers of ripe Merlot fruit, and a long, very
satisfying finish. It is one of the top Pomerols of this vintage.
Drink over the next 5–6 years. Last tasted, 1/85.

PETIT-VILLAGE (Unclassified) VERY GOOD

Production: 4,000–5,000 cases	Grape varieties: Merlot—80% Cabernet Sauvignon—10% Cabernet Franc—10%
Time spent in barrels: 18–20 months	Average age of vines: 28 years

Evaluation of present classification: The quality equivalent of a fifth-growth, particularly since 1978

Petit-Village is a Pomerol estate that is on the move. Since the 1970s when Bruno Prats, the dynamic owner of the famous Médoc estate, Cos d'Estournel, took over responsibility for the making of the wine, the quality has increased dramatically. Petit-Village now has the benefit of significant capital investment, a very dedicated owner, and state-of-the-art technology for producing wine. The result has been a succession of wines that have ranged in quality from good to exceptional.

The style of Petit-Village under Prats has been one that emphasizes the toasty, smoky character of new oak barrels, a fat, supple, blackcurrant fruitiness, and impeccably clean winemaking and handling. Recent vintages have the ability to age for 10–15 years, although they are fully ready to drink by age 6 or 7. Older vintages have generally proved to be disappointing, so wine enthusiasts are best advised to stick to vintages since 1978. Petit-Village is a Pomerol to buy as its price has not yet crept up to its rejuvenated quality level.

VINTAGES

1983—Quite supple, fat, and richly fruity, this full-bodied, dark ruby-
· colored wine is redolent with the aromas of blackberries and
86 toasty oak. On the palate, the wine is very precocious, sweet,
ripe, fleshy, and delicious. Anticipated maturity: 1989–2000.
Last tasted, 6/84.

1982—The best Petit-Village I have ever tasted, the 1982 has an exotic
· bouquet filled with spicy, smoky, oaky aromas. Quite full-
92 bodied, very fat, supple, and richly fruity, this big, dark-colored
wine has moderate tannins and will age very well despite its
youthful, precocious charm. It is a very impressive wine. Anticipated maturity: 1990–2005. Last tasted, 3/85.

1981—Definitely lighter and less concentrated than the powerful 1982
· and deeply fruity 1983, the 1981 Petit-Village does show a pre-
85 cocious, soft, ripe, fat, Merlot fruitiness, ripe, round tannins,
and a long, voluptuous finish. Anticipated maturity: 1986–1995.
Last tasted, 6/84.

1979—The 1979 Petit-Village does not have the concentration of the
· 1981, 1982, and 1983, but offers a ripe, moderately intense fruit-
84 iness, medium body, a spicy, smoky bouquet, and a pleasant
finish. Drink over the next 5–6 years. Last tasted, 2/83.

1978—Medium ruby, with a spicy, slightly herbaceous, oaky bouquet,
· the 1978 Petit-Village has supple, moderately concentrated,
83 fruity, berryish flavors, light tannin, and a soft, round finish.
Drink over the next 5 years. Last tasted, 4/84.

CLOS RENÉ (Unclassified)

VERY GOOD

Production: 6,800 cases	Grape varieties: Merlot—70% Cabernet Franc—30%
Time spent in barrels: 18–24 months	Average age of vines: 27 years

Evaluation of present classification: The quality equivalent of a fifth-growth

Clos René sits well to the west of the major châteaux of Pomerol, in an area just south of the appellation of Lalande-de-Pomerol. The wines made here tend to be open knit in style, quite fruity, supple, and easy to drink. While the style of Clos René is no exception to this rule, I have noticed a perceptible change, starting with the 1981, to a wine that is a bit bigger framed, darker colored, and a little more substantial and concentrated. Perhaps the counseling of Michel Rolland, a highly respected Libourne oenologist and also proprietor of Bon Pasteur, has made the difference at Clos René between a good, round, fruity Pomerol and a very good, more serious wine. Whatever the reason, there is no doubt that the vintages of the '80s have produced the best wines from Clos René in recent memory. Not being one of the Pomerols in great demand, Clos René remains very reasonably priced.

VINTAGES

1983—Quite successful, the 1983 Clos René is atypically dense, full-bodied, ripe, corpulent, and loaded with layers of fruit. Rather viscous and jammy, but intensely perfumed and decadently fruity, with plenty of tannin in the finish, this wine is very exciting. Anticipated maturity: 1988–1996. Last tasted, 6/84.
· 86

1982—Lush and quite rich and fruity, but surprisingly not as deep or as big as the 1983, the 1982 Clos René is a heady, supple, delicious wine, with some round, non-aggressive tannins in the finish. Anticipated maturity 1986–1994. Last tasted, 1/85.
· 86

1981—Supple, spicy, intensely fruity, with plenty of blackcurrant flavors, the 1981 Clos René is a lovely, richly textured wine, with medium to full body, and light to moderate tannin. Anticipated maturity: 1986–1992. Last tasted, 6/84.
· 84

1979—The 1979 Clos René is rather bland and straightforward, with average intensity, ripe berryish flavors, light body, and little tannin. This wine is ready to drink now. Last tasted, 6/83.
· 74

1978—The 1978 is a nicely concentrated, round, fruity wine that lacks
· some grip and complexity. However, it does offer quite ripe,
83 fruity flavors in a medium-bodied format. Drink over the next 4
years. Last tasted, 4/84.

1976—Diffuse, overripe, loosely knit, and quite fragile, the 1976 Clos
· René is a medium ruby-colored wine with some amber at the
73 edges. It has a sweet, candied flavor, and overly soft, disjointed
flavors. It was more attractive several years ago, and now is
beginning to fade. Drink up. Last tasted, 12/84.

1975—This is a typical 1975, tannic, still youthfully hard and closed,
· though somewhat less weighty, concentrated, and authoritative
80 than other wines from this vintage. The wine is moderately dark
in color, with the hard 1975-style tannins still quite assertive.
Anticipated maturity: 1987–1995. Last tasted, 5/84.

CERTAN-GIRAUD (Unclassified) VERY GOOD

Production: 1,900 cases	Grape varieties: Merlot—70% Cabernet Franc—30%
Time spent in barrels: 20–24 months	Average age of vines: 30 years
Evaluation of present classification: The quality equivalent of a fifth-growth	

With its immediate neighbors being Pétrus, Certan de May, and Vieux Château Certan, one can almost assume that the wines of Certan-Giraud have something special to offer. The vineyard, which is sandwiched in between these much more famous properties on Pomerol's famed plateau, does indeed produce high quality, typically rich, plump, fruity, Pomerol wine.

The wines of Certan-Giraud are clearly on a move upward in quality. They are round, supple, usually quick to mature wines, with an excellent ripe fruitiness, soft, round tannin, and a lush, savory texture. The vintages after 1979 have been markedly deeper and richer than were earlier efforts. The price/quality rapport is especially attractive, as Certan-Giraud is probably the least expensive Pomerol from the prestigious plateau section of this appellation.

VINTAGES

1983—One of the very top Pomerols in this vintage, Certan-Giraud is a
· dark ruby-colored wine, with a big, ripe black cherry bouquet,
89 interlaced with the scent of fresh garden herbs and overripe
tomatoes. Dense, unctuous, full-bodied, and moderately tannic, this is a rich, fat, deeply concentrated wine which will offer considerable pleasure. Anticipated maturity: 1988–1995. Last tasted, 3/85.

1982—The 1982 Certan-Giraud is an excellent wine, but it is one of the
· few Pomerols of this remarkable vintage that is eclipsed by the
88 1983. The wine is dark ruby, with a dense, ripe, rich, plummy
bouquet, full body,and excellent concentration. It has a lush, almost voluptuous finish with moderate tannins present. The 1982 is a precociously styled wine that will captivate tasters with its dazzling fruitiness for at least the next decade. Anticipated maturity: 1987–1995. Last tasted, 1/85.

1981—Not quite up to the quality of the 1982 and 1983, but still attrac-
· tive, fruity, and delicious, the 1981 Certan-Giraud is quite for-
84 ward and ready to drink. Dark ruby, with a moderately intense,
plummy bouquet, this medium- to full-bodied wine has very light tannins, and a round, lush finish. Drink over the next 5–6 years. Last tasted, 6/84.

LA GRAVE TRIGANT DE BOISSET (Unclassified) VERY GOOD

Production: 3,000 cases	Grape varieties: Merlot—90% Cabernet Franc—10%
Time spent in barrels: 16–20 months	Average age of vines: 25 years
Evaluation of present classification: The quality equivalent of a fifth-growth	

La Grave is another of the relatively obscure Pomerol estates that is making better and better wine. Owned by the meticulous and brilliant Christian Moueix, who directs the business affairs of his father's firm in Libourne, this wine should continue to grow in stature as the relatively young vineyard gets older and older.

La Grave, which is located just to the east of the Route Nationale 89 in the direction of Perigueux, is situated on gravelly, sandy soil, which results in wines that are a little lighter and less powerful than those from the Pomerol plateau.

All the recent vintages have been successful, with the 1982 being a classic. Normally, La Grave is a wine to drink after 5–6 years of bottle age. While not one of the most expensive Pomerols, neither is it one of the bargains of this appellation. However, given the increasing quality exhibited by this wine in recent vintages, this is a property to take more and more seriously.

VINTAGES

1983—A rather big, richly fruity wine for La Grave, the 1983 has impressive color, surprisingly good acidity for a 1983 Pomerol, a ripe, toasty, plummy fruitiness, and medium to full body. Anticipated maturity: 1988–1996. Last tasted, 3/85.
· 85

1982—A gorgeously ripe, richly scented Pomerol, the 1982 does not have the huge power and richness of some top Pomerols, but it does have considerable style and personality. Rich, quite concentrated, moderately tannic, and full-bodied, this is a sensual, lush Pomerol that will provide rewarding drinking for some time to come. Anticipated maturity: 1989–2000. Last tasted, 1/85.
· 88

1981—Dominated by the taste and smell of new oak barrels, the 1981 La Grave has elegant, ripe berry fruitiness, and finesse and grace rather than pure power. Moderate tannin is present, so 3–4 years of further cellaring seems warranted. Anticipated maturity: 1987–1995. Last tasted, 6/84.
· 83

1976—One of the most successful 1976 Pomerols, La Grave, which is fully mature, has a toasty, ripe fruity bouquet, soft, round, nicely concentrated flavors, and no noticeable tannins remaining. Drink over the next several years. Last tasted, 4/83.
· 84

LE PIN (Unclassified)

VERY GOOD

Production: 350 cases	Grape varieties: Merlot—88% Cabernet Franc—12%
Time spent in barrels: 18–20 months	Average age of vines: 23 years
Evaluation of present classification: The quality equivalent of a fifth-growth	

The Thienpont family, who owns the neighboring and very well-known Pomerol estate, Vieux Château Certan, acquired the miniature vineyard of Le Pin in 1979, and by their own admission are trying to make a Pétrus-like wine of great richness and majesty. The first vintages have Pomerol enthusiasts jumping with glee, as this looks to be a splendidly rich, but noticeably oaky, big-styled Pomerol. It is still too early to say if Le Pin will turn out to be one of the great wines of Pomerol, but the first several vintages look to be smashing.

VINTAGES

1983—The 1983 Le Pin is the third straight top-notch wine produced
· by this up-and-coming Pomerol estate. Similar to the rich, oaky,
89 concentrated 1982, but even more deep, this wine has a voluptuous texture, full body, a huge bouquet of spicy oak and black currants. Very impressive. Anticipated maturity: 1990–2000. Last tasted, 4/85.

1982—The 1982 Le Pin is very dark ruby with a sensational bouquet of
· ripe blackcurrants, and toasty, vanillin, spicy oak. It is a rich,
88 deeply concentrated wine, with excellent concentration and balance, and a full-bodied, moderately tannic finish. Young, muscular, and impressive, this is a wine to search out. Anticipated maturity: 1990–2000. Last tasted, 1/85.

1981—This is an opulent 1981, with a pronounced spicy, oaky, pene-
· trating bouquet interlaced with the scent of melted toffee and
88 ripe blackcurrants. On the palate, the wine is voluptuous, powerful, and rich. It is quite impressive and one of the leading Pomerols in this vintage. Anticipated maturity: 1990–2000. Last tasted, 10/84.

LA CROIX (Unclassified) — ABOVE AVERAGE TO GOOD

Production: 6,000 cases	Grape varieties: Merlot—60% Cabernet Franc—20% Cabernet Sauvignon—20%
Time spent in barrels: 20–24 months	Average age of vines: 35 years
Evaluation of present classification: The quality equivalent of a Grand Bourgeois	

La Croix is a reputable property in Pomerol, producing rather big, dark-colored, tannic, full-bodied wines that lack refinement and finesse. They do offer mouth-filling gustatory pleasure, and will repay the 6–10 years of cellaring that most of them need.

Owned by the Janoueix family, La Croix can be quite a good wine bargain.

VINTAGES

1983—La Croix made a very powerful wine in 1983, certain lots producing a wine with 14.8% alcohol. Very deep purple, with a dense, plummy, viscous, powerful presence on the palate, this full-bodied wine is quite massive, and should prove to be one of the top bargains of the vintage. Anticipated maturity: 1990–2000. Last tasted, 6/84.
· 86

1982—Another very successful wine, the 1982 La Croix is slightly less alcoholic than the big, massive 1983, but very dark in color, with layers of ripe, rich fruit, moderate tannin, and an impressive finish. Anticipated maturity: 1990–2005. Last tasted, 1/85.
· 86

1981—The 1981 La Croix has been an inconsistent performer. Some bottles have shown a deficiency in color, whereas others have a rich, ripe cherry texture, with full body and hefty weight. The score reflects the better bottlings. Anticipated maturity: 1986–1992. Last tasted, 11/84.
· 84

OTHER NOTABLE POMEROL PROPERTIES

NENIN (Unclassified)

Evaluation of present classification: The quality equivalent of a Grand Bourgeois

Nenin has a loyal following of wine enthusiasts, but I have never been able to quite figure out why. I was certainly taken by a bottle of 1947 I tasted in 1983, but aside from that splendid wine, I have always found Nenin to be rather good, but unfortunately somewhat coarse, rustic, and dumb.

The sizable vineyard of 65 acres produces 8,000-plus cases of wine from 50% Merlot, 30% Cabernet Franc, and 20% Cabernet Sauvignon. Nenin tends to be a firm, rather hard, chewy wine. The most successful vintages have included a good 1961, and very good 1966 and 1975. The 1981, 1982, and 1983, unless they magically develop in the bottle, seem especially austere, hard, and lacking generosity for Pomerols. However, this wine has its dedicated followers and I must applaud Nenin's moderate price.

GAZIN (Unclassified)

Evaluation of present classification: The quality equivalent of a Grand Bourgeois

Most commentators on Bordeaux have generally held Gazin in high regard, no doubt because the vineyard is ideally situated behind Pétrus in the northeast corner of the appellation. However, the track record for Gazin has been one of mediocrity throughout the '60s, '70s, and in the first several vintages of the '80s. One of the largest vineyards of Pomerol, covering 56 acres, Gazin produces 10,000 cases of wine from its vineyard planted with 75% Merlot, 20% Cabernet Franc, and 5% Cabernet Sauvignon. The wine is vinified very traditionally, but far too many good vintages, 1961, 1970, 1975, 1978, 1979, and 1981, have been dull, light, and one-dimensional wines. Most vintages have matured quite quickly, normally reaching maturity within 5–7 years.

Of the two most recent vintages, the 1982 is perhaps the best Gazin since the good, if uninspiring 1966, but even the 1982 is light and unexciting in the context of the vintage. The 1983 is supple, fruity, and attractive, but not what it potentially could be.

Strangely enough, Gazin is an expensive wine. Its historic reputation and strategic placement on the Pomerol plateau have served it well. However, consumers wanting a tasty, plump, succulent Pomerol are best advised to look elsewhere.

LAGRANGE (Unclassified)

Evaluation of present classification: The quality equivalent of a Grand Bourgeois

One rarely sees the wine of Lagrange, another of the properties owned and managed by the firm of Jean-Pierre Moueix. Lagrange is well located near the plateau of Pomerol, but the vineyard has been recently replanted significantly with the composition changed to 90% Merlot and 10% Cabernet Franc. With the increased reliance on more Merlot in making the wine, it is anticipated that Lagrange will become a more supple, softer style of wine. The wine, of which there are 2,000 cases produced, tends to be a rather brawny, densely colored Pomerol with significant power and tannins, but not much complexity. The 1970, 1975, and 1978 have all proved to be stubbornly big, brooding wines that have been slow to develop.

LA FLEUR GAZIN (Unclassified)

Evaluation of present classification: The quality equivalent of a Cru Bourgeois

La Fleur Gazin, situated between the two estates of Gazin and Lafleur, is produced by the firm of Jean-Pierre Moueix, which farms this property under a lease arrangement. The wine, a blend of 70% Merlot and 30% Cabernet Franc, is supple, round, and rather straightforward in style, but in highly successful vintages such as 1979 and 1982, it is very ripe, precocious, and interesting enough to merit serious consumer interest.

PLINCE (Unclassified)

Evaluation of present classification: The quality equivalent of a Grand Bourgeois

Plince is a solid Pomerol, fairly rich, hefty, spicy, and deep. Rarely complex, but usually very satisfying, Plince produces 2,500 cases of wine from a vineyard planted with 75% Merlot, 20% Cabernet Franc, and 5% Cabernet Sauvignon. The Moreau family, also owners of Clos L'Eglise, owns this property, but the commercialization is controlled by the Libourne firm of Jean-Pierre Moueix.

I have found Plince to be a consistently sound, well-made wine. Though it may never have the potential to be great, it seems to make the best of its situation. The 1981 is chunky, spicy and full. The 1982 is big, peppery, rich, and full, and the 1983 is similarly styled but lower in acidity.

Plince is an attractive wine value; it is well-vinified wine in a big, chunky style that seems capable of aging for 8–10 years.

TAILLEFER (Unclassified)

Evaluation of present classification: The quality equivalent of a Grand Bourgeois

Taillefer is home for another branch of the ubiquitous Moueix family; Bernard Moueix owns this very important estate on the edge of Libourne. It produces in excess of 10,000 cases of wine from a vineyard planted with 66% Cabernet Franc and 34% Merlot. Taillefer is a straightforward, fruity, medium- to full-bodied wine, without a great deal of complexity, but always soundly made, round, fruity, and capable of evolving for 7–10 years before losing its fruit. Recent vintages have rendered consistently sound, attractive, cleanly made wines, particularly the 1975, 1979, and 1982. Taillefer merits consideration as it is usually very fairly priced.

DOMAINE DE L'EGLISE (Unclassified)

Evaluation of present classification: The quality equivalent of a Cru Bourgeois

The wine of Domaine de L'Eglise is owned by the Bordeaux firm of Borie-Manoux, who acquired this 17-acre estate in 1972. Planted with 75% Merlot and 25% Cabernet Franc, I have generally found the wines of Domaine de L'Eglise to be plump, fruity, but somewhat dull and bland. The 1970, 1971, 1976, and 1978 left me wanting more for my money. The 1982 is better, but in this great vintage not terribly special. Domaine de L'Eglise is a wine to drink within its first 6–8 years of age, and tends to be overpriced and overrated.

TAILHAS (Unclassified)

Evaluation of present classification: The quality equivalent of a Grand Bourgeois

Located on the St.-Emilion border, Tailhas produces 5,000 cases of wine from a vineyard planted with 80% Merlot, 15% Cabernet Sauvignon, and 5% Cabernet Franc. It tends to be a rather full-bodied, robustly styled Pomerol with a good richness and weight, but a tendency toward blandness. The 1979 and 1981 are disappointing, the 1982 is an excellent wine, a dense, ripe, fat, chewy Pomerol which will provide enjoyment for the next decade. The 1983 is less interesting, but quite fruity, supple, concentrated, and precocious. Much of the production by Tailhas is sold in Europe, but it is beginning to receive an audience in America for its rich, chewy fruit, and good price/quality rapport.

LA VIOLETTE (Unclassified)

Evaluation of present classification: The quality equivalent of a Grand Bourgeois

A rather obscure Pomerol estate producing 1,800 cases of wines from a vineyard near the historic church in this appellation, La Violette is a wine made with 95% Merlot and 5% Cabernet Franc. It is inconsistent, but at its best La Violette can be a splendidly rich wine. The 1962 and 1967 were still exhibiting dense, ripe fruit when tasted in January 1985. Other vintages are less impressive, as this estate lacks the consistency of the very top Pomerols. However, the 1982 looks to be quite rich and dense, and must surely be the best La Violette since the 1967. The 1983, while less concentrated, is also a notable success for this property. Fortunately, the price of La Violette is not yet excessive.

VRAYE-CROIX-DE-GAY (Unclassified)

Evaluation of present classification: The quality equivalent of a Grand Bourgeois

This tiny property, just to the northeast of the Pomerol plateau near Lagrange and Lafleur, has the perfect location to produce high-quality wine. The production of 2,000 cases is made from a vineyard planted with 80% Merlot, 15% Cabernet Franc, and 5% Cabernet Sauvignon. The wine, like its surrounding neighbors', is very darkly colored, dense, powerful, and richly flavored and tannic. However, it does suffer from inconsistency and an inclination toward blandness. The 1982 is the best wine I have tasted from this estate, possessing an exotic, chocolatey, smoky, hickory-scented bouquet, and big, rich, jammy flavors.

CLOS L'EGLISE (Unclassified)

Evaluation of present classification: The quality equivalent of a Grand Bourgeois

One of the numerous châteaux in Pomerol with the word "*eglise*" in its name, Clos L'Eglise produces 2,300 cases of elegant, spicy, Médoc-like wine from close to 15 acres of vineyards planted with 60% Merlot, 20% Cabernet Franc, 10% Cabernet Sauvignon, and 10% Malbec.

The wine can be remarkably good. The 1964 is still superb, richly concentrated, ripe, and rich. The 1970 and 1971 were above average but not particularly exciting. However, the 1975, just tasted for the first time, was quite rich and special, and the 1982 looks to be very promising.

This is a property that can produce very fine, elegant, rich wines. While it is rarely seen in America, the price is modest and reasonable.

CLOS DU CLOCHER (Unclassified)

Evaluation of present classification: The quality equivalent of a Grand Bourgeois

A terribly underpublicized property that sits near the large church in Pomerol, Clos du Clocher's 1,600-case production rarely makes its way outside Europe. The vineyard, planted with 66% Merlot and 34% Cabernet Franc, produces a generously flavored, rather full-bodied wine that lacks some polish and finesse, but is quite attractive. The 1983 is good, the 1981 even better, and the 1982 surprisingly dense, concentrated, deeply fruity, and promising. In fact, the 1982 Clos du Clocher seems to be well above the quality level normally seen from this château. It might be a wine to serve blind to your guests for pure "shock" effect.

Clos du Clocher's wines are not inexpensive because the tiny production is eagerly gobbled up by enthusiastic fans of Pomerol wines.

CLINET (Unclassified)

Evaluation of present classification: The quality equivalent of a Cru Bourgeois

I have always found Clinet to be an unusually styled Pomerol, often rather austere and reserved, without the exuberant, fleshy, rich fruit for which Pomerols are so renowned. The choice of grapes at Clinet shows a high percentage (25%) of Cabernet Sauvignon, in addition to 60% Merlot, and 15% Cabernet Franc. The average production in a good year ranges between 3,000 and 4,000 cases. Most Clinets evolve in the bottle quite irregularly, and older vintages have provided more disappointments than pleasant surprises. Of the recent vintages, the 1978 is mediocre, the 1979 diluted and overcropped, the 1981 below average, and the 1982, from a great Pomerol vintage, barely acceptable.

Clinet is marketed aggressively in America, but represents very poor value for the money.

BEAUREGARD (Unclassified)

Evaluation of present classification: The quality equivalent of a Cru Bourgeois

A well-known Pomerol estate, Beauregard produces almost 6,000 cases of wine in a good year from a vineyard planted with 48% Merlot, 44% Cabernet Franc, 6% Cabernet Sauvignon, and 2% Malbec. This has never been a wine that has greatly impressed me. While it has a good reputation, the wine tends to be rather light in color and body for a Pomerol, with an atypical, pronounced herbaceous bouquet, probably a result of the unusually high percentage of Cabernet Franc used in the wine. Normally fully mature within 4–5 years of vintage, Beauregard is a very light-styled Pomerol which tends to be expensive, and therefore overvalued.

LA POINTE (Unclassified)

Evaluation of present classification: The quality equivalent of a Cru Bourgeois

La Pointe has been an irregular performer for me, sometimes round, fruity, simple, but generous, as in 1970, but far too frequently just boringly light and insubstantial. Certainly the 1975, 1976, 1978, and 1979 all were uncommonly deficient in the rich, chewy, supple, zesty fruit that one finds so typical of a good Pomerol. The production of 7,500 cases ensures that the wine is widely promoted. The blend chosen at La Pointe is 80% Merlot, 15% Cabernet Franc, and 5% Malbec. The owners have increased the percentage of Merlot significantly since the early '70s. All things considered, this is a very mediocre Pomerol, but the future may portend better things as the gifted Libourne oenologist, Michel Rolland, has recently been retained to provide advice on the vinification of La Pointe's wine.

BOURGNEUF-VAYRON (Unclassified)

Evaluation of present classification: The quality equivalent of a Cru Bourgeois

A relatively unknown wine, Bourgneuf has a large production of 6,000 cases. The vineyard sits just behind the famous estate of Trotanoy. The vineyard is planted with 80% Merlot and 20% Cabernet Franc. I have no notes on older vintages, but both the 1981 and 1982 proved to be good middle-of-the-road wines, with satisfying richness, power, interest, and aging potential of 5–8 years.

BONALGUE (Unclassified)

Evaluation of present classification: The quality equivalent of a Cru Bourgeois

Only 2,000 cases of Bonalgue are made, but the wine, a blend of 66% Merlot, 33% Cabernet Franc, and 1% Cabernet Sauvignon, has in recent vintages shown surprising strength and richness. It is not complex, but obviously well vinified, with a deep, black cherry fruitiness, and medium to full body. Both the 1981 and 1982 represent good values.

GOMBAUDE-GUILLOT (Unclassified)

Evaluation of present classification: The quality equivalent of a Cru Bourgeois

Unfortunately, my tasting experience with Gombaude-Guillot is quite limited. I can report an excellent, rich, tasty bottle of 1970, and a hard but promising bottle of 1975, but virtually all of this estate's production of 2,400 cases is sold directly to private customers in France. The vineyard is planted in an interesting mixture of 33% Merlot, 33% Cabernet Franc, and an abnormally high percentage of Malbec, 33%.

MOULINET (Unclassified)

Evaluation of present classification: The quality equivalent of a Cru Bourgeois

One of Pomerol's largest estates, Moulinet produces in excess of 7,500 cases of wine from a vineyard planted with 66% Merlot and 34% Cabernet Franc. The property is located in the most northwest section of the Pomerol appellation, near the large estate of de Sales. The soil in this area renders lighter-style Pomerols, and Moulinet is certainly one of the lightest. Unusually light in color and faintly perfumed, Moulinet is made in a very commercial style by the owners, the Armand Moueix family. At best, in vintages such as 1981 and 1982, it can be round, fruity, and elegant, but quite frequently the wine is rather bland and innocuous, although cleanly and consistently made.

LA CROIX DE GAY (Unclassified)

Evaluation of present classification: The quality equivalent of a Cru Bourgeois

Virtually unseen in America, La Croix de Gay produces over 5,000 cases of wine from a vineyard planted with 80% Merlot, 15% Cabernet Sauvignon, and 5% Cabernet Franc. The wine, although once reputed to be creamy, rich, and intensely flavorful, is now quite light, fruity, and obviously vinified in a style that warrants immediate drinking. With regard to the three major vintages of the '80s, they are all rather light, supple, and fruity, yet undeniably charming and attractive, The ideal picnic Pomerol, the 1983 is my pick of the trio of vintages between 1981 and 1983.

THE WINES OF ST.-EMILION

St.-Emilion is Bordeaux's most attractive tourist attraction. Some will even argue that the walled, medieval village of St.-Emilion, which is perched on several hills amongst a sea of vines, is France's most beautiful wine town.

The wine community of St.-Emilion is a very closely knit fraternity who maintain a fierce belief that their wines are the best in Bordeaux. They have always been sensitive and have felt slighted because the region was entirely omitted from the 1855 classification of the wines of the Médoc.

St.-Emilion is only a 40-minute drive from Bordeaux. The top vineyards are centered in two distinctive and geographically different parts of St.-Emilion. The vineyards called "*côtes* St.-Emilions" cover the limestone hillsides around the town of St.-Emilion. There are even a few vineyards located in the town. Most of St.-Emilion's best and most famous wines, Ausone, Belair, Canon, Magdelaine, L'Arrosée, Curé-Bon-Le-Madeleine, and Pavie, are located along these hillsides. Of the official 11 Premier Grand Cru properties of St.-Emilion, 8 have their vineyards on these limestone hillsides. The wines from the *côtes* vineyards are all unique and distinctive, but they share a firm, restrained, more austere character in their youth. However, with proper aging the youthful toughness gives way to wines of richness, power, and complexity.

Certainly Ausone with its impressive wine cellars carved out of the rocky hillside and steep vineyard filled with very old, gnarled vines is the most famous wine of the St.-Emilion *côtes*. This property was considered capable of making one of Bordeaux's best wines in the 19th century, but the wine of Ausone was quite shabby until 1976 when a new winemaking team was installed. Ausone tends to be different from the other *côtes* St.-Emilions. Tougher, more tannic, with an exotic, sweet bouquet, it has more of a Médoc austerity on the palate than many of its neighbors. Since 1976, Ausone has been impeccably vinified and cared for and in 1982 and 1983 produced incredibly great wines.

The only other *côtes* vineyards capable of achieving the complexity and sheer class of Ausone are Canon and Magdelaine. Canon's vineyard, like that of Ausone, sits on the limestone hillside. Canon has always had an excellent reputation, but has reached new heights under the leadership of Eric Fournier, who took over management of Canon in 1972. Canon is a powerful and rich wine for a *côtes* St.-Emilions. However, despite its excellent aging potential, it is a wine that matures quickly and is approachable long before that of Ausone.

Magdelaine is also a worthy challenger to Ausone. The vineyard, like that of Ausone and Canon, sits on the limestone hillside to the south of St.-Emilion. However, whereas Ausone and Canon use approximately 50% Cabernet Franc and 50% Merlot in their formula for making great wine, Magdelaine uses up to 80% Merlot for its wine. For that reason, Magdelaine tends to be a fleshier, rounder, creamier wine than either Ausone or Canon.

Of the other top *côtes* vineyards in St.-Emilion, L'Arrosée, not a Premier Grand Cru, but Grand Cru, has been making splendid wine since the early '60s and can often be counted on to produce one of the half-dozen best wines of St.-Emilion. L'Arrosée's wine lasts well, and it has a richness and highly aromatic bouquet that lead some to call it the best burgundy-like St.-Emilion of the *côtes* section.

Pavie and its sister château that sits further up the hillside, Pavie-Decesse, are both owned by one of the friendliest and kindest men in St.-Emilion, Jean Paul Valette. Pavie is the Premier Grand Cru, Pavie-Decesse the Grand Cru, and both have always been good, yet lighter, more elegant, easygoing styles of St.-Emilion. Valette has been trying

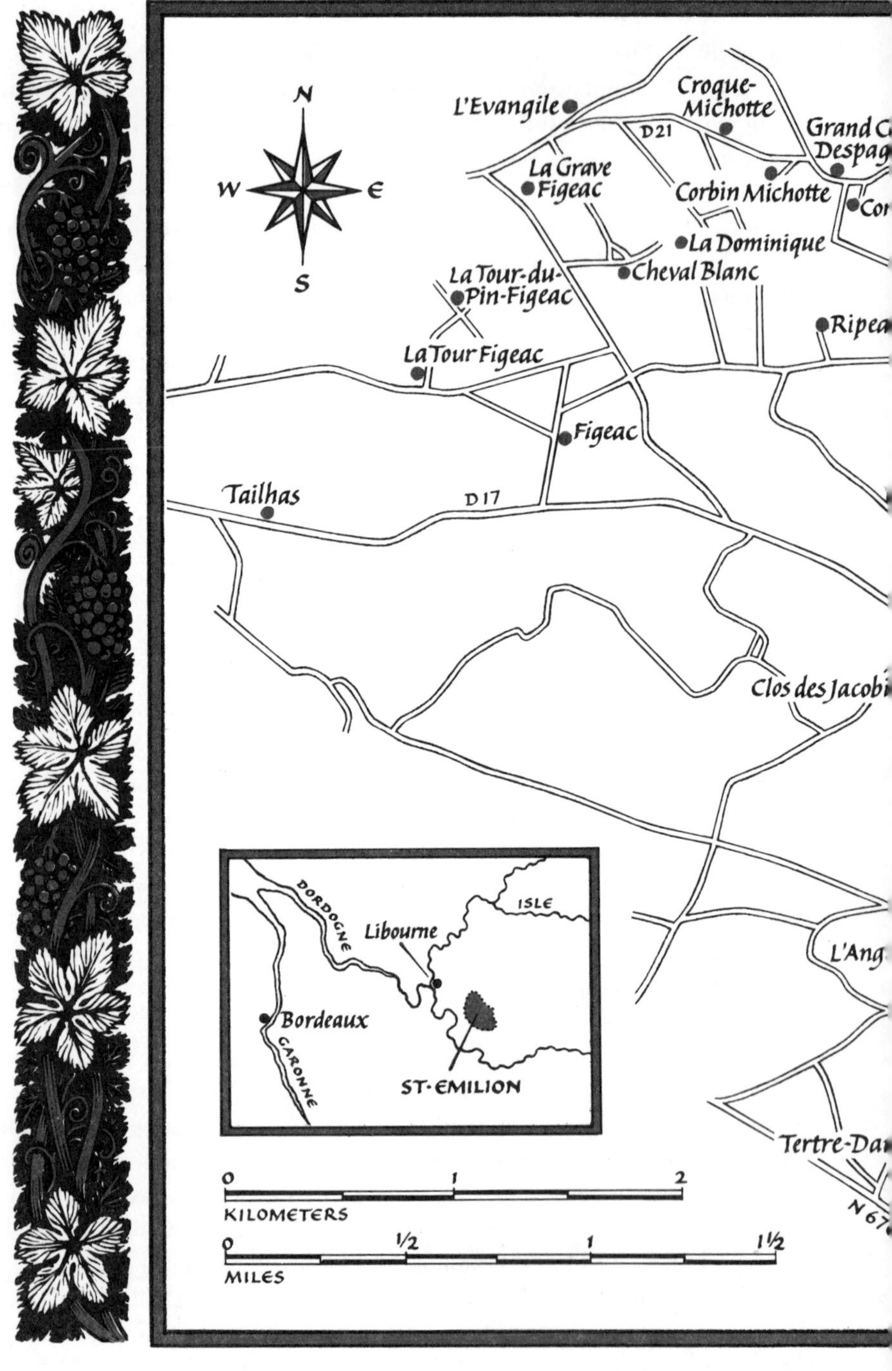

N
W
E
S
L'Evangile
Croque-
Michotte
D21
La Grave
Figeac
Corbin Michotte
La Dominique
Cheval Blanc
La Tour-du-
Pin-Figeac
La Tour Figeac
Figeac
Tailhas
D17
Clos des Jacobi
L'Ang
Tertre-Da
DORDOGNE
Libourne
ISLE
Bordeaux
GARONNE
ST-EMILION
0
1
2
KILOMETERS
0
1/2
1
1 1/2
MILES

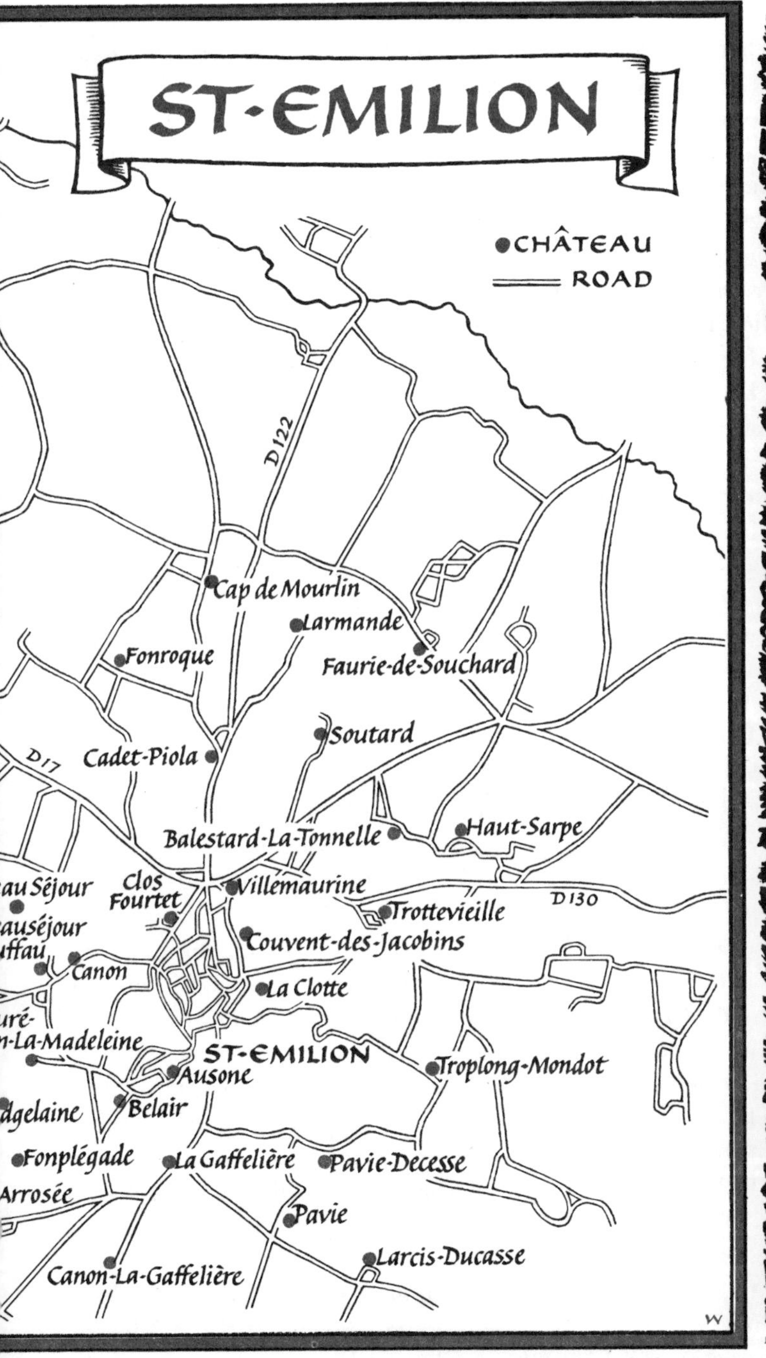
ST-EMILION
CHÂTEAU
ROAD
D122
Cap de Mourlin
Larmande
Fonroque
Faurie-de-Souchard
Soutard
D17
Cadet-Piola
Balestard-La-Tonnelle
Haut-Sarpe
Clos Fourtet
Villemaurine
Trottevieille
D130
Couvent-des-Jacobins
Canon
La Clotte
ST-EMILION
Ausone
Troplong-Mondot
Belair
Fonplégade
La Gaffelière
Pavie-Decesse
Pavie
Larcis-Ducasse
Canon-La-Gaffelière

to make richer, bigger wines, and in both 1982 and 1983 produced two of the finest wines ever made at these two estates.

Belair is of course the immediate neighbor of Ausone. It also shares the same owner and the same winemaking team. Like Ausone, Belair rarely produced memorable wines until 1976 when the "new regime" started. Lighter, more delicate, and earlier to mature than Ausone, Belair can be a classy, stylish, medium-weight St.-Emilion that has the potential to reach great heights in quality as it did in 1983.

Of the other famous *côtes* vineyards of St.-Emilion, a number of poor performers have just recently begun to turn things around and produce better and better wine. The Beauséjour estate of Duffau-Lagarrosse, and Clos Fourtet of André Lurton have both improved considerably in quality over the last half-dozen years. Clos Fourtet's style of wine is the more commercial of the two, having abandoned its hard, tannic, stern and unyielding style of a *côtes* St.-Emilion and now producing a modern supple, fruity, very easy to like and drink style of wine. Not so for Beauséjour, which has improved its quality but continues to emphasize the classic *côtes* style of St.-Emilion, tannic, firm, well colored, and very ageworthy.

The other Beauséjour estate on the western slopes of St.-Emilion is owned by Michel Bécot (Beau Séjour-Bécot) and the demotion of this estate from a Premier Grand Cru to Grand Cru in the new 1985 classification of St.-Emilion wines came as no surprise to this writer. This is a publicity-conscious estate, yet the quality of winemaking has been suspect and the wines often disappointing. However, the 1983 looked very promising.

Three other *côtes* St.-Emilions estates have the potential to produce one of St.-Emilion's best wines. The Premier Grand Cru La Gaffelière and two Grands Crus, L'Angélus and Curé-Bon-La-Madeleine, have the proper soil and vineyard exposition to make wonderful wines.

La Gaffelière has always been the most mysterious of the *côtes* St.-Emilions. The vineyard is superbly located. The wine is potentially lush, elegant, fruity and complex, but other than an excellent 1970 and promising 1982 and 1983, this is a wine that usually shows well in France, but after the ocean voyage to America, it frequently tastes tired, feeble, and short-lived.

One could say that L'Angélus went through a very mediocre period in the '60s and '70s. However, the first three vintages of the '80s have been reassuringly good. L'Angélus produces lush, supple, some would say commercial wines, but they have a fleshy, ripe, almost sweet berry fruitiness and taste more open knit and fleshy than most *côtes* St.-Emilions.

Curé-Bon is a wine I see all too infrequently, but one which can be very impressive. The vineyard is well situated between that of Canon and Ausone and the wine made is a big, forceful, dark, tannic, true classic *côtes* style.

The second section where St.-Emilion's best wines can be found is called the "*graves* plateau." Only 4 kilometers from the town of St.-Emilion, the soil in this area is, as the name implies, a gravelly bed intermixed with some clay and sand. The top properties here, Cheval Blanc, Figeac, La Dominique, La Grave Figeac, and Corbin, produce a lush, more velvety, voluptuous wine that shows quite well when young, and in the top vintages has excellent aging potential as well. These properties sit right on the southeastern border of Pomerol and often show the same lush, supple fruitiness as the two closest Pomerol estates of L'Evangile and La Conseillante.

Of these *graves* St.-Emilions, none is greater than Cheval Blanc. Even with the renaissance at Ausone, Cheval Blanc remains the quintessential St.-Emilion, opulent, decadently rich, exotic, surprisingly easy to drink when young, but capable of lasting 30–40 years in the great vintages. Cheval Blanc and Figeac are the only two Premiers Grands Crus from the *graves* section of St.-Emilion. Certainly La Dominique merits inclusion as well.

Cheval Blanc's vineyard is situated on deep gravelly soil with certain parts clay and sand as well as iron. Perhaps the most unique aspect of this wine is that nowhere else in Bordeaux does the Cabernet Franc grape reach such heights. Cheval Blanc can be almost overpoweringly rich, deep, and fruity in vintages such as 1964, 1975 and 1982, and this fact, no doubt, is why much of this wine is drunk before it ever achieves maturity. Figeac, the immediate neighbor of Cheval Blanc, is often compared to Cheval Blanc; however, Figeac is a very differently styled wine. With a rather high percentage of Cabernet Sauvignon (35%) for a St.-Emilion and much sandier soil than Cheval Blanc, Figeac tends to be a more herbaceous-scented, lighter wine. However, Figeac in its great vintages is a very fruity, soft, charming, concentrated wine which can be drunk when it is very young.

La Dominique, an impressive wine and up-and-coming estate, sits just to the north of Cheval Blanc. La Dominique produces excellent wine with lush richness, a deep fruitiness, plenty of body, and aging potential of 10–20 years. It is a wine that merits elevation to a Premier

Grand Cru. In some vintages, 1955, 1970, 1971 and 1982, this property can produce wine rivaling the best in St.-Emilion.

Two of the *graves* St.-Emilions that consistently produce deeply fruity, rich, dark-colored wines that sell for very reasonable prices are La Grave Figeac and Corbin. Shrewd consumers would do well to search these wines out.

It would be an oversimplification to think that the only fine wines of St.-Emilion come from either the *graves* plateau or *côtes* sections of this appellation. There are other portions of St.-Emilion that have slightly different soils and several properties in these sections of St.-Emilion are capable of producing excellent wine.

On the sand-covered slopes to the north of St.-Emilion, properties like Larmande, Cap de Mourlin, and Cadet-Piola are making excellent wine today. The plateau that fans out to the east of St.-Emilion has predominantly clay and sand soil with a limestone base. Soutard is the outstanding estate in this area. Trottevieille, one of the best-known St.-Emilion estates, is a consistent underachiever in this area. Two over-achievers are La Clotte and Balestard-La-Tonnelle, which are capable of producing excellent wines.

Lastly, one property that is in none of the above geographic areas of St.-Emilion but makes excellent wine is Clos des Jacobins, a property located a kilometer northwest of St.-Emilion.

St.-Emilion developed its own classification of wine quality in 1954. On paper, the system developed by St.-Emilion should be the best of all the Bordeaux wine classifications. The classification is based on reputation, soil analysis, and tasting, and unlike the 1855 Médoc classification, which has been eternally rigid and inflexible except for the elevation of Mouton-Rothschild in 1973, the St.-Emilion classification is supposed to be revised every 10 years, so that in theory top vineyards can be promoted and poorly run vineyards demoted. However, the first major revision in 1969 changed very little. The 1969 classification established a four-tiered hierarchy. The hierarchy that was in effect until 1985 established at the top level 12 Premiers Grands Crus Classés of which 2 were given recognition as the best. These were called Premiers Grands Crus Classés "A," and the remaining 10 Premiers Grands Crus Classés "B." The second rung of this ladder of quality was the Grands Crus Classés, of which there were 72. The third level of quality was for wines entitled to the status Grand Cru. Up until 1985, if the consumer did not read the label carefully, he or she may not have detected the omission of one key word, "Classés," which denoted the wines in this third grouping. The bottom level of St.-Emilion's quality hierarchy was for the wines that are only entitled to the appellation of St.-Emilion. Most of these wines are made by the large cooperatives.

What has this progressive system of quality meant for the wine consumer? Well, there is no doubt that this system has encouraged proprietors to produce higher-quality wine in the hope that better quality will result in a promotion to a higher rank. On the negative side, the commission that issued the new 1985 classification was unwilling to promote several ambitious properties making fine wine, and they have refused to demote several properties that have been notorious underachievers, given their reputation. For example, among the top 12 Premiers Grands Crus Classés in the 1969 classification, Beau Séjour-Bécot, Trottevieille, and La Gaffelière have over the last two decades consistently produced mediocre wine in most vintages. In the new classification of 1985, only Beau Séjour-Bécot was dropped down. However, the new 1985 classification (see pages 489–90) does simplify the St.-Emilion quality hierarchy a great deal. The subtle distinction between a Grand Cru Classé and Grand Cru has been eliminated. The new classification has only three levels of wine quality. At the top, there are 11 Premiers Grands Crus Classés with the demotion of Beau Séjour-Bécot. At the next level, which is now called Grand Crus Classés, there are 64 estates instead of 72. The third and last level are the generic St.-Emilions. Two excellently run properties, Soutard and L'Angélus, had applied for consideration for promotion from Grand Cru Classé to Premier Grand Cru Classé. Unfortunately, neither of these two wines was promoted in the new 1985 classification.

St.-Emilion produces wines that have enormous crowd appeal. Fleshy, quick-maturing, round, and generous, they are easy to like, easy to drink, and easy to understand. While the Premiers Grands Crus are expensive, many of the Grands Crus Classés are significantly undervalued and can represent excellent bargains.

Since quality of the soils, the winemaking, and the percentage of grapes planted in the vineyards are so diverse in St.-Emilion, it is exceedingly difficult to generalize about vintages in this vast appellation. Certainly the great vintages for St.-Emilion have been 1983 and 1982 (probably the two best vintages for this region in the post-World War II era), 1970, 1964, and of course 1961. Certainly the key to any excellent or great vintage for St.-Emilion is the healthy flowering and ripening to maturity of the Merlot and Cabernet Franc grapes, the two most important grapes for this region.

Since this area has an enormous number of wine-producing estates, I have emphasized in my tastings and in this chapter the Premiers

Grands Crus and Grands Crus Classés. It may be arbitrary and capricious, but given the sheer number of St.-Emilions that merit coverage from the two aforementioned categories, I have disregarded the generic St.-Emilions. Some of these wines can, in fact, be good, but they never have the consistency of the top estates.

A CONSUMER'S CLASSIFICATION OF THE CHÂTEAUX OF ST.-EMILION

OUTSTANDING

Cheval Blanc
Ausone

EXCELLENT

Figeac
Canon
Magdelaine

VERY GOOD

L'Arrosée
La Dominique
Pavie
Soutard
Cadet-Piola
Clos des Jacobins
Belair

GOOD

Clos Fourtet, L'Angélus, Corbin, La Gaffelière, Balestard-La-Tonnelle, Fonroque, Beauséjour (Duffau-Lagarrosse), Fonplégade, Curé-Bon-La-Madeleine, Larmande, Cap de Mourlin, La Grave Figeac, Croque-Michotte, Pavie-Decesse, La Tour-Figeac, Troplong-Mondot, Couvent-des-Jacobins, Haut-Sarpe, La Tour-du-Pin-Figeac, Monbousquet

AVERAGE

Trottevieille, Canon-La-Gaffelière, Beau Séjour-Bécot, Larcis-Ducasse

OTHER NOTABLE ST.-EMILION PROPERTIES

La Clotte, Corbin-Michotte, La Commanderie, Destieux, Faurie-de-Souchard, Fleur-Cardinale, Fombrauge, Grand-Corbin-Despagne, Haut Brisson, Haut Plantey, Ripeau, Tertre-Daugay, Villemaurine

CHEVAL BLANC (Premier Grand Cru Classé) OUTSTANDING

Production: 11,500–12,000 cases	Grape varieties: Cabernet Franc—66% Merlot—33% Malbec—1%
Time spent in barrels: 20 months	Average age of vines: 39 years

Evaluation of present classification: The quality equivalent of a first-growth

Cheval Blanc is undoubtedly one of Bordeaux's greatest and most unique wines. For most of this century it has sat alone at the top of St.-Emilion's hierarchy, representing the finest wine this appellation can produce. Since the renaissance began at Ausone in the mid-'70s, Cheval Blanc has had to share the limelight. Cheval Blanc is a very distinctive wine. Sitting right on the Pomerol border, in the St.-Emilion *graves* sector, with only a ditch separating its vineyards and those of L'Evangile and La Conseillante, it has for years been accused of making a wine which is as much a Pomerol as it is a St.-Emilion.

For me, Cheval Blanc is Cheval Blanc—it is like no Pomerol or St.-Emilion I have ever tasted. The distinctive choice of grape varieties used at Cheval Blanc, two-thirds Cabernet Franc and one-third Merlot, with a tiny parcel of old vines of Malbec, is very unusual. No other major château uses this much Cabernet Franc. But curiously, this grape reaches its zenith in Cheval Blanc's gravelly, sandy, clay soil, which is underpinned by a bed of iron rock, producing an extremely rich, ripe, intense, viscous wine.

Cheval Blanc is also unique in that the property has been in the same family's hands since 1852. The Fourcaud-Laussac family's current live-in owner is the towering Jacques Hébrard, who seems to be obsessed with taking Cheval Blanc's reputation to even greater heights.

The style of wine produced at Cheval Blanc has no doubt contributed to its immense popularity. Dark ruby in color, it is, in the very good vintages, an opulently rich and fruity wine, full-bodied, quite voluptuous and lush, and deceptively easy to drink when young. Many tasters, fooled by its cunning show of precocious charm, falsely assume it will not age well. In the big, rich vintages, Cheval Blanc can age exceptionally well, although one suspects that far too much of this wine is consumed long before its real majesty begins to show through.

As the tasting notes demonstrate, Cheval Blanc can produce a decadently rich wine of unbelievable depth and richness. In some vintages, however, it has been one of the most disappointing wines of the top "Big Eight" châteaux of Bordeaux. Recently, the quality of this wine seems to have become more consistent and brilliant with the increasing attention to detail provided by owner Jacques Hébrard. The three consecutive vintages of the early '80s, 1981, 1982, and 1983, are the finest Cheval Blanc trilogy since the splendid wines of 1947, 1948, and 1949.

VINTAGES

1983—Since Cheval Blanc has been one of a handful of wines I have consistently underrated in cask tastings, I was surprised to be so impressed with the 1983. Very dark ruby, with a powerful bouquet of ripe fruit, this wine is quite full-bodied, more harshly tannic than usual, but big-boned and deeply concentrated. One can expect Cheval Blanc's 1983 to be less charming in its youth than normal, but have a long, positive evolution. Anticipated maturity: 1995–2020. Last tasted, 3/85.
·
93

1982—At this level of near perfection, words hardly seem adequate. In its first 12 months in the cask, Cheval Blanc seemed not to have the greatness of the top wines of the vintage. In March and June of 1984, it was spectacular, and now, after six tastings in the bottle, it must surely be the greatest Cheval Blanc since the 1949. The color is quite deep and dark, but the bouquet is magnificent already. Exotic aromas of very rich, intense fruit interplay with caramel, vanillin, and coffee beans and seem to fill the room. On the palate, the wine is opulent, very, very concentrated, quite full-bodied, with layers and layers of unctuous, lush fruit that just lingers and lingers. There is plenty of tannin, but the immense concentration of fruit will cause many to drink this wine too young. Anticipated maturity: 1992–2015. Last tasted, 1/85.
·
98

1981—I had this wine several times from the barrel, and also twice in comparative tastings prior to bottling. I never gave it more than average marks. Tasted three times after bottling, it is a different wine, relatively rich, spicy, plummy, with soft, silky, layered flavors, good concentration, and moderate tannin. It can be drunk now, but ideally begs for 3–5 years of cellaring. I paid the price for my unkind, and unfortunately incorrect, assessment of this wine on my last visit to Cheval Blanc. I was bitten by the château's nasty little dog, and verbally blasted by the owner, Monsieur Hébrard. *C'est la vie!* Anticipated maturity: 1989–2000. Last tasted, 12/84.
·
90

1980—All things considered, the 1980 Cheval Blanc is a relative suc-
· cess for this mediocre vintage. Medium ruby, with a moderately
80 intense bouquet of herbal, cedary, fruity scents, this wine has medium body, adequate concentration, and a supple, soft finish. Anticipated maturity: 1985–1988. Last tasted, 4/84.

1979—The 1979 is a charming, elegant wine that lacks some depth and
· richness (because of the prolific yields), but shows moderately
84 intense, ripe plummy fruit, a cedary, herbaceous aroma, and soft, very forward, easygoing, round flavors. This is a lightweight but well-made Cleval Blanc that will age quickly. Anticipated maturity: 1986–1990. Last tasted, 3/85.

1978—This is a firmly built, deeply concentrated Cheval Blanc that
· curiously has not shown the precocious, fleshy, charming fruit
87 in its early life that this wine is famous for. The wine is quite dark ruby, with a relatively stubborn and backward bouquet suggestive of rich, ripe blackcurrant, mineral scents, and grilled nuts. On the palate, the wine is tannic, medium- to full-bodied, and admirably concentrated. It resembles the stylish, austere 1966, but is more concentrated. Anticipated maturity: 1988–2005. Last tasted, 4/84.

1977—Cheval Blanc had a disastrous year in 1977, with over 75% of
· the crop lost because of the poor weather. The resulting wine
65 should have been declassified. It is light in color, rather shallow in flavor, and has a nasty, harsh finish. Time will not help it. Last tasted, 7/83.

1976—In this vintage marked by extreme drought, heat, and hope-
· crushing rains at harvest time, Cheval Blanc has produced an
82 open-knit, somewhat overripe, roasted style of wine that is now fully mature. Medium ruby with some browning at the edge, the 1976 Cheval Blanc has a full-blown bouquet of ripe fruit and toasty oak. On the palate, the wine lacks its normal intense concentration, but shows round, somewhat diluted, but ripe, savory, fleshy, plummy, fruity flavors. Low in acidity and very soft, the 1976 Cheval Blanc should be drunk over the next 5 years, as it will not be long-lived. Last tasted, 11/84.

1975—The best Cheval Blanc of the decade of the '70s, the 1975,
· cunningly and deceptively drinkable when young, has continued
92 to put on weight and richness. It now looks like one of the best Cheval Blancs of the last 30 years. Dark ruby, with a very rich bouquet of roasted fruit, oak, and mineral scents, this big, full-bodied wine has considerable strength and weight to comple-

ment its tannic clout. A big, virile, large-scaled Cheval Blanc, it will last for a long time. Anticipated maturity: 1990–2020. Last tasted, 5/84.

1973—The 1973 Cheval Blanc has totally faded, and is now just a
· pale, washed-out wine, with a thin, diluted finish. Last tasted,
60 6/83.

1971—Somewhat of a disappointment, the 1971, while very good, has
· in the last several years begun to brown badly. Nevertheless,
84 the wine still has plenty of sweet fruit, a burnt, roasted character to its bouquet, and medium body. The 1971 is a good Cheval Blanc, which should be drunk over the next 5–6 years. Last tasted, 11/83.

1970—A better wine than the 1971, the 1970 is now fully mature, but
· can be held for at least 5–8 more years as it is in no danger of
86 falling apart. Medium to dark ruby with some browning, this wine has a cedary, burning tobacco-scented aroma, plump, ripe, round flavors which are nicely concentrated and show light tannins. The wine is medium- to full-bodied, supple and soft, and will be very pleasing to drink over the next decade. Last tasted, 11/83.

1967—Now in decline, the 1967 Cheval Blanc drank well between
· 1971–1978, but has begun to take on a decaying, leafy character
82 component in an otherwise tobacco-scented, plummy bouquet. In the mouth, the wine is soft and round, but fades quickly. Drink up! Last tasted, 2/83.

1966—A good rather than great effort from Cheval Blanc, the 1966 is
· now fully mature. Dark ruby with an amber edge, this is a re-
85 strained version of Cheval Blanc, with a stylish, reserved bouquet of mineral scents, blackcurrants, and spicy oak. On the palate, the wine is medium-bodied, moderately fleshy, but not as voluptuous or as concentrated as one expects Cheval Blanc to be in an excellent vintage. Anticipated maturity: 1985–1992. Last tasted, 11/84.

1964—Only Pétrus is better than Cheval Blanc in this vintage that
· proved to be very good to excellent for the wines of Pomerol,
95 Graves, and St.-Emilion, but disappointing (because of late rains) for the wines of the Médoc. Wonderfully rich and concentrated, this is one of the best Cheval Blancs produced since the monumental wines made by this château in 1947 and 1949. Very dark ruby, with a powerful yet restrained bouquet of ripe fruit, new wood, and gravelly, mineral scents, the wine is still young

and tannic, with layers and layers of ripe fruit. This heavyweight Cheval Blanc should be pure nectar in 4–5 years. Anticipated maturity: 1985–2000. Last tasted, 10/84.

1962—Compact, small-sized, and disappointing, the 1962 Cheval Blanc
·
78
has never been one of my favorite wines from this underrated vintage. Now in decline, losing its fruit and drying out, the 1962 is a light, pretty wine, with some charm, and round, gentle fruitiness. It is best drunk from large-format bottles as I suspect the regular-sized bottles are well past their prime. Last tasted, 2/79.

1961—I have consistently mistaken this wine for a great Graves in
·
94
tastings where it has appeared. Dark ruby with a rust-colored edge, this wine has a big, full-blown bouquet of burnt tobacco, and earthy, gravelly scents. On the palate, it is sweet, ripe, quite full-bodied, extremely soft and supple, and clearly at its apogee. I have noticed above-normal bottle variation with the 1961 Cheval Blanc, but the best bottles of this wine are marvelously rich, lush wines. However, they require drinking over the next 5–8 years. Last tasted, 12/83.

AUSONE (Premier Grand Cru Classé) — OUTSTANDING

Production: 1,800–2,200 cases	Grape varieties: Merlot—50% CabernetFranc—50%
Time spent in barrels: 16–20 months	Average age of vines: 50 years
Evaluation of present classification: Since 1976, the quality equivalent of a first-growth	

If the first-time visitor to Bordeaux had just one château and vineyard to visit, it should be the tiny Ausone property, perched on one of the hillsides outside the medieval walls of St.-Emilion.

Ausone has a spectacular location, made all the more startling because of its tiny vineyard of very old vines and the extensive limestone caves that house this property's wine cellar.

Ausone is named after the Roman poet Ausonius who lived between A.D. 320 and 395, and was a professor at the Bordeaux university. He was also known to have had a vineyard that is believed to have been closer to Bordeaux than St.-Emilion. While there are Roman ruins at Ausone, it is highly doubtful that Ausonius himself had anything to do with this particular vineyard.

Ausone is now owned jointly by the Dubois-Challon and Vauthier families, who can trace their ownership of Ausone back to 1800.

Despite the great historical significance of Ausone and the fact that it has one of the most splendid locations for making wine in all of Bordeaux, the record of wine quality has been quite mediocre, even poor, until 1976. The turnabout in quality was a result of the owners' bringing in a new *régisseur*, Pascal Delbeck, and agreeing to work more closely with the famous Libourne oenologist and winemaker at Pétrus, Jean-Claude Berrouet. After producing so many dry, tired, and feebly-colored wines in the '40s, '50s, and '60s, the new team turned out one excellent wine after another, starting with the outstanding 1976, which is one of the two best wines of Bordeaux in that vintage.

The minuscule production of Ausone makes it a wine that is almost impossible to find commercially. Even more rare than the famous Pomerol Pétrus, yet considerably less expensive, Ausone has a style that is totally different from St.-Emilion's other famous estate, Cheval Blanc.

From 1976 onward, the wines of Ausone have been characterized by a dark ruby color, a bouquet of ripe fruit, mineral scents, and spicy oak, and a firm, solidly tannic texture. No doubt the addition of 5–20% stems (which provide additional tannins and acidity) to the fermenting wine, as is done at Pétrus, has produced a notably more tannic wine that is meant to be cellared a long time.

VINTAGES

1983—One of the top dozen or so great successes of the vintage, Au-
• sone's 1983 is a powerful, rich, full-bodied wine with a higher
90 alcohol content than normal. Dark ruby, rich, and jammy, with
low acidity but great concentration, this wine should last 15–20 years, but be drinkable after its seventh or eighth birthday. Anticipated maturity: 1992–2005. Last tasted, 3/85.

1982—I was somewhat depressed when I tasted this wine from the
• bottle. I had thought it would be close to perfection. In my heart,
94 I think Ausone, in 15 years, will match the brilliant perfection
of the 1982 Pétrus and 1982 Mouton-Rothschild, but at present, it is the least approachable, most unyielding and backwardly dumb of the "Big Eight" of Bordeaux. However, its impressive dark ruby color, enormous power and richness, and brutal tannins all reek of greatness, as well as mandate long-term cellaring. In June 1984, I saw this huge wine beginning to close up after dazzling me four separate times before from the barrel. It

is very concentrated, very full-bodied, but absurdly backward. Anticipated maturity: 2000–2040. Last tasted, 1/85.

1981—This medium to dark ruby wine is very closed in, but shows good
· ripeness of fruit, a hard, tannic finnish, and medium weight and
82 body. It has good concentration, but is not in the same class as
the property's 1976 and 1978 wines, and is certainly a world apart from the legendary 1982 Ausone. The 1981 needs 10 years to soften and develop. Anticipated maturity: 1994–2010. Last tasted, 11/84.

1980—A lightweight wine from a lightweight vintage, the 1980 Ausone
· has medium-ruby color, a minor, straightforward bouquet of
75 plums and herbs, medium body, and average-intensity flavors.
Anticipated maturity: 1986–1992. Last tasted, 6/84.

1979—From the cask, I preferred the 1979 to the highly heralded 1978,
· but now that this vintage is in the bottle, the wine has closed up,
86 and seems unyielding and dumb. Dark ruby, with a spicy, tight
bouquet with hints of oak and ripe black cherries, this medium- to full-bodied wine seems surprisingly backward and austere. Will the marvelous fruit it exhibited when young outlive the tannins? Anticipated maturity: 1990–2000. Last tasted, 10/84.

1978—A classic Ausone, still backward and remarkably youthful, the
· 1978 has dark ruby color, an aroma of ripe fruit, as well as scents
87 of minerals and spicy oak. Full-bodied, with high tannins and a
long finish, this wine is obviously made for long-term cellaring. Anticipated maturity: 1990–2000.

1976—The finest Ausone of the '70s, and along with Lafite-Rothschild
· of Pauillac, one of the two outstandingly great wines of this
90 vintage, the 1976 Ausone is a very special wine. Surprisingly
dark-colored for the vintage, with a voluptuous, intense, very complex bouquet of ripe blackcurrant fruit and spices, this full-bodied, deeply fruity, concentrated wine has a long finish and plenty of tannins. It is quite a winemaking triumph for this vintage. Anticipated maturity: 1988–2000. Last tasted, 11/84.

1975—Rather pale-colored for a 1975, with a bouquet of fading fruit,
· and old, musty clothes, the 1975 Ausone has power and average
75 concentration of fruit, but seems to be prematurely drying out.
I have only tasted it once, so perhaps I was unlucky. Last tasted, 5/84.

1971—Light- to medium-ruby with a rust-colored edge, this pleasant
· yet insubstantial wine has a light perfume of spicy oak as well
78 as scents of minerals and decaying leafy vegetation. Not terribly

well concentrated, but adequately fruity in a savory, satisfying manner, the 1971 is a nice wine for drinking immediately. Last tasted, 3/83.

1970—Tasted alongside the 1971, the 1970 Ausone was lighter and its
· bouquet more fleeting. Brown at the edges, and beginning to dry
69 out, this medium-bodied wine is the poorest of the "Big Eight" of Bordeaux in this excellent vintage. Very disappointing. Last tasted, 3/83.

1967—A diluted, insipid bouquet is followed by a wine with bland,
· washed-out flavors, and significant browning to the color. Not a
65 complete failure, but extremely disappointing. Last tasted, 9/83.

FIGEAC (Premier Grand Cru Classé) — EXCELLENT

Production: 12,500 cases	Grape varieties: Cabernet Sauvignon—35% Cabernet Franc—35% Merlot—30%
Time spent in barrels: 20–22 months	Average age of vines: 37 years

Evaluation of present classification: The quality equivalent of a second-growth

This moderately large property of just over 90 acres that sits on the gravel plateau diagonally across the road from Cheval Blanc has generally been considered by most observers to produce St.-Emilion's second-best wine. The emergence of Ausone beginning with the 1976 vintage and the increased consumer awareness of the excellence of other St.-Emilions has meant that Figeac has had to contend with increased competition for its reputation as St.-Emilion's second-best wine.

Owned by the aristocratic-looking Thierry Manoncourt, Figeac makes a very popular style of wine that in the top vintages is much closer in style and quality to its fabulously expensive neighbor, Cheval Blanc, than the price difference would seemingly suggest. Usually quite darkly-colored, richly fruity, and precociously supple and charming, Figeac tends to show well young and mature very quickly, despite the fact of having the highest percentage of tannic and astringent Cabernet Sauvignon used in the blend of any major St.-Emilion. Most recent vintages have tended to be quite ready to drink by the time they are 5 or 6 years old, yet they have had the cunning ability to last well in the bottle for 10 to 20 years.

Figeac has had a good record in off-vintages; the 1977, 1974, and 1968, while hardly inspired wines, were considerably better than most of their peers. Figeac is a wine that I have had difficulty judging when it is less than a year old. At this infant stage the wine often seems thin, and too stalky and herbaceous, only to fill out and put on weight its second year in the cask, and it continues to develop well in the bottle. Perhaps the high percentages of Cabernet Sauvignon and Cabernet Franc from the vineyard's gravelly based soil account for this peculiar trend.

Figeac is generally priced at the level of the best Médoc second-growths, which is high, but seems fair and realistic given the quality of wines produced here.

VINTAGES

1983—Given my tendency to underestimate Figeac when young, I tend
· to think this wine will ultimately merit a higher score. From the
86 cask, it had a pronounced herbaceous aroma which may have
been due to the young Cabernet Franc vines. On the palate, the
1983 Figeac is soft, rich, and fruity, with fine quality, and is
moderately tannic. Anticipated maturity: 1988–1995. Last
tasted, 3/85.

1982—From the bottle, I was shocked at how good this wine has turned
· out to be. Very dark ruby, with a wonderfully fragrant bouquet
90 of cedar, ripe fruit, spicy oak, and subtle herbaceous scents. On
the palate, the wine resembles the 1982 Cheval Blanc, only
slightly less concentrated. Figeac has excellent concentration,
full body, a velvety, silky texture and excellent length. Despite
its precocious appeal, the moderate tannins suggest that cellaring
the wine until 1990 is warranted. This is clearly the best
Figeac since the outstanding 1964. Anticipated maturity: 1990–
2005. Last tasted, 1/85.

1981—Not terribly impressive, either from the cask or in the bottle, the
· 1981 Figeac tastes like a rather dull, commercial sort of wine. It
82 is herbaceous, very soft, velvety, and medium-bodied, with light
tannins and a low acidity that point to a rapid maturation. Anticipated
maturity: 1987–1992. Last tasted, 10/84.

1980—A successful wine in this mediocre vintage, the 1980 Figeac,
· already fully mature, has a pleasant, light-intensity, cedary,
78 spicy, fruity aroma, soft, easy, round flavors that are marked by
a slight vegetal element and a surprisingly adequate finish.
Drink over the next 3 years. Last tasted, 3/84.

1979—Now mature and fully ready to drink, the 1979 Figeac has a
· moderately intense bouquet of soft, spicy, cedary fruit, adequate
83 but unexceptional richness and concentration, medium body, and a soft finish, with no tannins present. Certainly good, but for Figeac's class and price, a bit disappointing. Drink over the next 5 years. Last tasted, 2/84.

1978—Early in its life, the 1978 Figeac seemed very fruity, soft, rather
· straightforward, and destined to be drunk young. Its evolution
85 in the bottle has been marked by a deepening of flavor and a more pronounced richness, and the emergence of more tannins and body. At present, this wine is more impressive than ever. Anticipated maturity: 1988–1998. Last tasted, 6/84.

1977—One of the few successes in this poor vintage, somehow Figeac
· has managed to produce a fruity, soft, and velvety wine, with
75 good body and adequate length. Drink over the next 2–3 years. Last tasted, 10/84.

1976—One of the top successes of the vintage, the 1976 Figeac has
· been consistently impressive in tastings. A big, deep, cedary,
86 ripe fruity bouquet shows good complexity. On the palate, this lush, rich, full-bodied wine avoids the soupy softness and diluted character of many wines produced in 1976. Round, concentrated, generous, and now fully mature, this is a lovely wine from the 1976 vintage. Drink over the next 5 years. Last tasted, 6/83.

1975—A typical Figeac—soft, fruity, and quite accessible when young,
· but age has shown the wine to exhibit increasing amounts of
89 depth, tannins, and body. Still not ready, the 1975 Figeac should prove to be the best wine produced by this estate between 1964 and 1982. Dark ruby with an amber edge, this full-bodied wine is loaded with rich, velvety blackcurrant fruit. It is quite rich and long on the palate. Anticipated maturity: 1986–2000. Last tasted, 5/84.

1974—Always a little stalky and too herbaceous, the 1974 Figeac was a
· good wine from this generally poor vintage. Nicely colored, this
75 medium-bodied wine has adequate fruit and a decent finish. Drink up as it is probably now fading. Last tasted, 3/79.

1971—I had always thought this wine lacking in richness and depth,
· and therefore disappointing in a vintage that was generally quite
84 good for the right-bank communes of St.-Emilion and Pomerol. Within the last year, I saw two examples of the 1971 Figeac that were ripe, roasted, deep, and deliciously fruity, making me won-

der about the abnormal degree of bottle variation. Fully mature, the good examples (reflected by the score) can be kept for 4–5 years. Last tasted, 12/84.

1970—Fully mature, with a big, deep, yet uncomplex bouquet of ripe
· plums with oaky scents, this full-bodied, lush, sweet wine has
86 been drinking nicely since the mid-1970s. Still dark ruby, with just a trace of tannin, this velvety, deeply fruity wine can be held for 5–6 more years. Last tasted, 10/83.

1966—A respectable effort from Figeac, nicely made, fruity, fragrant,
· with scents of ripe fruit and cedarwood, this wine was fully
85 mature when last tasted, yet has the stuffing and balance to age well until at least 1990. Not as big or as full-bodied as either the 1964 or 1970, the 1966 is elegant and quite attractive. Last tasted, 1/82.

1964—This has always been my favorite Figeac of the '60s, along with
· the 1961. It is not as classic as the 1975, but does offer an
90 opulent, rich, deep fruitiness, a velvety texture, and a sensational bouquet of cedar, roasted chestnuts, and ripe plums. It is a rich, smooth wine that has been at its peak for almost a decade without losing any of its marvelous fruit. However, don't tempt fate—it should be drunk up. Last tasted, 3/82.

1962—Still enjoyable, but beginning to lose its fruit and to brown sig-
· nificantly, the 1962 Figeac, a rather lightweight wine from this
80 estate, should be drunk up immediately. Last tasted, 7/80.

1961—Figeac's 1961 must be almost as good as Cheval Blanc in this
· legendary vintage. I have never tasted them together, but if
92 memory serves me right, I would give Cheval Blanc the edge. However, the Figeac is no ugly duckling. A very rich, cedary, spicy, exotic bouquet is quite special. On the palate, the wine is expansive, with layers of unctuous fruit, a slight touch of coarseness which keeps the score down a bit, and a wonderful finish. Fully mature and slightly brown, this wine should hold well for at least 5–7 more years. Last tasted, 3/81.

CANON (Premier Grand Cru Classé) EXCELLENT

Production: 8,500 cases	Grape varieties: Merlot—53% Cabernet Franc—40% Cabernet Sauvignon—4.7% Malbec—2.3%
Time spent in barrels: 20–22 months	Average age of vines: 35 years
Evaluation of present classification: The quality equivalent of a second-growth	

One of the *côtes* St.-Emilions, Canon has a splendid location on the western slopes of the town of St.-Emilion, where its vineyard is sandwiched in between other Premier Cru vineyards such as Belair, Magdelaine, Clos Fourtet, and Beauséjour.

Canon has been the property of the Fournier family since the 19th century, and the young, articulate Eric Fournier runs the property today. The wine produced makes no compromises. A very traditional, long fermentation cares little about consumers who want to drink supple Bordeaux wines. This is a tannic, powerful wine, built to last and last. It is marked by a pronounced oakiness which can, in lighter vintages, obliterate the fruit, and it is this overzealous yet expensive use of new oak that is my only criticism of Canon. It is a wine I adore, and in recent vintages such as 1979, 1982, and 1983, under the leadership of Eric Fournier, it has attained a quality that equals that of the St.-Emilions like Cheval Blanc and Ausone.

Canon is a splendidly rich, deep, and concentrated wine. Muscular and full-bodied, but when mature, richly fruity, cedary, and often magnificent, it remains a mystery why this wine is not better known, because it is certainly one of the top three or four St.-Emilions, yet is nowhere near these other wines in price.

VINTAGES

1983—From cask samples, the 1983 Canon was one of the very top wines of St.-Emilion, as well as of all Bordeaux. It is a notable successor to the sensational 1982. Very dark, with an aroma of rich, ripe black cherry fruit, fresh tobacco, and vanillin oak, this full-bodied, alcoholic, powerful, and tannic wine will take a good decade or more to reach maturity. Quite impressive. Anticipated maturity: 1995–2020. Last tasted, 3/85.
·
92

1982—From its inception, one could easily tell that the 1982 Canon was
· something special and sublime. The proprietor, Eric Fournier,
93 compares it to the 1929 and 1947 in style and richness, and while I have never tasted these wines, this wine is the greatest Canon I have had. Very dark ruby, with the great hallmark of this wonderful vintage (the astonishing richness in aroma) immediately apparent, the wine's bouquet of very ripe, rich blackcurrants, intermingled with vanillin oakiness, jumps from the glass. On the palate, the wine is extremely concentrated, quite rich and full-bodied, but also very, very tannic. This wine will require every bit of a decade to be even close to maturity and will last well into the next century. A monumental wine. Anticipated maturity: 1995–2010. Last tasted, 1/85.

1981—While Canon produced a very good wine in 1978 and 1979, a
· great, perhaps legendary wine in 1982, and an excellent one in
75 1983, it falls way short of my expectations in 1981. The château's obsession with new oak barrels has rendered a wine that from its birth was too light and fragile to absorb the full impact of the tannin and vanillin from new barrels. The wine is overly tannic, lean, and out of balance. Time may help, but don't count on it. Anticipated maturity: 1990–2000. Last tasted, 11/84.

1980—In this vintage I have found the 1980 Canon to have surprisingly
· good fruit, average color, but too oaky a bouquet. One would
72 call this a modest success for the vintage, yet I would like to see less of the annoying vegetal character and more of the pleasant, supple, blackcurrant fruitiness. Drink over the next 5 years. Last tasted, 3/84.

1979—One of the very top St.-Emilions in this vintage, Canon is im-
· pressively dark ruby in color, spicy, quite tannic and youthful,
86 but it exhibits very good concentration, depth, and body. Canon's 1979 is a young, muscular wine with obvious potential. Anticipated maturity: 1990–2005. Last tasted, 12/83.

1978—Similar to the 1979, only slightly fatter, with more of a fleshy,
· open-knit structure, the 1978 Canon still needs plenty of time in
86 the bottle to develop. Dark ruby with a hint of amber, this relatively big, tannic wine has evolved much slower than I expected. Anticipated maturity: 1990–2005. Last tasted, 12/83.

1976—Not one of my favorite Canons, the 1976 is diffuse, and lacks
· both depth and structure. Browning, and overly tannic and oaky
70 without supporting fruit for balance, this wine will only continue

to get more awkward. It should be drunk soon, if ever. Last tasted, 10/82.

1975—The 1975 Canon remains a mystery. A hulking, powerful wine,
· with very good color, a closed, tight bouquet, and ferociously
? tannic, hard flavors, this is a wine that remains totally closed and buttoned up. Only time will prove whether the fruit outlasts that tannin. This is the type of wine that is virtually impossible to judge. It either has a long way to go or no place to go. Anticipated maturity: 1995–2010. Tasted only once, 11/84.

1970—This is a good Canon, yet not nearly up to the quality that the
· young Eric Fournier, who took over direct management in 1972,
84 has produced in the period 1978–1983. Fully mature, somewhat lighter and less concentrated than expected, but fragrant and spicy, with a plummy, roasted character, there is little tannin remaining, so this lightweight Canon should be consumed immediately. Last tasted, 2/85.

1966—One of Canon's top efforts, this rich, intense, deeply concen-
· trated wine is still in top-notch shape, with a big, full-intensity
87 bouquet of ripe fruit and melted toffee. On the palate, the wine is in complete harmony, soft, rich, velvety, full-bodied, and quite fleshy. Drink over the next 5–7 years. Last tasted, 11/82.

1961—An excellent wine, deep, ripe, with a bouquet suggesting smoky,
· ripe fruit and grilled chestnuts, the 1961 Canon is quite full-
88 bodied, still youthfully deep ruby with an amber edge, a trifle austere for a 1961, but long, rich, and probably still evolving. Anticipated maturity: 1985–1995. Last tasted, 10/84.

MAGDELAINE (Premier Grand Cru Classé) EXCELLENT

Production: 4,500–5,000 cases	Grape varieties: Merlot—80% Cabernet Franc—20%
Time spent in barrels: 18–20 months	Average age of vines: 34 years
Evaluation of present classification: The quality equivalent of a second-growth	

Magdelaine, one of the *côtes* St.-Emilions, has been among the top St.-Emilions since the early '60s. Owned by the famous Libourne firm of Jean-Pierre Moueix, which acquired Magdelaine in 1952 and began an extensive replanting program, Magdelaine can now be expected to rival the best wines of St.-Emilion in top vintages.

It is a unique St.-Emilion in that such a high proportion of Merlot is used in its composition. One would therefore assume that the wine is soft, fleshy, and forward. It is not. Because of its long fermentation, and the addition of 20% stems to the fermenting juice, Magdelaine is quite a tannic wine that is always marked by the scent of new oak barrels.

Magdelaine is quite expensive. Its small production and popularity among connoisseurs ensures that it will cost at least the same as a top second-growth of the Médoc.

VINTAGES

1983—Impressive from the cask, but brutally tannic, backward, and
· aggressive, the 1983 Magdelaine has excellent color, very full
85 body, plenty of rich, ripe fruit and weight, but the ferocious tannins makes it reminiscent of the 1975. Anticipated maturity: 1996–2010. Last tasted, 3/85.

1982—If there has ever been a better Magdelaine produced, then I
· would like to taste it. This beautifully made wine is quite full-
92 bodied, very dark in color, with a powerful, rich, deeply concentrated, tannic personality, immense structure, and a sensationally opulent, oaky, richly fruity bouquet. Magdelaine has produced a great wine that has the potential to be even greater; this is a long-distance runner. Anticipated maturity: 1995–2020. Last tasted, 1/85.

1981—Here is an example of a wine that had a lovely, perfumed, soft,
· berry bouquet, and moderately intense flavors, yet because of
80 extensive oak aging, now tastes hard, astringent, tannic, and deficient in fruit. The color is very sound, the bouquet suggests vanillin, woodsy aromas, but on the palate, the wine is unyielding and ungenerous. Perhaps time will result in the fruit being unleashed. Anticipated maturity: 1990–2000. Last tasted, 11/84.

1979—Here is an example of a Magdelaine that behaves as if it were
· made with 80% Merlot. Quite accessible, with round, gentle,
84 forward, silky flavors, this medium-bodied wine shows good concentration and light tannins. Anticipated maturity: 1985–1991. Last tasted, 5/82.

1978—A very ripe wine, Magdelaine's 1978 is jammy and intensely
· fruity, with a round, generous, nicely concentrated texture. Per-
84 haps a little low in acidity, but generally well balanced, with a spicy, vanillin oakiness, this is a forward-styled Magdelaine which will be ready to drink soon. Anticipated maturity: 1985–1992. Last tasted, 5/82.

1975—This wine, like so many 1975s, has evolved at an incredibly slow pace. Still painfully backward, yet so, so promising, this big, dense, tannic wine has dark ruby color, a powerful, ripe plum and oak dominated bouquet, and almost abrasive tannins. Although gobs of fruit are present, Magdelaine's 1975 is recommended for the young and the patient. Anticipated maturity: 1992–2015. Last tasted, 4/79.
· 87

1970—Now beginning to shed its cloak of tannin, the 1970 Magdelaine is dark ruby, has a stylistic resemblance to the 1975 in power and tannic ferocity, but seems to have just a little more flesh and fruit. Quite full-bodied, big, rich, oaky, and spicy, this wine can be drunk now, but promises to be even better during the period 1987–2000. Last tasted, 9/80.
· 88

1967—Always one of the best examples of the 1967 vintage, Magdelaine has begun to fade, but still offers an interesting, chocolatey, cedary, minty bouquet, soft, rich, surprisingly deep flavors marred by a slight astringence. Drink it up. Last tasted, 2/85.
· 82

1962—A lovely success for the vintage, the 1962 Magdelaine has been mature for quite some time, but seems to be holding its fruit. A full-blown bouquet of cedary, herbal, spicy, ripe fruit is altogether impressive. Round generous flavors show good body, no tannins, and despite the brown color at the edges, this wine still has plenty of life. Drink over the next 5 years. Last tasted, 1/81.
· 85

1961—The plague of severe bottle variation among old vintages is well exemplified by this wine. Two bottles tasted in the mid-1970s seemed tired and close to senility. Just recently, a bottle proved sensationally rich, exotic, and intense, with layers of ripe fruit and a superb bouquet. The score reflects the well-preserved bottle. Drink over the next 7–10 years. Last tasted, 6/82.
· 91

L'ARROSÉE (Grand Cru Classé) — VERY GOOD

Production: 5,000 cases	Grape varieties: Merlot—50% Cabernet Sauvignon—35% Cabernet Franc—15%
Time spent in barrels: 18–20 months	Average age of vines: 40 years

Evaluation of present classification: Should be upgraded to a St.-Emilion Premier Grand Cru; the quality equivalent of a fourth-growth

One of the least-known or publicized wines of St.-Emilion, L'Arrosée, which sits on the slopes or *côtes* of St.-Emilion, is destined to become more famous as the high quality of its wine becomes better known.

Owned since 1910 by the Rodhain family, the estate is today managed by François Rodhain. The wine was unfortunately sold off in bulk to the local St.-Emilion cooperative for over three decades because the property had no winemaking facilities. Now the entire production is made and bottled at the château.

My experience with L'Arrosée is limited, but what I have seen has been immensely impressive. The style of the wine is unique. Fleshy, yet firm and powerful, fragrant, as well as rich and full, it is a wine with plenty of character and a style that seems to recall a southern Médoc property such as La Lagune.

The price of L'Arrosée has not yet caught up with the quality, so this is a wine for Bordeaux enthusiasts to search out.

VINTAGES

1983—A brawny, powerful, concentrated, wine, the 1983 L'Arrosée has
· a big, rich bouquet of ripe black cherries and spice. Full-bodied,
88 tannic, and high in alcohol, one can taste the great ripeness this vineyard attained in 1983. Anticipated maturity: 1993–2003. Last tasted, 3/85.

1982—The dark-ruby color, the intense, rich bouquet of spicy oak, the
· explosive blackberry fruit, the full-bodied, lush, deep, very con-
90 centrated feel on the palate, and the round, ripe, high level of tannins present are all telltale characteristics of this very special vintage. The bouquet is fragrant and some might say very burgundian. This is a rich, yet supple, spicy wine, with plenty of extract and a wonderful texture. Anticipated maturity: 1990–2000. Last tasted, 2/85.

1981—A classically proportioned wine of power and balance, the 1981
· L'Arrosée is one of the top wines of St.-Emilion in this vintage.
86 Dark ruby, with an intense perfume of ripe black cherries and spicy oak, this full-bodied wine is powerful, rich, quite tannic, and should have quite a future. Anticipated maturity: 1990–2000. Last tasted, 6/84.

1978—This is one of the very best St.-Emilions of this vintage. Many
· wines became too ripe in the very late harvest of 1978, but
87 L'Arrosée is extremely well structured and vinified. Dark ruby, with some amber at the edge, this wine has a deep, rich, ripe

fruity, oaky bouquet that suggests a Médoc more than a St.-Emilion. On the palate, the wine is full-bodied, quite concentrated, tannic, beefy, and long in the finish. It is a big, substantial wine, with a long way to go. Anticipated maturity: 1986–1992. Last tasted, 1/85.

1970—Quite youthful, even after 14 years, this big, full-bodied wine
· has a dark-ruby color, with some amber at the edge, a spicy,
86 oaky, black cherry bouquet, full body, tightly knit flavors, and a rich, long finish. L'Arrosée is just beginning to shed its tannins and open up. Impressive. Anticipated maturity: 1986–1994. Last tasted, 6/84.

1964—Now fully mature, but in no danger of declining, this wonderfully
· fragrant wine has a big, rich, deep bouquet that develops in the
87 glass. The wine is quite fleshy, concentrated and rich, with a chewy texture, substantial weight, and a surprising amount of alcohol. Drink over the next 5 years. Last tasted, 6/84.

LA DOMINIQUE (Grand Cru Classé) — VERY GOOD

Production: 6.500 cases	Grape varieties: Merlot—76% Cabernet Sauvignon—8% Cabernet Franc—8% Malbec—8%
Time spent in barrels: 18–22 months	Average age of vines: 22–25 years

Evaluation of present classification: Should be upgraded to a St.-Emilion Premier Cru; the quality equivalent of a fourth-growth

La Dominique is a vivid example of an estate that clearly merited promotion in the new 1985 classification of the wines of St.-Emilion. However, it was left as a Grand Cru Classé. This property, while lacking the glamor and reputation of a great property such as Cheval Blanc or Figeac, is making consistently fine wines that rival and even surpass many of the other top wines of St.-Emilion.

La Dominique is named after the island of the Dominican Republic, where, apparently, one of this property's former owners had lived and made a fortune. Since 1969, La Dominique has been run with meticulous attention to detail and an obsessive commitment to quality by Clément Fayat. Fayat, a wealthy builder who lives in the Médoc in an up-and-coming wine-producing property called Pichon, brought in the highly respected Libourne oenologist, Michel Rolland, to oversee the vinification and care of this wine. The result has been a succession of very good vintages for this property, led by a superb 1971 (one of the top wines of that vintage) and the sensational 1982.

La Dominique's vineyard sits next to Cheval Blanc on a sandy, gravelly, clay subsoil base. The wine is lighter than Cheval Blanc, but always highly aromatic, richly fruity, and moderately tannic. The use of new oak barrels (about one-third are new each year) is prevalent here.

La Dominique's wines remain considerably undervalued, but all that will change once the wine world learns of the quality here.

VINTAGES

1983—The third consecutive successful wine in this wonderful trilogy
· for La Dominique, the 1983, while not a match for the heavenly
85 1982, is still a very good, well-structured, flavorful, full-bodied wine, with plenty of class. Slightly more rustic and alcoholic than usual, this tannic wine has plenty of rich fruit. Anticipated maturity: 1990–2000. Last tasted, 3/85.

1982—La Dominique makes consistently fine wines, but as anyone
· knows who has tasted either the 1955 or 1971, the property can
90 on occasion make something truly divine. The 1982 is such a wine, which from its earliest days in the cask showed such a remarkable perfume and majestic flavors that it could be nothing less than sensational when released. Very dark in color, with an opulent bouquet of toasty vanillin oak and rich, ripe fruit, this full-bodied wine is packed with layers of intense, velvety fruit. The finish seems to last several minutes, as this wine captures the magical essence of the 1982 vintage. Anticipated maturity: 1988–2000. Last tasted, 1/85.

1981—La Dominique's 1981, while no match for the château's extraor-
· dinary 1982 wine, is a complex, medium-weight, nicely balanced
84 wine, with a tight but promising bouquet of new oak, ripe fruit, and herbal scents. Well made, this medium-bodied wine needs 2 years to show all its charms. Anticipated maturity: 1986–1994. Last tasted, 11/84.

1980—A success given the vintage in 1980, La Dominique produced a
· supple, fruity wine, with a slightly herbaceous, vegetal quality
78 to its bouquet. On the palate, the wine displays good fruit, medium body, and a soft, pleasant finish. Drink over the next 4 years. Last tasted, 6/84.

1979—I have never been a great admirer of this wine. Consistently
· lean, austere, and lacking generosity, it is an acceptable wine
75 with an attractive bouquet, but for La Dominique, a disappointment. Time may yield some hidden fruit, but I would not gamble on it. Anticipated maturity: 1985–1990. Last tasted, 12/83.

1978—Now drinking beautifully, this lovely, ripe, fleshy, very fruity La
· Dominique has a cedary, spicy, ripe fruity bouquet, medium to
84 full body, light tannins, and a soft, savory, long finish. This is an extremely elegant, supple wine that will keep and continue to drink well over the next 5 years. Last tasted, 6/84.

1976—A trifle loosely knit (as most 1976s are), but La Dominique has
· managed to produce a wine that avoids the soupy softness and
83 unstructured feel of many wines of this vintage. A ripe, cedary, oaky, spicy bouquet is fully developed. On the palate, the wine is soft, nicely concentrated, and expansive. This is a delightful medium-weight wine for drinking over the next 2–3 years. Last tasted, 2/84.

1975—A typical 1975, hard, astringent, promising, but obnoxiously
· backward and tannic, this wine remains closed and slightly
82 dumb, but shows very good color, a hint of ripe, cedary, plummy fruit in its nose, and weight and length in the finish. Will the fruit last? Anticipated maturity: 1988–2000. Last tasted, 2/84.

1971—This is the kind of wine that one sip of can make a skeptic of La
· Dominique an instant devotee. A sensational wine for La Domi-
90 nique, the 1971 is not only the best St.-Emilion, but one of the top wines of the vintage. Quite dark ruby with a very concentrated, jammy, rich bouquet of ripe berry fruit, this wine is lush and silky, with layers of ripe fruit and a great finish. This is certainly one of the sleepers of the vintage. Drink over the next 5 years. Last tasted, 10/83.

1970—The 1970 is a very attractive, mature St.-Emilion that is in no
· danger of falling apart, but is best drunk up over the next several
85 years. Medium ruby with some amber, this wine is soft, fragrant, ripe, and very nicely concentrated, with a velvety, good finish. Drink up. Last tasted, 2/84.

PAVIE (Premier Grand Cru Classé) VERY GOOD

Production: 14,000–16,000 cases	Grape varieties: Merlot—55% Cabernet Franc—25% Cabernet Sauvignon—20%
Time spent in barrels: 20–24 months	Average age of vines: 40 years

Evaluation of present classification: The quality equivalent of a fifth-growth, particularly since 1979

Pavie has the largest vineyard of all the St.-Emilion Premiers Grands Crus. With a production seven times the size of one of its neighbors, Ausone, and twice that of the adjacent vineyard, La Gaffelière, Pavie's wines are widely known throughout the world.

The vineyard is superbly situated just to the southeast of St.-Emilion (a 5-minute drive), on the eastern section of the hillsides of the town. Therefore, it is one of the *côtes* St.-Emilions.

Pavie is now owned and run by Jean Paul Valette, who has been at Pavie since 1967 (after giving up ranching in Chile). He is one of St.-Emilion's friendliest proprietors, and his friendliness, as well as the fact that Pavie has some of the region's most interesting limestone caves for storing wine, make this a must stop for tourists to the area.

Pavie, despite its large production and popularity, has not been a top performer among the St.-Emilion first-growths. In many vintages the wine has been too light and feebly colored, with a tendency to brown and mature at an accelerated pace. Valette has been aware of these problems, and one can easily detect a move to a more strongly concentrated, deeper colored, fuller-bodied Pavie with the vintages of 1979 on. This is not to suggest that all of the wines of Pavie produced before 1979 were insipid and weak, but far too many vintages, for example, 1976, 1975, 1974, and 1966, were well below acceptable standards. But this period of inconsistency is apparently behind the château. The famous oenologist Emile Peynaud is now taking an active interest in the fermentation of Pavie, and recent vintages have gone from one strength to another.

Pavie is fairly priced for a Premier Grand Cru Classé St.-Emilion. The large production has guaranteed that the price has remained realistic.

VINTAGES

1983 · 86 —A difficult wine to assess, the 1983 Pavie, tasted several times from the cask, was brutally tannic, severe, astringent, and just too aggressive to be sure about. Certainly the color is dark ruby, and the wine has very good weight and concentration, but this tough wine might turn out like some 1975s and have an excess of tannin, although its recent showing in March 1985 seemed to suggest that the requisite concentration of fruit was present. Anticipated maturity: 1993–2005. Last tasted, 3/85.

1982 · 89 —I doubt that Pavie can make a better wine than it did in 1982. It is very dark in color, with a closed, but powerful, rich, ripe bouquet of briary fruit and toasted almonds. In the mouth, the wine is uncommonly rich and full for Pavie, with excellent concentration, mouth-puckering tannins, and a full decade and a half of cellaring necessary to reach full maturity. It is a wonderfully structured, very deep, profound Pavie. For the patient. Anticipated maturity: 1995–2010. Last tasted, 1/85.

1981 · 82 —This vintage of Pavie seems to be developing faster than I expected. A classy and complex bouquet of spicy, vanillin oak and ripe cherries is quite attractive. In the mouth, the wine is medium-bodied, flavorful, a little lean and hard, but elegant and capable of further improvement. Anticipated maturity: 1988–1995. Last tasted, 4/84.

1979 · 85 —Along with the 1982, this is one of the best Pavies in over a decade. The 1979 has surprisingly dark ruby color, with a toasty, almost smoky, berryish bouquet, medium to full body, good power and weight, and moderate tannins. Anticipated maturity: 1988–1996. Last tasted, 12/84.

1978 · 78 —A loose, open-knit style of wine, the 1978 Pavie lacks concentration, structure, and firmness, but offers a sweet, ripe (possibly overripe) Merlot fruitiness, and one-dimensional charm. I also detected a vegetal quality to the bouquet. Drink over the next 3–4 years. Last tasted, 4/82.

1976 · 56 —Quite disappointing, the 1976 Pavie is an insipid, dull, diluted wine, with marginal flavor interest, a vegetal, overly spicy, woody aroma and pale, shallow flavors. Last tasted, 9/80.

1975 · 72 —A minor wine in this vintage, the 1975 Pavie exhibits sweet, ripe, lightly concentrated, Merlot fruity flavors, medium body, and surprisingly little tannin. A compact, little wine, the 1975 Pavie should be drunk over the next several years. Last tasted, 5/84.

1971—The 1971 Pavie is a graceful, well-balanced, fruity, soft, elegant
· wine that always impressed me as among the most restrained
81 and subdued of the 1971 St.-Emilions. Now beginning to lose its fruit, this medium-bodied wine still has charm and finesse, but it is displayed in an understated way. Drink up. Last tasted, 2/79.

1970—Produced in a period when Pavie was obviously in a perfor-
· mance slump, the 1970 Pavie is a notable success for the
84 vineyard. Not terribly complex, but chunky, straightforward, and "four-square" as I suspect Michael Broadbent would say, this wine has a roasted, ripe cherry bouquet, and full, oaky, yet one-dimensional flavors. It is a good effort. Drink over the next 4 years. Last tasted, 2/83.

1967—Not retasted in a long time, I have always enjoyed the 1967 Pavie
· and thought it to be one of the underrated wines of this vintage.
82 Probably past its peak, this wine has a wonderful, smooth, graceful, supple texture, with no hard edges, and an enjoyable, oaky, ripe bouquet. Drink up. Last tasted, 3/76.

1966—Consistently inferior and rather disturbingly light-colored and
· shallow, this wine has been fully mature for over a decade, and
64 is no doubt now close to total senility. Pavie is a major disappointment of the vintage. Last tasted, 11/78.

1961—Certainly a good wine, with an open-knit, spicy, cedary, mature,
· fruity bouquet, the 1961 Pavie, viewed in the context of the
81 vintage, is a disappointment. Lacking the telltale personality traits of this vintage (often fabulous richness and concentration), this medium-bodied wine should be consumed immediately, as the brown color and absence of tannins clearly suggest. Last tasted, 12/83.

SOUTARD (Grand Cru Classé) — VERY GOOD

Production: 6,500 cases	Grape varieties: Merlot—70% Cabernet Franc—25% Cabernet Sauvignon—5%
Time spent in barrels: 18–24 months	Average age of vines: 43 years

Evaluation of present classification: Should be upgraded to a St.-Emilion Premier Cru; the quality equivalent of a fifth-growth

Soutard is highly prized in the Benelux countries, but the wine is terribly ignored in America. The vineyard and lovely château are located just to the northeast of St.-Emilion on a limestone plateau. Quite traditionally made, Soutard can easily lay claim to producing some of St.-Emilion's most backward and long-lived wines, particularly in great vintages such as 1964, 1975, and 1982.

Although only one-third new oak barrels are used each year, I have always found this wine marked by the scent and aroma of vanillin oakiness. In addition, it usually stands out among other St.-Emilions because of its very dark color and tannic ferocity, which can be abrasive when the wine is young.

Soutard, owned by the Comte Jacques des Ligneris, is one of St.-Emilion's best-kept secrets. Consequently, the price has remained moderate. However, this is a wine that only collectors willing to cellar it for a decade or more should take a serious interest in.

VINTAGES

1982—The 1982 is an old-style St.-Emilion made to last and last. It
· belongs to enthusiasts who have the patience to lay it away for a
87 decade or more. The 1982 is typically huge, backward, almost abrasively tannic. However, this wine, which is now quite closed, has a broodingly dark color, excellent richness, ripeness, and weight on the palate, and will no doubt receive a higher score circa 2000, but it is brutally tannic now. Anticipated maturity: 2000–2025. Last tasted, 1/85.

1981—The 1981 is closed in, but shows ripe, spicy, plummy fruit, a
· tight, firm structure, and plenty of weight and richness. Soutard
84 has made an impressive wine in 1982, but once again one must have patience. Anticipated maturity: 1995–2005. Last tasted, 6/84.

1979—A very successful 1979, but unlike most wines from this vintage,
· Soutard is backward and quite tannic, with a deep ruby color,
84 and a big-framed structure. It is still raw, undeveloped, and tasting like a barrel sample rather than a 5-year-old wine. Anticipated maturity: 1990–2005. Last tasted, 6/84.

1978—Totally different in style from the 1979, the 1978 Soutard tastes
· much softer, riper, has more mid-range fruit, full body, rela-
84 tively low acidity, and a good, lush, moderately tannic finish. For Soutard, this wine will develop much more quickly than normal. Anticipated maturity: 1988–1998. Last tasted, 6/84.

1975—A very impressive wine, the 1975 Soutard is still youthfully dark
· ruby, with rich, savory, ripe, full-bodied flavors, plenty of
87 mouth-coating tannins, and a long finish. This is a big, typical
Soutard which will continue to evolve very slowly. Anticipated
maturity: 1990–2005. Last tasted, 10/84.

1966—Not as big nor as intense as one might expect, the 1966 Soutard
· is fully mature, has a dark color with some brown at the edge, a
82 ripe, harmonious, sweet palate impression, and some light tannins in the finish. Surprisingly elegant and lighter than expected,
this vintage of Soutard should be drunk over the next 2–3 years.
Last tasted, 6/81.

1964—One of Soutard's really top-class wines, the 1964, an especially
· good vintage for St.-Emilion, has a voluptuous, rich, intense,
87 velvety texture that is layered with fruit. Medium- to full-bodied
with a big, creamy, ripe, fruity bouquet, this dense yet extremely well-balanced wine will last, but ideally should be drunk
over the next 4–5 years. Last tasted, 5/84.

CADET-PIOLA (Grand Cru Classé) VERY GOOD

Production: 3,000 cases	Grape varieties: Merlot—51% Cabernet Sauvignon—28% Cabernet Franc—18% Malbec—3%
Time spent in barrels: 18 months	Average age of vines: 22 years

Evaluation of present classification: Should be upgraded to a St.-Emilion Premier Cru; the quality equivalent of a Médoc fifth-growth

It must be the small production of Cadet-Piola that has kept this wine's quality relatively secret for so long a time. Cadet-Piola, which is neither a *côtes* St.-Emilion nor a *graves* St.-Emilion, is just half a kilometer north of the town. It sits on a rocky outcropping with a splendid view overlooking St.-Emilion.

The owners, the Jabiol family, are conservative winemakers who produce a black-ruby-colored, rich and intense, full-bodied wine that over the last decade has outperformed many of the more famous and more expensive Premiers Grands Crus. Cadet-Piola is a great value, and perhaps consumer demand will result in more of this estate's wine being exported.

VINTAGES

1983—Not the success of the wonderful 1982, however, the 1983 Cadet-
· Piola is still a darkly colored, ripe, full-bodied, admirably con-
85 structed St.-Emilion with plenty of concentration, balance, and
power. Anticipated maturity: 1990–1998. Last tasted, 3/85.

1982—A real sleeper of the vintage, this wine has excellent structure
· and some spicy new oak in its bouquet that nicely complements
87 the oodles of ripe black cherries and chocolate aromas present.
Full-bodied, quite concentrated, very tannic and very deep, this
big wine is impeccably made and will age very well. Anticipated
maturity: 1990–2005. Last tasted, 1/85.

CLOS DES JACOBINS (Grand Cru Classé) VERY GOOD

Production: 4,000 cases	Grape varieties: Merlot—47% Cabernet Franc—45% Cabernet Sauvignon—8%
Time spent in barrels: 18–20 months	Average age of vines: 30–32 years

Evaluation of present classification: Should be upgraded to a St.-Emilion Premier Cru; the quality equivalent of a fifth-growth

The large *négociant* firm of Cordier acquired this lovely little château northwest of St.-Emilion in 1964. Unlike the firm's famous Médoc properties, Talbot and Gruaud-Larose, Close des Jacobins, despite increasingly high-quality wines, gets very little publicity, and is undoubtedly Cordier's least-known great wine. It has been remarkably consistent over the last decade, producing a wine that is deeply colored, rich, round, creamy, and plummy, with oodles of ripe fruit, and an absence of astringent, aggressive tannins. Clos des Jacobins is terribly undervalued.

VINTAGES

1983—One of the top successes of the appellation in this very good, yet
· very irregular vintage, the 1983 Clos des Jacobins is quite dark
87 ruby, with an intense, supple, blackberry fruitiness, a lush, ripe,
creamy, fat texture, moderate tannins, plenty of alcoholic
punch, and a long finish. It should mature quickly. Anticipated
maturity: 1988–1996. Last tasted, 3/85.

1982—Certainly the best Clos des Jacobins I have ever tasted, the 1982
· has an unbelievably rich, ripe, jammy bouquet that is just filled
89 with blackberry fruit. On the palate, the wine is full-bodied, sweet, and ripe, with layers of voluptuous fruit. This is a soft, decadently fruity wine that is succulent and delicious. Anticipated maturity: 1988–1998. Last tasted, 1/85.

1981—The 1981 is a success for the vintage; however, this vintage of
· Clos des Jacobins gets overwhelmed in the company of the re-
86 markable 1982 and big-styled 1983 wines. The 1981 is precociously soft and intensely fruity, with a complex cedary, herbaceous bouquet, medium body, and lush, nicely concentrated tannins. Drink over the next 6–7 years. Last tasted, 11/84.

1979—Fully mature, this wine lacks the great concentration of the
· vintages of the '80s, but is fat, juicy, and spicy, with a smooth,
84 graceful, lush fruitiness, medium body, and light tannins. Drink over the next 4 years. Last tasted, 1/82.

1978—Another top-notch success for the vintage and the appellation,
· the 1978 Clos des Jacobins has a fine dark color, a rich black-
86 berry bouquet, medium to full body, a beefy, rather weighty feel on the palate, and round, ripe, moderate tannins. Very appealing when young, the 1978 Clos des Jacobins has also aged well. Drink over the next 5–7 years. Last tasted, 3/82.

1976—This is a notably good wine from a vintage that has provided
· quite a few disappointments. Fully mature, this fleshy, open-
83 knit style of St.-Emilion has good concentration for the vintage, a very supple, smooth texture, and no tannins in the soft finish. It is quite mature, so don't hesitate to drink it up. Last tasted, 9/80.

1975—Now entering its mature period, where it should remain for 5–8
· years, the 1975 Clos des Jacobins, despite a higher level of
87 tannins than usual for this estate, still shows the rich, glossy, fat fruitiness that makes this wine so appealing. Full-bodied, succulent, and showing good depth, this is one of the few major 1975s that can be drunk now. It will hold for at least another 3–4 years. Last tasted, 5/84.

BELAIR (Premier Grand Cru Classé) VERY GOOD

Production: 4,500	Grape varieties: Merlot—60% Cabernet Franc—40%
Time spent in barrels: 20–22 months	Average age of vines: 38 years

Evaluation of present classification: The quality equivalent of a fifth-growth, particularly since 1979

Belair, like so many other properties in Bordeaux, has just recently come out of a prolonged period of mediocre performance. This property had a great reputation in the 19th century (and its history can be traced back to the 14th century). The tiny vineyard of Belair is owned by the Dubois-Challon family, who are also co-proprietors of Ausone, Belair's next-door neighbor. The level of wine quality at Belair has followed that of Ausone. The rehabilitation and renaissance of Ausone started with the 1976 vintage, and it was during this time that higher-quality wines from Belair began to be produced. The same team that makes Ausone —Pascal Delbeck, Marcel Lanau, and Jean-Claude Berrouet—are also the main brain trust at Belair, and as the tasting notes demonstrate, this wine has gotten better and better with each passing vintage. In style, one might assume that because of the vineyard's location on the *côtes* next to Ausone, with which it shares the same winemakers, Belair would resemble Ausone. It does not. The wine is lighter, less concentrated and powerful, softer, and earlier to mature. Thankfully, it is also significantly less expensive.

VINTAGES

1983 —In my cask tastings of the 1983 St.-Emilions, Belair, along with
· Cheval Blanc, Ausone, and Canon, stood out among the top
89 wines of this vintage. Surprisingly powerful and rich for Belair, with excellent color, a deep, ripe, tannic, full-bodied texture, this is a rather big-styled wine that should prove to be the longest-lived Belair in over 20 years. Quite impressive. Anticipated maturity: 1993–2005. Last tasted, 3/85.

1982 —As good as Belair is in 1982, it will have to take a back seat to
· the lovely, rich, "*très grand vin*" in 1983. Nevertheless, the 1982
87 is dark ruby, with a very attractive, plummy, ripe, fruity, almost truffle-like aroma. Medium- to full-bodied, with good concentration, moderate tannins, and a velvety, supple finish, this wine

will provide very stylish, balanced drinking. Anticipated maturity: 1989–2000. Last tasted, 1/85.

1981—The 1981 is, as the Bordelais would enthusiastically say, "a
· finesse wine with plenty of elegance." Light, fruity, soft, this
74 medium-ruby-colored wine has a pleasing texture, some hard tannins in the finish, and seems unlikely to gain much in flavor or depth after another 2 years in the bottle. More impressive from the cask, the final bottled Belair is quite mediocre. Anticipated maturity: 1986–1992. Last tasted, 2/85.

1979—The first really good Belair in almost 20 years, the 1979 has an
· attractive perfumed quality of ripe blackcurrant fruit, some
85 spicy oak, and (I believe) violets. On the palate, the wine is medium-bodied, with a lush, precocious fruitiness, and light tannins. This is a deliciously soft, fruity, very elegant wine to drink over the next 6 years. Last tasted, 4/84.

1978—This is an attractive wine that is a trifle too light and fleeting on
· the palate, but does offer soft, pleasant, easygoing fruity flavors,
78 and it also finishes well. Drink over the next 5–6 years. Last tasted, 5/81.

1976—The 1976 is respectable, but perhaps it could have been better,
· given the excellence of Ausone in this vintage. Rather light, soft,
75 fruity, and sweet, with the obvious overripe quality of the vintage displayed, the 1976 Belair has no tannin discernible. It should be drunk over the next several years for its straightforward charm. Last tasted, 6/82.

1975—I have found this wine to be hollow and lacking fruit, with an
· excess of tannin present. Medium ruby with some brown at the
70 edges, this medium-bodied wine has a dusty, sparse texture, a leathery, hard bouquet, and a short, harsh finish. It appears to be one of the 1975s in which the tannin content significantly outnumbers the fruit. Last tasted, 5/84.

1971—Quite meagerly endowed, without much bouquet, this little wine
· has a brownish color, dry, astringent, hard flavors, and no
65 charm. One rarely sees top properties today producing wines at this level of quality. Last tasted, 9/78.

1970—Adequately colored with just a shade of brown, the 1970 Belair
· is hard, spicy, and finishes with a coarseness and bitterness. It
68 is an atypical 1970. Last tasted, 7/81.

1967—Extremely poor, the 1967, from a vintage which was generally
· better for St.-Emilion and Pomerol than the Médoc, is brown in
55 color, with pale, coarse, diluted flavors. Last tasted, 4/80.

1966—Thin, sharp, acidic flavors dominate the palate. The fruit is
· fading, and the wine has only wood and alcohol in the finish.
60 Belair is a major disappointment in this vintage. Last tasted, 4/80.

CLOS FOURTET (Premier Grand Cru Classé) GOOD

Production: 5,500–6,000 cases	Grape varieties: Merlot—60% Cabernet Sauvignon—20% Cabernet Franc—20%
Time spent in barrels: 18 months	Average age of vines: 22 years

Evaluation of present classification: Should be downgraded to a Grand Cru Classé; the quality equivalent of a Grand Bourgeois Exceptionnel

It is unfortunate that the most interesting thing about the estate of Clos Fourtet is the extensive underground wine cellars that are among the finest in the Bordeaux region. This winery, like a number of highly respected but overrated St.-Emilion Premiers Grands Crus, has been making wine over the last two decades that is good, but not up to the standards of its classification. The wines have been plagued by a bland, dull, chunky, dry, astringent fruitiness, and a curious habit of getting older without getting better. They simply have not developed well in the bottle.

This property is on the *côtes* of St.-Emilion, almost at the entrance to St.-Emilion, opposite the Place de L'Eglise and Hôtel Plaisance. Over the last few years, the ubiquitous Lurton family (owners of numerous châteaux throughout Bordeaux) have made significant renovations to the winery, and have retained the services of Emile Peynaud, the famed oenologist, to get things just right. The results look promising rather than spectacular. Certainly, the new style of Clos Fourtet, which commenced with the 1978 vintage, is a more supple, more overtly fruity, less tannic, and easier wine to comprehend and enjoy, but it has not yet shown the quality and character of the wines that have preceded it in this section.

VINTAGES

1983—Cask samples of this wine consistently exhibited a one-dimen-
· sional, soft, light-intensity fruitiness, medium body, hardly any
78 tannin, and a short finish. Unless this wine mysteriously finds

some concentration and flesh, this is not one of the top wines in 1983 from St.-Emilion. Anticipated maturity: 1986–1990. Last tasted, 3/85.

1982—Another St.-Emilion estate that has long been in the throes of
· mediocrity, the 1982 Clos Fourtet is the most satisfying wine
86 produced by this estate in well over 20 years. Dark ruby, with a full-blown bouquet of vanillin oakiness and ripe, rich, berry fruit, this full-bodied wine has a forward, precocious, rich, supple fruitiness that coats the palate and lingers and lingers. One suspects that this wine will be drinkable soon but will hold well. Drink between 1988 and 1996. Last tasted, 1/85.

1981—Another medium-weight 1981 St.-Emilion, the Clos Fourtet has
· high-intensity fruit, but the wood flavors dominate the frail com-
80 position of the wine. A nice, ripe cherry component indicates good ripeness of the grapes, but the wood tannins are entirely too pronounced. Anticipated maturity: 1986–1989. Last tasted, 5/83.

1979—The 1979 is a good example of a wine that shows that Clos
· Fourtet's wines are on an upswing in quality. The 1979 is quite
82 dark in color, with attractive, ripe fruit, medium to full body, and a good, clean finish. The wine's bouquet has opened, and this precocious wine should be drunk over the next 2–4 years. Last tasted, 6/84.

1978—The first wine in a line of good, rather than superb Clos Fourtets,
· the 1978 has settled down nicely in the bottle and reveals allur-
84 ing scents of blackcurrants, an open-knit, soft, ripe fruity texture, medium body, and a good finish with moderate tannins present. Quite successful for a 1978 St.-Emilion, this wine should be drunk over the next 4–5 years. Last tasted, 5/83.

1975—This wine seems to have lost its fruit and dried out, revealing an
· excess of tannins, and a charmless, hollow structure. Last
70 tasted, 5/84.

1971—Well colored for a 1971, but it has very little bouquet, a dull,
· tough, bland fruitiness, and very astringent tannin in the finish.
70 There is just not enough fruit to balance the tannin. It is also beginning to fade badly. Last tasted, 2/79.

1970—The 1970 has the same personality traits as the 1971. Even
· though it is a bigger, riper wine, it is one-dimensional, slightly
72 coarse, tannic, and just tastes boring. Last tasted, 8/78.

L'ANGÉLUS (Grand Cru Classé) GOOD

Production: 11,000–12,500 cases

Grape varieties:
Cabernet Franc—60%
Merlot—40%

Time spent in barrels: 16–18 months

Average age of vines: 25 years

Evaluation of present classification: The quality equivalent of a Grand Bourgeois Exceptionnel

L'Angélus has always been a St.-Emilion that has had great popular appeal. With a large production, much of it exported, its lovely label, and charming, supple style of wine, L'Angélus has been able to build a strong following among enthusiasts of the wines of St.-Emilion.

However, an objective evaluation of the vintages and quality of wine produced at L'Angélus in the '60s and '70s will show a wine that starts off when young with a charming fruity intensity, then proceeds to disintegrate in a matter of a few short years. This has all been changed in the '80s. The well-known Bordeaux oenologist, Pascal Ribereau Gayon, was brought in to provide consultation, and he insisted that the property age the wine in oak casks, of which one-third should be new each vintage. Previously, the wine had been aged in vats and saw no oak aging at all.

The results have been stunning. No doubt the young proprietor, Hubert de Bouard, is also making a much stricter selection of only the best lots for the final wine. L'Angélus applied for elevation to Premier Grand Cru status in the new 1985 classification of the wines of St.-Emilion. This was denied, but based on the vintages of the '80s, L'Angélus seems to have increased its quality significantly.

The style of the new L'Angélus is one that still emphasizes early drinkability, with its intense, rich, supple, fat fruitiness. However, the wine is now much deeper colored, more concentrated, and has more supportive tannins to help it age better. Certainly the two fine wines of 1982 and 1983 are woth looking at; however, older vintages must be approached with extreme caution, as many of these wines have fallen completely apart.

VINTAGES

1983—From the cask, this wine was magnificent. Densely colored, very
· concentrated, exuberantly fruity, L'Angélus is a wonder just to
87 smell the ripeness and taste the richness of the layers of lush

fruit. Potentially, this wine looks to be the best of the last three vintages of L'Angélus. Anticipated maturity: 1989–1996. Last tasted, 3/85.

1982—I had higher hopes for this wine, which may have been exces-
· sively fined or filtered. Compared to the numerous barrel sam-
85 ples I saw, the bottled wine is significantly lighter in color and less concentrated. Nevertheless, it is no ugly duckling. Extremely precocious, supple, very fruity, and lush, this is a sumptuous wine that lacks some backbone, but offers the prospect of delicious drinking over the next 7–8 years. Last tasted, 2/85.

1981—After an extended period of mediocrity, the young Hubert de
· Bouard has taken full charge of L'Angélus, and is making gigan-
84 tic strides forward in quality. The new 1985 classification of the wines of St.-Emilion refused to elevate L'Angélus, but if one looks at the remarkable turnaround at L'Angélus, a very good 1981 and 1982, and great 1983, and if this type of quality continues, L'Angélus will be due for promotion when the next classification comes out in 1995. The 1981 is lush, fruity, fat, and concentrated. It should be drunk over the next 8 years. Last tasted, 1/85.

1979—The 1979 has a vegetal, very herbaceous bouquet that is a trifle
· unusual, not to mention unpleasant. On the palate, this wine is
72 very light, diffuse, medium-bodied and quite shallow and feeble, Drink up. Last tasted, 2/81.

1978—A typical pre-1981 L'Angélus, the 1978 is light, fully mature,
· beginning to exhibit plenty of brown in its color and to lose its
75 fruit. It is pleasant and charming in a light, picnic sort of style. It must be drunk. Last tasted, 3/83.

1976—The 1976 L'Angélus is a total disaster, light, pale, no fruit, no
· character, no charm—just alcohol and distant flavors of fruit.
55 Last tasted, 6/80.

1975—The 1975 is a very poor wine, brown in color with an old, decay-
· ing, leafy vegetal aroma, and hardly any ripe fruity intensity.
50 This wine is unacceptably poor in what was an excellent if somewhat irregular vintage for the wines of Bordeaux. Last tasted, 5/84.

CORBIN (Grand Cru Classé) GOOD

Production: 6,500 cases	Grape varieties: Merlot—66% Cabernet Franc—34%
Time spent in barrels: 20 months	Average age of vines: 25 years
Evaluation of present classification: The quality equivalent of a Grand Bourgeois Exceptionnel	

Corbin is clearly a property of which to take note. My first experience with this wine was at a dinner party where the 1970 was served blind. It was an immensely enjoyable, round, full-bodied, concentrated, delicious wine with plenty of fruit. Since then I have made it a point to follow this estate closely. In great vintages like 1970, 1975, and 1982, this wine can rival the best St.-Emilions. Its problem has been inconsistency from year to year.

Corbin sits on the *graves* plateau near the Pomerol border. The administrator is Madame Blanchard-Giraud, who also manages the up-and-coming high-quality Pomerol estate, Certan-Giraud. The style of wine here, which seems to be at its best in hot, sunny years, is one in which the wine is quite dark in color, very fat, ripe, full-bodied, and quite concentrated. Unfortunately, Corbin is a moderately expensive wine since it has long been very poular in the Benelux counties and Great Britain. Consequently, demand has always guaranteed that supplies of Corbin will be scarce.

VINTAGES

1983—From the cask, this wine was big, jammy, fat, alcoholic, and
• quite a mouthful. Almost black in color, with excellent extract,
86 this wine should turn out to be quite a chewy, corpulent mouthful of St-Emilion. Anticipated maturity: 1989–1996. Last tasted, 3/85.

1982—In very good vintages, Corbin can be excellent. The 1982 prom-
• ises to be even better than the lovely 1970. Quite dark ruby, with
87 a full-blown, ripe blackcurrant, toasty bouquet, this full-bodied wine has excellent concentration, moderate tannins, and excellent balance and length. Still youthfully jammy, and tasting very much like a barrel sample, this wine should be drunk between 1990–2000. Last tasted, 1/85.

1978—Now mature, the 1978 is a big, juicy, fat, ripe, richly fruity wine,
· with plenty of soft, velvety fruit, full body, and an alcoholic yet
84 long finish. Drink over the next 5 years. Last tasted, 2/84.

1975—Not quite the size and dimension of the two big wines Corbin
· produced in 1982 and 1983, the 1975 is richly fruity, has full
86 body, moderate tannins, and a very good finish. The wine is just entering its mature plateau, where it should remain for at least 4–6 years. Last tasted, 5/84.

1970—A wonderfully fragrant, round, generous, richly fruity wine, the
· 1970 Corbin is a textbook example of what a well-vinified St.-
86 Emilion is all about. This wine was fully mature when last tasted in 1979, so it should be drunk up. Last tasted, 3/85.

Production: 8,500 cases	Grape varieties: Merlot—65% Cabernet Franc—25% Cabernet Sauvignon—10%
Time spent in barrels: 20–22 months	Average age of vines: 42 years

Evaluation of present classification: Should be downgraded to a Grand Cru Classé; the quality equivalent of a Grand Bourgeois Exceptionnel

La Gaffelière is a perplexing wine to evaluate. The vineyard and château sit on the southerly slopes of St.-Emilion, so this is one of the *côtes* St.-Emilions. The wine was well made in the decade of the '60s, with the 1961 starting the decade well enough and the 1970 beginning the next decade with what has unfortunately been La Gaffelière's best wine in the last 20 years.

Everything looks perfect for making excellent wine at La Gaffelière. Curiously named after a medieval leper colony that inhabited this site, La Gaffelière is an impeccably kept property with spotless stainless steel fermentation tanks, a high percentage of old vines, and a very traditional vinification aimed at obtaining concentrated, tannic wines. Yet, after the production of the superb 1970, the estate went into a slump for reasons that have yet to be ascertained. Certainly the wines of the subsequent vintages in the '70s (except for the 1975) have been rather light and feeble, and have reached full maturity within several years of the vintage. Given the high price charged for a bottle of La Gaffelière, this property probably has the worst quality/rapport ratio of any Premier Grand Cru St.-Emilion. Yet the potential for excellence is here, and the vintages of the '80s, although hardly breathtaking examples of St.-Emilion at its best, are improvements upon the mediocre wines produced in the '70s.

VINTAGES

1983—In early cask tastings, this was certainly not one of the stars of
· the vintage, but it should be a good wine, clearly better than
84 many of the recent below-par efforts from this property. Medium
dark ruby, with a good bouquet of crushed berry fruit, this medium-bodied, elegant, moderately tannic wine will be at its best between 1989–1995. Last tasted, 3/85.

1982—La Gaffelière is a classic case of a highly reputed wine rarely
· living up to its potential. I was about ready to give up on La
? Gaffelière in 1982 after seeing its lackluster performances in
several tastings. However, last year it began to show excellent richness and depth in tastings where it appeared. From the bottle, it seems to be reverting back to its form of its first year in the cask, which was less than impressive. Tasted at the château, it seems considerably more impressive and richer than examples tasted on this side of the Atlantic. Has the transatlantic voyage negatively affected this wine? Judgment reserved. Last tasted, 3/85.

1981—A respectable showing for La Gaffelière, the 1981, while disap-
· pointing for one of St.-Emilion's best, is acceptably fruity,
78 round, plump, and light. It offers charm and attractiveness if
drunk over the next 3 years. Last tasted, 2/84.

1979—Light to medium ruby, with an undistinguished, rather light-
· intensity berrylike bouquet and lightish, shallow flavors, this
74 1979 is very soft, fully mature, and should be drunk soon. Last
tasted, 11/83.

1978—Disappointingly light, bland, dull and insufficiently concen-
· trated, the 1978 La Gaffelière is a pleasant quaffing wine, but
70 lacks concentration and character. It is fully mature and will not
hold for more than 4–5 years. Last tasted, 10/83.

1975—Quite a lightweight for the vintage and now fully mature, this
· medium-ruby-colored wine has a spicy, minty, plummy bouquet,
80 medium body, light tannins, and good balance. It should be
drunk over the next 3–4 years. Last tasted, 5/84.

1971—Very mature and on the edge of cracking up. This wine has an
· attractive perfumed quality with decent fruit, medium body, a
80 silky texture, and supple, pleasant finish. Drink up. Last tasted, 4/82.

1970—A favorite of mine, the 1970 La Gaffelière is this property's best
· wine over the period 1961–1983. A lovely, complex bouquet of
87 grilled nuts, oak, and ripe, plummy fruit is first-rate. On the palate, the wine is lighter than many 1970s, but has layers of soft, velvety fruit and a clean, well-balanced finish. Drink up. Last tasted, 2/83.

1966—A straightforward sort of wine, La Gaffelière's 1966 is lean,
· austere, with some elegance and charm, but is compact and
78 rather one-dimensional. It is fully mature. Drink up. Last tasted, 10/78.

1964—Diffuse, shallow, awkward flavors seem to struggle with each
· other. The medicinal, bizarre bouquet suggests something went
60 afoul during the making of this wine. Last tasted, 4/80.

1961—Another classic case of La Gaffelière not performing up to the
· standards of the vintage, the 1961, while attractively fruity and
83 showing some signs of the vintage's ripeness, power, and concentration, is beginning to dry out and show some faulty vinification characteristics such as volatile acidity. Last tasted, 12/83.

BALESTARD-LA-TONNELLE (Grand Cru Classé) GOOD

Production: 5,500 cases	Grape varieties: Merlot—70% Cabernet Franc—15% Cabernet Sauvignon—10% Malbec—5%
Time spent in barrels: 12–14 months	Average age of vines: 30 years

Evaluation of present classification: The quality equivalent of a Grand Bourgeois Exceptionnel

I have always regarded Balestard-La-Tonnelle as the Lynch-Bages of St.-Emilion. This property, owned by Jacques Capdemourlin, like Lynch-Bages in Pauillac, produces a densely colored, big, deep, rich and chewy style of wine. It sometimes gets a little too big and alcoholic for its own good, but this is an immensely enjoyable style of St.-Emilion that can normally be drunk after 5 or 6 years of bottle age, yet has no problem living for 10 or more years.

Balestard has been especially successful since 1970 and given the realistic price Jacques Capdemourlin charges for his wine, this is one of St.-Emilion's great bargains. It is also a wine that should appeal to poets, since the property takes its name from the 15th-century French poet François Villon, who in one of his poems referred to the "divine nectar of Balestard."

VINTAGES

1983—A huge wine that may be too big for some tasters, the 1983
· Balestard has a black ruby color, a ripe, full-blown bouquet of
86 plums and tarry, truffle scents on the palate. On the palate, the
wine is very powerful, very tannic, extremely dense, and quite alcoholic. This is a mammoth old-style wine that is reminiscent of some of the heavyweight Bordeaux wines from the 1947 vintage. Anticipated maturity: 1990–1995. Last tasted, 3/85.

1982—Always one of the most chewy and fleshy St.-Emilions, the 1982
Balestard-La-Tonnelle is a hulking, beefy, full-tilt St.-Emilion
85 with impressive color, a big, jammy, concentrated feel on the
palate, and a toasty, tarry, plummy bouquet. Power rather than finesse is the rule here. Drink between 1987–1996. Last tasted, 1/85.

1981—I have always liked the uncomplicated fleshy texture and rich
· fruitiness of Balestard. The 1981 is best drunk young, within 6–
84 8 years of the vintage, before its powerful, fruity gusto has lost
its zest. The 1981 is straightforward, generous, full-bodied, with plenty of fruit and interest. Anticipated maturity: 1986–1992. Last tasted, 10/84.

1978—Now mature, the 1978 Balestard is a richly fruity, soft, gener-
· ously flavored, full-bodied wine with plenty of appeal. It should
84 be drunk over the next 5 years. Last tasted, 2/83.

1976—Not as concentrated or as powerful as Balestard normally is, the
· 1976 is a trifle flabby and diffuse. Nevertheless, it is a soft,
78 foursquare, one-dimensional wine with plenty of punch. Drink
up. Last tasted, 9/80.

1975—This is certainly the best Balestard that I have encountered.
· Quite concentrated and powerful, but better balanced and less
87 alcoholic than the big, jammy 1982 and 1983 wines, the 1975 has
a complex bouquet of ripe plums and spicy oak. Full-bodied,

rich, and moderately tannic, this wine can be drunk now or held for another 5 years. Last tasted, 3/84.

1971—Beginning to show a generous amount of browning at the edges,
· this plump, fat, slightly sweet wine has always shown good ripe-
82 ness and a rich, open-knit, plummy fruitiness. It requires drinking up. Last tasted, 5/83.

1970—A very good wine from Balestard, the 1970 is full-bodied, very
· dark ruby, fragrant, chewy, and rich on the palate and has a
84 long, somewhat alcoholic finish. This is a big, rich, succulent,
fully mature St.-Emilion that will continue to drink well for another 3–4 years. Last tasted, 8/82.

FONROQUE (Grand Cru Classé) GOOD

Production: 8,000 cases	Grape varieties: Merlot—70% Cabernet Franc—30%
Time spent in barrels: 16–18 months	Average age of vines: 38 years
Evaluation of present classification: The quality equivalent of a Grand Bourgeois Exceptionnel	

Fonroque is located in an isolated location north and west of St.-Emilion. The vineyard is owned by the highly respected Libourne firm of Jean-Pierre Moueix. While the Moueix name is more commonly identified with such famous estates of St.-Emilion and Pomerol as Pétrus, Trotanoy, and Magdelaine, the wine of Fonroque usually represents an excellent value, as well as being an interesting and distinctive style of wine that is always vinified properly.

In style it tends to be of the robust, rich, tannic, full-bodied school of St.-Emilions. It can take aging quite well, and in good vintages actually needs cellaring of at least 5–6 years.

VINTAGES

1983—A typical Fonroque, broodingly dark with a high tannin content,
· this wine has layers of ripe fruit, is quite full-bodied, and should
85 have quite a future. Anticipated maturity: 1990–1998. Last
tasted, 3/85.

1982—The 1982 Fonroque is made in an open-knit style, with an in-
· tensely fruity, spicy, plummy fruitiness. This full-bodied wine
85 has dark ruby color, a velvety texture, and a soft, generous

finish. It is a big, plump, decadently fruity wine with plenty of ripe tannins. Drink over the next 5 years. Last tasted, 1/85.

1981—A chunky sort of wine, the 1981 Fonroque has an open-knit,
· fruity, oaky, earthy bouquet, a rustic, rich, full-bodied texture,
84 and good length. Drink over the next 5–6 years. Last tasted, 6/84.

1979—A precociously styled Fonroque, easy to drink, soft, not as pow-
· erful or as concentrated as usual, but pleasant and fully mature.
74 Drink up. Last tasted, 4/83.

1978—A trifle clumsy and awkward when young, this full-bodied,
· nicely concentrated wine has developed well in the bottle. A
81 spicy, ripe plummy bouquet, soft, fat, chewy flavors and some light tannin in the finish. Drink over the next 3–4 years. Last tasted, 4/83.

BEAUSÉJOUR (DUFFAU-LAGARROSSE)

(Premier Grand Cru Classé) GOOD

Production: 3,500–4,000 cases	Grape varieties: Merlot—50% Cabernet Franc—25% Cabernet Sauvignon—25%
Time spent in barrels: 18–20 months	Average age of vines: 15 years

Evaluation of present classification: Should be downgraded to a Grand Cru Classé; the quality equivalent of a Grand Bourgeois Exceptionnel

There are two Beauséjour estates in St.-Emilion. Both are located on the *côtes* of St.-Emilion. Both are among the *crème de la crème* of St.-Emilion's hierarchy, that being Premiers Grands Crus. The other Beauséjour, owned by the Bécot family, was demoted in the new 1985 classification to a Grand Cru Classé, but the status of this Beauséjour has remained unchanged. Both estates have produced terribly overrated wines and have been living off their reputations for too long.

This Beauséjour, owned by the Duffau-Lagarrosse family, is the better of the two and has shown hints of turning things around starting with the 1982 vintage. Despite the fact that Beauséjour has produced a series of uninspiring wines, the price for such mediocrities has remained surprisingly high.

VINTAGES

1983—From cask samples, this wine showed good color, a tight yet
· promising bouquet of rich, ripe cranberry fruit and smoky oak,
85 medium to full body, firm, rather significant tannins, and a long
finish. It should be good. Anticipated maturity: 1990–2000. Last
tasted, 3/85.

1982—Normally one of the poorest performers among the first-growth
· St.-Emilions, Beauséjour has turned in a very special perfor-
87 mance in 1982. Dark ruby, with a moderately intense bouquet of
ripe black cherries, oak, and caramel. On the palate, the wine
is medium- to full-bodied, with relatively supple, expansive, rich
flavors, and moderate tannins. Not a powerhouse 1982, but generously full and quite promising. Anticipated maturity: 1990–
2000. Last tasted, 1/85.

1981—Medium ruby with a firm, astringent, and tough personality. I
· admire the wine's tight structure, but only wish that there were
82 a little more fruit and depth. Anticipated maturity: 1990–1996.
Last tasted, 11/84.

1979—Inexcusably light, feeble, frail and lacking the richness and con-
· centration one expects from wines of this class, Beauséjour's
74 1979 has no tannin, so it is best consumed now. Last tasted,
7/83.

1978—A bigger, richer, more substantial wine than the pale 1979, the
· 1978, despite more flesh and weight, is flawed by a very metallic,
61 bizarre bouquet that seems atypical and foreign. If you can get
past the smell, the wine shows good structure and fruit. Last
tasted, 7/83.

1976—A satisfactory effort from Beauséjour, the 1976 has some ripe,
· concentrated fruit, medium body, a little structure, and a
70 charming, fruity bouquet. Not a big wine, but cleanly made and
pleasant. Drink up. Last tasted, 7/83.

1970—Extremely thin, hard, acidic flavors show none of the character
· of the 1970 vintage. Shockingly diluted and hollow; one cannot
60 possibly speculate what could have gone wrong with this wine.
Last tasted, 7/83.

1964—In a year in which many St.-Emilions excelled, Beauséjour pro-
· duced an insipid, dull, weakly colored, fruitless wine which has
62 no charm or appeal. Quite disappointing. Last tasted, 7/83.

FONPLÉGADE (Grand Cru Classé) GOOD

Production: 9,500 cases	Grape varieties: Merlot—66% Cabernet Franc—34%
Time spent in barrels: 18 months	Average age of vines: 25 years

Evaluation of present classification: The quality equivalent of a Grand Bourgeois Exceptionnel

I have always wondered why Fonplégade is so underregarded as a top estate of St.-Emilion. The vineyard is well located in the *côtes* just below the famous estate of Magdelaine. The production is significantly large enough to receive good distribution, and the quality and style of the wines so appealing that it is mystifying why this wine has not caught on more in this country.

Fonplégade is owned by the Armand Moueix family. The style of wine produced at Fonplégade is supple, fat, darkly colored and quite full-bodied, while being intensely fruity as well. It is a cunning wine that shows so well young that most wine enthusiasts tend to think it will not keep. While it may not have the aging potential of wines such as Cheval Blanc, Ausone, Canon, Pavie, and Magdelaine, it will keep for at least 10 years, if well stored.

Fonplégade is a consistently successful wine that is usually very fairly priced.

VINTAGES

1982—Reminiscent of this estate's lovely 1970 and 1975 wines, the 1982 has good dark ruby color, a moderately intense bouquet of roasted chestnuts, and ripe fruit. On the palate, the wine is medium- to full-bodied, shows good, ripe tannin, fine length, and aging potential of 8–12 years. Anticipated maturity: 1989–2000. Last tasted, 1/85.
· 84

1981—The 1981 is not as robust as some of this château's previous efforts, but displays good color, a spicy, almondy, plummy bouquet, and soft, nicely textured flavors. Drink over the next 5 years. Last tasted, 4/84.
· 82

1976—Starting to show the telltale signs of old age (e.g., a brown color), the 1976 Fonplégade is still drinking well with a rich, ripe berryish bouquet, soft, creamy, pleasant, round flavors, and no tannins in the finish. Drink up. Last tasted, 4/84.
· 80

1975—Fully mature, but holding nicely, the 1975 Fonplégade is a fat
· plummy, very fruity wine that has good body, a fleshy texture,
83 and an alcoholic, soft finish. Drink over the next 4–5 years. Last
tasted, 3/83.

1970—This is a typical Fonplégade—fat, very fruity, succulent, and
· immensely satisfying rather than cerebral or complex. While it
84 still continues to offer a mouthful of corpulent St.-Emilion, it is
now beginning to lose its fruit and should be drunk up. Last
tasted, 12/82.

1961—Still alive and well, the 1961 Fonplégade has no discernible tan-
· nins left, but plenty of viscous, ripe, savory, supple fruit, full
86 body, and a long, silky, velvety finish. Drink up. Last tasted,
7/81.

CURÉ-BON-LA-MADELEINE (Grand Cru Classé) GOOD

Production: 1,500 cases	Grape varieties: Merlot—80% Cabernet Franc—10% Malbec—10%
Time spent in barrels: 18–24 months	Average age of vines: 30 years

Evaluation of present classification: The quality equivalent of a Grand Bourgeois Exceptionnel

This tiny estate has a splendid location on the *côtes* of St.-Emilion, sandwiched in between the famous vineyards of Canon, Belair, and Ausone. It is a wine with a very good reputation, but one that is rarely seen in America and only occasionally appears in my tastings. My experience is extremely limited with Curé-Bon-La-Madeleine, but what I have seen of this wine has been generally a powerful, quite intense, alcoholic, rather big St.-Emilion.

VINTAGES

1981—With the exception of Cheval Blanc, there are not that many
· 1981 St.-Emilions that I have found particularly exciting, but
84 Curé-Bon, if not exactly exciting, is a full-bodied, chewy, darkly
colored wine, with a robust personality, moderate tannins, and
a good finish. Not complex, but it is quite attractive. Anticipated
maturity: 1988–1994. Last tasted, 3/83.

1979—Very ripe, soft, fat, and sweet, this wine has an expansive bouquet of ripe Merlot fruit, spicy oak, and broad, rich, viscous, somewhat alcoholic flavors. Dark ruby, and still moderately tannic, this wine should be drunk between 1986 and 1993. Last tasted, 1/85.
· 85

1978—One of the most successful St.-Emilions, the 1978 Curé-Bon is just beginning to shed its tannic cloak and reveal spicy, plummy, ripe Merlot scents and aromas. On the palate, the wine shows good power and concentration, and more firmness than most wines of St.-Emilion in this vintage. Anticipated maturity: 1986–1992. Last tasted, 1/85.
· 86

1976—The 1976 is a very successful effort from Curé-Bon. Dark ruby with just a trace of brown, this well-made wine has a rich, plummy, cedary, leather-scented bouquet, broad, velvety, rich and supple flavors, and light tannins. Fully mature, it has held up much better than many wines of this vintage. Drink up. Last tasted, 1/85.
· 84

LARMANDE (Grand Cru Classé) GOOD

Production: 7,500–9,000 cases	Grape varieties: Merlot–65% Cabernet Franc—30% Cabernet Sauvignon—5%
Time spent in barrels: 16–18 months	Average age of vines: 35 years
Evaluation of present classification: The quality equivalent of a Grand Bourgeois Exceptionnel	

Larmande is one of those vineyards that is on an upward course in quality. The estate is not yet well known, but I predict that once the quality of recent vintages becomes more widely known, Larmande will become a St.-Emilion very much in demand because the price has not kept pace with the quality.

Larmande is located just to the northeast of St.-Emilion, near the two much more famous estates of Cadet-Piola and Soutard. The property is owned by the Mèneret-Capdemourlin family, who since 1975 have invested large sums of money in this estate. A new winery has been built with stainless steel fermentation tanks, the eminent Emile Peynaud has been brought in to look after the vinification, and approximately one-third new oak casks are purchased each year for aging the wine.

This commitment to quality is evident in each new vintage of Larmande. The wine has gone from strength to strength since 1978, and this is a property that Bordeaux wine enthusiasts must take very seriously.

VINTAGES

1983—From cask samples, the 1983 Larmande was even better than the very fine 1982. Quite big, rich, full-bodied, and very tannic, this deeply colored, powerfully built Larmande should prove to be quite a good wine. Anticipated maturity: 1989–1996. Last tasted, 6/84.
· 87

1982—One of the best run and managed Grand Cru St.-Emilions, Larmande has been making very fine wine since 1977. The 1982 has excellent potential and should be cellared for at least 4–5 years. Quite dark ruby, with a plummy, cedary, spicy bouquet, rich, full-bodied flavors, very good concentration, and moderate tannins. Anticipated maturity: 1988–1994. Last tasted, 2/85.
· 86

1981—The lightest and most elegant of the three good vintages of the early '80s, Larmande's 1981 has medium ruby color, a ripe, moderately intense, plummy, slightly herbaceous bouquet, medium body, good concentration, and a fine, crisp, clean finish. Anticipated maturity: 1987–1991. Last tasted, 6/84.
· 83

1980—A success given the trying vintage conditions, Larmande's 1980 is fairly light and supple, but shows a fragrant, light-intensity bouquet of herbs, oak, and cherry fruit, medium body, and soft, pleasant flavors. Drink over the next 2 years. Last tasted, 6/84.
· 75

1978—Now fully mature, yet clearly capable of being held for 2–4 more years, the 1978 Larmande is a very stylish, elegant, fruity wine, with medium body, a fine, cedary, herbaceous, plummy bouquet of moderate intensity, and nicely balanced, medium-bodied flavors. Drink over the next 4 years. Last tasted, 6/84.
· 82

CAP DE MOURLIN (Grand Cru Classé) — GOOD

Production: 6,500–7,000 cases	Grape varieties: Merlot–65% Cabernet Franc—30% Cabernet Sauvignon—5%
Time spent in barrels: 18–24 months	Average age of vines: 25 years

Evaluation of present classification: The quality equivalent of a Grand Bourgeois Exceptionnel

Up until 1983, there were two Grand Cru St.-Emilions with the same Cap de Mourlin label—two separate estates—one owned by Jean Capdemourlin and the other by Jacques Capdemourlin. Their respective estates of 23 and 20 acres have been united since 1983, and the confusion consumers encountered in the past between these two different wines will cease to exist with the 1983 vintage.

The difference between the two wines has been marginal. I have always seen more of the "Jacques" on the market and in tastings have identified that Cap de Mourlin with a chunky, robust, full-bodied style of wine that lacked finesse but offered plenty of power and fleshy fruit. The "Jean" has had a reputation for being less robust, more silky and supple, yet my experience with it is so limited that I have no opinion whether these observations about the "Jean" are correct.

From the 1983 vintage on, every Cap de Mourlin label will bear the name "Jacques Capdemourlin."

VINTAGES

1983—The first vintage produced from the combined estates under the
· management of Jacques Capdemourlin, the 1983 is an uncom-
85 monly powerful, dense, black colored wine that is reminiscent of some of the huge mountain-styled California Cabernet Sauvignons of the mid-'70s. Massive on the palate, with an unbelievable density of viscous fruit, this huge, full-bodied, very tannic wine is a trifle too high in alcohol and too low in acidity to get higher marks, but it is quite a corpulent mouthful of wine. Anticipated maturity: 1989–1995. Last tasted, 1/85.

1982—(Jacques) In this vintage, the "Jacques" is peppery, somewhat
· herbaceous, rich, full-bodied, very concentrated and deep, with
84 a long, deep finish. Perhaps a little too robust and fleshy, it is still quite enjoyable. Drink over the next 8 years. Last tasted, 1/85.

1982—(Jean) The 1982 "Jean" is a better-balanced wine, with a lovely
· bouquet of black cherries and spicy oak. On the palate, the wine
85 is full-bodied, velvety, and quite precocious. Drink over the next 8 years. Last tasted, 1/85.

1981—(Jacques) A deeply colored wine, the 1981 Cap de Mourlin is
· quite chunky, fruity, soft, and robust. It lacks complexity and
82 finesse, but has oodles of power and authority. Drink over the next 5–6 years. Last tasted, 9/84.

LA GRAVE FIGEAC (Unclassified) GOOD

Production: 1,500–2,000 cases	Grape varieties: Merlot—75% Cabernet Franc—25%
Time spent in barrels: 18–20 months	Average age of vines: 40 years

Evaluation of present classification: The quality equivalent of at least a Grand Bourgeois Exceptionnel

This is a tiny gem of a property near Cheval Blanc on the Pomerol border. I have tasted only three vintages of this wine, so I am hesitant to place it higher in the hierarchy of quality in this book. However, based on what I have seen, this is a splendidly rich wine, with an opulence and concentration that is usually associated only with the top properties of St.-Emilion. In style, it reminds me of a rich Pomerol. Given its remarkably low price, this is a wine that merits a thorough search of the market.

VINTAGES

1983—Absolutely sensational from the cask, this big, rich, concentrated, full-bodied wine could easily be confused with one of the better Premiers Grands Crus of St.-Emilion. Decadently fruity, black ruby in color, with oodles of ripe blackberry fruit, moderately ripe tannins, and a super finish, this is quite a stunning wine. Anticipated maturity: 1988–1994. Last tasted, 1/85.
· 89

1982—Sitting opposite Cheval Blanc, this estate has produced a very lush, rich, full-bodied, deeply concentrated St.-Emilion that, while drinking well now, promises to be even better in 5 years. Very dark colored, with a rich blackcurrant bouquet and a velvety texture, this wine was one of the great values of the vintage. As excellent as the 1982 is, the 1983 is superior. Anticipated maturity: 1988–1994. Last tasted, 11/84.
· 87

1981—This is a delicious St.-Emilion, big, concentrated, fleshy, richly fruity, savory, and spicy. Full-bodied, with light to medium tannins, this wine is quite a lovely mouthful for drinking over the next 5–6 years. Last tasted, 11/84.
· 84

CROQUE-MICHOTTE (Grand Cru Classé) GOOD

Production: 6,000 cases	Grape varieties: Merlot—80% Cabernet Franc—20%
Time spent in barrels: 12-14 months	Average age of vines: 25–28 years

Evaluation of present classification: The quality equivalent of a Grand Bourgeois

Croque-Michotte is a wine that is frequently seen in Great Britain, Switzerland, and the Benelux countries rather than America. The open-knit, fleshy, precocious, rather alcoholic style of Croque-Michotte offers considerable appeal.

The vineyard of Croque-Michotte is well situated in the *graves* section of the St.-Emilion appellation, not far from the Pomerol border. The wine produced here is normally fully ready to drink within the first 5 or 6 years of a vintage and it rarely improves beyond its seventh or eighth birthday.

VINTAGES

1983—From the cask, this fat, jammy, viscous, alcoholic wine showed
· considerable concentration and weight, but lacked acidity and
80 finished with an alcoholic hotness. It appears to be a big, rather
clumsy wine. Anticipated maturity: 1986–1990. Last tasted,
1/85.

1982—The 1982 Croque-Michotte is full-bodied, very flavorful and
· fleshy, cleanly made, ripe, savory, and ready to drink. In many
85 ways, a textbook, full-bodied St.-Emilion that should be drunk
over the next 6–7 years. Last tasted, 1/85.

1978—Starting to fade and to lose its freshness and grip, this soft,
· mellow wine has a soft, medium-bodied texture, average con-
75 centration, and a pleasant yet tiring alcoholic finish. Drink up.
Last tasted, 2/84.

PAVIE-DECESSE (Grand Cru Classé) GOOD

Production: 3,000–3,500 cases

Grape varieties:
Merlot–60%
Cabernet Franc—25%
Cabernet Sauvignon—15%

Time spent in barrels: 20–22 months

Average age of vines: 34 years

Evaluation of present classification: The quality equivalent of a Grand Bourgeois

Since 1971, this small estate has been owned by Jean Paul Valette, the proprietor of the Premier Grand Cru Pavie, which sits several hundred feet further down the hill below Pavie-Decesse. This is a *côtes* St.-Emilion, and the quality at this estate has followed that of its bigger, more famous sibling, Pavie. Consequently, after some mediocre wines in the '70s, the vintages from 1979 on have promised much higher quality.

Because Pavie and Pavie-Decesse are adjacent vineyards and have the same winemaker, there is an inclination to believe that the wines are similar. They are not. Pavie-Decesse is a less fleshy, more tannic, and significantly more austere wine than Pavie.

VINTAGES

1983—This looks to be a very good Pavie-Decesse, provided one is willing to invest the time necessary for it to mature. Quite tannic, with plenty of ripe, concentrated fruit, as well as high alcohol, this big, virile, tough, and brawny wine is quite aggressive, yet also very, very promising. Anticipated maturity: 1993–2000. Last tasted, 3/85.
· 86

1982—Pavie-Decesse has turned in its best performance in decades in 1982. Big, rich aromas of ripe fruit and toasty oak jump from the glass. On the palate, the wine is full-bodied, tannic, and quite concentrated. Anticipated maturity: 1990–2005. Last tasted, 1/85.
· 86

1981—A very elegant, medium-weight wine, with a spicy, oaky, soft fruity bouquet and round, supple flavors, the 1981 Pavie-Decesse will drink delightfully for the next 5–6 years. Last tasted, 6/84.
· 81

LA TOUR-FIGEAC (Grand Cru Classé) GOOD

Production: 6,000 cases

Grape varieties:
Merlot—60%
Cabernet Franc—40%

Time spent in barrels: 10–12 months

Average age of vines: 20 years

Evaluation of present classification: The quality equivalent of a Grand Bourgeois

This modestly sized estate adjacent to the two most famous *graves* St.-Emilions, Cheval Blanc and Figeac, was once part of the latter château's estate. In 1879 it split away from Figeac, and since then has produced a wine under its own label. The Franco-German ownership does an excellent job of producing a commercial yet interesting style of wine. It is consistently well colored, fat, supple, intensely fruity, and ready to drink when released. It rarely repays keeping beyond 5–6 years.

VINTAGES

1983—This is an uncomplicated style of St.-Emilion, but few can deny its charm and appeal. Dark ruby, with an open-knit bouquet of black cherry fruit, this medium- to full-bodied wine has soft, velvety, fat, fruity flavors, a long, smooth finish, and a heady alcohol content. Drink over the next 4–5 years. Last tasted, 1/85.
· 84

1982—A deeply colored wine, the 1982 La Tour-Figeac is loaded with jammy, blackcurrant fruit, has a full-bodied, lush, velvety texture, moderate tannins, and good length. It is a very satisfying, well-made, fleshy style of St.-Emilion that will provide great enjoyment over the next 4–6 years. Last tasted, 1/85.
· 85

1981—A shade lighter and less concentrated than either the 1982 or 1983, the 1981 La Tour-Figeac has a ripe berryish, lovely bouquet, supple, soft, quite fruity flavors, medium body, and no tannins. Drink over the next 2–3 years. Last tasted, 1/85.
· 84

1978—Still very darkly colored, this wine appears fully mature, with an open-knit, crushed blackberry bouquet, jammy, rich, yet soft flavors, medium body, and plenty of alcoholic kick in the finish. Drink over the next 1–3 years. Last tasted, 1/85.
· 85

TROPLONG-MONDOT (Grand Cru Classé) GOOD

Production: 12,000–14,000 cases

Grape varieties:
Merlot—65%
Cabernet Franc—15%
Cabernet Sauvignon—10%
Malbec—10%

Time spent in barrels: 20–22 months

Average age of vines: 32 years

Evaluation of present classification: The quality equivalent of a Grand Bourgeois

Troplong-Mondot is a rather large St.-Emilion estate located about one kilometer southeast of the town. The property has a good reputation, and certainly some of the older vintages that I have tasted, the 1962, 1964, and 1970, have justified the interest in this St.-Emilion. However, since 1975 I have generally found the wines to be dull and quite one-dimensional. Much of the large production is exported to Belgium. Since 1975, Troplong-Mondot's style has been fairly light without the depth and character one expects from a St.-Emilion. My feeling is that the wine is quite commercially produced for immediate consumption, as few of the recent vintages appear to have the concentration and stuffing to last more than 5–6 years. This a rather unfortunate trend in view of the quality and character of the older vintages of Troplong-Mondot.

VINTAGES

1982—Refreshingly fruity, forthright, and attractive, this medium-bodied wine is surprisingly light for the vintage, has some tannins, a soft, supple, berryish fruitiness, and finishes slightly sweet. It is a commercial wine for drinking over the next 3–5 years. Last tasted, 1/85.
· 81

1981—Not much different from the 1982, the 1981 is perhaps less fleshy, ripe, and concentrated, but it has a light- to medium-bodied feel on the palate, soft, fruity flavors, and some light tannins in the finish. Drink over the next 3–4 years. Last tasted, 1/85.
· 79

1979—The 1979 is an attractively fruity, soft, ripe, moderately rich wine, with good body and concentration, a supple, round, easy-going texture, and warm, soft finish. Quite ready to drink, this wine will make pleasant drinking over the next 2–3 years. Last tasted, 3/83.
· 82

1978—Ready to drink, this wine is soft, supple, medium-bodied, with a loose-knit structure, moderately intense, jammy fruit, light
75 tannins, and some alcohol showing through in the finish. Drink up. Last tasted, 1/82.

1976—Disturbingly brown in color, the 1976 Troplong-Mondot lacks concentration and fruit, and since it seems to be cracking up at
65 the seams, it is best drunk up as soon as possible. Last tasted, 2/83.

COUVENT-DES-JACOBINS (Grand Cru Classé) GOOD

Production: 3,500–4,000 cases	Grape varieties: Merlot—65% Cabernet Franc—25% Cabernet Sauvignon—9% Malbec—1%
Time spent in barrels: 18–20 months	Average age of vines: 30 years
Evaluation of present classification: The quality equivalent of a Grand Bourgeois	

Couvent-des-Jacobins, named after the 13th-century Dominican monastery built on this site, is an up-and-coming estate that is meticulously run by the Joinaud-Borde family, who have owned the property since 1902.

The vineyards are immediately adjacent to the town of St.-Emilion, on a sandy, clay soil of the *côtes* that produces darkly colored, rich, fairly alcoholic wines of substance and character. I have tasted only three vintages of Couvent-des-Jacobins, but all of those wines showed well and were moderately priced.

VINTAGES

1983—Nearly as concentrated and as deep as the 1982, the 1983 Couvent-des-Jacobins is soft, supple, quite fruity, medium-
85 bodied, well colored, and destined to mature quite rapidly. It tasted very stylish and elegant in 1985. Anticipated maturity: 1987–1991. Last tasted, 3/85.

1982—This is a top-notch effort from this little-known property, which should not be confused with the separate Cordier St.-Emilion
85 château, Clos des Jacobins. The 1982 Couvent has impressive dark ruby color and a complex berry bouquet of cedary, slightly herbaceous, richly fruity scents. On the palate, this big wine is

deep, rich, and full-bodied, with 5–8 years of further evolution. However, it can be drunk now. This is a very interesting, somewhat precociously styled St.-Emilion. Anticipated maturity: 1986–1993. Last tasted, 1/85.

1981—The 1981 represents a muscular effort from Couvent-des-
· Jacobins. I have found this wine a trifle austere and hard, with
78 an above-average bouquet of herbaceous, fruity aromas, and flavors that are tannic and lean. Time will help, but this will not be an especially interesting wine. Anticipated maturity: 1987–1992. Last tasted, 11/84.

HAUT-SARPE (Grand Cru Classé) GOOD

Production: 5,500–6,000 cases	Grape varieties: Merlot—60% Cabernet Franc—30% Cabernet Sauvignon—10%
Time spent in barrels: 20–22 months	Average age of vines: 35 years
Evaluation of present classification: The quality equivalent of a Grand Bourgeois	

Haut-Sarpe is a reliable St.-Emilion owned by the Libourne *négociant* firm of J. Janoueix. The château, which is one of the most beautiful of the region, sits to the northeast of St.-Emilion next to the highly regarded estate of Balestard-La-Tonnelle. The style of wine produced here is darkly colored, rustic, generously flavored, usually firmly tannic. In good vintages, the wine should be cellared for 5–6 years.

VINTAGES

1982—Haut-Sarpe is showing even better from the bottle than from the
· cask. A darkly colored wine, with a tight but promising bouquet
85 of ripe blackberry fruit and some spicy oak, the 1982 Haut-Sarpe is a muscular, moderately big wine, with very good concentration, moderate tannin, and quite good balance. Anticipated maturity: 1990–2000. Last tasted, 1/85.

1981—The bouquet is closed, but this tightly knit wine shows a good
· concentration of ripe fruit, firm tannins, medium to full body,
83 and a long finish. Quite well made, this wine, from the impeccably run estate of Haut-Sarpe, could use 3–5 years of cellaring. Anticipated maturity: 1988–1993. Last tasted, 6/84.

1978—Ready to drink, Haut-Sarpe's 1978 is a straightforwardly fruity,
· well-colored wine that has medium body and an earthy, plummy
82 bouquet. Drink over the next 2–3 years. Last tasted, 6/83.

LA TOUR-DU-PIN-FIGEAC (Grand Cru Classé) GOOD

Production: 4,000–4,500 cases

Grape varieties:
Merlot–66%
Cabernet Franc—34%

Time spent in barrels: 16–22 months

Average age of vines: 33 years

Evaluation of present classification: The quality equivalent of a Grand Bourgeois

There are two estates called La Tour-du-Pin-Figeac. One is owned by the Giraud family and that property makes quite mediocre wine. The other estate, owned by the Armand Moueix family, makes much better wine and it is that estate that is reviewed here. La Tour-du-Pin-Figeac is situated on a sandy, clay, gravelly soil base on the Pomerol border between Cheval Blanc and La Tour-Figeac.

The wine of La Tour-du-Pin-Figeac is made in a straightforward, fleshy, fruity style, with good body, and an aging potential of 6–8 years. Few vintages of this wine will improve beyond their eighth birthday.

VINTAGES

1982—One of the best efforts in years from this property, the 1982 is
· dark ruby, with an attractive, ripe berryish, spicy bouquet. On
85 the palate, the wine is silky, velvety, medium- to full-bodied, with light to moderate tannins, and a good, lush finish. Anticipated maturity: 1986–1993. Last tasted, 1/85.

1981—Soft and fleshy, with a moderately intense, perfumed bouquet,
· the La Tour-du-Pin-Figeac is tasting quite precocious, with
82 good, solid fruit, plenty of body, and moderate tannin. Not complex, but it is very agreeable. Drink over the next 4 years. Last tasted, 6/83.

1979—Approaching maturity, this medium ruby wine has a spicy, ripe
· berryish bouquet, round, moderately concentrated flavors and
82 light tannin in the finish. This wine will present charming drinking over the next 2–4 years. Last tasted, 1/83.

1976—Beginning to fade and lose its fruit, the 1976 La Tour-du-Pin-
· Figeac shows a lot of brown in the color, washed-out, dull fruity
67 flavors, and a short finish. Last tasted, 11/82.

MONBOUSQUET (Unclassified) GOOD

Production: 14,000–15,000 cases	Grape varieties: Merlot—60% Cabernet Franc—40%
Time spent in barrels: 18 months	Average age of vines: 28 years

Evaluation of present classification: The quality equivalent of a Cru Bourgeois

This large estate is the pride and joy of the Querre family, who produce a deliciously fruity, supple, commercial style of St.-Emilion that has immense appeal and is always fairly priced.

The wine tends to be ready to drink when released, and while it rarely improves after 5 or 6 years of bottle age, some vintages (1970, 1975) of Monbousquet have proved they can live for over a decade.

VINTAGES

1982—I have always enjoyed the frank, open-knit fruitiness of Alain
· Querre's wines. They are immediately appealing, soft, savory,
75 and flavorful. This is an average-quality wine, but in the context
of the vintage, a disappointment. Yes, the color is dark, there is
weight and power, but the wine has a one-dimensional, grapey
character, and bland, dull flavors. Last tasted, 11/84.

1981—A lightweight St.-Emilion that has barely enough fruit to cover
· its structure, this medium-ruby-colored wine has a light, fairly
74 innocuous bouquet, easy, light intensity, soft flavors, and a short
finish. Drink over the next 2–3 years. Last tasted, 2/83.

1978—A good effort from Monbousquet, the 1978 has a fragrant, open-
· knit, cherry-fruit bouquet, with a touch of vanillin spice. Round,
80 moderately concentrated, supple, and cleanly made, this is an
enjoyable style of quaffing St.-Emilion to drink over the next
several years. Last tasted, 10/81.

1975—One of my favorite Monbousquets, this wine, which has always
· been one of the most precocious 1975s, is still drinking very
83 nicely. Medium ruby with some amber at the edge, this lush,
velvety wine has ample fruit, and a good, generous, clean finish.
Drink up. Last tasted, 6/83.

TROTTEVIEILLE (Premier Grand Cru Classé) AVERAGE

Production: 5,000 cases	Grape varieties: Merlot—50% Cabernet Franc—25% Cabernet Sauvignon—25%
Time spent in barrels: 18 months	Average age of vines: 32 years

Evaluation of present classification: Should be downgraded to a St.-Emilion Grand Cru Classé; the quality equivalent of a Cru Bourgeois

One of the celebrated Premiers Grands Crus of St.-Emilion, Trottevieille's vineyard is located east of St.-Emilion in a relatively isolated spot on clay and limestone soil. Since 1949, it has been the property of the well-known firm of Bordeaux *négociants*, Borie-Manoux. This firm also owns Batailley, the fifth-growth Pauillac, and Domaine de L'Eglise, a Pomerol of some repute.

Trottevieille is a wine with which I have had many disappointing experiences. For some time now the property has been producing wine that is among the most mediocre of St.-Emilions and is an embarrassment for a Premier Grand Cru. The reasons for this lack of success are not apparent. When tasting the wine, it lacks concentration and character, is often disturbingly light and dull, and in some vintages seems poorly vinified. These problems lead me to conclude that the management of the property is sloppy, and that the château does not make a rigid selection of its best lots for selling under the Trottevieille label. The 1979 and 1982 are the only two recent vintages that merit attention as Trottevieille is a terribly overrated and overpriced wine. Despite this, its status in the new 1985 classification of the wines of St.-Emilion remained unchanged.

VINTAGES

1983—In comparative tastings against the other St.-Emilion Premiers
· Grands Crus, Trottevieille came off as one of the weaker wines
? of the vintage. Decently colored, but a stewed, rather bizarre bouquet and diffuse, awkward flavors showed little promise of anything exciting. Anticipated maturity: 1986–1992. Last tasted, 3/85.

1982—Despite being one of St.-Emilion's most overrated properties,
· Trottevieille's 1982 is what one would expect of this estate.
86 Heretofore, the property has turned out some disappointingly

light, diluted wines. Certainly the best Trottevieille in over 25 years, this dark-colored wine is quite tannic, quite fleshy, and concentrated. Anticipated maturity: 1990–2000. Last tasted, 11/84.

1981—Lacking color, fruit, body, and uncommonly bizarre to smell,
· this is a feeble, lightweight wine that has no substance to it.
70 Disappointing. Last tasted, 4/84.

1979—A strong effort from Trottevieille, the 1979 shows good color, a
· medium- to full-bodied, nicely concentrated feel on the palate,
84 moderate tannin, and good ripeness. This is a rare success for
this estate. Anticipated maturity: 1985–1990. Last tasted, 2/84.

1978—Quite frail, beginning to brown, and seeming on the edge of
· cracking up, this loosely knit, shallow, lean wine has little to
64 offer. Last tasted, 2/84.

1976—A failure, the 1976 Trottevieille was apparently picked when the
· grapes were overripe and waterlogged. No structure, with a wa-
55 tery, jammy quality, and unusually harsh finish, this is a most
unattractive wine. Last tasted, 9/80.

1975—There is certainly not much to get excited about here. Light,
· underendowed, medium-bodied, and tannic, or, as several En-
70 glish wine writers would say, "not enough flesh to cover the
bones." Last tasted, 5/84.

1971—Completely dead, this brown-colored wine has lost its fruit, and
· offers only tart acidity, alcohol, and old, oaky scents and flavors.
55 Last tasted, 2/78.

CANON-LA-GAFFELIÈRE (Grand Cru Classé) AVERAGE

Production: 11,000 cases	Grape varieties: Merlot—65% Cabernet Franc—30% Cabernet Sauvignon—5%
Time spent in barrels: 12–16 months	Average age of vines: 22 years

Evaluation of present classification: The quality equivalent of a Cru Bourgeois

Another of the *côtes* St.-Emilions, although much of this vineyard is on flat land rather than the St.-Emilion hillsides, Canon-La-Gaffelière is a widely promoted château that offers light, bland, mediocre wines for surprisingly high prices. The German owners here admit that they want to produce a supple wine for immediate consumption, yet one would like to see a little more character and generosity in the wine, given its price. Canon-La-Gaffelière rarely improves after 3–4 years in the bottle, and should you by chance be confronted with a wine from this estate older than 7 or 8 years, remember the odds are stacked against its still being fresh, fruity, and attractive.

VINTAGES

1983—Light, supple, fruity, spicy and ready to drink, the 1983 Canon-
· La-Gaffelière shows a medium-bodied, spicy, easygoing charm
82 and light tannins. Drink over the next 5 years. Last tasted, 3/85.

1982—This is the best Canon-La-Gaffelière that I have tasted. Soft,
· ripe, round, generous, fruity flavors, medium body, and light
83 tannins suggest drinking this wine over the next 4 years before
it loses its exuberance. Last tasted, 1/85.

1981—A rather hollow wine, without adequate fruit to balance the oak
· and tannins, the 1981 Canon-La-Gaffelière should be drunk over
72 the next several years before it becomes further unbalanced.
Last tasted, 2/83.

1979—Ready to drink, the 1979 Canon-La-Gaffelière is soft, slightly
· herbaceous, medium-bodied, pleasantly fruity, but undistin-
75 guished. Last tasted, 2/84.

1978—The 1978 is fully mature, and given this wine's inclination to
· behave like a burgundy and die quickly, it is best drunk up.
75 Light ruby with some browning, this round, soft, fruity wine is
quite one-dimensional and light, but cleanly made. Last tasted,
2/84.

1976—Premature senility afflicted this wine in 1979. Even then it was
· brown, stalky, diluted, and astonishingly unpleasant. Now it
50 must be completely shot. Last tasted, 12/79.

1971—When last tasted in 1978, this wine was thin, decrepit, too her-
· baceous and watery, and totally unrepresentative of a St.-
50 Emilion in a vintage that produced a considerable number of
flavorful wines. Last tasted, 1/78.

BEAU SÉJOUR-BÉCOT (Grand Cru Classé) AVERAGE

Production: 9,000 cases	Grape varieties: Merlot—60% Cabernet Franc—20% Cabernet Sauvignon—20%
Time spent in barrels: 12–18 months	Average age of vines: 22 years
Evaluation of present classification: The quality equivalent of a Cru Bourgeois	

There used to be two Beauséjour Premiers Grands Crus in St.-Emilion. The Bécot-owned Beau Séjour (now written in two words to avoid confusion) continues to produce disappointing wine, notwithstanding major capital investments in this property and the use of Bordeaux's famed oenologist, Emile Peynaud, to oversee the vinification. If the wines cannot be accused of being poor, they are dull, simple, one-dimensional wines that taste eviscerated and stripped of concentration, as if they had been overly fined or filtered. Apparently, the committee that did the 1985 classification of St.-Emilion wines also thought something was amiss, because this is the only Premier Grand Cru to be demoted.

Beau Séjour is on the *côtes* of St.-Emilion, and spends large sums of money to promote its wines. However, until the quality improves considerably, this is often a wine to pass by.

VINTAGES

1983—The best example of Beau Séjour from Bécot that I have tasted.
· The 1983 exhibits surprisingly good color, a ripe raspberry, oaky
86 bouquet, lush, concentrated, soft flavors, and medium to full body. Given the usually mediocre performance of this property, the 1983 is an encouraging effort. Anticipated maturity: 1988–1995. Last tasted, 3/85.

1982—In the context of the vintage, this is hardly an inspiring wine,
· but for Beau Séjour it is a minor success, and undoubtedly an
78 improvement over some of the distressingly mediocre wines of the last decade. Straightforwardly fruity, one-dimensional, and medium-bodied, this is an enjoyable, moderately intense wine that should be consumed over the next 4–5 years. Last tasted, 1/85.

1981—Suspiciously light in color, with an innocuous, barely discernible
· bouquet of fruit, the 1981 seems to be overly oaky, as well as
70 hollow and lean. Quite disappointing. Last tasted, 9/84.

1979—For its class and obviously for its price, this skinny little wine
· leaves a lot to be desired. Medium ruby, with a simple, oaky,
72 light-intensity, cherry bouquet, medium body, and tannic, short
flavors which tail off in the mouth, this wine is palatable, but
outclassed by numerous generic St.-Emilions made by the
town's cooperative. Last tasted, 11/82.

1978—A respectable effort from Beau Séjour, the 1978, which is fully
· mature, is fruity, plummy, soft, adequately concentrated, and
78 medium-bodied. There is no bitterness in the finish, and the
wine has decent balance. Drink up. Last tasted, 10/82.

1976—Now totally faded and dried out, the 1976 has a vegetal, barn-
· yard aroma, soft, diluted flavors, medium body, and a very short
62 finish. Last tasted, 10/83.

1975—An acceptable wine was produced by Beau Séjour in 1975. Me-
· dium ruby, with an emerging bouquet of cherries and oak, this
75 wine has tight, hard, tannic flavors, medium body, and a good
finish. Anticipated maturity: 1987–1993. Last tasted, 5/84.

1971—Probably the best wine from this estate in the '70s, this vintage
· resulted in a soundly made wine, with an open-knit, plummy,
80 oaky bouquet, soft, spicy, medium-bodied flavors that show
good ripeness with light tannins present in the finish. Drink over
the next 1–3 years. Last tasted, 12/84.

1970—Tired and too tannic for its meager intensity of fruit, this lean,
· compact Beau Séjour will only deteriorate further. Last tasted,
65 5/84.

LARCIS-DUCASSE (Grand Cru Classé) AVERAGE

Production: 4,500 cases	Grape varieties: Merlot—70% Cabernet Franc—20% Cabernet Sauvignon—10%
Time spent in barrels: Aged in vats 18 months	Average age of vines: 25–30 years

Evaluation of present classification: The quality equivalent of a Cru Bourgeois

Larcis-Ducasse sits on the *côtes* of St.-Emilion, southeast of the town, its vineyard abutting that of Pavie. This wine seems to have a good reputation, but I have been quite unimpressed by most recent vintages, which have consistently displayed a lean, austere, skinny taste and structure. The property refuses to use oak casks, preferring to age the wine in vats until they deem it ready for bottling. Given its rather high price, someone must like Larcis-Ducasse a great deal more than I do.

VINTAGES

1983—Larcis-Ducasse showed very poorly at a comparative tasting of
· St.-Emilions in June 1984, where I ranked it last out of 20 wines.
? Until it is bottled, I will reserve judgment.

1982—I suspect I will never forget the 1945 Larcis-Ducasse, a monu-
· mental wine even in that great vintage. That wine caused me to
80 take an active interest in vintages of Larcis-Ducasse, yet I continue to be underwhelmed by them. The 1982, like most recent vintages, is cleanly made, but not terribly deep. This is a medium-bodied, moderately fruity wine to drink over the next 5 years. Last tasted, 1/85.

1981—I continue to wait for this property to turn things around. The
· 1981 is too angular, and lacks flesh, generosity, and fruit. This
75 is another so-so wine for near-term drinking, from an estate that has a good reputation. Drink over the next 5 years. Last tasted, 6/84.

1979—Medium ruby, with a spicy, fruity aroma of moderate intensity,
· this Larcis-Ducasse has average to above average intensity fla-
78 vors that are plainer scaled than other St.-Emilions. The wine does have some underlying firmness and texture. Anticipated maturity: 1985–1989. Last tasted, 11/83.

1978—Quite mediocre, this pale-colored, lightweight wine has a bou-
· quet suggestive of strawberry and cherry fruit. On the palate,
72 there is not much to find but short, shallow, watery flavors, with some tannin and dry oaky flavors in the finish. Drink up. Last tasted, 9/82.

OTHER NOTABLE ST.-EMILION PROPERTIES

There are hundreds of châteaux in the St.-Emilion appellation, and if I have been arbitrary in my selection, it is because I firmly believe that those that have been reviewed either produce the finest wine, or are widely promoted and recognized in commercial channels. There are, however, a few more châteaux that merit attention. I do not have many tasting notes on these properties, but they are listed here for having given me a pleasant experience in the vintages noted.

LA CLOTTE (Grand Cru Classé)

Evaluation: Should be maintained

This wine is rarely seen outside of France since only 2,000 cases are produced. I have a sentimental spot for this agreeable, soft, fruity, fleshy, lightly styled St.-Emilion since the owners of one of my favorite restaurants in St.-Emilion, the Logis de la Cadène, also own the vineyard. This is a wine to drink within 6–7 years of the vintage. I have fond memories of the 1978, 1975, and 1971.

CORBIN-MICHOTTE (Grand Cru Classé)

Evaluation: Should be maintained

A typical, fat, plummy, deeply colored *graves* St.-Emilion, which is best 5–6 years after the vintage. Approximately 3,000 cases are produced from 65% Merlot, 30% Cabernet Franc, and 5% Cabernet Sauvignon. 1983, 1982, and 1975 stand well above the rest.

LA COMMANDERIE (Unclassified)

Evaluation: Should be upgraded to a Grand Cru Classé

Located near Cheval Blanc, this tiny property produces about 1,500 cases; 84% Merlot, 11% Cabernet Franc, and 5% Cabernet Sauvignon. The vintages of the mid and late '70s were rather heavy wines. 1982 is very good, and the 1983 was fabulous from the cask.

DESTIEUX (Unclassified)

Evaluation: Should be upgraded to a Grand Cru Classé

Located in the satellite commune of St.-Hippolyte, Destieux makes an attractive, plummy, fleshy, open-knit wine, with good concentration and plenty of alcohol; 4,000 cases are from 66% Merlot and 34% Cabernet Franc. The 1981 is good and ready to drink, the 1982 is fat and supple, but deeper, and the 1983 is the best of this typically fleshy, supple trio. They are best drunk within 5–6 years.

FAURIE-DE-SOUCHARD (Grand Cru Classé)

Evaluation: Should be maintained

The Jabiol family, who make the excellent Cadet-Piola, also own this vineyard planted with 65% Merlot, 27% Cabernet Franc, and 8% Cabernet Sauvignon. I have good notes on the 1970 and 1971, but the vintages in the '80s have left me unmoved.

FLEUR-CARDINALE (Unclassified)

Evaluation: Should be maintained

This St.-Emilion produces almost 4,000 cases of wine: 70% Merlot, 15% Cabernet Franc, and 15% Cabernet Sauvignon. Soft, very fruity, yet deep and velvety, the 1982 is especially attractive, and the 1983 looks to be a success as well. A wine to drink in its youth.

FOMBRAUGE (Unclassified)

Evaluation: Should be maintained

With a large production of over 20,000 cases, this wine is widely seen both in Europe and America. Made from a typical St.-Emilion blend of 60% Merlot, 30% Cabernet Franc, and 10% Cabernet Sauvignon, it tends to be light, sound, and fruity, but relatively simple. These are very commercial wines at reasonable prices. Both the 1982 and 1983 exhibited plenty of flavor and interest as well as higher quality and should be drunk over the next 5–6 years.

GRAND-CORBIN-DESPAGNE (Grand Cru Classé)

Evaluation: Should be maintained

Another of the St.-Emilion châteaux with the name Corbin, this large estate of over 200 acres produces 15,000 cases of rather stern, darkly colored, full-bodied wine from a vineyard planted with 60% Merlot, 25% Cabernet Franc, and 15% Cabernet Sauvignon. Little of the production makes its way to this country. I had an impressive 1975, a disappointing 1976, and a 1983 cask sample that looked promising.

HAUT BRISSON (Unclassified)

Evaluation: Should be upgraded to a Grand Cru Classé

Haut Brisson's vineyard is planted on very gravelly soil with 66% Merlot and the remaining 34% a field mixture of Cabernet Franc and Cabernet Sauvignon; production in 1983 was almost 10,000 cases. My experience is limited, but I found both the 1982 and 1983 to be very well made, clean, stylish, ripe, fruity, moderately concentrated, with ample body. Both wines should be drunk over the next 5–6 years.

HAUT PLANTEY (Unclassified)

Evaluation: Should upgraded to a Grand Cru Classé

Haut Plantey in St.-Laurent des Combes, produces an uncomplicated St.-Emilion with plenty of crowd appeal. Both the 1982 and 1983 showed ripe, fat, plummy, chewy textures, and a good concentration of fruit with an aging potential of 5–7 years. The vineyard produces 4,500 cases from 70% Merlot, 28% Cabernet Franc, and 2% Cabernet Sauvignon.

RIPEAU (Grand Cru Classé)

Evaluation: Should be maintained

Ripeau makes close to 5,000 cases in the *graves* section of St.-Emilion with 40% Merlot, 40% Cabernet Franc, and 20% Cabernet Sauvignon. This property has plenty of potential, but has been inconsistent. Since 1978, the quality has been more even as Ripeau has turned in very good efforts in 1978, 1982, and 1983. This is an attractive, open-knit, medium-weight St.-Emilion best drunk within 8 years of the vintage.

TERTRE-DAUGAY (Grand Cru Classé)

Evaluation: Should be maintained

One of St.-Emilion's oldest estates, this property completely lost credibility. In 1978, the owner of La Gaffelière purchased the property and made significant improvements. It will take time to totally rebound, but both the 1982 and 1983 look promising. The production of 5,000 cases is made from a blend of 60% Merlot, 25% Cabernet Franc, and 15% Cabernet Sauvignon.

VILLEMAURINE (Grand Cru Classé)

Evaluation: Should be downgraded

Villemaurine is one of St.-Emilion's most interesting vineyards. The property gets its name from an 8th-century army of invading Moors who supposedly set up camp on this site, which was called Ville Maure, the City of Moors, by the French. In addition, Villemaurine has enormous underground cellars that merit considerable tourist interest. As for the wine, it is considerably less interesting. In good, abundant years, close to 5,000 cases of wine are made from a blend of 70% Merlot and 30% Cabernet Sauvignon. Despite increasing promotional claims by the proprietor, Robert Giraud, also a major *négociant*, that Villemaurine's quality is improving, I have found the wines to lack richness and concentration, to be rather diffuse, hard and lean, and to have little character. I tasted mediocre wines from 1983 and 1982, below average in 1981, 1978, and 1975.

THE WINES OF SAUTERNES AND BARSAC

The Sauternes and Barsac wine-producing regions are located a short 40-minute drive south from downtown Bordeaux. They are the dinosaurs of Bordeaux. Labor intensive and expensive to produce, the sweet wines of Barsac and Sauternes have huge climatic and manpower problems to overcome almost every year. Additionally, for almost three decades, the producers have had to confront a dwindling demand for these luscious, sweet, sometimes decadently rich and exotic wines because of the consumer's growing demand for drier wines. Given the fact that it is rare for a given decade to produce more than three excellent vintages for these wines, the producers in this charming, rural, viticultural region have become increasingly pessimistic that their time has passed. Château owners have changed at a number of properties, more and more vineyards are producing a dry white wine to help ease

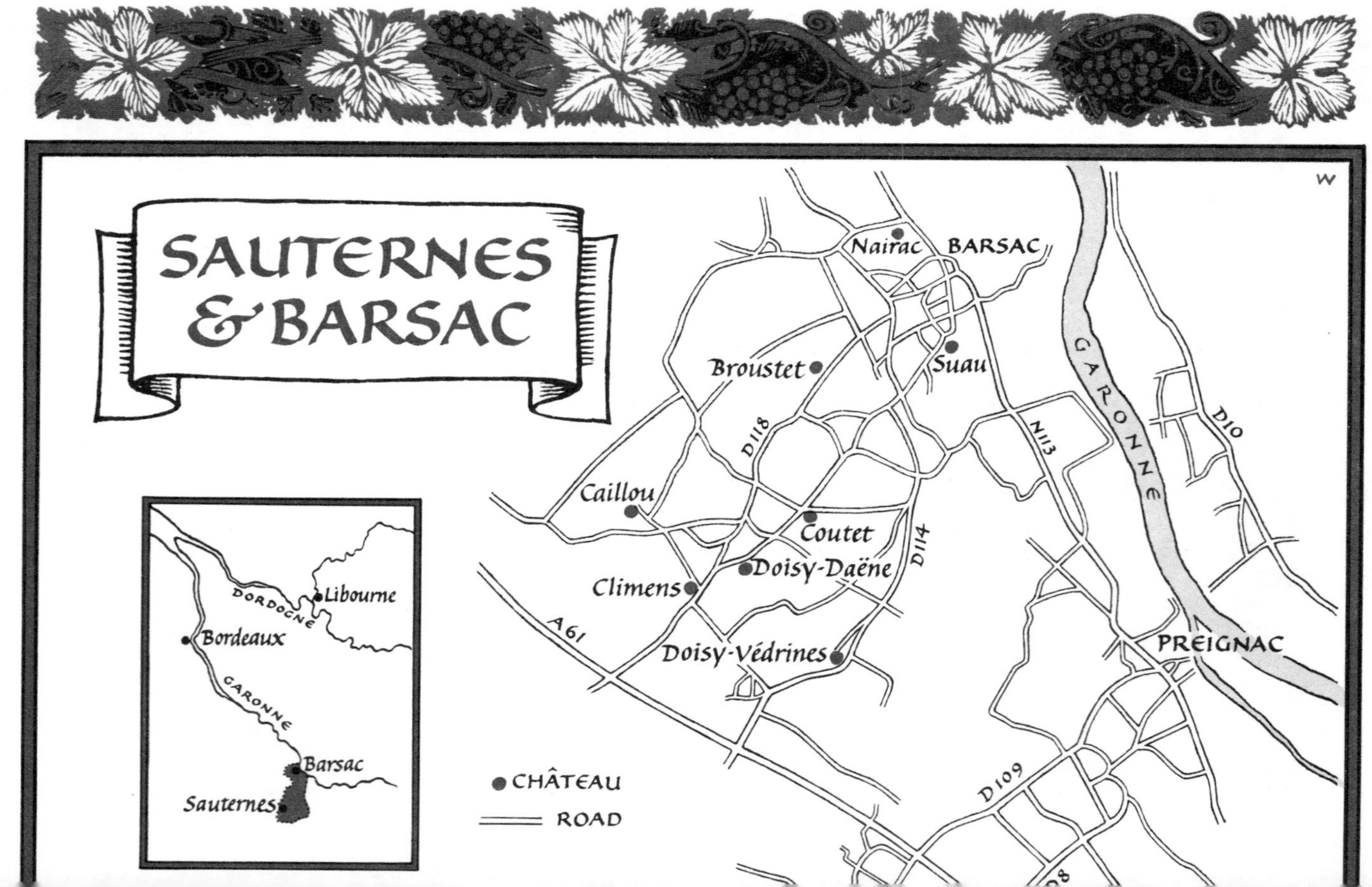
SAUTERNES & BARSAC
W
Nairac
BARSAC
Suau
Broustet
D118
N113
GARONNE
D10
Caillou
Coutet
D114
Climens
Doisy-Daëne
Doisy-Védrines
A61
PREIGNAC
D109
CHÂTEAU
ROAD
Libourne
DORDOGNE
Bordeaux
GARONNE
Barsac
Sauternes

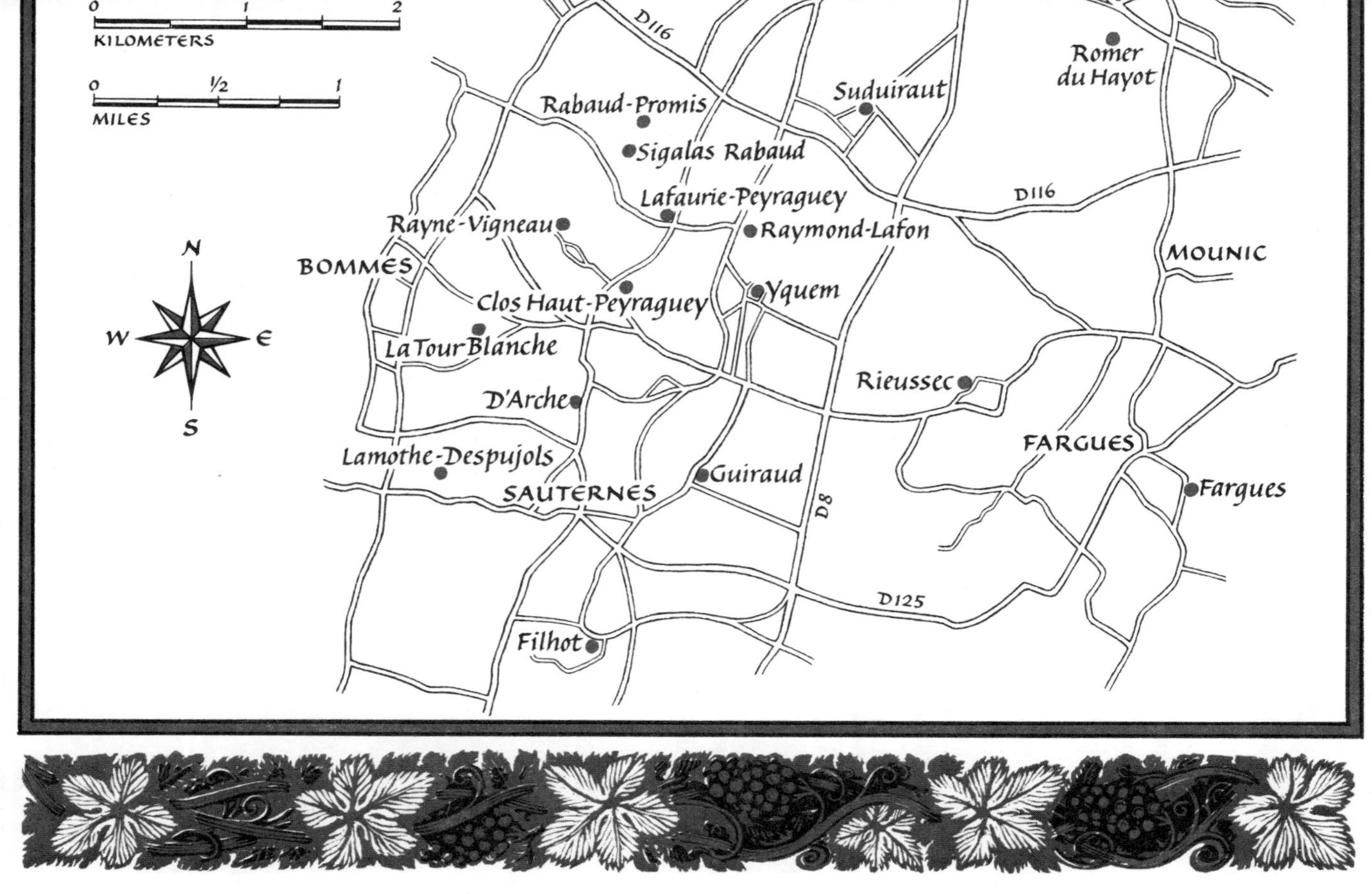
0
1
2
KILOMETERS
0
½
1
MILES
N
W
E
S
D116
Rabaud-Promis
Sigalas Rabaud
Suduiraut
Romer du Hayot
Lafaurie-Peyraguey
Raymond-Lafon
D116
Rayne-Vigneau
BOMMES
MOUNIC
Clos Haut-Peyraguey
Yquem
La Tour Blanche
Rieussec
D'Arche
FARGUES
Lamothe-Despujols
Guiraud
Fargues
SAUTERNES
D8
D125
Filhot

cash flow problems, and at one classified-growth property, Château de Myrat, the owner simply gave up after the 1975 vintage and tore out all his vines, saying it was no longer profitable to produce this type of wine.

Yet surprisingly, most growers continue. They know they make one of the most remarkable wines in the world, and they hope that "Mother Nature," good luck, and an increasing consumer awareness of their products will result in accelerated demand and appreciation of these white wines, which remain France's most undervalued and underappreciated great wines.

No one doubts that the winemakers of Barsac and Sauternes face the most forbidding odds for producing successful wines. The hopes and fears regarding the outcome of a vintage normally begin at the time most of the red wine-producing appellations to the north have commenced or even finished their harvests. It is during the latter half of September that Mother Nature begins to unfold the climatic conditions that will be important for the vintages of this region. The climate in Barsac and Sauternes is normally misty, mild, and humid at this time of year. The humid, misty, damp mornings and sunny, dry afternoons encourage the growth of a mold called *Botrytis cinerea.* This mold attacks each ripe, mature grape individually, devouring the grape skin and causing the grape to die and become dehydrated. Curiously, it causes a superconcentration of the grape's juice, which becomes considerably higher in sugar than normal. This happens without any loss of acidity.

This process is erratic and time-consuming. It can often take as long as one or two months for a significant portion of the white grapes to become infected by the botrytis mold. For this reason, the great wines of this region can only be made by an arduous, time-consuming, labor intensive process of sending teams of pickers into the vineyard to pick the afflicted grapes grape by grape rather than bunch by bunch. The best estates have their pickers descend on the vineyard up to half a dozen times over this period, which usually occurs throughout October and November. The famous Château d'Yquem often sends its pickers through the vineyard *ten* separate times. As expensive and time-consuming as it is, the most hazardous risk of all is the weather. Heavy rains, hailstorms, or frost, all common meteorological developments for Bordeaux in late fall, can transform a promising vintage into a disaster.

Since the conditions for making great wine are so different for Barsac and Sauternes, it is not surprising that what can be a great vintage for the red wines of Bordeaux can be mediocre for the sweet white wines from this area. Nineteen eighty-two and 1961 are two vintages in point.

Both are undeniably great years for the red wines, but for the sweet wines of Barsac and Sauternes, the vintages are average at best. In contrast, 1980, 1967, and 1962 are three vintages for Barsac and Sauternes that most observers would consider very good to superb. With the exception of 1962, these vintages were less successful for most of the red wines of Bordeaux.

Like the red wines of the Médoc, the wines of Barsac and Sauternes were considered important enough to be classified into quality groupings in 1855. The hierarchy (see p. 487) established Yquem as the best of the region, and it was called a "Premier Grand Cru Classé." Following Yquem were "Premiers Crus Classés" (now 11 as a result of several vineyards being partitioned), and 14 "Deuxièmes Crus Classés" (now 12 because one has ceased to exist and two others have merged).

From a consumer's perspective, two unclassified Cru Bourgeois estates, Raymond-Lafon and de Fargues, are making exquisite wines that rival all of the best estates' wines except for Yquem. However, they were not included in the 1855 classification. Additionally, there are a number of first-growths and second-growths that simply cannot afford to make wine the traditional way, utilizing numerous crews of pickers working sporadically over a four- to eight-week period. They do not merit their current status, and have been downgraded in my evaluations of the châteaux of this region.

As for Château d'Yquem, it towers (both literally and figuratively) above the other estates of this region, producing a splendidly rich, distinctive, unique wine. In my opinion, it is Bordeaux's greatest single wine. Whereas the official first-growths of the Médoc have worthy challengers every year who produce wine often as impressive, and whereas the right-bank trio of Cheval Blanc, Ausone, and Pétrus can in some vintages be matched by the brilliance of other estates in their respective appellations, Yquem never has a challenger. This is not because top Barsac and Sauternes properties such as Climens, Rieussec, or Suduiraut don't produce excellent wine, but rather that Yquem produces a wine at such an extravagantly expensive level of quality that it is commercial madness for any other property to even attempt to emulate the wine that Yquem can produce.

A CONSUMER'S CLASSIFICATION OF THE CHÂTEAUX OF SAUTERNES AND BARSAC

OUTSTANDING

Yquem

EXCELLENT

Climens, Rieussec, de Fargues, Suduiraut, Raymond-Lafon, Gilette

VERY GOOD

Coutet, Lafaurie-Peyraguey, Nairac, Sigalas Rabaud

GOOD

Guiraud, Rayne-Vigneau, Broustet, Bastor-Lamontagne, Doisy-Védrines, Doisy-Daëne

OTHER NOTABLE SAUTERNES AND BARSAC PROPERTIES

Caillou, d'Arche, Filhot, Clos Haut-Peyraguey, Lamothe-Despujols, de Malle, Rabaud-Promis, Romer du Hayot, Suau, La Tour Blanche

YQUEM (Premièr Grand Cru Classé) OUTSTANDING

Production: 5,000–6,000 cases
Grape varieties: Semillon—80%, Sauvignon Blanc—20%
Time spent in barrels: 42 months
Average age of vines: 25 years
Evaluation of present classification: Should be maintained

Yquem is located in the heart of the Sauternes region. It sits magnificently atop a small hill overlooking the surrounding vineyards of many of the Premiers Crus Classés.

Since 1785, this estate has been in the hands of just one family. Comte Alexandre de Lur Saluces is the most recent member of this family to have responsibility for managing this vast estate of 427 acres, having taken over from his uncle in 1968.

Yquem's greatness and uniqueness certainly result from a number of factors. First, it has a perfect location that is said to have its own microclimate. Second, Yquem has an elaborate drainage system that was installed by the Lur Saluces family; it includes over 60 miles of pipes. Third, there is a fanatical obsession at Yquem to produce only the finest wines, regardless of financial loss or trouble. It is this last factor that is the biggest reason why Yquem is so superior to its neighbors.

At Yquem, they proudly boast that only one glass of wine per vine is produced. The grapes are picked at perfect maturity, one by one, by a group of 150 pickers who frequently spend 6–8 weeks at Yquem, and go through the vineyard a minimum of four separate times. In 1964 they canvassed the vineyard thirteen separate times, only to have harvested grapes that were deemed unsuitable. Yquem decided to produce no wine in that vintage. Few winemaking estates are willing or financially able to declassify the entire crop. In addition to 1964, no wine was produced at Yquem in 1972 and 1974.

Yquem has unbelievable aging possibilities. Because it is so rich, opulent, and sweet, much of it is drunk before it ever reaches its tenth birthday. However, Yquem almost always needs 15–20 years to show its best, and the great vintages will be fresh and decadently rich for as long as 40–50 years. The greatest Yquem I ever drank was the 1921, served in November 1983. It was remarkably fresh and alive, with a luxuriousness and richness I shall never forget.

This passionate commitment to quality does not stop in the vineyard. The wine is aged for at least three years in new oak casks, at a loss of 20% of the total crop volume due to evaporation. Even when the Comte Lur Saluces deems the wine ready for bottling, a severe selection of only the best casks is made. In excellent years, such as 1975, 1976, and 1980, 20% of the barrels were eliminated. In difficult years, such as 1979, 60% of the wine is declassified, and in the troublesome vintage of 1978, 85% of the wine was declared unworthy of being sold as Yquem. To my knowledge, no other property has such a ruthless selection process. Yquem is also never filtered, for fear of removing some of its richness.

Yquem also produces a dry wine called "Y." It is a distinctive wine, with a bouquet not unlike that of Yquem, but oaky and dry to taste and usually very full-bodied and quite alcoholic. The 1979 and 1981 are two of the most successful vintages for "Y." It, unlike Yquem, is a wine to drink in its youth.

Yquem, unlike other famous Bordeaux wines, is not sold "en primeur," or as a wine future. The wine is usually released four years after the vintage at a very high price, but given the labor involved, the risk, and the brutal selection process, it seems to be one expensive wine that deservedly merits the price.

VINTAGES

1981—The 1981 is certainly an outstanding Yquem, but it will not be
· considered one of this property's greatest efforts. Light golden,
90 with a moderately intense bouquet of spicy, vanillin oak, fresh melons, and tropical fruit, this full-bodied Yquem has average acidity, a plump, viscous, somewhat precocious feel on the palate, and is remarkably long and clean in the finish. It will develop rapidly for an Yquem. Anticipated maturity: 1991–2010. Last tasted, 3/85.

1980—1980 is a perfect example of a vintage that was much better for
· the sweet wines of Barsac and Sauternes than it was for the red
93 wines. Yquem produced its greatest wine since the twin titans of 1975 and 1976. Medium golden, with a big, opulent, honeyed, oaky, flowery, tropical fruit bouquet, this wine is quite rich and concentrated, has very good acidity, a lot of botrytis, and a stunning finish. It is a great success. Anticipated maturity: 1995–2020. Last tasted, 1/85.

1979—This is an immensely attractive Yquem, yet it seems to be miss-
· ing something. It is light golden, with Yquem's typically oaky,
88 spicy, buttery, ripe bouquet, but slightly more reserved than usual. On the palate, this full-bodied wine is intense, well balanced, and long, but falls just a trifle short in the finish. This Yquem is not as powerful or as rich as this wine can be in the top vintages. Anticipated maturity: 1992–2010. Last tasted, 1/85.

1978—1978 was an extremely difficult year for the wine producers in
· Sauternes and Barsac. Unlike the red wine producers who had
87 a late, excellent harvest, the weather was not humid enough for the formation of the noble rot, and while the wines are rich, full-bodied, and viscous, they lack character and often taste dull. Yquem's 1978 is one of the best wines produced in the appellation. It is rich and honeyed, with excellent concentration, plenty of alcohol and body. Unfortunately, it does not have the majestic bouquet and complex flavors and aromas that can only result from rampant botrytis-infected grapes. Anticipated maturity: 1988–2000. Last tasted, 1/85.

1977—In what was a miserable vintage, Yquem managed to produce a
· toasty, ripe, pineapple, buttery-scented wine with a predomi-
85 nant oaky character that is somewhat amazing given the climatic conditions. 70% of the crop was eliminated in 1977, and the result is a wine that may well turn out to be almost as good as

the underrated 1973. Anticipated maturity: 1988–2000. Last tasted, 2/84.

1976—A sensational vintage for Yquem, very rich and concentrated,
· with a superb bouquet of honeyed fruit, spicy oak, melons and
94 pineapples, this full-bodied, viscous, luscious wine seems to have everything going for it. Moderate acidity suggestes that this wine will develop earlier than the 1975. Anticipated maturity: 1988–2015. Last tasted, 12/84.

1975—A textbook vintage for Yquem, the 1975 remains potentially one
· of the greatest Yquems of our time, but it continues to develop
96 at a snail's pace. Medium golden, with a remarkably rich yet elegant bouquet of ripe fruit, vanillin oak, and tropical aromas of coconut and melons, this rich, full-bodied wine has impeccable balance, excellent acidity, and astonishing power and finesse. It has a staggering finish that seems to last and last. A monumental effort. Anticipated maturity: 1990–2030. Last tasted, 12/84.

1973—Surprisingly successful in what was a mediocre vintage for the
· wines of this region, the 1973 Yquem is a trifle overly oaky and
86 too spicy, but has very good concentration, less sweetness and botrytis than in vintages like 1975 and 1976, but is well balanced, fat, and long on the palate. Now fully mature, it should be drunk over the next 5–8 years. Last tasted, 3/84.

1971—This is an outstanding Yquem, but I have been plagued by bad
· bottles in tastings, which I hope is only attributable to poor
92 storage and handling of the wine. The top bottles show plenty of ripe, concentrated, tropical fruit and botrytis. Full-bodied, deep golden in color, with a spicy, caramel, toasted *rôti*, fat flavor, this big, rich wine is developing quite quickly for a Yquem. Drink over the next 15 years. Last tasted, 2/84.

1970—Somewhat less evolved than the 1971, and for me always a shade
· less interesting and complex, the 1970 Yquem is an extremely
90 big, rich, full-bodied, fairly alcoholic Yquem with significant flavor interest as well as crisp acidity. Unlike the 1971, which is close to peak maturity, this wine has a long way to go. Impressive, but not yet showing all of its potential. Anticipated maturity: 1990–2025. Last tasted, 11/84.

1967—Based solely on the strength of what is unquestionably a great
· Yquem, many have concluded that 1967 was a superb vintage
96 for Sauternes. The truth is that 1967 was a very good but irregular vintage. As for Yquem, it is close to perfection. Medium

amber golden with a full-intensity bouquet of vanillin spice, honey, ripe pineapples, and coconut, this intense, very ripe. unctuous Yquem has layers of sweet, opulent fruit, excellent balance, and a hefty, powerful finish. Almost too rich to be served with food, this wine should be drunk alone as a dessert. It can be drunk over the next 20 years. Last tasted, 11/84.

1966—The 1966 is a very good wine, but for Yquem it is quite mediocre.
· Not nearly as rich and intense as one would expect, this wine is
85 still big, a trifle clumsy, and too oaky, but quite enjoyable. Drink
over the next 10 years. Last tasted, 1/82.

1962—This is an excellent, even outstanding Yquem, but I must admit
· to being less impressed by it than others who have ecstatically
90 called it one of the greatest Yquems produced. It is rich and
honeyed, with a spicy, oaky, tropical fruit aroma, rich butterscotch, toasted fruit, and caramel flavors, and an astringent, dry, slightly coarse finish which, for me, keeps it from getting higher marks. Last tasted, 11/82.

1961—1961 was only a mediocre vintage for the Barsacs and Sauternes;
· however, the sales of these wines have long been helped by the
84 greatness of this vintage for the red wines of Bordeaux. I have
consistently found Yquem's 1961 to be a big, out-of-balance wine, with a burnt character to the bouquet, and overly oaky, aggressive flavors that lack this estate's ripeness and great richness. The wine is now beginning to dry out and become more awkward. Drink up. Last tasted, 4/82.

CLIMENS (Premier Cru Classé) EXCELLENT

Production: 6,000 cases	Grape varieties: Semillon—85% Sauvignon Blanc—15%
Time spent in barrels: 24 months	Average age of vines: 38 years
Evaluation of present classification: Should be maintained	

The wine of Climens will never quite challenge the supremacy of Yquem. However, Climens produces a stylish, elegant, racy sort of wine from the Barsac area just north of Sauternes. For sheer class, elegance, and interest, I find it the second-best wine of this region.

Climens is currently owned by Lucien Lurton, the well-known proprietor of a bevy of Bordeaux estates, most notably the second-growth Brane-Cantenac in Margaux. He acquired Climens in 1971, and has continued to make Climens in a very classic manner. Both the fermentation and aging of the wine occur in oak casks and the yield per hectare at Climens is rather conservative. While groups of pickers carry out four separate pickings in the vineyard, the grapes are picked in bunches rather than the laborious one-grape-at-a-time procedure practiced at Yquem.

While Climens is the richest wine of the Barsac region, it never has the strength, viscosity, richness, or power of Yquem, or several of the other Sauternes such as Suduiraut, Rieussec, and de Fargues.

What it does offer is tremendous balance, a racy, crisp acidity, and a lightness that makes it among the easiest wines of this region to match with food. Climens is best drunk between 8 and 15 years after a vintage, but the great vintages of this wine last considerably longer. Climens is often notably successful in the "off" vintages.

VINTAGES

1983—Tasted from a cask sample, the wine was rich and concentrated,
· but seemed awkward and a trifle loosely knit. Nevertheless, the
87 hallmark of this vintage, the stunning ripeness and botrytis, are
plentiful in ample amounts. A very good to excellent Climens, but unless it develops more structure, it will not surpass the lighter and impeccably made and structured 1980, or the wonderful duo of wines from 1975 and 1976. Anticipated maturity: 1987–1998. Last tasted, 6/84.

1982—Only tasted twice, but on each occasion Climens did not show
· the crisp acidity and structure that one has come to expect from
80 this property. Somewhat diffuse, sweet, and flabby, without
enough counterbalancing acidity, this is a wine that will no doubt mature quite quickly. Anticipated maturity: 1985–1990. Last tasted, 6/84.

1980—1980 is a wonderful vintage for Climens, which has produced an
· outstanding Barsac. An exotic bouquet of tropical fruit, pineap-
90 ples, and melons is really top-class. On the palate, the wine is
rich, yet never heavy or cloyingly sweet, with rather crisp, rich, medium-bodied, lush, velvety, ripe fruity flavors. This is a superb effort from Climens. Anticipated maturity: 1986–1996. Last tasted, 2/85.

1979—A success for Climens, this pale golden-colored wine with a
· greenish tint is less concentrated and affected by botrytis than
85 the 1980. Lighter and drier, but still relatively rich, this stylish
and graceful wine has great flexibility for a Barsac in that it can

be matched with a dessert or served to open a meal. Drink over the next 7–8 years. Last tasted, 2/85.

1978—The 1978 Climens is slightly more concentrated than the 1979,
· but like the 1979 it lacks the extra dimension that botrytis gives
86 these wines. Because of the weather conditions, little botrytis formed in this vintage. The 1978 is a plump, well-concentrated wine, with a fat, fruity concentration, moderate sweetness, full body, and a top-class bouquet of grilled nuts, flowers, and candied apples. This is quite an elegant wine. Drink over the next 5–6 years. Last tasted, 2/85.

1977—Climens produced a very respectable wine from this poor vin-
· tage. Light golden with a green tint, the wine lacks richness and
80 depth, but offers surprisingly crisp, fresh, tropical fruit flavors, good elegance, and a style not unlike a good dry Graves. Drink up. Last tasted, 3/84.

1976—Quite fat and advanced in evolution for Climens, the 1976 is
· drinking gorgeously now. Charmingly fruity, with an expansive
87 bouquet of ripe fruit, fresh honey, a vanillin oakiness, and some subtle herbal notes, this medium-bodied wine has average acidity, and a plump, soft texture. Drink over the next 4–7 years. Last tasted, 2/83.

1975—Still remarkably youthful and closed, the 1975 Climens has a
· light golden color and a tight bouquet of coconut, flowers, and
89 ripe fruit. On the palate, it is impeccably balanced, displaying crisp acidity, excellent richness, and an alcoholic, rich, very, very long finish. Rather full-bodied and powerful for Climens, this wine will age for 20–30 years. Anticipated maturity: 1988–2010. Last tasted, 2/85.

1973—One of the top successes in a vintage that produced such light-
· weight wines, the 1973 Climens should be drunk now before its
84 freshness and crisp, lively, fruity intensity disappears. Rather dry for a Barsac, and medium-bodied, this wine has good acidity and enough flavor to merit interest. Last tasted, 3/84.

1972—I was shocked at how good this wine was when I first tasted it at
· Climens in March 1984. 1972 was a dreadful year, but Climens
80 managed to produce a wine with good ripeness, some hints of botrytis, a fleshy texture, and sound balance. Drink up. Last tasted 4/84.

1971—I have had some of the fabled old vintages of Climens like the
· 1947, but the 1971 remains my all-time favorite. It is a classic
93 Climens, powerful yet restrained, rich and opulent, yet also del-

icate. This wine has superb balance, a long, lively, crisp finish, and moderate sweetness kept light and delightful by excellent acidity; it is one of the finest Barsacs I have ever tasted. Drink over the next 6–10 years. Last tasted, 4/84.

1970—The 1970 is an adequate wine, but I have always felt the wine
· was a bit dull, and a little clumsy and heavy. Its pale gold color
70 is nice enough, but this rather light-styled Climens lacks grip, and as the English say, "attack." It seems to be an uninspired winemaking effort. Drink up. Last tasted, 5/82.

1967—Perhaps I am not lucky and have never seen a top-flight bottle
· of the 1967, but I have generally found this wine to be powerful
83 and richly concentrated, but not the best-balanced example of Climens. Nevertheless, it is full and mouth-filling, and if the finish is a little coarse and unpolished, the wine is still quite satisfying. Drink up. Last tasted, 12/79.

1962—Beginning to deepen in color and take on an amber golden color,
· the 1962 Climens must certainly be the best Climens of the '60s.
89 A fragrant, roasted bouquet of melted caramel and brown sugar sautéed in butter is captivating. On the palate, the wine has rich, luscious, unctuous flavors that have remained crisp and lively because of good acidity. It is a worthy challenger to the Yquem in 1962. Drink up. Last tasted, 1/85.

RIEUSSEC (Premier Cru Classé) EXCELLENT

Production: 6,500 cases	Grape varieties: Semillon—75% Sauvignon Blanc—24% Muscadelle—1%
Time spent in barrels: 12–30 months	Average age of vines: 23 years
Evaluation of present classification: Should be maintained	

Rieussec sits on a hill just about one kilometer east of Yquem. It is one of the great wines of the Sauternes region, and since 1975 has been particularly consistent as well as excellent. The architect of Rieussec's consistency has been Albert Vuillier, who has also made Rieussec his home. However, in 1984 Vuillier sold Rieussec to the same Rothschild family who owns the famous Lafite-Rothschild in Pauillac. It is assumed that high-quality wines will continue to be produced here.

Rieussec's style is one of power and almost roasted richness. The wine is usually quite deeply colored, and generally alcoholic, with excellent viscosity. Rieussec, like several other estates in Barsac and Sauternes, produces a tiny amount of decadently rich, intensely concentrated wine under a "*Crème de Tête*" label. Should you ever come across this rare, unctuous nectar, don't hesitate to give it a try. Rieussec also produces a dry wine called "R." Such wines help cash flow problems considerably, and "R" is one of the most popular and best of the dry Sauternes. The 1982 is quite a successful "R," and the 1983 even better.

VINTAGES

1983—Light golden with just the slightest tint of green, the 1983 Rieus-
· sec, from an excellent year for Sauternes, is certainly one of this
94 property's greatest wines. Quite well structured with excellent acidity, and a deep, long, rich, full-bodied, viscous texture, this wine, despite its richness and power, is neither heavy nor cloying. It has gorgeous balance and a very long, lingering, spectacular finish. One of the great successes of the vintage. Anticipated maturity: 1990–2005. Last tasted, 1/85.

1982—A maligned vintage for the sweet white wines of Bordeaux,
· Rieussec has, through a very strict selection process, turned out
82 a lovely, fruity, spicy, lighter-styled wine with medium body and delicate tropical fruit flavors. Drink over the next 5–6 years. Last tasted, 3/84.

1981—One of the top 1981s, Rieussec must certainly be among the best
· Sauternes of this vintage. A very fragrant, spicy, richly fruity
86 bouquet intermingled with scents of apricots and melting butter is top-class. On the palate the wine is quite well balanced, fairly big and rich, and already showing well. Drink over the next 6–8 years. Last tasted, 3/84.

1980—Somewhat dull and a trifle heavy, Rieussec's 1980 is a good,
· relatively rich, spicy, full-bodied wine that shows rather high
80 acidity, some botrytis, and adequate flavor intensity. However, it is not one of the leaders in this vintage. Drink over the next 5 years. Last tasted, 3/84.

1979—This vintage does not have the intensity and richness of vintages
· such as 1981 or 1983, but does offer an elegant, well-made, less
84 powerful wine that is light enough to be served as an *apéritif*. Drink over the next 5 years. Last tasted, 3/84.

1978—The 1978 Rieussec just missed the mark. While quite good, it is
· not special. Slightly too alcoholic, a trifle too heavy and over-
82 blown, this wine has a nice honeyed character and rich, unc-

tuous flavors, but shows little botrytis. Drink up. Last tasted, 6/84.

1976—1976 is one of the most controversial vintages of Rieussec. Very
· dark amber gold in color, some observers have said it has oxi-
90 dized and is falling apart. Despite the dark color, the remarkable taste seems to suggest that this wine has a way to go. I think it is simply a very big, old-style Sauternes. Incredibly rich and full-bodied, with a honeyed luscious texture and extremely intense flavors, this exotic, hugely proportioned wine (15% alcohol) can be served *only* as a dessert. The yield at Rieussec in 1976 was 2.5 hectoliters per hectare, which is approximately one-half a glass of wine per vine. This is a bold, rather overblown style of Sauternes, but I love it. Drink over the next 10 years. Last tasted, 3/84.

1975—Remarkably youthful looking, and seemingly unevolved since it
· was first released, this is a powerful, quite concentrated and
90 rich Sauternes, with decades of life ahead of it. Lemony, tropical fruity, and vanillin oaky aromas titillate the olfactory glands. Tight, yet rich, full-bodied flavors show marvelous balance and richness. Anticipated maturity: 1990–2015. Last tasted, 3/84.

1971—Now fully mature, the 1971 Rieussec has a light-intensity,
· honeyed, ripe apricot, oaky nose, a ripe, sweet, full-bodied feel
85 on the palate, and a crisp, spicy finish. Drink over the next 5–6 years. Last tasted, 10/80.

1970—A little heavier to taste, and a bit less elegant than the 1971, the
· 1970 is a corpulent, rich, sweet mouthful of viscous, chewy Sau-
82 ternes. The moderately amber gold color is a sign of approaching maturity, but this wine has the acidity and overall balance to drink nicely for at least another decade. Last tasted, 6/83.

1967—Rieussec made a very fine 1967. Not having tasted it for some
· time, I suspect this wine has been fully mature since the mid-
84 1970s. It is rather lighter in style and body than some of the more recent vintages of Rieussec, but richly fruity and spicy, with a roasted or grilled nut aroma. Last tasted, 9/79.

DE FARGUES (Unclassified) EXCELLENT

Production: 850–1,000 cases	Grape varieties: Semillon—80% Sauvignon Blanc—20%
Time spent in barrels: 36 months	Average age of vines: 20 years

Evaluation of present classification: Should be upgraded to a Premier Cru Classé

In 1472, 300 years before the Lur Saluces family acquired the famous Château d'Yquem in 1785, they owned Château de Fargues. While de Fargues has never been classified, the quality of the wine produced here is brilliant. Still owned by the Lur Saluces family, it receives virtually the identical winemaking care that Yquem does. In recent vintages, de Fargues has often been the second-best wine produced in the Sauternes region, and when it is tasted blind, most tasters, including most experts, think it is an Yquem.

Interestingly, the vineyard of de Fargues is located well to the east of Yquem's, and the harvest here occurs an average of 10 days later than at Yquem. Additionally, the yield is less than at Yquem, causing some to say that if Yquem's tiny yield per vine equals only one glass of wine, the yield of a vine at de Fargues is equal to only two-thirds of a glass.

De Fargues's resemblance to Yquem is uncanny and given the price charged for de Fargues, approximately half that paid for a bottle of Yquem, it is quite a bargain. Unfortunately, the production of de Fargues is tiny, thereby reducing the opportunity for many wine enthusiasts to taste this wine, which while jokingly called Yquem, Jr., is very close in quality to Yquem, Sr.

VINTAGES

1981—Quite rich and concentrated, with a ripe, oaky, toasted bouquet,
· this full-bodied, viscous, quite sweet and alcoholic wine has
88 more than a casual resemblance to Yquem. Medium golden in color, and very precocious for the vintage, this wine will probably develop quite quickly, given its low acidity. Anticipated maturity: 1987–1994. Last tasted, 1/85.

1980—A great vintage for de Fargues, the 1980 from this estate is very
· powerful, opulent, and exotic. A bouquet of coconuts, apricots,
91 grilled almonds, and spicy oak is quite sensational. In the mouth, the wine is decadently rich, full-bodied, and remarkably

similar in taste, texture, and viscosity to Yquem. The 1980 is an outstanding success for de Fargues. Anticipated maturity: 1989–2000. Last tasted, 1/85.

1979—Less powerful and rich than normal, the 1979 de Fargues is light
· golden, with a toasty, lemony, fruity, oaky bouquet, medium to
85 full body, some botrytis, good acidity, and a clean, spicy, rich, alcoholic finish. Drink over the next 10 years. Last tasted, 3/84.

1976—A full-blown *crème brûlée* aroma, intermingled with scents of
· caramel and apricots, is quite powerful. Very full-bodied, with
90 viscous, sweet, ripe flavors of tropical fruit, this big, robust, yet surprisingly mature wine is quite delicious now, but will hold and hopefully improve for at least a decade. Last tasted, 9/84.

1975—Along with the 1980, the 1975 is one of the finest de Fargues
· ever produced. It has the Yquem-like bouquet of coconuts,
91 grilled nuts, ripe exotic fruit, and spicy oak. On the palate, the 1975 is much tighter-structured and less evolved than the 1976. It has a lighter golden color and more acidity, but every bit as much concentration and richness. Anticipated maturity: 1987–2005. Last tasted, 3/84.

1971—Incredibly rich, unctuous, fat, spicy, and chewy, this huge wine
· offers oodles of coconut, apricot and almond flavors, viscous
90 fruitiness, huge body, and a head-spinning alcohol content. Fully mature, this is a big, old-style, intense Sauternes. Drink up. Last tasted, 12/80.

SUDUIRAUT (Premier Cru Classé) — EXCELLENT

Production: 8,500 cases	Grape varieties: Semillon—80% Sauvignon Blanc—20%
Time spent in barrels: 24 months	Average age of vines: 28 years
Evaluation of present classification: Should be maintained	

Just down the road from Yquem, abutting Yquem's vineyards on the north, is the large, beautiful estate of Suduiraut. Suduiraut can be one of the great wines of Sauternes. For example, the 1959 and 1967 are really staggering examples of Suduiraut's potential. Both are very rich, luscious wines that in blind tastings can often be confused with Yquem. However, I have always been perplexed by the shocking inconsistency in quality of the wines from this estate. In the first half of the decade of the '70s, Suduiraut produced several wines well below acceptable standards. Apparently some of the criticism caught up with the Paris-based owners, the Fonquernie family, who put their best foot forward with the fantastic 1976 and hired a new *maître de chai*, Pierre Pascaud, in 1978. Now, all things at Suduiraut seem to be in good order as the wines have been consistently successful.

When Suduiraut is good, it is very, very good. In its great vintages, the wine needs a decade to be at its best, but will keep easily for 25 years. Richly colored, quite perfumed, and decadently rich, Suduiraut, while less consistent than properties like Climens and Rieussec, appears to be back in top form in the mid-'80s.

VINTAGES

1983—This looks to be an excellent Suduiraut. Tasted from the cask,
· it had medium golden color, and a very honeyed, rich floral
87 bouquet. Full-bodied on the palate, but not overly done, or too alcoholic and sweet as some of these wines have a tendency to become, this is a rather elegant, graceful Suduiraut with plenty of character. Anticipated maturity: 1990–2005. Last tasted, 1/85.

1982—The 1982 vintage, while great for Bordeaux's red wines, was
· hardly very special for the sweet wines. However, the 1982 Su-
90 duiraut is a smashing success. Pierre Pascaud thinks it is the best since the great 1967 or 1959. Only the grapes harvested before the rains fell were used, and the result is a very concentrated, deep, luscious, honeyed wine, with outstanding concentration, great length, the buttery, viscous richness that Suduiraut is famous for, and superb balance. If it had just a trifle more botrytis character, it would be perfect. Anticipated maturity: 1990–2010. Last tasted, 1/85.

1981—A very attractive, elegant Suduiraut that does not have the rich-
· ness of the 1982 or 1983, but is agreeably forward, spicy and
84 ripe, with less power and concentration than normal, but clearly well made and moderately sweet. Drink over the next 5–6 years, as it will not be long-lived. Last tasted, 3/84.

1979—One of the top 1979s, Suduiraut has produced an uncommonly
· rich, deep, powerful wine for this vintage. The wine is medium
86 golden, with a ripe, toasty, caramel-and-apricot-scented bouquet, full body, plenty of viscous fruit, and a long finish. Last tasted, 3/84.

1978—A down-scaled version of the 1979, the 1978 is elegant, less
· sweet, and significantly less rich, with medium body, and an
83 elegant, fairly light texture for a Suduiraut, and good acidity.
Drink over the next 5–6 years. Last tasted, 3/84.

1976—For me, the greatest Suduiraut of the '70s, and really the only
· wine I have seen from this estate that resembles the magnificent
92 1959 that this property produced. Medium to dark amber gold,
this full-bodied, full-tilt wine has a very intense bouquet of vanillin oak, ripe pineapples, and melting caramel. Quite full-bodied, very deep, viscous and concentrated, this is a decadently opulent Suduiraut with enormous presence in the mouth. Anticipated maturity: 1986–2005. Last tasted, 12/84.

1975—Produced when Suduiraut was in a slump, this wine, from an
· excellent vintage, has good ripeness, but is shockingly light and
78 a little too simple and one-dimensional for a top-rated estate.
The finish also leaves a lot to be desired. Drink up. Last tasted, 6/82.

1971—Pleasant, but light and rather meagerly endowed, the 1971 Su-
· duiraut, while agreeable and quite palatable, is a disappoint-
75 ment for a wine from this estate. I have not tasted it recently,
but this wine is probably in decline. Last tasted, 2/78.

1970—A good Suduiraut, but despite its concentration and depth, it
· tastes flabby, overly alcoholic, and just too one-dimensional.
80 Drink up. Last tasted, 8/81.

1969—Surprisingly rich, fruity, and mouth-filling, the 1969 Suduiraut
· is one of a number of 1969 Sauternes that turned out consider-
78 ably better than their red wine siblings. Drink up. Last tasted,
6/77.

1967—A classic vintage for Suduiraut, this rich, full-bodied, expansive,
· viscous, fully mature wine has a wonderful honeyed, almond,
89 caramel-scented bouquet, rich, sweet, deep, succulent flavors,
full body, and a muscular, aggressive finish. The 1967 is perhaps not a match for the 1959 or 1976, but it is certainly the best wine produced at this château in between these two vintages. Drink over the next 5–8 years. Last tasted, 11/82.

RAYMOND-LAFON (Unclassified) EXCELLENT

Production: 400–1,000 cases	Grape varieties: Semillon—80% Sauvignon Blanc—20%
Time spent in barrels: 36–40 months	Average age of vines: 15 years
Evaluation of present classification: Should be upgraded to a Premier Cru Classé	

Raymond-Lafon is a name to watch in the Sauternes district, particularly if one is looking for a wine that is close to the brilliance and majestic richness of Yquem for less than half the price of a bottle of Yquem.

This small estate abuts Yquem's vineyard and has had an excellent reputation. The 1921 Raymond-Lafon was considered even better than Yquem's wine in that great vintage. I have never tasted the 1921 Raymond-Lafon, but the single greatest Sauternes I have ever drunk was the Yquem of that vintage. However, the estate of Raymond-Lafon fell into neglect, and it was not until 1972 that Pierre Meslier, the manager of Yquem, purchased this vineyard and began to slowly rebuild this wine's once fabulous reputation.

With a tiny yield per hectare that is even less than Yquem's, and with the same grape blend and winemaking techniques and the same ruthless selection procedure, Raymond-Lafon has already produced a succession of splendid Sauternes beginning with a great 1975 and just recently concluding with a monumental 1983.

Raymond-Lafon looks to be well on the road to becoming one of the great classic wines of Sauternes. The wine is hard to find because of the tiny production, but well worth a special search of the marketplace.

VINTAGES

1983—From cask samples, this wine was magnificent. Light golden,
· with a wonderfully pure tropical fruit aroma of ripe pineapples
93 and melons, this decadently rich, full-bodied, viscous wine has layers of viscous, sweet fruit, an astonishing finish, and excellent balancing acidity. Anticipated maturity: 1990–2015. Last tasted, 1/85.

1982—In this rain-plagued harvest, Raymond-Lafon bottled only 33%
· of its production, and all of that from grapes picked prior to the
86 rain. The wine is fat, very fruity, sweet and rich, with good

botrytis, a full-bodied, rich, velvety texture, and low to moderate acidity. This vintage of Raymond-Lafon should develop fairly quickly. Anticipated maturity: 1987–1997. Last tasted, 1/85.

1981—Because of low acidity, I predict a rapid evolution for the 1981
· Raymond-Lafon. A glorious bouquet of spicy, vanillin oak,
87 lemony, honeyed, pineapple fruit, and floral scents is intense and expansive. On the palate, the wine is quite fat, succulent, rich and sweet, with high alcohol, and a soft, supple, long, clean finish. Drink over the next 10 years. Last tasted, 1/85.

1980—1980 was a great vintage for Raymond-Lafon, as it also was for
· Yquem and de Fargues, two other properties that proprietor
90 Pierre Meslier looks after. A full-intensity bouquet of ripe tropical fruit and spicy oak is followed by an unctuous, powerful, very rich, full-bodied wine, with layers of fruit, refreshingly high, crisp acidity, and a decade of evolution ahead of it. Anticipated maturity: 1988–2005. Last tasted, 6/84.

1978—Nineteen seventy-eight was a good, but hardly special vintage
· for the wines of Sauternes. However, the 1978 Raymond-Lafon
89 gets my nod as the best sweet wine of this vintage. It lacks the high-level botrytis found in vintages such as 1975 and 1980, but shows beautifully textured, viscous, velvety flavors, full body, a refreshing lemony acidity, and a clean, crisp finish. This is not the biggest Raymond-Lafon, but it is certainly one of the most graceful. Anticipated maturity: 1987–2000. Last tasted, 1/85.

1975—Like many Sauternes from this vintage, Raymond-Lafon has
· been slow to develop. Light golden with a green tint, this lus-
90 cious, rich, creamy wine has a tight but expansive bouquet of very ripe fruit. Full-bodied, rich and sweet, yet tightly knit because of good acidity, this big, rich wine has enormous potential. Anticipated maturity: 1990–2005. Last tasted, 10/83.

GILETTE (Unclassified) EXCELLENT

Production: 3,000 cases	Grape varieties: Semillon—85% Muscadelle—15%
Time spent in barrels: None; aged in tanks for a minimum of 20 years	Average age of vines: 25–30 years

Evaluation of present classification: Should be upgraded to a Premier Cru Classé

Gilette is one of the most unusually run properties in the Sauternes region. Not that the wine is odd, because it is one of the finest made in Sauternes despite the fact that Gilette was not classified. However, what is bizarre and unbelievable in today's harsh world of commercial realities is that Gilette's proprietor, Christian Médeville, holds his sweet wines for over 20 years in vats prior to bottling them. For example, he just bottled the 1955 in 1984, 29 years after the vintage. The fact that his wines are excellent and have a honeyed maturity has caused some of France's leading restaurateurs, like Pierre Troisgros, to beat a path to his door to purchase his old vintages of Sauternes.

Gilette's best wines are called "*Crème de Tête,*" and are extremely well-balanced, remarkably well-preserved wines, with plenty of viscous, fruity flavors, and deep amber golden colors. The following are the three vintages of Gilette that have been released for sale by M. Médeville over the last several years.

VINTAGES

1955—*Crème de Tête*—Fully mature, but still astonishingly fresh and
· alive, the 1955 Gilette is deep golden in color, with a rich,
87 honeyed bouquet, full body, and a ripe, long finish. It can probably last another 10–15 years. Last tasted, 6/84.

1953—*Crème de Tête*—Slightly less rich and fat than the 1955, the 1953
· is spicy and oaky, with a bouquet suggesting melted caramel
86 and ripe pineapples. Full-bodied, still fresh and lively, this unctuous, rich wine is quite impressive. Drink over the next 10 years. Last tasted, 6/84.

1950—*Crème de Tête*—Quite fat and sweet, with excellent ripeness,
· full body, and a long, deep, velvety finish, this wine is a revela-
89 tion given its age. A big, heavyweight Sauternes that will last for 15–20 more years. Last tasted, 1/85.

COUTET (Premier Cru Classé) — VERY GOOD

Production: 8,000 cases	Grape varieties: Semillon—80% Sauvignon Blanc—15% Muscadelle—5%
Time spent in barrels: 30 months	Average age of vines: 25 years

Evaluation of present classification: Should be maintained

Coutet has always been one of the leading as well as one of the largest estates of Barsac. Famous for an elegant, less sweet, less powerful wine, Coutet is usually well made, stylish, and probably a more flexible wine with a variety of food dishes than many of the intense, superconcentrated wines that this region produces in abundance.

Coutet does produce a tiny amount of incredibly rich, unctuous wine that is rarely seen commercially, but is worth mentioning because it may be this region's finest wine, including that of Yquem. In certain vintages, Coutet produces a special cuvée called "*Cuvée Madame*" made from the oldest vines and most botrytized grapes; it is one of the most remarkably rich and unctuous wines produced anywhere. Between 1943 and 1981 it appeared only in 1943, 1949, 1950, 1959, 1971, 1975, and 1981. Approximately 1,000 bottles (three barrels) of this wine are made, but should you ever see it, don't hesitate to try it because the *Cuvée Madame* of Coutet is pure nectar. The 1971 and 1981 vintages of *Cuvée Madame*, along with the 1921 Yquem, represent the three greatest sweet wines from this region that I have ever tasted. As for Coutet, the recent vintages of 1978–1982 have seemed particularly light and a little disappointing for this property.

Coutet also produces a dry wine that is very fresh, attractively priced, and best drunk when quite young.

VINTAGES

1983—Coutet's 1983 showed extremely well from the cask. Not the
· biggest, most concentrated, or most luscious Coutet, this wine
87 gets high marks because of its undeniable elegance, breed, class, and fresh, lively feel on the palate. The flavors show excellent ripeness, and the wine's refreshing crispness makes this an exceptionally enjoyable, non-filling Barsac. Anticipated maturity: 1987–2000. Last tasted, 1/85.

1981—Surprisingly mature and ready to drink, the 1981 Coutet is an
· agreeable wine, but lacks richness and complexity. What it does
78 offer is straightforward, fruity, lemony, melon aromas, and moderately sweet, somewhat short flavors. Drink up. Last tasted, 6/84.

1980—A good but rather uninspired effort from Coutet, the 1980 lacks
· richness and depth, even for the lighter-scaled wines of Coutet.
80 Nevertheless, the wine is perfect as an *apéritif* Barsac, and can do double duty with lighter, not too sweet desserts. Drink over the next 5–7 years. Last tasted, 6/84.

1979—The 1979 is one of the better efforts from Coutet in this period
· when the property may have been slightly off its normally top
83 form. Light golden, with a spicy, lemony, floral, fruity bouquet, this wine is elegant, has medium weight, and is clean and crisp in the mouth. Drink over the next 4–5 years. Last tasted, 7/82.

1978—Quite light, and a little insubstantial, this medium-bodied, mod-
· erately sweet Coutet is fruity and pleasant, but shows little evi-
75 dence of botrytis and seems to tail off in the mouth. Drink over the next 3–4 years. Last tasted, 5/82.

1976—One of the best Coutets of the '70s, the 1976 is a relatively big
· Coutet, with a surprising amount of alcohol (15%), a ripe apricot,
86 spicy, floral, lemon-scented bouquet, full body, fat, succulent flavors, and Coutet's personality trademark, crisp, fresh acidity. Drink over the next decade. Last tasted, 3/83.

1975—Every bit as good as the more open-knit and expressive 1976,
· the 1975 is lighter and more typically Coutet in its proportions,
86 with a graceful, fresh taste, very good concentration, and years of evolution ahead of it. Anticipated maturity: 1986–1992. Last tasted, 2/84.

1971—Probably as good as Coutet can get (except for this vintage's
· sublime *Cuvée Madame*), the 1971 is a gorgeous example of a
87 Barsac that is not that powerful, but has an authoritative presence in the mouth and wonderful, fresh, crisp acidity that admirably balances the apricot, honeyed flavors. Drink over the next 5 years. Last tasted, 9/81.

1970—Rather undistinguished, the 1970 Coutet seems diluted, with a
· bizarre, tarry, vegetal aroma, and little depth. Last tasted, 2/79.
72

1967—In this very fine vintage for the wines of Barsac and Sauternes,
· Coutet is a disappointment. Extremely light and a little herba-
70 ceous, this is more akin to a dry Graves than a sweet wine. Last tasted, 12/80.

LAFAURIE-PEYRAGUEY (Premier Cru Classé) VERY GOOD

Production: 4,500 cases	Grape varieties: Semillon—85% Sauvignon Blanc—10% Muscadelle—5%
Time spent in barrels: 24 months	Average age of vines: 32 years
Evaluation of present classification: Should be maintained	

Lafaurie-Peyraguey is one of the less-renowned wines of Sauternes but this will change when the wines of 1981 and 1983 are tasted by wine enthusiasts.

Lafaurie-Peyraguey has been owned since 1913 by the Cordier family, who are well known throughout the wine world for their high-quality range of wines, particularly the two St.-Julien estates of Talbot and Gruaud-Larose. However, the quality of these wines has always been much more highly regarded than that of Lafaurie-Peyraguey.

My experience with older vintages of this Sauternes has been that they are often too light and feeble, and at other times too heavy and dull. But, starting with the 1979, the wines of Lafaurie-Peyraguey have strengthened considerably in character, with more richness, body, and depth. It seems clear that the Cordier firm is making an all-out effort to restore confidence in this neglected estate in Sauternes.

VINTAGES

1983—This was fantastic from the cask. The staff at Cordier have every
· right to be happy with their splendidly concentrated, complex
92 wine, which is certainly the best Lafaurie-Peyraguey I have tasted. Tremendous intensity, viscous, ripe and layered with honeyed apricot-flavored fruit, this unctuous wine is not tiring or heavy to drink, but lively and effusively fruity. Anticipated maturity: 1987–2000. Last tasted, 3/85.

1982—Much lighter than the 1983, with little botrytis evident, the 1982
· is quite fresh and fruity, with aromas of melons and flowers
84 present. On the palate, the wine is medium-bodied, moderately sweet, spicy, and cleanly made. Drink over the next 5–7 years. Last tasted, 6/84.

1981—Quite exceptional, the 1981 Lafaurie/Peyraguey exhibits ripe
· apricot aromas, a rich, chewy, viscous texture, good acidity, and
88 a long, sweet, fat finish. This wine shows considerable botrytis, and is clearly one of the top efforts in this vintage. Anticipated maturity: 1987–1997. Last tasted, 6/84.

1980—Not quite up to the top-quality wines produced in 1983 and 1981,
· the Lafaurie-Peyraguey is still quite well turned out. Medium in
84 weight for a Sauternes, with a good, ripe pineapple, spicy fruitiness, this wine has average acidity, suggesting that cellaring of 2–4 years is warranted. Last tasted, 3/83.

1979—The 1979 is the first in a line of successful Lafaurie-Peyraguey
· wines that seem to have taken on greater richness as the Cordier
85 firm has moved to upgrade the quality. A lovely pineapple,

spicy-scented bouquet is quite attractive. The wine displays good botrytis, good acidity, moderate sweetness, and a crisp, clean finish. Drink over the next 5 years. Last tasted, 3/82.

1976—There is really nothing wrong with this wine, but is seems one-
· dimensional and innocuous and clearly lacks character and
75 depth. It is a minor Sauternes. Drink up. Last tasted, 11/82.

1975—A very atypical Sauternes, the 1975 has an olive-like, earthy
· aroma that seems slightly unclean and unripe. On the palate,
67 the wine is light, surprisingly thin, and finishes quite poorly.
Something clearly went wrong in 1975 for Lafaurie-Peyraguey.
Last tasted, 12/80.

1970—The 1970 is pleasant and agreeable, but very short on the palate,
· and not very sweet or concentrated. It is disappointing for a
74 Sauternes of this class. Last tasted, 12/80.

NAIRAC (Deuxième Cru Classé) VERY GOOD

Production: 2,000 cases	Grape varieties: Semillon—90% Sauvignon Blanc—6% Muscadelle—4%
Time spent in barrels: 36 months	Average age of vines: 15–20 years
Evaluation of present classification: Should be upgraded to a Premier Cru Classé	

Nairac is one of the most meticulously and passionately operated Barsac estates. In 1971 the property was purchased by American-born Tom Heeter and his French wife, Nicole Tari. Heeter apprenticed at the red-wine-producing property Giscours (in the Margaux appellation), where he met his wife, a member of the Tari winemaking family. The celebrated Emile Peynaud was brought in to provide oenological advice, and Nairac seems well on the way to producing some of the best wines of Barsac, at a quality level well above its Deuxième Cru classification.

Nairac is a relatively big-styled, oaky, ripe, concentrated wine for a Barsac. To say that it is impeccably made is an understatement. No compromises are made here, and this is clearly demonstrated by the fact that no Nairac was made in 1977 and 1978, and in 1979, 60% of the crop was deemed unworthy to be sold under the Nairac label.

Nairac represents a good value, and should be sought out by consumers looking for a very good Barsac at a reasonable price.

VINTAGES

1982—Probably the most successful Barsac of the vintage, Nairac's
· 1982 exhibits a light golden color, a spicy pineapple and vanillin
84 oaky bouquet, medium to full body, and surprisingly good concentration and length. It is a nice, medium-weight Barsac for drinking over the next 5–7 years. Last tasted, 1/85.

1981—Certainly good, but like many 1981s Nairac's wine lacks the
· botrytis character that gives the great vintages of this region so
83 much character. Perhaps a little too plump, and with a tendency toward dullness, this medium- to full-bodied wine has average acidity and 4–6 years of evolution ahead of it. Anticipated maturity: 1988–1996. Last tasted, 11/84.

1980—Nairac's 1980 is a well-balanced, light golden-colored wine that
· shows a good level of botrytis, a spicy, tropical fruit, oaky bou-
84 quet, medium body, soft acidity, and a fat, tasty finish. It seems to be very close to full maturity. Drink over the next 5–8 years. Last tasted, 11/84.

1979—A good Barsac, rather light for Nairac, but elegant, adequately
· concentrated, with a crisp, clean, moderately sweet finish.
83 Drink over the next 7–8 years. Last tasted, 11/84.

1976—One of the best Nairacs, the 1976 has a powerful, oaky, ripe
· fruity bouquet and strong vanillin, spicy, oaky notes. On the
86 palate, the wine is full-bodied, long, lush, quite concentrated and has a high level of botrytis. Drinking well now, it should continue to evolve for at least another 5–6 years. Last tasted, 11/84.

1975—Lighter in style than the 1976, with less power and obvious
· appeal, the 1975 Nairac has a quiet, introverted charm, with a
84 fresh, lively fruitiness, good acidity and presence on the palate, and a long, moderately sweet finish. It is quite well made. Drink over the next 5–6 years. Last tasted, 11/84.

SIGALAS RABAUD (Premier Cru Classé) — VERY GOOD

Production: 2,500 cases	Grape varieties: Semillon—75% Sauvignon Blanc—25%
Time spent in barrels: None; aged in vats	Average age of vines: 33 years

Evaluation of present classification: Should be maintained

The wines of Sigalas Rabaud are rarely seen these days. Yes, the production is small, but the dwindling interest in sweet wines from Barsac and Sauternes has clearly hurt the less-renowned names of these regions more than the celebrated châteaux.

The style of wine produced at Sigalas Rabaud is significantly lighter, and at its best, more elegant and graceful than many of its overblown, richer, more alcoholic peers. Interestingly, it is not aged at all in oak barrels, but rather in cement and stainless steel vats. For that reason, I always find Sigalas Rabaud to have one of the most exuberantly fruity bouquets and tastes, which would no doubt please more wine enthusiasts than some of the aggressively alcoholic, thick, viscous, oaky giants that are made in Sauternes.

Sigalas Rabaud is most definitely a wine to drink young, before it attains the age of 7 or 8 years. Since it is lighter and less alcoholic, it is a more flexible Sauternes with food than many others.

VINTAGES

1983—Potentially the best Sigalas Rabaud since 1967, the 1983 has a
· wonderfully fruity bouquet suggestive of pineapples, surprising
86 depth and concentration, an unctuous quality, and crisp, fresh
acidity. It is a very fruity, moderately sweet, well-knit Sauternes. Anticipated maturity: 1987–1997. Last tasted, 1/85.

1982—The 1982 is a middle-of-the-road Sauternes, with good fruit,
· medium body, and a pleasant finish, but like so many 1982s, it
75 has no complexity. Drink over the next 3–4 years. Last tasted,
1/85.

1981—Light but charming, with a fragrant, fruity, herbaceous, almost
· flowery bouquet, the 1981 seems to be a typically proportioned,
80 medium-weight wine from Sigalas Rabaud, Drink over the next
4–5 years. Last tasted, 6/84.

1980—Rather one-dimensional and dull, the 1980 is light, not very
· concentrated, and missing the usual fruity intensity and charm
75 that this wine frequently offers. Drink up. Last tasted, 2/84.

1979—Quite appealing in a lighter, more refreshing manner, the 1979
· Sigalas Rabaud has a moderately intense, fruity, minty, spicy
78 bouquet, medium body, not much botrytis, but crisp acidity, and
some sweetness. It is a charming Sauternes. Drink over the next 5 years. Last tasted, 9/83.

1976—Light, fruity and typically Sigalas Rabaud, this medium-bodied
· wine has a light perfume of pineapple fruit, good acidity, and
80 moderately sweet, nicely balanced flavors. Fully mature, it

should be drunk over the next 5 years. Last tasted, 7/80.

1975—Highly touted by the château, this wine has more in common
· with a German *Auslese* from the Mosel than a Sauternes. Flow-
75 ery, rather simple and compact, this lean, atypical Sigalas Rabaud is also suffering from an intrusive amount of sulfur dioxide.
Last tasted, 4/82.

1971—This is another lightweight effort from Sigalas Rabaud, but it is
· graceful and fruity, with a honeyed, fruity bouquet that is clean
82 and fresh. Medium body, moderately sweet flavors, and crisp
acidity are admirably balanced. Drink up. Last tasted, 3/81.

1967—Just beginning to lose its fruit and freshness, this has always
· been one of my favorite vintages of Sigalas Rabaud. The antith-
84 esis of a powerhouse, oaky, viscous Sauternes, the 1967 is moderately sweet and has a honeyed bouquet of pineapples.
Medium-bodied and concentrated, but surprisingly light, this is
a textbook example of Sigalas Rabaud. Drink up. Last tasted,
1/85.

GUIRAUD (Premier Cru Classé) — GOOD

Production: 10,000 cases	Grape varieties: Semillon—50% Sauvignon Blanc—45% Muscadelle—5%
Time spent in barrels: 24–30 months	Average age of vines: 28 years
Evaluation of present classification: Should be maintained	

Guiraud is one of the largest estates of the Sauternes district, covering almost 300 acres, of which 178 are planted with vines. Curiously, the estate produces a red wine with the Bordeaux Supérieur appellation, and of course a dry Sauternes called "G."

The sweet wine of Guiraud is undergoing a metamorphosis of sorts. In 1981 an ambitious Canadian, Hamilton Narby, purchased the estate and made bold promises that Yquem-like techniques of individual grape picking, barrel fermentation, and long aging in new oak barrels would be employed at Guiraud. Consequently, Bordeaux wine enthusiasts, particularly the nectar lovers, have taken great interest in the goings-on at Guiraud in the hopes that Narby will deliver on his promises. If the 1983 is any example of his commitment, then Guiraud will be a name to watch out for.

VINTAGES

1983—Cask samples of this wine showed marvelous potential. Light
· golden, with a ripe, intense bouquet of apricots and pineapples,
88 with a whiff of vanillin oakiness, this full-bodied, lush, rich wine
has excellent concentration, superb balance, and apparently
quite a future. Anticipated maturity: 1988–2005. Last tasted,
3/85.

1982—Rather big and ponderous on the palate, with a sticky, viscous
· fruitiness that comes too close to being ponderous and heavy,
78 and lacking finesse and sufficient acidity to give the wine crispness, this effort from Guiraud has plenty of richness, but is tiring
to drink. Last tasted, 6/84.

1981—An attractively fruity bouquet shows aromas of new oak, some
· spice, a herbal element, and some pineapple fruit. On the pal-
80 ate, the wine is fruity and medium- to full-bodied, but lacks
complexity and dimension. Drink over the next 3–4 years. Last
tasted, 6/84.

1980—Surprisingly dull, and too aggressively oaky, the 1980 Guiraud
· tastes fruity but flat. Drink up. Last tasted, 6/84.
75

1979—Firm and rather closed, with a reticent bouquet of fresh oranges
· and vanillin spices, this medium- to full-bodied wine has good
84 acidity, and good concentration and length. Anticipated maturity: 1986–1992. Last tasted, 3/84.

1976—Dark amber gold in color, this wine has a roasted, ripe fruity
· bouquet suggestive of sautéed oranges and almonds. On the
87 palate, the wine is full-bodied, sweet and rich, but seemingly
still young and unevolved. In a way, the 1976 Guiraud is perplexing; the bouquet seems mature, the taste suggests youth.
Impressive, but what direction is it going? Last tasted, 3/84.

1975—Significantly lighter in color than the 1976, the 1975 Guiraud has
· a honeyed bouquet of peach- and orange-like scents, intermin-
86 gled with the scent of new oak. On the palate, the wine is fat,
full-bodied, with hints of almonds, butter, and caramel. This is
a rich, full-bodied, quite impressive Guiraud. Drink over the
next decade. Last tasted, 9/82.

RAYNE-VIGNEAU (Premier Cru Classé) GOOD

Production: 16,500 cases	Grape varieties: Semillon—65% Sauvignon Blanc—30% Muscadelle—5%
Time spent in barrels: 30–36 months	Average age of vines: 27 years
Evaluation of present classification: Should be downgraded to a Deuxième Cru Classé	

Rayne-Vigneau is a very large Sauternes estate that sits to the west of Yquem's vineyards. It is the most commercial of Premiers Crus Classés in Sauternes. The yield per acre at Rayne-Vigneau is quite high, and while the general quality of the wine is above average, one can easily tell that it is not among the top rank of Barsacs and Sauternes, and it should be downgraded to a Deuxième Cru Classé should any objective new evaluation of the Sauternes classification take place.

VINTAGES

1983—Light aromas of pineapples and some faint botrytis emerge with
· breathing from this simply proportioned Sauternes. In the
82 mouth, the wine shows good ripeness, a pleasant, velvety, creamy texture, medium sweetness, and crisp acidity. In the context of the vintage, this is an uninspiring wine, but for Rayne-Vigneau, a good effort. Drink over the next 5–6 years. Last tasted, 1/85.

1982—One-dimensional, fruity, sweet flavors offer little complexity,
· but do exhibit pleasing ripeness and adequate, balancing acid-
75 ity. Drink over the next 5 years. Last tasted, 1/85.

1981—Soft, fruity, moderately sweet flavors show average concentra-
· tion, and some alluring scents of grilled almonds and pineapples,
75 but this wine has a diluted finish, and just not enough stuffing and concentration to warrant much interest. Last tasted, 2/85.

1979—A straightforward, fruity, rather sweet wine, without much bo-
· trytis, but showing solid, underripe flavors of peaches and mint.
74 Typically light, and lacking muscle and concentration, the 1979 Rayne-Vigneau should be drunk over the next 2–3 years for its freshness. Last tasted, 6/83.

1976—For a 1976, this is a lightweight wine, but it does have a good,
· ripe apricot fruitiness, medium body, and a decent, moderately
78 sweet finish. One is tempted to say that this is a nice picnic
Sauternes. Last tasted, 2/84.

1975—A disappointing effort, the 1975 has excessively high acidity, a
· lean, austere, ungenerous texture, and light, vegetal, washed-
65 out flavors. One wonders what could have gone afoul in this
excellent vintage? Last tasted, 6/84.

1971—Hot alcohol tends to intrude on this wine's soft, delicate pine-
· apple fruitiness and medium-bodied texture. It will only become
75 more unbalanced. Drink up. Last tasted, 2/80.

BROUSTET (Deuxième Cru Classé) GOOD

Production: 2,000–4,000 cases	Grape varieties: Semillon—63% Sauvignon Blanc—25% Muscadelle—12%
Time spent in barrels: 20 months	Average age of vines: 38 years
Evaluation of present classification: Should be maintained	

Broustet is one of the rarely encountered and least-known Barsacs. The property is owned by Eric Fournier, who is more widely known as the owner of the excellent *côtes* St.-Emilion, Canon. Broustet is a fairly robust Barsac, but I have not seen as many vintages of it as I would have liked. Certainly, Fournier has been tough when it comes to quality controls; no Broustet was produced in 1977, 1976, or 1964.

VINTAGES

1980—A successful vintage for Broustet, the 1980 is chunky, shows
· good botrytis, creamy pineapple fruitiness, and a soft, ripe, gen-
82 erous finish. Drink over the next 4 years. Last tasted, 1/85.

1978—Quite aggressively oaky, the 1978 Broustet has clean, crisp, ripe
· fruity flavors behind a wall of oak. On the palate, the wine is
80 relatively full-bodied, but seems a little hollow and less succulent and sweet than it should be. Big and oaky, but a little more
fleshy ripe fruit would have made a big difference. Anticipated
maturity: 1986–1992. Last tasted, 2/84.

1975—The best Broustet I have tasted, the 1975 is a rather powerful
· wine with a luscious pineapple, peachy, appley sweet fruitiness,
85 medium to full body, and a medium-bodied feel on the palate.

The long, lively finish is surprisingly crisp. Drink over the next 5–6 years. Last tasted, 4/82.

1971—Beginning to fade and lose its freshness and vigor, the 1971
· Broustet is spicy, a touch too oaky, but medium- to full-bodied
78 with good concentration and slightly sweet flavors. Drink up.
Last tasted, 4/78.

BASTOR-LAMONTAGNE (Unclassified) — GOOD

Production: 8,000–9,000 cases	Grape varieties: Semillon—80% Sauvignon Blanc—20%
Time spent in barrels: 36 months	Average age of vines: 20 years
Evaluation of present classification: Should be upgraded to a Deuxième Cru Classé	

Bastor-Lamontagne makes a shockingly good Sauternes on a sizable property of 208 acres located halfway between Barsac and Sauternes. Given its lack of notoriety and astonishingly low price, this is clearly a property in which consumers should take a more active interest.

VINTAGES

1983—A voluptuous, lush, luscious wine with oodles of ripe, botrytized
· pineapple fruit, medium- to full-bodied texture, and a long, rich,
87 silky finish—all combine to titillate the palate. Bastor-
Lamontagne is rather precocious, but so tasty. Drink over the next 10 years. Last tasted, 1/85.

1982—Bastor-Lamontagne has made a shockingly good wine in 1982.
· It is a lovely, richly fruity, moderately sweet, well-balanced Sau-
85 ternes with plenty of character. The wine is forward and quite
ready now, but promises to be even better in 4–5 years. The Bastor-Lamontagne is an unlikely candidate for fame in this vintage. Last tasted, 1/85.

1980—The aroma of ripe pineapples and fresh melons is quite apparent
· in this medium-weight wine with a lush, nicely concentrated
82 personality. Not as good as the 1982 or 1983, this is still a notable
effort from what is Sauternes's best-priced estate bottled wine. Drink over the next 3 years. Last tasted, 1/84.

1976—Bastor-Lamontagne is quite a success in this very fine vintage
· for the wine of Barsac and Sauternes. Fully mature, but capable
85 of holding, this unctuous, ripe, orange-and-apricot-scented and

flavored wine has plenty of body to go along with its excellent flavor. Drink up. Last tasted, 2/83.

1975—A lemony, buttery, tropical-fruit-scented bouquet, ripe medium-
· to full-bodied flavors, and good crisp acidity all complement
85 each other in this moderately sweet, well-structured wine. The 1975 Bastor-Lamontagne is still holding nicely and can be drunk over the next 3–4 years. Last tasted, 2/83.

DOISY-VÉDRINES (Deuxième Cru Classé) GOOD

Production: 1,500–2,500 cases	Grape varieties: Semillon—80% Sauvignon Blanc—20%
Time spent in barrels: 24 months	Average age of vines: 27 years
Evaluation of present classification: Should be maintained	

This Barsac estate is well placed just to the southeast of the two most famous Barsacs, Climens and Coutet. Unfortunately, the tiny production of sweet Doisy-Védrines precludes many wine enthusiasts from ever discovering how good this wine can be. Most wine drinkers probably know the dry white and red table wine produced by this estate much better. It is called Chevalier de Védrines and is a delightful commercial wine that is equally good in either white or red. As for the sweet wine, Doisy-Védrines is a much fatter, richer, more intense wine than the wine of Doisy-Daëne, its next-door neighbor. Doisy-Védrines is a wine that is usually at its best 5–7 years after the vintage, but will age considerably longer, particularly in the top vintages.

VINTAGES

1980—A fat, spicy, apricot, coconut-scented bouquet is quite captivat-
· ing. On the palate the wine is quite ripe, very sweet, almost
84 jammy and marmalade-like, with a good, sweet, alcoholic finish. It lacks a little finesse, but the 1980 Doisy-Védrines exhibits plenty of fruit and a chewy texture. Drink over the next 4–5 years. Last tasted, 2/85.

1978—Charming but lighter in style than normal, the 1978 lacks botry-
· tis, but has fresh, clean, lemony, pineapple fruitiness and de-
80 cent finish. Drink over the next 3–4 years. Last tasted, 2/82.

1976—In many respects a typically chunky, fat, corpulent Doisy-
· Védrines, the 1976 shows plenty of ripe, viscous honeyed fruit,
84 good botrytis, full body, and enough acidity to keep the wine

from tasting cloyingly sweet or heavy. Drink over the next 5 years. Last tasted, 9/82.

1975—A rather unforthcoming nose in no way suggests the richness
· and depth of this rather intense, full-bodied, ripe, very fruity
85 Doisy-Védrines. Unctuous, luscious flavors of apricots and melons are admirably balanced by spicy oak. Drink over the next 5 years. Last tasted, 12/83.

DOISY-DAËNE (Deuxième Cru Classé) GOOD

Production: 4,000 cases	Grape varieties: Semillon—100%
Time spent in barrels: 12 months	Average age of vines: 30 years
Evaluation of present classification: Should be maintained	

One of the most ambitiously and innovatively run estates in Bordeaux, Doisy-Daëne produces a very fine Barsac that seems to be underrated in the scheme of Barsac/Sauternes realities. While I would not rate it a Premier Cru Classé, it is certainly one of the leaders among the Deuxièmes Crus Classés. The proprietor of Doisy-Daëne, Pierre Dubourdieu, also produces one of the better dry wines of the region, Doisy-Daëne Sec. Five thousand cases of this full and refreshing, vibrant, fruity, and best of all, very inexpensive wine are produced each year. Apparently not content with two white wines, Dubourdieu also produces what is one of the better red wines of this region. It is called Chantegril, and while it is entitled only to an Appellation Bordeaux, the 1982 was of remarkably high quality, and as good as a Grand Bourgeois in the Médoc.

Doisy-Daëne's sweet wine is surprisingly enjoyable when young, causing many tasters to think that it will not age. However, the 1924 and 1955 I drank in 1984 were still fresh, lively, and full of fruit. Doisy-Daëne is generally very fairly priced, so when the property excels it can offer a very fine quality/price rapport.

VINTAGES

1983—Doisy-Daëne finished its harvest one month after Yquem, and
· has possibly produced this property's finest wine in over two
90 decades. A big, ripe bouquet of pineapples, peaches, and spring flowers is very attractive. On the palate, the wine is concentrated, full-bodied, and unctuous, without being too heavy or

alcoholic. Excellent acidity suggests a long, eventful evolution. Anticipated maturity: 1990–2010. Last tasted, 1/85.

1982—One of the better 1982s, ripe and fruity, with the taste of fresh
· oranges, this medium-bodied Doisy-Daëne has good length, a
82 fresh, lemony acidity, moderate sweetness, and a solid finish. Drink over the next decade. Last tasted, 1/85.

1981—Somewhat light, and perhaps dominated by oak to an extreme,
· this fruity, soft, moderately concentrated wine has little botrytis
78 and a short finish. Drink over the next 7–10 years. Last tasted, 1/85.

1980—Surprisingly advanced on the nose, the 1980 Doisy-Daëne has a
· light golden color, an aromatic floral-and-pineapple-scented
82 bouquet, soft, moderately sweet, fat, plump flavors, and just enough acidity to keep the wine from feeling heavy. Drink over the next 5 years. Last tasted, 6/84.

1979—A tightly knit, restrained rendition of Doisy-Daëne, the 1979
· exhibits very good ripeness, a rich, full-bodied texture, plenty of
84 vanillin, oaky aromas, and good acidity. Anticipated maturity: 1988–2000. Last tasted, 4/85.

1978—Not a terribly impressive vintage, but this wine made from
· grapes picked very late in November shows less intensity than
83 the 1979, has an elegant, fruity, spicy nose, firm, sweet flavors, and good, firm acidity. Drink over the next 7–8 years. Last tasted, 6/84.

1975—Some disturbing sulfur aromas in the bouquet seem to con-
· stantly appear in bottles of this wine. On the palate, the wine is
78 rich and creamy, with a honeyed, pineapple fruitiness, and a succulent, sweet finish. The taste is considerably better than the bouquet. Drink up. Last tasted, 11/82.

OTHER NOTABLE SAUTERNES AND BARSAC PROPERTIES

CAILLOU (Deuxième Cru Classé)

Production: 1,500 cases	Grape varieties: Semillon—90% Sauvignon Blanc—10%
Time spent in barrels: 36 months	Average age of vines: 22 years
Evaluation of present classification: Should be maintained	

Caillou is a modest Barsac estate that sells virtually all of its production directly to private customers. The vineyard just northwest of that of Climens produces a fairly light, fruity, elegant but perhaps too understated style of wine that is best drunk up within 6 or 7 years of the vintage. However, the wine can age, and the proprietor, Joseph Bravo, keeps rather substantial stocks of older vintages to prove this point. From a consumer's point of view, this is an interesting property to visit because it has a handsome twin-towered château and an array of old vintages for sale at modest prices. Two recent vintages I have enjoyed include the 1975 and 1970.

D'ARCHE (Deuxième Cru Classé)

Production: 4,500 cases	Grape varieties: Semillon—80% Sauvignon Blanc—15% Muscadelle—5%
Time spent in barrels: 24–36 months	Average age of vines: 20 years
Evaluation of present classification: Should be maintained	

This little-known Sauternes estate can make solid and reliable wines that represent good value. The vineyard sits just north of the village of Sauternes next to the overrated Premier Cru estate of La Tour Blanche. D'Arche's rich, botrytized 1980, stylish, powerful, but restrained 1975, and graceful but light 1971 all stand out among recent vintages. The 1978, 1979, and surprisingly, the 1970 are mediocre wines. However, the 1983 looks to be the finest d'Arche made in several decades. It is a powerful, rich, rather heavy style of Sauternes.

FILHOT (Deuxième Cru Classé)

Production: 6,500 cases	Grape varieties: Semillon—65% Sauvignon Blanc—32% Muscadelle—3%
Time spent in barrels: None; 30 months in vats	Average age of vines: 22 years
Evaluation of present classification: Should be maintained	

Filhot has the potential to be one of the best Deuxième Crus produced. However, a lack of consistency and some rather mediocre efforts in the late '70s kept me from placing it higher in the ratings. The wine is differently styled from most Sauternes. Because of the rather high percentage of Sauvignon Blanc, this is a fruitier, more aromatic and lighter, more delicate wine. The wine is aged in vats to accentuate its fruitiness and freshness. The 1981, 1980, and 1978 all have left me underwhelmed, although the 1979 did show Filhot's light, lemony, pineapple fruitiness, medium body, and freshness to its advantage. However, the two vintages to watch for from Filhot are 1975 and 1976. If the 1975 is good, the 1976 is excellent, with an apricot scent and full, rich, ripe flavors. Filhot is relatively inexpensive, so when one is fortunate enough to find a good vintage, it is quite a bargain.

ROMER DU HAYOT (Deuxième Cru Classé)

Production: 4,000 cases	Grape varieties: Semillon—70% Sauvignon Blanc—30%
Time spent in barrels: None	Average age of vines: 28 years
Evaluation of present classification: Should be maintained	

I have generally enjoyed the wines of Romer du Hayot, a small Sauternes estate of just over 30 acres located near the beautiful Château de Malle. The style of wine produced here emphasizes a fresh fruity character, medium body, and moderate sweetness. The wine sees no aging in barrels, so its exuberant fruitiness is not masked by spicy, vanillin oaky aromas and flavors.

While it is a lighter-styled Sauternes, it has plenty of interest and generally ages well for 4–7 years. The 1983, 1979, 1976, and 1975 were all very successful years for Romer du Hayot. Fortunately, the price asked for this unknown property is quite reasonable.

LAMOTHE-DESPUJOLS (Deuxième Cru Classé)

Production: 1,800 cases	Grape varieties: Semillon—70% Sauvignon Blanc—20% Muscadelle—10%
Time spent in barrels: 24 months, 12 of which are in vats	Average age of vines: 47 years
Evaluation of present classification: Should be maintained	

This tiny estate, located just to the west of the village of Sauternes, produces a very commercial style of wine that is meant to be drunk when released. Not too sweet or too dry, light- to medium-bodied without much complexity or interest, Lamothe's wines, to their credit, are usually cleanly made and technically correct. The 1975 is the best vintage from the decade of the '70s, exhibiting light but proper pineapple fruity flavors, medium body, and a light finish that is rather drier than normal.

One confusing characteristic of Lamothe's wines is the proprietor's predilection for changing the design of the label with certain vintages. To complicate consumer recognition of this wine even more, there will be another Château Lamothe Sauternes wine starting with the 1981 vintage. A separate estate altogether, the other Lamothe is owned by the Guignaud family.

DE MALLE (Deuxième Cru Classé)

Production: 4,500–5,000 cases	Grape varieties: Semillon—75% Sauvignon Blanc—22% Muscadelle—3%
Time spent in barrels: Aged in vats and barrels for 30 months	Average age of vines: 18 years
Evaluation of present classification: Should be maintained	

Along with the fortress-like Château d'Yquem, Château de Malle is a showpiece property in Sauternes. Well worth a tourist's visit, this gorgeous château also has wonderful gardens. This is a large estate that produces a dry, oak-aged white wine called M. de Malle, a dry red wine called Cardaillan, and a Sauternes under the secondary label, Ste.-Hélène. However, the real interest is the sweet Sauternes produced here—light, fruity, not too sweet, but cleanly made and in good vintages very elegant and graceful. The 1983 tasted from the cask stands above the other recent vintages for its richness, depth, and length on the palate.

SUAU (Deuxième Cru Classé)

Production: 1,500 cases	Grape varieties: Semillon—60% Sauvignon Blanc—33% Muscadelle—7%
Time spent in barrels: 12 months	Average age of vines: 22 years
Evaluation of present classification: Should be maintained	

The tiny estate of Suau, tucked away on a back road of Barsac, is largely unknown. Much of the production is sold directly to consumers and while the quality is not bad, it is not terribly exciting either. Two vintages of Suau that possess an extra measure of richness are the 1975 and 1980, but the 1978, 1979, and 1981 seem to be rather flabby, dull, commercial wines with cloying sweetness.

CLOS HAUT-PEYRAGUEY (Premier Cru Classé)

Production: 2,000 cases

Grape varieties:
Semillon—83%
Sauvignon Blanc—15%
Muscadelle—2%

Time spent in barrels: 15–20 months

Average age of vines: 28 years

Evaluation of present classification: Should be downgraded to a Deuxième Cru or Cru Bourgeois

This estate produces an acceptable Sauternes, but the wine is not up to the standard of a Premiers Crus. The wine is quite light for a Sauternes, often annoyingly high in acidity, and on occasion shows an overly zealous use of sulfur dioxide, which can give it the infamous "rotten egg" smell. Of the recent vintages tasted, only the 1976 stands out as deserving interest from Sauternes enthusiasts.

LA TOUR BLANCHE (Premier Cru Classé)

Production: 6,200 cases

Grape varieties:
Semillon—72%
Sauvignon Blanc—25%
Muscadelle—3%

Time spent in barrels: 24 months

Average age of vines: 25 years

Evaluation of present classification: Should be downgraded to a Deuxième Cru

La Tour Blanche in Sauternes is owned and operated by the French Ministry of Agriculture. In 1855 it was ranked second behind Yquem, and this fact has always been advantageous for the sale of this property's wines. Despite the temptation to criticize it because it is state run, the truth is that the wines are not what they should be. Clearly, the quality here does not justify its exalted status.

Perhaps I have been unlucky, but a close examination of this estate's wines show them to be rather characterless. light, meagerly endowed Sauternes that do not stand the test of time. The best recent vintage is 1975, but it is hardly an inspired effort.

RABAUD-PROMIS (Premier Cru Classé)

Production: 7,500 cases

Grape varieties:
Semillon—80%
Sauvignon Blanc—18%
Muscadelle—2%

Time spent in barrels: None; aged in vats

Average age of vines: 20 years

Evaluation of present classification: Should be downgraded to a Deuxième Cru or Cru Bourgeois

Until 1952, Rabaud-Promis was part of the huge Rabaud estate. In that year a division took place and there are now two Rabaud estates, Rabaud-Sigalas and Rabaud-Promis. Both are entitled to the Premier Cru status, but Rabaud-Promis hardly merits such recognition, given the quality of the wine produced here. The wine is sold directly to consumers and bottled only upon demand. Consequently, vintages have a way of sitting longer than they should in vats, apparently not receiving as much supervision as is necessary. The results are often flawed wines with stale, musty aromas, amazingly high acidity, and a lack of the succulent, sweet fruit that makes Sauternes famous. The 1978 and 1979 are very light, somewhat tart wines that seem uncharacteristically dry and acidic for Sauternes. The 1976 has shown reasonably well in tastings, but the 1971 is old, stale, and oxidized.

THE SATELLITE APPELLATIONS OF BORDEAUX

There are very large quantities of wine produced in a bevy of other lesser-known appellations of Bordeaux. Most of these wines are widely commercialized in France, but have met with little success in America because of this country's obsession with luxury names and prestigious appellations. For the true connoisseur, the wines of Bordeaux's satellite appellations can in fact represent outstanding bargains, particularly in top vintages like 1982 and 1983 where excellent climatic conditions and the improved use of modern techology by many of these estates resulted in a vast selection of wines at prices that rarely exceed a few pounds a bottle.

On recent trips to France I have spent considerable time tasting the wines from the satellite communes of Bordeaux in an all-out effort to try to discover who's who in these obscure appellations. In this section, I have listed the top estates from the major satellite appellations of Bordeaux and I unhesitatingly recommend these wines to Bordeaux wine enthusiasts looking for sensational values from this area. I have tasted all of the wines from these estates in the vintages 1981, 1982, and 1983. The estates mentioned in this chapter represent only a small percentage of the total number of properties I evaluated, but I believe the ones listed are producing the finest wine in their respective appellations.

These satellite appellations are listed in order of my opinion of their overall ability to produce high-quality wine.

CANON-FRONSAC

Canon-Fronsac in five or ten years will have a reputation as good as St.-Emilion or Pomerol. Everything is present to make fine wines except the financial investment in this region and the modern technology. The appellation of Canon-Fronsac is located a short five-minute drive northwest of the city of Libourne. Beautifully situated on rolling hills overlooking the Dordogne River, the limestone-based soil here produces rather darkly colored, somewhat big and stern wines with plenty of character. Despite this region's close proximity to Pomerol, the *vignerons* of Canon-Fronsac have yet to share the same wealth and popularity that wine producers in Pomerol have finally realized. Most of the lovely châteaux in Canon-Fronsac are run down and their proprietors pitifully poor and obviously undercapitalized. This is all about to change, however.

The famous Libourne firm of Jean-Pierre Moueix, which in the last 20 years has taken Pomerol and its top property Pétrus from obscurity to worldwide fame, has begun to take considerable interest in the wines of Canon-Fronsac, realizing the excellent potential for this region that, climatically and geographically, has it all.

The Canon-Fronsac wines resemble in style both the wines of St.-Emilion and Pomerol, but tend to be tougher, more aggressively tannic wines. The general red grape varieties, Merlot and Cabernet Franc, are widely planted in Canon-Fronsac and one sees more Malbec here than in any other Bordeaux appellation.

A CONSUMER'S CLASSIFICATION OF THE CHÂTEAUX OF CANON-FRONSAC

VERY GOOD

Canon De Brem, Canon

GOOD

Vray-Canon-Boyer, Rouet, Bodet, Mazeris-Bellevue

AVERAGE

Mazeris, Vincent, Vrai-Canon-Bouché, Junayme

At present, the two outstanding wines of Canon-Fronsac are Canon de Brem and Canon.

Canon de Brem produces 3,200 cases of very darkly colored wine that is very full-bodied, usually quite tannic, and always rather concentrated. It tends to be a robust, virile wine rather than an elegant, supple wine. The 1982 is very good and the 1983 good.

Canon is the other top wine of this appellation. This property is run by Christian Moueix of the firm of Jean-Pierre Moueix, and the wine produced there is supple, richly fruity, and expertly vinified. Both the 1982 and 1983 are top successes. The production of Canon is 4,000 cases per year.

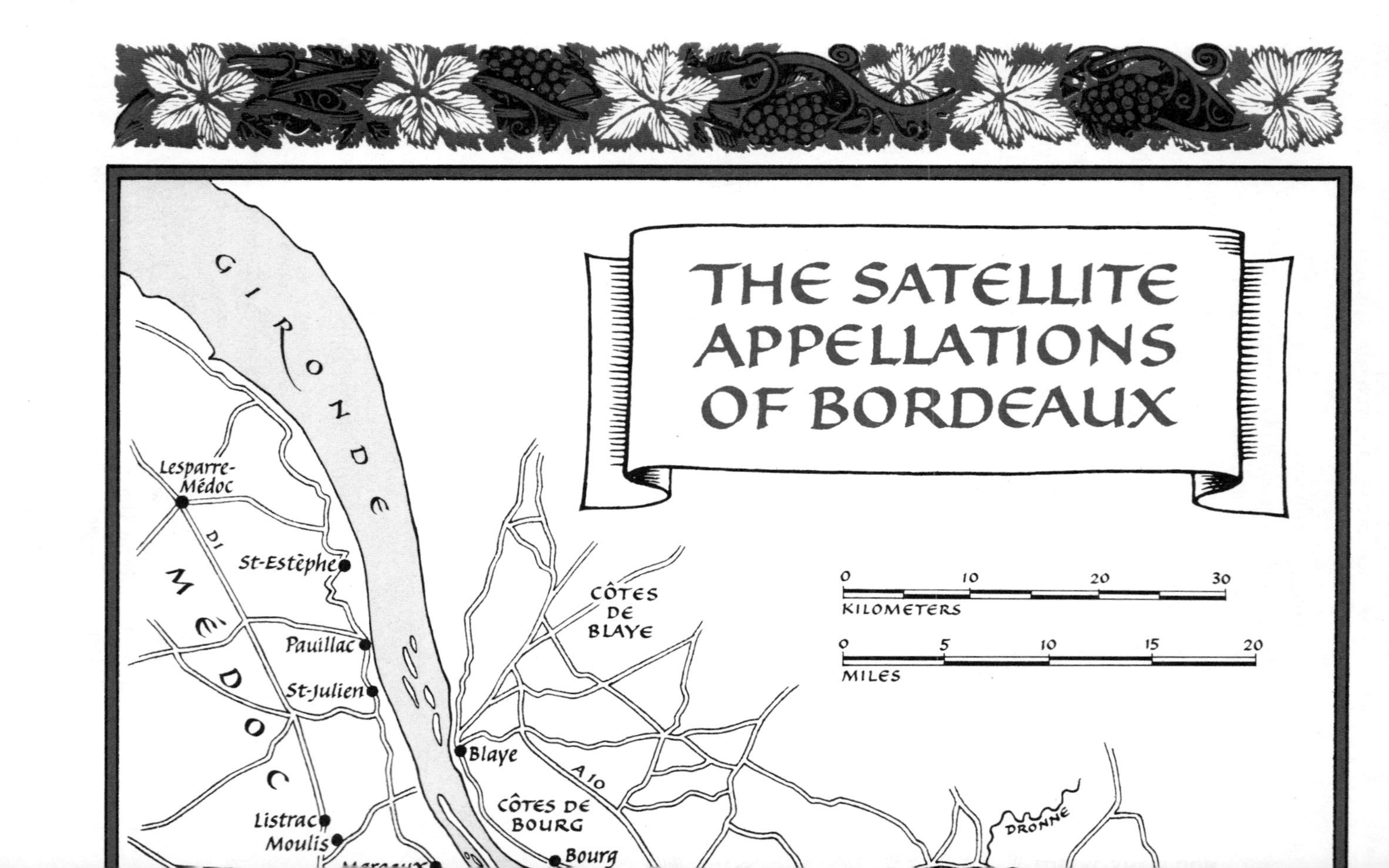

THE SATELLITE APPELLATIONS OF BORDEAUX
0
10
20
30
KILOMETERS
0
5
10
15
20
MILES
GIRONDE
Lesparre-Médoc
D1
MÉDOC
St-Estèphe
Pauillac
St-Julien
Listrac
Moulis
Blaye
CÔTES DE BLAYE
A10
CÔTES DE BOURG
Bourg
DRONNE

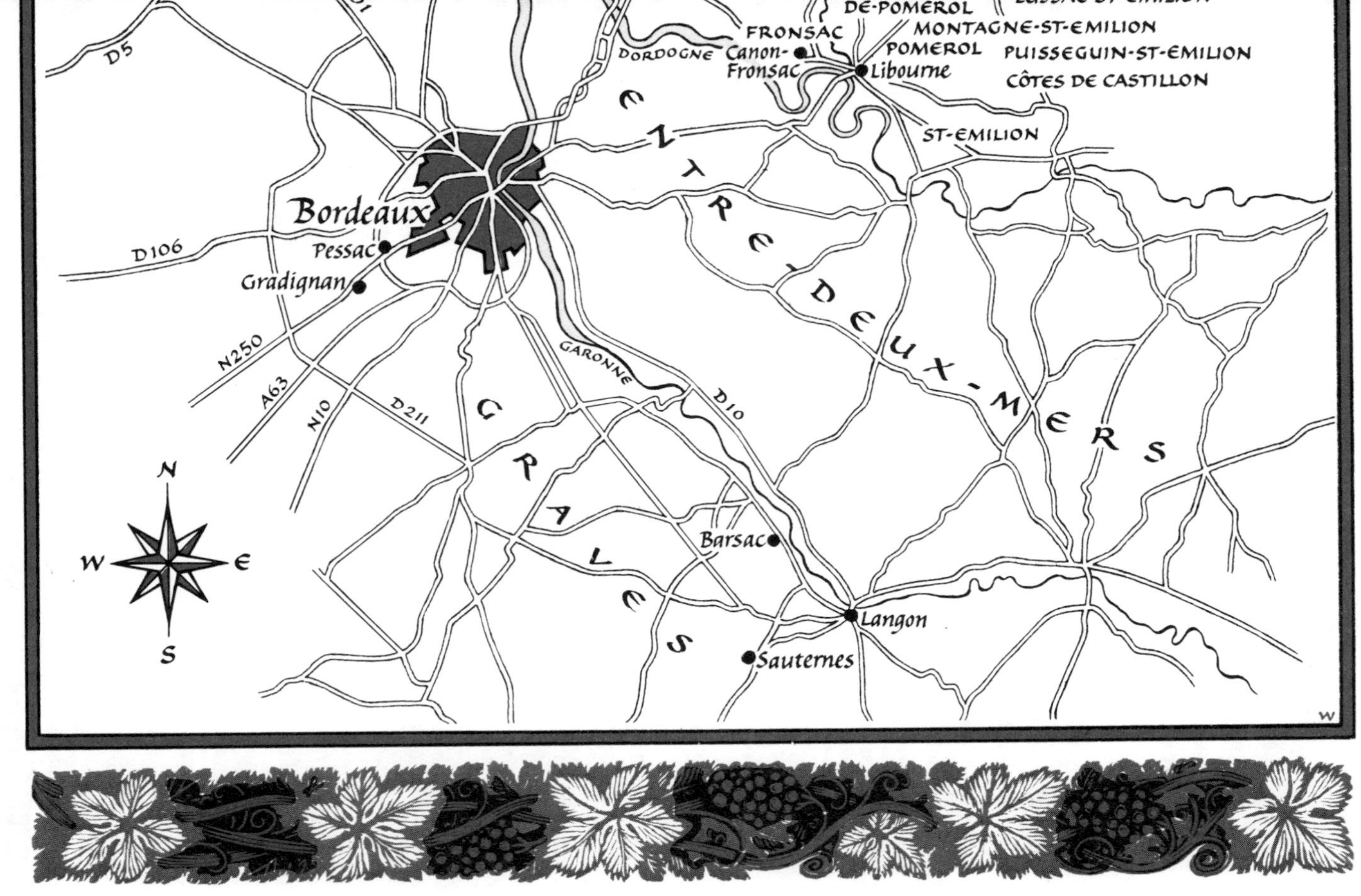

LUSSAC-ST-EMILION
DE-POMEROL
MONTAGNE-ST-EMILION
POMEROL
PUISSEGUIN-ST-EMILION
CÔTES DE CASTILLON
FRONSAC
Canon-Fronsac
Libourne
DORDOGNE
ST-EMILION
D5
D1
D106
Bordeaux
Pessac
Gradignan
N250
A63
N10
D211
GARONNE
D10
ENTRE-DEUX-MERS
GRAVES
Barsac
Langon
Sauternes
N
W
E
S

Of the other Canon-Fronsacs, Vray-Canon-Boyer is probably the best, although its style of wine is quite fleshy, tannic, and robust. I have enjoyed Bodet in vintages such as 1975 and 1970, but I thought the 1982 disappointing. Rouet can make supple, fruity wines, but they are generally lighter than the other Canon-Fronsacs.

LALANDE-DE-POMEROL

Lalande-de-Pomerol is a satellite commune located just to the north of Pomerol. There are quite a few good estates in Lalande-de-Pomerol producing a darkly colored, plump, richly fruity wine not unlike that of the second tier of Pomerol estates. Since many Lalande-de-Pomerol estates already have an enthusiastic following in Europe, the prices of these wines, while modest and fair, are rarely bargains.

A CONSUMER'S CLASSIFICATION OF THE CHÂTEAUX OF LALANDE-DE-POMEROL

VERY GOOD

Bel-Air, Belles-Graves, Tournefeuille, Grand-Ormeau

GOOD

Garraud, Haut-Chatain, Clos des Templiers, Haut-Surget, Moncets

AVERAGE

Brouard, Laborde, La-Croix-St.-André, Perron, Teysson

The top four wines of Lalande-de-Pomerol all share similar characteristics. They are darkly colored, plummy, ripe, medium- to full-bodied wines with a limited aging potential of 6–8 years. All these properties made very good wines in 1982, and Bel-Air and Belles-Graves were also quite successful in 1983. Belles-Graves in particular may be a property to watch very carefully as the last vintages of this wine have been truly excellent.

Right below these four top Lalande-de-Pomerols are five estates, Garraud, Haut-Chatain, Clos des Templiers, Haut-Surget, and Moncets, that are producing chunky, solid, amply endowed wines that have been consistently good over recent vintages. Of these estates, Garraud has been the most consistent from vintage to vintage, but Haut-Chatain, Clos des Templiers, Haut-Surget, and Moncet are all capable of producing robust, full-flavored wines in top vintages such as 1975, 1982, and 1983.

FRONSAC

Fronsac is adjacent to Canon Fronsac on the lower-lying sections of the hills of this bucolic region to the northwest of Pomerol. The wines are not as consistently good as those of Canon-Fronsac, or as fleshy and succulent as the top wines of Lalande-de-Pomerol. However, there are several notable estates in Fronsac that produce very good quality wine.

A CONSUMER'S CLASSIFICATION OF THE CHÂTEAUX OF FRONSAC

VERY GOOD

La Dauphine

GOOD

La Rivìere, Villars, Clos du Roy

AVERAGE

Mayne-Vieil, Magondeau, Trois-Croix, de Carles, Richelieu, Puyguilhem

The top wine of Fronsac is La Dauphine. This estate produces 8,000 cases of relatively rich, deeply colored wine with a blackcurrant taste and spicy, tarry bouquet. This wine has been particularly fine in vintages such as 1970, 1975, 1978, 1982, and 1983.

After La Dauphine there is a drop in quality. La Rivière is probably next, and this property makes a supple, rich, and fruity Fronsac with 1978, 1982, and 1983 being the best among the recent vintages. La Rivière is even better known for its splendid château and gorgeous setting along the Dordogne River. Both Clos du Roy and Villars produce well-made, supple, fruity Fronsacs with good concentration and character.

CÔTES DE BOURG

The Côtes de Bourg sits on the wrong side of the Gironde River. On the other side of the Gironde, just a 5-minute boat ride away, is the world famous commune of Margaux. The Côtes de Bourg is congested with modestly sized estates producing straightforward, uncomplicated wine that is meant to be drunk within the first 3–5 years of the vintage. The better estates that sit on the slopes overlooking the Gironde tend to make a fuller-bodied, richer wine, but few Côtes de Bourg wines will retain their fresh, exuberant fruitiness past their fifth birthday. The wines here are generally a blend of Merlot and Cabernet Franc, although some Cabernet Sauvignon is planted. For consumers wanting honest wines at very low prices, the Côtes de Bourg has plenty to offer.

A CONSUMER'S CLASSIFICATION OF THE CHÂTEAUX OF THE CÔTES DE BOURG

VERY GOOD

Tayac "Cuvée Prestige"

GOOD

de Barbe, Brûle Sécaille, Rousset, Tayac, de Thau, Mercier, Rousselle, Les Heaumes, Guerry, Caruel, Croûte Courpon

AVERAGE

Conilh, La Grave, Montaigut, Coubet, Le Breuil, Peychaud, Haut-Guiraud, Genibon, Gazin, Dumezil, L'Hospital

If all the good Côtes de Bourg wines are characterized by an obviously fruity character and one-dimensional charm, one wine must stand above the rest for its uniqueness and character. Tayac's special reserve *cuvée* called "*Cuvée Prestige*" in vintages like 1975, 1978, and 1982 is possibly as good as a Médoc fifth-growth. It is an especially big, rich, full-bodied wine with at least an 8–10-year life expectancy. It is an atypical Côtes de Bourg.

As for the other wines, all of the châteaux listed above in the "good" category produce distinctively fruity, clean, supple wines that are at their best in vintages such as 1982 and 1983. They are perfect wines for drinking within 4–5 years of the vintage, and one only wishes that more restaurants and consumers would avail themselves of these supple, soft, fruity, well-made wines.

PREMIÈRES CÔTES DE BLAYE

The Côtes de Blaye consists of the northernmost appellations located on Bordeaux's right bank just to the north of the Côtes de Bourg. Not surprisingly, this area produces similarly fruity, soft, pleasant and agreeable wines that represent great values to the wine enthusiast, not the wine collector or snob.

There are fewer noteworthy estates in Blaye than in Bourg, but several estates here do an especially fine job if it is intensely fruity, supple, ready-to-drink wines you are looking for.

A CONSUMER'S CLASSIFICATION OF THE CHÂTEAUX OF PREMIÈRES CÔTES DE BLAYE

GOOD

La Tonnelle, Haut-Sociando

AVERAGE

Barbé, Grolet, Bellevue, Maine-Guyon, Les Chaumes, Lardière, Chante-Alouette

The two outstanding estates of Blaye are La Tonnelle and Haut-Sociando. La Tonnelle produces a lovely, berry-scented, richly fruity wine that can be drunk young or aged for 2–4 years. The 1982 and 1983 are both very successful. Haut-Sociando is a spicier, more peppery and larger-framed wine with generally good color and a hefty, mouth-filling presence. It too is very successful in both 1982 and 1983.

PUISSEGUIN-ST.-EMILION

Puisseguin-St.-Emilion is, as the name suggests, a satellite commune of St.-Emilion. It is not the only one, but it has several estates that are producing noteworthy wines. In style and taste, the wines of Puisseguin-St.-Emilion resemble down-scaled versions of St.-Emilions. They are rarely complex, but rather tasty, fleshy, and chunky wines that are best drunk within their first 6–7 years of life.

A CONSUMER'S CLASSIFICATION OF THE CHÂTEAUX OF PUISSEGUIN-ST.-EMILION

GOOD

Durand Laplaigne, Vieux-Château-Guibeau, Bel Air

AVERAGE

Teyssier, Soleil, de Mole, Cassat, La Tour Guillotin, Laurets, Roc de Boissac, Beauséjour, La-Croix-de-Mouchet

In my tastings of the 1981, 1982, and 1983 Puisseguin-St.-Emilions, two wines consistently stood far and above the pack. Durand Laplaigne and Vieux-Château-Guibeau both seemed better made, more fruity and concentrated than all the other wines except for Bel Air. While the 1982s were clearly superior to each property's 1981s, I thought the 1983 Durand Laplaigne and 1983 Vieux-Château-Guibeau were even better than those properties' 1982s. These generous, fruity wines are best consumed over the next 4 years.

LUSSAC-ST.-EMILION

Another of the satellite appellations of St.-Emilion, Lussac can produce sound, reliable wines at very reasonable prices. They are similar in style and character to the wines of Puisseguin.

A CONSUMER'S CLASSIFICATION OF THE CHÂTEAUX OF LUSSAC-ST.-EMILION

GOOD

Cap de Merle, Villadière, Carteyron, Courlat, du Lyonnat

AVERAGE

de Barbe-Blanche, La Tour de Ségur, Bel-Air, Lucas, de Bellevue, La Tour de Grenet, de Tabuteau, des Vieux Chênes

My tastings have left me convinced that 5 estates in Lussac-St.-Emilion produce good, reliable, chunky, fruity wines of character. Cap de Merle gets my nod as the best performer in the 1981, 1982, and 1983 vintages, followed by a lighter but still pleasant Villadiére, a spicy, light-styled Carteyron, a fairly robust, well-proportioned Courlat, and a graceful, fruity, nicely made du Lyonnat.

The wines of Lussac-St.-Emilion should never cost more than 5 to 6 dollars a bottle and given the quality of the aforementioned estates, they represent good values.

MONTAGNE-ST.-EMILION

Not far from the *graves* section of northern St.-Emilion and Pomerol is the satellite commune of Montagne-St.-Emilion. There are a number of soundly made, round, rather straightforward wines here, but 3 properties stand out.

A CONSUMER'S CLASSIFICATION OF THE CHÂTEAUX OF MONTAGNE-ST.-EMILION

VERY GOOD

Roudier

GOOD

Maison Blanche, Vieux-Château-St.-André

AVERAGE

Calon, Chevalier St.-Georges, Bonneau, Beauséjour, Gilet, Montaiguillon, des Tours, Barraud, de Maison Neuve, Négrit

Roudier is owned by Jacques Capdemourlin, who also owns several Grands Crus Classés Châteaux in St.-Emilion. His style of wine is one that emphasizes richness, fullness, and a big, chewy texture. Roudier has all of these characteristics. While it may not compare favorably with his two St.-Emilion estates, Balestard-La-Tonnelle and Cap de Mourlin, Roudier is certainly the best Montagne-St.-Emilion. The 1982 and 1983 are particularly robust and flavorful wines. A 1964 tasted in spring 1985 was also marvelous and showed no signs of decay.

Maison Blanche also makes fine wine in Montagne-St.-Emilion, and I have immensely enjoyed that property's rather rich and flavorful 1979, 1981, and 1982.

Lastly, Vieux-Château-St. André should prove to be a property well worth keeping an eye on. Both the 1981 and 1982 were graceful, fruity, well-made wines, and the owner and winemaker here is none other than Jean-Claude Berrouet, the brilliant oneologist who vinifies the wine at the famous estates of Pétrus and Trotanoy in Pomerol.

CÔTES DE CASTILLON

Just to the east of Puisseguin-St.-Emilion is the appellation called Côtes de Castillon. These wines are very inexpensive and there are 3 estates here that produce deliciously round, fruity, medium-bodied, well-made wines.

A CONSUMER'S CLASSIFICATION OF THE CHÂTEAUX OF THE CÔTES DE CASTILLON

GOOD

de Pitray, La Terrasse, de Belcier

AVERAGE

Fontbaude, La Fourquerie, Lamour, Blanzac, Beynat, Moulin Rouge

Pitray, La Terrasse, and Belcier all produce well-colored, round, fruity wines that lack complexity, but offer good body, plenty of chunky fruit, and a clean, solid bouquet. They are all best drunk within the first 5–6 years of their lives, and they represent exceptional wine values since they are usually priced well under 5 dollars a bottle. The 1982s and 1983s of Pitray and La Terrasse are especially good wines.

ENTRE-DEUX-MERS

This vast wine-producing region which lies between the Dordogne and Garonne Rivers produces an ocean rather than a river of red and white wine. Most of it is fairly innocuous and bland, but some examples of Entre-Deux-Mers wine can be pleasant, agreeable, and refreshing. The white wines carry the appellation "Entre-Deux-Mers," and the red wines the appellation "Bordeaux" or "Bordeaux Supérieur."

It is impossible to provide any sort of classification of the properties here, but two estates have stood out in my tastings of the wines from this region. André Lurton's Bonnet produces soft and delicious red and white wines, and Rémy Greffier's Launay produces a fresh, crisp, very lovely dry white wine that can have an uncanny resemblance to a Médoc white Graves.

4: THE BORDEAUX WINE CLASSIFICATIONS

Bordeaux wines, in the minds of the wine trade and the wine consumer, are only as good as their official placement in one of the many classifications of wine quality. These classifications of wine quality have operated both for and against the consumer. Those few châteaux fortunate enough to "make the grade" have had guaranteed to them various degrees of celebrity status and respect. They have been able to set their price according to what their peers charged, and have largely been the only châteaux to be written about by wine writers. As this book demonstrates, these top châteaux have not always produced wine becoming of their status in the official French wine hierarchy. As for the other châteaux, many have produced excellent wine for years, but because they were not considered of classified growth quality in 1855, or 1955, or 1959 (the dates at which the major classifications of wine quality occurred), they have received significantly less money for their wines, and significantly less attention, particularly from writers.

Yet it is the excellent wine produced from some of these lesser-known châteaux that represents potential gustatory windfalls for the wine consumer.

THE 1855 CLASSIFICATION OF THE WINES OF THE MÉDOC

Of all the classifications of wine quality in Bordeaux, it is the 1855 classification of the wines of the Médoc that is by far the most important of these historical categorizations of Bordeaux wine quality. Among the thousands of châteaux in the Bordeaux region, 60 châteaux and wine-making estates in the Médoc and one in the Graves region were selected on the basis of their selling price and vineyard condition. Since 1855, only one change has occurred to the classification. In 1973, Château Mouton-Rothschild was elevated to first-growth status. The 1855 classification,[1] which established a five-tiered pyramid with originally 4 (now 5 as the result of the elevation of Mouton-Rothschild) First-Growths, 14 Second-Growths, 14 Third-Growths, 10 Fourth-Growths, and 18 Fifth-Growths, while being a good general guide to the quality of some of the best Bordeaux wines, has numerous deficiencies that are chronicled in detail throughout this book.

While the classification of the wines of the Médoc dealt with red-wine-producing estates, there was also a classification in 1855 of the estates in the Sauternes/Barsac region south of the city of Bordeaux that produce sweet, white wines.[2] One estate, Château d'Yquem, was rated first, followed by 18 other châteaux divided equally into two groupings, "Premiers Crus" and "Deuxièmes Crus."

The other classifications of Bordeaux wine quality are much more modern-day creations, yet are no more accurate or reliable than the 1855 classification. In 1959, the wines of the Graves region immediately south of the city of Bordeaux were classified.[3] Thirteen châteaux that

[1] See page 485: Bordeaux Wine: The Official Classification of 1855
[2] See page 487: Sauternes-Barsac: The Official Classification of 1855
[3] See page 487: Graves: 1959 Official Classification

produced red wine were given classified or "Cru Classé" status. Eight châteaux that produced white wine were classified. In 1955 the wines of St.-Emilion were classified into two categories, "Premiers Grands Crus Classés," or first great growths, and "Grands Crus Classés." This was followed by some corrections to the 1955 classification in 1959 and a revised classification in 1969.[4] The 1985 classification appears on pages 485–90.

Pomerol, the smallest of the major Bordeaux wine districts, just northwest of St.-Emilion, has never had a classification of the wine quality of its châteaux. The lack of any categorization of Pomerol's wines has certainly not deterred quality. The most expensive and sought-after wine of all Bordeaux is Pétrus, and it is a Pomerol. In addition to Pétrus, there are at least another dozen châteaux in this district that fetch prices for their wines that are equivalent to any one of the Médoc's famous second-growths.

There is still another classification of Bordeaux wines that merits significant attention. It is the classification of the so-called Crus Bourgeois of the Médoc. Pejoratively called "*petits châteaux*" by many, these numerous, small, moderate, and large-sized properties have never had the prestige or glory of the famous classified growths. Regardless of how high the quality of winemaking was, or how carefully the vineyards were managed and cared for, the Crus Bourgeois have for years been considered minor wines. In fact, many of them are, but there are increasing numbers of these châteaux that make wine on a very high level of excellence, comparable to a Médoc classified growth. Furthermore, they represent outstanding value and quality to knowledgeable wine consumers.

There were several unsuccessful attempts in the early half of the century to get an effective organization to promote the virtues of the Médoc's hundreds of lesser known châteaux. A classification was accomplished in 1932 that listed 444 Cru Bourgeois châteaux, broken down into three categories. There are 6 "Crus Bourgeois Superieurs Exceptionnels," 99 "Crus Bourgeois Superieurs," and 339 "Crus Bourgeois."

Over the following decades many of these vineyards were absorbed by adjacent properties or went out of the winemaking business. In an

[4] See page 488: St.-Emilion: 1955 Official Classification

effort to update this classification, new rankings were issued in 1966 by an organization of the Bourgeois châteaux called the Syndicate of Crus Bourgeois. The most recent result has been an updated list of 128 châteaux issued in 1978.[5] Eighteen châteaux were given "Crus Grands Bourgeois Exceptionnels" status, 41 are entitled to the title "Crus Grands Bourgeois" and 69 are designated as "Crus Bourgeois."

The selection process utilized by the Syndicate left open a number of questions regarding the overall validity of the 1978 classification. First, only members of the Syndicate were entitled to be recognized in the classification. For example, highly respected Cru Bourgeois châteaux such as de Pez in St.-Estèphe and Gloria in St.-Julien refused to join the Syndicate and are therefore excluded from its official rankings. In short, there is no question that while the current classification of the Crus Bourgeois is of some benefit, the exclusion of at least 10 well-known Crus Bourgeois producing top-quality wine, merely on the grounds that they refused to become members of the Syndicate, leaves a lot to be desired.

While Bordeaux has an elaborate "ranking" system for its multitude of wine-producing châteaux, it is true that many of the châteaux clearly merit their placement, but many don't. In addition, there are quite a few châteaux that have not been officially recognized at all but make very fine wine year in and year out.

These historic classifications of wine quality were employed both to promote Bordeaux wines and establish well-delineated quality bench-marks. The classification system was based on the vineyard's soil base and reputation. However, owners and winemakers change, and whereas some famous Bordeaux estates consistently make the best wine possible given the year's climatic conditions, others, because of negligence, incompetence, or just greed, produce mediocre and poor wine that hardly reflects their official pedigree.

The Bordeaux classifications are looked at in this book only from a consumer's or buyer's perspective. The quality of wine produced by a vineyard over the period 1961–1983 has been thoroughly examined. A qualitative analysis rather than historical analysis of each major and many serious lesser known estates has been conducted, focusing on (1) the style and overall quality of the wine, (2) the wine's relative quality and record of quality over the period 1961–1983, and (3) its relative value.

The judgments, the commentaries, and the evaluations of the wines

[5] See page 490: The Crus Bourgeois of the Médoc: The 1978 Syndicate's Classification

in this book are mine. They have been made on the basis of my extensive comparative tastings and numerous trips to Bordeaux since 1970. While no one will argue with the premise that the enjoyment of wine is strictly a personal and subjective matter, it is important to note that critical wine tasting at either the amateur or professional level without prejudice usually results in general agreement as to the greatest and worst wines. There are indeed quality benchmarks for Bordeaux wines, as there are for all the world's finest wines, and this book is intended to be a guide to those Bordeaux vineyards that establish the benchmarks not only for quality, but also value.

BORDEAUX WINE: THE OFFICIAL CLASSIFICATION OF 1855

FIRST-GROWTHS *(Premiers Crus)*

Château Lafite-Rothschild	*Pauillac*
Château Latour	*Pauillac*
Château Margaux	*Margaux*
Château Haut-Brion *	*Pessac, Graves*

SECOND-GROWTHS *(Deuxièmes Crus)*

Château Mouton-Rothschild **	*Pauillac*
Château Rausan-Ségla	*Margaux*
Château Rauzan-Gassies	*Margaux*
Château Léoville-Las Cases	*Saint-Julien*
Château Léoville-Poyferré	*Saint-Julien*
Château Léoville-Barton	*Saint-Julien*
Château Durfort-Vivens	*Margaux*
Château Lascombes	*Margaux*
Château Gruaud-Larose	*Saint-Julien*
Château Brane-Cantenac	*Cantenac-Margaux*
Château Pichon-Longueville Baron	*Pauillac*
Château Pichon Lalande	*Pauillac*
Château Ducru-Beaucaillou	*Saint-Julien*
Château Cos d'Estournel	*Saint-Estèphe*
Château Montrose	*Saint-Estèphe*

* This wine, although a Graves, was universally recognized and classified as one of the four First-Growths.

** This wine was decreed a First-Growth in 1973.

THIRD-GROWTHS *(Troisièmes Crus)*

Château Giscours	*Labarde-Margaux*
Château Kirwan	*Cantenac-Margaux*
Château d'Issan	*Cantenac-Margaux*
Château Lagrange	*Saint-Julien*
Château Langoa-Barton	*Saint-Julien*
Château Malescot Saint-Exupéry	*Margaux*
Château Cantenac-Brown	*Cantenac-Margaux*
Château Palmer	*Cantenac-Margaux*
Château La Lagune	*Ludon-Haut-Médoc*
Château Desmirail	*Margaux*
Château Calon-Ségur	*Saint-Estèphe*
Château Ferrière	*Margaux*
Château Marquis d'Alesme-Becker	*Margaux*
Château Boyd-Cantenac	*Cantenac-Margaux*

FOURTH-GROWTHS *(Quatrièmes Crus)*

Château St.-Pierre	*Saint-Julien*
Château Branaire	*Saint-Julien*
Château Talbot	*Saint-Julien*
Château Duhart-Milon	*Pauillac*
Château Pouget	*Cantenac-Margaux*
Château La Tour-Carnet	*Saint-Laurent-Haut-Médoc*
Château Lafon-Rochet	*Saint-Estèphe*
Château Beychevelle	*Saint-Julien*
Château Prieuré-Lichine	*Cantenac-Margaux*
Château Marquis-de-Terme	*Margaux*

FIFTH-GROWTHS *(Cinquièmes Crus)*

Château Pontet-Canet	*Pauillac*
Château Batailley	*Pauillac*
Château Grand-Puy-Lacoste	*Pauillac*
Château Grand-Puy-Ducasse	*Pauillac*
Château Haut-Batailley	*Pauillac*
Château Lynch-Bages	*Pauillac*
Château Lynch-Moussas	*Pauillac*
Château Dauzac	*Labarde-Margaux*
Château Mouton-Baronne-Philippe	*Pauillac*

Château du Tertre	*Arsac-Margaux*
Château Haut-Bages-Libéral	*Pauillac*
Château Pédesclaux	*Pauillac*
Château Belgrave	*Saint-Laurent-Haut-Médoc*
Château de Camensac	*Saint-Laurent-Haut-Médoc*
Château Cos Labory	*Saint-Estèphe*
Château Clerc-Milon-Rothschild	*Pauillac*
Château Croizet-Bages	*Pauillac*
Château Cantemerle	*Macau-Haut-Médoc*

SAUTERNES-BARSAC: THE OFFICIAL CLASSIFICATION OF 1855

FIRST GREAT GROWTH

Château d'Yquem

FIRST GROWTHS

Château Guiraud
Château La Tour-Blanche
Château Lafaurie-Peyraguey
Château de Rayne-Vigneau
Château Sigalas-Rabaud
Château Rabaud-Promis
Clos Haut-Peyraguey
Château Coutet
Château Climens
Château Suduiraut
Château Rieussec

SECOND-GROWTHS

Château d'Arche
Château Filhot
Château Lamothe
Château de Myrat*
Château Doisy-Védrines
Château Doisy-Daëne
Château Suau
Château Broustet
Château Caillou
Château Nairac
Château de Malle
Château Romer Du Hayot

GRAVES: 1959 OFFICIAL CLASSIFICATION

CLASSIFIED RED WINES OF GRAVES

Château Haut-Brion	*Pessac*
Château Bouscaut	*Cadaujac*
Château Carbonnieux	*Léognan*
Domaine de Chevalier	*Léognan*
Château de Fieuzal	*Léognan*
Château Haut-Bailly	*Léognan*

* No longer in existence.

Château La Mission-Haut-Brion	*Pessac*
Château La Tour-Haut-Brion	*Talence*
Château La Tour-Martillac	*Martillac*
Château Malartic-Lagravière	*Léognan*
Château Olivier	*Léognan*
Château Pape-Clément	*Pessac*
Château Smith-Haut-Lafitte	*Martillac*

CLASSIFIED WHITE WINES OF GRAVES

Château Bouscaut	*Cadaujac*
Château Carbonnieux	*Léognan*
Domaine de Chevalier	*Léognan*
Château Couhins	*Villenave-d'Ornon*
Château La Tour-Martillac	*Martillac*
Château Laville-Haut-Brion	*Talence*
Château Malartic-Lagravière	*Léognan*
Château Olivier	*Léognan*
Château Haut-Brion *	*Pessac*

ST.-EMILION: 1955 OFFICIAL CLASSIFICATION

FIRST GREAT GROWTHS *(Saint-Emilion—Premiers Grands Crus Classés)*

(A) Château Ausone
Château Cheval Blanc
(B) Château Beau Séjour-Bécot
Château Beauséjour-Duffau-Lagarrosse
Château Belair
Château Canon
Château Figeac
Clos Fourtet
Château La Gaffelière
Château Magdelaine
Château Pavie
Château Trottevieille

GREAT GROWTHS *(Saint-Emilion—Grands Crus Classés)*

Château l'Angélus
Château l'Arrosée
Château Baleau
Château Balestard-la-Tonnelle
Château Bellevue
Château Bergat
Château Cadet-Bon
Château Cadet-Piola
Château Canon-la-Gaffelière
Château Cap de Mourlin
Château Cap de Mourlin
Château Chapelle Madeleine
Château-le-Chatelet

* Added to the list in 1960.

Château Chauvin
Château Coutet
Château Couvent-des-Jacobins
Château Croque-Michotte
Château Curé-Bon
Château Dassault
Château Faurie-de-Souchard
Château Fonplégade
Château Fonroque
Château Franc-Mayne
Château Grand-Barrail-Lamarzelle-Figeac
Château Grand-Corbin
Château Grand Corbin-Despagne
Château Grand-Mayne
Château Grand-Pontet
Château Grandes-Murailles
Château Guadet-Saint-Julien
Château Haut-Corbin
Clos des Jacobins
Château Jean Faure
Château La Carte
Château La Clotte
Château La Cluzière
Château La Couspaude
Château La Dominique
Clos La Madeleine
Château La Marzelle
Château La Tour-Figeac
Château La Tour-du-Pin-Figeac
Château La Tour-du-Pin-Figeac
Château Laniotte
Château Chapelle-de-la-Trinité
Château Larcis-Ducasse
Château Larmande
Château Laroze
Château Lasserre
Château Le Couvent
Château Le Prieuré
Château Matras
Château Mauvezin
Château Moulin du Cadet
Château l'Oratoire
Château Pavie-Decesse
Château Pavie-Macquin
Château Pavillon-Cadet
Château Petit-Faurie-de-Souchard
Château Ripeau
Château Saint-Georges-Côte-Pavie
Clos Saint-Martin
Château Sansonnet
Château Soutard
Château Tertre-Daugay
Château Trimoulet
Château Trois-Moulins
Château Troplong-Mondot
Château Villemaurine
Château Yon-Figeac

ST.-EMILION: 1985 OFFICIAL CLASSIFICATION

PREMIERS GRANDS CRUS CLASSÉS

Ausone
Cheval Blanc
Beauséjour (Duffau-Lagarrosse)
Belair
Canon
Clos Fourtet
Figeac
La Gaffelière
Magdelaine
Pavie
Trottevieille

GRANDS CRUS CLASSÉS

L'Angélus
L'Arrosée
Balestard-La-Tonnelle
Beau Séjour
Bellevue
Bergat
Berliquet
Cadet-Piola
Canon-La-Gaffelière
Cap de Mourlin
Le Chatelet
Chauvin
Clos des Jacobins
Clos La Madeleine
Clos St.-Martin
La Clotte
La Clusière
Corbin
Corbin-Michotte
Couvent-des-Jacobins
Croque-Michotte
Curé-Bon
Dassault
La Dominique
Faurie-de-Souchard
Fonplégade
Fonroque
Franc-Mayne
Grand Barrail Lamarzelle Figeac
Grand Corbin Despagne
Grand Corbin
Grand Mayne
Grand Pontet
Guadet-St. Julien
Haut-Corbin
Haut-Sarpe
Laniote
Larcis-Ducasse
Lamarzelle
Larmande
Laroze
Matras
Mauvezin
Moulin-du-Cadet
L'Oratoire
Pavie-Decesse
Pavie-Macquin
Pavillon-Cadet
Petit-Faurie-de-Souchard
Le Prieuré
Ripeau
Sansonnet
St.-Georges-Côte-Pavie
La Serre
Soutard
Tertre-Daugay
La Tour-du-Pin-Figeac
La Tour-Figeac
Trimoulet
Troplong-Mondot
Villemaurine
Yon-Figeac

THE CRUS BOURGEOIS OF THE MÉDOC: THE 1978 SYNDICATE'S CLASSIFICATION

CRUS GRANDS BOURGEOIS EXCEPTIONNEL

d'Agassac (Ludon)
Andron-Blanquet (Saint-Estèphe)
Beau-Site (Saint-Estèphe)
Capbern Gasqueton (Saint-Estèphe)
Caronne-Sainte-Gemme (Saint-Laurent)

Chasse-Spleen (Moulis)
Cissac (Cissac)
Citran (Avensan)
Le Crock (Saint-Estèphe)
Dutruch-Grand-Poujeaux (Moulis)
Fourcas-Dupré (Listrac)
Fourcas-Hosten (Listrac)
Du Glana (Saint-Julien)
Haut-Marbuzet (Saint-Estèphe)
De Marbuzet (Saint-Estèphe)
Meyney (Saint-Estèphe)
Phélan-Ségur (Saint-Estèphe)
Poujeaux (Moulis)

CRUS GRANDS BOURGEOIS

Beaumont (Cussac)
Bel-Orme (Saint-Seurin-de-Cadourne)
Brillette (Moulis)
La Cardonne (Blaignan)
Colombier-Monpelou (Pauillac)
Coufran (Saint-Seurin-de-Cadourne)
Coutelin-Merville (Saint-Estèphe)
Duplessis-Hauchecorne (Moulis)
La Fleur Milon (Pauillac)
Fontesteau (Saint-Sauveur)
Greysac (Bégadan)
Hanteillan (Cissac)
Lafon (Listrac)
De Lamarque (Lamarque)
Lamothe-Cissac (Cissac)
Larose-Trintaudon (Saint-Laurent)
Laujac (Bégadan)
Liversan (Saint-Sauveur)
Loudenne (Saint-Yzans-de-Médoc)
Mac-Carthy (Saint-Estèphe)
De Malleret (Le Pian)
Martinens (Margaux)
Morin (Saint-Estèphe)
Moulin à Vent (Moulis)
Le Meynieu (Vertheuil)
Les Ormes de Pez (Saint-Estèphe)
Les Ormes Sorbet (Couquèques)
Patache d'Aux (Bégadan)
Paveil de Luze (Soussans)
Peyrabon (Saint-Sauveur)
Pontoise-Cabarrus (Saint-Seurin-de-Cadourne)
Potensac (Potensac)
Reysson (Vertheuil)
Ségur (Parempuyre)
Sigognac (Saint-Yzans-de-Médoc)
Sociando-Mallet (Saint-Seurin-de-Cadourne)
Du Taillan (Le Taillan)
La Tour de By (Bégandan)
La Tour du Haut-Moulin (Cussac)
Tronquoy-Lalande (Saint-Estèphe)
Verdignan (Saint-Seurin-de-Cadourne)

CRUS BOURGEOIS

Aney (Cussac)
Balac (Saint-Laurent)
La Bécade (Listrac)
Bellerive (Valeyrac)
Bellerose (Pauillac)
Les Bertins (Valeyrac)
Bonneau (Saint-Seurin-de-Cadourne)
Le Boscq (Saint-Christoly)
Du Breuilh (Cissac)

La Bridane (Saint-Julien)
De By (Bégadan)
Cailloux de By (Bégadan)
Cap Léon Veyrin (Listrac)
Carcanieux (Queyrac)
Castéra (Cissac)
Chambert (Saint-Estèphe)
La Clare (Saint-Estèphe)
Clarke (Listrac)
La Closerie (Moulis)
De Conques (Saint-Christoly)
Duplessis-Fabre (Moulis)
Fonpiqueyre (Saint-Sauveur)
Fonréaud (Listrac)
Fort Vauban (Cussac)
La France (Blaignan)
Gallais-Bellevue (Potensac)
Grand-Duroc-Moulin (Pauillac)
Grand-Moulin (Saint-Seurin-de-Cadourne)
Haut-Bages-Monpelou (Pauillac)
Haut-Canteloup (Couquèques)
Haut-Garin (Bégadan)
Haut-Padargnac (Pauillac)
Houbanon (Prignac)
Hourton-Ducasse (Saint-Sauveur)
De Labat (Saint-Laurent)
Lamothe-Bergeron (Cussac)
Le Landat (Cissac)
Landon (Bégadan)
Larivière (Blaignan)
Lartigue de Brochon (Saint-Seurin-de-Cadourne)
Lassalle (Potensac)
Lavalière (Saint-Christoly)
Lestage (Listrac)
Mac-Carthy-Moula (Saint-Estèphe)
Monthil (Bégadan)
Moulin de la Roque (Bégadan)
Moulin Rouge (Cussac)
Panigon (Civrac)
Pibran (Pauillac)
Plantey de la Croix (Saint-Seurin de-Cadourne)
Pontet (Blaignan)
Ramage-la-Batisse (Saint-Sauveur)
Romefort (Cussac)
La Roque de By (Bégadan)
De la Rose Maréchale (Saint-Seurin-de-Cadourne)
St.-Bonnet (Saint-Christoly)
St.-Roch (Saint Estéphe)
Saransot (Listrac)
Soudars (Avensac)
Tayac (Soussans)
La Tour Blanche (Saint-Christoly)
La Tour du Haut-Caussan (Blaignan)
La Tour du Mirail (Cissac)
La Tour Saint-Bonnet (Saint-Christoly)
La Tour Saint-Joseph (Cissac)
Des Tourelles (Blaignan)
Vernous (Lesparre)
Vieux-Robin (Bégadan)

WHO'S ON FIRST?

The 1855 classification of the wines of the Médoc and the subsequent classifications of the wines of Graves and St.-Emilion created a rigid hierarchy that, to this day, dictates how much a consumer must spend for a bottle of classified-growth Bordeaux. Ironically, these historic classifications, which were created in an attempt to classify the quality of Bordeaux wine, are of little relevance with respect to determining the quality of wine produced by a specific château. At most, these classifications should be regarded by both the wine connoisseur and novice as informational items of historical significance only.

The following is my classification of the top 103 wines of Bordeaux divided into the same five-tiered hierarchy that was used in 1855. It is based on the performance of these châteaux from 1961–1983. More weight has been given to the direction the property is heading and the quality of wine produced from 1975–1983 than what the property may have done in the 1961–1974 period. This is done simply because today is the golden age of Bordeaux. Bordeaux is prosperous, and more properties are making better wine with better facilities and advice than ever before.

There are 103 properties in my classification. Since I have included the wines of all the major appellations of Bordeaux, especially St.-Emilion, Pomerol, and Graves, that were excluded (except for Haut-Brion), the number of top classified growths is larger than the 61 that made the grade in 1855.

This classification is, of course, my own, but I can say that I have tasted all of these producers' wines from all of the significant vintages, not once, but numerous times. In addition, I have visited the great majority of these properties, and have studied their placement in this classification intensely. Nothing I have stated is arbitrary, but it is a personal judgment based on years of tasting and years of visiting Bordeaux. Furthermore, I think I can say it was done with no bias. Some of the proprietors with whom I have had some very difficult times over the years are included as first-growths. Some of the owners whom I personally like and respect have not done well. That is the risk, but in the end, I hope this consumer's look at the top estates in Bordeaux serves a constructive purpose for those properties who feel unfairly demoted, while I hope those that have won acclaim and recognition here will continue to do what it takes to make the best wine.

MY CLASSIFICATION OF THE TOP CHÂTEAUX OF BORDEAUX

FIRST-GROWTHS (15)
Ausone (St.-Emilion)
Cheval Blanc (St.-Emilion)
Ducru-Beaucaillou (St.-Julien)
Gruaud-Larose (St.-Julien)
Haut-Brion (Graves)
Lafite-Rothschild (Pauillac)
Latour (Pauillac)
Léoville-Las Cases (St.-Julien)
Margaux (Margaux)
La Mission-Haut-Brion (Graves)
Mouton-Rothschild (Pauillac)
Palmer (Margaux)
Pétrus (Pomerol)
Pichon Lalande (Pauillac)
Trotanoy (Pomerol)

SECOND-GROWTHS (15)
Canon (St.-Emilion)
Certan de May (Pomerol)
La Conseillante (Pomerol)
Cos d'Estournel (St.-Estèphe)
Branaire-Ducru (St.-Julien)
L'Evangile (Pomerol)
Figeac (St.-Emilion)
Giscours (Margaux)
Lafleur (Pomerol)
La Lagune (Ludon)
Latour à Pomerol (Pomerol)
Léoville-Barton (St.-Julien)
Lynch-Bages (Pauillac)
Magdelaine (St.-Emilion)
Montrose (St.-Estèphe)

THIRD-GROWTHS (11)
Beychevelle (St.-Julien)
Boyd-Cantenac (Margaux)
Cantemerle (Macau)
Domaine de Chevalier (Graves)
Grand-Puy-Lacoste (Pauillac)
d'Issan (Margaux)
Lafleur-Pétrus (Pomerol)
Langoa-Barton (St.-Julien)
La Tour-Haut-Brion (Graves)
Talbot (St.-Julien)
Vieux Château Certan (Pomerol)

FOURTH-GROWTHS (10)
L'Arrosée (St.-Emilion)
Calon-Ségur (St.-Estèphe)
La Dominique (St.-Emilion)
Gloria (St.-Julien)
Haut-Bailly (Graves)
Lascombes (Margaux)
Léoville-Poyferré (St.-Julien)
de Pez (St.-Estèphe)
Prieuré-Lichine (Margaux)
St.-Pierre (St.-Julien)

FIFTH-GROWTHS (52)
Batailley (Pauillac)
Belair (St.-Emilion)
Bon Pasteur (Pomerol)
Brane-Cantenac (Margaux)
Brillette (Moulis)
Cadet-Piola (St.-Emilion)
Camensac (Haut-Médoc)
Cantenac-Brown (Margaux)
Certan-Giraud (Pomerol)
Chasse-Spleen (Moulis)
Clerc-Milon-Rothschild (Pauillac)
Clos des Jacobins (St.-Emilion)
Clos-René (Pomerol)
Duhart-Milon-Rothschild
Durfort-Vivens (Margaux)
L'Eglise Clinet (Pomerol)
L'Enclos (Pomerol)
Fonbadet (Pauillac)
Les Forts de Latour (Pauillac)
Fourcas-Hosten (Listrac)
Le Gay (Pomerol)
Grand-Puy-Ducasse (Pauillac)
La Grave Trigant de Boisset (Pomerol)
Kirwan (Margaux)
Haut-Bages-Libéral (Pauillac)
Haut-Batailley (Pauillac)
Lafon-Rochet (St.-Estèphe)
Haut-Marbuzet (St.-Estèphe)
Lanessan (Haut-Médoc)
La Louvière (Graves)
Malescot St.-Exupéry (Margaux)
Maucaillou (Moulis)
Meyney (St.-Estèphe)
Mouton-Baronne-Philippe (Pauillac)
Les Ormes-de-Pez (St.-Estèphe)
Pape-Clément (Graves)
Pavie (St.-Emilion)
Pavillion Rouge de Margaux
Petit-Village (Pomerol)
Pichon Baron Longueville
Le Pin (Pomerol)
Pontet-Canet (Pauillac)
Potensac (Médoc)
Poujeaux (Moulis)
Pouget (Margaux)
Rausan Ségla
Rauzan-Gassies (Margaux)
Rouget (Pomerol)
de Sales (Pomerol)
Sociando-Mallet (Haut-Médoc)
Soutard (St.-Emilion)
du Tertre (Margaux)

THE SECONDARY LABELS OF THE MAJOR BORDEAUX CHÂTEAUX

Many châteaux, particularly in the Médoc, bottle part of their production under a secondary label. Sometimes this wine can share many of the same characteristics as the "grand vin" that is bottled under the château's own name. These wines normally sell for one-half the price of the primary label. The wine in the bottle usually represents wine from younger vines and lots that were just not considered good enough to merit the château's own label. In particular, these first-growths that have second labels make excellent wine under these names. Certainly Les Forts de Latour and Pavillon Rouge de Château Margaux are as good as most classified growths. Among the other châteaux, some of the better *deuxièmes vins* are Marbuzet, Reserve de la Comtesse, La Croix, and Clos du Marquis.

FIRST-GROWTHS

Haut-Brion—Bahans-Haut-Brion
Lafite-Rothschild—Moulin des Carruades
Latour—Les Forts de Latour
Margaux—Pavillon Rouge de Château Margaux

SECOND-GROWTHS

Brane-Cantenac—Domaine de Fontarney and Notton
Cos d'Estournel—de Marbuzet
Ducru-Beaucaillou—La Croix
Duforts-Vivens—Domaine de Curé Bourse
Gruaud-Larose—Sarget de Gruaud-Larose
Lascombes—La Gombaude
Léoville-Las Cases—Clos du Marquis
Léoville-Poyferré—Moulin-Riche
Pichon Lalande—Reserve de la Comtesse
Montrose—Demereaulemont

FOURTH-GROWTHS

Duhart-Milon—Moulin de Duhart
Prieuré-Lichine—de Clairfont
Talbot—Connétable Talbot
La Tour-Carnet—Sire de Camin

FIFTH-GROWTHS

Grand-Puy-Lacoste—Lacoste-Borie
Haut-Batailley—La Tour L'Aspic
Lynch-Bages—Haut-Bages-Averous

5: THE ELEMENTS FOR MAKING GREAT BORDEAUX WINE

Traditionalists often wax poetically about "the good ole days" and that "they just don't make Bordeaux the way they used to." In fact, for Bordeaux wines, times have never been better, both climatically and financially. Moreover, the quality of winemaking in Bordeaux has never been higher. The greatest wines ever made in Bordeaux are those that are produced today.

The most prominent factor about the best red and white wines of Bordeaux is their remarkable longevity. In great years, the aging potential of these wines is unequaled by any other table wines produced in the world. Even in lesser vintages, the wines often need a good 5–8 years to develop fully. The reasons? In order of importance: the grape varieties, the soil, the climate, and the methods of winemaking that are discussed in the sections that follow.

BORDEAUX GRAPES FOR RED WINE

For red wines there are three major grape varieties planted and two minor varieties that have largely now fallen out of favor. The choice of grape varieties used for making Bordeaux wine has a profound influence on the style of wine that is ultimately produced. Hundreds of years of practice have allowed specific winemaking châteaux to select only the grape varieties that do best on their soil.

For red wines in the Médoc, if one were to give an average formula for a percentage of grapes planted at a majority of the Médoc châteaux, it would be 60% to 65% Cabernet Sauvignon, 10% to 15% Cabernet Franc, 20% to 25% Merlot and 3% to 8% Petit Verdot. Each château has its own best formula for planting its vineyards, some preferring to use more Merlot, some, more Cabernet Sauvignon or Cabernet Franc, and some, more Petit Verdot. However, the two most important grapes for a highly successful vintage in the Médoc are Cabernet Sauvignon and Merlot. The Cabernet is more widely planted in the Médoc simply because it ripens well and flourishes in the gravelly, well-drained soil that exists in the top vineyards there. The Merlot is popular because, when blended with the tannic, tough, deeply colored Cabernet Sauvignon, it offers softness, flesh, and suppleness to balance out the rougher texture of the Cabernet Sauvignon. If a château uses a high percentage of Cabernet Sauvignon in its blend, in all likelihood the wine will be densely colored, big, full-bodied, tannic, and very ageworthy. On the other hand, if a high percentage of Merlot is used in the blend, then in most cases suppleness and precocious charm are the preferred personality traits. In the Médoc, Cabernet Franc is also used in small percentages. Cabernet Franc lacks the color of Cabernet Sauvignon and Merlot, but does offer complex, aromatic components that the Bordelais call finesse. The Petit Verdot is planted in very small percentages because it ripens very late and in most vintages rarely achieves full maturity. It is however, often used by those châteaux who often use a high percentage of Merlot. The Petit Verdot provides the hard, tannic backbone to those wines that would otherwise be soft as a result of a high concentration of Merlot.

Each of these four major red grape varieties ripens at a different time. The Merlot is always the first grape to blossom and to become fully mature. Cabernet Franc is second, followed by Cabernet Sauvignon and Petit Verdot. Few wine consumers realize that spring frost and varying weather patterns at different times during the growing season can seriously affect some of these grape varieties, while sparing others. The production from the Merlot grape, because of its early ripening characteristic, is frequently curtailed by spring frost. In addition, Merlot is the grape most susceptible to rot from moist or damp weather conditions since its skin is less tough and less resistant to disease than that of the Cabernet Sauvignon or Petit Verdot. This fact alone can be critical for the success of châteaux with extensive Merlot plantations, as late-season rains have on more than one occasion washed out the late-picking properties with vineyards dominated by Cabernet Sauvignon, while the vineyards of Merlot plantings have already been harvested under optimum conditions. When one asks why the Merlot-based wines, such as Pétrus and Trotanoy, were so successful in 1964 as compared to the disappointing Cabernet Sauvignon–based wines, such as Mouton-Rothschild and Lafite-Rothschild, the answer is because the Merlot crop was harvested in perfect weather conditions long before the Cabernet crop, which was drenched and diluted by torrential rains.

On the right bank of the Gironde River are the two principal appellations of St.-Emilion and Pomerol. Here, significantly higher percentages of the Merlot grape and Cabernet Franc grape are planted. Much of the soil of these two appellations is less well drained and frequently heavier because of a significant clay content. The Cabernet Sauvignon is not fond of such soils and accordingly smaller amounts of it are planted, unless the vineyard is situated on a particularly well-drained, gravelly soil base, as a few are in these two appellations. The Merlot takes well to this type of heavy clay soil and surprisingly so does the Cabernet Franc. There are many exceptions, but in St.-Emilion the standard formula for grape varieties is close to 50% Merlot and 50% Cabernet Franc with Cabernet Sauvignon mixed in various percentages. In Pomerol, Merlot is clearly the key. Except for a handful of estates, such as Clos L'Eglise and Vieux Château Certan, little Cabernet Sauvignon is planted. The average vineyard's composition in Pomerol would be 70% to 80% Merlot and the balance, Cabernet Franc.

Consequently, it is not surprising to find wines from these two regions maturing faster and being generally fruitier, more supple, and fatter than those of the Médoc.

In the Graves region, the soil is extremely gravelly as the name implies, thereby affording excellent drainage. As in the Médoc, the Cabernet Sauvignon is favored, but one sees more Cabernet Franc and Merlot in Graves, with wines that are usually lighter as a result. However, in rainy years, the Graves wines often turn out better than all the others simply because of the outstanding drainage the vineyards have in this region. The 1974 vintage is a classic case in point.

The advantage of knowing such things about the percentage of grape varieties planted at a particular château is that one can predict with some degree of certainty which areas may have performed better than others before even the critics begin issuing their tasting judgments. This can be done simply by knowing the climatic conditions leading up to and during the harvest and matching those conditions against how the different grape varieties perform under such conditions.

Rarely does Bordeaux have a perfect vintage for all four red-wine grape varieties. Over recent vintages, the Merlot crop was devastated in 1984 by a poor flowering, but the Cabernet Sauvignon crop was harvested and ripened under healthy conditions. Not surprisingly, the 1984 is considered a Médoc year. In 1983 and 1982, all the grape varieties ripened superbly, although in 1982 the Merlot and Petit Verdot were said to have been perfect, wherein in 1983 it was the Cabernet Sauvignon that growers raved about.

CABERNET SAUVIGNON—A grape that is highly pigmented, very astringent and tannic that provides the framework, strength, dark color, character, and longevity for the wines in a majority of the vineyards in the Médoc. It ripens late, is resistant to rot because of its thick skin, and has a pronounced blackcurrant aroma which is sometimes intermingled with subtle herbaceous scents that take on the smell of cedarwood with aging. Virtually all Bordeaux châteaux blend Cabernet Sauvignon with other red grape varieties. In the Médoc, the average percentage of Cabernet Sauvignon in the blend ranges from 40% to 85%, in Graves, 40% to 60%, in St.-Emilion 10% to 50%, and in Pomerol, 0% to 20%.

Examples of wines with very high percentages of Cabernet Sauvignon: Latour Pauillac (80%), Haut-Bages-Libéral Pauillac (78%), Mouton-Rothschild Pauillac (85%), du Tertre Margaux (80%), and d'Issan Margaux (80%).

MERLOT—Utilized by virtually every château in Bordeaux because of its ability to provide a round, generous, fleshy, supple alcoholic wine, Merlot ripens, on an average, one to two weeks earlier than Cabernet Sauvignon. In the Médoc, this grape reaches its zenith in several Médoc châteaux that use high percentages of it (Palmer and Pichon Lalande), but its fame is in the wines it renders in Pomerol where it is used profusely. In the Médoc, the average percentage of Merlot in the blend ranges from 5% to 45%. In Graves, it ranges from 20% to 40%, in St.-Emilion, 25% to 60%, and in Pomerol, 35% to 98%. Merlot produces wines lower in acidity and tannin than Cabernet Sauvignon, and, as a general rule, wines with a high percentage of Merlot mature faster than wines with a high percentage of Cabernet Sauvignon.

Examples of wines with very high percentages of Merlot are Pétrus Pomerol (95%), Trotanoy Pomerol (85%), Latour à Pomerol Pomerol (80%), L'Enclos Pomerol (80%), Coufran Médoc (85%).

CABERNET FRANC—A relative of Cabernet Sauvignon that ripens slightly earlier, Cabernet Franc, (called Bouchet in St.-Emilion and Pomerol), is used in small to modest proportions to add complexity and bouquet to a wine. Cabernet Franc has a pungent, often very spicy, sometimes weedy, olive-like aroma. It does not have the fleshy, supple character of Merlot, nor the astringence, power, and color of Cabernet Sauvignon. In the Médoc, an average percentage of Cabernet Franc used in the blend is 0–30%, in Graves, 5–25%, in St.-Emilion, 25–66%, in Pomerol, 5–50%.

Examples of wines with a very high percentage of Cabernet Franc: Cheval Blanc St.-Emilion (66%), Lafleur Pomerol (50%), La Conseillante Pomerol (45%), Ausone St.-Emilion (50%).

PETIT VERDOT—A useful, but generally difficult red grape because of its very late ripening characteristics, Petit Verdot provides intense color, mouth-gripping tannins, and high sugar and thus high alcohol when it ripens fully, as it did in 1982 and 1983 in Bordeaux. When unripe, it provides a nasty, sharp, acidic character. In the Médoc, few châteaux use more than 5% in the blend. In Graves, St.-Emilion, and Pomerol, very little Petit Verdot now exists.

Examples of wines with a very high percentage of Petit Verdot: Pichon Lalande Pauillac (8%), Langoa-Barton St.-Julien (8%), Léoville-Barton St.-Julien (8%), Marquis d'Alesme Margaux (13%), Palmer Margaux (10%).

MALBEC—The least-utilized red grape (also called Pressac in St.-Emilion and Pomerol) of the major varietals, Malbec has fallen into disfavor and in most vineyards has now been replanted with one of the more favored grapes. Its future in Bordeaux's best vineyards seems doubtful.

Examples of wines with a high percentage of Malbec: Pichon Baron Longueville Pauillac (2%), Lafon Rochet St.-Estèphe (2%), La Tour-Martillac Graves (4%).

BORDEAUX GRAPES FOR WHITE WINE

Bordeaux produces both dry and sweet white wine. There are usually only three grape varieties used, Sauvignon Blanc and Semillon for both dry and sweet wine, and Muscadelle, which is used sparingly for the sweet wines.

SAUVIGNON BLANC—Used for making both the dry white wines of Graves and the sweet white wines of the Barsac/Sauternes region, Sauvignon Blanc renders a very distinctive wine with a pungent, somewhat herbaceous aroma, and crisp, austere flavors. Among the dry white Graves, a few châteaux employ 100% Sauvignon Blanc, but most blend it with Semillon. Less Sauvignon Blanc is used in the winemaking blends in the Sauternes region than in Graves.

Examples of dry Graves with a high percentage of Sauvignon Blanc: Smith-Haut-Lafitte (100%), Malartic-Lagravière (100%), La Louvière (85%), Domaine de Chevalier (70%).

Examples of sweet Sauternes with a high percentage of Sauvignon Blanc: Guiraud (45%), Filhot (32%), Romer du Hayot (30%), Sigalas Rabaud (25%).

SEMILLON—Very susceptible to the famous noble rot called botrytis which is essential to the production of excellent, sweet wines, Semillon is used to provide a rich, creamy, intense texture to both the dry wines of Graves and the rich, sweet wines of Sauternes. Semillon is quite fruity when young, and wines with a high percentage of Semillon seem to take on weight and viscosity as they age. For these reasons, higher percentages of Semillon are used in making the sweet wines of the Sauternes/Barsac region than in producing the white wines of Graves.

Examples of dry Graves wines with a high percentage of Semillon: Laville-Haut-Brion (60%), de Fieuzal (40%), Haut-Brion (50%), Olivier (65%).

MUSCADELLE—The rarest of the white wine grapes planted in Bordeaux, Muscadelle is a very fragile grape that is quite susceptible to disease, but when healthy and mature, produces a wine with an intense flowery, perfumed character. It is used only in tiny proportions by châteaux in the Sauternes/Barsac region. It is not used at all by the white wine producers of Graves.

Examples of sweet Sauternes wines with a high percentage of Muscadelle: Broustet (12%), Coutet (5%), Rayne-Vigneau (5%).

SOIL

It is not unusual to hear Bordeaux's best winemakers say that the "wine is made in the vineyard," not the winery. It is interesting to compare the traditional attitude in California where the primary considerations for making quality wine have been the region's climatic profile, the expertise of the winemaker, and the availability of high technology to sculpture the wine. While a growing number of California wineries are beginning to pay greater attention to soil, few Bordelais will argue with the premise that the greatness of their wine is a result of the soil, or "*terroir*," and not the winemaker or vinification equipment.

The famous Médoc area of Bordeaux is a triangular land mass, bordered on the west by the Atlantic Ocean, on the east by the wide

Gironde River, and on the south by the city of Bordeaux. The top vineyards of the Médoc stretch out on the eastern half of this generally flat land on slightly elevated slopes facing the Gironde River. The soil is largely unfit for any type of agriculture other than grape growing. It is extremely gravelly and sandy, and the subsoil of the Médoc ranges from heavy clay soil (producing heavier, less fine wines) to lighter chalk and gravels (producing finer, lighter wines).

In the Graves region south of the city of Bordeaux, the name of the region no doubt reflects the very rocky soil, which is even more deeply embedded with gravel than in the Médoc. This contributes to the unique flavor that some commentators have suggested is a mineral-like, earthy taste in the wines of this region. The regions of St.-Emilion and Pomerol are situated 20 miles to the east of the city of Bordeaux. St.-Emilion has two distinctive soil bases. Around the charming and medieval city of St.-Emilion are the châteaux which are said to sit on the "*côtes*" or hillsides. These hillsides were once the sides of a river valley, and the soil is primarily chalk, clay, and limestone. Some of the famous châteaux that sit on the *côtes* of St.-Emilion include Ausone, Canon, Pavie, and Belair. Several miles to the northwest of St.-Emilion is the "*graves*" section of St.-Emilion, a gravelly, sandy outcropping bordering the Pomerol appellation. The St.-Emilion châteaux located in this *graves* area produce a different style of wine, more fleshy, more fruity, more accessible than the austere, tannic, and reserved wines produced from vineyards on the limestone, chalk, and clay hillsides of the town of St.-Emilion. Two of the best-known châteaux in the area of St.-Emilion are Cheval Blanc and Figeac. Of course, exceptions in style within each sub-region exist, but in broad terms, there are two distinct types of St.-Emilion wines, a *graves* style and a *côtes* style, and the style is a direct result of the soil base the vines are planted in.

In Pomerol, which borders the *graves* section of St.-Emilion, the soil composition is quite similar, yet variations exist. Pomerol's most famous estate, Pétrus, sits on an elevated plateau which has a unique, rather heavy clay soil unlike any other vineyard in Pomerol. It is this fact alone at Pétrus that is credited for producing Bordeaux's most massive, concentrated, and rich wine.

The very gravelly soil that is the predominate geological character of the Bordeaux vineyards operates as an excellent drainage system, as well as being permeable enough for the vines' roots to penetrate deep into the subsoil for nutrients, water, and minerals.

The subtle differences in soil composition and their effect on the style and personality of the wine are best exemplified by three examples of adjoining vineyards. On the border of the Médoc communes of Pauillac and St.-Julien, three highly respected properties, the first-growth Latour, the second-growth St.-Julien, Léoville-Las Cases, and the second-growth Pauillac, Pichon Baron, sit together with each one's vineyard contiguous to the other. The yield from the vineyards, the percentage of each vine planted, the method of making the wine, the average age of the vines, the types of grape varieties, and finally, the time the wine spends aging in the cask is not dramatically different for all three châteaux. However, all three wines are totally different in taste, style, texture, and in their evolution. All three have totally different soil bases. The main vineyards of Léoville-Las Cases are planted in very gravelly soil atop a sandstone subsoil, Latour's vineyards are composed of very deep gravel beds, and Pichon Baron's vineyards are significantly less gravelly, with a much higher proportion of clay in the soil.

In Pomerol, one has only to compare the vineyard of that appellation's most famous wine, Pétrus, which is planted in heavy clay soil rich in iron, with the soil of its immediate neighbor, La Fleur Pétrus, which has little clay, but much more sand and gravel. Both wines could not, despite almost exactly the same vinifications by the same people, be more different.

Soil is undoubtedly a very important factor in the character and diverse style of Bordeaux wines. It is not, in my opinion, as the Bordelais would have one believe, the only element necessary to make a great wine. The importance of a hospitable climate, conservative viticultural practices whereby the use of fertilizers is kept to a minimum, aggressive pruning procedures, and of course, the careful vinification and handling of the wine are all significant factors in the making of great wine. Even with the finest technology, a great winemaking team, and the best, well-drained, gravelly soil, great wine can not be made without a cooperative climate that produces fully mature ripe grapes.

CLIMATE

The great vintages of Bordeaux have always been characterized by growing seasons that have been abnormally hot, dry, and sunny. The excellent and great vintages of Bordeaux such as 1921, 1929, 1945, 1947, 1949, 1959, 1961, 1970, and 1982 have all shared several distinctive climatic characteristics—heat, sunshine, and drought-like conditions. Several prominent Bordeaux château proprietors, who have recently claimed that disastrous vintages such as 1968, 1965 and 1963 will never occur again because of the technological winemaking advances, seem to forget that good wine cannot be made from unripe, vegetal-tasting grapes. Bordeaux, like any major viticultural area, must have plenty of sunshine, dry weather, and heat in order to produce excellent wine.

When the Bordeaux châteaux have to wait until October to harvest their grapes rather than September, it is usually a sign that the growing season has been abnormally cool and even worse, wet. A review of the greatest vintages in Bordeaux reveals that the commencement date of the harvest almost always occurs in September.

1921—September 15
1929—September 26
1945—September 13
1947—September 19
1949—September 27
1953—October 1
1959—September 20
1961—September 22
1970—September 27
1975—September 22
1978—October 7
1982—September 13
1983—September 26

In comparison, here are the commencement dates of the harvests for some of Bordeaux's most notoriously bad vintages:

1951—October 9
1954—October 10
1956—October 14
1957—October 4
1963—October 7
1965—October 2
1968—September 20
1972—October 7

The pattern would appear to be obvious. Great years are characterized by plentiful amounts of sunshine, heat, and dry weather. Under such conditions the grapes ripen steadily and quickly, and the harvests begin early. Poor years are a result of inadequate supplies of these precious natural commodities. The grapes never ripen fully and are picked in either an unripe or a rain-diluted condition.

There are several notable exceptions to the climatic patterns for excellent and poor vintages. Nineteen fifty-three was a moderately late harvest (October 1) that produced excellent red wines. More recently, 1978 (October 7) and 1979 (October 3) were all late-October harvest years that produced very good to excellent wines. These successful late harvests in Bordeaux in recent years have been a result of beneficial "Indian summer" weather conditions and a growing tendency by Bordelais to attempt to obtain what they call *surmaturité*. The old rule that governed the harvest in Bordeaux was the so-called 100-day rule which dictated harvesting the grapes 100 days after the flowering. Now, in an effort to make wines full-bodied, richer, and lower in acidity, the 100-day custom has grown to 110 or even 120 days. This new trend in Bordeaux may well result in many more excellent October harvests, such as 1978 and 1979, than in the past when an October harvest often meant poor quality.

The climatic patterns leading to excellent vintages for red wines in Bordeaux have no application to the production of the sweet white wines made in the Sauternes/Barsac regions. Great vintages in this region require a combination of misty, humid mornings and dry, sunny afternoons. This daily pattern of climatic events enables the noble rot (botrytis) to begin to develop on the grapes. It is interesting that each grape succumbs to the botrytis infection on a different timetable. Some grapes quickly become totally infected, others not until weeks later. The key to the great, luscious, sweet wines of this area is an extended period of alternating humidity and dry heat that permits the botrytis infections to take place. During this period, the château must harvest the infected grapes by hand numerous times if the highest quality is to be achieved, for it is the botrytis infection that causes the remaining grape juice to be intensely concentrated, and imparts to it the distinctive smell and flavor of a late harvest, decadently rich, sweet wine. Of course, the harvest for the sweet wines of Barsac/Sauternes almost always takes place long after the red wine grapes have been picked and made into wine in the Médoc, Graves, St.-Emilion and Pomerol. It also occurs when Bordeaux's weather becomes the most risky, late October and November.

A week or more of a deluge can destroy the chances for a successful crop in Sauternes and Barsac. More often than not, the grape crop is damaged by late season rains that wash the noble rot from the grapes, and also cause other grapes to swell, thus diminishing their intensity. In the last 14 years, only 1971, 1975, 1976 and 1983 have been uniformly excellent growing seasons for the sweet wine producers of this region.

THE VINIFICATION AND ÉLEVAGE OF BORDEAUX WINES

The production of red wine is the process in which the freshly harvested grapes are crushed and then processed into wine. The steps are as follows: (1) picking, (2) destemming and crushing, (3) pumping into fermentation tanks, (4) fermenting of grape sugar into alcohol, (5) macerating or keeping the grape skins and pips in contact with the grape juice for additional extract and color, (6) racking or transferring the wine to small 55-gallon barrels or large tanks for the secondary or malolactic fermentation to be completed, (7) putting the wine in oak barrels for aging, and (8) bottling the wine.

In Bordeaux, the average harvest takes three weeks or more to complete for the dry white and red wines. For the sweet wines, the harvest can take as long as two months to complete. The white wine grapes used for making the dry wines ripen earliest and are picked first. This is followed by the red grape Merlot, and then the other red grape varieties, Cabernet Franc, Cabernet Sauvignon, and lastly, Petit Verdot. The fact that the Merlot ripens earliest makes it an interesting fact to monitor. In 1964 and 1967, the châteaux that had extensive plantings of Merlot, primarily those in St.-Emilion and Pomerol, harvested early and their vineyards produced much better wines than the châteaux in the Médoc who had to wait for their Cabernet to ripen and were caught by fall rains. In such a year when significant rains damage the overall crop quality, the early pickers, normally the right-bank communes of St.-Emilion and Pomerol, will have completed most of their harvest. As vintages such as 1964 and 1967 attest, they may have succeeded brilliantly whereas their counterparts in the Médoc have had to deal with bloated, rain-swollen Cabernet Sauvignon grapes and, therefore, mediocre or poor quality wine.

MAKING THE RED WINE

When the grapes arrive, few châteaux today employ the traditional and laborious hand sorting of the grapes prior to their entrance into the destemmer-crusher machine. One major château that continues to adhere to this procedure is Palmer, a third-growth Margaux. Palmer feels hand sorting is mandatory if top-quality wines are to be made.

Most châteaux claim to get the best results by instructing their pickers to remove and discard damaged or unhealthy grape bunches in the vineyard. Certainly the need for careful picking of grapes exists every year, but in vintages where there has been extensive rot in the vineyards, the most reputable châteaux have the pickers make a very severe selection (called a *triage*) in which the damaged berries are removed from each bunch at the time of picking.

The first decision the winemaker must make is whether the grapes are to be partially destemmed or totally destemmed. Today the great majority of the châteaux destem completely. This policy is in keeping with Bordeaux's current passion to make rich, supple wines that can be drunk young but will age. Several notable châteaux continue to throw a percentage of stems into the fermentation tank with the crushed grapes. Both Pétrus, which uses between 10% and 30% stems, and Ausone, which uses 20% stems, believe that adding them produces a tougher wine that will age better and longer.

The opponents of adding the stems argue that they add a vegetal coarseness to a wine, soak up some of the color-giving material, and can add too much tannin to the wine.

Once the grapes have been destemmed by an apparatus the French call a *fouloir égrappoir*, the partially crushed berries are pumped into tanks for the commencement of the fermentation.

Today, the trend in Bordeaux is to replace the large, old, oak and cement fermentation vats with stainless steel temperature-controlled tanks. They are especially easy to clean and easy to control the temperature, an element that is especially important when the grapes are harvested in torridly hot conditions as in 1982. Despite the increasing numbers of properties that have converted to stainless steel tanks, the traditional large oak *cuves* and concrete *cuves* are still the most widely used.

Of the most famous Bordeaux properties, Latour, Haut-Brion, and Ausone use stainless steel, Lafite, Mouton, and Margaux use oak, and Cheval Blanc and Pétrus use cement. While stainless steel may be easier to use, great vinyards managed by meticulous winemakers have proved that great wine can be made in either oak, cement, or steel fermentation tanks.

Once the grapes have been put into the vat, the wild yeasts that inhabit the vineyard, and in many cases additional cultured yeasts, begin the process called fermentation—the conversion of the grape sugars into alcohol. At this critical point, the temperature of the fermenting juice must be monitored with extreme care, and how hot or how cold the fermentation is does indeed affect the resulting style of the wine. Most Bordeaux winemakers ferment a red wine at 25° to 30° C. Few châteaux allow the temperature to exceed 30° C. Several of those that do include Pétrus, Mouton-Rothschild, Domaine de Chevalier, and Haut-Brion. These properties allow the fermentation to go up to 32°–33° C. The higher temperatures are aimed at extracting as much color and tannins as possible from the grape skins. The risk of a temperature in excess of 35° C is that acetic bacteria will grow and flourish. It is these acetic bacteria that cause a wine to take on a flawed, vinegary smell. An additional danger at fermentation temperatures in excess of 35° C is that the natural yeasts will be destroyed by the heat, and the fermentation will stop completely, causing what is referred to as a "stuck fermentation." As a general rule, the châteaux that ferment at high temperatures are normally aiming for high-extract, rich and tannic wines. Those châteaux that ferment at cooler temperatures, of 25° C or less, usually are trying to achieve a lighter, fruitier, less tannic style of wine. However, for châteaux that ferment at high temperatures, constant vigilance is mandatory. Fermentation tanks must be watched 24 hours a day, and if a dangerously high temperature is reached, the grape juice must be cooled immediately. With stainless steel tanks, this can be done rather simply by running cool water over the outside of the tanks. For concrete and wooden tanks, the wine must be siphoned off and run through cooling tubes.

During the vinification, a cap or "*chapeau*" is formed, as a result of the solid materials, grape skins, stems, and pips rising to the top of the fermentation tank. Winemakers must be careful to keep the cap moist, even submerged in some cases, to encourage additional extractive material to be removed from the color- and tannin-giving skins. Additionally, the cap must be kept wet so as to prevent bacterial growth. The pumping of the fermented wine juice over the cap is called the "*remontage*" in French and "pumping over the cap" in English.

When the fermentation begins, the winemaker must make another critical decision that will influence the style of the wine. To chaptalize or not? Chaptalization is the addition of sugar to increase the alcohol content. It is employed widely in Bordeaux because this region rarely has a vintage where perfect grape ripeness and maturity are obtained. In most years, the grapes do not have sufficient natural sugar contents to produce wines with 12% alcohol. Therefore, the Bordeaux châteaux aim to increase the alcohol content by 1–2 degrees. Only in years such as 1961, 1970, 1982, and 1983 has little or no chaptalization been necessary because of the superb ripeness achieved by the grapes in these years.

After the total grape sugar (and added sugar if necessary) has been converted to alcohol, the primary or alcoholic fermentation is completed. It is at this stage that one of the most important winemaking decisions must be made. The winemaker must decide how long to macerate the grape skins with the wine which has just been made. The length of the maceration period has a direct bearing on whether the wine will be rich, well colored, tannic, and long-lived, or supple, precocious, and ready to drink soon. At most major Bordeaux châteaux the maceration period is 7 to 14 days, making the average total time the wine spends in contact with the skins about 21 days. This period is called the *cuvaison.*

Well-known châteaux that adhere to a particularly long *cuvaison* of more than 20–21 days include Pétrus, Trotanoy, Cos d'Estournel, Montrose, Branaire, Lafite-Rothschild, Léoville-Barton, and Palmer.

Well-known châteaux that adhere to a particularly short *cuvaison* of less than 15 days include Figeac, Rauzan-Gassies, and Prieuré-Lichine. Following the *cuvaison,* the new infant wine is transferred off its lees, which are composed of the grape skins and pips, called the "*marc,*" into clean tanks or wood barrels. This free-run juice is called the "*vin de goutte.*" The skins are then pressed and the resulting press wine, or "*vin de presse,*" is a heavily pigmented, tannic, chewy, coarse wine that will, in many instances, be eventually blended back into the free-run wine juice. Some winemakers, not wanting a firm, tannic wine, refuse to use any press wine in the blend. Others, who want to add a little muscle and firmness to their wines, will add 10–20%. Some winemakers desirous of a robustly styled, intense wine will blend it all back in with the free-run *vin de goutte*. In most cases, the decision to utilize the press wine is conditioned on the type of wine the vintage produced. In a year such as 1975 or 1982, the addition of press wine would, in most cases, make the wine too tannic and robust. In light vintages where the quality of the free-run juice lacks strength, firmness and color, for example 1973 and 1980, more of the highly pigmented, tannic press wine will be used.

The secondary fermentation, or malolactic fermentation, in which the tart malic acidity is converted into softer, creamier, lactic acidity, is the next step in the evolution of the young red wine. In some châteaux, the malolactic fermentation occurs simultaneously with the alcoholic fermentation, but at most properties the malolactic takes place over a period of months, usually October following the harvest through the end of January. In certain years, the malolactic may continue through spring and summer following the vintage, but this is quite unusual. Malolactic fermentation is especially critical for red wines because it adds roundness and character.

The use of new versus old oak barrels for wine aging has been hotly debated in winemaking circles. In Bordeaux, the famous first-growths, Lafite-Rothschild, Mouton-Rothschild, Latour, Margaux, and Haut-Brion, and the famous trio from the right-bank communes of St.-Emilion and Pomerol, Cheval Blanc, Ausone, and Pétrus, use 100% new oak barrels for virtually every vintage. For the other well-run châteaux, 20% to 33% new oak barrels per vintage seems to produce a comfortable marriage of fruit, tannin, and oak. Unquestionably, the higher the percentage of new oak barrels used, the richer the wine has to be not to be overwhelmed by the oaky, vanillin aromas and flavors. For example, many of the wines from the 1973 and 1980 vintages that produced light yet fruity wines were simply not big enough or rich enough wines to handle aging in the new oak barrels they received. New barrels impart a significant tannin content, as well as vanillin oakiness to a wine, and therefore they must be used judiciously. One of the side effects of Bordeaux's modern-day prosperity from the success of recent vintages is the tremendous investment in new winery equipment, and, in particular, new barrels. Overuse of new oak can obliterate the fruit of a wine, and while the huge massive fruit and concentration of wines from a vintage like 1982 can easily handle the exposure to plenty of new oak, my tastings of the more delicate, less intense and concentrated 1981s have frequently left me wondering whether too much new oak cooperage was doing more harm than good.

One of the remarkable aspects of a red Bordeaux wine is its long sojourn in small oak barrels. In most vintages, this period of aging will take from 12 months to as long as 24 to 30 months. This period of barrel aging has been shortened noticeably over the last several decades. Bordeaux winemakers have tried to capture more fruit and freshness in their wines, and to reduce the risk of oxidation or overly woody, dry, tannic wines from too much exposure to wood. The great majority of Bordeaux châteaux now bottle their wine in late spring and early summer of the second year after the harvest. For example, the 1980 and 1981 Bordeaux wines were bottled from May through July in 1982 and 1983 respectively. It is rare for a châteaux to bottle in late fall or the following winter, as was the practice 20 years ago. Several prominent châteaux that do bottle later than the others include Lafite-Rothschild, Latour, Pétrus, and Calon-Ségur, all of whom rarely bottle unless the wine has had at least 24 months in small oak casks.

The period of cask aging will be shorter in vintages like 1981, 1979, or 1976 where the wines lack great concentration and depth of character, and will be longer in years such as 1975, 1982, and 1983 where the wines are very full, rich, highly pigmented, and concentrated. The principle is simple; lighter, frailer wines can easily be overwhelmed by oak aging, whereas robust, virile, rich wines need and can take significantly more exposure to oak casks. However, there is no question that the practical and commercial realities of the Bordeaux wine business now dictate that the wine will be bottled within two years of the harvest in all but the most unusual circumstances.

During the aging period in oak barrels, the new wine is racked four times the first year. Racking is an essential step necessary for clarifying the wine. This process involves transferring the clear wine off its deposit or "lees" that have precipitated to the bottom of the barrel. If racking is not done promptly or carefully, the wine will take on a smell of rotten eggs as a result of hydrogen sulfide emissions that come off the lees. The rackings are an intensely laborious process, but the French theory is that it is these lees, or solids that float in the wines and which eventually fall to the bottom of the barrel, that are the substance and material that give Bordeaux wines their remarkable aromatic and flavor complexity.

One of the most significant new technological developments in this area, and one used now by at least two major châteaux in Bordeaux,

Cos d'Estournel in St.-Estèphe and de Fieuzal in Graves, is the filtration of the new wine prior to its placement in barrels. This process, employed widely in California, removes the solids from the wine and results in a clearer wine that needs to be racked significantly less—only one time the first year. The proponents of this process such as Cos d'Estournel's proprietor, Bruno Prats, argue that they get a cleaner, purer wine that does not have to be handled as much, and therefore is less prone to oxidation. Critics of such a procedure argue that the process strips the wine of its solids and therefore deprives the wine of the important elements necessary for the wine to achieve complex aromas and flavors. The critics claim that such a procedure is only a labor-saving procedure. Since Cos d'Estournel makes superb wine, the effectiveness of the procedure will be left to time to determine.

While the red wine rests in barrels, all châteaux carry out another procedure designed to ensure that the wine is brilliant, clean, and free of hazy, suspended colloidal matter when bottled. It is called fining. Fining, which has traditionally been done with egg whites that function to attract and trap suspended solids in the barrel of wine and then drop to the bottom of the barrel with the other solids that have been precipitated, must be done carefully. Wines that are overly fined lose body, length, concentration, and character. Today, fining is often done immediately prior to bottling, in large tanks. Additionally, many châteaux have abandoned the traditional egg whites in favor of more efficacious substances like bentonite and gelatin. In Bordeaux, rarely is a wine fined more than twice for fear of removing too much flavor at the expense of absolute clarity.

In addition to the careful vinification and handling of the young red wine, one of the common characteristics at the best-run châteaux in Bordeaux is an extremely rigid selection process for determining which wine will be bottled under the château's name, and which wine will be bottled under a secondary label, or sold in bulk to a cooperative or broker in Bordeaux. The best châteaux make their first selection in the vineyard. For example, the wine from young vines (normally those under 7 or 8 years old) is vinified separately from the wine from old vines. The difference to even a neophyte taster between wine produced from 25-year-old vines and a wine from 5-year-old vines is remarkable. Young vines may produce a well-colored wine, but the wine rarely has the depth or rich concentrated character of a wine from older vines. For that reason, the top châteaux never blend in wine from the younger section of the vineyard with the wine from the older vines.

There are a number of châteaux that refuse to discriminate between old and new vines, and the quality of their wines frequently suffers as a result.

In addition to the selection process in the vineyard, the best châteaux also make a strict selection of the finished wine, normally in January or February following the vintage. At this time, the winemaking staff, together with the consulting oenologist, and in many cases the owner, will taste all the different lots of wine produced in the vintage, and then decide which lots or *cuvées* will go into the château's wine, and which lots will be bottled under a secondary label, or sold off in bulk. This procedure is also accompanied by the *assemblage*, wherein the best lots of wine are blended together, including the blending of the different red grape varieties, Merlot, Cabernet Sauvignon, Cabernet Franc, and Petit Verdot. It is no coincidence that the châteaux that make the most severe selections frequently produce the best wines of Bordeaux. Virtually all châteaux make their *assemblage* in January or February following the vintage, but two major châteaux, Palmer and Cheval Blanc, wait until early spring, preferring to evaluate a more evolved wine.

Unless there is something unusual that occurs in the barrel (a dirty barrel that causes bacterial spoilage is the most common problem) during the aging process, called *élevage*, the wine will be transferred from the barrel to the fermentation tanks, given its last fining, and then bottled at the château.

The idea of bottling the wine at the château (it is designated on the label with the words "*mise en bouteille au château*") is a rather recent development. Until the 1960s, many of the Bordeaux châteaux routinely sent barrels of their wine to brokers in Bordeaux, and merchants in Belgium or England where the wine would be bottled. Such a practice was fraught with the potential for not only fraud, but for sloppy handling of the wine as a result of poor, unsanitary bottling facilities.

Now, the châteaux all have modern bottling facilities, and all the classified growths, as well as the great majority of Crus Bourgeois, bottle their own wine. The bottling of the château's entire production in a given vintage can take from one month to almost three months at the largest properties. Yet one of the distinctive characteristics of Bordeaux wine is that each château's production for a given year is bottled within this time frame. This guarantees to the consumer that, given the same treatment and cellar storage, the wine should be relatively consistent from bottle to bottle.

At the time of the bottling operation, the winemaker has one last decision to make that will influence the style (and perhaps the quality) of the wine. More and more châteaux have begun to purchase German-made, sophisticated micropore filter machines to run their wine through to remove any solids or other colloidal particles that may have escaped the various racking procedures and finings. Some châteaux believe that filtration is essential for a healthy, clean bottle of wine, whereas others claim that it is totally unnecessary, and robs and strips the wine of body, flavor, and potential life.

Who is right? There is ample authority to support both sides in the filtration versus non-filtration argument. Certainly, the current fear on the part of retailers, restaurateurs, wholesalers, importers, and the wine producers themselves that wine consumers think that sediment in a wine is a sign of a flawed wine has tragically caused many châteaux to overreact and run their wines through very fine, tight micropore filters that undoubtedly eviscerate the wine. Fortunately, the major châteaux have been content to do just a slight, coarse polishing filtration, aimed at removing large colloidal suspensions, or have simply refused to filter the wine at all, hoping the fickle consumer will learn one day that a sediment, or "*dépôt*" as the French say, is in reality one of the healthiest signs in an older bottle of Bordeaux.

Prominent châteaux that adamantly refuse to conduct any type of filtration on their wine include Palmer, Margaux, Latour, Pichon Lalande, Mouton, Montrose, Ducru-Beaucaillou, Grand-Puy-Lacoste, Léoville-Barton, La Lagune, La Mission-Haut-Brion (prior to the 1983 vintage), Pétrus, Trotanoy, Ausone, Lynch-Bages, Canon, Pavie, and Magdelaine.

Prominent châteaux that run the wine through a filtration machine prior to bottling include Haut-Brion, Domaine de Chevalier, Cos d'Estournel, Lafite-Rothschild, Gruaud-Larose, Talbot, Branaire, Cheval Blanc, Figeac, Giscours, Brane-Cantenac, Léoville-Poyferré, and Trottevieille.

Since filtration of wine is a relatively recent trend in oenology, and since most of the châteaux in both groupings above make excellent wine, only time in the bottle will tell whether filtration robs a wine of richness, complexity, and life as its opponents argue.

Once the wine is bottled, the châteaux usually refuse to release the wine for shipment until it has rested for 2 to 4 months. The theory is that the bottling operation churns up the wine so much that the wine is shocked, and requires at least several months to recover. My tastings of immediately bottled Bordeaux have often corroborated this fact.

MAKING THE WHITE WINE

There are significant differences in the making of red Bordeaux and white Bordeaux. Like the best white wines made throughout the world, the winemaker must emphasize crispness and freshness in white winemaking, or the wine will taste stale or heavy.

In the Graves region, the dry white wines are fermented at temperatures of 18°–20° C, which is much cooler than those utilized for the red wines. Most of the Graves châteaux ferment the wine in tanks, although a few properties continue to ferment the wine in oak casks. The finished wine is normally bottled in the spring following the vintage. Some châteaux age the wine in oak casks, while others ferment and age the wine completely in tanks, with the wine seeing no oak aging whatsoever.

Prominent producers of dry white Graves that oak age their white wines are Haut-Brion, Laville-Haut-Brion, Malartic-Lagravìere, Domaine de Chevalier, and Carbonnieux.

Prominent producers of dry white Graves that tank age their white wines are La Tour-Martillac, and Couhins-Lurton.

With regard to the sweet wines of Barsac and Sauternes, the harvesting of this grape has already been explained. The vinification of these wines is not unlike that for the white Graves. The wines are fermented at low temperatures of 18°–20° C, but unlike the dry white wines of Graves, most of the major châteaux of Barsac/Sauternes ferment in oak casks and age the wine in oak barrels from one to as long as three and a half years in the case of properties like Yquem and de Fargues.

6: A USER'S GUIDE TO BORDEAUX: CELLARING AND SERVING

Bordeaux, like any fine wine, has to be stored properly if it is to be served in a healthy condition when mature. All wine enthusiasts know that subterranean wine cellars that are vibration free, dark, damp, and kept at a constant 55° F are considered perfect for wine. However, few of us have our own castle with such accommodations for our beloved wines. While such conditions are the ideal, Bordeaux wines will thrive and develop well in other conditions, too. I have tasted many old Bordeaux wines from closet and basement cellars that reach 65°–70° F in the summer, and the wines have been perfect. In cellaring Bordeaux keep the following rules in mind and you are not likely to be disappointed with a wine that has gone prematurely over the hill.

RULE 1

Do try to guarantee that the wine is kept as cool as possible. The upper safe limit for long-term cellaring of 10 years or more is

68°–70° F, but no higher. Wines kept at such temperatures will age a bit faster but they will not age badly. If you can somehow get the temperature down to 65° F or below, you will never have to worry about the condition of your wines. At 55° F, the ideal temperature, the wines actually evolve so slowly that your grandchildren will probably benefit from the wines more than you. As for temperature, constancy is highly prized and any changes in temperature should occur slowly. As for white wines, they are much more sensitive to less than ideal cellar temperatures. Therefore, while the dry white wines of Bordeaux should be kept at temperatures as close to 55° F as possible, the bigger, more alcoholic, sweet white wines of Barsac and Sauternes can age quite well at cellar temperatures up to 65°–68° F.

RULE 2

Be sure the storage area is odor free, vibration free, and dark. A humidity level of 50% to 80% is ideal. Above 80% is fine for the wine, but the labels will become moldy and deteriorate. A humidity level below 50% can cause the corks to become very dry, and be potentially life-threatening to your wines.

RULE 3

Bordeaux wines from vintages that produced powerful, rich, concentrated, full-bodied wines travel and age significantly better than wines from vintages that produced lightweight wines. For example, the oceanic voyage for Bordeaux can be traumatic for wines from vintages such as 1971, 1976, 1977, and 1980. The wines from these vintages, less concentrated, less tannic, and more fragile, often suffer considerably more from travel to this country than big, rich, tannic, full-bodied wines such as 1970, 1975, 1978, 1982, and 1983. When you decide which Bordeaux wines to cellar, keep in mind that the fragile wines will develop much faster under ideal storage conditions.

RULE 4

When buying new vintages of Bordeaux to cellar, I personally recommend buying the wine as soon as it appears on the market, assuming of course you have tasted the wine and like it. The reason for this is that few wine merchants, importers, wholesalers, or distributors care about how wine is stored. This attitude, that wine is just another spirit and that like whiskey or beer can be left standing upright, exposed to dramatic extremes of temperature, as well as to damaging light, is fortunately changing as more knowledgeable wine people assume positions of control in major wineshops. However, far too many fine wines are damaged early in their life by terrible storage conditions, so the only way a wine enthusiast can prevent such tragedies from happening is to assume custody and control over the wine as early in its life as possible. This means acting early to secure your wines.

There are no secrets or formalities to serving Bordeaux. All one needs is a good corkscrew, a clean, odor-free decanter, and a sense of order as to how Bordeaux wines should be served and whether the wine should breathe.

Bordeaux wines do throw a sediment, particularly after they have attained 6 or 7 years of age. This mandates decantation—the procedure where the wine is poured into a clean decanter to separate the brilliant wine from the dusty particles that have precipitated to the bottom of the bottle. First, older bottles of Bordeaux should be removed carefully from storage so as not to disturb them and make the wine cloudy. Decanting can be an elaborate procedure, but all one needs is a clean, soap- and odor-free decanter and a steady hand. If you lack a steady hand, consider buying a decanting machine, which is a wonderful, albeit expensive invention for making decanting fun, easy, and highly effective. Most important of all, be sure to rinse the decanter with unchlorinated well or mineral water regardless of how clean you think it is. A decanter or wine glass left sitting in a china closet or cupboard acts as a wonderful trap for room and kitchen odors that are invisible, but rear their off-putting smells when the wine is poured into the decanter or glass. In addition, many glasses have an invisible soapy residue left in them from less than perfect dishwasher rinses and maids. I can't begin to tell you how many dinner parties I have attended where the wonderful, cedary, blackcurrant bouquet of a 15- or 20-year-old Pauillac was flawed by the smell of dishwater detergents or some stale kitchen smell that accumulated in the glass between uses.

Assuming you have decanted the wine into a clean decanter, you should also consider the temperature at which the wine should be served, whether you should allow the wine to breathe, and if you are serving several Bordeaux wines, the order of presentation.

The breathing or airing of a Bordeaux wine is rather controversial. Some connoisseurs adamantly claim that breathing is essential, while others claim it is simply all nonsense. Who is right? I have done numerous comparisons with wines to see if breathing works or doesn't. I still don't know the answers, if in fact they indeed exist, but here are my observations. The art of decanting a Bordeaux wine is probably all the pre-serving breathing most wines need. I have found that when serving young, muscular, rich, tannic vintages of Bordeaux, 20–90 minutes of breathing can sometimes result in a softer wine. However, the immediate gush of intense fruitiness that often spills forth when the wine is opened and decanted does subside a bit. So for the big, rich wines of Bordeaux, breathing is often a trade-off—you get some softening of the wine, but you also lose some of the wine's fruity aromas. With lighter weight, less tannic Bordeaux wines I have found extended breathing to be detrimental to their enjoyment. Such wines are more fragile and often less endowed, and prolonged breathing tends to cause them to fade. With respect to older vintages of Bordeaux, decanting only 15–20 minutes is usually all that is necessary. With lightweight, older vintages and very, very old vintages, I recommend opening the wine, decanting it, and serving it immediately. Once an old wine begins to fade it can never be resuscitated.

There are always exceptions to such rules and I can easily think of 1945s and even a few 1961s that seemed at their peak 4–5 hours after decantation rather than the 20–25 minutes that I have suggested here. However, it is always better to err on the side of needing more time to breathe and let the guest swirl and aerate the wine in the glass, than to wait too long and then serve a wine that was magnificently scented when opened and decanted but has lapsed into a comatose state by the time it is served.

The serving temperature of wine is also a critical aspect of serving Bordeaux. I am always surprised how many times I am given a great Bordeaux wine that is too warm. Every wine book talks about serving fine red wines at room temperature. In America's overly warm and generously heated dining rooms, room temperature is often 75°–80° F, a temperature that no fine red Bordeaux cares for. A Bordeaux served at such a temperature will often taste flat and flabby, and its bouquet will be diffuse and unfocused. The alcohol content will also seem higher than it should be. The ideal temperature for red Bordeaux is 67°–68° F, and for a white Bordeaux, 55°–60° F. If your best wines cannot be served at this temperature, then you are doing them a great injustice. If a red Bordeaux must be put in an ice bucket for 10 minutes to lower its temperature, then do it. I have often requested on a hot summer day in Bordeaux or the Rhône Valley that my Pomerol or Châteauneuf du Pape be chilled for 10 minutes rather than drink it at a temperature of 80° F.

Lastly, the effective presentation of Bordeaux wines at a dinner party will necessitate a sense of order. The rules here are easy to follow. Lighter weight Bordeaux wines or wines from light vintages should always precede richer, fuller wines from great vintages. If such an order is not followed, the lighter, more delicate wines will taste pale after a rich, full-bodied wine has been served. For example, to serve a delicate 1979 Margaux like d'Issan after a 1975 Lynch-Bages or 1979 Pétrus would be patently unfair to the d'Issan. Another guideline is to serve the wines in order from youngest to oldest. This should not be blindly applied, but younger, more astringent wines should precede older, more mellow, mature wines.

A PERSONAL BORDEAUX WINE COLLECTION FOR £1,000, £2,000, AND £4,000

The following Bordeaux wines are personal choices representing outstanding quality for the price. The wines and prices are based on December 1985 prices and availability, which as you know are subject to change. At the conclusion is a list of the Bordeaux wines that I personally consider the best value for your money in 1986.

A £1,000 BORDEAUX WINE COLLECTION

(9 cases and 8 bottles of wine)

DRY RED WINE

For optimum drinking between 1986–1992

1983 La Tonnelle (12)	£48
1982 Tayac (12)	£45
1982 La Louvière (12)	£72

For optimum drinking between 1990–2000

1982 Clos des Jacobins (6)	£85
1982 La Dominique (6)	£72
1982 L'Arrosée (6)	£72

1982 La Tour de By (6) £25

1982 Potensac (6) £32
1983 La Grave-Figeac (6) £42
1982 Haut-Bages-Libéral (6) £46
1982 Pichon Lalande (12) £212
1982 Léoville-Barton (12) £142

DRY WHITE GRAVES
1985 Pontac-Monplaisir (6) £17

A SWEET SAUTERNES
1983 Bastor-Lamontagne (6) £30

TWO SPECIAL-EVENT WINES FOR THE YEAR 2000
1982 L'Evangile (1) £30
1982 Latour à Pomerol (1) £30

A £2,000 BORDEAUX WINE COLLECTION
(14 cases and 4 bottles)

For optimum drinking between 1986–1992
1979 Pichon Lalande (6) £64
1979 Gruaud-Larose (6) £52
1980 Giscours (6) £40
1980 Léoville-Barton (6) £40
1980 Pichon Lalande (6) £43

For optimum drinking between 1990–2010
1982 Cos d'Estournel (12) £214
1982 Calon-Ségur (12) £178
1982 Canon (12) £192
1982 Branaire-Ducru (12) £142
1982 Léoville-Barton (12) £142
1982 Pavie (6) £90
1982 Petit-Village (12) £160
1983 Cantemerle (12) £142
1983 d'Angludet (12) £60
1983 d'Issan (12) £90
1983 Prieuré-Lichine (12) £90

A DRY WHITE GRAVES
1983 La Louvière (6) £44

A SWEET SAUTERNES
1983 Rieussec (8) £120

TWO SPECIAL-EVENT WINES FOR THE YEAR 2000

1982 Certan de May (1) £40
1982 Margaux (1) £42

A £4,000 BORDEAUX WINE COLLECTION

(16 cases of wine)

For optimum drinking between 1986–1992

1976 Branaire-Ducru (6)	£44
1976 Haut-Bages-Libéral (6)	£42
1983 Haut-Marbuzet (6)	£54
1979 Haut-Bailly (6)	£42
1979 Talbot (6)	£44
1976 La Lagune (6)	£52
1982 de Sales (12)	£86

For optimum drinking between 2000–2020

1982 Margaux (12)	£600
1982 Cheval Blanc (12)	£650
1982 Haut-Brion (12)	£580
1982 Latour (6)	£358

For optimum drinking between 1990–2005

1976 Lafite-Rothschild (6)	£285
1980 Margaux (6)	£108
1981 Pichon Lalande (6)	£176
1979 Giscours (12)	£114
1979 du Tertre (12)	£114
1982 Léoville-Barton (12)	£142
1982 Léoville-Poyferré (12)	£158
1979 Trotanoy (12)	£232
1979 Palmer (12)	£215

A DRY WHITE GRAVES

1983 Domaine de Chevalier (6) £108

A SWEET SAUTERNES

1980 or 1981 de Fargues (12) £250

When only a high quality/value relationship is considered, the following are the wines for you.

BORDEAUX'S TOP WINE VALUES

St.-Estèphe
Haut-Marbuzet
Meyney
de Pez
Marbuzet

Pauillac
Haut-Batailley
Fonbadet
Haut-Bages-Libéral

St.-Julien
Branaire-Ducru
Gruaud-Larose
Talbot
Léoville-Barton
Hortevie
St.-Pierre
Clos du Marquis

Margaux
du Tertre
d'Angludet
d'Issan

Médoc & Haut-Médoc
Chasse-Spleen
Sociando-Mallet
Potensac
Lanessan
La Rose-Trintaudon
La Tour St.-Bonnet

Lalande-de-Pomerol
Belle Graves
Grand Ormeau
Clos des Templiers

Graves
Haut-Bailly
La Louvière
Pique-Caillou
Cheret-Pitres

Sauternes/Barsac
Bastor Lamontagne
Doisy-Daëne

Pomerol
de Sales
L'Enclos
Rouget

St.-Emilion
La Dominique
L'Arrosée
Clos des Jacobins
Balestard-La-Tonnelle
Cadet-Piola
La Grave-Figeac

Côtes de Bourg
Tayac
La Grolet

Côtes de Blaye
La Tonnelle
Haut-Sociando

Fronsac & Canon-Fronsac
Canon

Premières Côtes de Bordeaux
Pitray

BUYING BORDEAUX WINE FUTURES: THE PITFALLS AND PLEASURES

The purchase of wine, already fraught with plenty of pitfalls for the consumer, becomes immensely more complex and risky when one enters the wine futures' sweepstakes.

On the surface, buying wine futures is nothing more than investing money in a case or cases of wine at a predetermined future price long before the wine is bottled and shipped. You invest your money in wine futures on the assumption that the wine will appreciate significantly in price between the time you purchase the future and the time the wine has been bottled and imported to England. Purchasing the right wine, from the right vintage, in the right international financial climate, can represent significant savings. On the other hand, it can be quite disappointing to invest heavily in a wine future only to witness the wine's arrival 18 to 24 months later at a price equal to or below the future price and to discover the wine to be inferior in quality as well.

For years, future offerings have been largely limited to Bordeaux wines, although they are seen occasionally from other regions. In Bordeaux, during the spring following the harvest, the estates or châteaux offer for sale a portion of their crops. The first offering, or *première tranche*, usually offers a good indication of the trade's enthusiasm for the new wine, the prevailing market conditions, and the ultimate price the public will have to spend.

Those brokers and *négociants* who take an early position on a vintage frequently offer portions of their purchases to retailers to make available publicly as a "wine future." These offerings are usually made to the retail shopper in the first spring, summer or autumn immediately following the vintage. For example, the highly regarded 1985 Bordeaux vintage was offered as wine futures to the consumer in spring 1986. Purchasing wine at this time is not without risks. Wine in its infancy is difficult to evaluate, and goes through so many different stages of development that extreme care must be exercised by professional tasters to get a broad and accurate view of the vintage quality. When wine futures are offered for sale, there is generally little independent consumer information available to prospective buyers. While retailers unabashedly declare any future offering as an opportunity to purchase "great wine from a great vintage," only a handful of serious merchants ever take the trouble to visit Bordeaux to sample the new wine. Most perfer to rely on the heavy propaganda issued by the Bordeaux wine trade at this time to convince their clients to buy wine futures.

In short, the consumer must satisfactorily resolve several issues prior to making a commitment to purchase a wine future.

Is the financial climate such that the wine will be at least 15 to 30 percent more expensive when it arrives on the market in 18 to 24 months? If no, then you are better off investing your money elsewhere.

In the particular vintage that is being offered as "futures," which areas and specific châteaux produced the finest wines? This information can only be obtained by consulting reliable, independent sources who have sampled a broad range of wines from the different regions and have a proven track record for reliability in assessing young Bordeaux vintages.

Recent history regarding purchasers of Bordeaux futures has revealed a number of interesting trends. First, anyone who purchased the "blue chip" Bordeaux wines in a good vintage at their opening price levels in the spring following the vintage has seen the prices for these wines appreciate significantly in value. The blue chips of Bordeaux include the famous "Big 8" châteaux which are Haut-Brion in Graves, Marguax in Margaux, Lafite-Rothschild, Mouton Rothschild and Latour in Pauillac, Pétrus in Pomerol, and Chevel Blanc and Ausone in St. Emilion. Over the last decade, investing in these wines in such outstanding vintages as 1982, 1978, and 1975 has proved to be a fabulous wine investment. Even in the good to very good vintages such as 1983, 1981, 1979, and 1976, these wines have represented attractive buys as wine futures. Of course, in poor or mediocre vintages such as 1977, 1980, and 1984, they would not have merited buying as a wine future.

These eight châteaux are not the only blue chip Bordeaux wines to look for as wine futures. There is a group of wines that are collectively referred to as "super seconds." Some are in fact second growths in the famous 1855 Classification of the Wines of the Médoc. However, others are unclassified Pomerols, or wines that are of such outstanding quality that collectors the world over seek them out because of their high quality level. In reality, many of these blue chip wines are as good as the first growths but sell for significantly less money. These super seconds include La Mission-Haut-Brion in Graves, La Lagune in Ludon, Palmer in Margaux, Ducru-Beaucaillou, Léoville Las Cases, Léoville Poyferré, Gruaud-Larose and Beychevelle in St. Julien, Pichon Lalande, Lynch-Bages and Grand-Puy-Lacoste in Pauillac, Cos D'Estournel in St. Estèphe, Trotanoy, Lafleur, Latour à Pomerol, L'Evangile, La Conseillante in Pomerol, and Canon, Figeac and Magdelaine in St. Emilion. In summary, these are the twenty-eight blue chip Bordeaux wines that are consistently among the very finest wines produced year in and year out and merit significant interest as wine futures. From their opening for *première tranche* prices, these wines in the top vintages usually escalate significantly in cost, sometimes coming on the market at two, even three times the price they sold for as wine futures. The key factor is simply the quality of the vintage. The greater the vintage, the greater the interest in and demand for these wines will be, and in turn, this causes the prices to escalate as demand escalates. No vintage in recent decades has illustrated this point more so than the 1982 Bordeaux vintage, a classic case of the wisdom of buying the top Bordeaux wines as early as possible.

As for the 1982s, they have jumped in price at an unbelievable pace, outdistancing the appreciation in value of any previous Bordeaux vintage. The first growths of 1982 were offered to consumers in late Spring, 1983 at prices of £300 to £350 for wines like Lafite-Rothschild, Latour, Mouton-Rothschild, Haut-Brion, and Cheval Blanc. By autumn, 1985, the Chevel Blanc had jumped to £400–£600, the Mouton to £700–£900, and the rest to £650–£700. This is a significant price increase for wines so young, but it reflects the insatiable world wide demand for a great vintage of Bordeaux. Rare, limited production wines like the Pomerols have skyrocketed in price. Pétrus has clearly been the top performer in terms of increasing in price; it jumped from an April, 1983 future price of £450 per case to an autumn 1985 price of £2,500. This is absurd given the fact that this particular wine won't be close to maturity until the year 2000. Other top 1982 Pomerols such as Trotanoy, Certan de May, and L'Evangile have doubled and tripled in price.

The huge demand for 1982 Bordeaux futures and tremendous publicity surrounding this vintage led many to assume that 1983 Bordeaux wine futures would do a repeat performance. To think so is to ignore the lessons of vintages such as 1978, 1979, and 1981. Nineteen eighty-three is a very good Bordeaux vintage. For some wines, a tiny minority in reality, it is a great vintage. Of the hundreds of Bordeaux châteaux offered by merchants as wine futures, only around three dozen wines were worth buying on a future basis.

In determining whether to buy Bordeaux futures or not, you should carefully consider the following points.

1. Are you buying potentially excellent or great wines in an outstanding vintage of Bordeaux? The greater the vintage, the greater your chances of making a smart purchase will be. The crop size of the vintage is also an important consideration. However, the huge crop of 1982 did little to keep prices stable.
2. Are you going to save money? You should consider the current international monetary situation. Is the pound getting stronger or weaker? What is the direction of the French franc? What kind of return could your money fetch if it were invested in a bank's interest bearing account rather than in Bordeaux futures?
3. If you have a fondness for the wines from estates with tiny productions, for example Pomerols and St. Emilions, you may want to buy these wines on a future basis simply to guarantee that you will have a case of these wines when they are bottled 18–24 months after the vintage and shipped to the market.
4. If you are buying Bordeaux futures, are you concentrating on the twenty-eight blue chip properties that were itemized earlier? In any given vintage, there are certain wines produced that are particularly stunning but are not among the twenty-eight blue chip Bordeaux properties I have enumerated (e.g. 1983 Cantemerle or 1982 La Dominique). However, your knowledge of these facts depends on your access to valid and independent information about the top wines of the vintage which you should have before you invest significantly in Bordeaux futures. To invest without a thorough understanding of the strength and quality of the vintage is asking for trouble.
5. Have you followed closely the preliminary barrel tasting reports from the professional wine tasters who have experience and a good track record of reliability?
6. Have you chosen a reputable wine merchant who has dealt in Bordeaux futures in the past and has a record of delivering the wines that were sold to his clients?

Keeping all these factors in mind, my strategy for buying 1983 Bordeaux futures would have been as follows. First, 1983 was a great vintage for only a handful of Margaux wines, a few Pauillac wines, and a handful of St.-Emilion and Pomerol wines. It was a great vintage for almost all the wines of Barsac and Sauternes. Therefore, selectivity would have been critical. If I had bought 1983 Bordeaux futures, the wines I would have purchased in spring 1984 when they were first offered would have been Margaux, Pichon Lalande, Cantemerle, Lafite-Rothschild, Cheval Blanc, Ausone, Canon, L'Evangile, Lafleur, and Latour à Pomerol. These ten wines satisfy all of the issues I raised previously. They are great wines and they were significantly more expensive when they were released in spring 1986. The three St.-Emilions and three Pomerols were produced in extremely limited quantities so, by buying them as wine futures, I was certain of being able to obtain these hard-to-find wines. I would also have purchased several Sauternes such as Rieussec and Doisy Daëne because of the greatness of the vintage in this region. You might notice that Cantemerle is not one of my blue chip Bordeaux wines, and you would be right. However, armed with the knowledge that Cantemerle made one of its greatest wines ever in 1983, I was prepared to invest heavily in it because of its greatness in this given vintage.

Lastly, should you decide to enter the futures market, be sure you know the other risks involved. The merchant you deal with could go bankrupt, and your unsecured sales slip would make you one of probably hundreds of unsecured creditors of the bankrupt wine merchant hoping for a few pence on your investment. Another risk is that the supplier in Bordeaux the merchant deals with could go bankrupt or be fraudulent. You may get a refund from the wine merchant, but you won't get your wine. Therefore, be sure to deal only with a wine merchant who has dealt in selling wine futures before and one who is financially solvent. And finally, buy wine futures only from a wine merchant who has received confirmed commitments as to the quantities of wine he or she will receive. Some merchants sell Bordeaux futures to consumers before they have received commitments from their suppliers. Be sure to ask for proof of the merchant's allocations. If you don't, then the words *caveat emptor* could have special significance to you.

For many Bordeaux wine enthusiasts, buying wine futures of the right wine, in the right vintage, at the right time guarantees that they have liquid gems worth four or five times the price they paid for the wine. For many Bordeaux enthusiasts it is the only way in which to buy great or excellent vintages. But one must be aware of the risks involved. Having a total picture of the international financial and wine markets, anticipating the demand that will exist for the vintage being offered, and having access to top quality information about the vintage will insure that your choices for Bordeaux wine futures are the best that can be made.

7: A GLOSSARY OF WINE TERMS

acetic—Wines, no matter how well made, contain quantities of acetic acid. If there is an excessive amount of acetic acid, the wine will have a vinegary smell.

acidic—Wines need natural acidity to taste fresh and lively, but an excess of acidity results in an acidic wine that is tart and sour.

acidity—The acidity level in a wine is critical to its enjoyment and livelihood. The natural acids that appear in wine are citric, tartaric, malic, and lactic. Wines from hot years tend to be lower in acidity, whereas wines from cool, rainy years tend to be high in acidity. Acidity in a wine preserves the wine's freshness and keeps the wine lively.

aftertaste—As the term suggests, the taste left in the mouth after one swallows is the aftertaste. This word is a synonym for length or finish. The longer the aftertaste lingers in the mouth (assuming it is a pleasant taste), the finer the quality of the wine.

aggressive—Aggressive is usually applied to wines that are either high in acidity or harsh tannins, or both.

angular—Angular wines are wines that lack roundness, generosity, and depth.

Wine from poor vintages or wines that are too acidic are often described as being angular.

aroma—Aroma is the smell of a young wine before it has had sufficient time to develop nuances of smell that are then called its bouquet. The word aroma is commonly used to mean the smell of a relatively young, unevolved wine.

astringent—Wines that are astringent are not necessarily bad or good wines. Astringent wines are harsh and coarse to taste, either because they are too young and tannic and just need time to develop or because they are not well made. The level of tannin in a wine contributes to its degree of astringence.

austere—Wines that are austere are generally not terribly pleasant wines to drink. An austere wine is a hard, rather dry wine that lacks richness and generosity. However, young, promising Bordeaux can often express itself as austere, and aging of such wine will reveal a wine with considerably more generosity than its youthful austerity suggested.

balance—One of the most desired traits in a wine is good balance, where the concentration of fruit, level of tannins, and acidity are in total harmony. Well-balanced wines are symmetrical and tend to age gracefully.

barnyard—An unclean, farmyard, fecal aroma that is imparted to a wine because of unclean barrels or generally unsanitary winemaking facilities.

berrylike—As this descriptive term implies, wines, particularly Bordeaux wines that are young and not overly oaked, have an intense berry fruit character that can suggest blackberries, raspberries, black cherries, mulberries, or even strawberries and cranberries.

big—A big wine is a large-framed, full-bodied wine with an intense and concentrated feel on the palate. Bordeaux wines in general are not big wines in the same sense that Rhône wines are, but the top vintages of Bordeaux produce very rich, concentrated, deep wines.

blackcurrant—A pronounced smell of the blackcurrant fruit is commonly associated with red Bordeaux wines. It can vary in intensity from faint to very deep and rich.

body—Body is the weight and fullness of a wine that can be sensed as it crosses the palate. Full-bodied wines tend to have a lot of alcohol, concentration, and glycerine.

Botrytis cinerea—The fungus that attacks the grape skins under specific climatic conditions (usually interchanging periods of moisture and sunny weather). It causes the grape to become superconcentrated because it causes a natural dehydration. *Botrytis cinerea* is essential for the great sweet white wines of Barsac and Sauternes.

bouquet—As a wine's aroma becomes more developed from bottle aging the aroma is transformed into a bouquet, which is hopefully more than just the smell of the grape.

brawny—A hefty, muscular, full-bodied wine with plenty of weight and flavor, although not always the most elegant or refined sort of wine.

briary—I usuually think of California Zinfandel rather than Bordeaux when the term briary comes into play. Briary denotes that the wine is aggressive and rather spicy.

brilliant—Brilliant relates to the color of the wine. A brilliant wine is one that is clear, with no haze or cloudiness.

browning—As red wines age, their color changes from ruby/purple, to dark ruby, to medium ruby, to ruby with an amber edge, to ruby with a brown edge. When a wine is browning it is usually fully mature and is not likely to get better.

cedar—Bordeaux reds often have a bouquet that suggests either faintly or overtly the smell of cedarwood. It is a complex aspect of the bouquet.

chewy—If a wine has a rather dense, viscous texture from a high glycerine content it is often referred to as being chewy. High-extract wines from great vintages can often be chewy.

closed—The term closed is used to denote that the wine is not showing its potential, which remains locked in because it is too young. Young Bordeaux often close up about 12–18 months after bottling, and depending on the vintage and storage conditions, remain in such a state for several years to more than a decade.

complex—One of the most subjective descriptive terms used, a complex wine is a wine that the taster never gets bored with and finds interesting to drink. Complex wines tend to have a variety of subtle scents and flavors that hold one's interest in the wine.

concentrated—Fine wines, whether they are light, medium- or full-bodied, should have concentrated flavors. Concentrated denotes that the wine has a depth and richness of fruit that gives it appeal and interest. Deep is a synonym of concentrated.

corked—A "corked" wine is a flawed wine that has taken on the smell of cork as a result of an unclean or faulty cork. It is perceptible in a bouquet that shows no fruit, only the smell of a musty cork.

deep—Essentially the same as concentrated, the word deep expresses the fact that the wine is rich, full of extract, and mouth-filling.

delicate—As this word implies, delicate wines are light, subtle, understated wines that are prized for their shyness rather than extroverted robust character. White wines are usually more delicate than red wines. Few Bordeaux can properly be called delicate.

diffuse—Wines that smell and taste unstructured and unfocused are said to be diffuse. Often when red wines are served at too warm a temperature they become diffuse.

dumb—A dumb wine is also a closed wine, but the term dumb is used in a more pejorative sense. Closed wines may only need time to reveal their richness and intensity. Dumb wines may never become any better.

earthy—This term may be used in both a negative and a positive sense; however, I prefer to use earthy to denote a positive aroma of fresh, rich, clean soil. Earthy is a more intense smell than woodsy or truffle scents.

elegant—Although more white wines than red are described as being elegant, lighter-styled, graceful, well-balanced Bordeaux wines can be elegant.

exuberant—Like extroverted, somewhat hyper people, wines too can be gushing with fruit, and seem nervous and intensely vigorous.

fat—When Bordeaux gets a very hot year for its crop, and the wines attain a super sort of maturity, they are often quite rich and concentrated with low to average acidity. Often such wines are said to be fat, which is a prized commodity. If they become too fat, that is a flaw and they are then called flabby.

flabby—A wine that is too fat or obese is a flabby wine. Flabby wines lack structure and are heavy to taste.

fleshy—Fleshy is a synonym for chewy, meaty, or beefy. It denotes that the wine has a lot of body, alcohol, and extract, and usually a high glycerine content. Pomerols and St.-Emilions tend to be fleshier wines than Médocs.

floral—With the exception of some Sauternes, I rarely think of Bordeaux wines as having a floral or flowery aspect to their bouquets or aromas. However, wines like Riesling or Muscat do have a flowery component.

forward—A wine is said to be forward when its charm and character are fully revealed. While it may not be fully mature yet, a forward wine is generally quite enjoyable and drinkable. Forward is the opposite of backward.

focused—Both a fine wine's bouquet and flavor should be focused. Focused simply means that the scents, aromas, and flavors are precise and clearly delineated. If they are not, the wine is like an out-of-focus picture: diffuse, hazy, and problematic.

fresh—Freshness in both young and old wines is a welcome and pleasing component. A wine is said to be fresh when it is lively and cleanly made. The opposite of fresh is stale.

fruity—A very good wine should have enough concentration of fruit so that it can be said to be fruity. Fortunately, the best Bordeaux wines will have more than just a fruity personality.

full-bodied—Wines rich in extract, alcohol, and glycerine are full-bodied wines.

green—Green wines are wines made from underripe grapes, and lack richness and generosity as well as having a vegetal character. Green wines were often made in Bordeaux in poor vintages such as 1972 and 1977.

hard—Wines with abrasive, astringent tannins or high acidity are said to be hard. Young vintages of Bordeaux can be hard, but they should never be harsh.

harsh—If a wine is too hard it is said to be harsh. Harshness in a wine, young or old, is a flaw.

herbaceous—Many wines have a distinctive herbal smell that is generally said to be herbaceous. Specific herbal smells can be of thyme, lavender, rosemary, oregano, fennel, or basil.

hollow—A synonym for shallow; hollow wines are diluted and lack depth and concentration.

honeyed—A common personality trait of sweet Barsacs and Sauternes, a honeyed wine is one that has the smell and taste of bees' honey.

hot—Rather than mean that the temperature of the wine is too warm to drink, hot denotes that the wine is too high in alcohol and therefore leaves a burning sensation in the back of the throat when swallowed. Wines with alcohol levels in excess of 14.5% are often hot.

jammy—When Bordeaux wines have a great intensity of fruit from excellent ripeness they can be jammy, which is a very concentrated, flavorful wine with superb extract. In great vintages such as 1961 and 1982, some of the wines are so concentrated that they are said to be jammy.

leafy—A leafy character in a wine is similar to a herbaceous character only in that it refers to the smell of leaves rather than herbs. A wine that is too leafy is a vegetal or green wine.

lean—Lean wines are slim, rather streamlined wines that lack generosity and fatness but can still be enjoyable and pleasant.

lively—A synonym for fresh or exuberant, a lively wine is usually a young wine with good acidity and a thirst-quenching personality.

long—A very desirable trait in a fine Bordeaux is that it be long in the mouth. Long (or length) relates to a wine's finish, meaning that after you swallow the wine, you sense its presence for a long time. (Thirty seconds to several minutes is great length.)

lush—Lush wines are velvety, soft, richly fruity wines that are both concentrated and fat. A lush wine can never be an astringent or hard wine.

massive—In great vintages where there is a high degree of ripeness and superb concentration, some wines can turn out to be so big, full-bodied and rich that they are called massive. Great wines, such as the 1961 Latour and Pétrus and the 1982 Pétrus, are textbook examples of massive wines.

meaty—A chewy, fleshy wine is also said to be meaty.

mouth-filling—Big, rich, concentrated wines that are filled with fruit extract and are high in alcohol and glycerine are wines that tend to texturally fill the mouth. A mouth-filling wine is also a chewy, fleshy, fat wine.

nose—The general smell and aroma of a wine as sensed through one's nose and olfactory senses is often called the wine's nose.

oaky—Most top Bordeaux wines are aged from 12 months to 30 months in small oak barrels. At the very best properties, a percentage of the oak barrels are new, and these barrels impart a toasty, vanillin flavor and smell to the wine. If the wine is not rich and concentrated, the barrels can overwhelm the wine, making it taste overly oaky. However, when the wine is rich and concentrated and the winemaker has made a judicious use of new oak barrels, the results are a wonderful marriage of fruit and oak.

off—If a wine is not showing its true character, or is flawed or spoiled in some way, it is said to be "off."

overripe—An undesirable characteristic; grapes left too long on the vine become too ripe, lose their acidity, and produce wines that are heavy and imbalanced. This happens much more frequently in hot viticultural areas than in Bordeaux.

oxidized—If a wine has been excessively exposed to air during either its making or aging, the wine loses freshness and takes on a stale, old smell and taste. Such a wine is said to be oxidized.

peppery—A peppery quality to a wine is usually noticeable in many Rhône wines which have an aroma of black pepper and a pungent flavor. It occasionally appears in some Bordeaux wines.

perfumed—This term usually is more applicable to fragrant, aromatic white wines than to red Bordeaux wines. However, some of the dry white wines and sweet white wines can have a strong perfumed smell.

plummy—Rich, concentrated wines can often have the smell and taste of ripe plums. When they do, the term plummy is applicable.

ponderous—Ponderous is often used as a synonym for massive, but in my usage a massive wine is simply a big, rich, very concentrated wine with balance, whereas a ponderous wine is a wine that has become heavy and tiring to drink.

pruney—Wines produced from grapes that are overripe take on the character of prunes. Pruney wines are flawed wines.

raisiny—Late-harvest wines that are meant to be drunk at the end of a meal can often be slightly raisiny, which in some ports and sherries is desirable. However, in dry Bordeaux wines a raisiny quality is a major flaw.

rich—Wines high in extract, flavor, and intensity of fruit are described as being rich.

ripe—A wine is ripe when its grapes have reached the optimum level of maturity. Less than fully mature grapes produce wines that are underripe, and overly mature grapes produce wines that are overripe.

round—A very desirable character of wines, roundness occurs in fully mature Bordeaux that have lost their youthful, astringent tannins, and also in young Bordeaux that are low in tannin and acidity and are meant to be consumed young.

savory—A general descriptive term which denotes that the wine is round, flavorful, and interesting to drink.

shallow—A weak, feeble, watery or diluted wine lacking concentration is said to be shallow.

sharp—An undesirable trait; sharp wines are bitter and unpleasant with hard, pointed edges.

silky—A synonym for velvety or lush, silky wines are soft, sometimes fat, but never hard or angular.

smoky—Some wines, either because of the soil or because of the barrels used to age the wine, have a distinctive smoky character. In Bordeaux, some of the Graves wines occasionally are smoky.

soft—A soft wine is one that is round and fruity, low in acidity, and has an absence of aggressive, hard tannins.

spicy—Wines often smell quite spicy with aromas of pepper, cinnamon, and other well-known spices. These pungent aromas are usually lumped together and called spicy.

stale—Dull, heavy wines that are oxidized or lack balancing acidity for freshness are called stale.

stalky—A synonym for vegetal, but used more frequently to denote that the wine has probably had too much contact with the stems and the result is a green, vegetal, or stalky character to the wine.

supple—A supple wine is one that is soft, lush, velvety, and very attractively round and tasty. It is a highly desirable characteristic as it suggests that the wine is harmonious.

tannic—The tannins of a wine, which are extracted from the grape skins and stems, are, along with a wine's acidity and alcohol, its lifeline. Tannins give a wine firmness and some roughness when young, but gradually fall away and dissipate. A tannic wine is one that is young and unready to drink.

tart—Sharp, acidic, lean, unripe wines are called tart. In general, a red Bordeaux that is tart is not pleasurable.

thick—Rich, ripe, concentrated wines that are low in acidity are often said to be thick.

thin—A synonym for shallow, a thin wine is an undesirable characteristic meaning that the wine is watery, lacking in body, and just diluted.

tightly knit—Young wines that have good acidity levels, good tannin levels, and are well made are called tightly knit, meaning they have yet to open up and develop.

toasty—A smell of grilled toast can often be found in wines because the barrels the wines are aged in are charred or toasted on the inside.

tobacco—Many red Graves wines have the scent of fresh burning tobacco. It is a distinctive and wonderful smell in wine.

unctuous—Rich, lush, intense wines with layers of concentrated, soft, velvety fruit are said to be unctuous. In particular, the sweet wines of Barsac and Sauternes are unctuous.

vegetal—An undesirable characteristic; wines that smell and taste vegetal are usually made from unripe grapes. In some wines a subtle vegetable garden smell is pleasant and adds complexity, but if it is the predominant characteristic, it is a major flaw.

velvety—A textural description and synonym for lush or silky, a velvety wine is a rich, soft, smooth wine to taste. It is a very desirable characteristic.

viscous—Viscous wines tend to be relatively concentrated, fat, almost thick wines with a great density of fruit extract, plenty of glycerine, and high alcohol content. If they have balancing acidity, they can be tremendously flavorful and exciting wines. If they lack acidity, they are often flabby and heavy.

volatile—A volatile wine is one that smells of vinegar as a result of an excessive amount of acetic bacteria present. It is a seriously flawed wine.

woody—When a wine is overly oaky it is often said to be woody. Oakiness in a wine's bouquet and taste is good up to a point. Once past that point the wine is woody and its fruity qualities are masked by excessive oak aging.

SELECTED BIBLIOGRAPHY

Benson, Jeffrey, and Alastair MacKenzie. *Sauternes.* London: Sotheby, Park, Bernet Publications, 1979.

———. *The Wines of St.-Emilion and Pomerol.* London: Sotheby, Park, Bernet Publications, 1983.

Bespaloff, Alexis. *The New Signet Book of Wine.* New York: New American Library, 1985.

Broadbent, Michael. *Complete Guide to Wine Tasting and Wine Cellars.* New York: Simon and Schuster, 1984.

———. *The Great Vintage Wine Book.* London: Mitchell Beazley Publishers, Ltd., and New York: Alfred A. Knopf, 1980.

Coates, Clive. *Claret.* Portland, U.K.: Century Publishing Co., Ltd., 1982.

Dovaz, Michel. *Encyclopédie des Crus Classés du Bordelais.* Paris: Julliard, 1981.

Duijker, Hubrecht. *Les Bons Vins de Bordeaux.* New York: Crown Publishers, 1983.

———. *The Great Wine Châteaux of Bordeaux.* New York: Hastings House Publishers, 1975.

Enjalbert, Henri. *Les Grands Vins de Saint-Emilion, Pomerol et Fronsac*. Paris: Bardi, 1983.

Féret, C. *Bordeaux et ses Vins*. Bordeaux: Féret et Fils, 1982.

Gayon, Jean Ribereau, and Emile Peynaud. *Sciences et Techniques de la Vigne*. Paris: Dunod, 1971.

Ginestet, Bernard. *Côtes de Bourg*. Paris: Jacques Legrand S.A., 1984.

———. *Margaux*. Paris: Jacques Legrand S.A., 1984.

———. *Pomerol*. Paris: Jacques Legrand S.A., 1984.

———. *Saint-Julien*. Paris: Jacques Legrand S.A., 1984.

Johnson, Hugh. *The Modern Encyclopedia of Wine*. New York: Simon and Schuster, 1983.

———. *The World Atlas of Wine*. New York: Simon and Schuster, 1982.

Lichine, Alexis. *The New Encyclopedia of Wines and Spirits of France*. New York: Alfred A. Knopf, 1981.

Penning-Rowsell, Edmund. *The Wines of Bordeaux*. 5th ed. San Francisco: Penguin Books, 1985.

Peppercorn, David. *Bordeaux*. Winchester, Mass.: Faber and Faber, 1982.

Peynaud, Emile. *Le Gout du Vin*, Paris: Dunod, 1980.

Schneider, Steven. *The International Album of Wine*. New York: Holt, Rinehart and Winston, 1977.

Spurrier, Steven, and Michel Dovaz. *Academie du Vin Wine Course*. Portland, U.K.: Century Publishing Co., Ltd., 1983.

Sutcliffe, Serena. *André Simon's Wines of the World*. 2nd ed. London: MacDonald Futura Publishers, 1981.

———. *Great Vineyards and Winemakers*. London: MacDonald Futura Publishers, 1981.

Harry Waugh's Wine Diaries. London: Christies' Wine Publications, 1975, 1976, 1978, 1981.

INDEX TO THE WINES OF BORDEAUX

About the Author

Robert Parker gave up a career in law to devote himself full time to evaluating and writing about wine. In 1978 in founded *The Wine Advocate*. He lives with his wife, Pat, and various bassett hounds in Parkton, Maryland.

MUCH OF THE MATERIAL IN THIS BOOK is based upon tastings and research done in conjunction with the publishing of *The Wine Advocate*, an independent consumer's guide to fine wines, which is issued six times a year. A one-year subscription to *The Wine Advocate* costs $28.00, and interested readers may obtain a free sample copy of *The Wine Advocate* or a subscription by writing to *The Wine Advocate*, 1002 Hillside View, Parkton, MD 21120.